Autodesk Revit 2024 Home Design

K Prathima

For resource files, contact us at:

revit.tutorialbook@gmail.com

Table of Contents

Scope of this Book

The ***Autodesk Revit 2024 Home Design*** book helps users to learn Revit in a project-based approach. It is written for students and designers who are interested to learn Autodesk Revit to create residential plans. The topics covered in this book are as follows:

- Part 1, "Modeling", helps you to create walls, floors, columns, roofs, kitchen and bathroom fixtures, and ceilings.

- Part 2, "Creating Views", teaches you to create elevation and section views.

- Part 3, "Publishing," teaches you to create and publish renderings and drawings sheets.

Part 1: Modeling

In this part, you learn to do the following:

- ***Starting Revit 2024***
- ***Creating and Managing Levels***
- ***Creating Walls and Footings***
- ***Creating Doors and Opening***
- ***Placing Windows***
- ***Creating Floors***
- ***Creating Columns and Beams***
- ***Creating Roofs***
- ***Adding Kitchen and Bathroom Fixtures***
- ***Creating Ceilings***
- ***Add Lights and Electrical Fixtures***

Tutorial 1: Starting Revit 2024

- Click **Start > Autodesk** > **Revit 2024** icon on the taskbar.
- To start a new document, click the **New** button in the **Models** section of the **Home** page.
- On the **New Project** dialog, click the **Browse** button to open the **Choose Template** dialog.
- Click the **Up one level** icon next to the **Look in** drop-down. Next, double-click on the **English – Imperial** folder.
- Select the **default** template, and then click **Open**.
- Select the **Project** option from the **Create new** section. Click **OK** to create a new project.

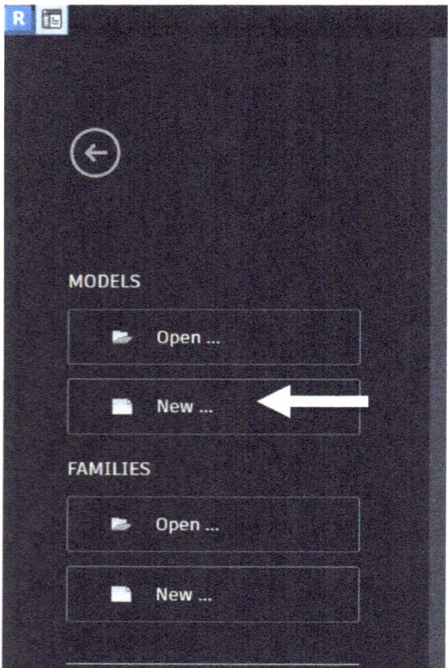
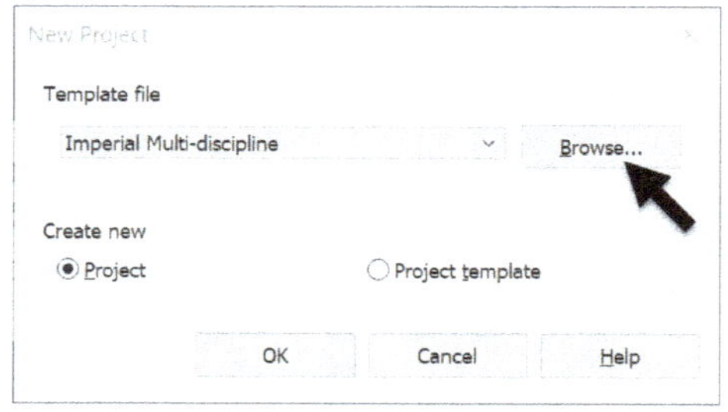
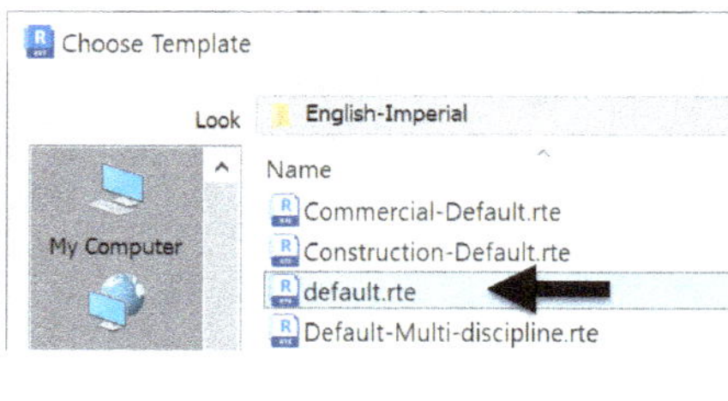

The components of the Revit user interface are shown in the figure given next:

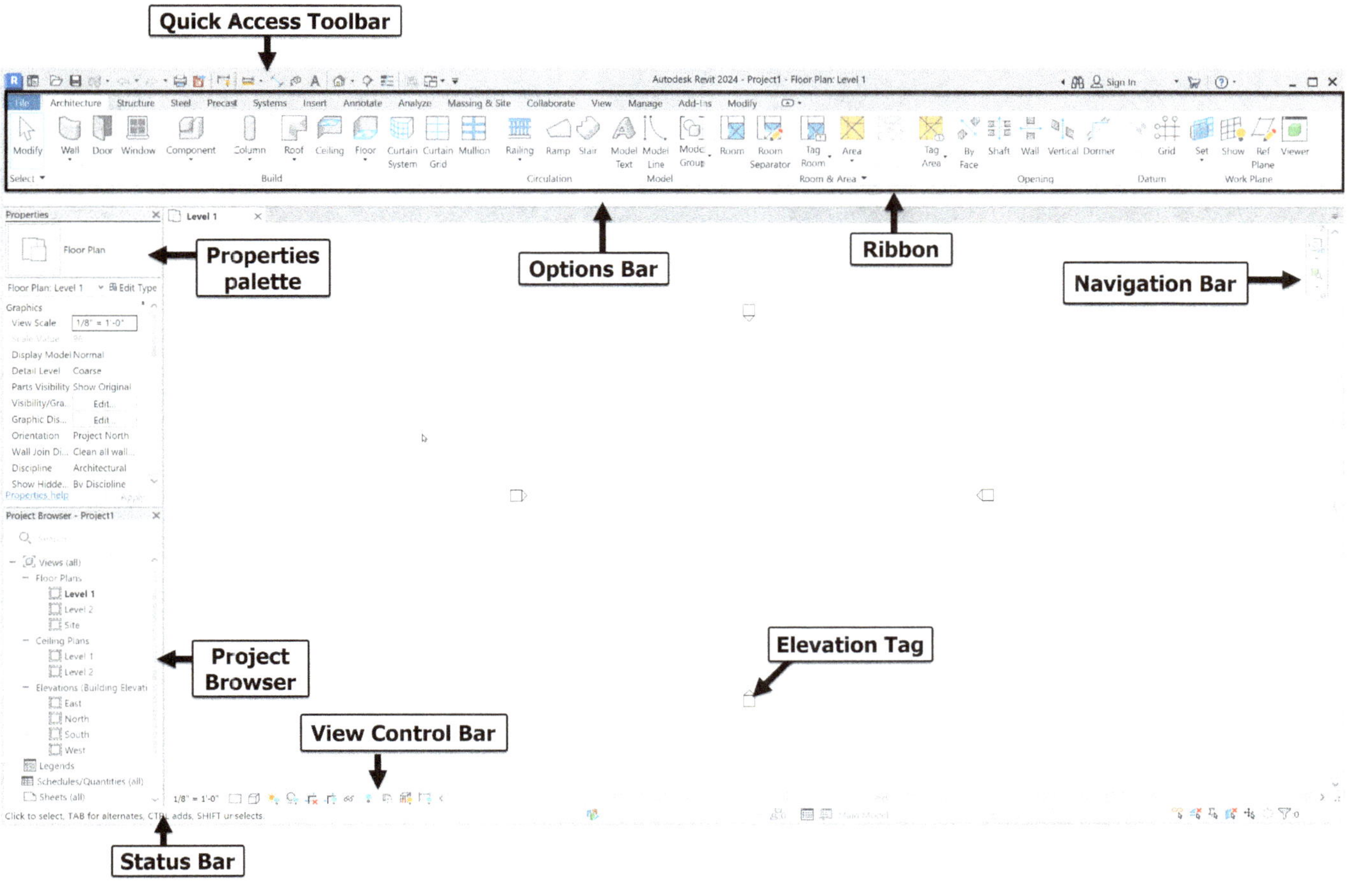

Tutorial 2: Creating and Managing Levels

Creating levels is one of the first things that you will do when setting up a new project. The levels define the height at which you create objects in the Revit model. If you have multiple levels in a Revit model, it indicates that you can create objects at multiple heights. The levels are displayed under the **Floor Plans** and **Ceiling Plans** nodes in the **Project browser**. You can view the levels in the graphics window by clicking anyone of the elevations in the elevations node.

- In the Project Browser, double-click the **South** option under the **Elevations (Building Elevation)** node.

- On the Navigation Bar, click **Zoom** drop-down > **Zoom in Region**.

- Specify the first and second corners of the zoom window, as shown; the names and dimensions of the levels are displayed in full.

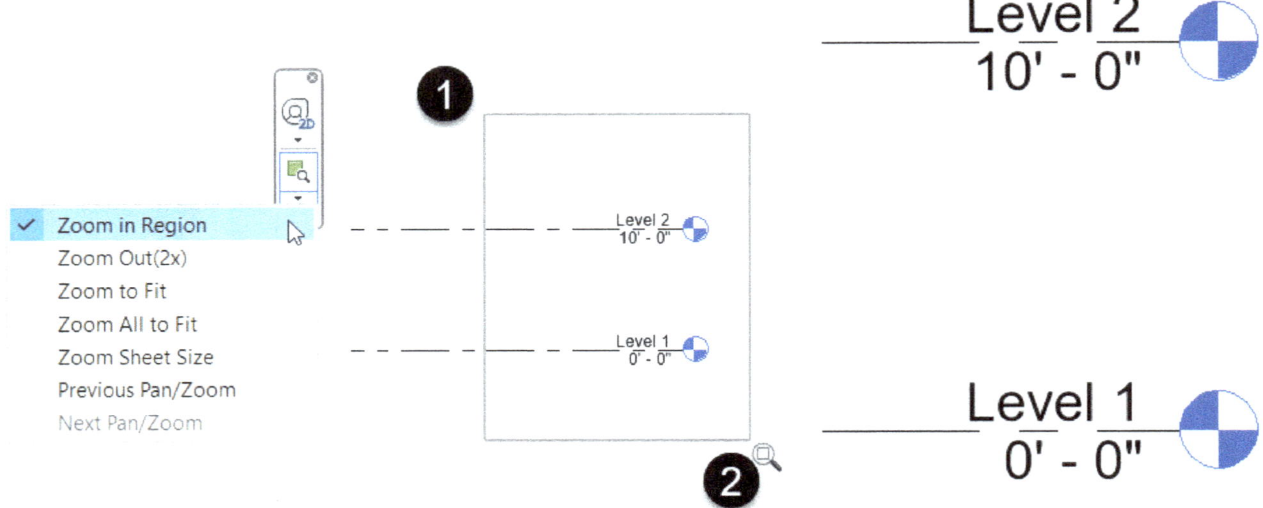

- Right-click and select **Cancel**.
- Select the level 1 and click on its name. Next, type **FIRST FLOOR** and click in the graphics window.
- Click **Yes** on the **Confirm Level Rename** message box.

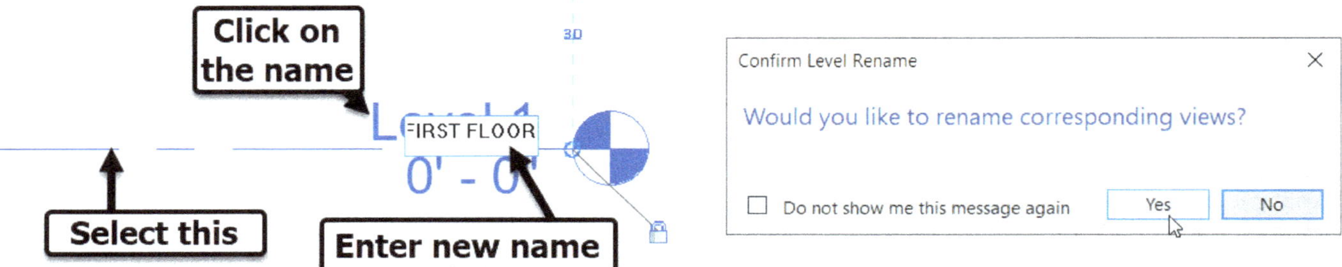

- Likewise, change the name of the Level 2 to TOP. Notice that the level names are updated in the **Floor Plans** and **Ceiling Plans** nodes in the Project Browser.

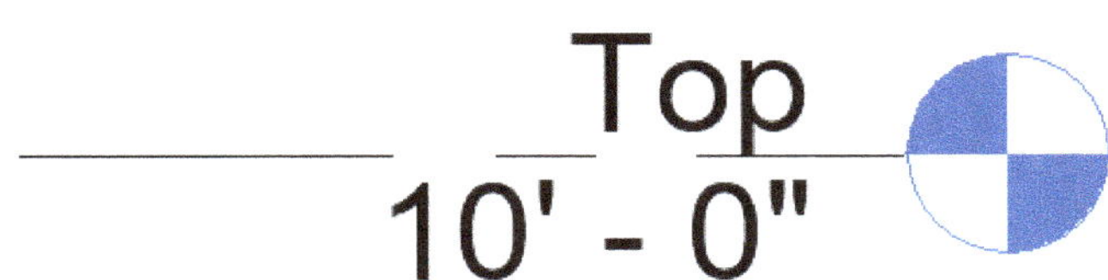

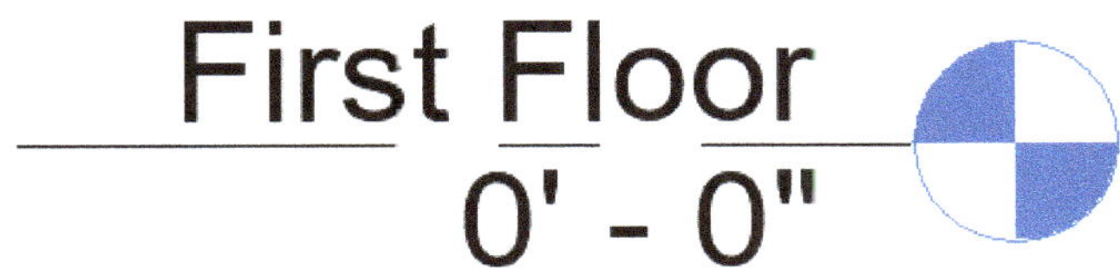

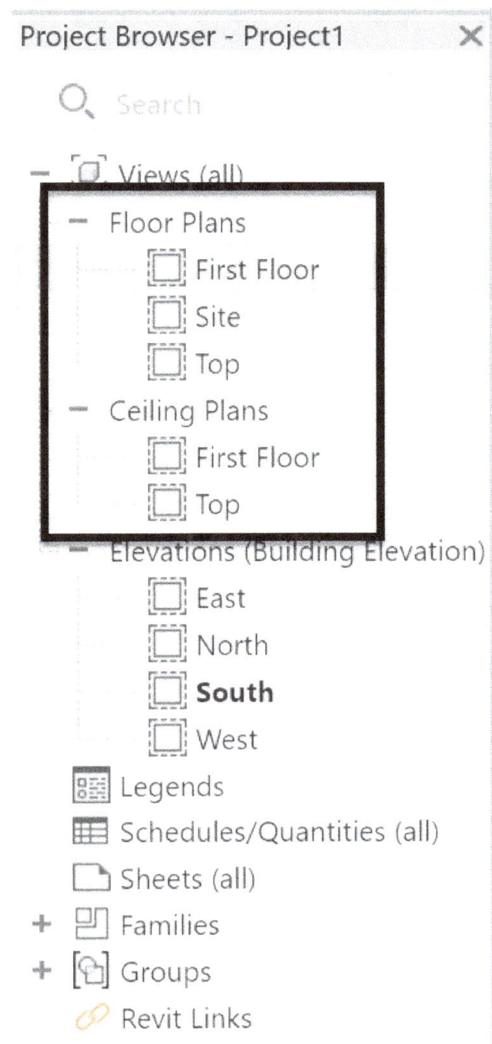

- Select the first floor and click on its dimension. Next, type **1'10 ½"**, and then click in the graphics window; the height of the first floor level is updated automatically.

- On the Navigation Bar, click **Zoom** drop-down > **Zoom All to Fit**.

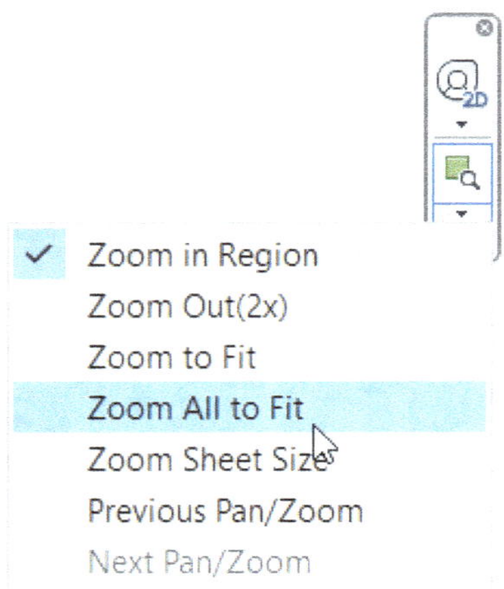

- On the ribbon, click **Architecture > Datum > Level**.
- On the Options Bar, make sure that the **Make Plan View** option is checked. Click the **Plan View Types** button.
- Deselect the **Structural Plan** option on the **Plan View Types** dialog and click **OK**.

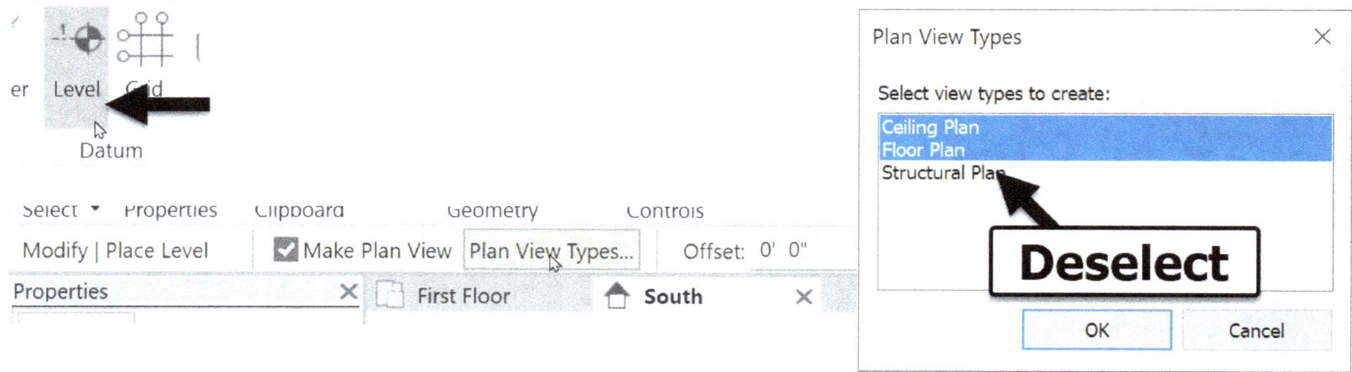

- Next, move the pointer near to the left end point of the FIRST FLOOR level; the extension line appears.
- Move the pointer downward along the extension line and click to specify the start point of the level.
- Move the pointer toward right up to the right end of the first floor level. Notice the extension line from the right end of the first floor level.
- Click to create a new level.

- Likewise, create another level, as shown. Next, press ESC to end the level creation.

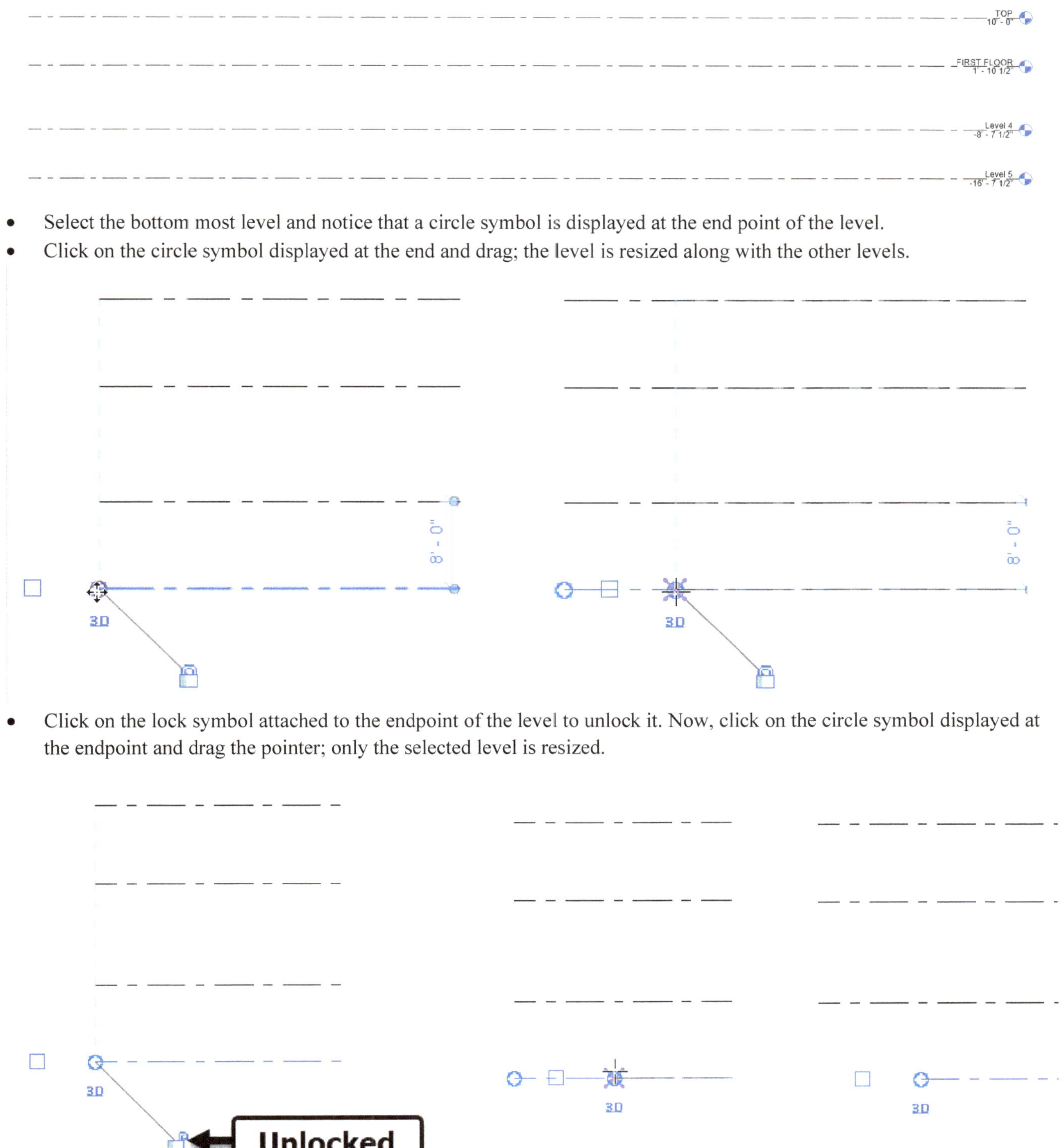

- Select the bottom most level and notice that a circle symbol is displayed at the end point of the level.
- Click on the circle symbol displayed at the end and drag; the level is resized along with the other levels.

- Click on the lock symbol attached to the endpoint of the level to unlock it. Now, click on the circle symbol displayed at the endpoint and drag the pointer; only the selected level is resized.

- Again, click on the circle symbol and drag the pointer toward left. Release when an extension line appears from the endpoint of the other level; the levels are locked again and the lock symbol appears.

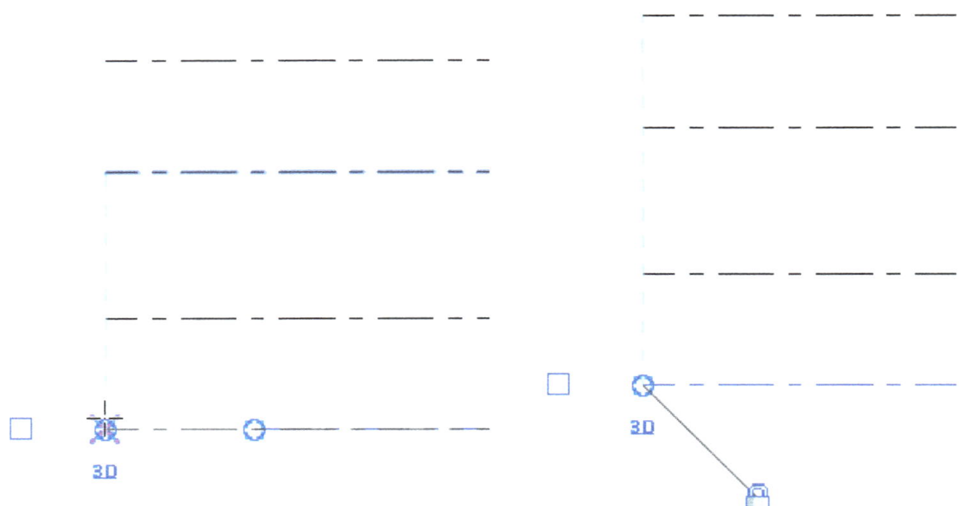

In addition to that, you can hide or show the annotations by using the checkboxes displayed at the endpoints of the level.

*   Change the names and dimensions of the two levels, as shown.

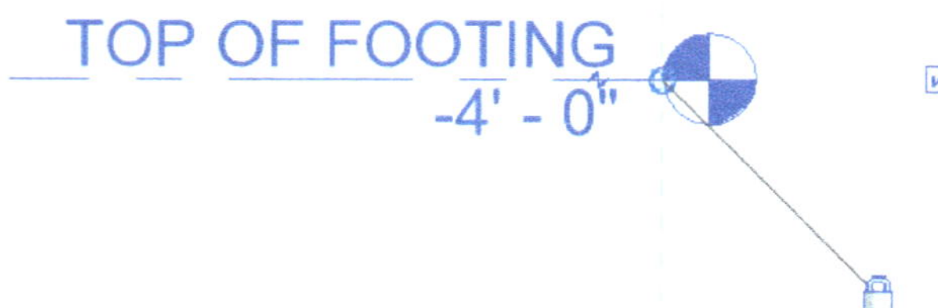

*   Select the TOP OF FOUNDATION level and click the Add elbow symbol displayed on it; an elbow is added to the level.
*   Click and drag the grips displayed on the elbow to change its length.

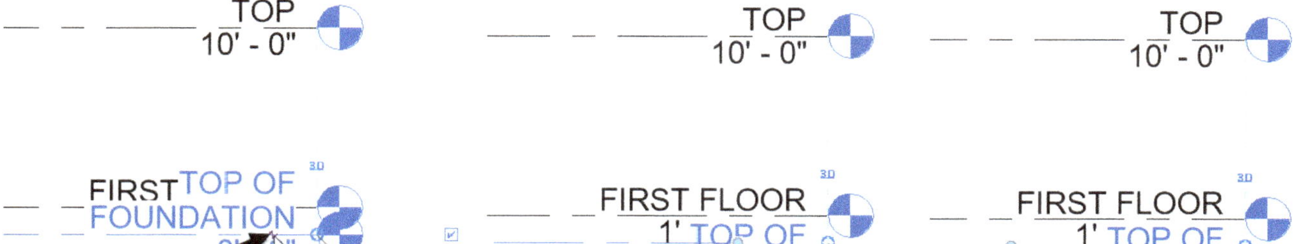

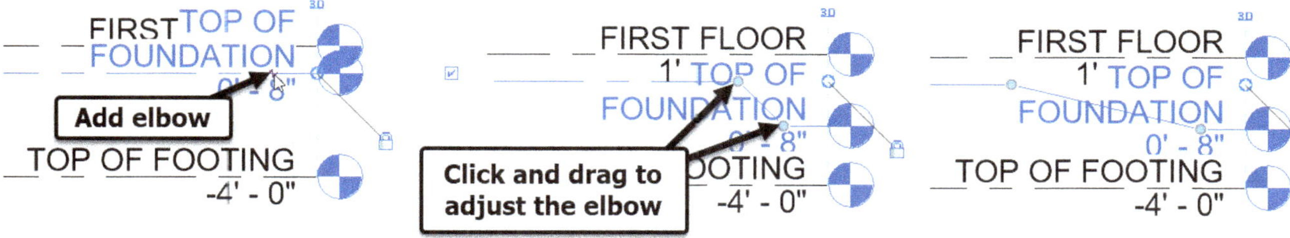

- Likewise, add elbows to the FIRST FLOOR and TOP OF FOOTING levels, as shown.

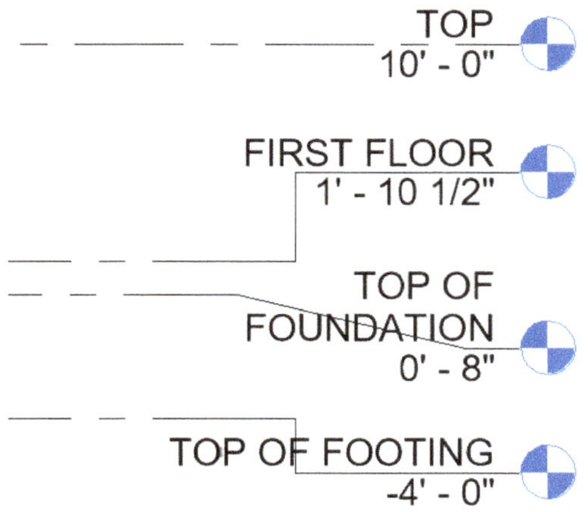

- On the Navigation Bar, click **Zoom** drop-down > **Zoom All to Fit**.

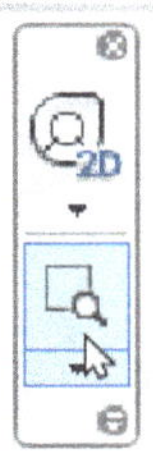

Saving the Document

- Click the **Save** icon on the **Quick Access Toolbar**.

- On the **Save As** dialog, use the **Save in** drop-down to define the location of the drawing.

- Click the **Create New Folder** icon on the **Save Drawing As** dialog. Enter Revit Architectural Design as the folder. Next, double click on the folder.

- Type **Tutorial_Project** in the **File name** box, and click **Save**.

Tutorial 3: Creating Walls and Footings

Revit offers many tools to create walls. Now, you learn to create walls using various tools.

Creating Exterior walls

- Double-click on the **TOP OF FOUNDATION** under the **Floor Plans** node in the **Project Browser**.
- On the ribbon, click **Architecture** tab > **Build** panel > **Wall** drop-down > **Wall Architectural**.

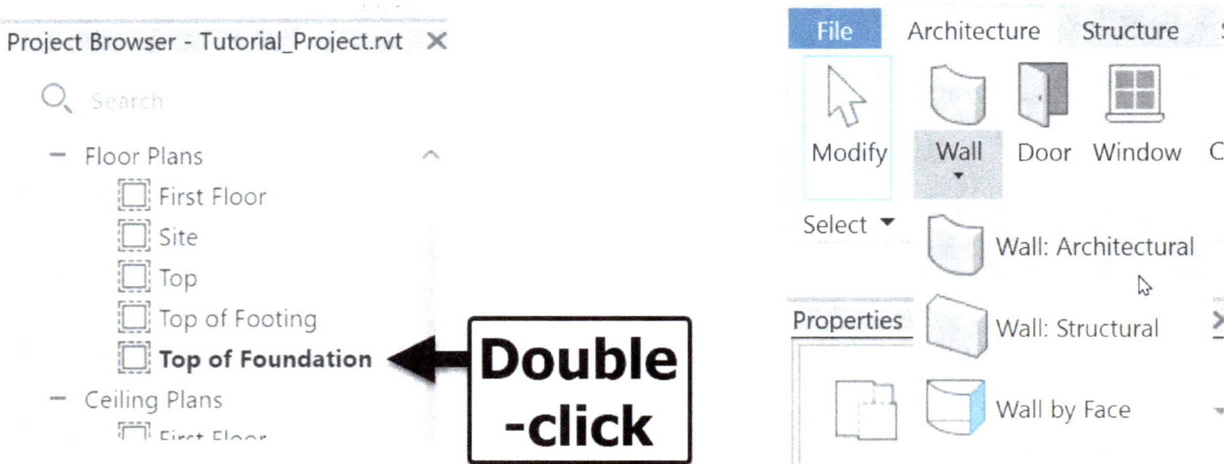

- On the **Properties** palette, select **Generic – 6"** wall from the **Basic Wall** drop-down.
- Click the **Edit Type** icon on the **Properties** palette.
- Click the **Preview** button located at the bottom left corner of the **Type Properties** dialog.

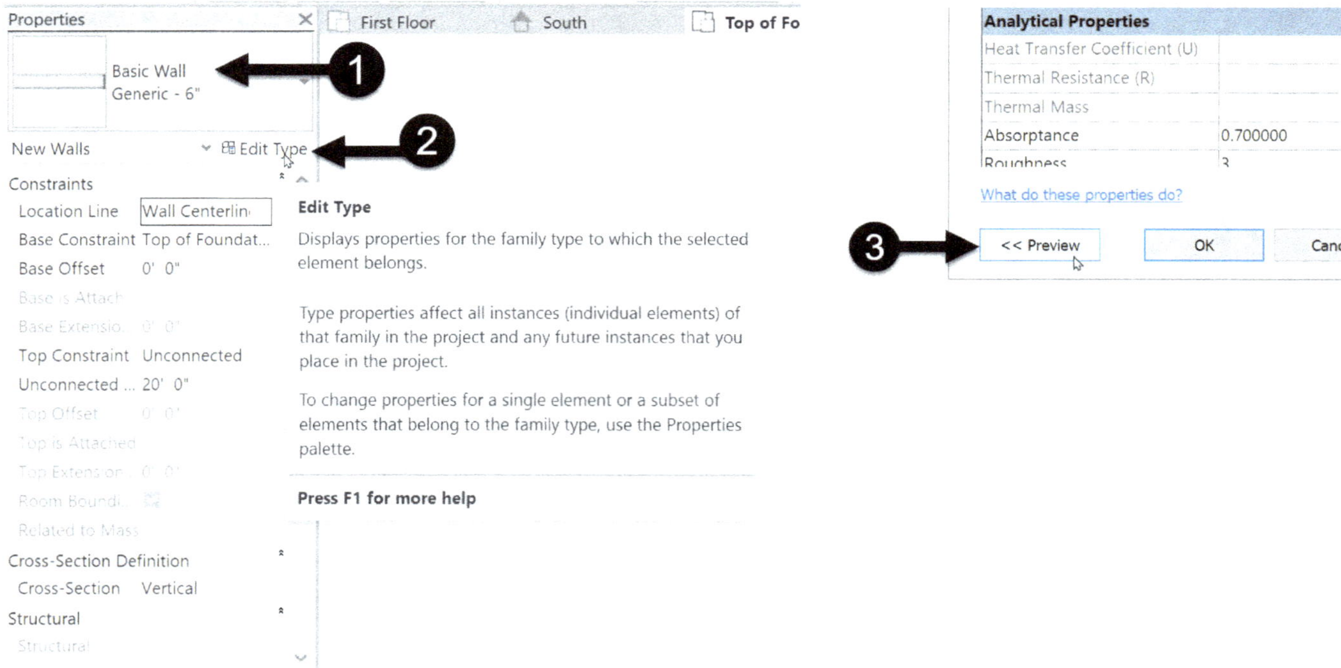

- On the **Type Properties** dialog, select **View > Section: Modify type attributes**; the section view of the wall is displayed.

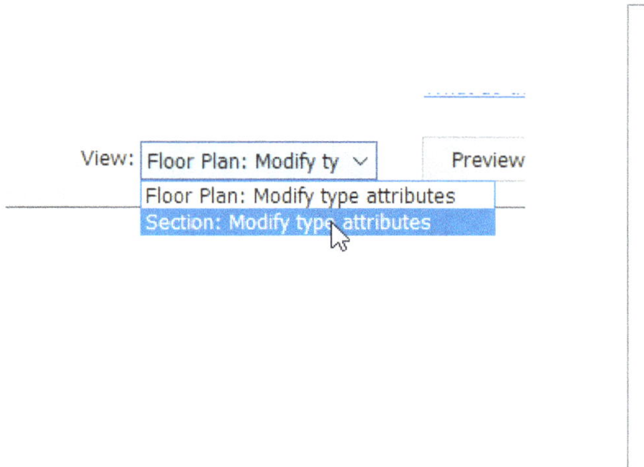

Next, you need to create a new wall type.

- Click the **Duplicate** button next to the **Type** drop-down. Next, type **New Exterior** in the **Name** box and click **OK**.

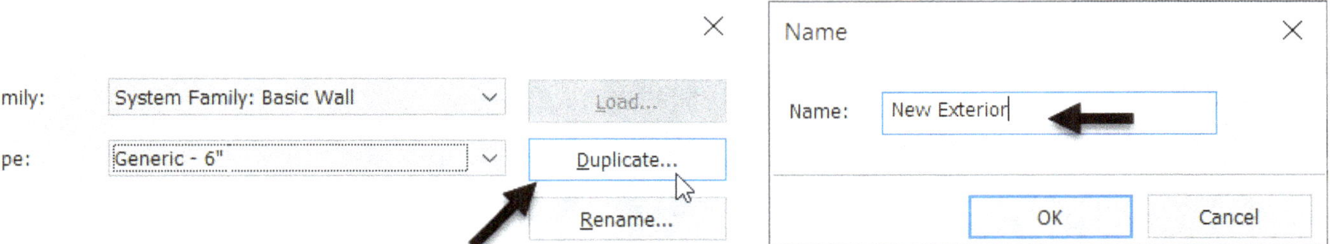

- Click the **Edit** button next to the **Structure** parameter; the **Edit Assembly** dialog appears. Notice that there is only one layer called **Structure [1]** in the table.
- Click in the **Material** column of the **Structure[1]** layer. Next, click the **Browse** button to display the **Material Browser** dialog.

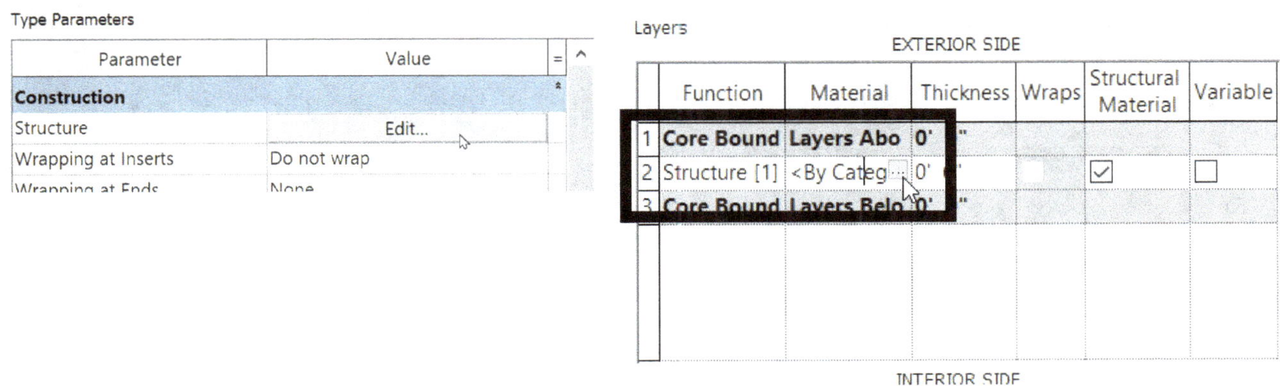

- Type **CMU** in the search box, and then select the **Concrete Masonry Units** material from the search results. Next, click **OK**.

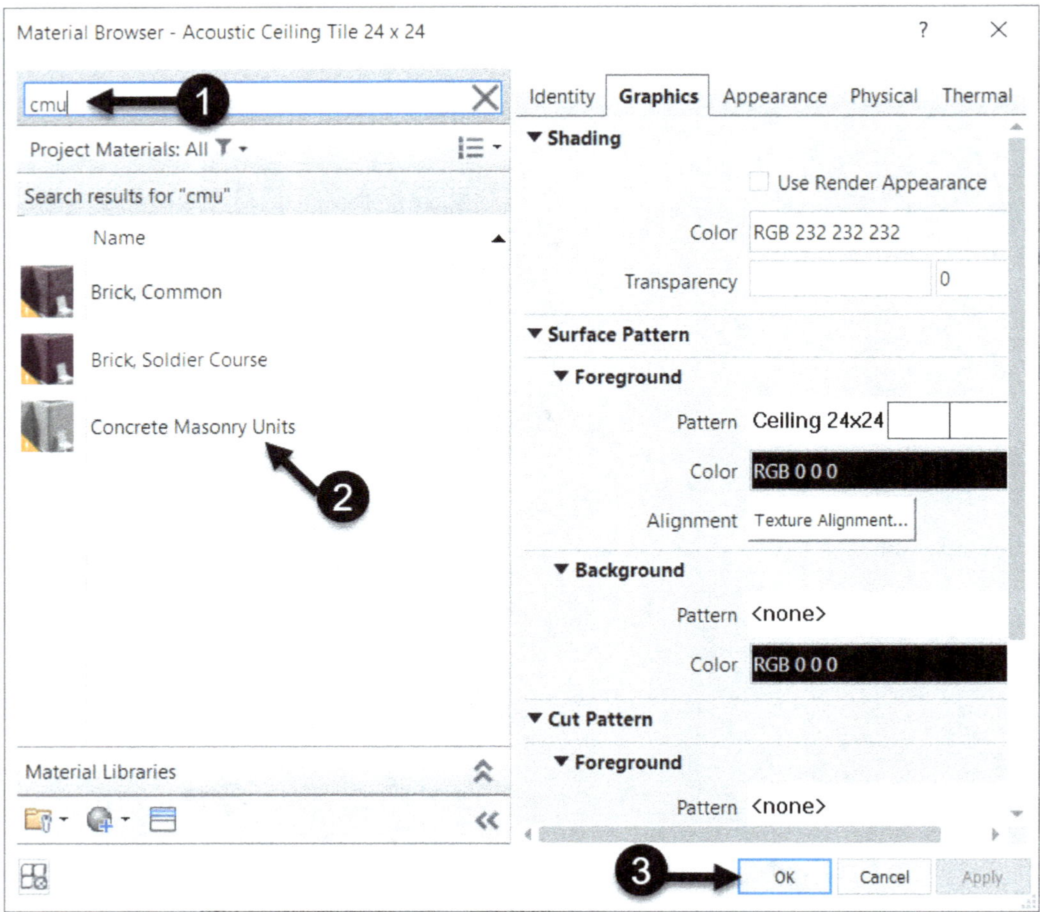

Next, you need to add the insulation layer to the wall.

- Click the **Insert** button in the **Layers** section; a new layer is added between the core boundaries. You need to move the newly added layer outside the core boundaries.
- Select the newly added layer and click the **Up** button.
- Click in the **Function** column of the newly created layer, and then select **Thermal/Air Layer** from the drop-down.

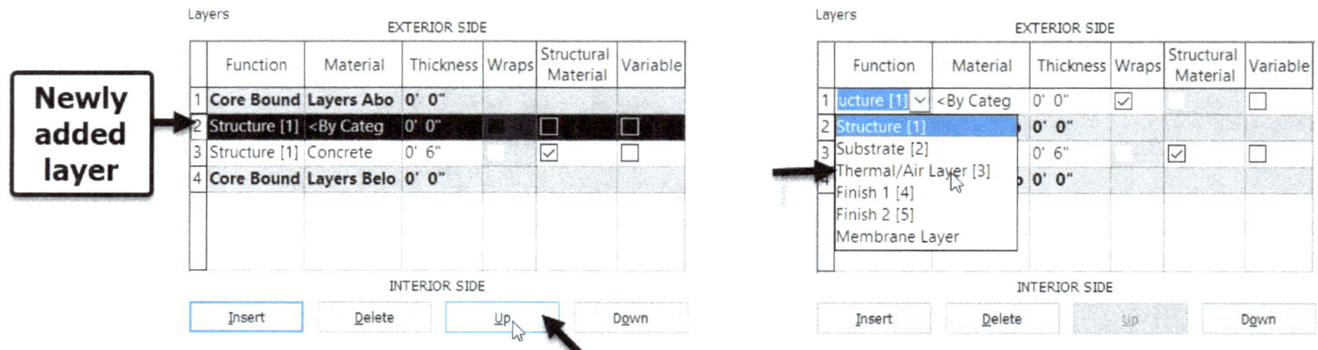

- Type **1"** in the **Thickness** column of the **Thermal/Air Layer**.
- Click in the **Material** column of the **Thermal/Air** layer. Next, click the **Browse** ⋯button to display the **Material Browser** dialog.
- Type **insulation** in the search box of the **Material Browser** dialog, and then select the **EIFS, Exterior Insulation**

material. Next, click **OK**.

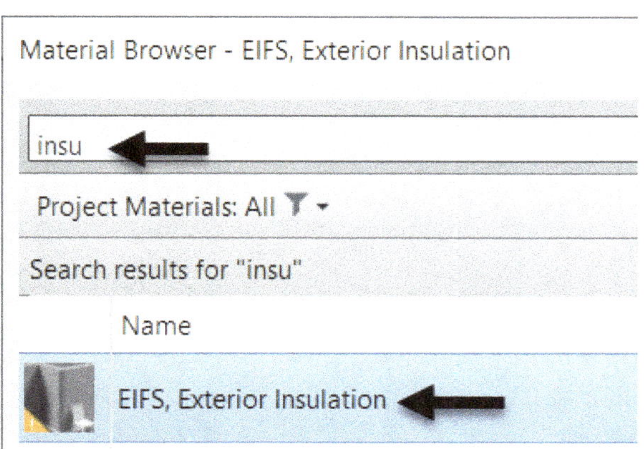

- Click the **Insert** button twice to add two more layers.
- Click in the **Function** column of the newly created layers, and then select **Finish 1** and **Finish 2** from the drop-downs.

Layers

	Function
1	Finish 1 [4]
2	Finish 2 [5]
3	Thermal/Air Layer [3]
4	**Core Boundary**
5	Structure [1]
6	**Core Boundary**

- Select the **Finish 2[5]** layer and click the **Down** button until the layer is moved to the bottom below the **Core Boundary**.

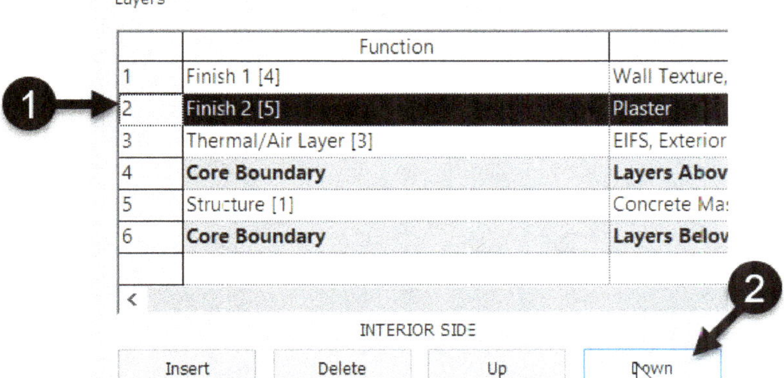
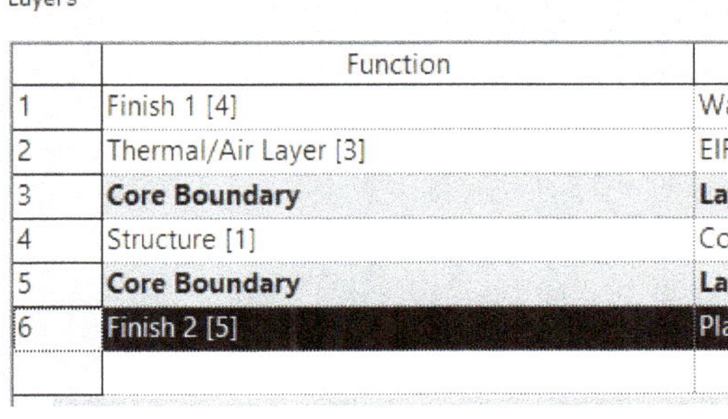

- Click in the **Material** column of the **Finish 1[4]** layer. Next, click the **Browse** ⋯button to display the **Material Browser** dialog.
- Expand the **Material Libraries** panel by clicking the arrows pointing in the upward direction.
- On the **Material Libraries** panel, expand **Home > AEC Materials > Plaster**.

- Scroll to the **Wall Texture, Stucco** material and click the **Adds material to document** icon.

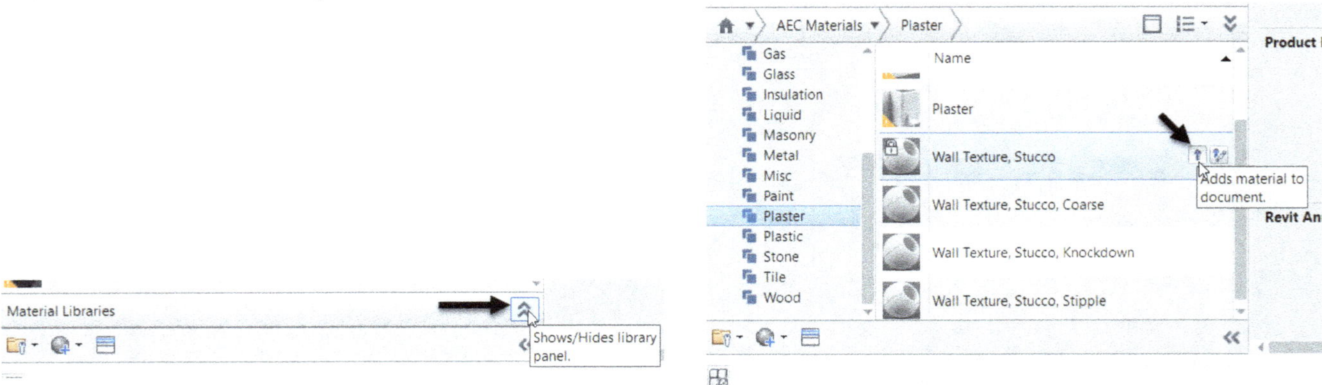

- Likewise, add the **Plaster** material to the document.

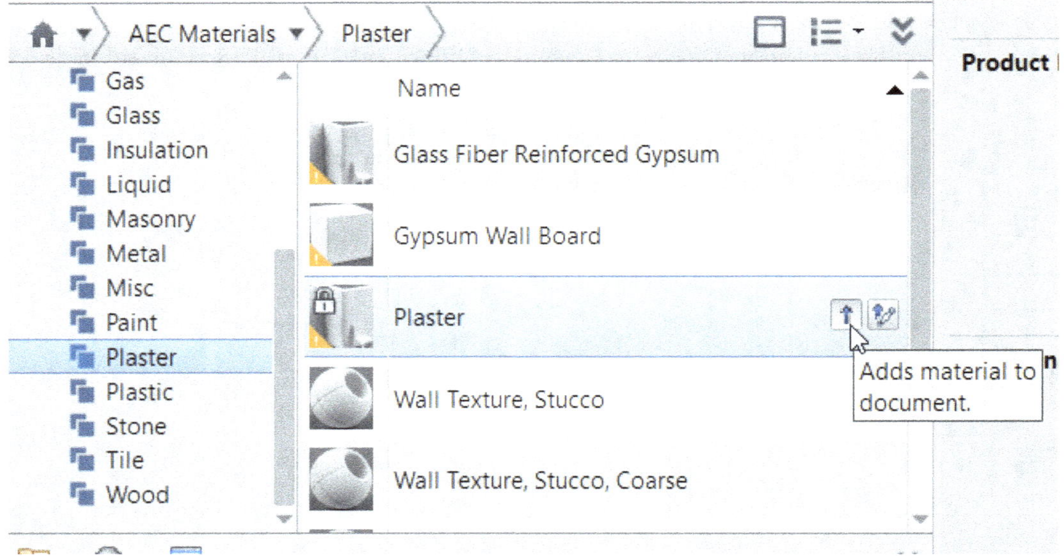

- Type **stucco** in the search bar, and then select the **Wall Texture, Stuccco** from the search results. Next, click **OK**.

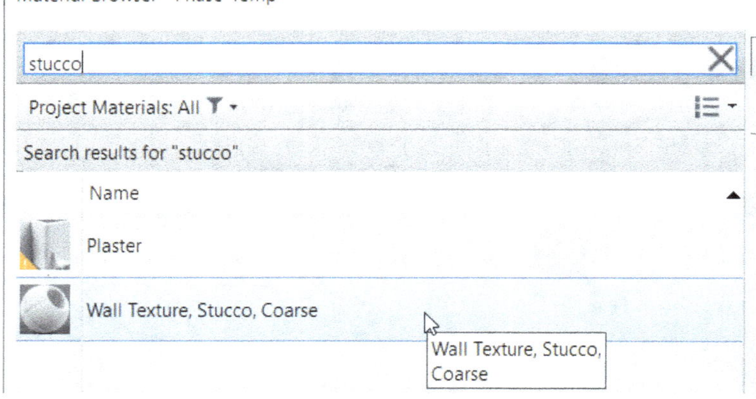

- Likewise, change the material of the **Finish 2 [5]** layer to **Plaster**.
- Change the **Thickness** values of the **Finish 1[4]** and **Finish 2[5]** layers to **0' 0 3/8"**. Next, click **OK**.

Layers

	Function	Material	Thickness
1	Finish 1 [4]	Wall Texture, Stucco, Coar	0' 0 3/8"
2	Thermal/Air Layer [3]	EIFS, Exterior Insulation	0' 1"
3	**Core Boundary**	**Layers Above Wrap**	**0' 0"**
4	Structure [1]	Concrete Masonry Units	0' 6"
5	**Core Boundary**	**Layers Below Wrap**	**0' 0"**
6	Finish 2 [5]	Plaster	0' 0 3/8"

- Select **Type > New Exterior** on the **Type Properties** dialog and click **OK**.

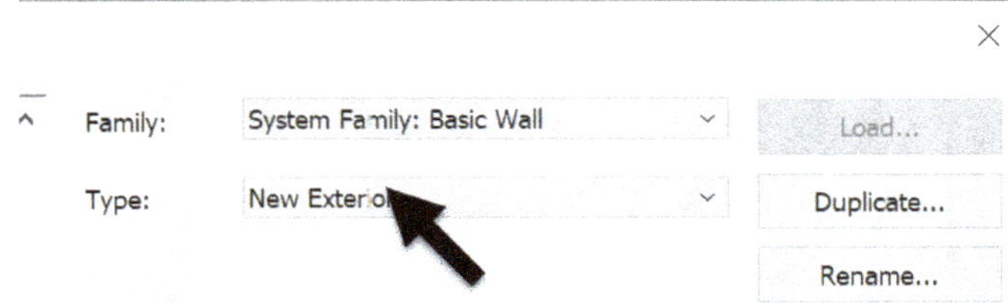

Next, you need to specify the height of the wall.

- On the Options Bar, select **Height** from first drop-down. Next, select **TOP** from next drop-down.
- Select **Location Line > Core Face Exterior**, and then check the **Chain** option.

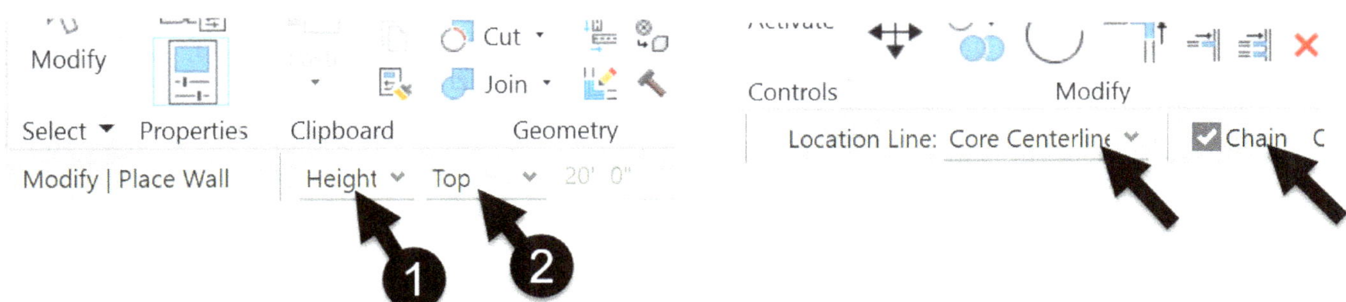

- Specify the start point somewhere near the top-right corner, as shown.

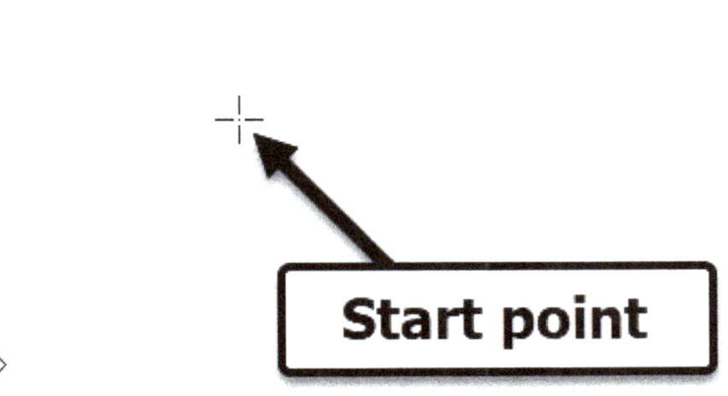

- Move the pointer horizontally toward right and type 15. Press ENTER to create a horizontal wall of ten feet length.
- Move the pointer vertically downward and type 6. Next, press ENTER to create a vertical wall.

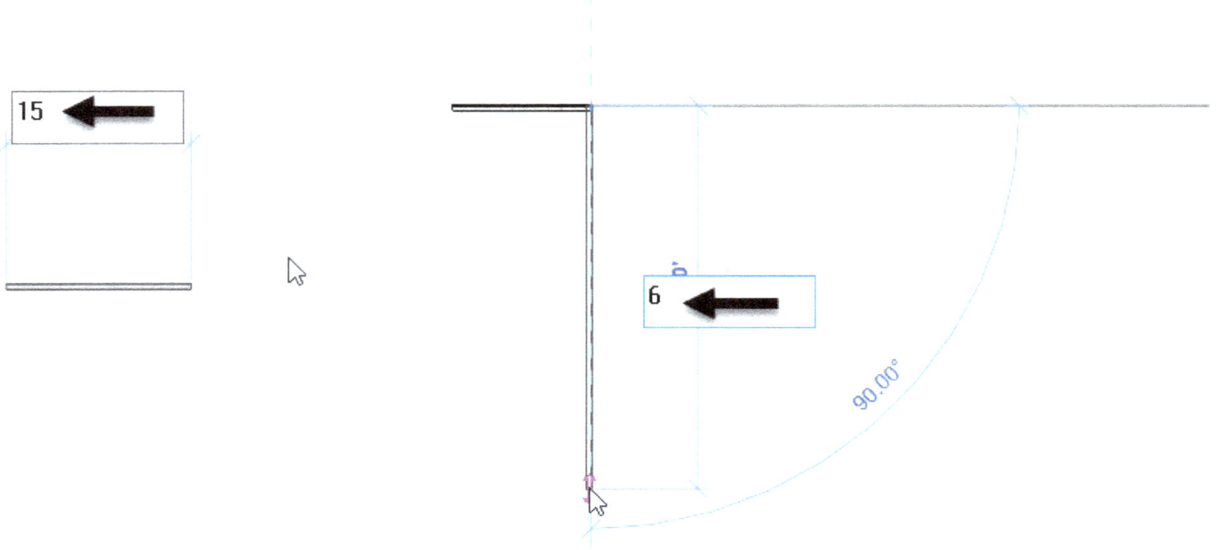

- Move the pointer horizontally toward right, type 52'6", and then press ENTER.

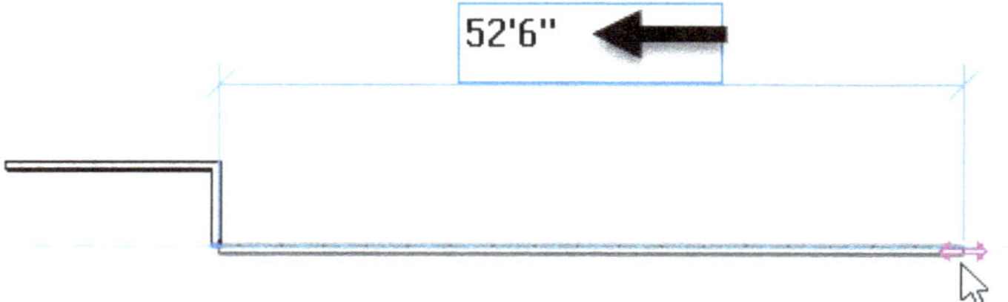

- Move the pointer vertically upward, type 9, and then press ENTER.

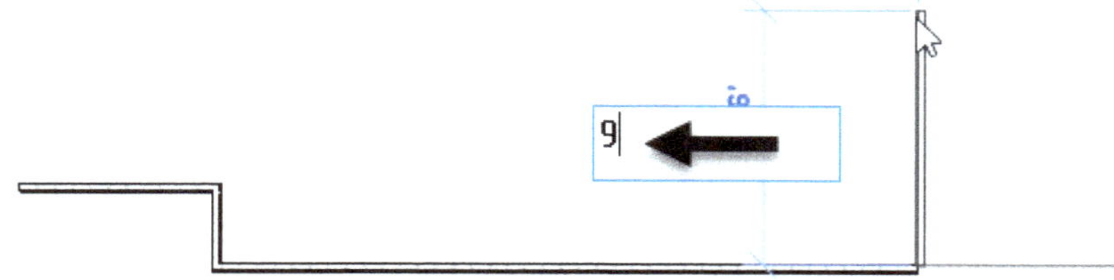

- Move the pointer horizontally toward right, type 18, and then press ENTER.

- Move the pointer vertically downward, type 64'6", and then press ENTER.

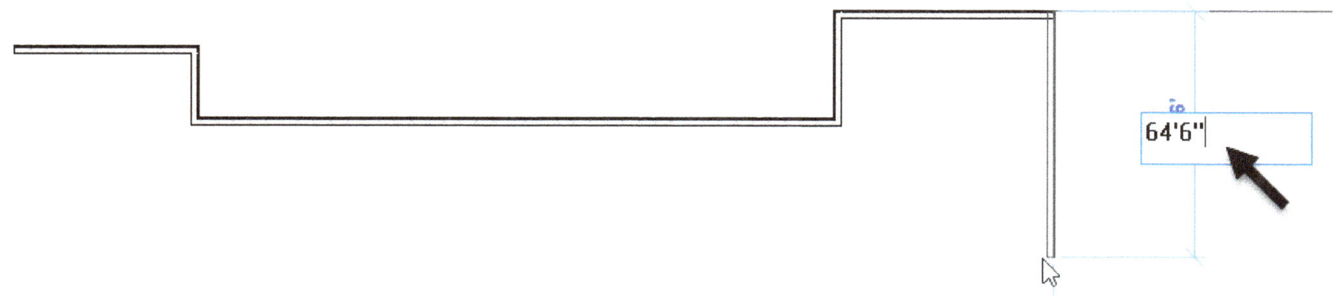

- Move the pointer horizontally toward left, type 27, and then press ENTER.
- Move the pointer vertically upward, type 31'5", and then press ENTER.

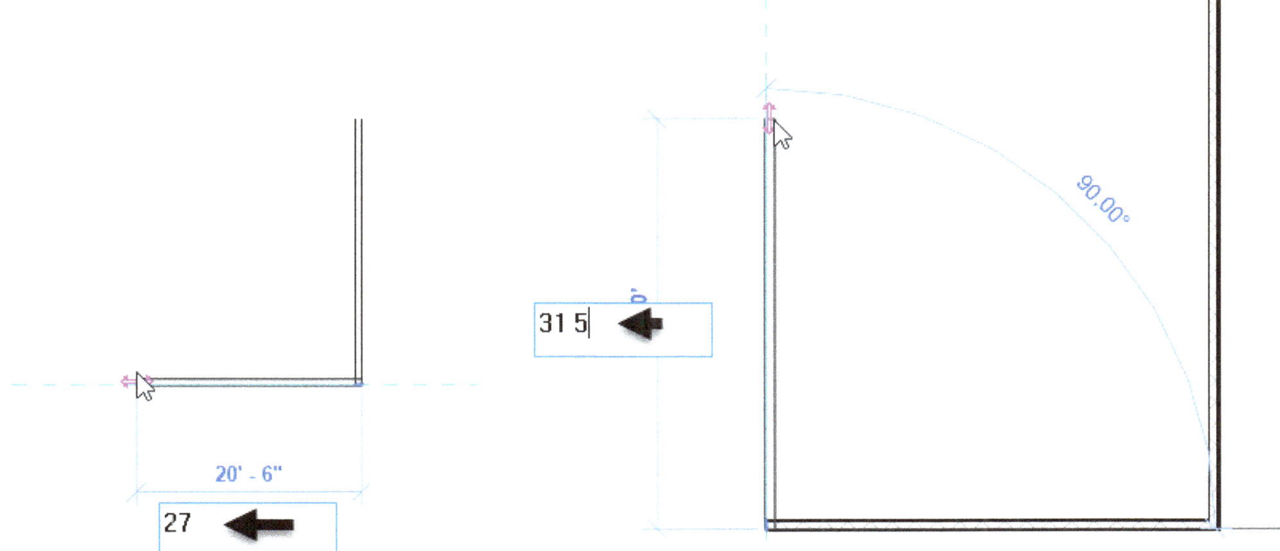

- Move the pointer horizontally toward left, type 43'6", and then press ENTER.

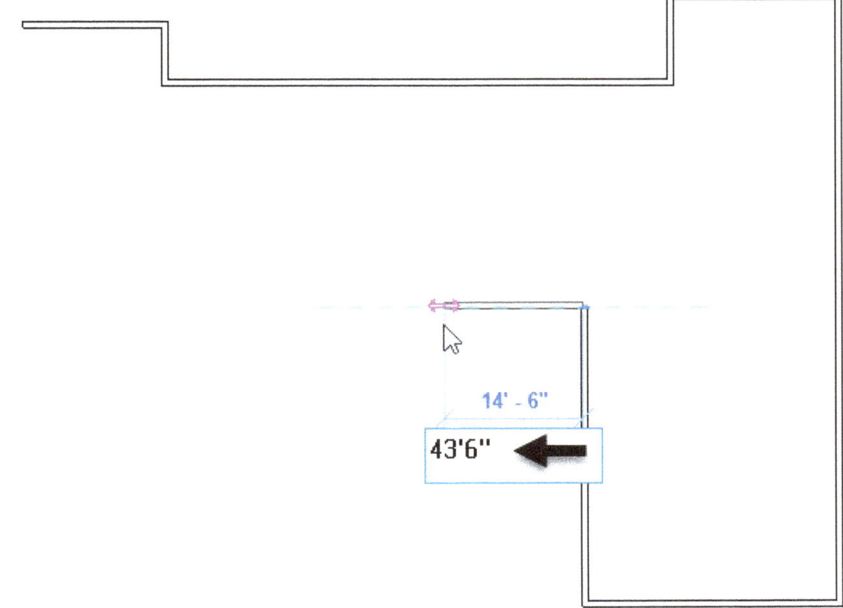

- Move the pointer vertically upward, type 2, and then press ENTER.

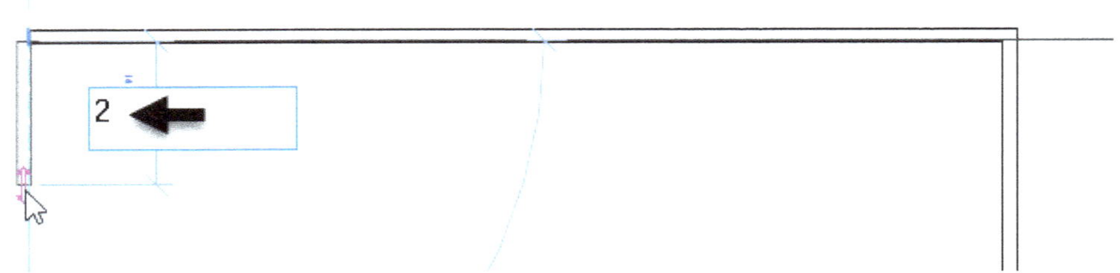

- Move the pointer horizontally toward left and notice the extension line from the start point of the first wall. Next, click to create the horizontal line.
- Move the pointer vertically upward and select the start point of the first wall.

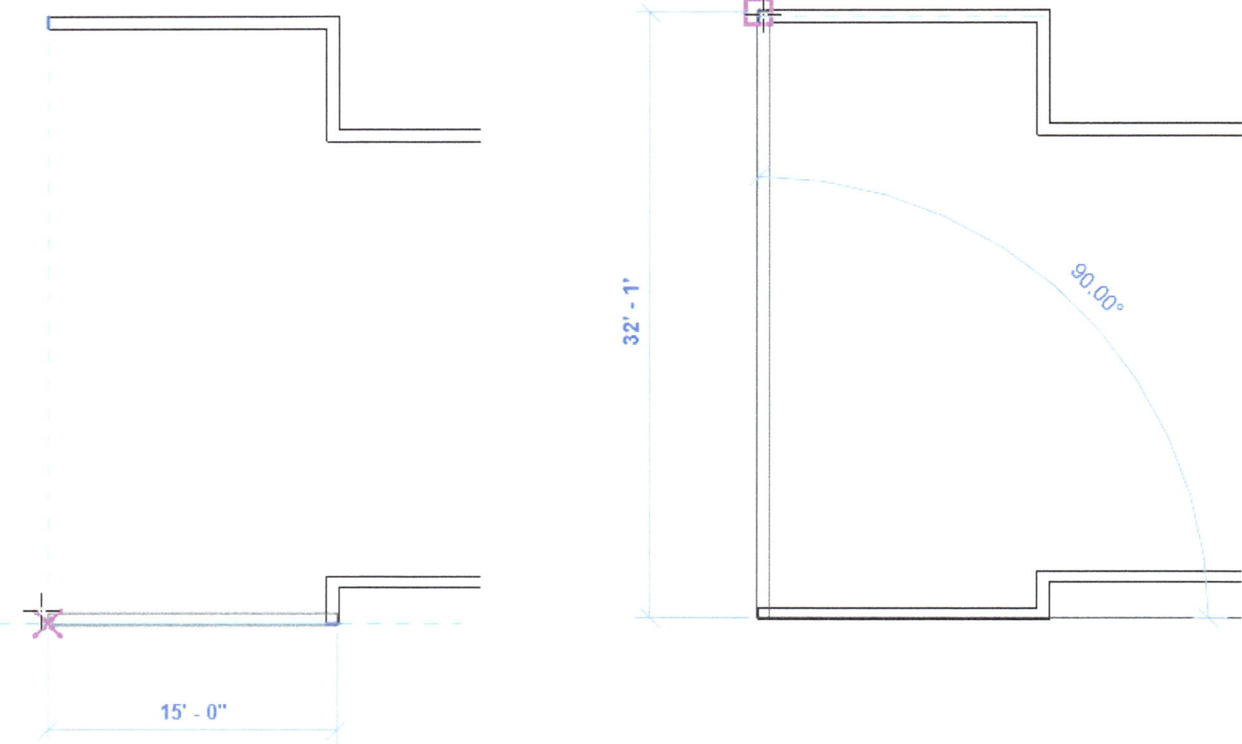

Notice that a closed corner is created.

- Click the **Default 3D View** icon on the Quick Access Toolbar; the 3D view of the model is displayed.

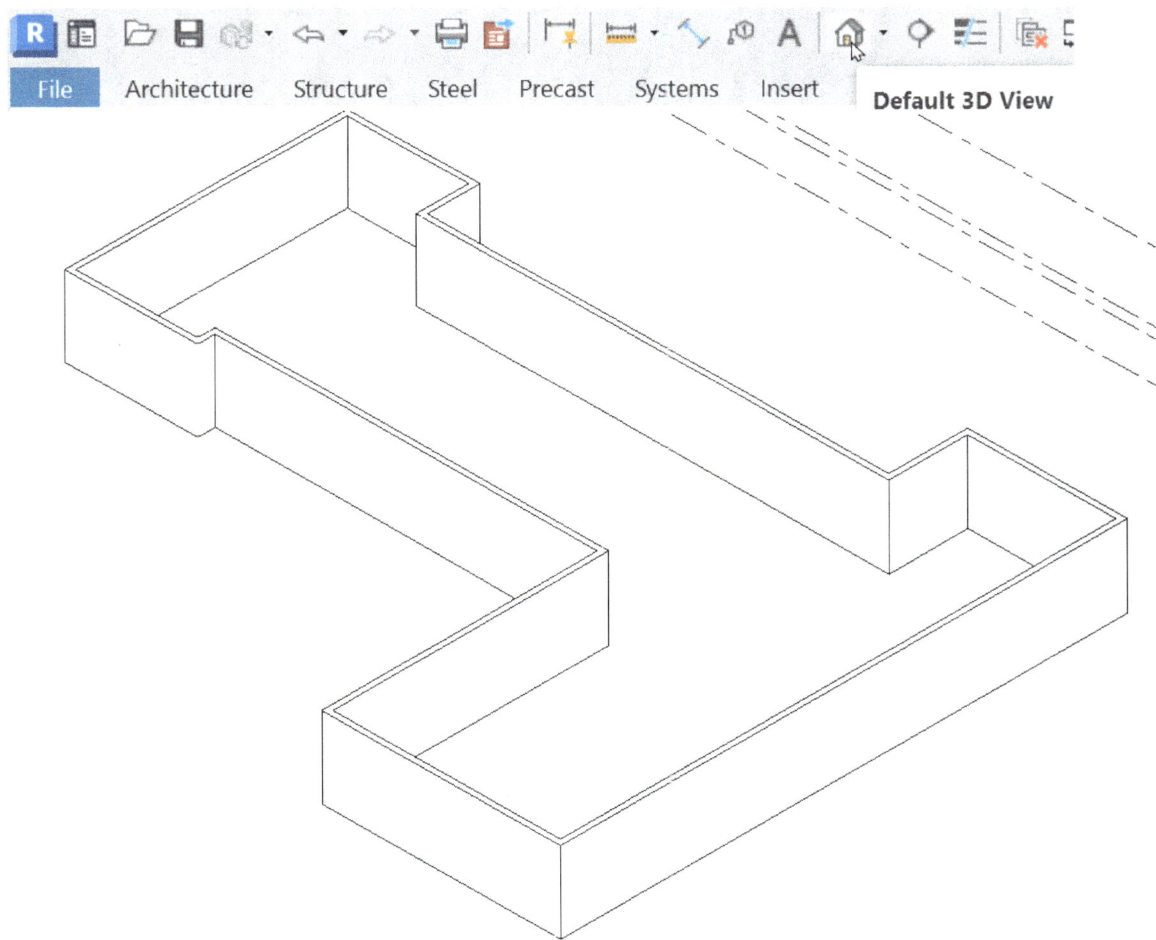

Creating Interior walls

- Double-click on the **First Floor** under the **Floor Plans** node in the **Project Browser**.

- On the ribbon, click **Architecture** tab > **Build** panel > **Wall** drop-down > **Wall Architectural**.
- On the **Properties** palette, select **Interior – 4 7/8" Partition (1-hr)** wall from the **Basic Wall** drop-down.

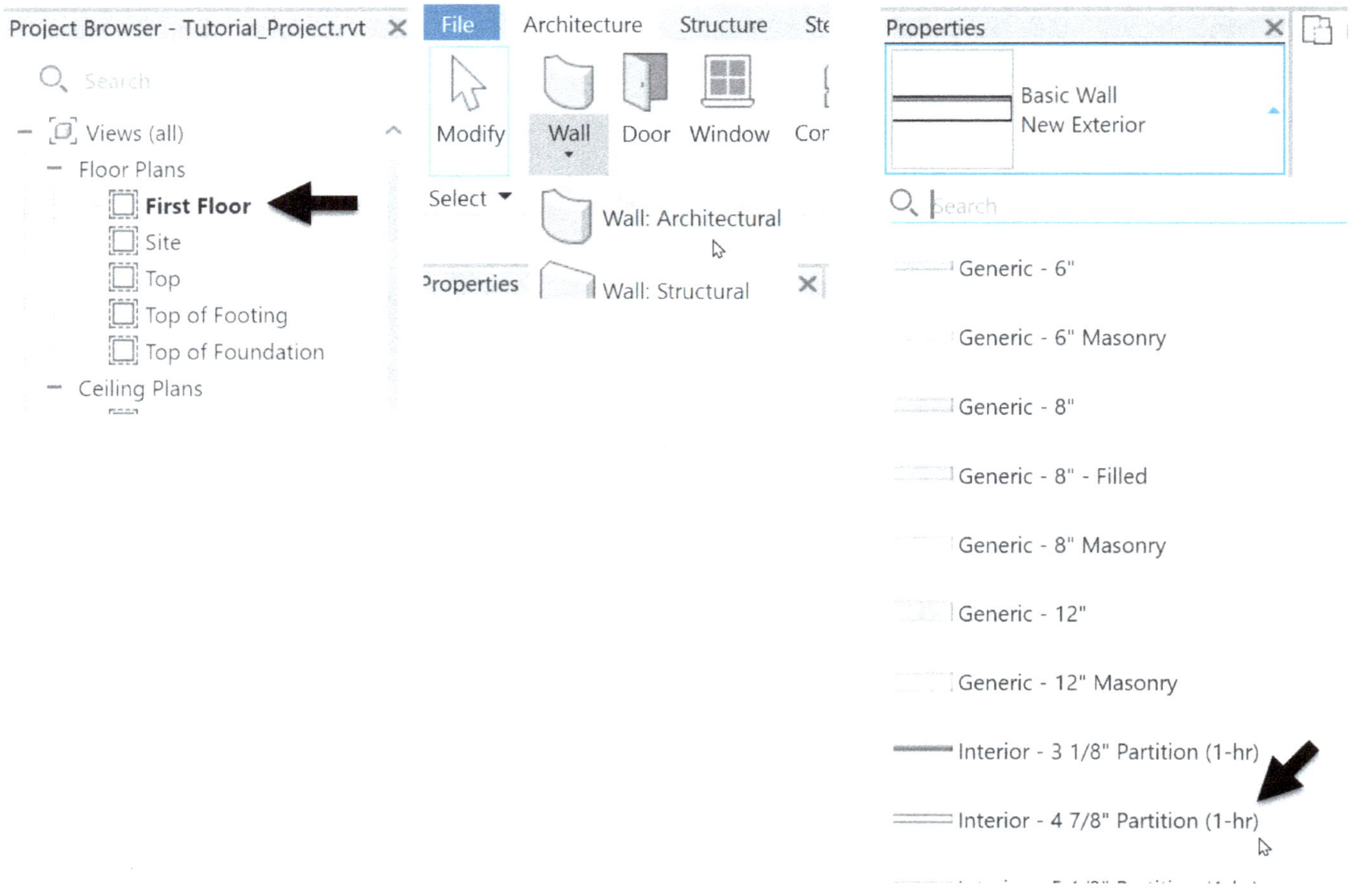

- On the Options Bar, select **Height** from the first drop-down. Next, select **TOP** from the next drop-down.
- Select **Location Line > Finish Face: Interior**, and then check the **Chain** option.

- Place the pointer in the left portion of the floor plan, and then roll the mouse wheel in the forward direction; the left portion of the floor plan is zoomed-in.
- Select the inner corner point of the walls, as shown.
- Move the pointer downward and select the other corner point, as shown.
- Right-click and select **Cancel**; the interior wall is merged with the exterior walls.

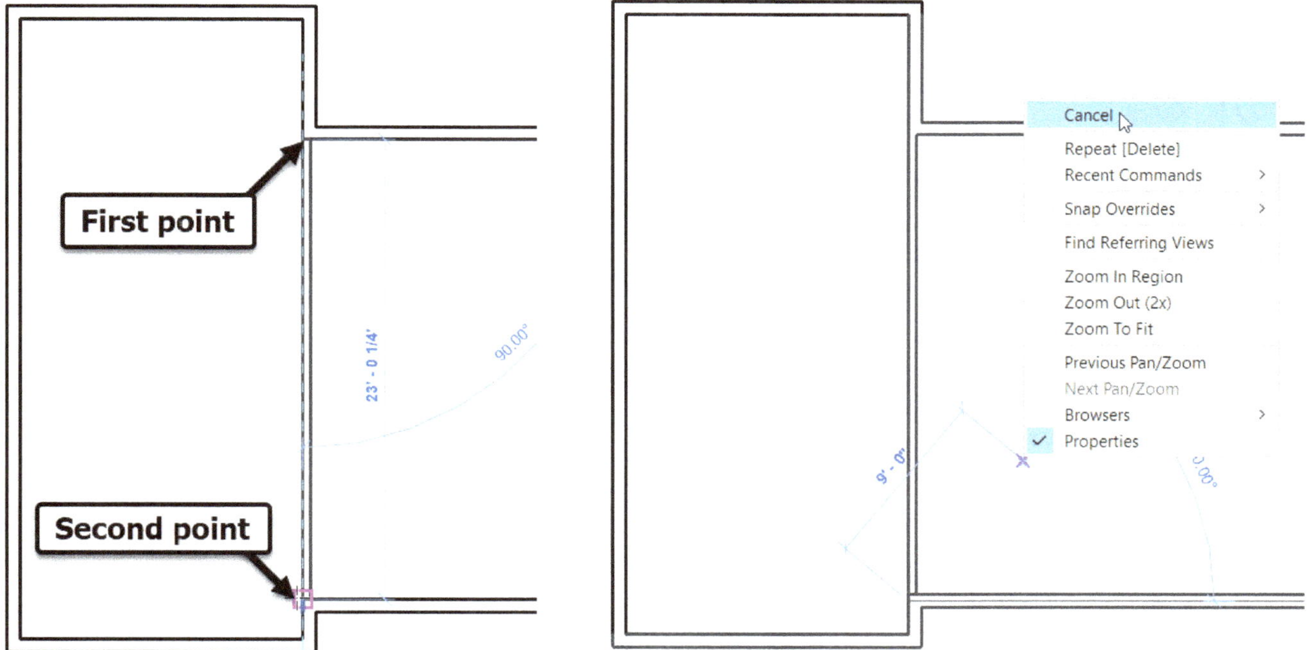

- Place the pointer near the intersection of the horizontal and vertical walls at the top-left corner, as shown. Notice that a dashed vertical line is displayed.
- Move the pointer along the dashed vertical line. Next, type 19 and press ENTER; the start point of the bathroom wall is specified.

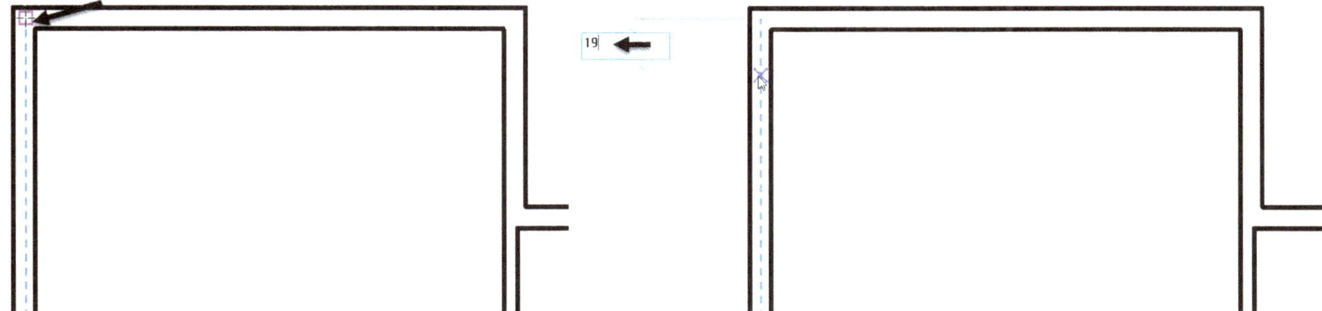

- Move the pointer horizontally toward right, type 23 and press ENTER.
- Move the pointer vertically upward and click on the exterior wall, as shown. Next, press ESC.

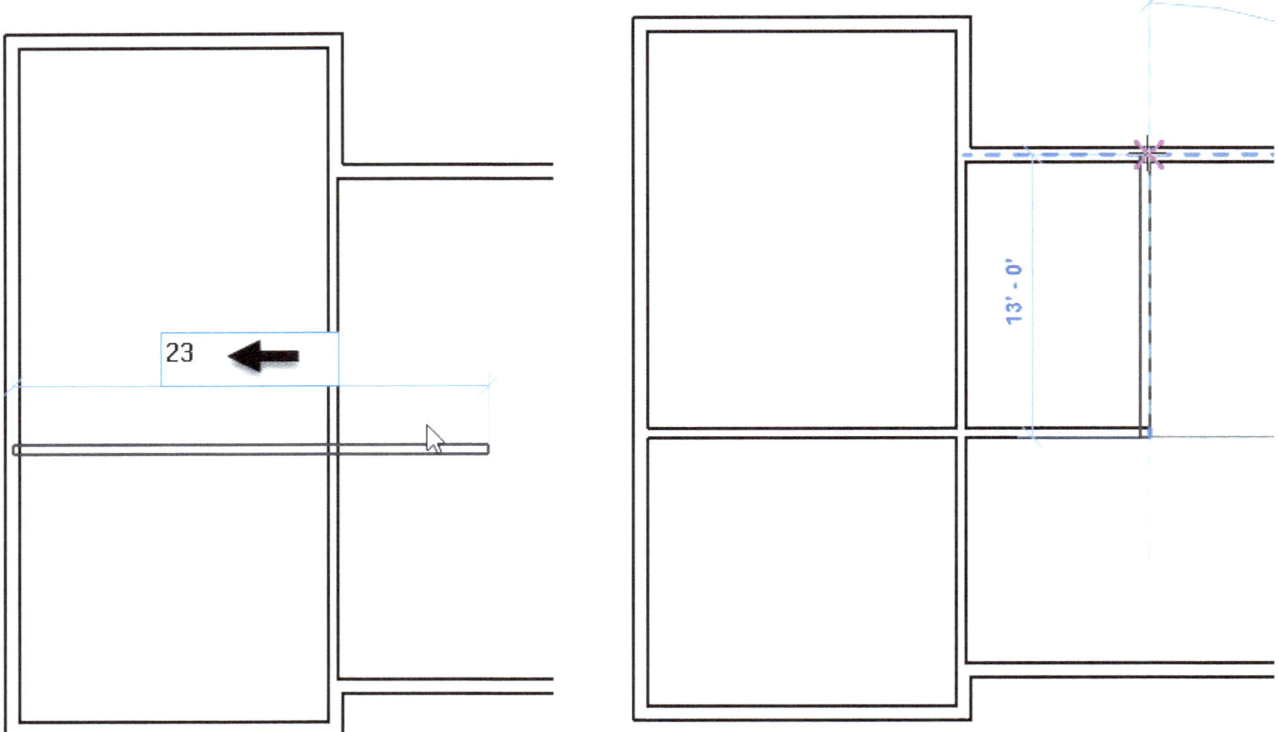

- On the ribbon, click **Modify > Modify > Offset**. Next, type **8** in the **Offset** box of the Options Bar.
- Click on the left edge of the interior wall, as shown. A new wall is created offset to the selected wall.

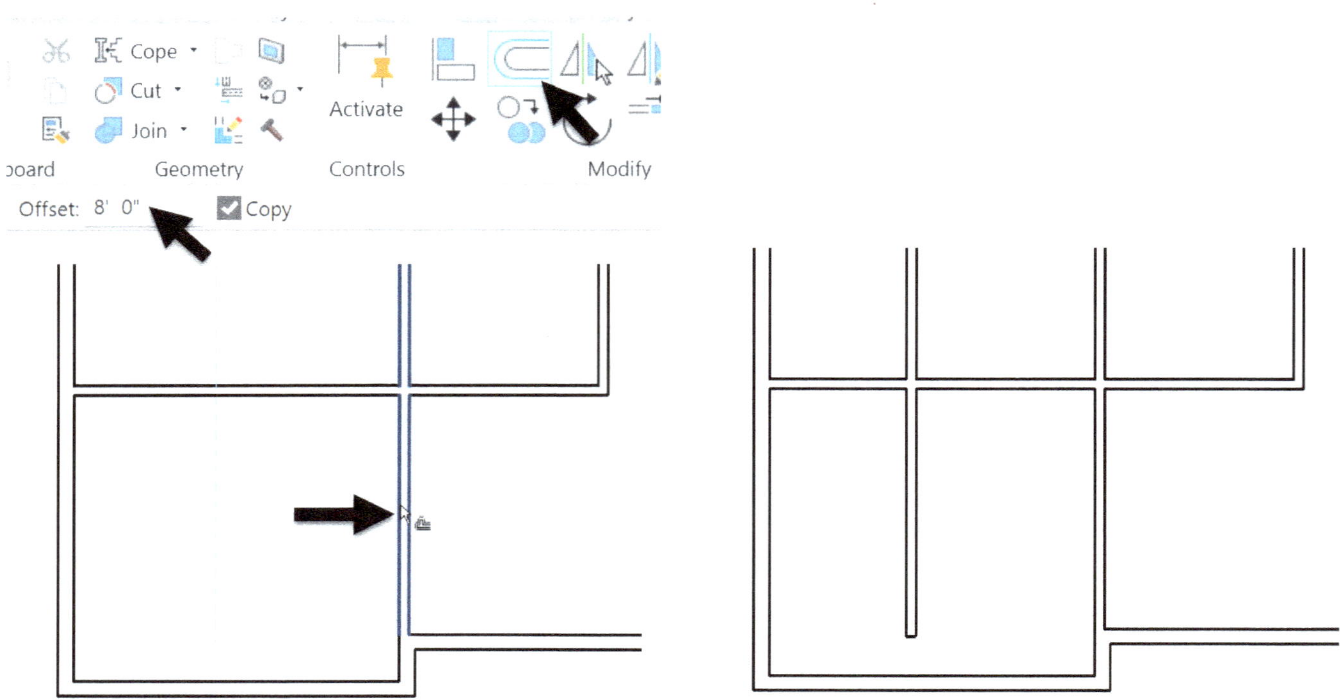

- Type **6** in the **Offset** box available on the Options Bar. Next, select the inner edge of the horizontal wall, as shown.

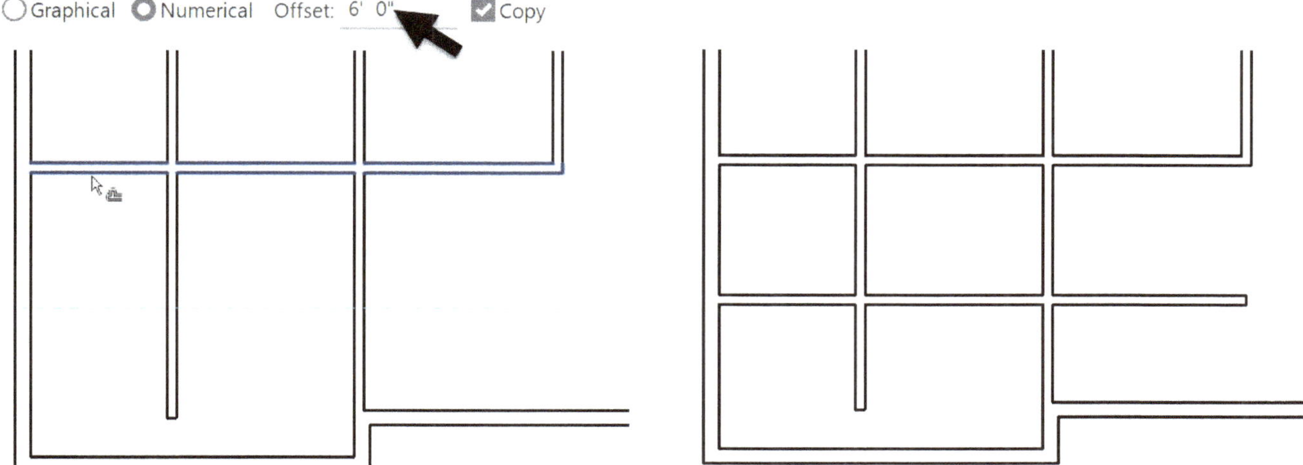

- On the ribbon, click **Modify** tab > **Modify** panel > **Trim/Extend to Corner (TR)**.
- Select the portion of the two walls intersecting with each other.

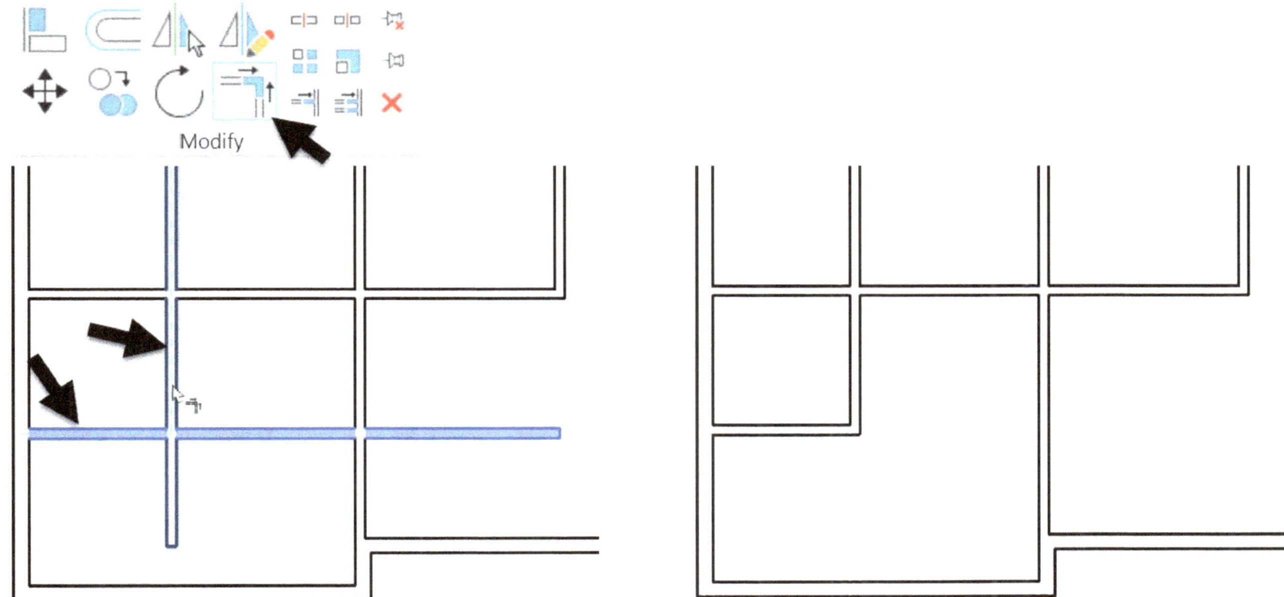

- On the ribbon, click **Modify** tab > **Modify** panel > **Trim/Extend Single Element** .
- Select the horizontal edge of the wall, as shown. The trimming boundary is defined.
- Select the lower portion of the vertical wall; the vertical wall is trimmed up to the selected edge.

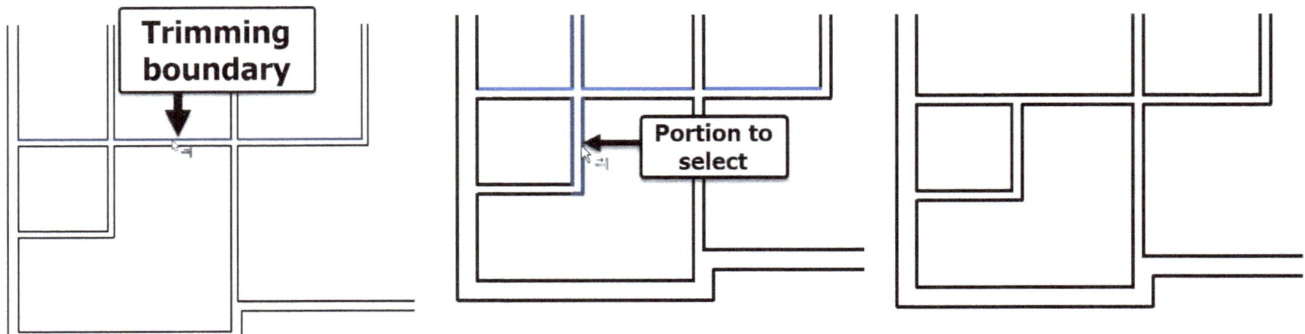

- On the ribbon, click **Modify > Modify > Offset** . Next, type **27** in the **Offset** box of the Options Bar.
- Click on the right edge of the interior wall, as shown. A new wall is created offset to the selected wall.

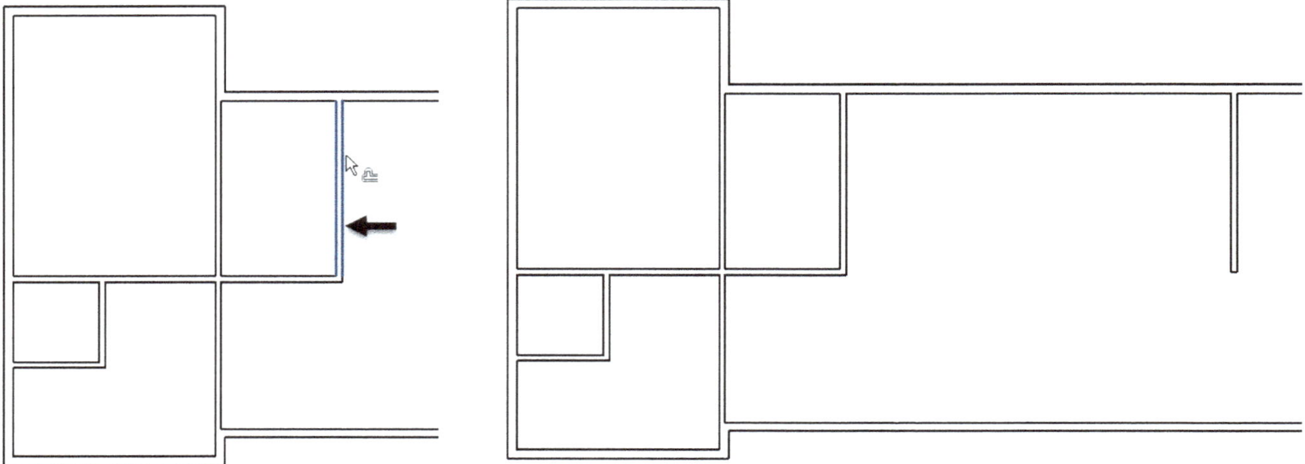

- On the ribbon, click **Modify** tab > **Modify** panel > **Trim/Extend Single Element** .
- Select the horizontal edge of the exterior wall, as shown. The extension boundary is defined.
- Select the newly created vertical wall; the vertical wall is extended up to the select edge.

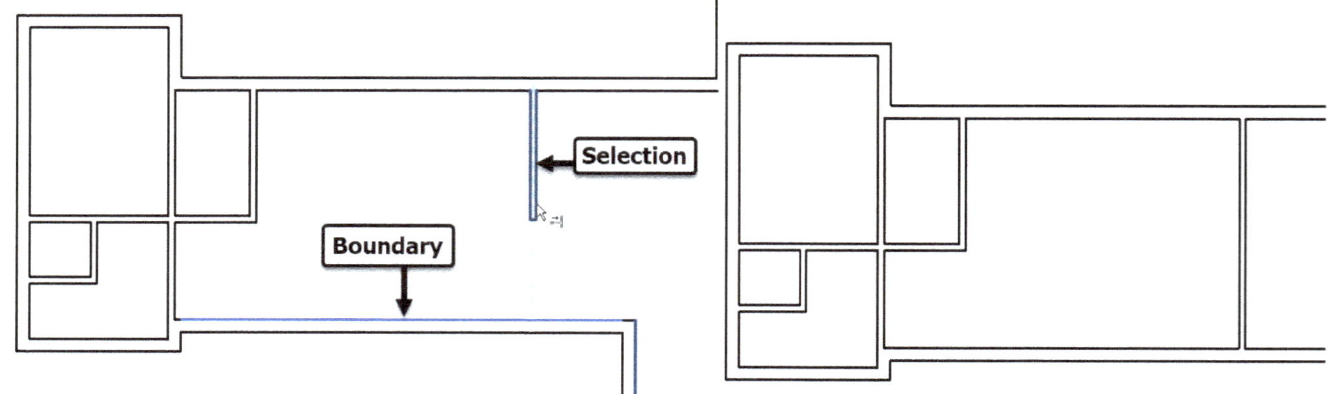

- On the ribbon, click **Architecture** tab > **Build** panel > **Wall** drop-down > **Wall: Architectural** .
- On the **Properties** palette, select **Interior – 4 7/8" Partition (1-hr)** wall from the **Basic Wall** drop-down.

- Place the pointer on the inner corner of the vertical wall, shown.
- Move the pointer along the inner vertical edge in the upward direction. Next, type 24 and press ENTER; the start point of the wall is specified.
- Move the pointer horizontally toward right, type 18 and press ENTER.

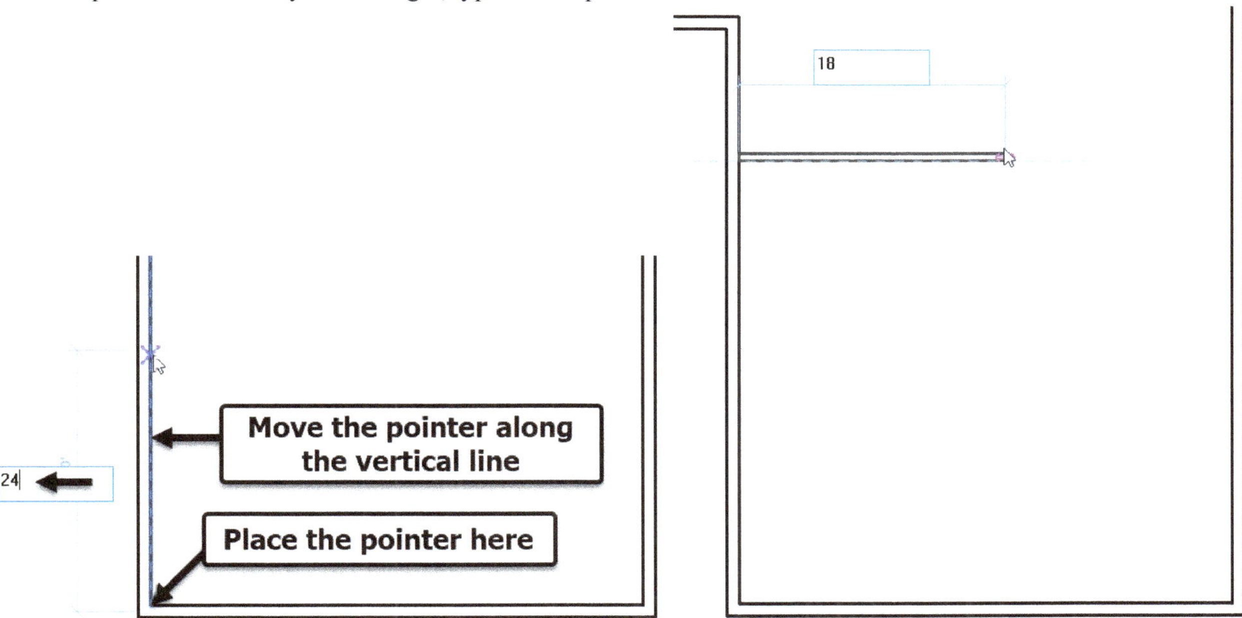

- Move the pointer vertically upward, type 3, and then press ENTER.
- Move the pointer horizontally toward right and click on the exterior wall, as shown.

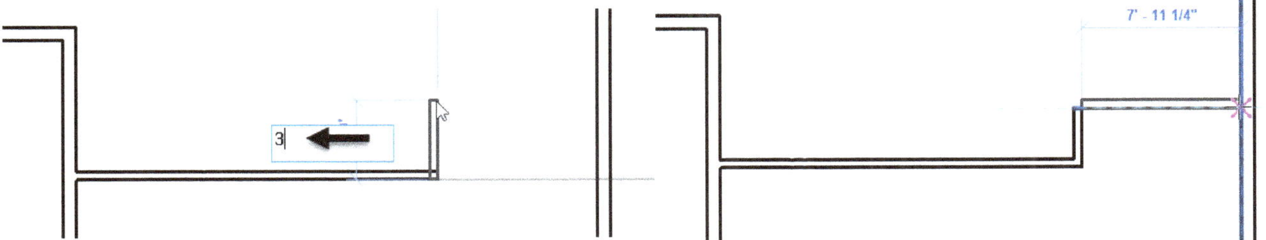

- On the ribbon, click **Modify > Modify > Offset**. Next, type **5' 9"** in the **Offset** box of the Options Bar.

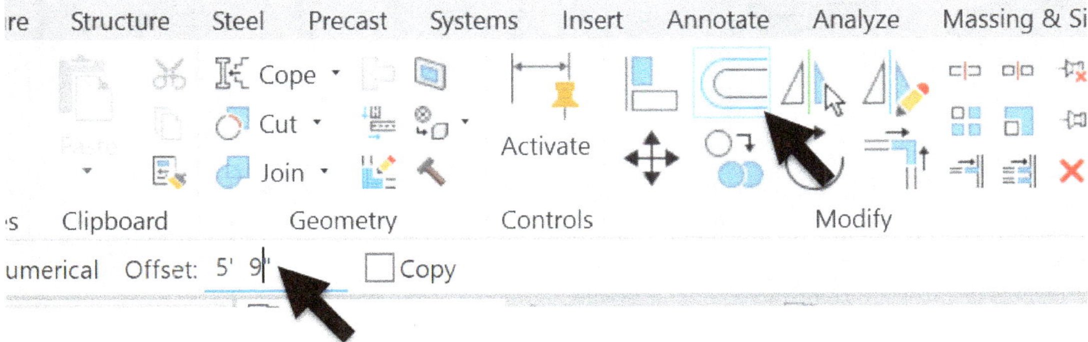

- Click on the left edge of the interior wall, as shown. A new wall is created offset to the selected wall.

- On the ribbon, click **Modify** tab > **Modify** panel > **Trim/Extend Single Element** .
- Select the horizontal edge of the exterior wall, as shown. The extension boundary is defined.
- Select the newly created vertical wall; the vertical wall is extended up to the selected edge.

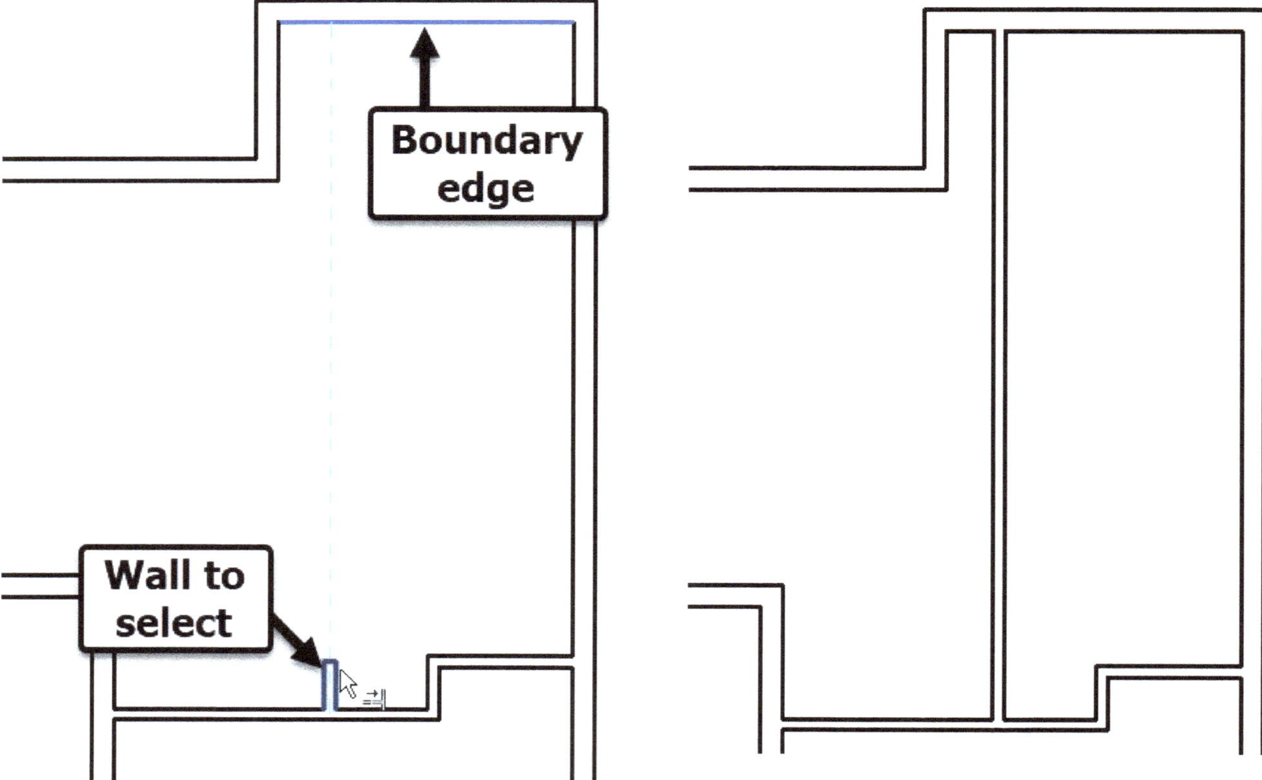

- On the ribbon, click **Architecture** tab > **Build** panel > **Wall** drop-down > **Wall Architectural** .
- On the **Properties** palette, select **Interior – 4 7/8" Partition (1-hr)** wall from the **Basic Wall** drop-down.
- Select the corner point of the exterior wall, as shown.
- Move the pointer horizontally toward right and click on the wall, as shown. Next, press ESC.

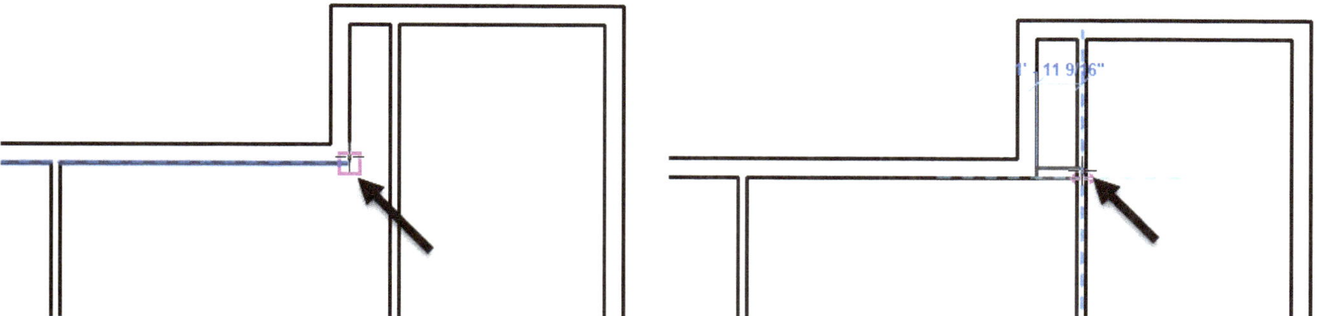

- Select the corner point of the exterior wall, as shown.
- Move the pointer vertically upward, type 2'3".
- Move the pointer horizontally toward right and click on the wall, as shown. Next, press ESC.

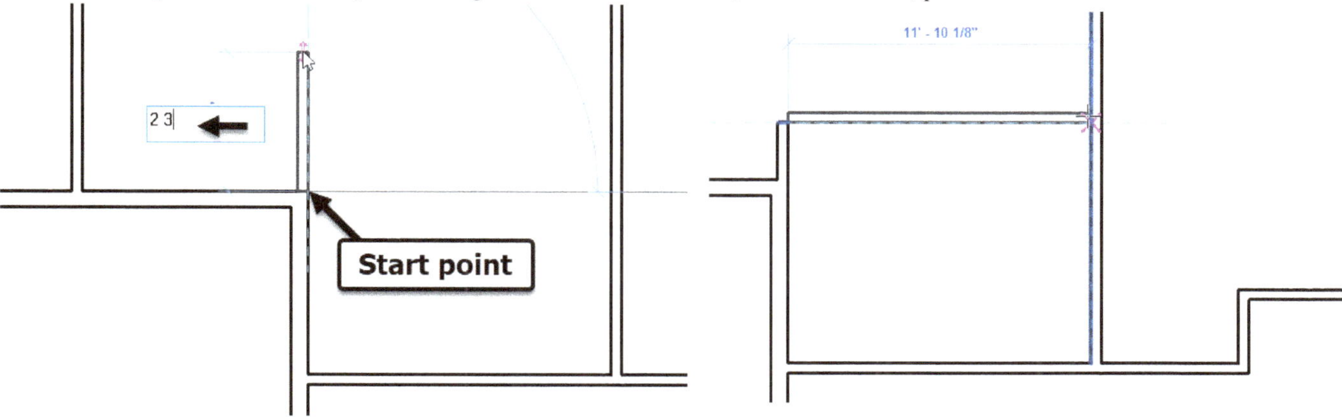

- On the ribbon, click **Architecture** tab > **Build** panel > **Wall** drop-down > **Wall Architectural**.
- On the **Properties** palette, select **Interior – 4 7/8" Partition (1-hr)** wall from the **Basic Wall** drop-down.
- Place the pointer on the inner corner of the wall, as shown.
- Move the pointer along the horizontal edge toward the right. Next, type 9' 6" and press ENTER; the start point of the wall is specified.

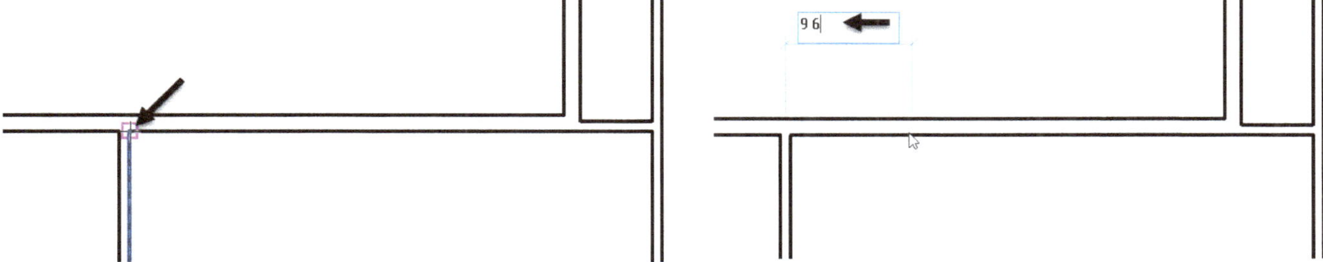

- Move the pointer vertically downward, type 15, and then press ENTER.
- Move the pointer horizontally toward right, type 6'3", and then press ENTER.

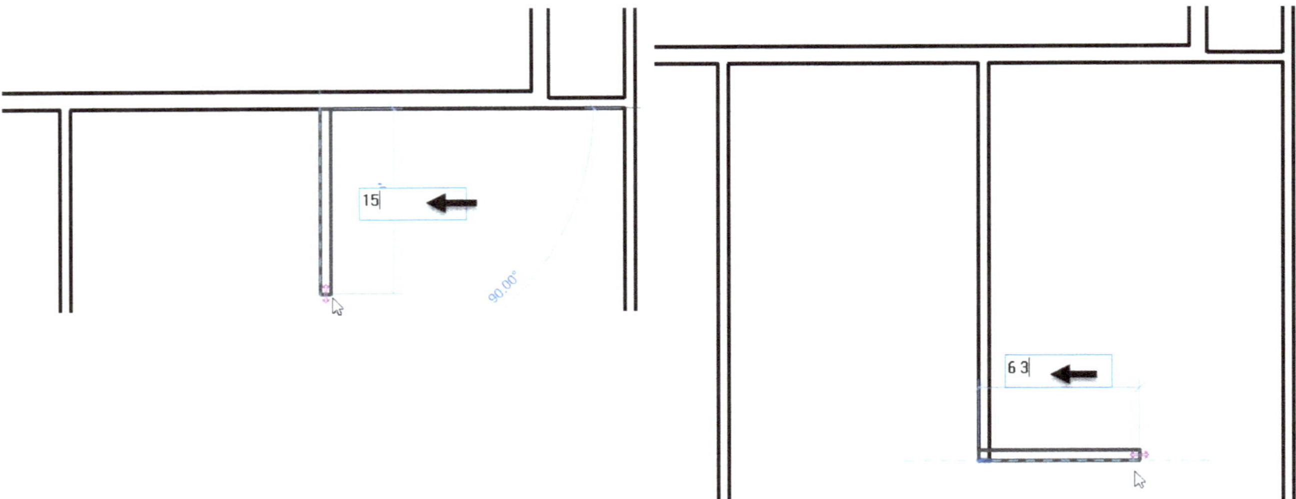

- Move the pointer vertically upward, type 8'4", and then press ENTER.
- Move the pointer horizontally toward right and click on the vertical wall. Next, press ESC.

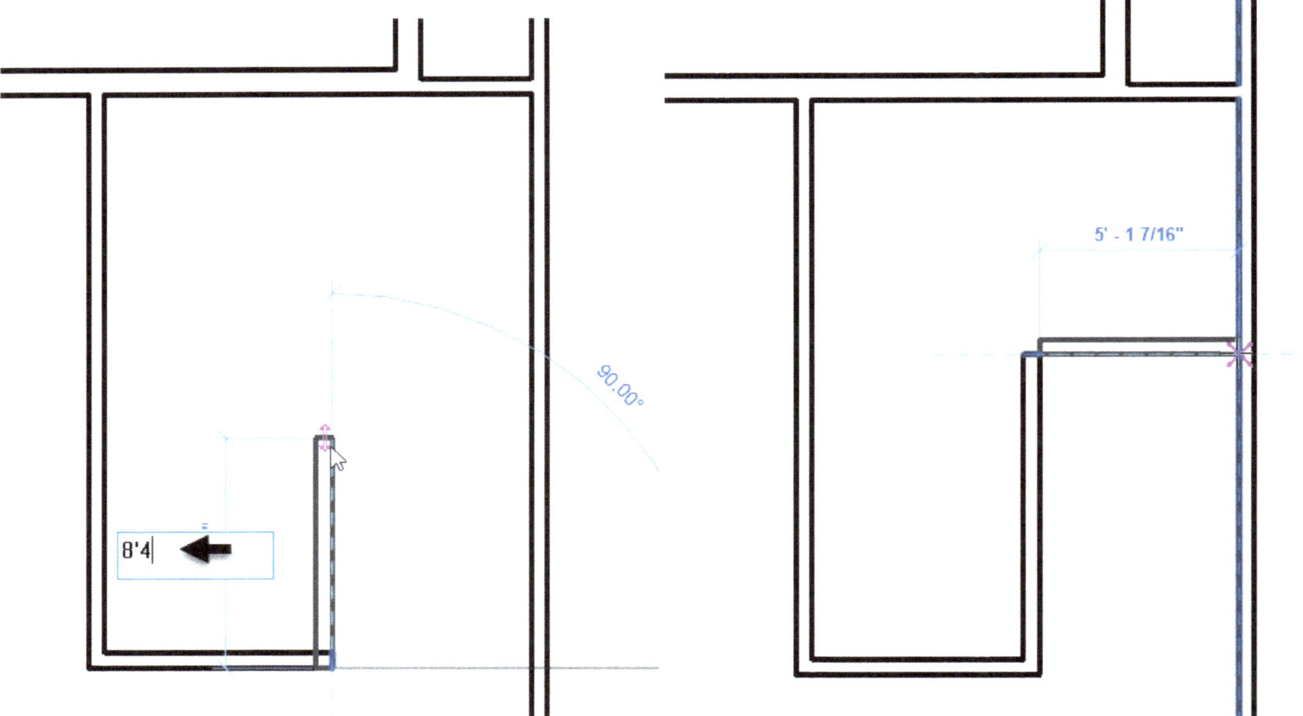

- On the ribbon, click **Architecture** tab > **Build** panel > **Wall** drop-down > **Wall Architectural**.
- On the **Properties** palette, select **Interior – 4 7/8" Partition (1-hr)** wall from the **Basic Wall** drop-down.
- Place the pointer on the inner corner of the exterior wall, as shown.
- Move the pointer along the vertical edge. Next, type 15' 3" and press ENTER; the start point of the wall is specified.

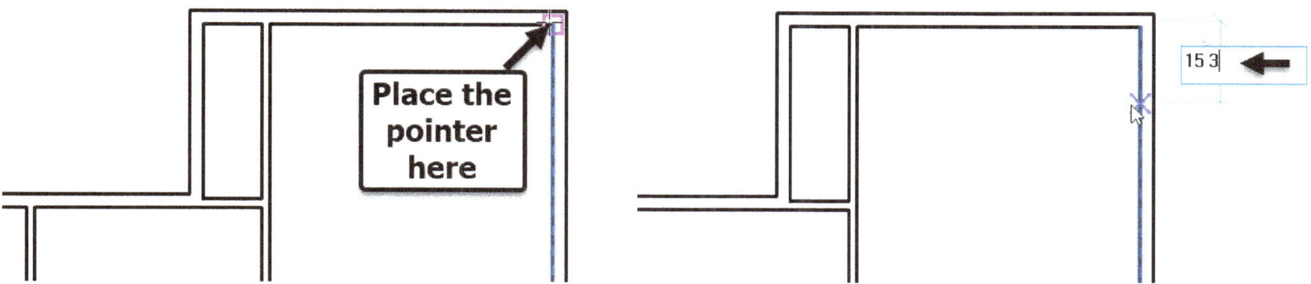

- Move the pointer toward left, type 9, and then press ENTER.
- Move the pointer downward, type 10, and then press ENTER.
- Move the pointer toward right and click on the exterior wall, as shown. Press ESC.

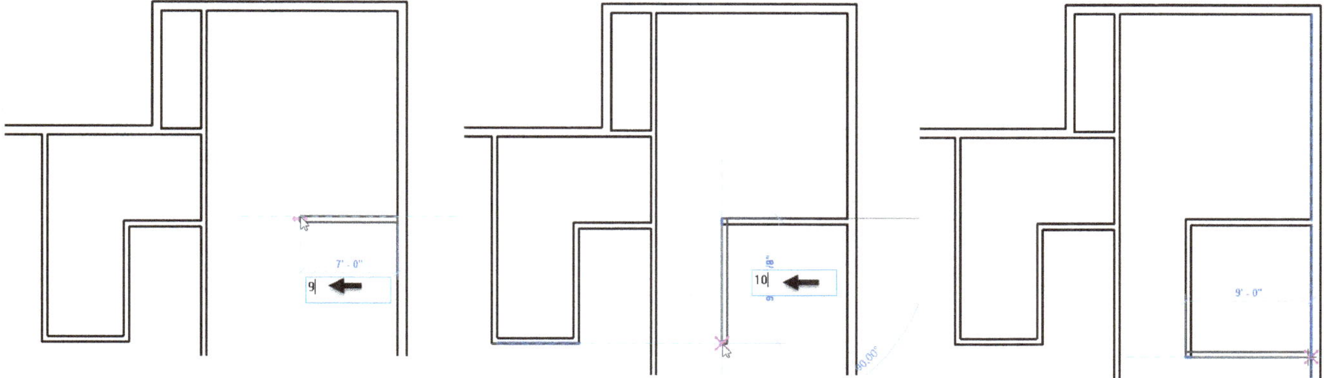

- On the ribbon, click **Modify > Modify > Offset**. Next, type **1' 9"** in the **Offset** box of the Options Bar.
- Click on the lower edge of the interior wall, as shown. A new wall is created offset to the selected wall.

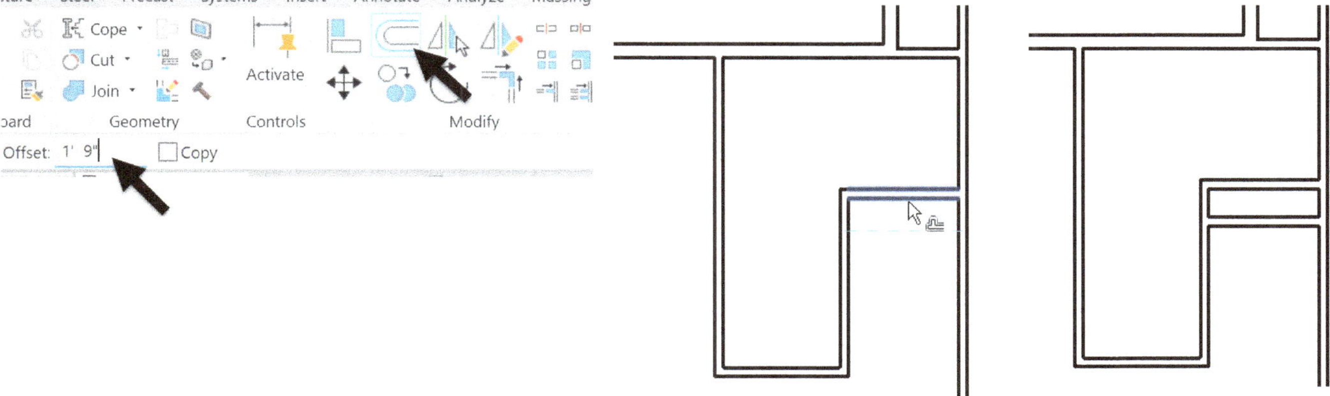

- On the ribbon, click **Architecture** tab > **Build** panel > **Wall** drop-down > **Wall Architectural**.
- On the **Properties** palette, select **Interior – 4 7/8" Partition (1-hr)** wall from the **Basic Wall** drop-down.
- Select the endpoint of the interior wall, as shown.
- Move the pointer toward left and click on the vertical wall, as shown. Next, press ESC.
- Select the endpoint of the interior wall, as shown.
- Move the pointer toward right and click on the vertical wall, as shown. Next, press ESC.

- On the ribbon, click **Modify > Modify > Offset**. Next, type **4** in the **Offset** box of the Options Bar.
- Click on the lower edge of the interior wall, as shown. A new wall is created offset to the selected wall.

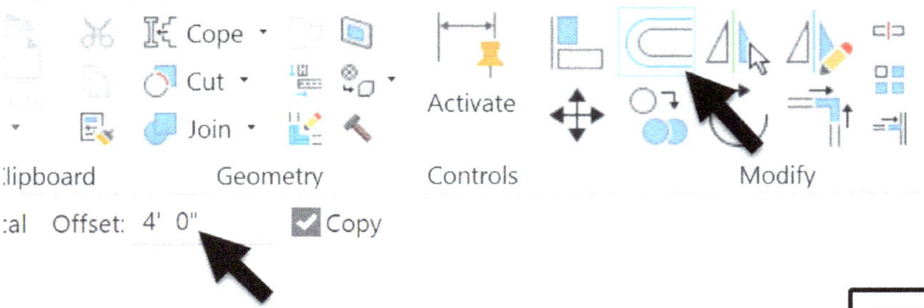

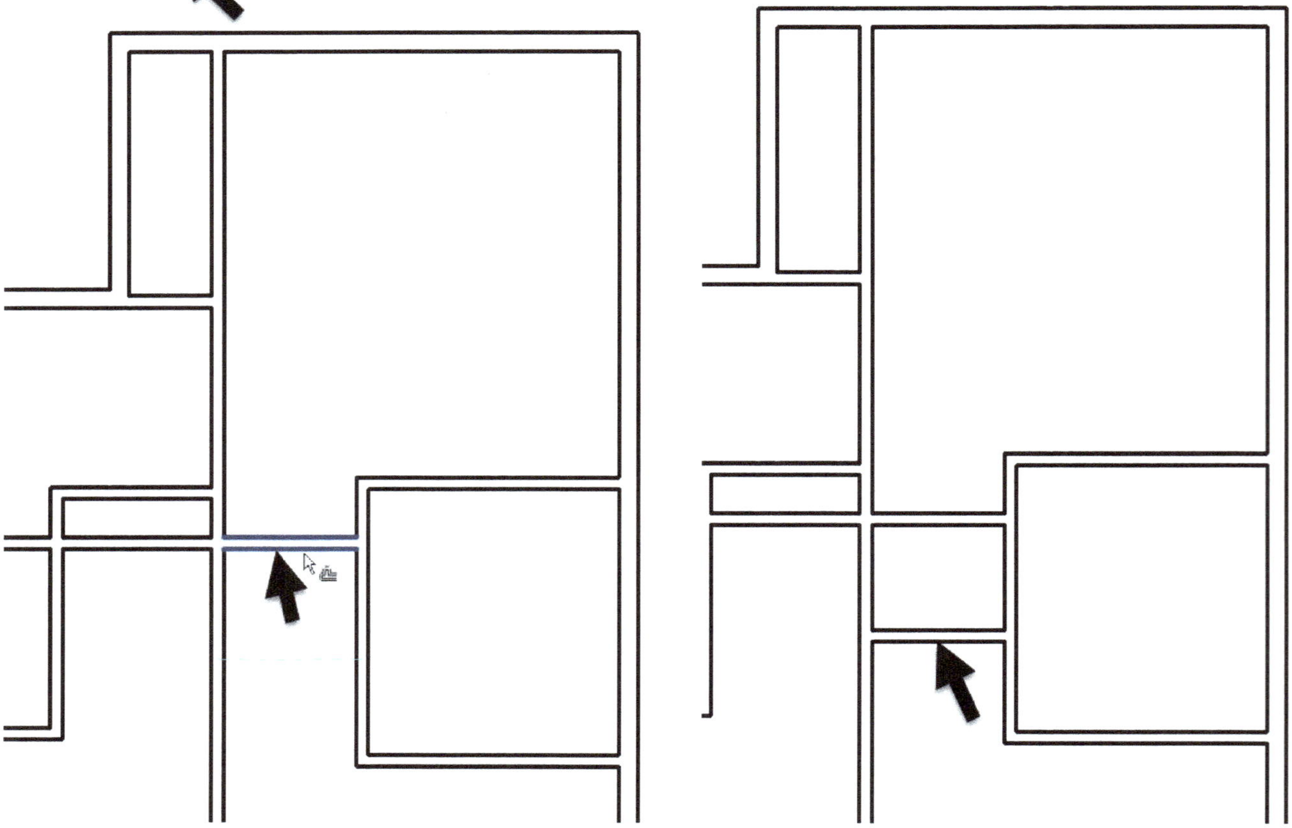

- On the ribbon, click **Modify > Modify > Split Element**. Next, click on the vertical interior wall, as shown.

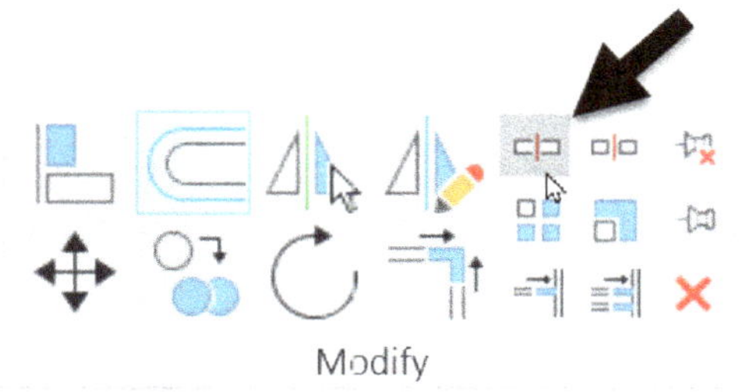

Modify

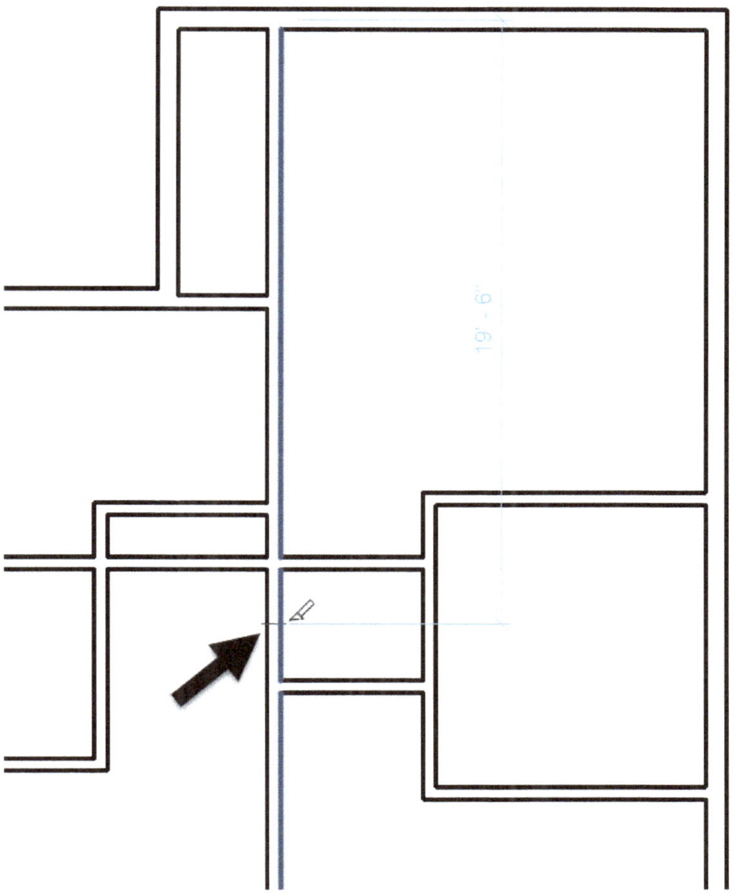

- On the ribbon, click **Modify** tab > **Modify** panel > **Trim/Extend to Corner (TR)**  .
- Select the portions of the two walls intersecting with each other, as shown.

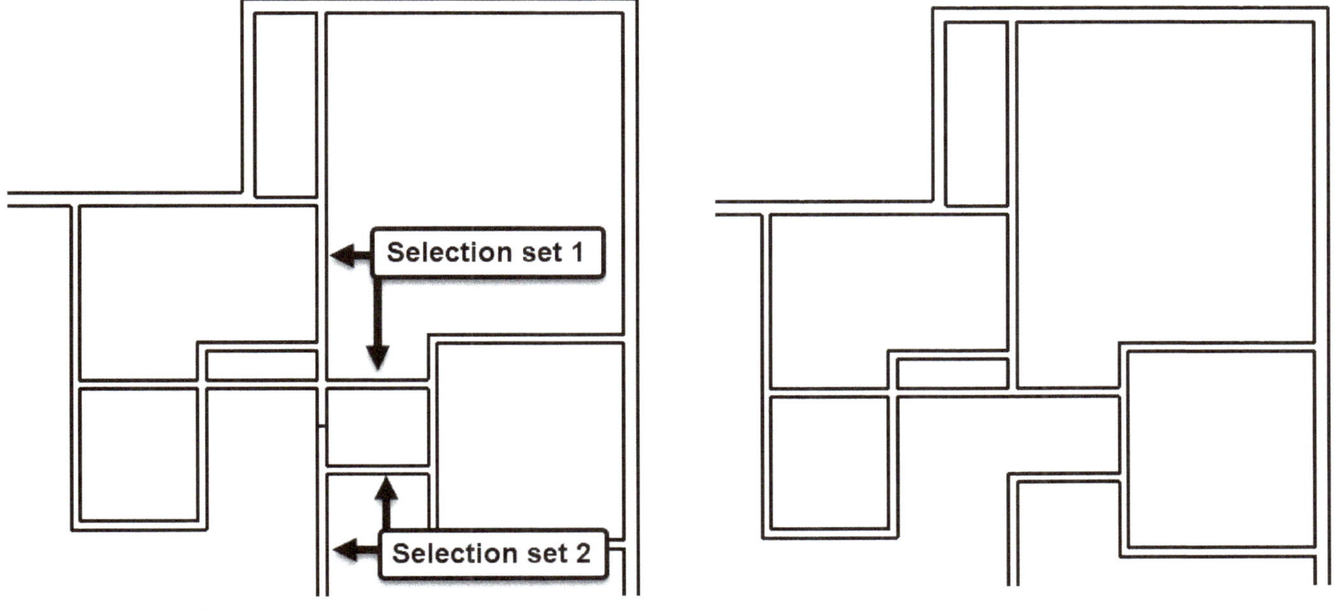

Creating the Foundation walls

- Double-click on the **TOP OF FOUNDATION** under the **Floor Plans** node in the **Project Browser**.
- On the ribbon, click **Architecture** tab > **Build** panel > **Wall** drop-down > **Wall Structural**.
- On the **Properties** palette, select **Basic Wall Foundation – 12" Concrete** from the **Basic Wall** drop-down.

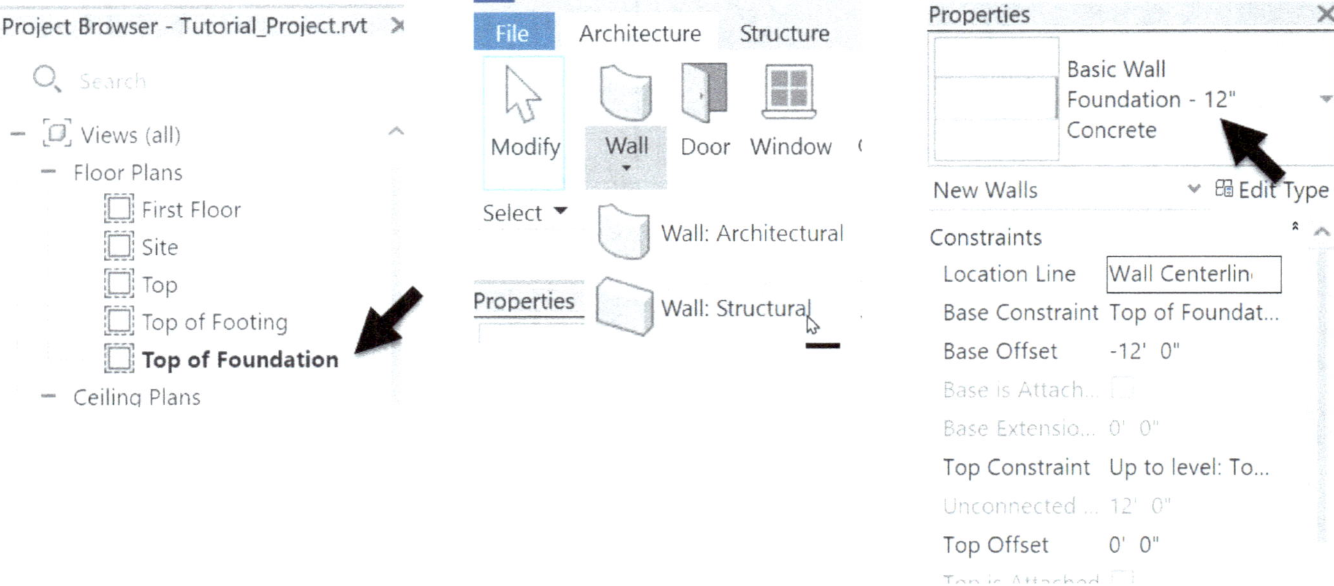

- Select **TOP OF FOUNDATION** from the **Floor Plan** drop-down available on the **Properties** palette.
- Select **Detail Level > Fine** from the bottom of the graphics window.
- On the ribbon, click **View** tab > **Graphics** panel > **Thin Lines**; the edges of the model are displayed as thin lines.

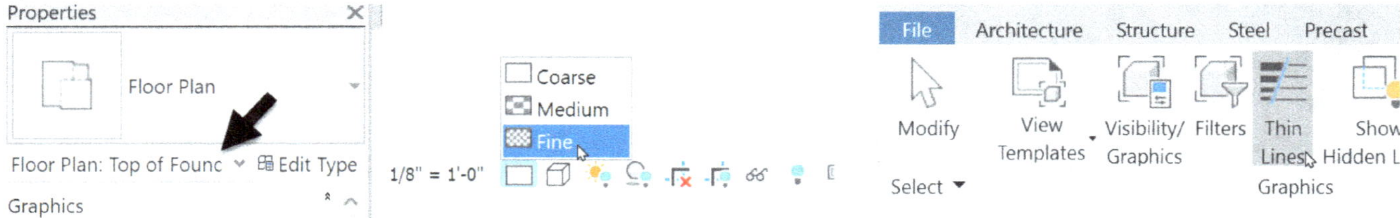

- On the **Properties** palette, scroll to the **Extents** section and click the **Edit** button next to the **View Range** parameter.
- On the **View Range** dialog, select **Level > Unlimited**. Next, click **OK**.

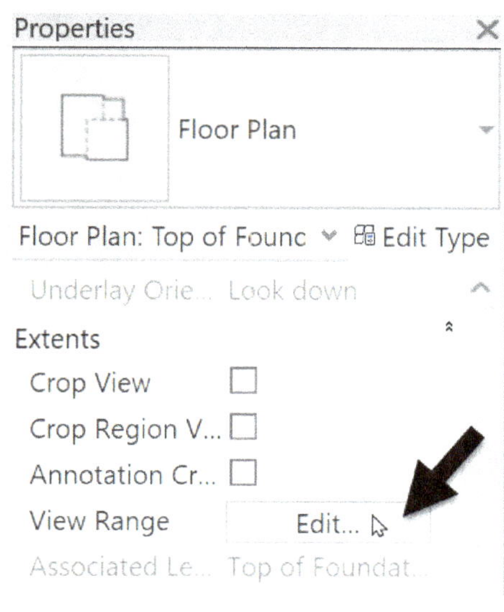

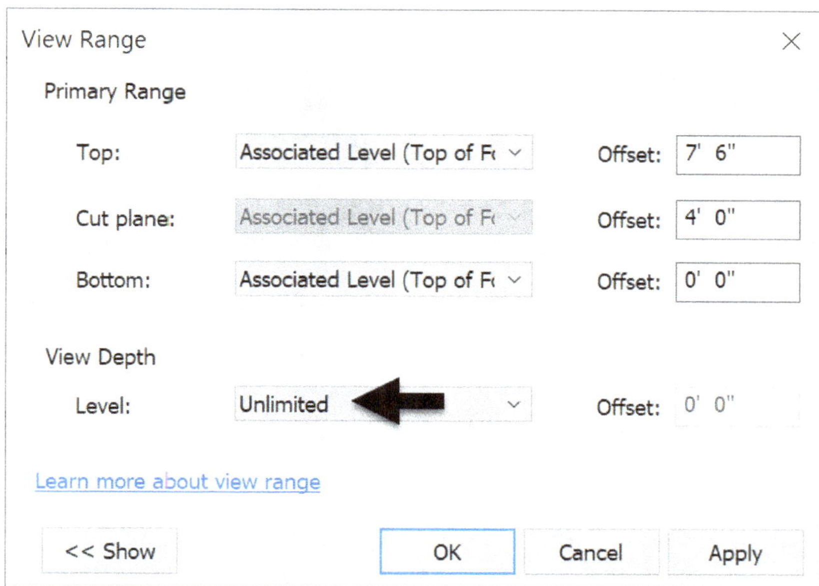

- On the Options Bar, select **Depth** drop-down > **TOP OF FOOTING**. Next, select **Location Line > Finish Face: Exterior**.

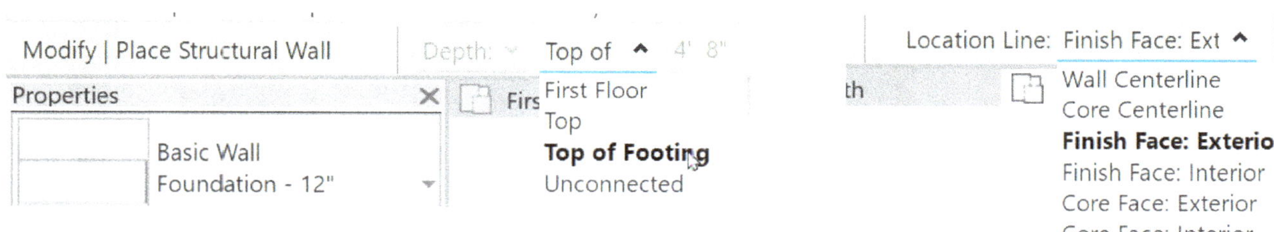

- Type **0' 2 1/8"** in the **Offset** box on the Options Bar.

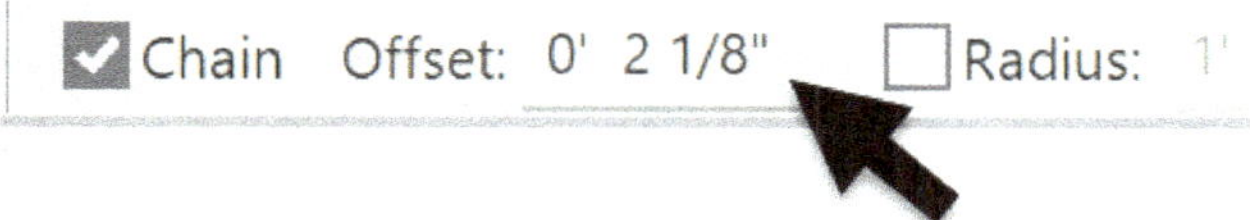

- Zoom to the top-left corner of the floor plan and select the top-left corner point of the walls.

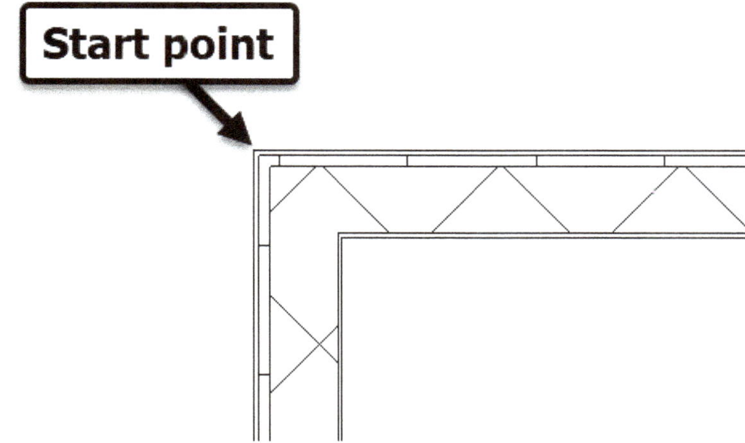

- Move the pointer toward right and select the other corner points, as shown. Next, select the start point and Press ESC.

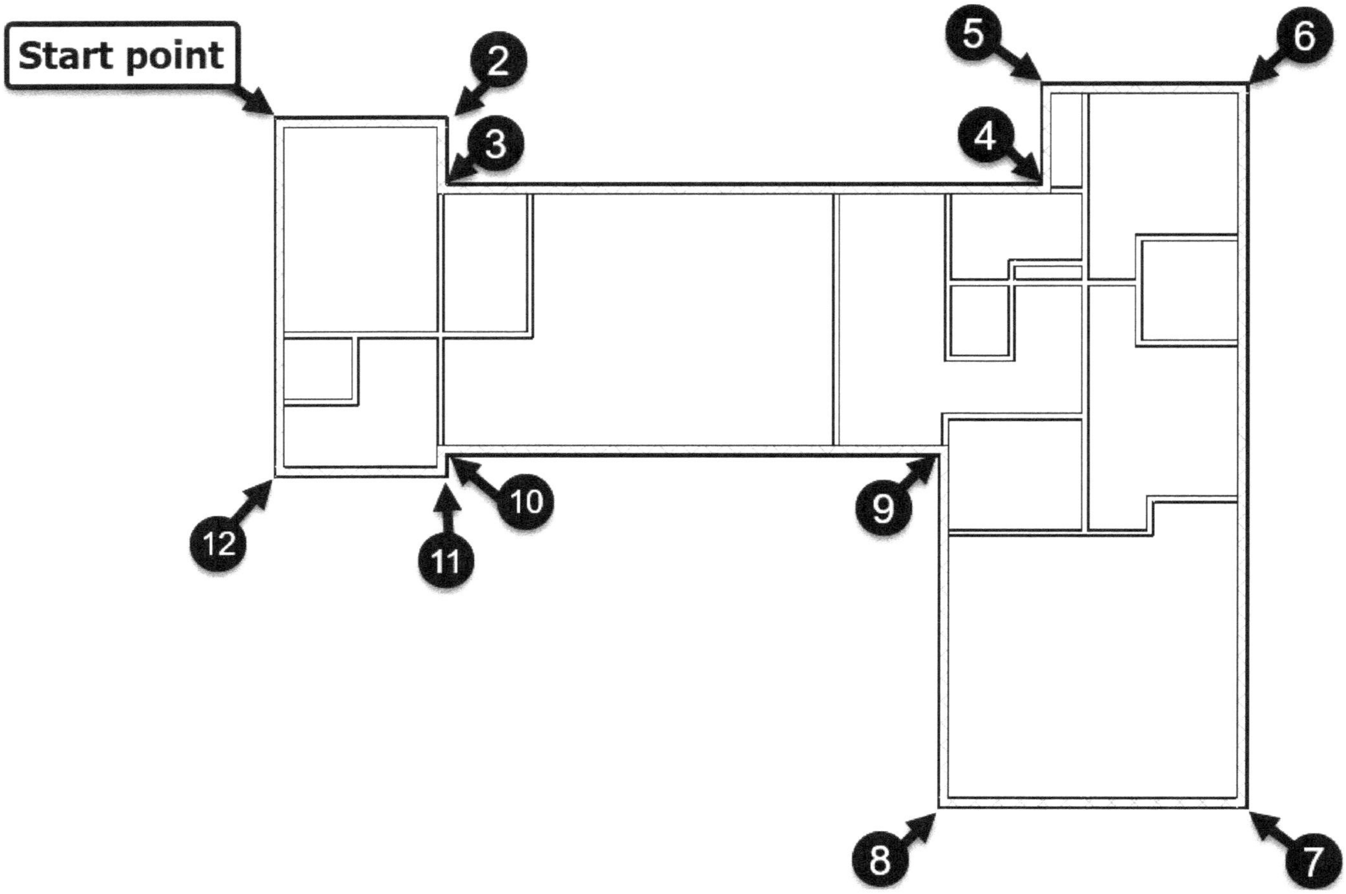

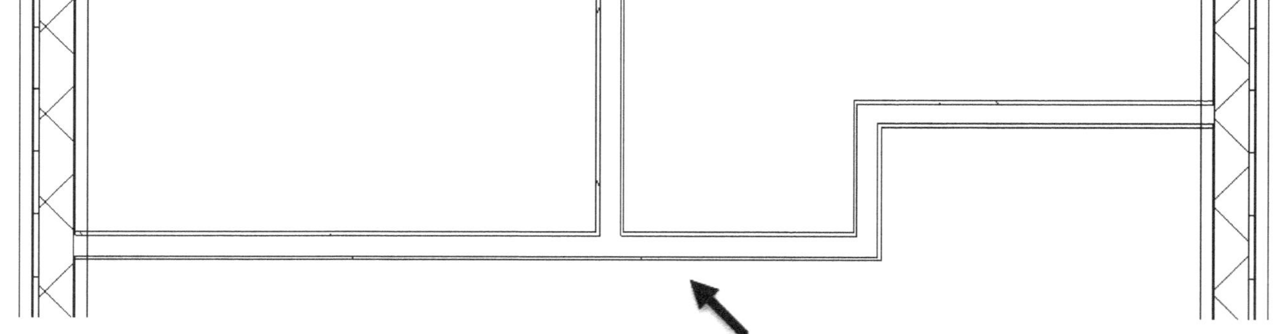

- Zoom to the interior wall near the garage area, as shown.

- On the ribbon, click **Architecture** tab > **Build** panel > **Wall** drop-down > **Wall Architectural**.
- On the ribbon, click **Modify|Place Lines** tab > **Draw** panel > **Pick Lines**.
- On the Options Bar, select **Depth** drop-down > **TOP OF FOOTING.**
- On the Options Bar, select **Location Line > Wall Centerline**. Next, type 0'0" in the **Offset** box.

- Place the pointer on the interior wall and select the dotted line passing through its center.

- Likewise, select the dotted lines passing through the centers of the interior walls, as shown. Next, press ESC.

- Click the **Default 3D View** icon on the Quick Access Toolbar; the 3D view of the walls is displayed.

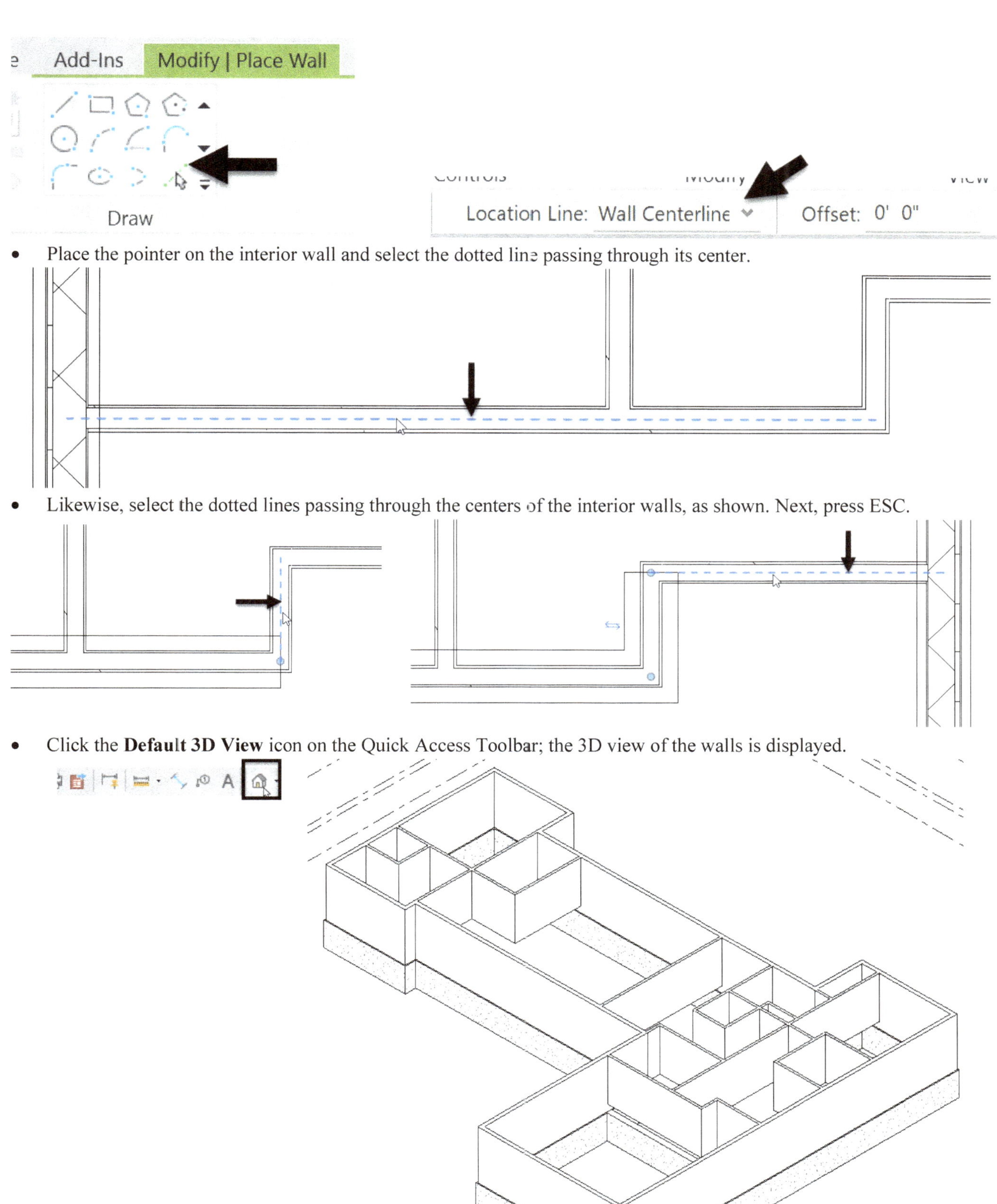

- Zoom to the interior wall near the garage area and notice the gap between the interior and the foundation walls.

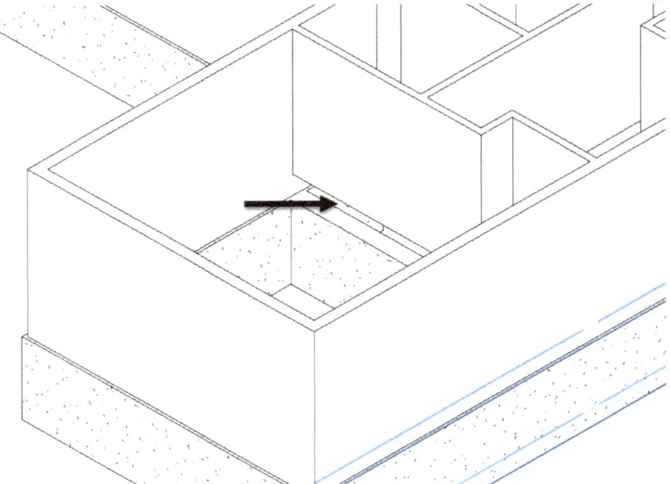

- Press and hold the CTRL key and select the three interior walls, as shown.
- On the **Properties** palette, select **Base Constraint > TOP OF FOUNDATION** under the **Constraints** section.
- Click in the graphics window and notice that the gap is closed.

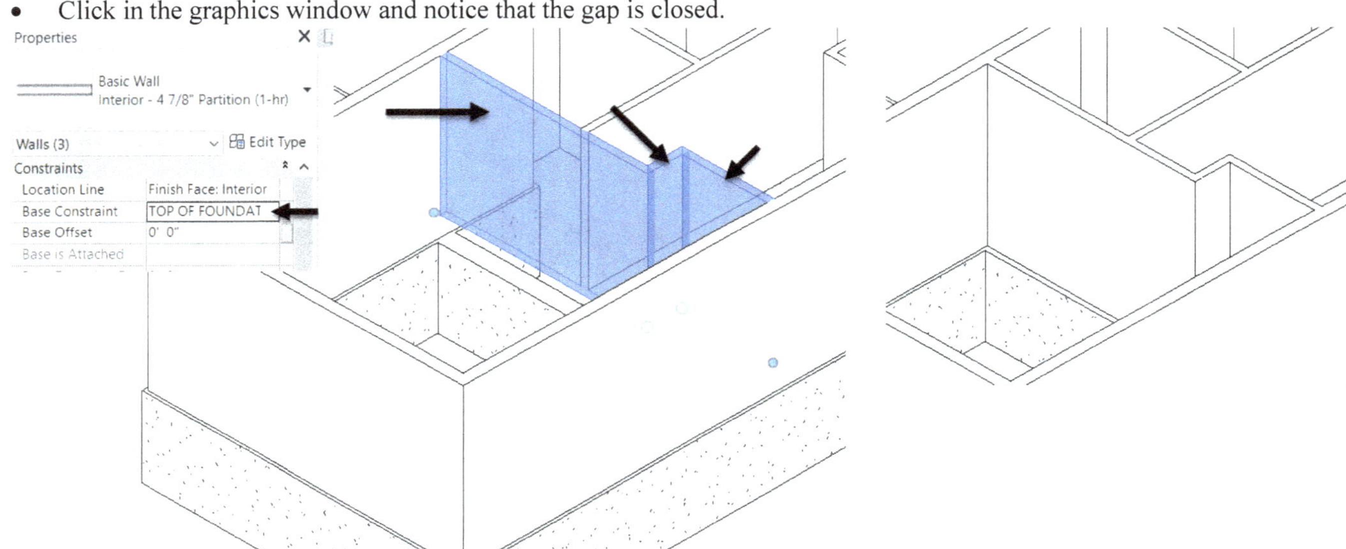

The height of the garage foundation wall is generally less than that of the main foundation. Now, you need to reduce the height of the garage foundation wall.

- On the ribbon, click **Modify** tab > **Modify** panel > **Split Element** .
- Click near the top edges of the side foundation walls of the garage, as shown. Press ESC twice.

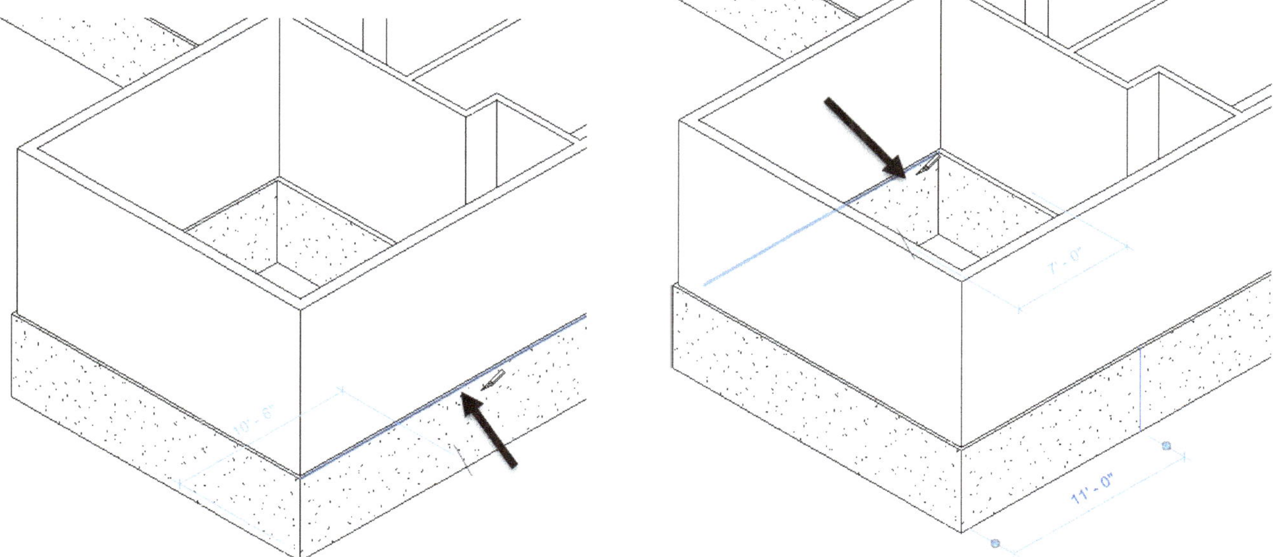

- Press and hold the CTRL key and select the three foundation walls, as shown.
- On the **Properties** palette, type 2 in the **Base Offset** box; the selected foundation walls are offset from the top of the footing.

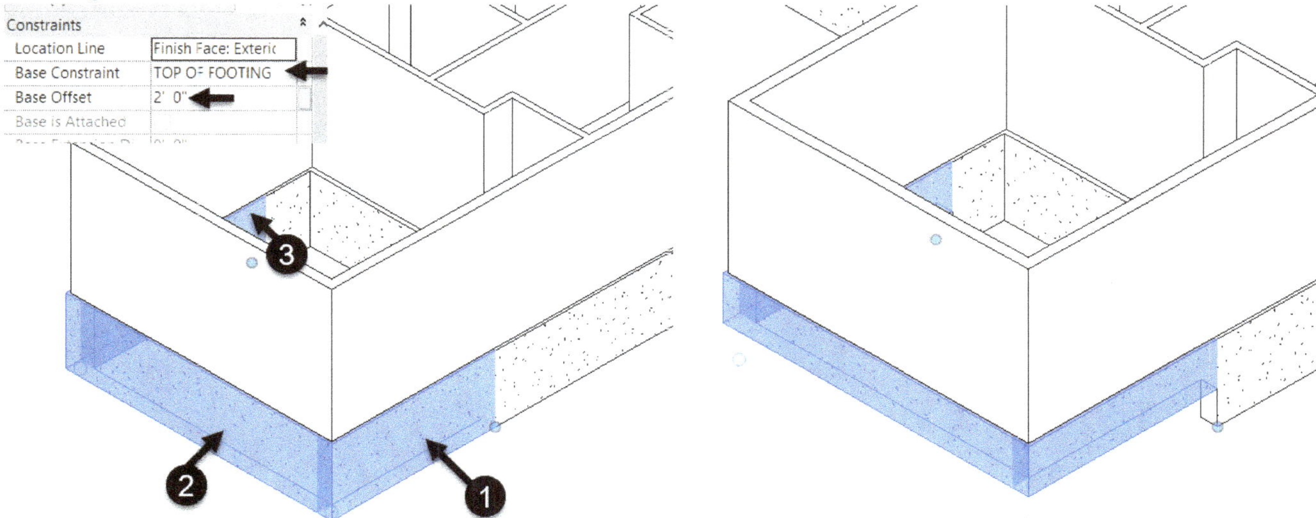

- Press ESC to deselect the foundation walls.
- Click on the top-left corner of the ViewCube, as shown; the orientation of the model is changed.

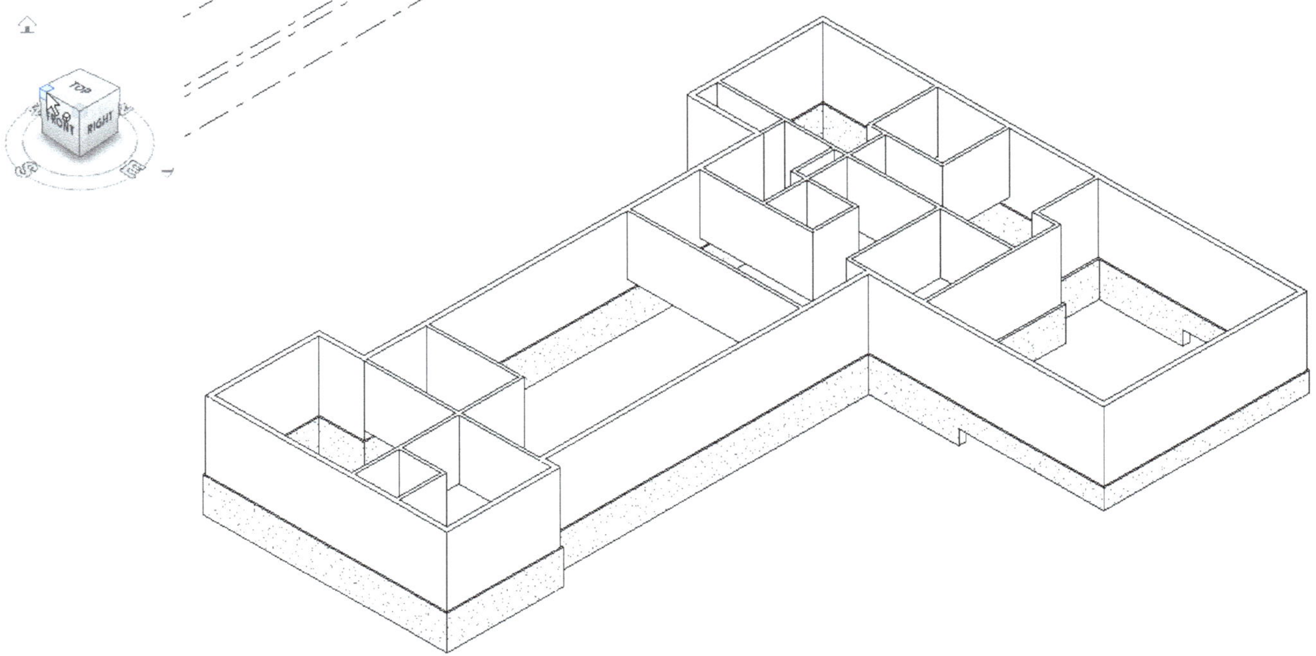

- Press and hold the CTRL key and select the three walls, as shown.
- Click the **Temporary Hide/Isolate** icon at the bottom of the graphics window. Next, select the **Hide Element** option.

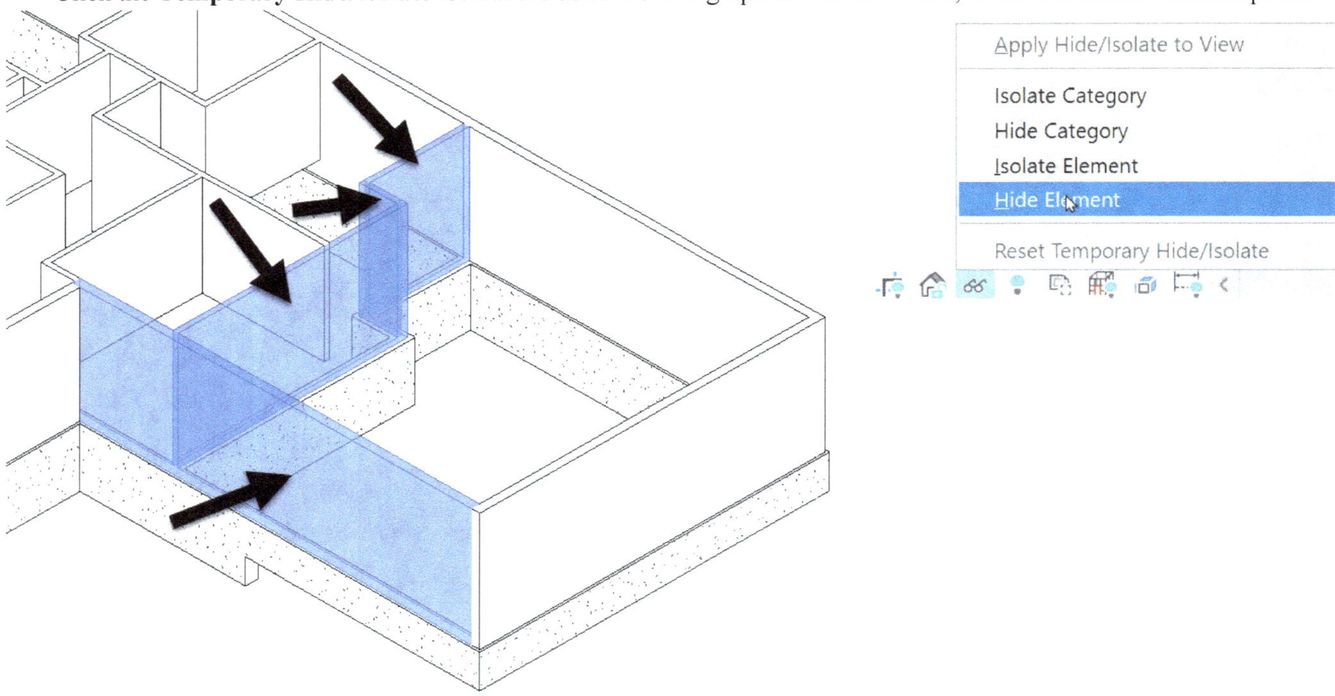

- On the ribbon, click **Modify** tab > **Modify** panel > **Trim/Extend to Corner (TR)**.
- Select the portions of the two walls intersecting with each other.
- Likewise, select the portions of the two walls, as shown.

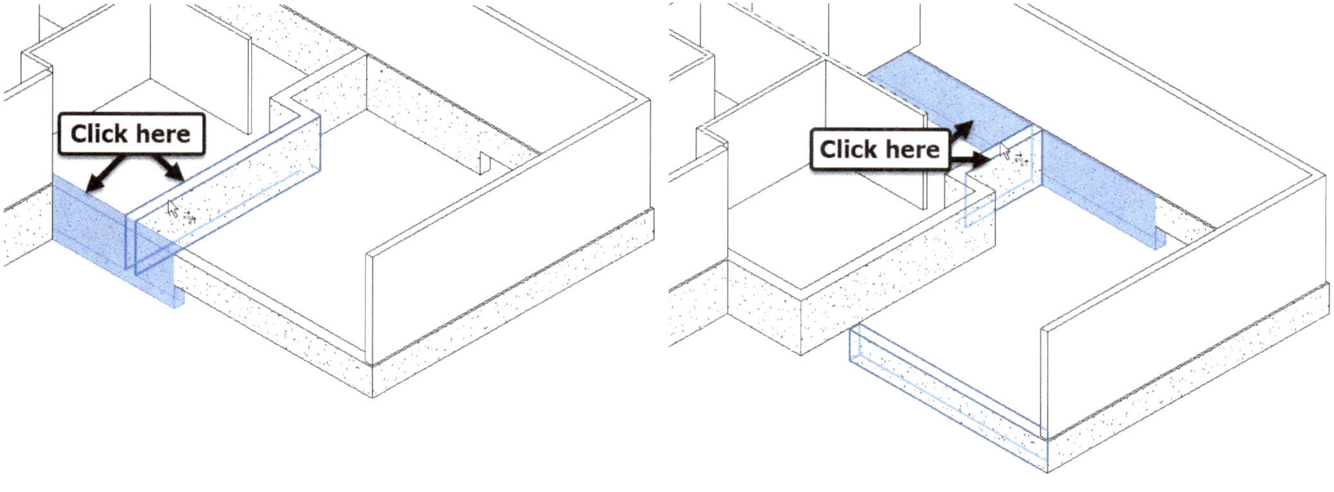

- On the ribbon, click **Modify** tab > **Modify** panel > **Trim/Extend Single Element** .
- Select the face of the foundation wall, as shown. The boundary is defined.
- Select the foundation wall of the garage, as shown; the wall is extended up to the selected face.

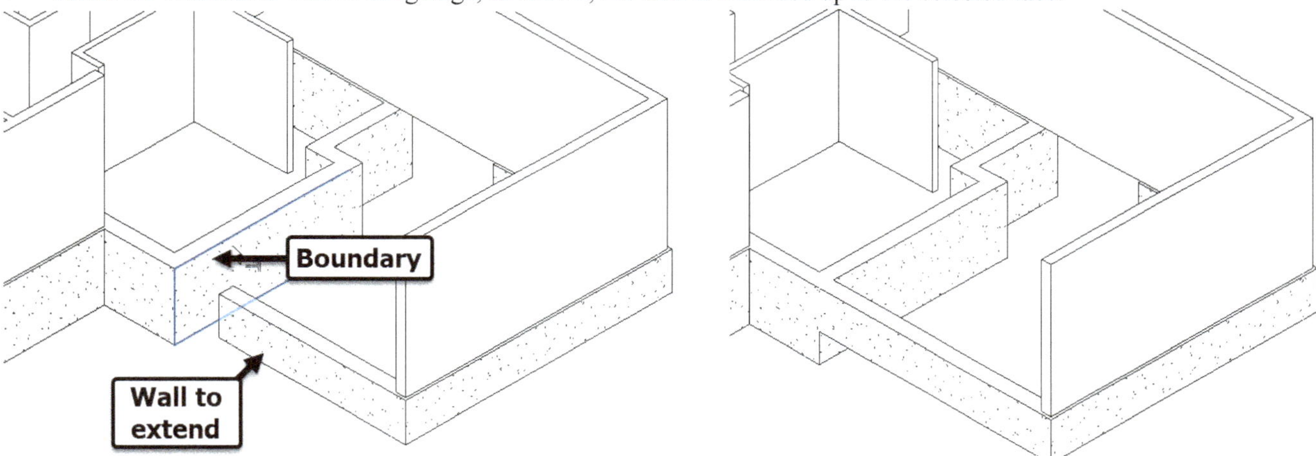

- Select the face of the foundation wall, as shown. The boundary is defined.
- Select the foundation wall of the garage, as shown; the wall is extended up to the selected face.

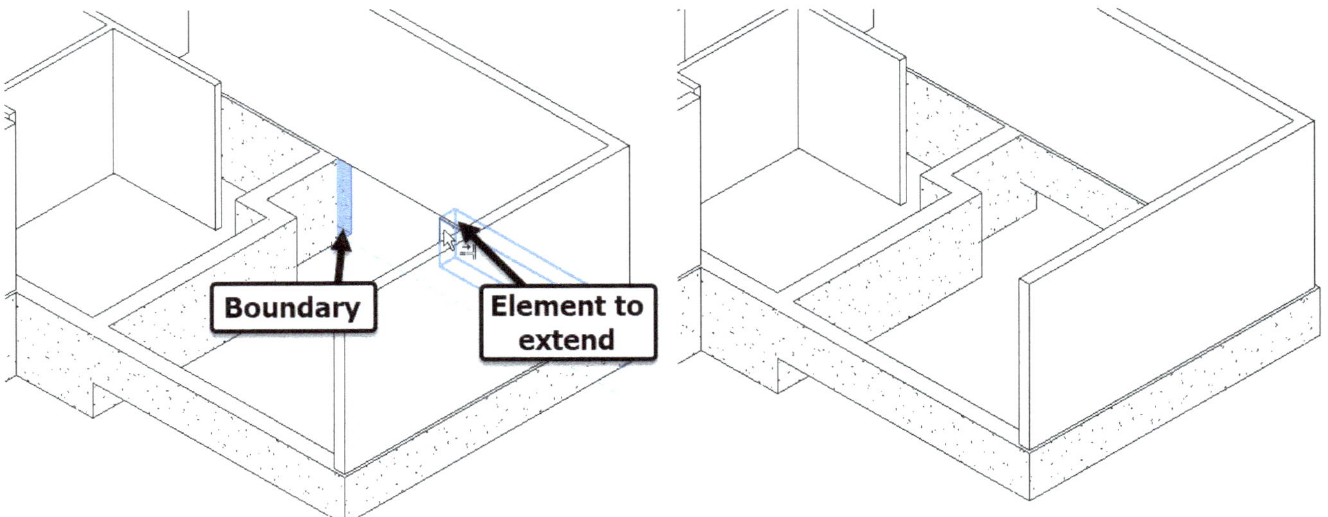

- Click the **Temporary Hide/Isolate** icon at the bottom of the graphics window. Next, select the **Reset Temporary Hide/Isolate** option.

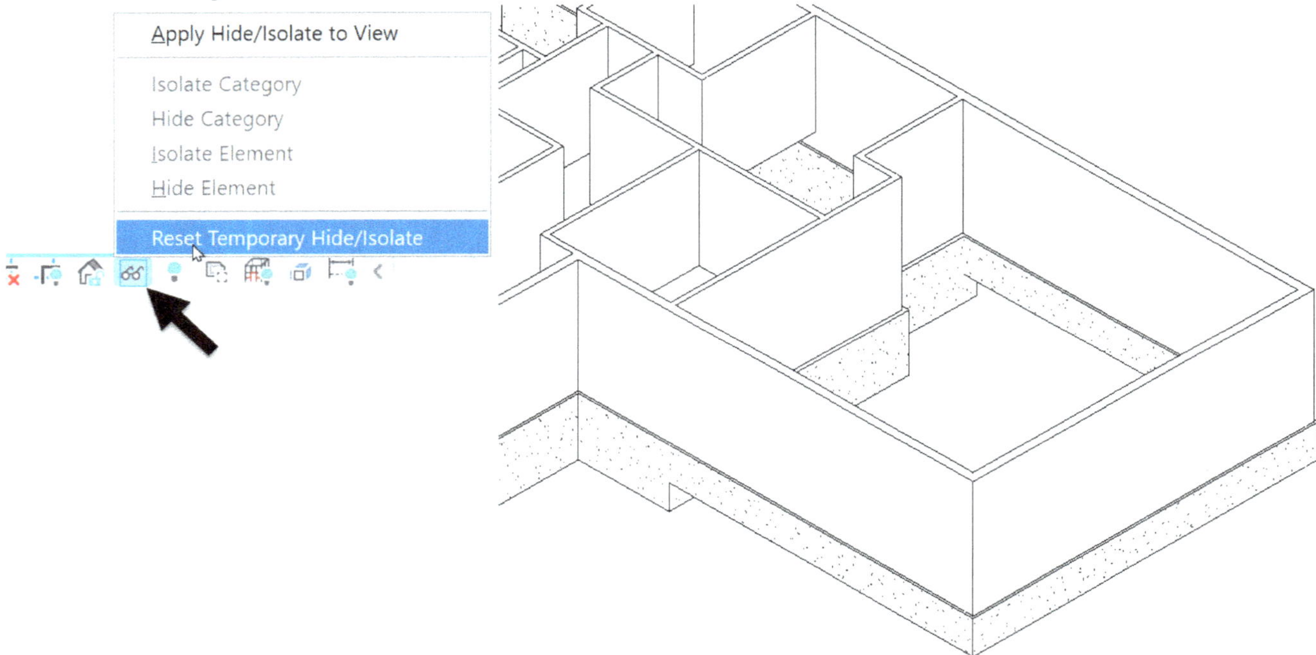

Creating the Footings

- Click the lower corner point between the left and front faces of the ViewCube. The bottom face of the model is displayed.

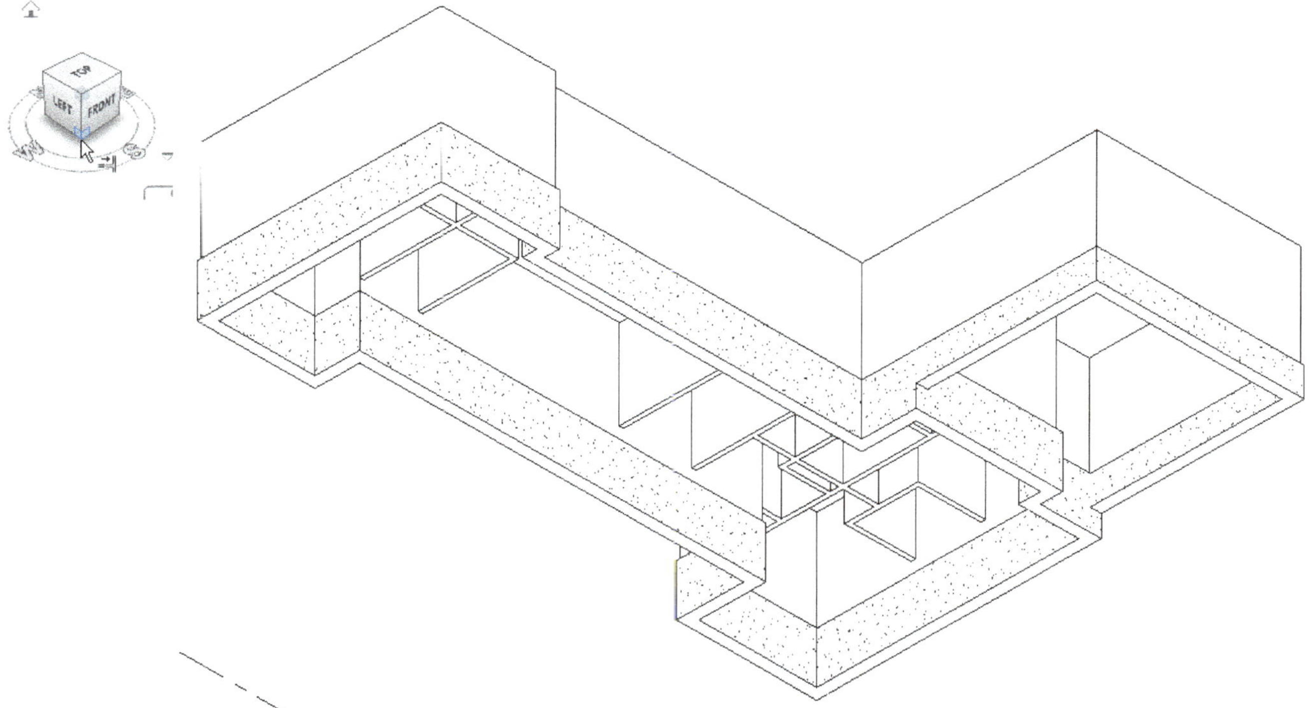

- On the ribbon, click **Structure** tab > **Foundation** panel > **Wall**.
- Select the **Bearing Footing – 36" x 12"** from the **Wall Foundation** drop-down on the **Properties** palette.

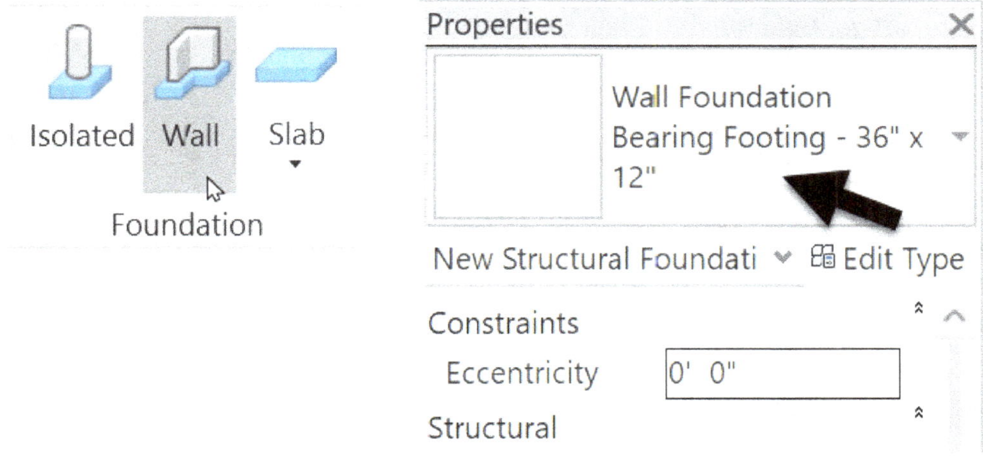

- Select all the bottom faces of the foundation walls, as shown. Press ESC.

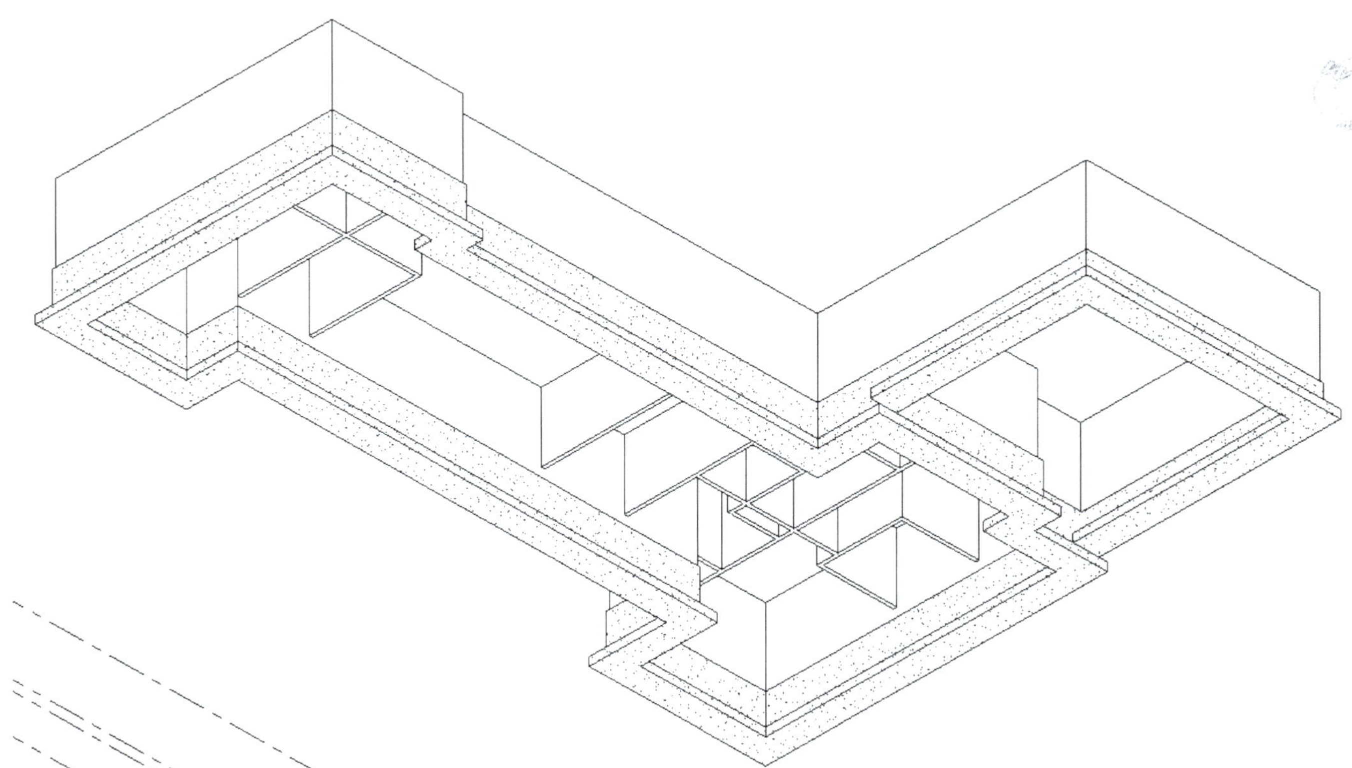

- Click the **Home** icon near the ViewCube; the orientation of the model is changed.

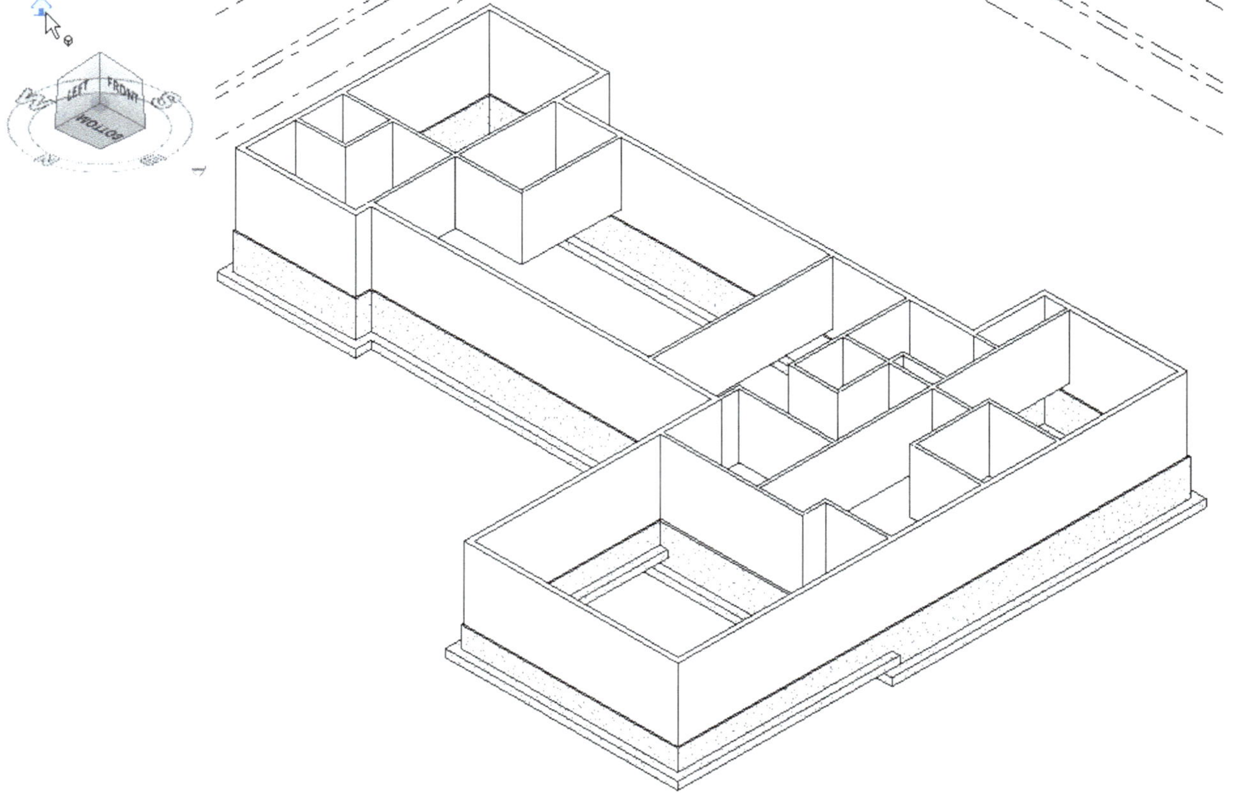

Tutorial 4: Creating Doors and Openings

- Double-click on the **TOP OF FOUNDATION** under the **Floor Plans** node in the **Project Browser**.
- On the **Properties** palette, scroll to the **Extents** section and click the **Edit** button next to the **View Range** parameter.
- On the **View Range** dialog, select **Level > Associated Level** Next, click **OK**.
- On the ribbon, click **Architecture** tab > **Build** panel > **Door**.
- Click the drop-down available at the top of the **Properties** palette; notice that only the Single Flush doors are available to be inserted into the drawing. If you want to insert a double-door, you need to load the respective library into the current project. The procedure to load a library is explained in the steps given next.

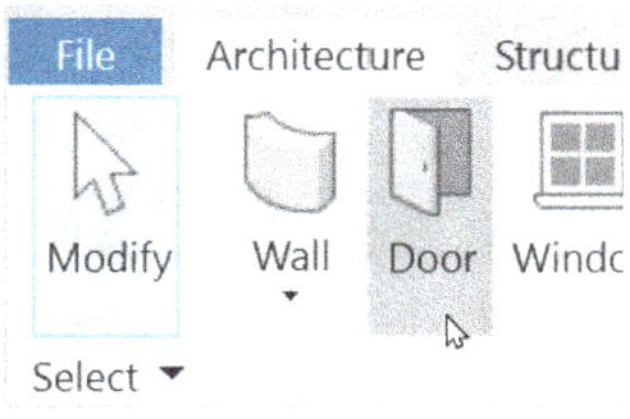

- On the ribbon, click **Modify|Place Door** tab > **Mode** panel > **Load Family**.
- Go to **Local Disc C > Program Data > Autodesk > RVT 2024 > Libraries > English imperial (or metric or other base) > Doors > Residential**. Next, double-click on **Door-Exterior-Double-Full Glass-Wood_Clad**.

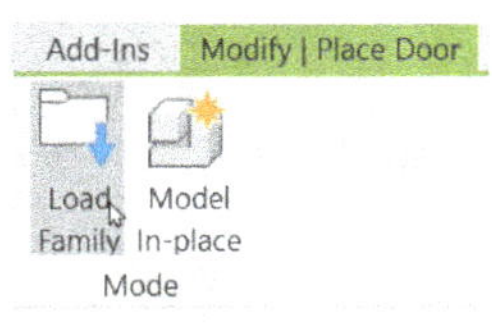
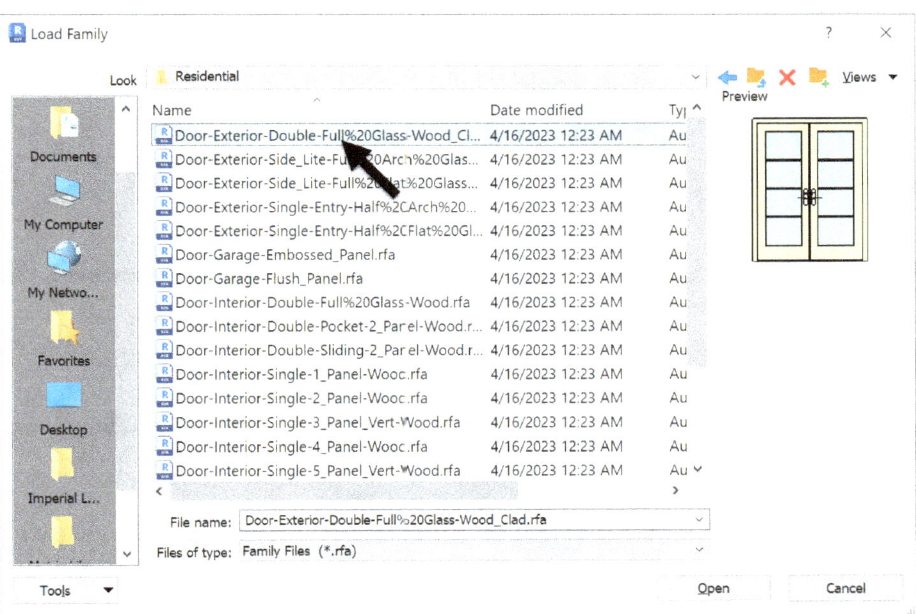

- On the **Specify Types** dialog, select the 70" x 80" door type, and then click **OK**.

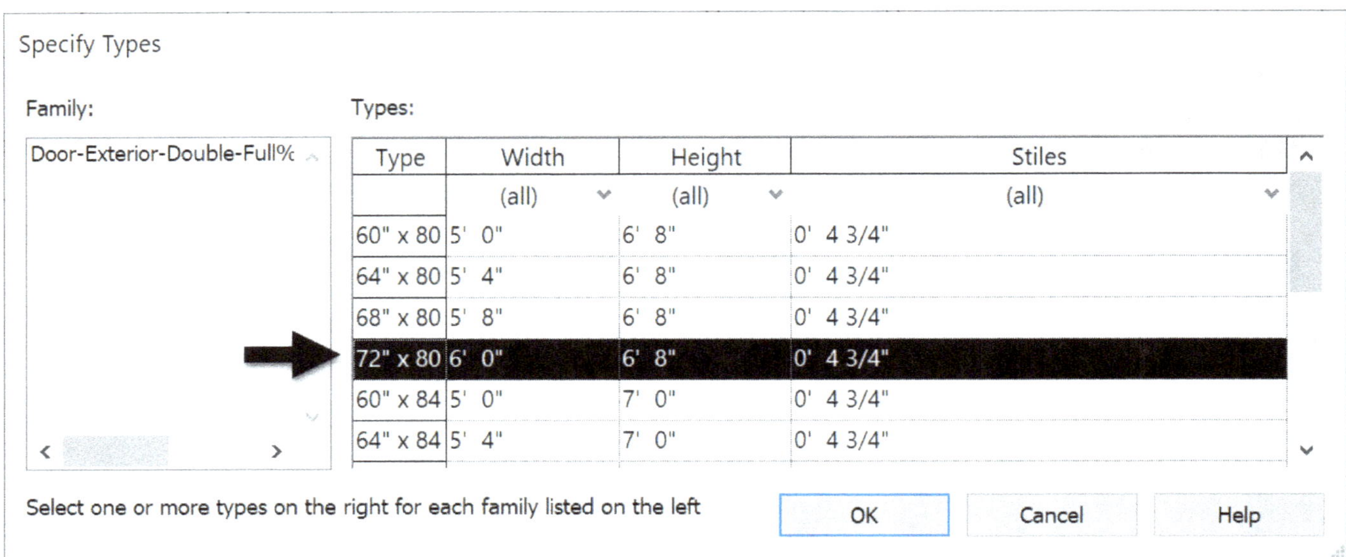

- On the **Properties** palette, select **Door-Exterior-Double-Full Glass-Wood_Clad 72" x 80"** door from the **Basic Door** drop-down.
- Zoom to the front portion of the drawing, as shown.

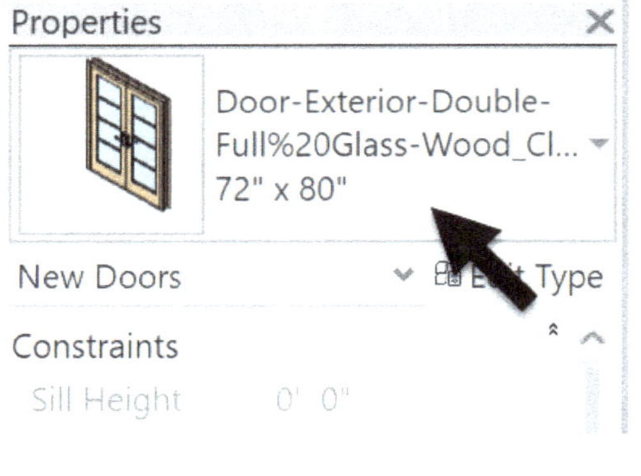

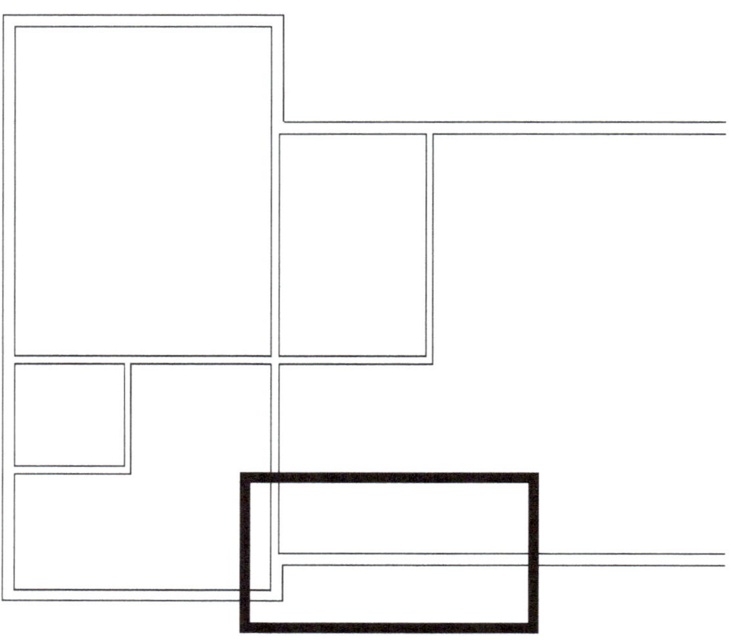

- Place the pointer on the inner edge of the exterior wall at the location, as shown. Next, click to place the double-door.
- Click on the dimension between the adjacent wall and the door. Next, type 3' 8" in the edit box and press ENTER. Next, press ESC.

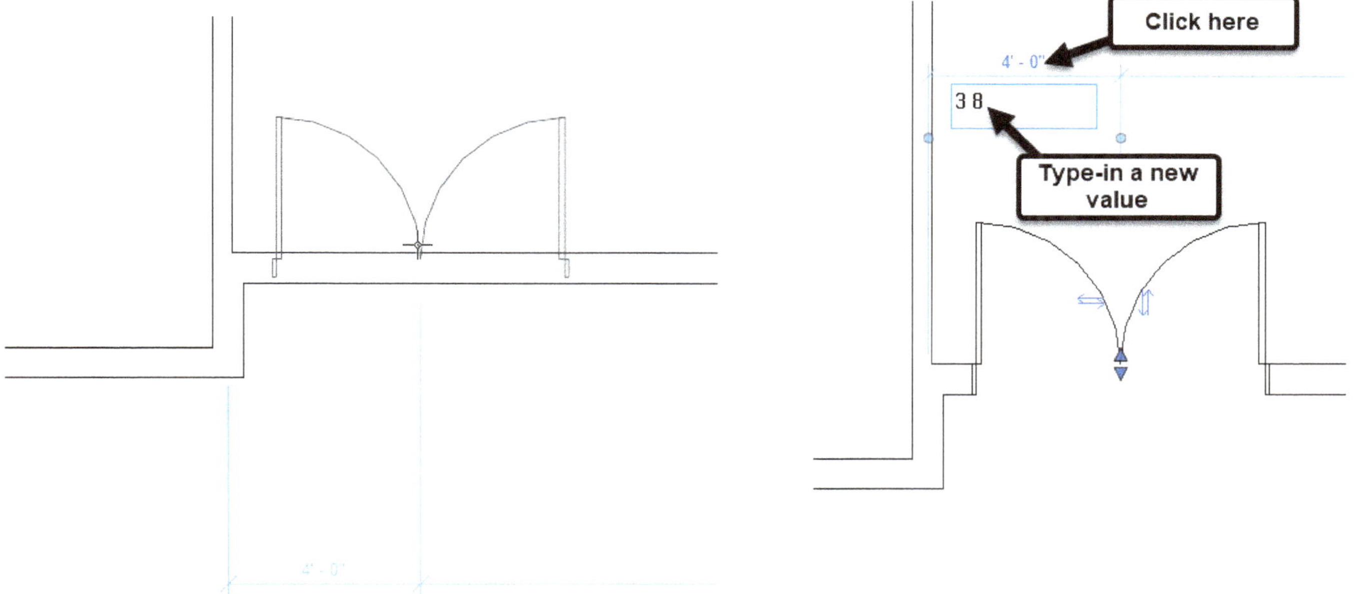

- On the **Properties** palette, select **Single-Flush 36" x 80"** door from the **Basic Door** drop-down.
- Zoom to the back portion of the drawing.
- Place the pointer on the inner edge of the bedroom wall, as shown. Next, click to position the door.
- Click on the dimension between the adjacent wall and the door. Next, type 2' 6" in the edit box and press ENTER.

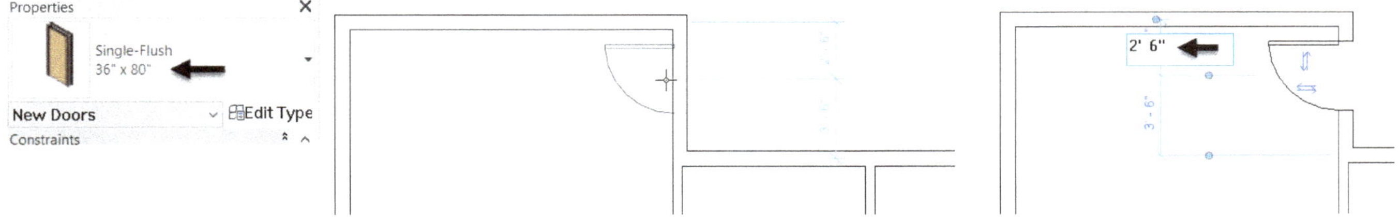

- Zoom to the garage portion of the drawing.
- Place the pointer on the inner edge of the interior wall, as shown. Next, press the SPACEBAR on your keyboard to flip the door.

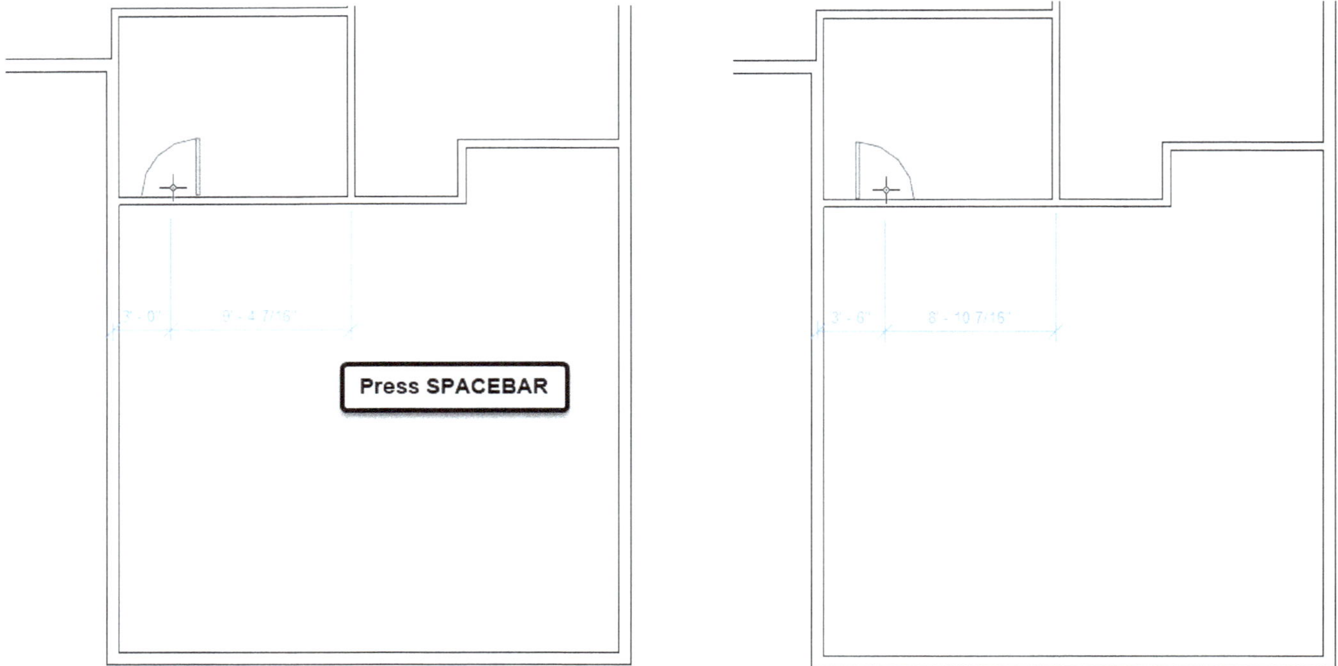

- Click to position the door. Click on the dimension between the adjacent wall and the door. Next, type 3 in the edit box and press ENTER.

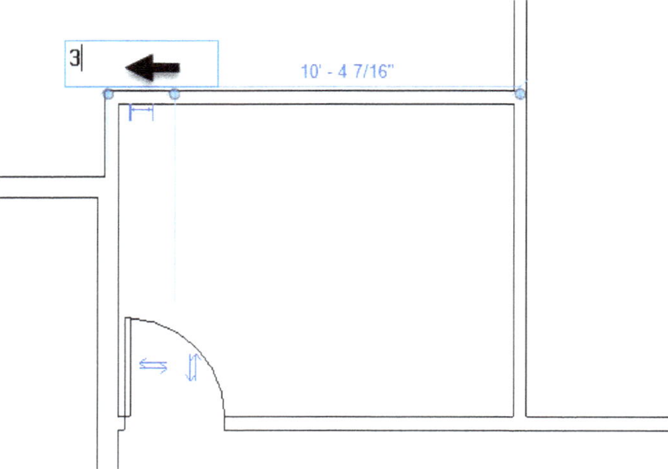

- Place the pointer on the inner edge of the exterior wall, as shown. Next, press the SPACEBAR on your keyboard to flip the door.
- Click to position the door. Click on the dimension between the adjacent wall and the door. Next, type 2 in the edit box and press ENTER.

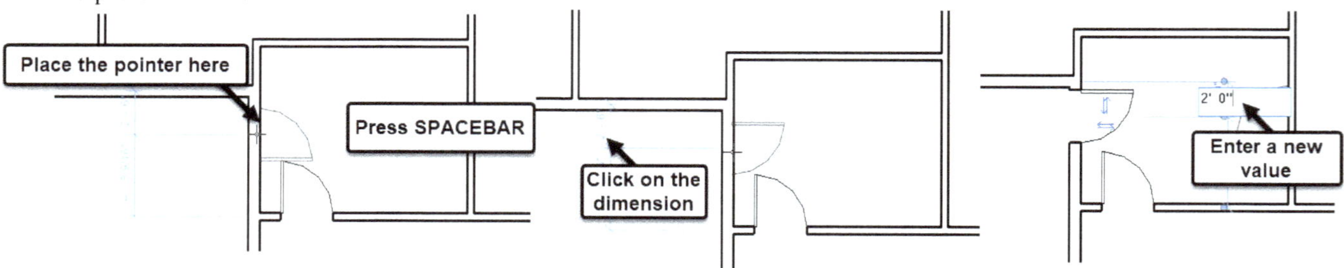

- On the **Properties** palette, select **Single-Flush 32" x 84"** door from the **Basic Door** drop-down.

- Place the doors at the locations, as shown.

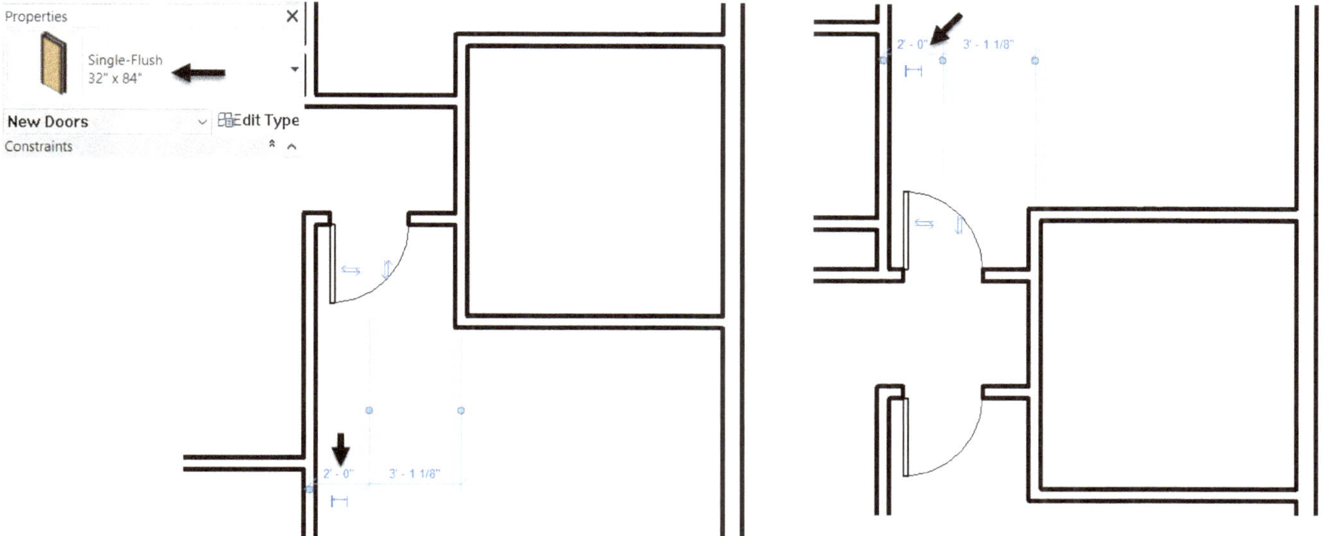

- On the **Properties** palette, select **Single-Flush 30" x 80"** door from the **Basic Door** drop-down.
- Place the doors at the locations, as shown.

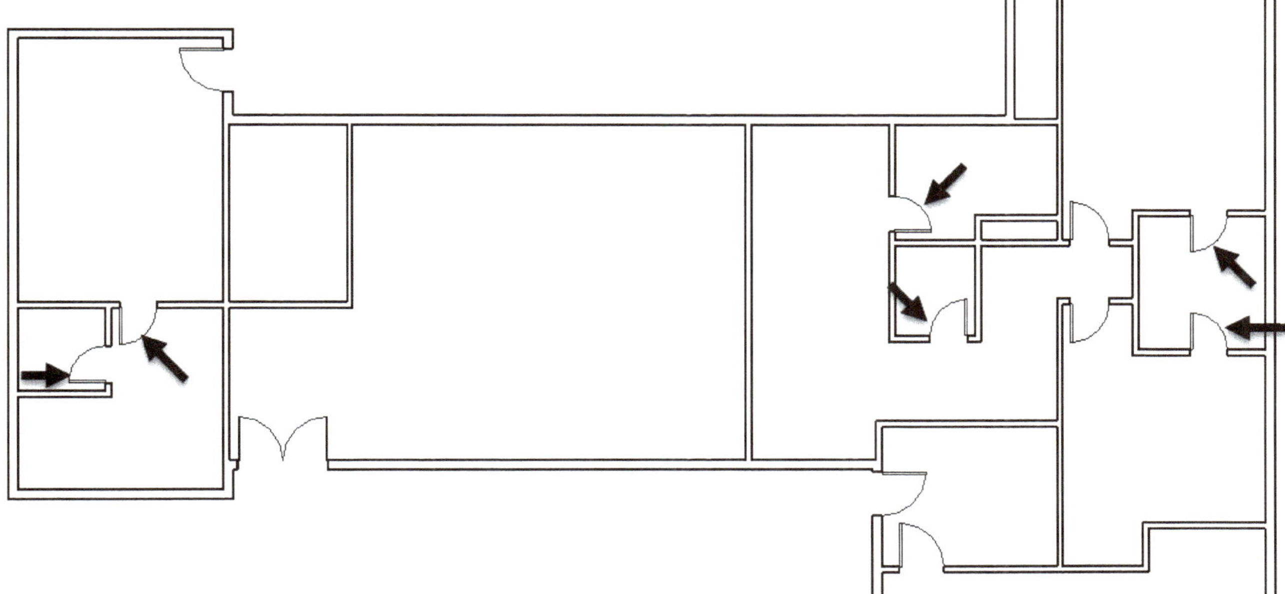

Next, you need to place a sliding glass door at the back side. However, the required door family is not available in the Revit Content Library. You need to download it from https://market.bimsmith.com/

- Open an Internet Browser and type *https://market.bimsmith.com* in the address bar. Next, create a new free user account, and then type **Ultra Series Sliding Patio Doors Garden Aire 4 Wide** in the search bar.
- Select the **Ultra Series Sliding Patio Doors Garden Aire 4 Wide** family from the search results.

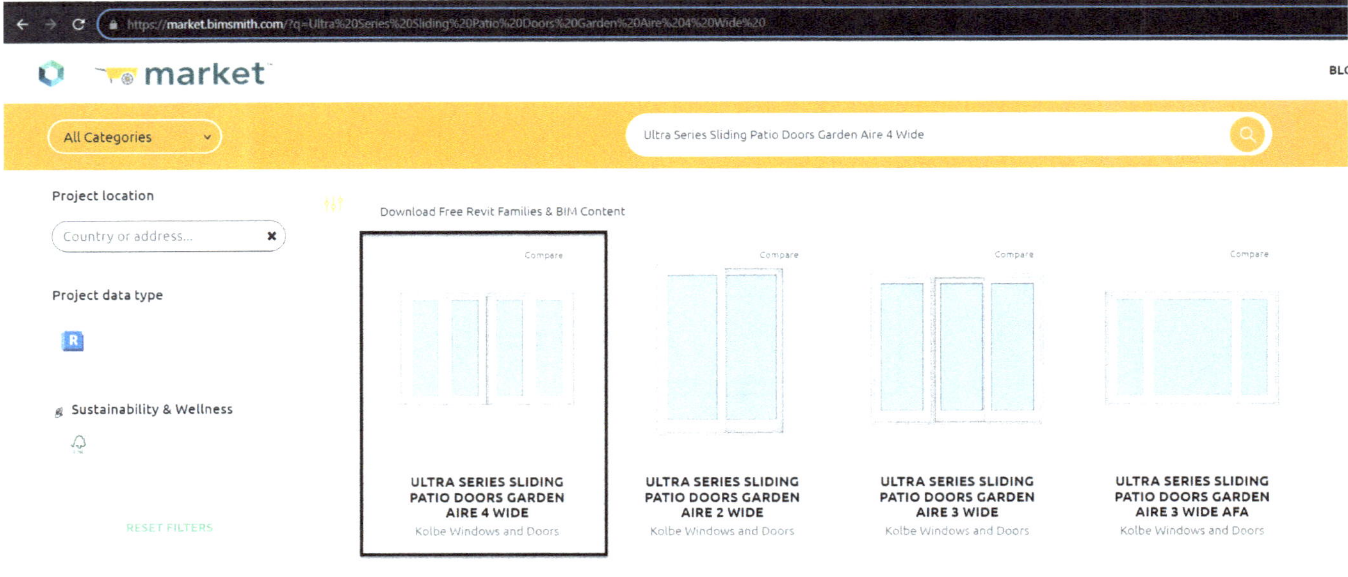

- Click the **Download** button located at the top-left corner of the webpage.
- Unzip the downloaded file to a desired location on your computer. Next, double-click on the **Door-Entrance-Kolbe-Ultra_Series_Garden-Aire_Sliding_Patio_Doors-4Wide** revit family file.

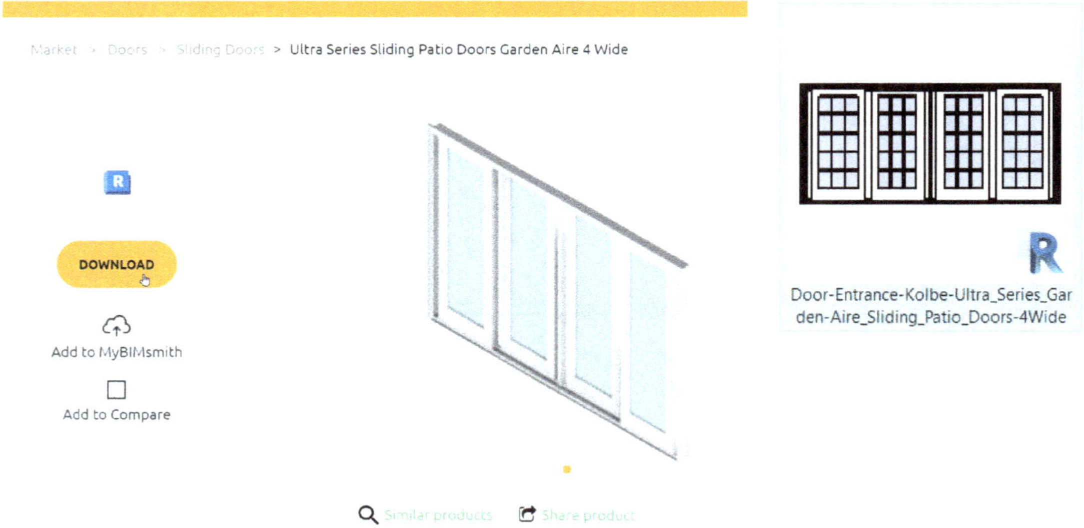

- Click **Upgrade the Model** on the **Model Upgrade** message box; the model upgrades to the new version and is opened in a new tab.
- On the ribbon, click **Create > Family Editor > Load into Project and Close**.

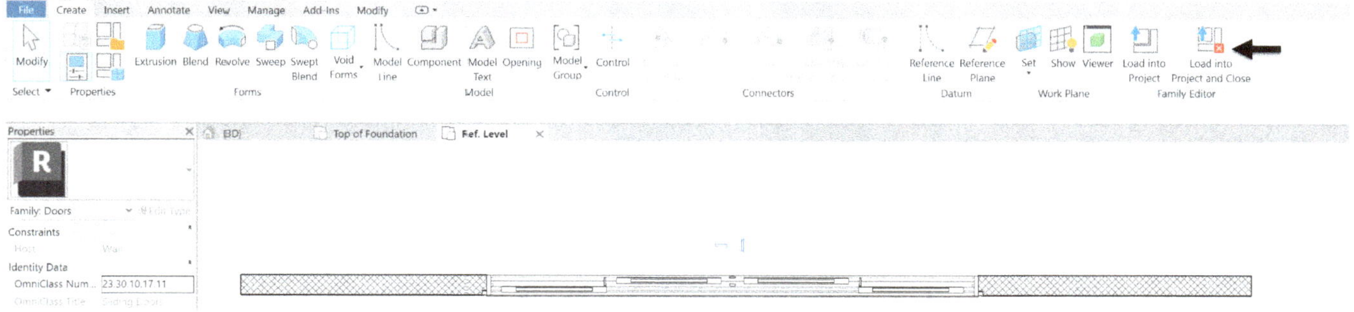

- On the ribbon, click **Architecture** tab > **Build** panel > **Door** .
- Click the drop-down available at the top of the **Properties** palette, and then select **Door-Entrance-Kolbe Ultra_Series_Garden-Aire_Sliding_Patio_Doors-4Wide**.
- Place the pointer on the inner edge of the exterior wall located on the back side.

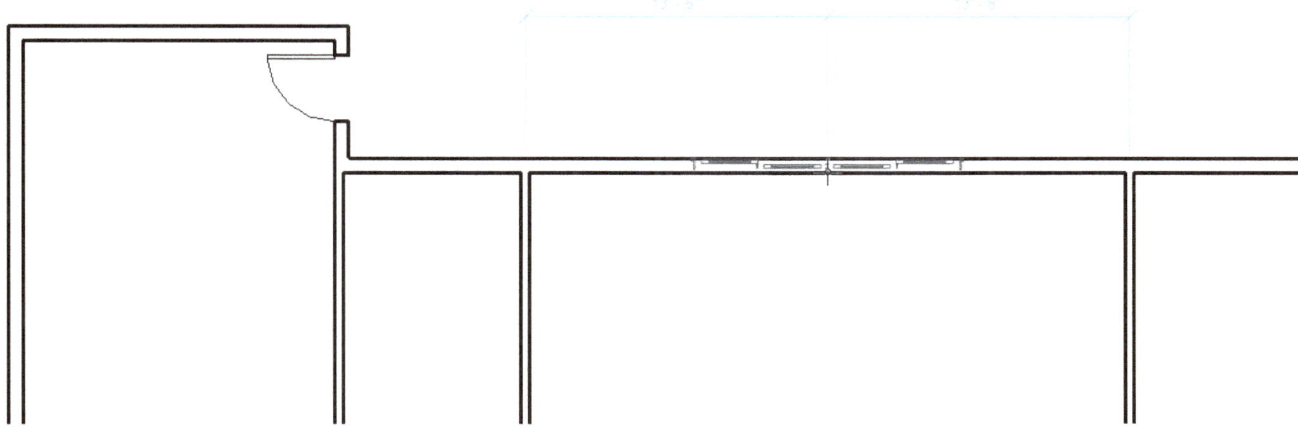

- Click to position the sliding door. Next, change anyone of the positioning dimensions to 13'6".

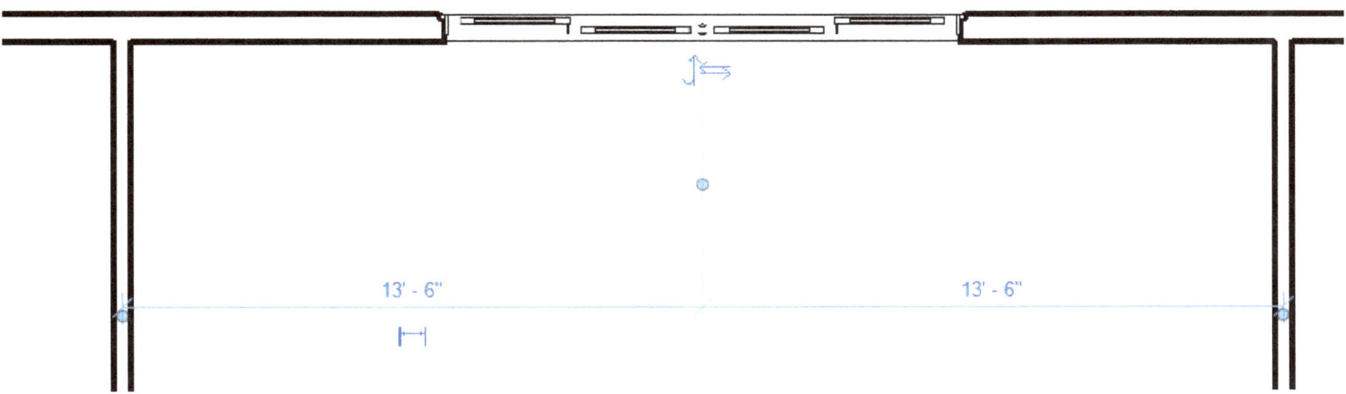

- On the ribbon, click **Modify|Place Door** tab > **Mode** panel > **Load Family** .
- Go to **Local Disc C > Program Data > Autodesk > RVT 2024 > Libraries > English imperial (or metric or other base) > Doors > Residential**. Next, double-click on **Door-Interior-Double-Sliding-2_Panel-Wood**.
- On the **Specify Types** dialog, select the **48" x 80"** door type from the **Types** list. Next, click **OK**.

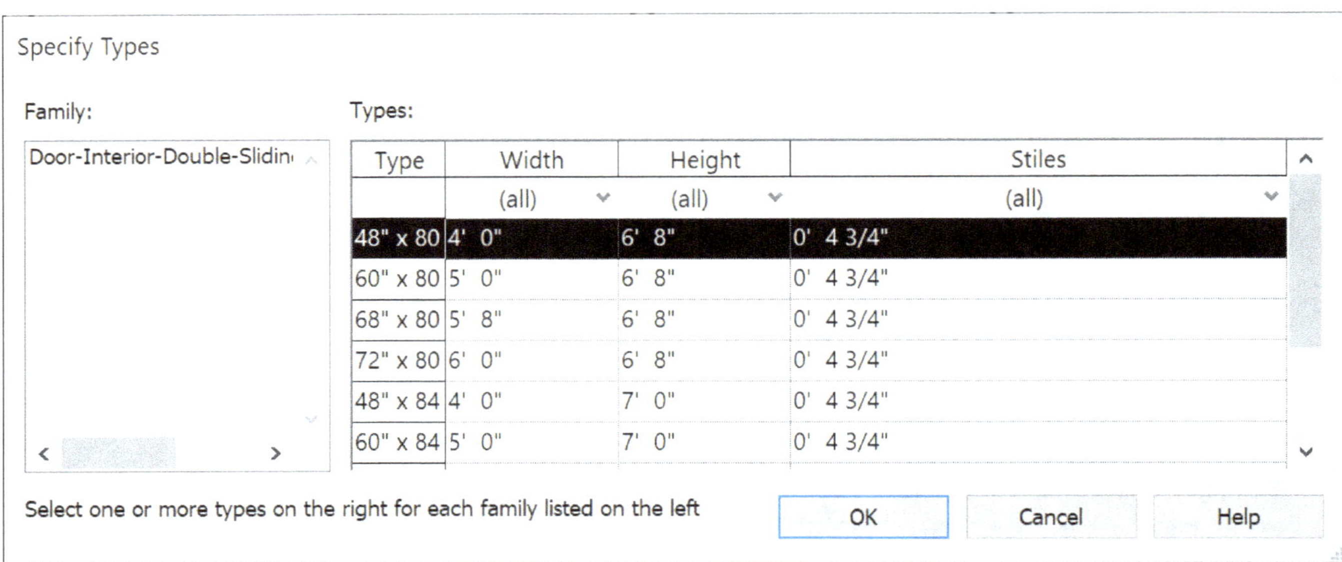

Type	Width	Height	Stiles
(all)	(all)	(all)	(all)
48" x 80	4' 0"	6' 8"	0' 4 3/4"
60" x 80	5' 0"	6' 8"	0' 4 3/4"
68" x 80	5' 8"	6' 8"	0' 4 3/4"
72" x 80	6' 0"	6' 8"	0' 4 3/4"
48" x 84	4' 0"	7' 0"	0' 4 3/4"
60" x 84	5' 0"	7' 0"	0' 4 3/4"

- Place the sliding door at the locations, as shown.

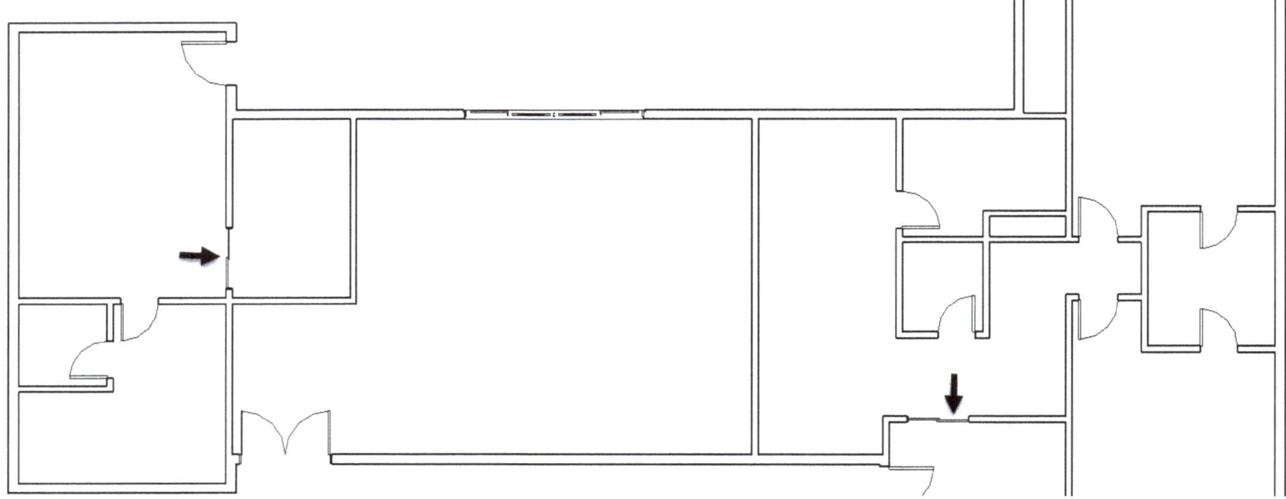

- Go to *https://market.bimsmith.com*, and then type **Bi-Fold Door** in the search bar.
- Select the **BI-FOLD DOOR** family from the search results.
- Click on the **Revit** icon and then click the **Download** button located at the top-left corner of the webpage.
- Unzip the downloaded file to a desired location on your computer. Next, double-click on the **Bifold-4 Panel** revit family file.

- Click **Upgrade the Model** on the **Model Upgrade** message box; the model upgrades to the new version and is opened in a new tab.

- On the ribbon, click **Create > Family Editor > Load into Project and Close** .
- Click the drop-down available at the top of the **Properties** palette, and then select **Bifold-4 Panel 48" x 84"**.
- Place the pointer on the lower edge of the interior wall, as shown. Click to position the door.

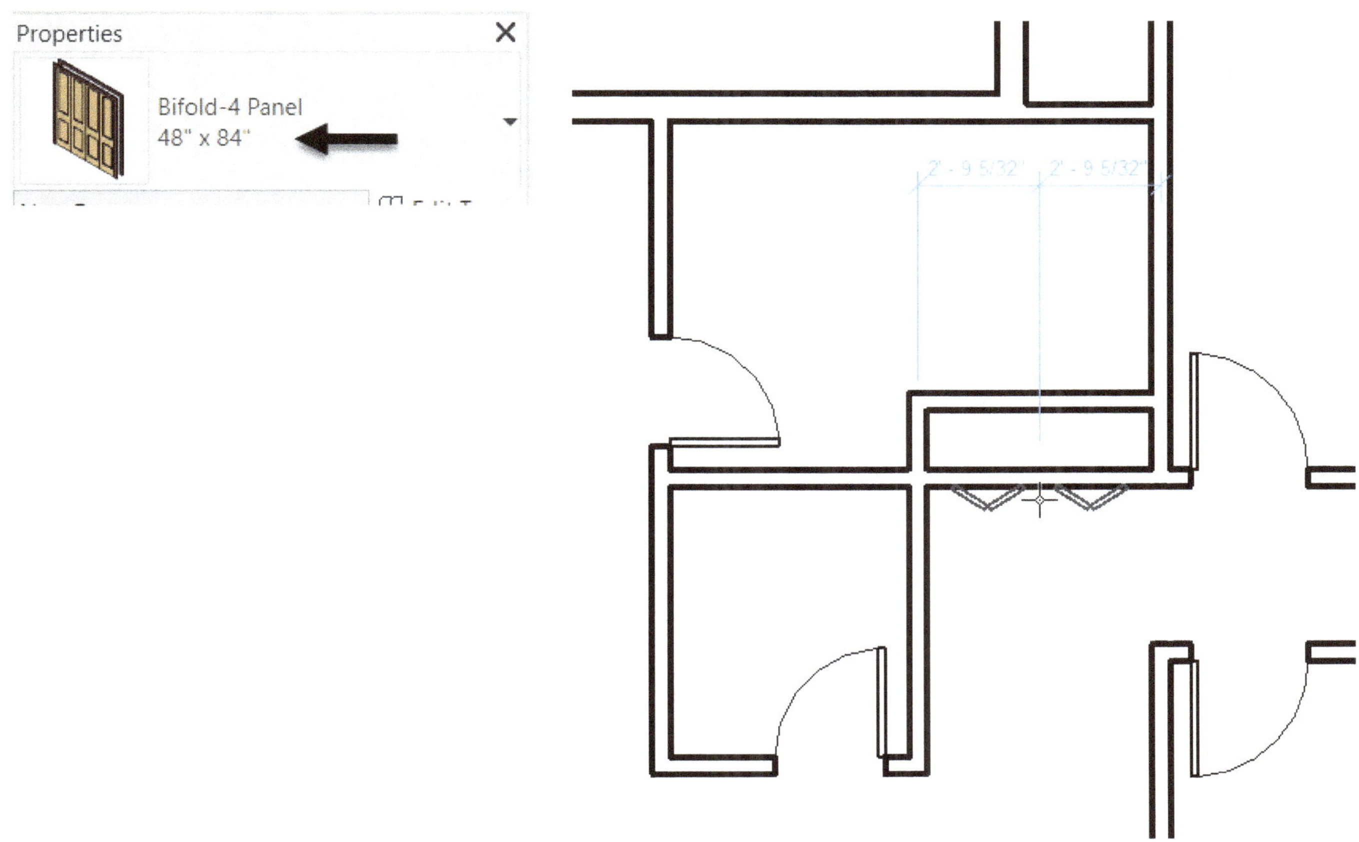

- Click the drop-down available at the top of the **Properties** palette, and then select **Bifold-4 Panel 72" x 84"**.
- Position the Bi-fold door at the location, as shown.

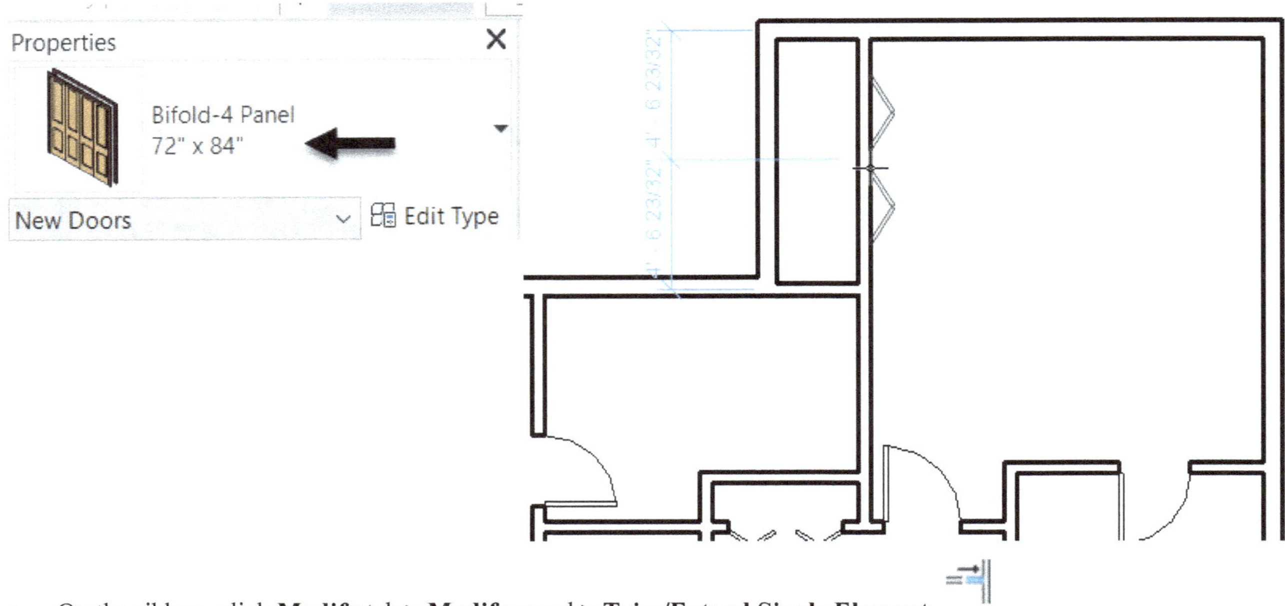

- On the ribbon, click **Modify** tab > **Modify** panel > **Trim/Extend Single Element**.
- Select the edge of the wall, as shown. The boundary is defined.
- Select the wall; the wall is extended up to the selected edge.

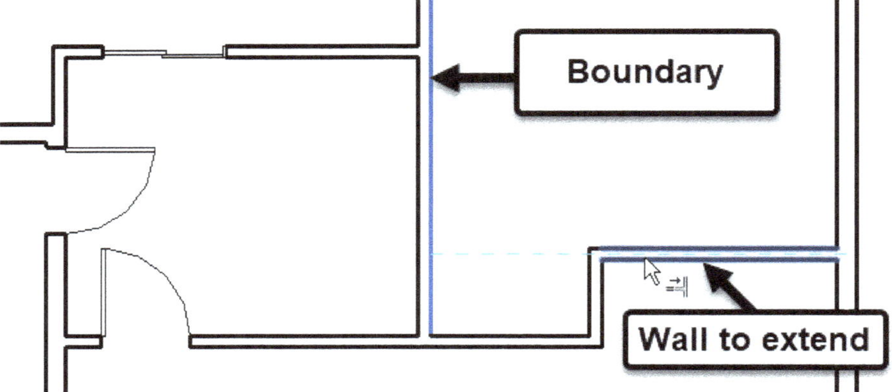

- On the ribbon, click **Architecture** tab > **Build** panel > **Door**.
- Click the drop-down available at the top of the **Properties** palette, and then select **Bifold-4 Panel 48" x 84"**.
- Position the Bi-fold door at the location, as shown.

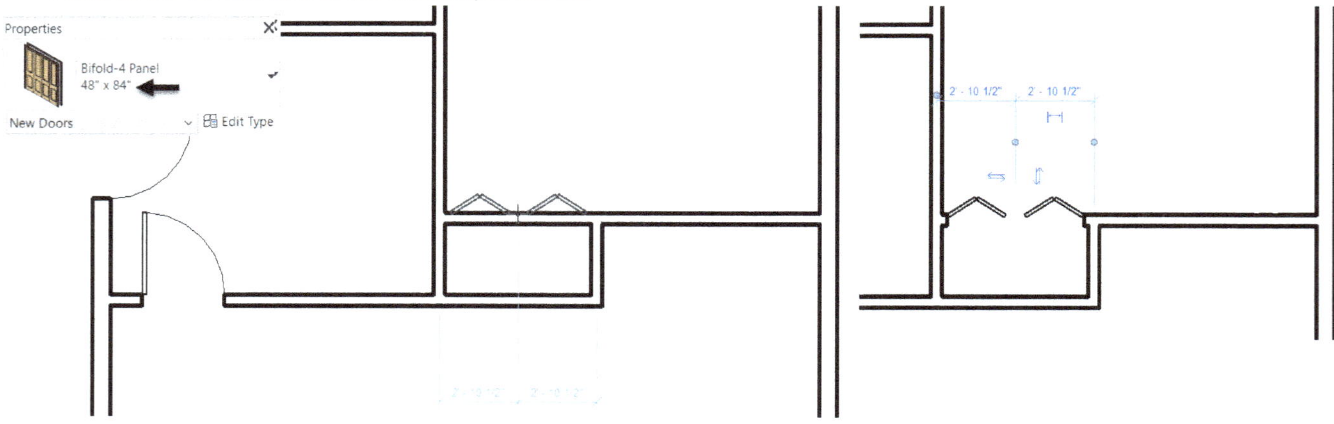

- On the ribbon, click **Modify|Place Door** tab > **Mode** panel > **Load Family**.

- Go to **Local Disc C > Program Data > Autodesk > RVT 2024 > Libraries > English imperial (or metric or other base) > Doors > Residential**. Next, double-click on **Door-Garage-Embossed_Panel**.
- Click the drop-down available at the top of the **Properties** palette, and then select **Door-Garage-Embossed_Panel 192" x 84"**.
- Click on the outer horizontal edge of the garage wall, as shown. Next, press ESC.
- Click the **Default 3D View** icon on the Quick Access Toolbar and notice that the garage door is placed at height above the bottom of the wall. You need to adjust the Sill Height of the garage door such that the garage door is placed at the Site level.

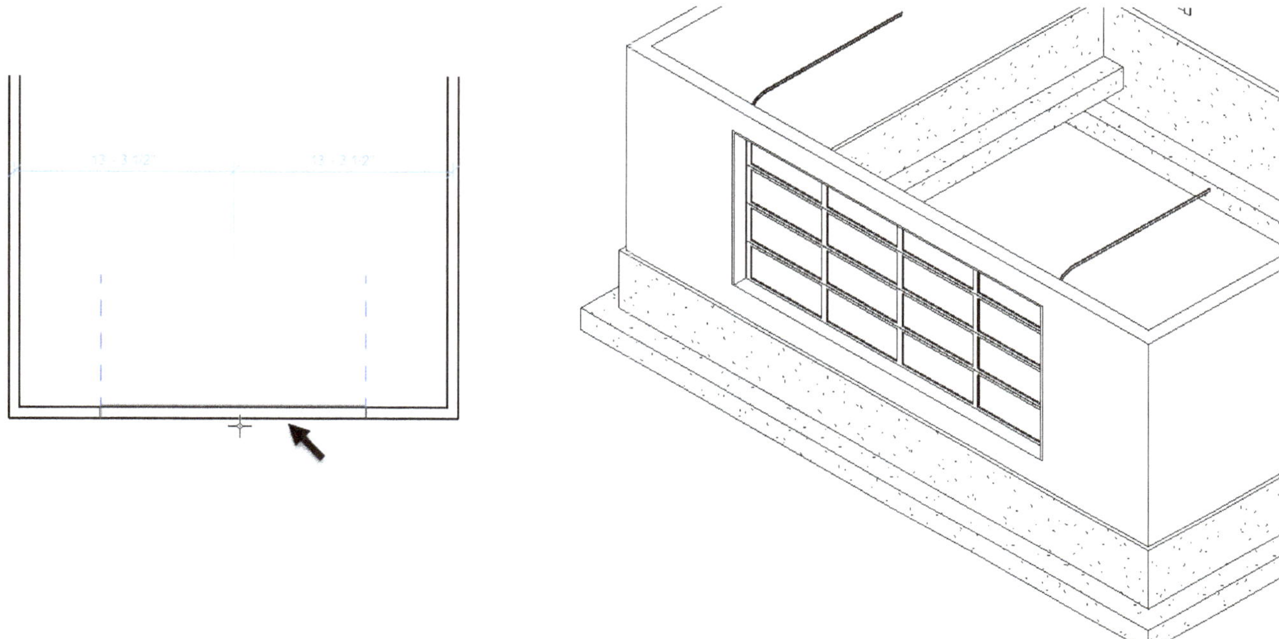

- Select **First Floor** from the **Level** drop-down under the **Constraints** section of the **Properties** palette.
- Select the garage door and type **1' 10 ½"** in the **Sill Height** box. Next, press ESC.

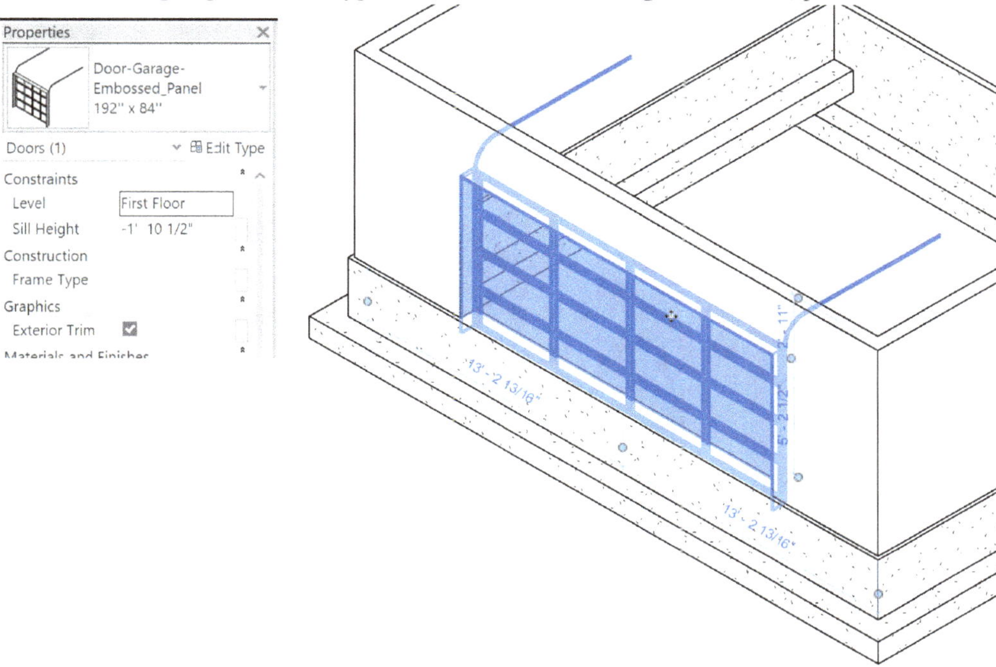

Next, you need to remove material from the foundation wall so that the door will not intersect with it.

- Select the foundation wall intersecting with the garage door.
- On the ribbon, click **Modify|Wall** tab > **Mode** panel > **Edit Profile**.
- Click on the front face of the ViewCube to change the orientation of the model.

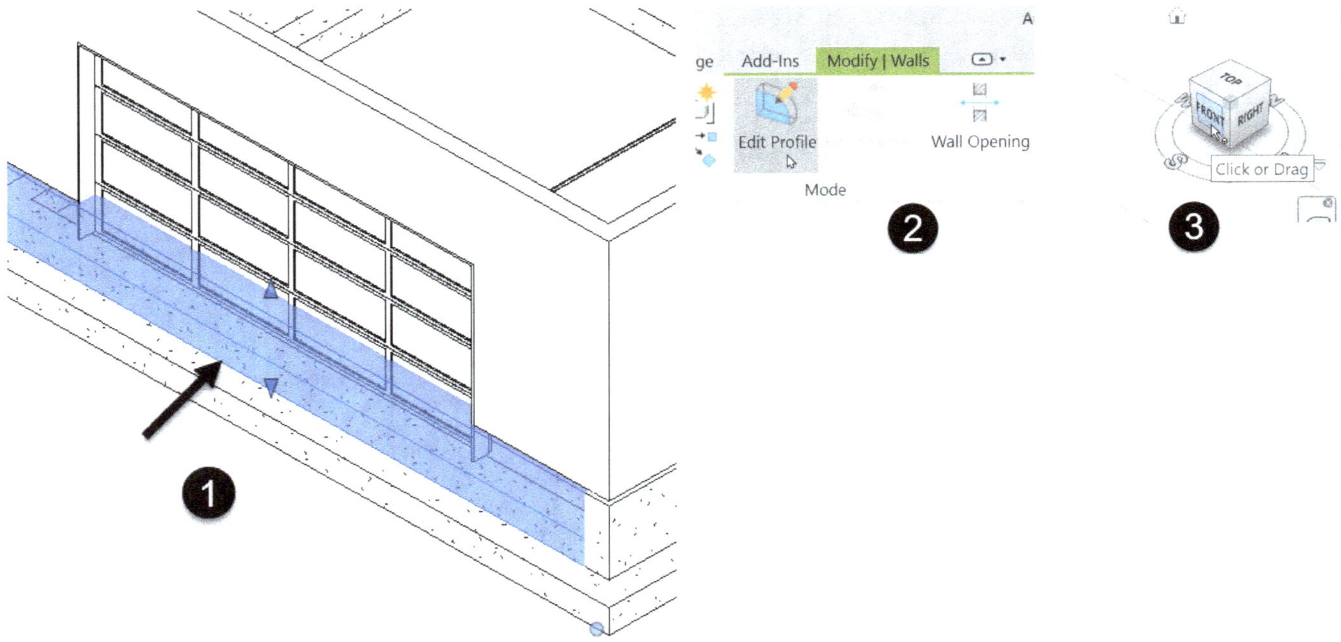

- On the ribbon, click **Modify|Wall** > **Edit Profile** tab > **Draw** panel > **Line**.
- Select the intersection and corner points of the lower portion of the garage door, as shown. Next, press ESC twice.

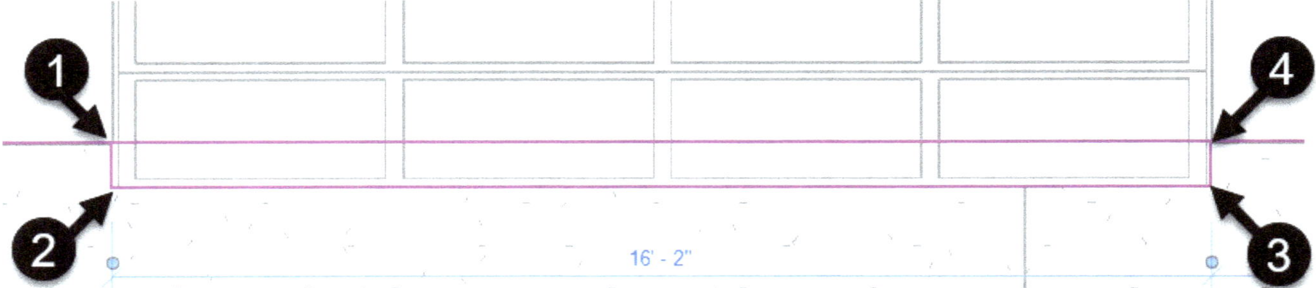

- Select the top horizontal line of the foundation wall, as shown. Next, drag the right endpoint of the selected line.

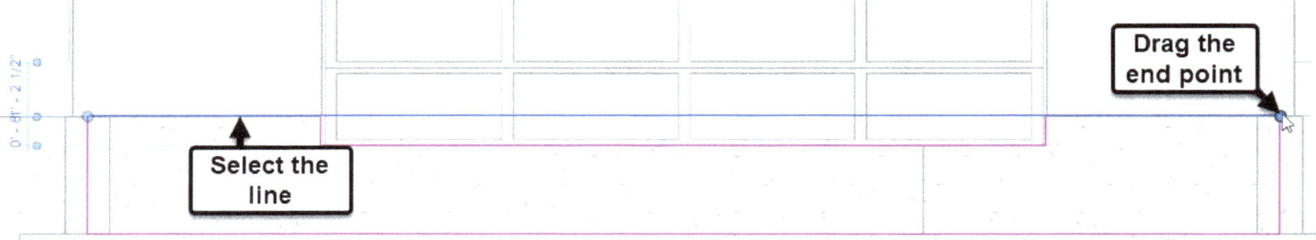

- Release the pointer on the endpoint of the left vertical line, as shown.
- Click the **Unjoin Elements** button on the **Autodesk Revit 2024** message box.

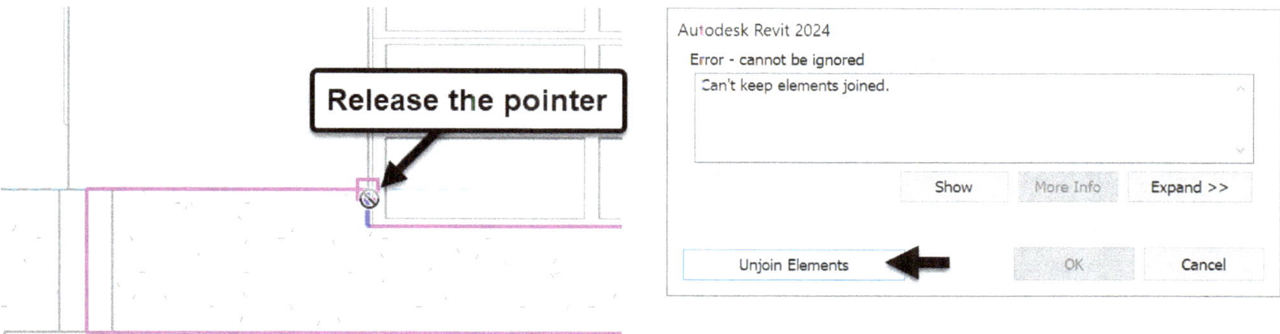

- On the ribbon, click **Modify|Wall** > **Edit Profile** tab > **Draw** panel > **Line**. Next, create a line, as shown.
- On the ribbon, click **Modify|Wall** > **Edit Profile** tab > **Mode** panel > **Finish Edit Mode**.

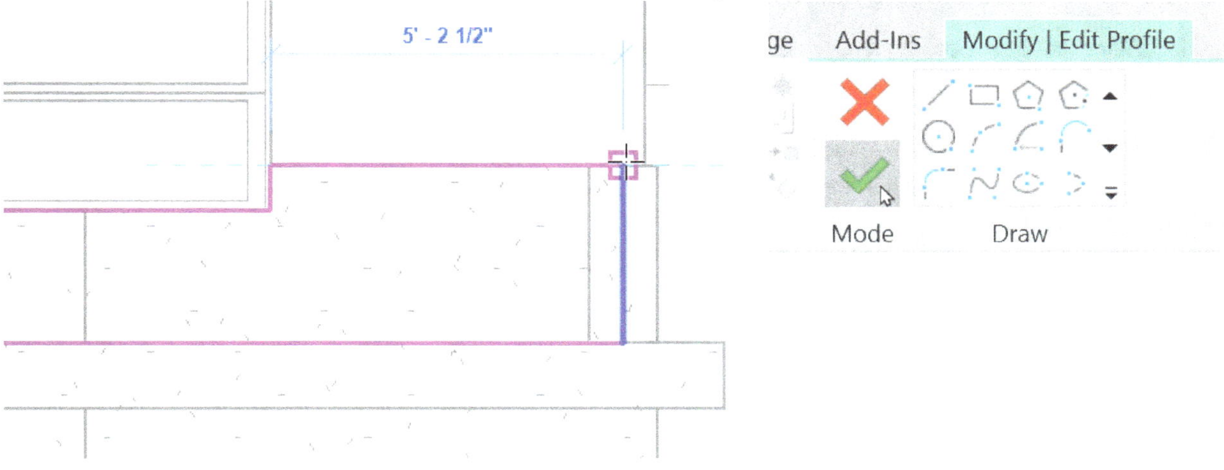

Next, you need to create a door opening for the kitchen wall.

- Double-click on the FIRST FLOOR level under the **Floor Plans** node.
- Select the kitchen wall and click the **Edit Profile** icon on the **Mode** panel of the **Modify|Walls** ribbon tab.

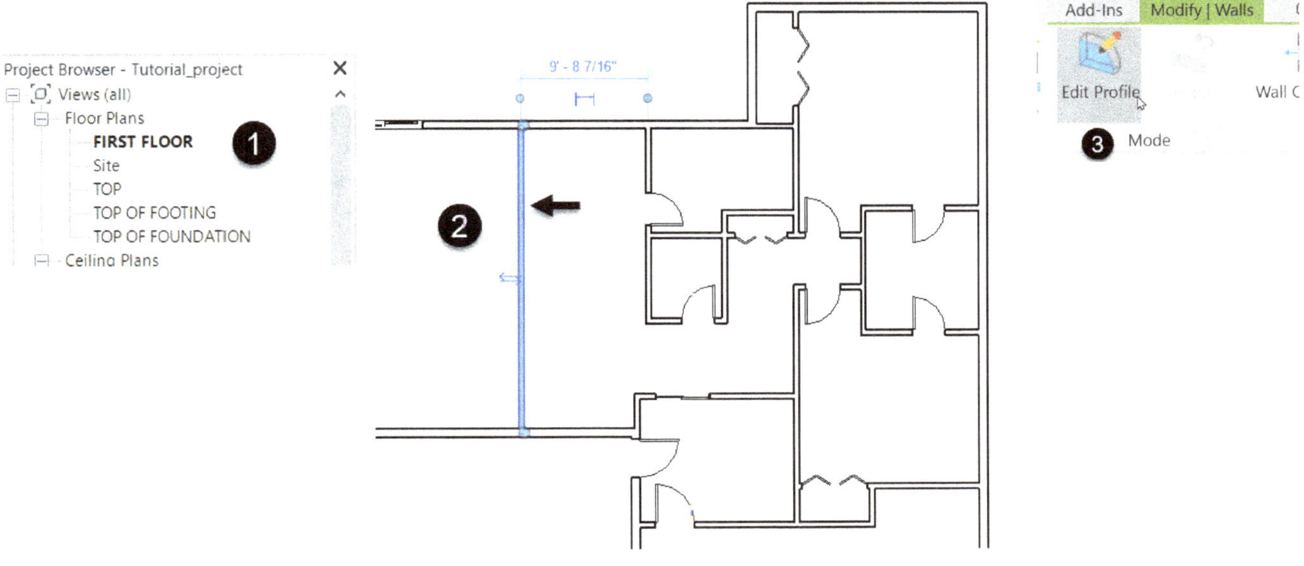

- Select the **Elevation:East** from the **Go To View** dialog, and then click the **Open View** button.
- On the ribbon, click **Modify|Wall** tab > **Modify** panel > **Offset**. Next, type 3'8" in the **Offset** box available on the Options bar.
- Click on the right-side of the left vertical line of the wall.
- Click on the left-side of the right vertical line of the wall.

- Type 7 in the **Offset** box and select the left vertical line.
- Click on the upper side of the lower horizontal line, as shown.

- On the ribbon, click **Modify|Wall** tab > **Modify** panel > **Trim/Extend to Corner (TR)**.
- Select the portions of the vertical and horizontal lines to form corners, as shown.
- Click the **Unjoin Elements** button.

- On the ribbon, click **Modify|Wall** tab > **Draw** panel > **Line**.
- Close the gap by selecting the lower endpoints of the vertical lines, as shown.

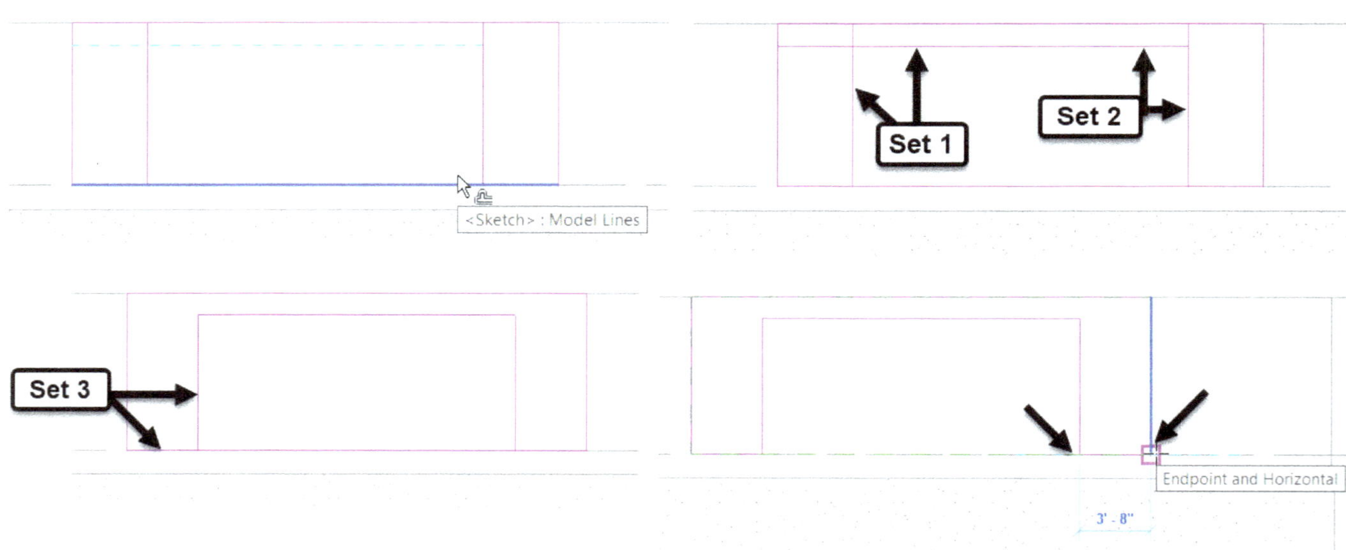

- On the ribbon, click **Modify|Wall** > **Edit Profile** tab > **Mode** panel > **Finish Edit Mode**.
- Click the **Default 3D View** icon on the Quick Access Toolbar.

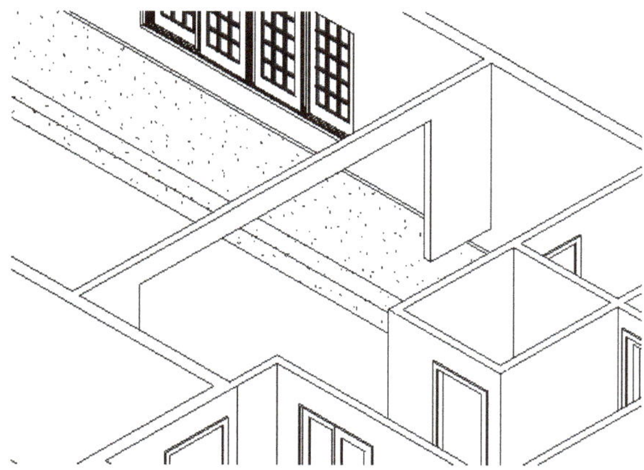

Tutorial 5: Placing Windows

- Double-click on the **TOP OF FOUNDATION** under the **Floor Plans** node in the **Project Browser**.
- On the ribbon, click **Architecture** tab > **Build** panel > **Window**.
- Click the drop-down available at the top of the **Properties** palette, and then select Fixed 24" x 48" window.
- Type **3** in the **Sill Height** box; it defines the height at which the window will be placed.

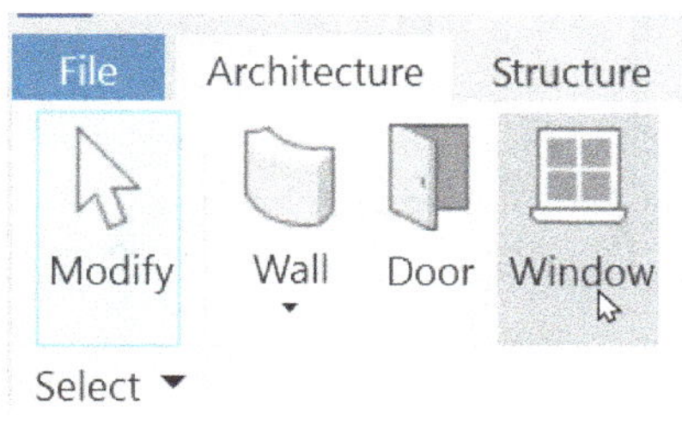
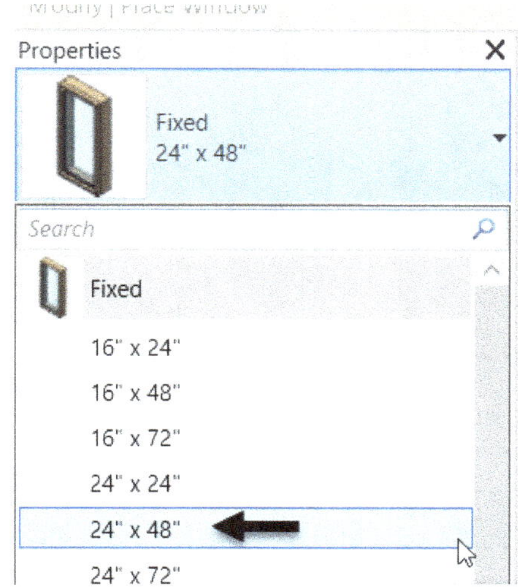
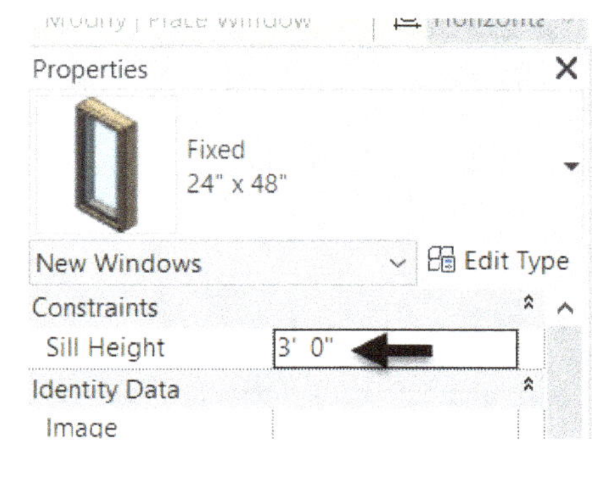

- Zoom to the bathroom area near the bottom-left corner, as shown.
- Place the pointer near the outer edge of the exterior wall, as shown. Next, click to position the window.
- Click the dimension displayed between the window and the adjacent wall. Next, type 2 and press ENTER.

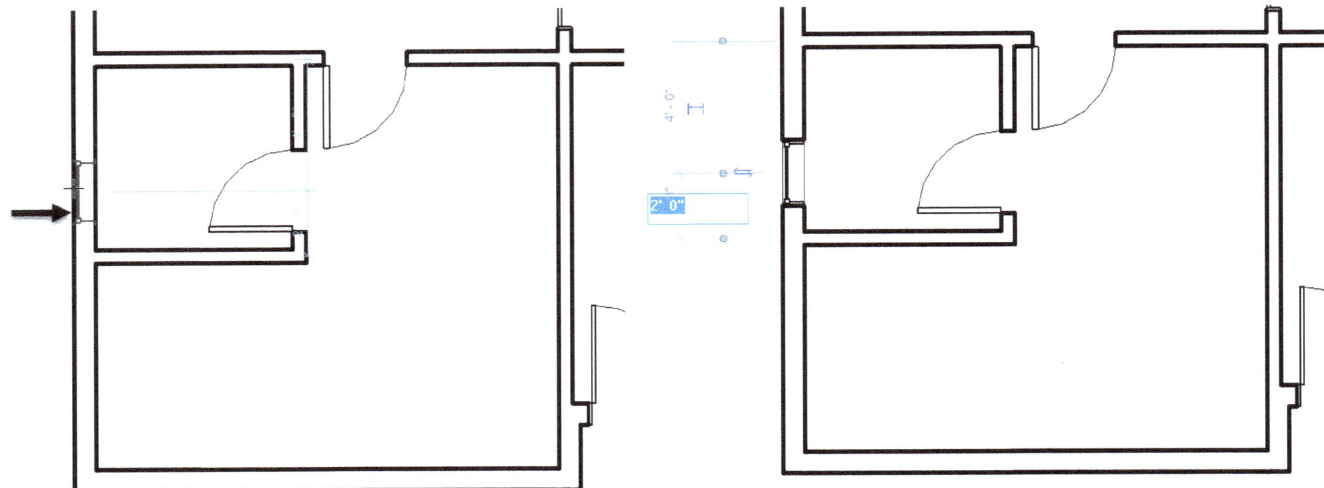

- Likewise, place the fixed windows at the locations, as shown.

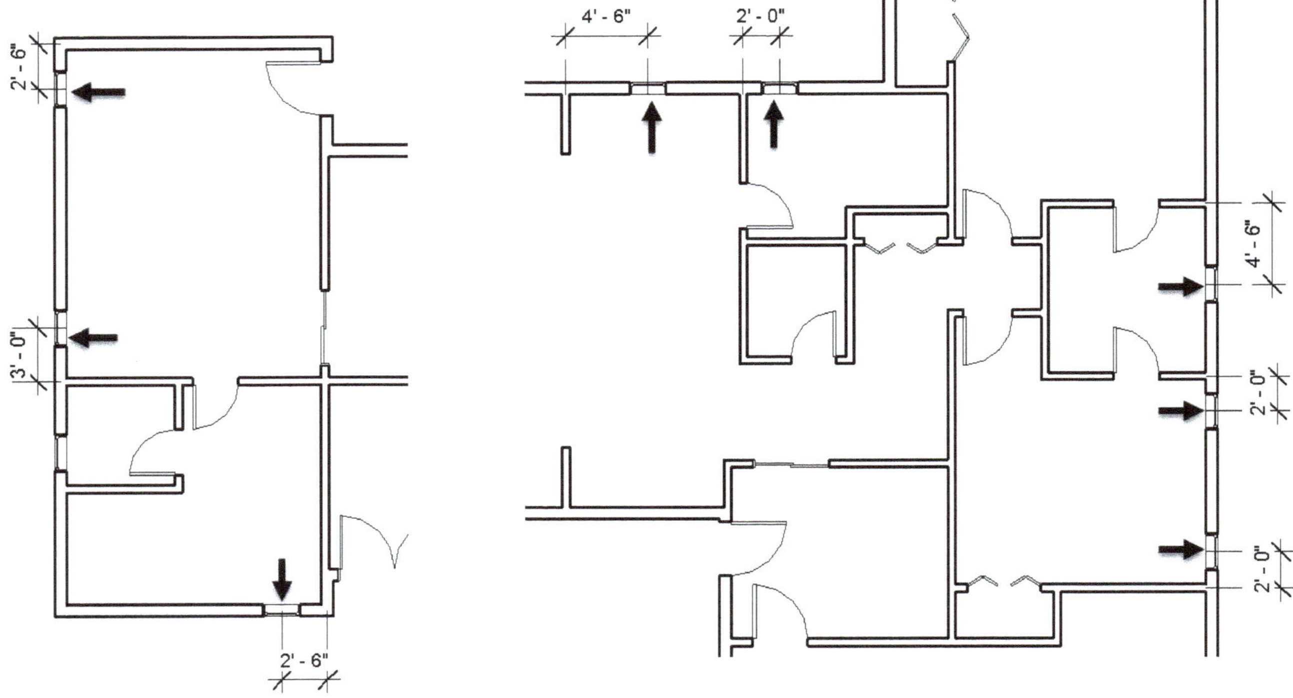

- On the ribbon, click **Architecture** tab > **Build** panel > **Window** .
- On the ribbon, click **Modify|Place Door** tab > **Mode** panel > **Load Family**.
- Go to **Local Disc C > Program Data > Autodesk > RVT 2024 > Libraries > English imperial (or metric or other base) > Windows**. Next, double-click on **Window-Casement-Double**.
- On the **Specify Types** dialog, select the 57" x 48" type, and then click **OK**.

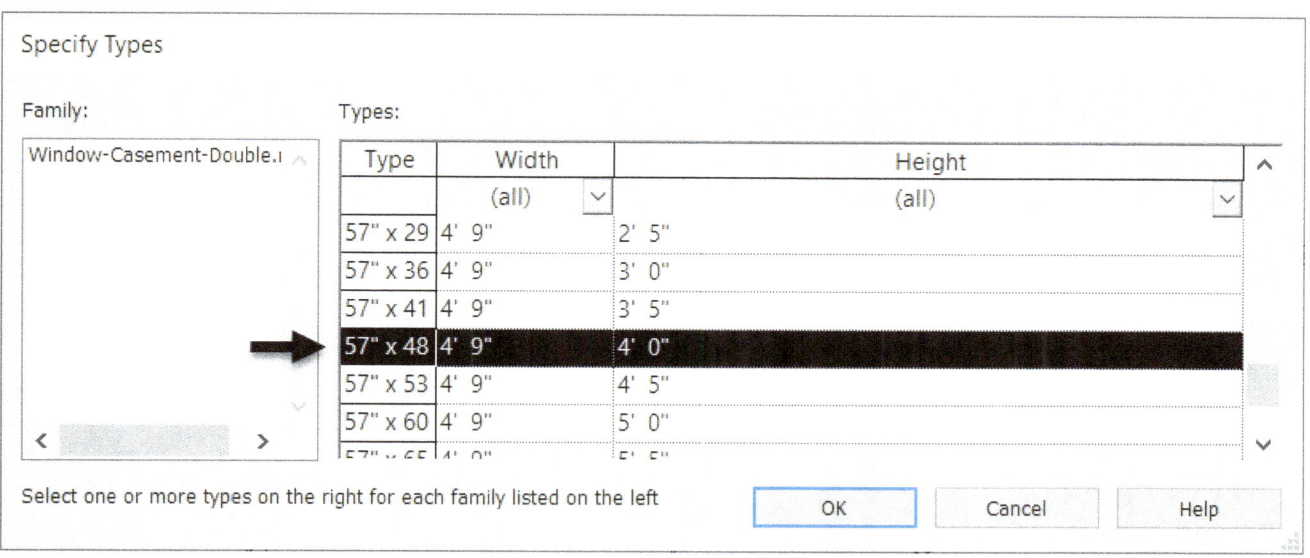

- Select the **Overwrite the existing version** option.
- On the **Properties** palette, select **Window-Casement-Double 57" x 48"** door from the **Basic window** drop-down.
- Type **2** in the **Sill Height** box and place the windows at the locations shown in figure.

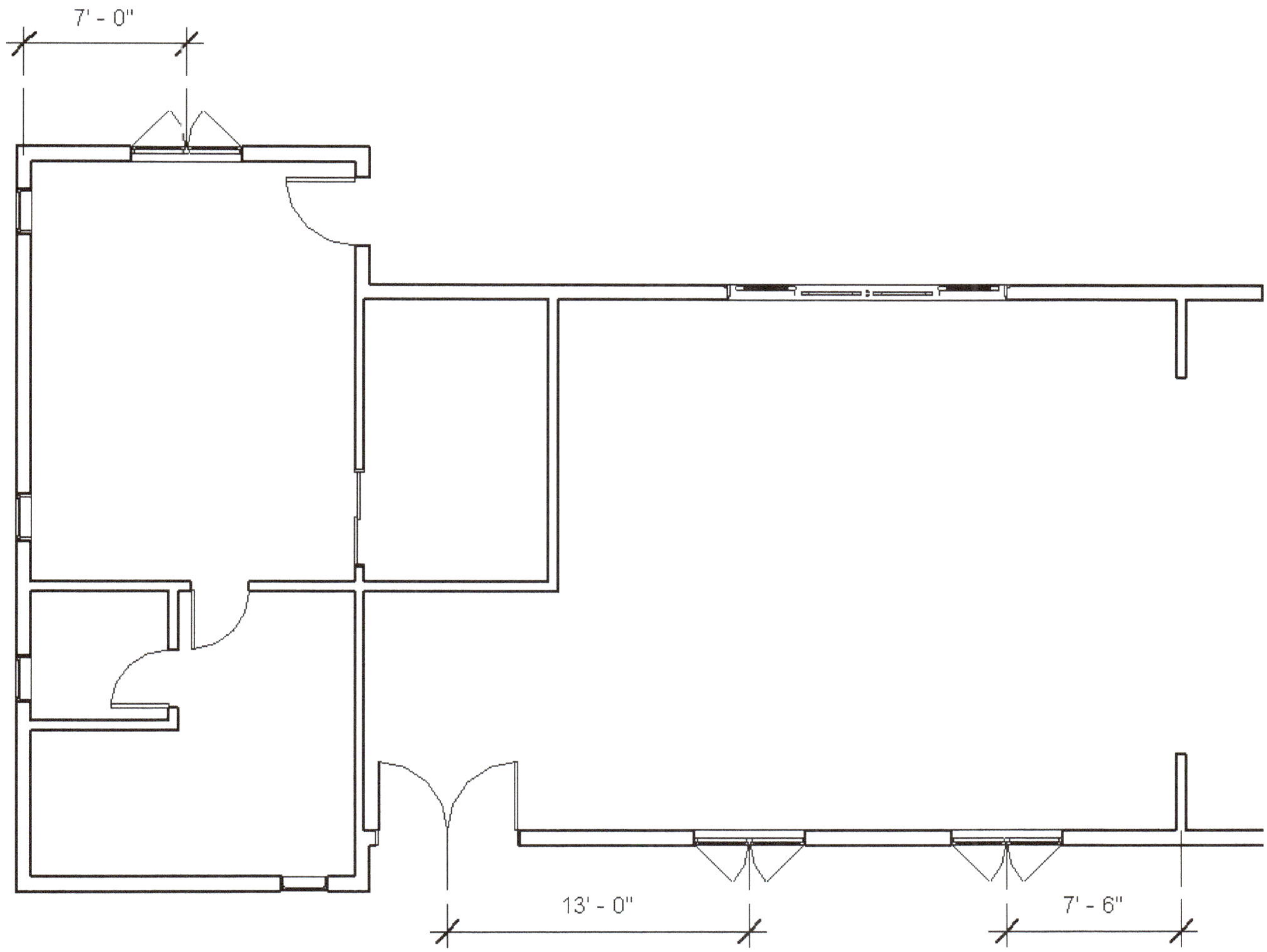

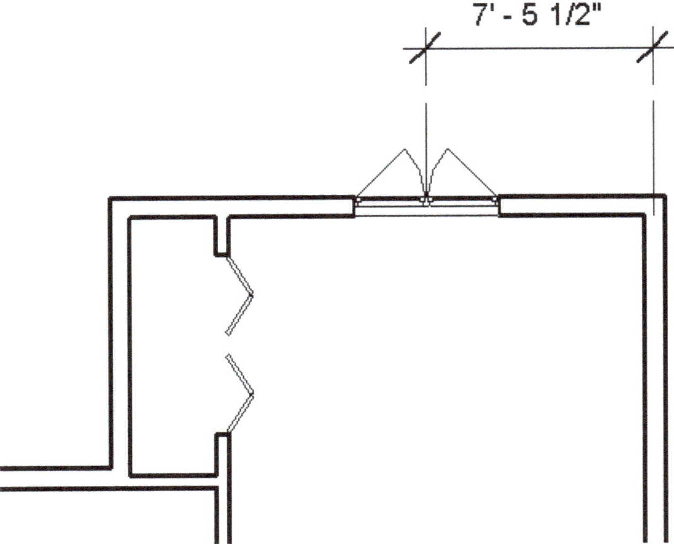

- On the ribbon, click **Architecture** tab > **Build** panel > **Window**.

- On the ribbon, click **Modify|Place Door** tab > **Mode** panel > **Load Family**.
- Go to **Local Disc C > Program Data > Autodesk > RVT 2024 > Libraries > English imperial (or metric or other base) > Windows**. Next, double-click on **Window-Casement-Triple**.
- On the **Specify Types** dialog, select the 85" x 60" type, and then click **OK**.
- On the **Properties** palette, select **Window-Casement-Triple 85" x 60"** door from the **Basic window** drop-down.
- Type **2** in the **Sill Height** box and place the window on the garage wall, as shown in figure.

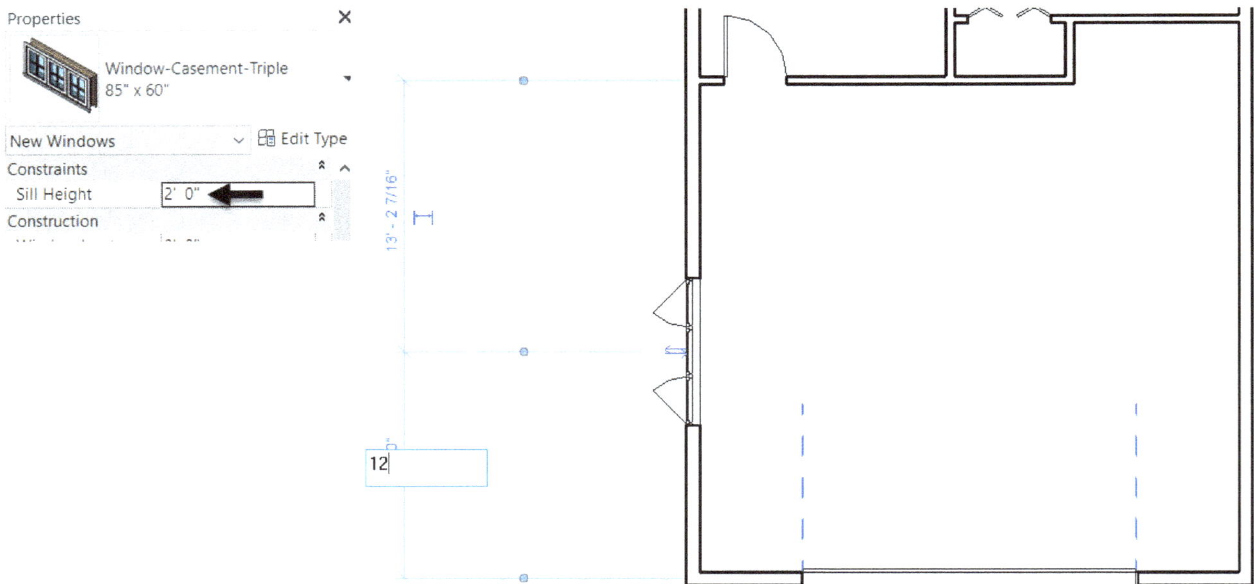

Tutorial 6: Creating Floors

In a project, you need to first create a structural floor, and then create a finished floor on top of it.

Creating the Structural Floor

- Double-click on the **First Floor** under the **Floor Plans** node in the **Project Browser**.
- On the **View Control Bar** located at the bottom of the drawing area, click the **Detail Level** icon, and select the **Medium** option.

- On the ribbon, click **Architecture** tab > **Build** panel > **Floor** drop-down > **Floor: Structural** (or) click **Structure** tab > **Structure** panel > **Floor** drop-down > **Floor: Structural**.
- On the Properties palette, from the **Type Selector**, select the **Generic – 12"** floor type.
- Click the **Edit Type** icon on the **Properties** palette.

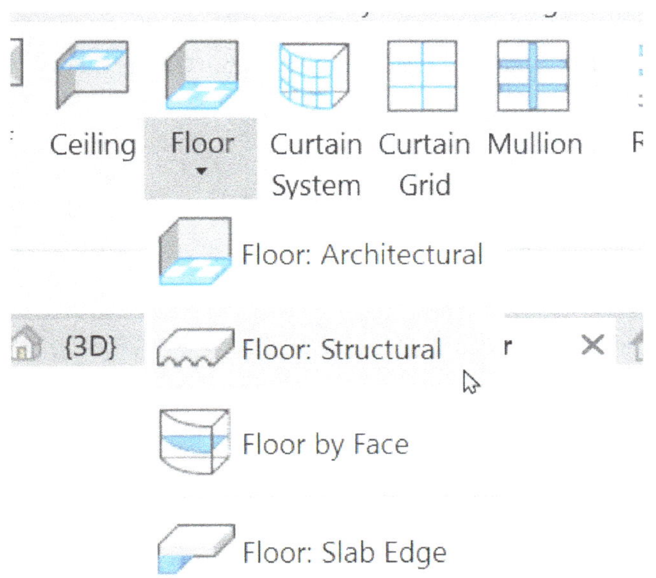

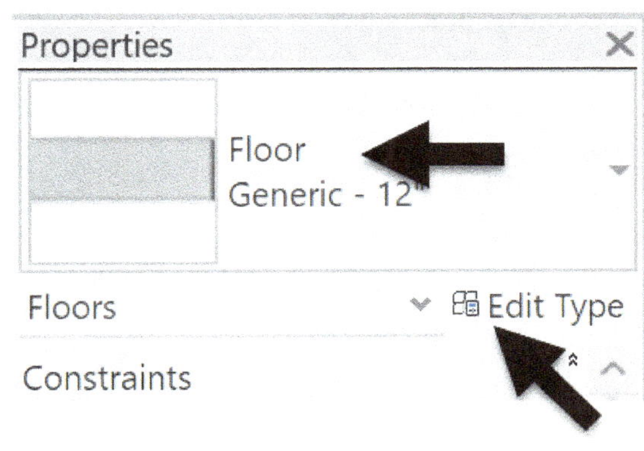

- Click the **Preview** button located at the bottom left corner of the **Type Properties** dialog.
- Click the **Duplicate** button next to the **Type** drop-down. Next, type **New Concrete - 12"** in the **Name** box and click **OK**.

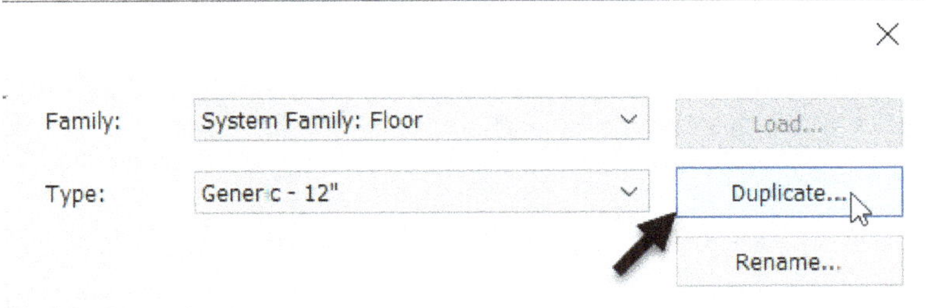

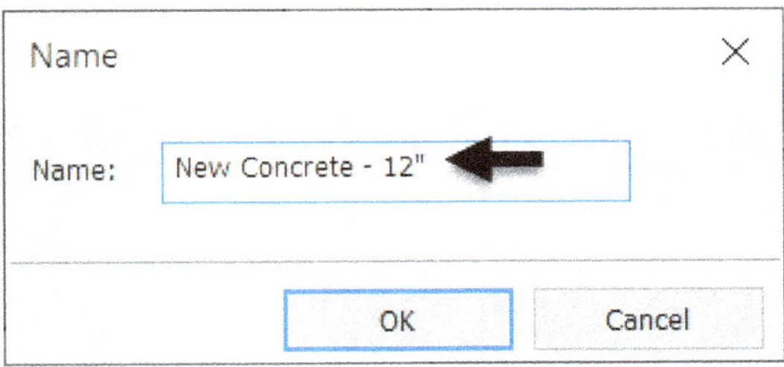

- Click the **Edit** button next to the **Structure** parameter; the **Edit Assembly** dialog appears. Notice that there is only one layer called **Structure [1]** in the table.
- Click in the **Material** column of the **Structure[1]** layer. Next, click the **Browse** button to display the **Material Browser** dialog.

Layers

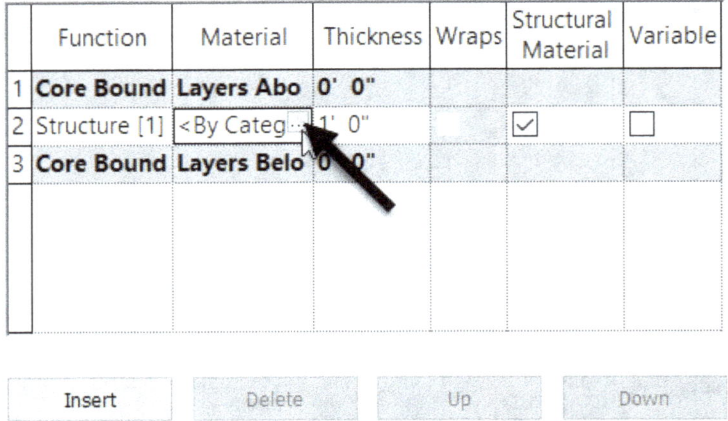

	Function	Material	Thickness	Wraps	Structural Material	Variable
1	**Core Bound**	**Layers Abo**	0' 0"			
2	Structure [1]	<By Categ	1' 0"		☑	☐
3	**Core Bound**	**Layers Belo**	0' 0"			

Insert	Delete	Up	Down

- Type **Concrete** in the search box, and then select the **Concrete, Lightweight** material from the search results. Next, click **OK** thrice.
- Make sure that the **Boundary Line** and **Pick Walls** icons are selected on the **Draw** panel of the **Modify|Create Floor Boundary** ribbon tab.

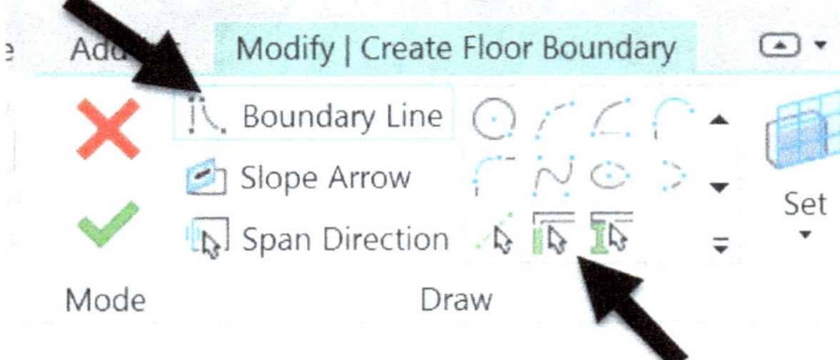

- Zoom to the top-left portion of the floor plan. Next, select the outer core boundary of the horizontal exterior wall, as shown.

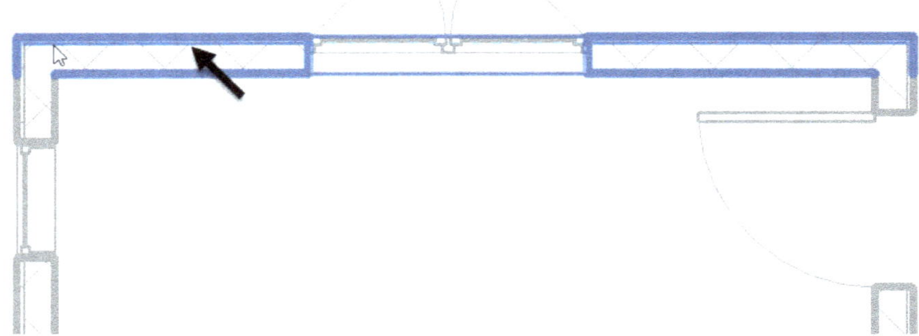

- Likewise, select the outer core boundaries of the exterior walls, as shown.

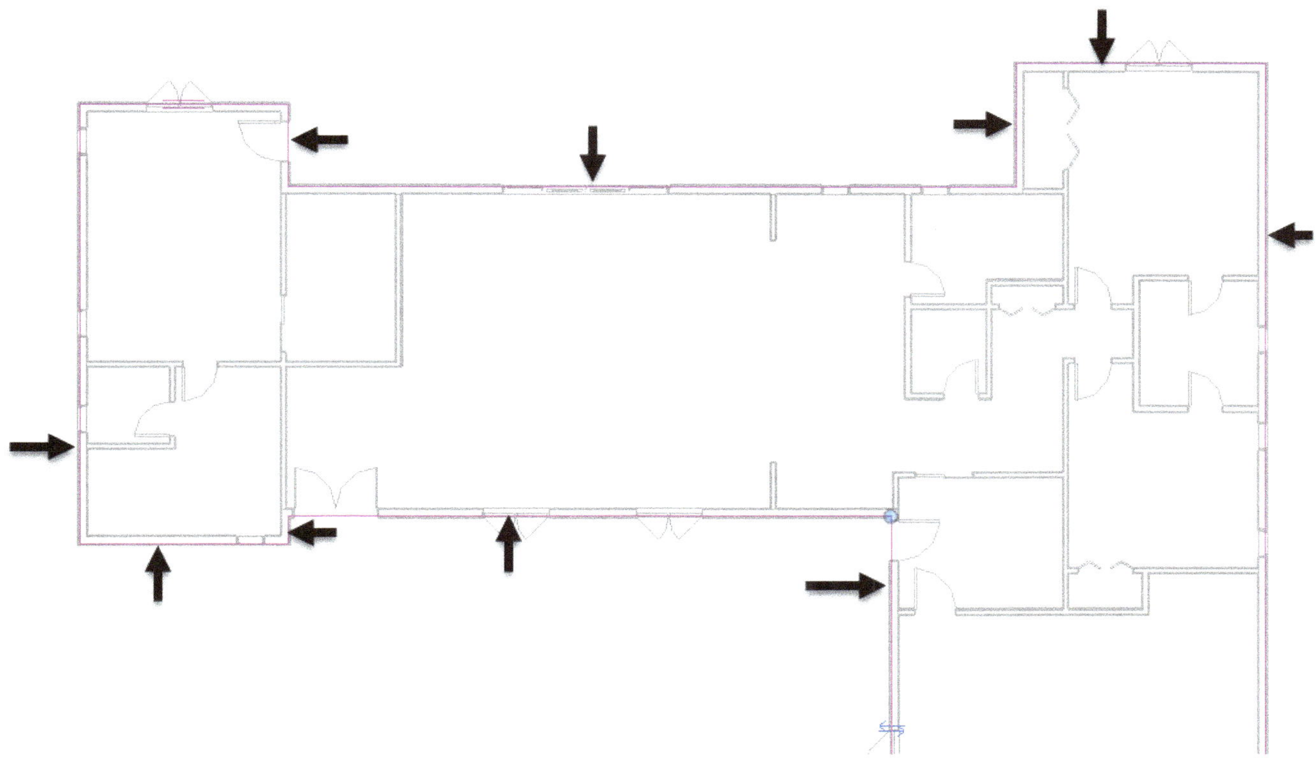

- Zoom to the interior wall near the garage area and select the outer edges, as shown.

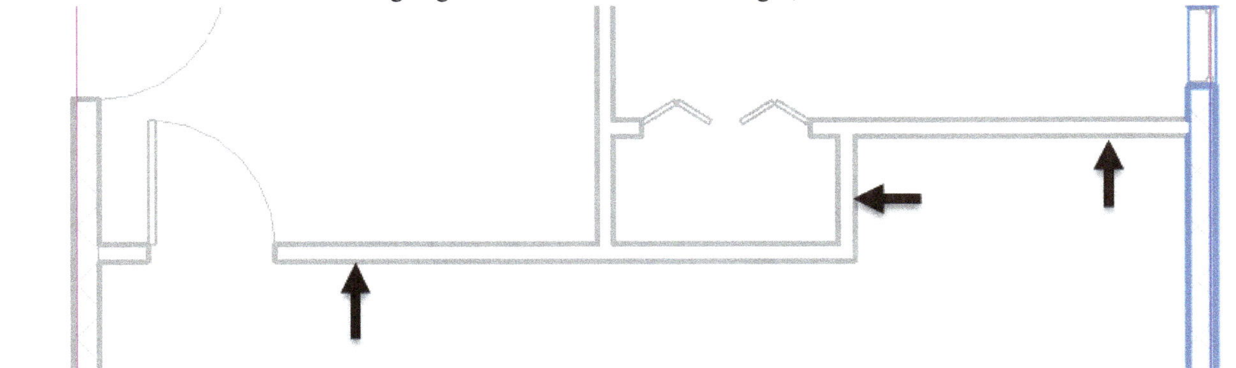

- Click the **Trim/Extend to corner (TR)** icon on the **Modify** panel of the **Modify|Create Floor Boundary** ribbon tab.
- Select the boundaries to form corners, as shown.

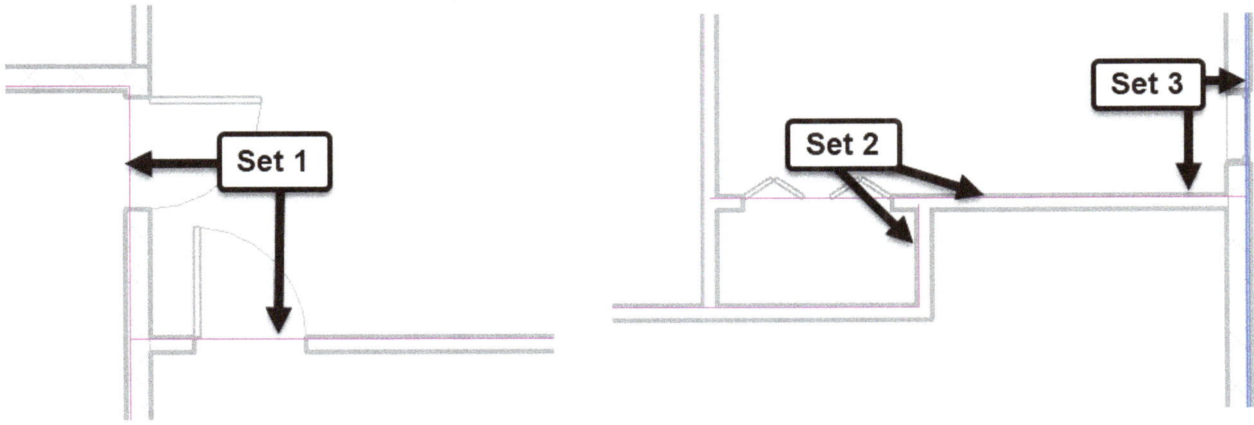

- Click the **Finish Edit Mode** ✓ icon on the **Mode** panel of the **Modify|Create Floor Boundary** ribbon tab. A message pops up showing that the floor/roof overlaps the highlighted wall. Click **Yes** to join geometry and cut the overlapping volume out of the wall.

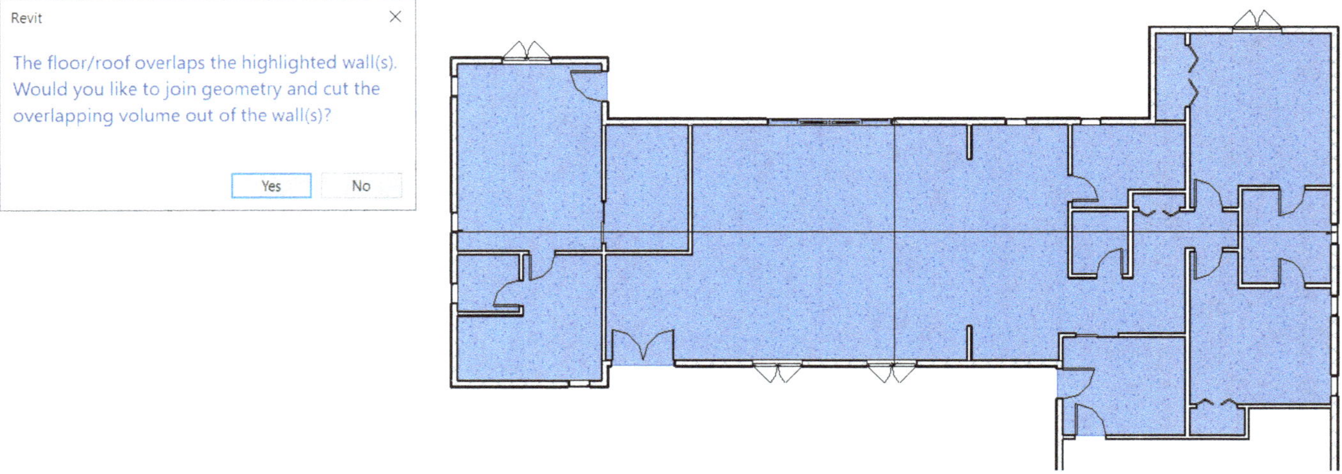

- On the ribbon, click **View** tab > **Create** panel > **Section**. Next, specify the first and second point of the section plane, as shown.

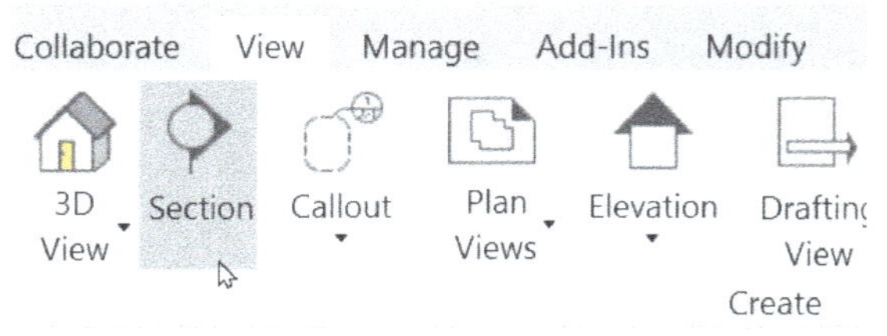

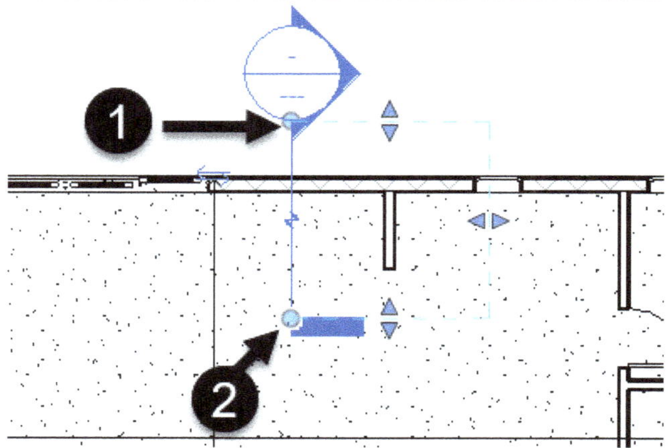

- In the Project Browser, expand the **Sections (Building Section)** node and double-click on **Section 1**.
- On the **View Control Bar** located at the bottom of the drawing area, click the **Detail Level** icon, and select the **Fine** option.

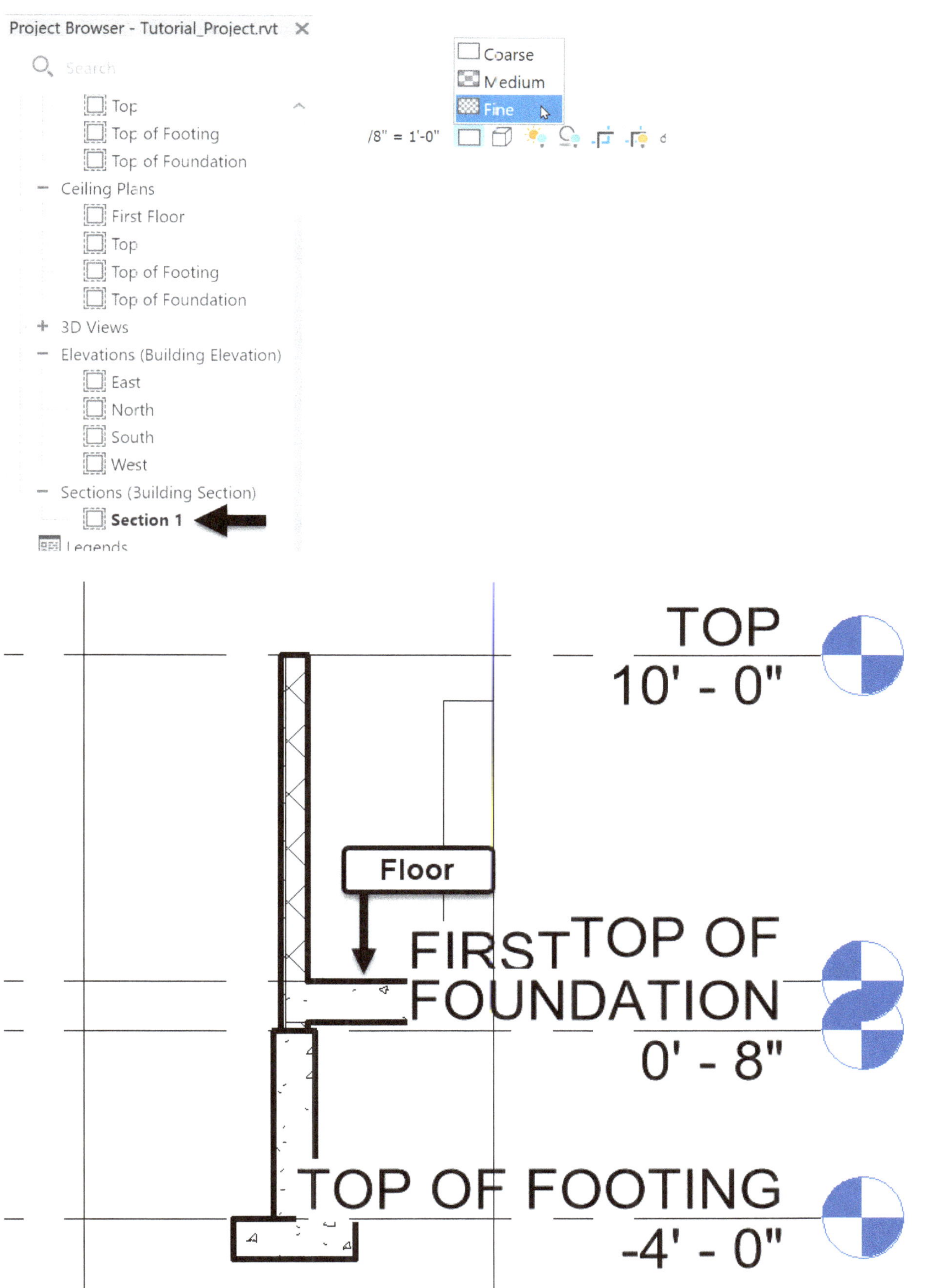

Project Browser - Tutorial_Project.rvt
Search
Top
Top of Footing
Top of Foundation
Ceiling Plans
First Floor
Top
Top of Footing
Top of Foundation
3D Views
Elevations (Building Elevation)
East
North
South
West
Sections (Building Section)
Section 1
Legends
Coarse
Medium
Fine
/8" = 1'-0"
TOP
10' - 0"
Floor
FIRST TOP OF
FOUNDATION
0' - 8"
TOP OF FOOTING
-4' - 0"

- Click the **Default 3D View** icon on the Quick Access Toolbar; the 3D view of the model is displayed.

Creating other floor types

- On the ribbon, click **Architecture** tab > **Build** panel > **Floor** drop-down > **Floor: Architectural**  .
- On the Properties palette, from the **Type Selector**, select the **New Concrete – 12"** floor type.
- Click the **Edit Type** icon on the **Properties** palette.
- Click the **Duplicate** button next to the **Type** drop-down. Next, type **Concrete - 4"** in the **Name** box and click **OK**.
- Click the **Edit** button next to the **Structure** parameter; the **Edit Assembly** dialog appears. Notice that there is only one layer called **Structure [1]** in the table.
- Click in the **Thickness** column of the **Structure[1]** layer. Next, type **0' 4"** and click **OK** twice.

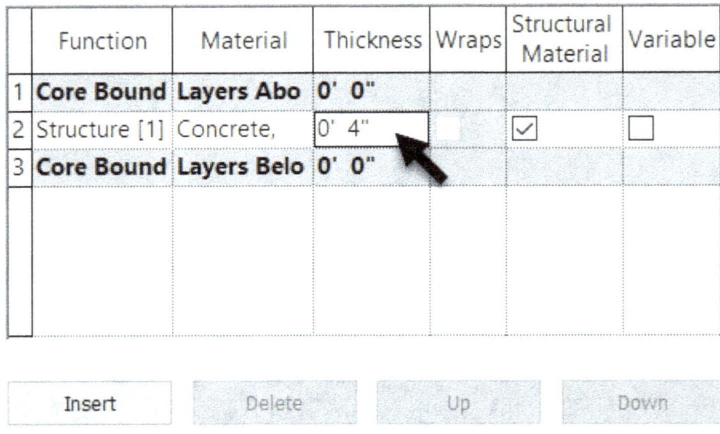

- On the **Properties** palette, from the **Type Selector**, select the **Wood Joist 10"– Ceramic Tile** floor type.
- Click the **Edit Type** icon on the **Properties** palette.
- Click the **Duplicate** button next to the **Type** drop-down. Next, type **Ceramic Tile** in the **Name** box and click **OK**.
- Click the **Edit** button next to the **Structure** parameter; the **Edit Assembly** dialog appears.
- Move the **Finish 1 [4]** and **Finish 2 [5]** layers down inside the Core Boundaries.
- Delete the two Structure layers.

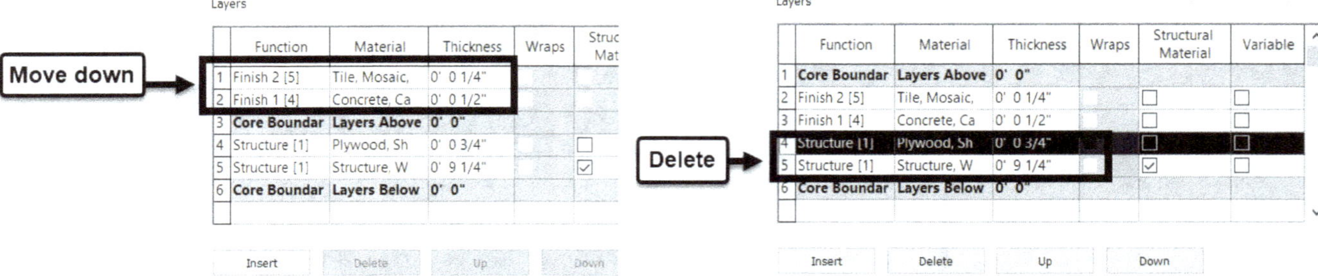

- Click **OK**.

Layers

	Function	Material	Thickness	Wraps	Structural Material	Variable
1	**Core Boundary**	**Layers Above**	**0' 0"**			
2	Finish 2 [5]	Tile, Mosaic,	0' 0 1/4"		☐	☐
3	Finish 1 [4]	Concrete, Cast	0' 0 1/2"		☐	☐
4	**Core Boundary**	**Layers Below**	**0' 0"**			

<table>
<tr><td>Insert</td><td>Delete</td><td>Up</td><td>Down</td></tr>
</table>

- Select the **Wood Joist 10"– Wood Finish** from the **Type** drop-down.
- Click the **Duplicate** button next to the **Type** drop-down. Next, type **Wood Finish** in the **Name** box and click **OK**.
- Click the **Edit** button next to the **Structure** parameter; the **Edit Assembly** dialog appears.
- Move the **Finish 1 [4]** layer down inside the Core Boundaries.
- Delete the two Structure layers.

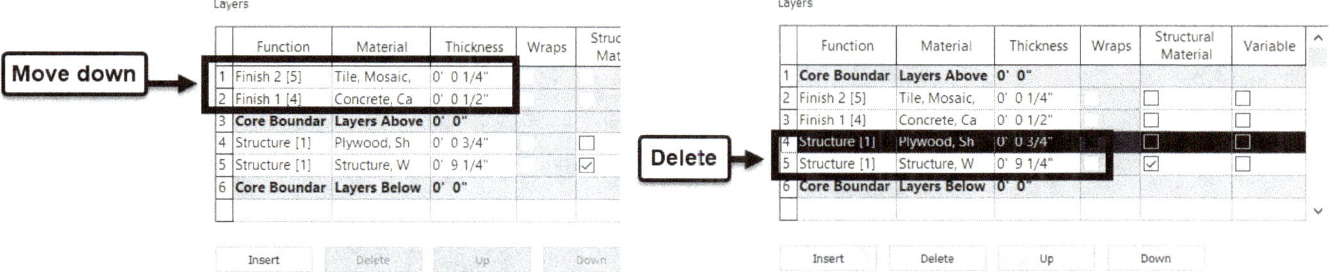

- Click **OK** twice.

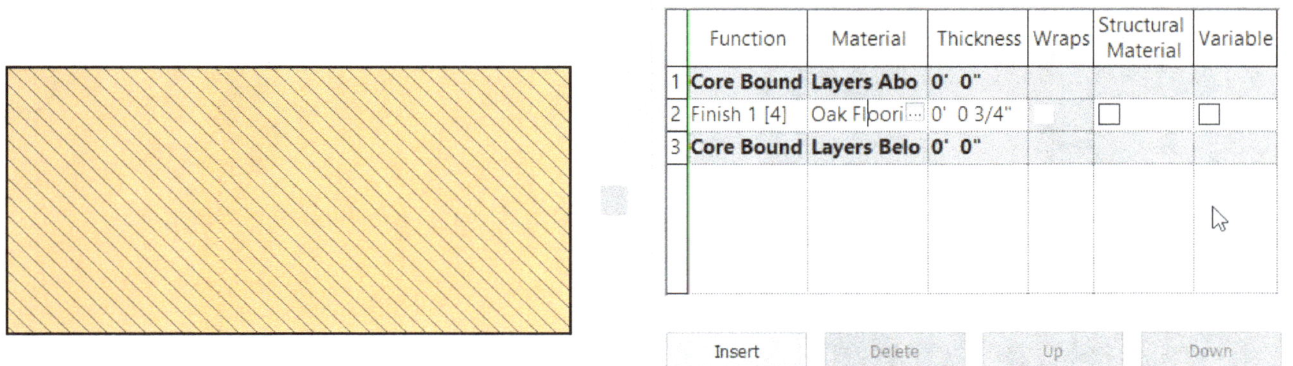

- Double-click on the **First Floor** under the **Floor Plans** node in the **Project Browser**.
- On the **Properties** palette, from the **Type Selector**, select the **Wood Finish** floor type.
- Select **Level > FIRST FLOOR**, and then click the **Edit Type** button. Notice that the **Default Thickness** of the Wood Finish floor is ¾". Click **OK** on the **Type Properties** dialog.
- Type ¾" in the **Height Offset From Level** box.
- Activate the **Boundary Line** and **Line** icons on the **Draw** panel of the **Modify|Create Floor Boundary** ribbon tab.

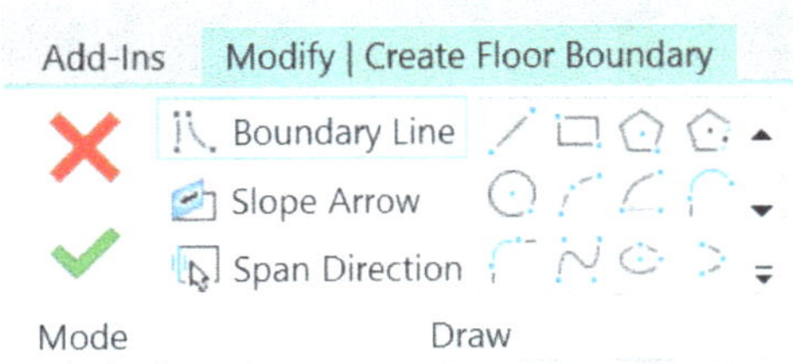

- Zoom to the top-left portion of the floor plan. Next, select the corner point of the exterior wall, as shown.

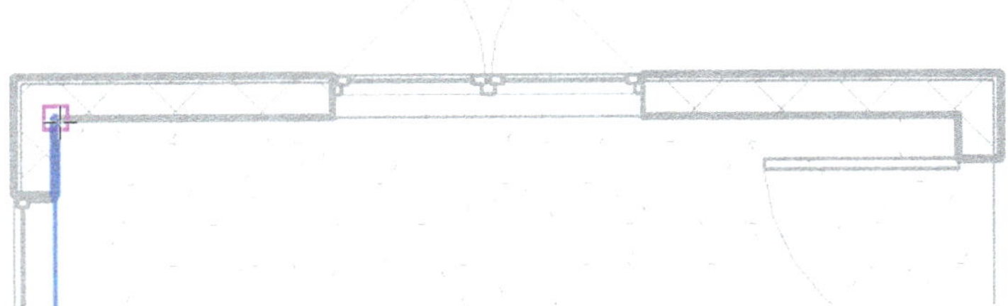

- Likewise, select the other corner points, as shown.

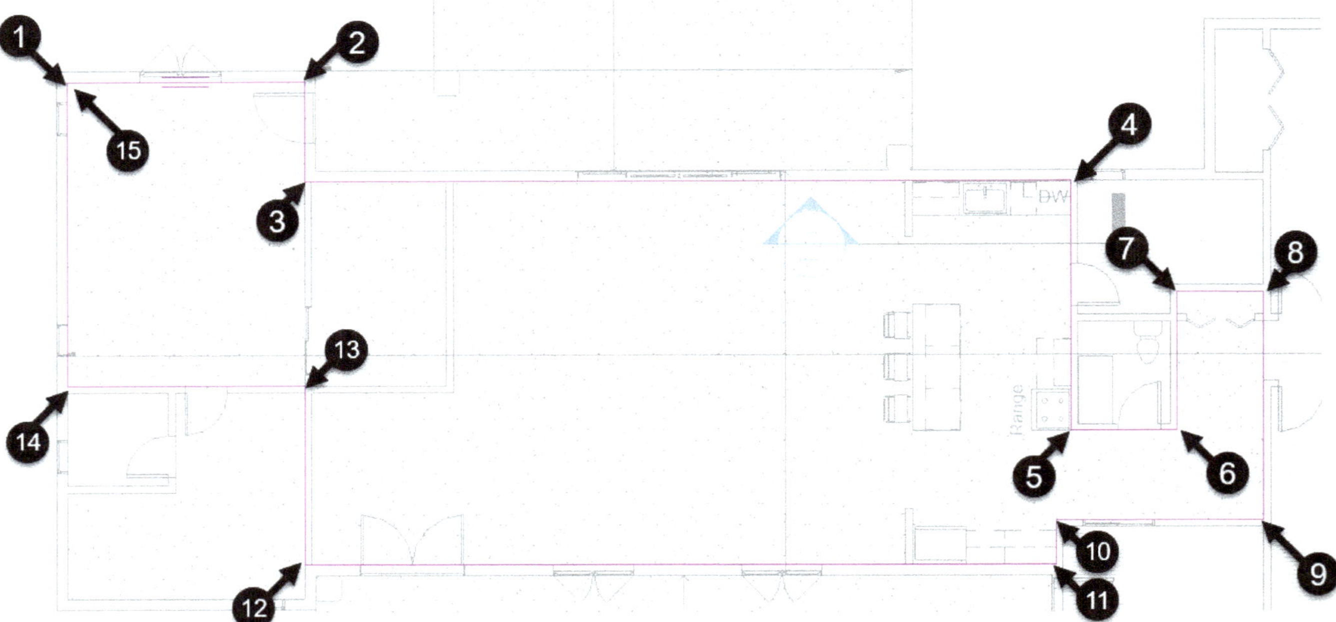

- Click the **Finish Edit Mode** ✔ icon on the **Mode** panel of the **Modify | Create Floor Boundary** ribbon tab.

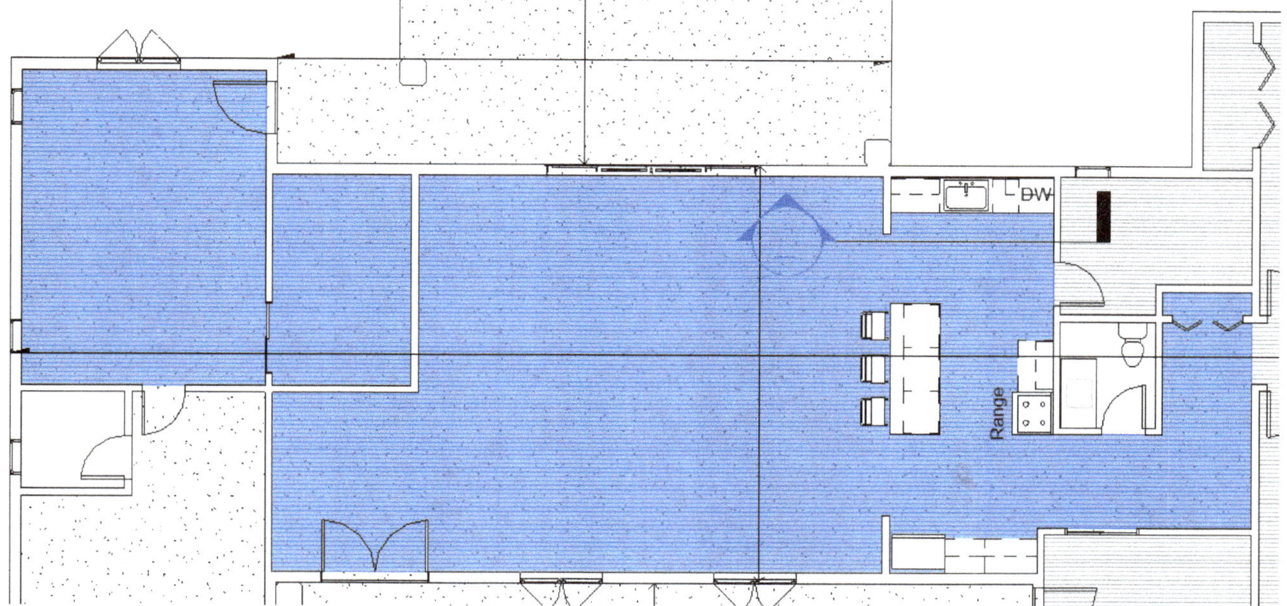

- On the ribbon, click **Architecture** tab > **Build** panel > **Floor** drop-down > **Floor: Architectural** .
- On the **Properties** palette, from the **Type Selector**, select the **Wood Finish** floor type.
- Activate the **Boundary Line** and **Line** icons on the **Draw** panel of the **Modify|Create Floor Boundary** ribbon tab.
- Select the lower-left corner of the interior wall near the garage, as shown.

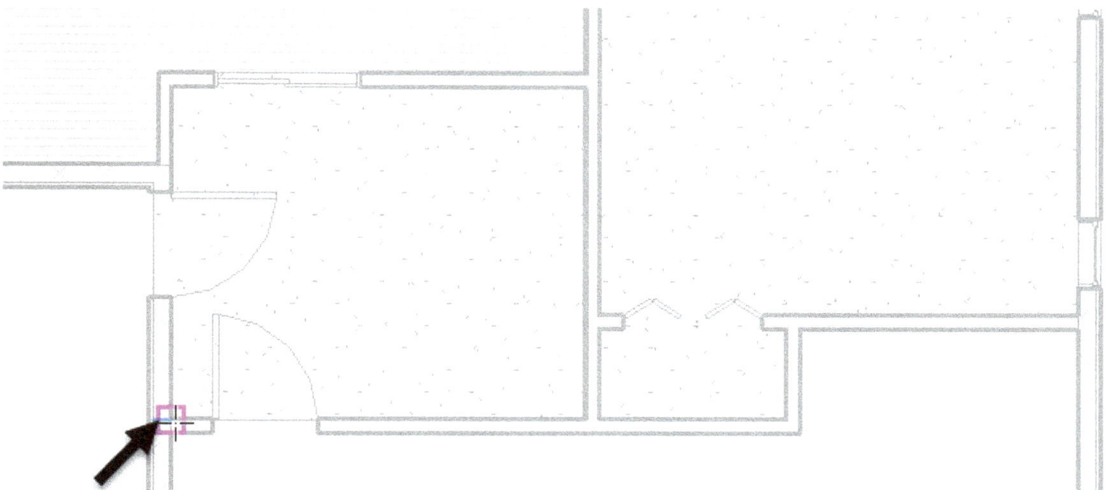

- Select the other corner points of the walls, as shown.

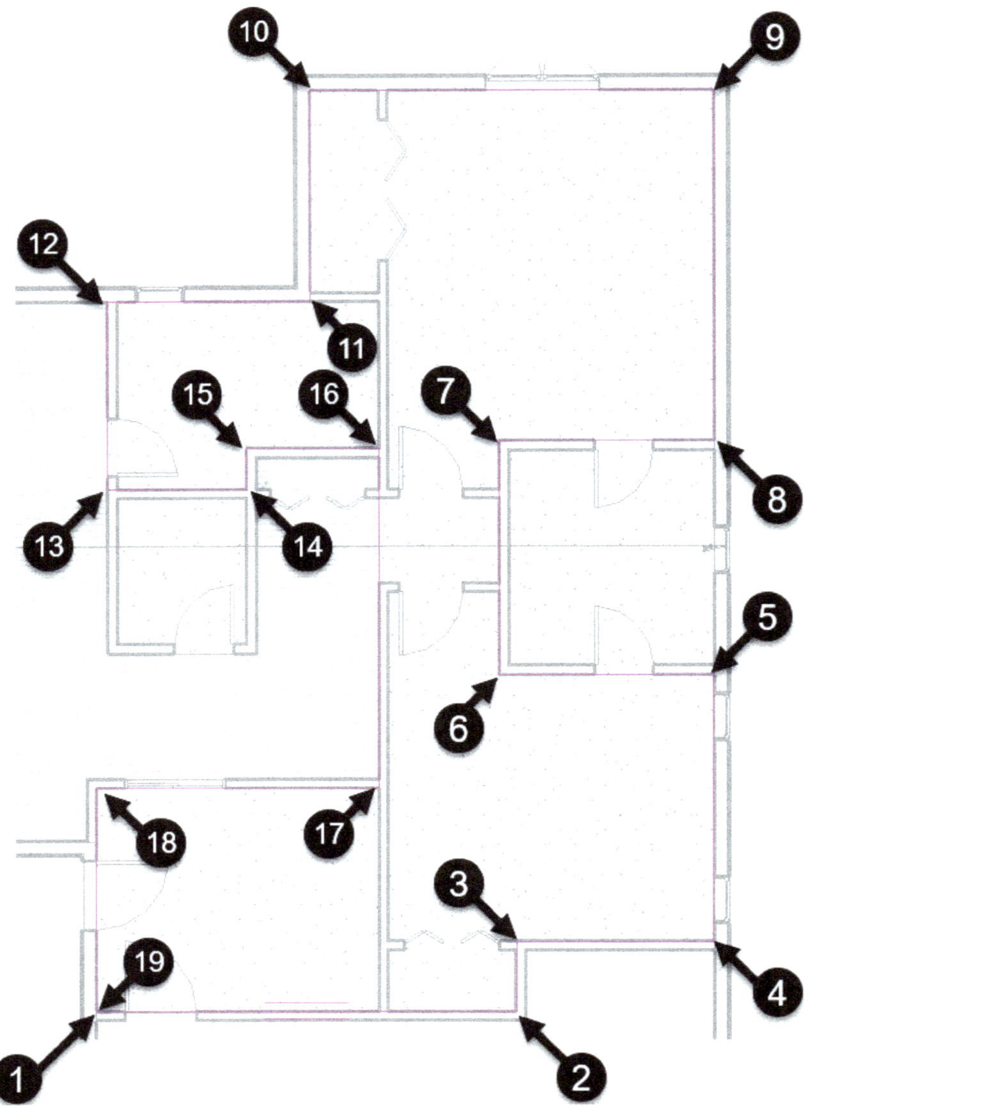

- Click the **Finish Edit Mode** ✔ icon on the **Mode** panel of the **Modify | Create Floor Boundary** ribbon tab.

Next, you need to add ceramic tile flooring to bathrooms

- On the ribbon, click **Architecture** tab > **Build** panel > **Floor** drop-down > **Floor: Architectural**.
- On the **Properties** palette, from the **Type Selector**, select the **Ceramic Tile** floor type.
- Activate the **Boundary Line** and **Rectangle** icons on the **Draw** panel of the **Modify|Create Floor Boundary** ribbon tab.

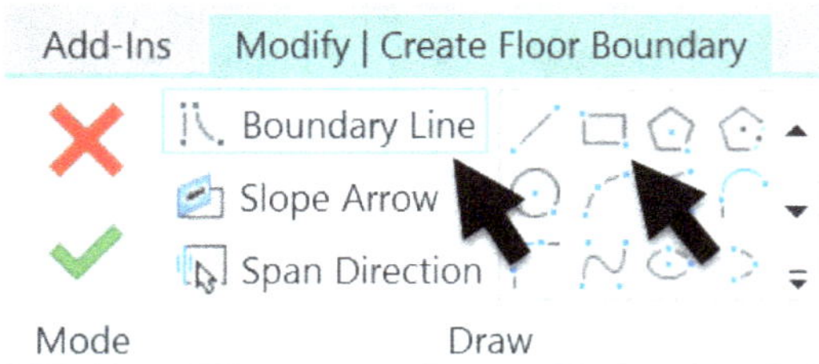

- Zoom to the bathroom area on the left side and specify the first and second corner of the rectangle, as shown.

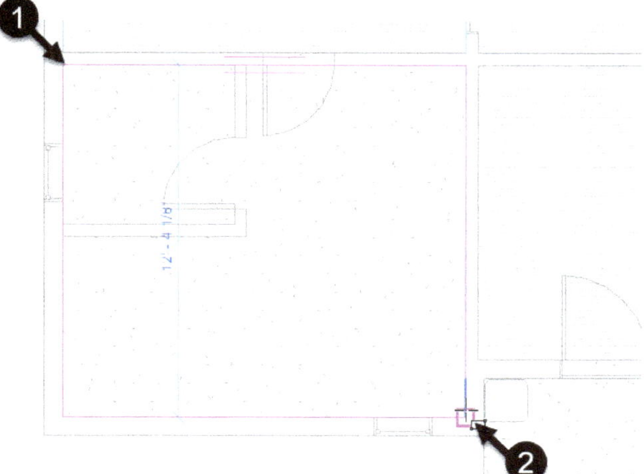

- Likewise, create two more rectangles, as shown.

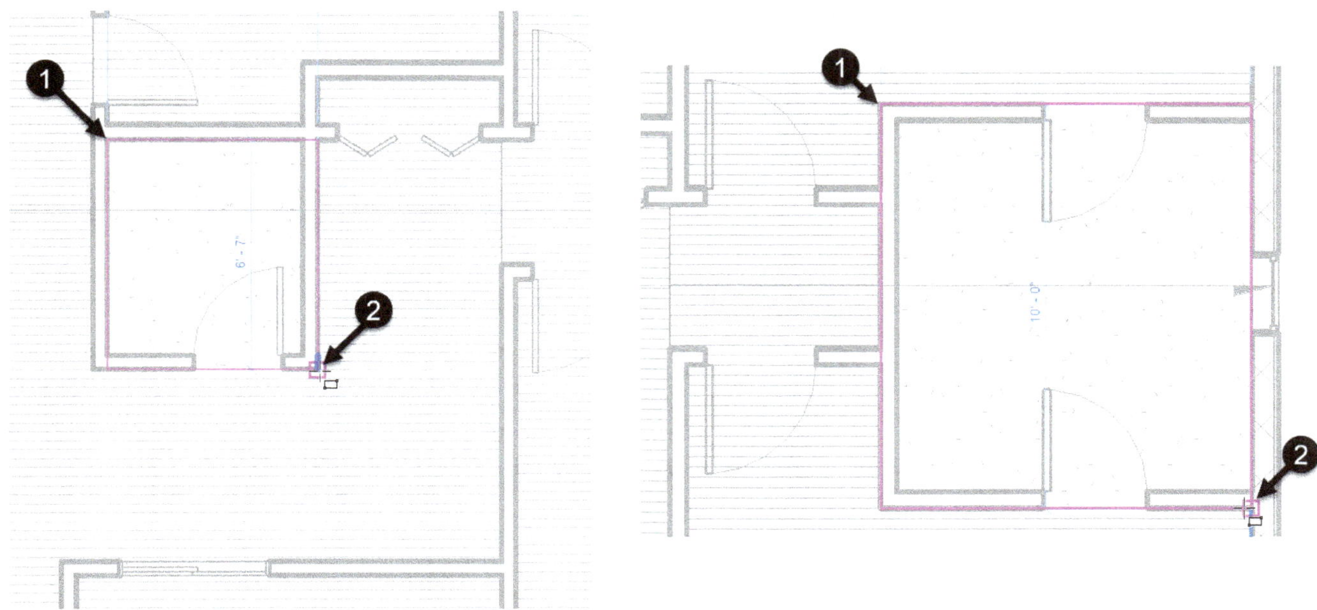

- Click the **Finish Edit Mode** icon on the **Mode** panel of the **Modify | Create Floor Boundary** ribbon tab.

Creating the Foundation Floor

- Double-click on the **TOP OF FOOTING** under the **Floor Plans** node in the **Project Browser**.
- On the ribbon, click **Architecture** tab > **Build** panel > **Floor** drop-down > **Floor: Stuctural**.
- On the **Properties** palette, from the **Type Selector**, select the **Concrete – 4"** floor type.

- Make sure that the **Boundary Line** and **Pick Walls** icons are selected on the **Draw** panel of the **Modify|Create Floor Boundary** ribbon tab.
- Zoom to the top-left portion of the floor plan. Next, select the inner edge of the horizontal exterior wall, as shown.

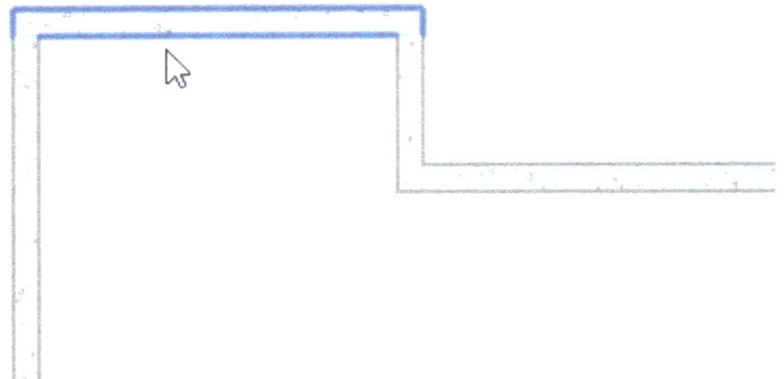

- Likewise, select the inner edges of the exterior walls, as shown.

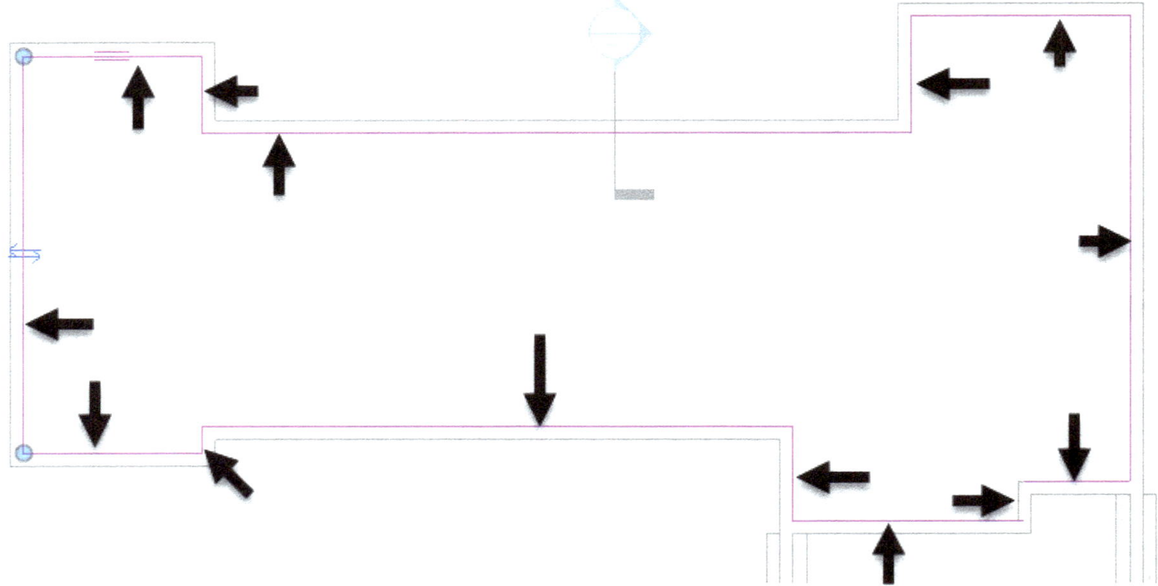

- Click the **Finish Edit Mode** ✓ icon on the **Mode** panel of the **Modify | Create Floor Boundary** ribbon tab.

Creating the Garage Floor

- Double-click on the **TOP OF FOUNDATION** under the **Floor Plans** node in the **Project Browser**.
- On the ribbon, click **Architecture** tab > **Build** panel > **Floor** drop-down > **Floor: Stuctural**.
- On the **Properties** palette, from the **Type Selector**, select the **Concrete – 4"** floor type.
- Make sure that the **Boundary Line** and **Pick Walls** 🖎 icons are selected on the **Draw** panel of the **Modify | Create Floor Boundary** ribbon tab.
- Zoom to the top-left portion of the garage. Next, select the inner edge of the foundation wall, as shown.
- Select the inner edge of the horizontal foundation wall, as shown.

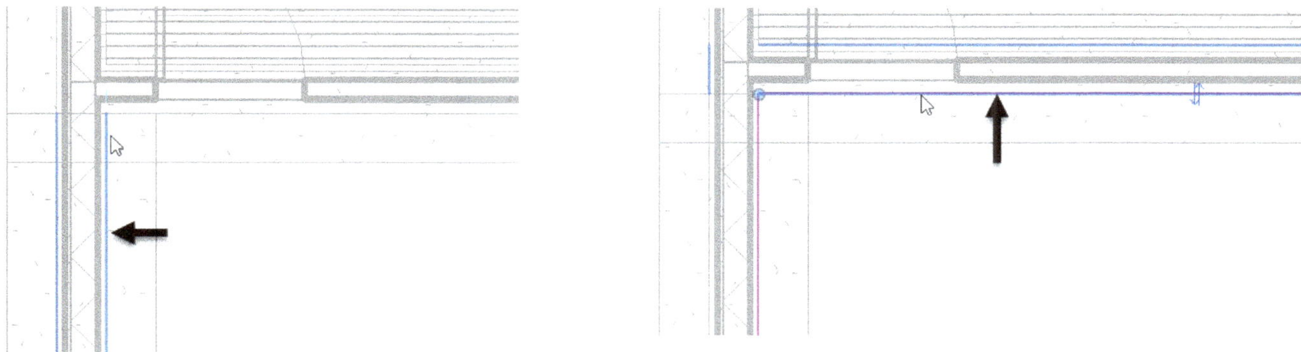

- Likewise, select the inner edges of the other foundation walls of the garage, as shown.

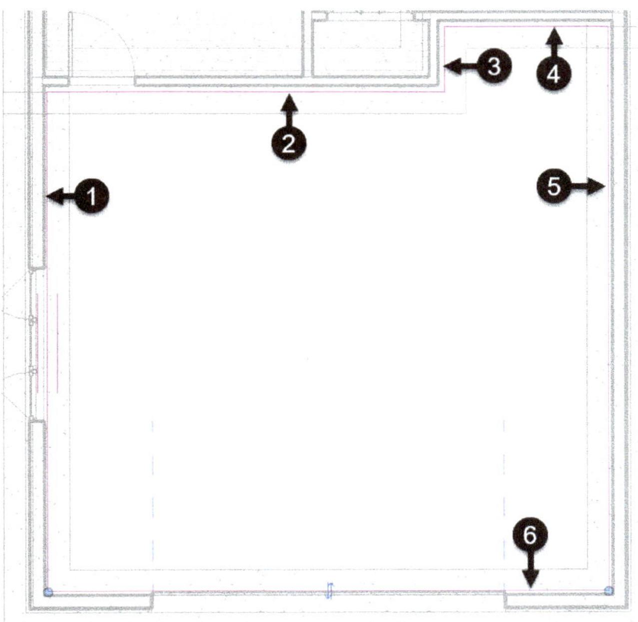

- Click the **Slope Arrow** icon on the **Draw** panel of the **Modify|Create Floor Boundary** ribbon tab.
- Specify the first point of the slope arrow by selecting the intersection point on the inner edge of the foundation wall.
- Move the pointer vertically downward and select a point on the floor boundary, as shown.

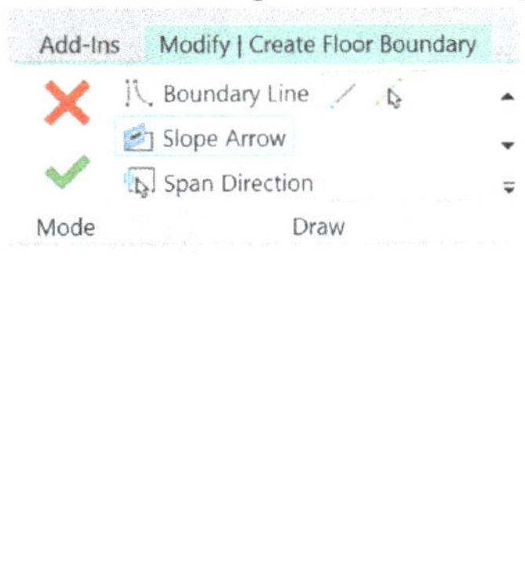

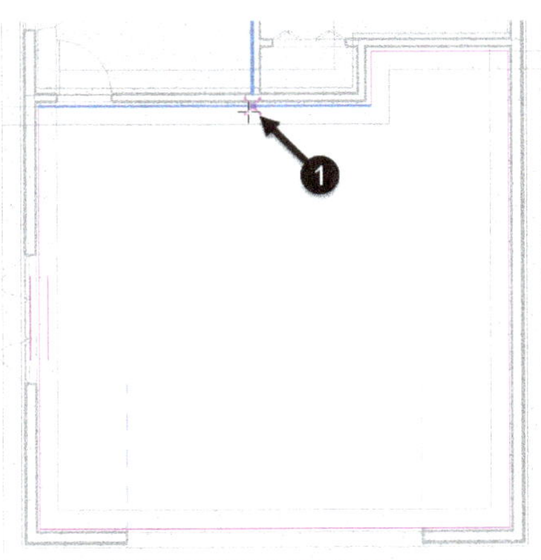

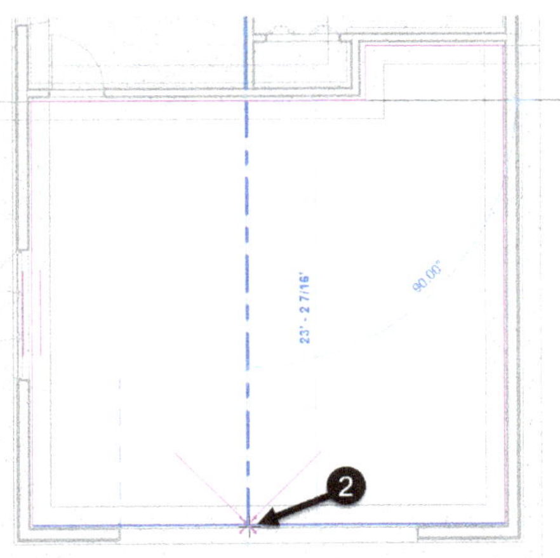

- In the **Properties** palette, type **-5"** and **-8"** in the **Height Offset at Tail** and **Height Offset at Head** boxes, respectively.

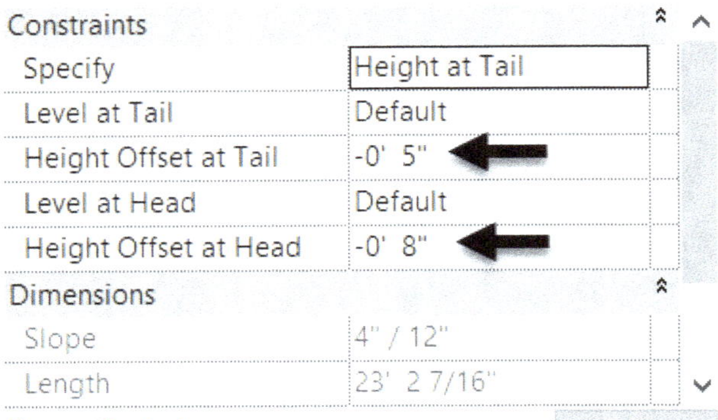

- Click the **Finish Edit Mode** icon on the **Mode** panel of the **Modify | Create Floor Boundary** ribbon tab.
- Click the **Attach** button.
- Create a section across the garage floor. Next, right-click on the section line, and then select **Go to View**; notice that the slope is applied to the floor.

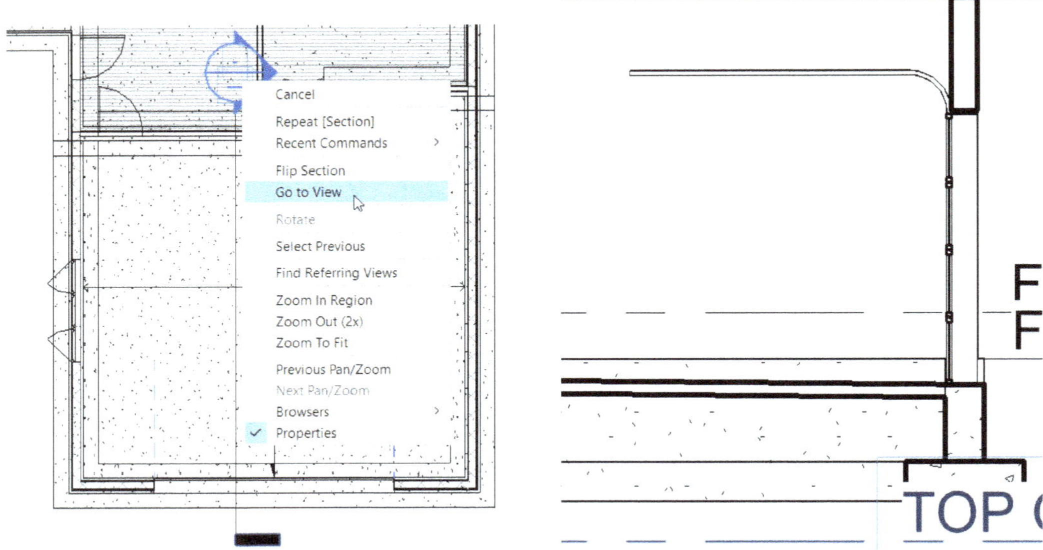

Creating the Front Porch and Back Porch

- Double-click on the **FIRST FLOOR** under the **Floor Plans** node in the **Project Browser**.
- On the ribbon, click **Architecture** tab > **Build** panel > **Floor** drop-down > **Floor: Stuctural**.
- On the Properties palette, from the **Type Selector**, select the **Concrete – 4"** floor type.
- Type **-4"** in the **Height Offset From Level** box
- Make sure that the **Boundary Line** and **Line** icons are selected on the **Draw** panel of the **Modify|Create Floor Boundary** ribbon tab.
- Zoom to the top-left corner of the floor plan and select the corner point, as shown.
- Move the pointer toward right, type **7** and press ENTER.

- Move the pointer upward, type 6 and press ENTER.
- Move the pointer toward right and place the pointer on the endpoint of the kitchen wall, as shown.
- Move the pointer upward and notice that a dotted line is displayed. Click to create a horizontal line.

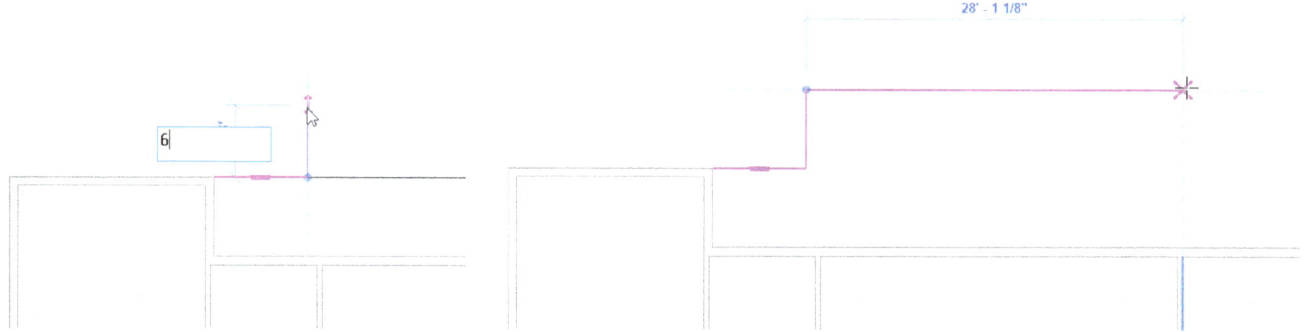

- Move the pointer vertically downward and click on the external edge of the outer wall.
- Move the pointer toward left and select the corner point, as shown.

- Move the pointer upward and select the start point of the sketch to close the boundary.

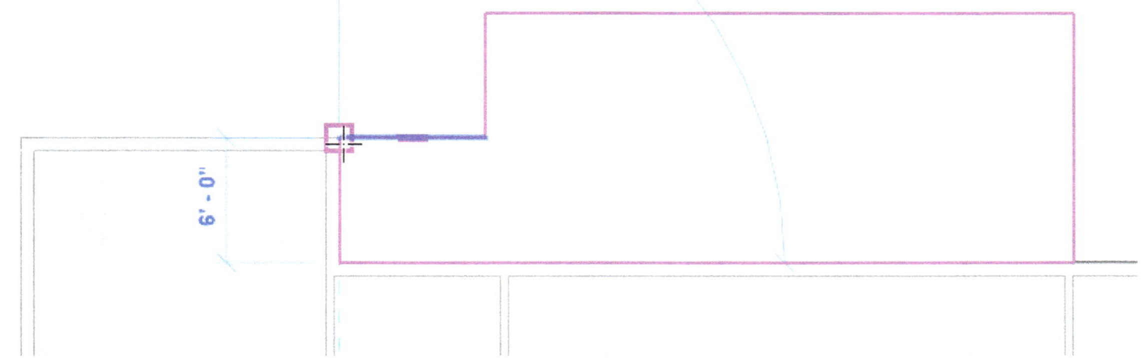

- Click the **Slope Arrow** icon on the **Draw** panel of the **Modify|Create Floor Boundary** ribbon tab.
- Specify the first point of the slope arrow by selecting the midpoint on the outer edge of the exterior wall.
- Move the pointer vertically upward and select a point on the horizontal line of the boundary, as shown.

- On the **Properties** palette, select **Specify > Slope**. Next, type **0** in the **Height Offset at Tail** box.
- Type **-1/8"/12"** in the **Slope** box under the **Dimensions** section.

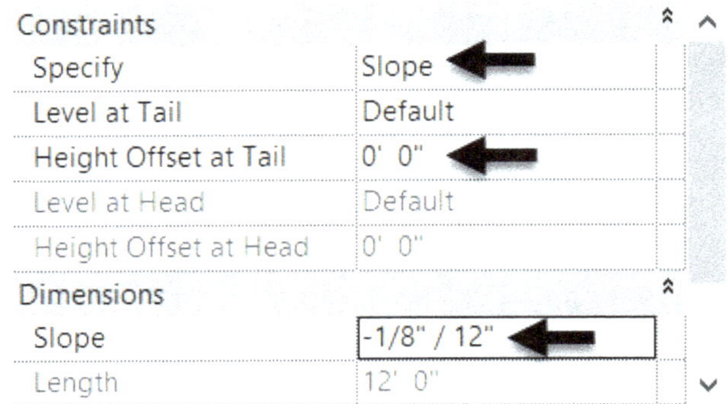

- Click the **Finish Edit Mode** ✔ icon on the **Mode** panel of the **Modify | Create Floor Boundary** ribbon tab.
- On the ribbon, click **Architecture** tab > **Build** panel > **Floor** drop-down > **Floor: Stuctural**.
- On the Properties palette, from the **Type Selector**, select the **Concrete – 4"** floor type.
- Make sure that the **Boundary Line** and **Rectangle** ⬒ icons are selected on the **Draw** panel of the **Modify|Create Floor Boundary** ribbon tab.
- Zoom to the front portion of the floor plan and select the corner point, as shown.
- Move the pointer toward right and select the outer edge of the garage wall, as shown. Next, press ESC twice.

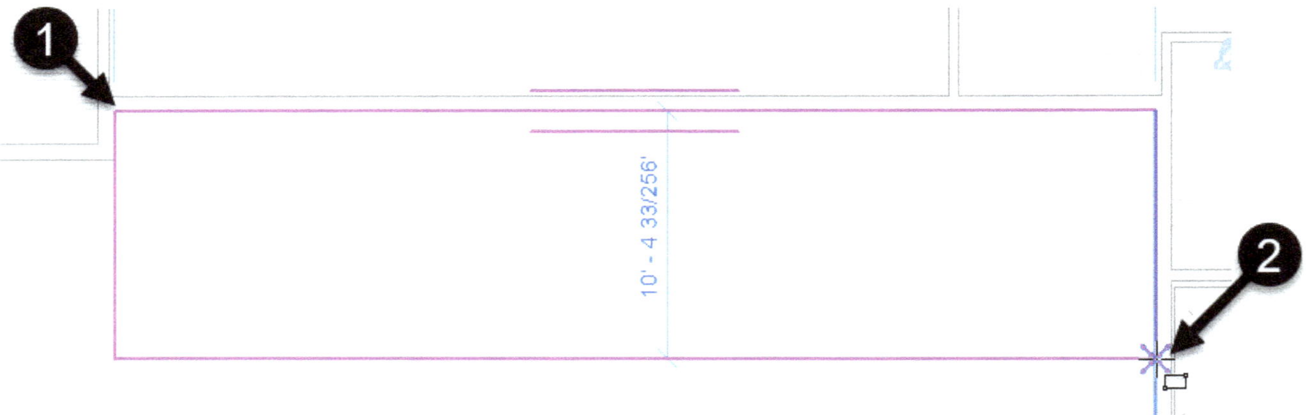

- Select the lower horizontal line of the rectangle and click the vertical dimension displayed. Next, type **8'4"** and press ENTER.

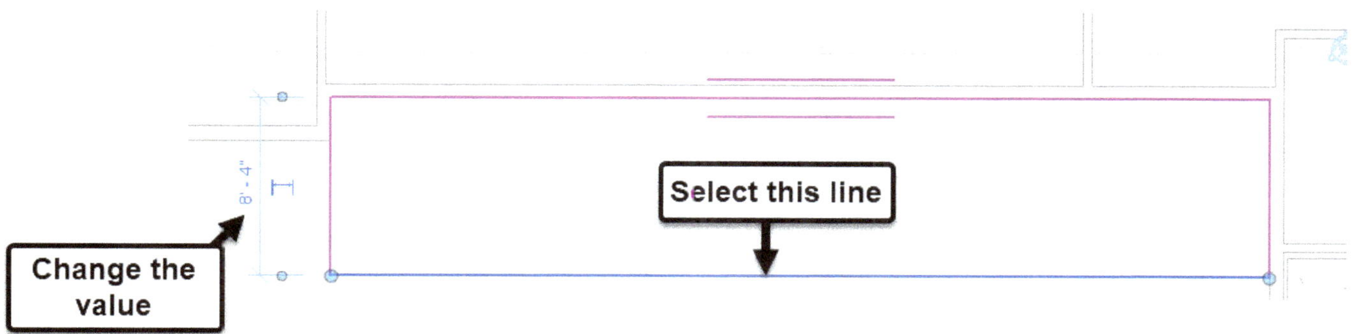

- Click the **Slope Arrow** icon on the **Draw** panel of the **Modify|Create Floor Boundary** ribbon tab.
- Specify the first point of the slope arrow by selecting the midpoint on the outer edge of the exterior wall.
- Move the pointer vertically downward and select the midpoint on the horizontal line of the boundary, as shown.

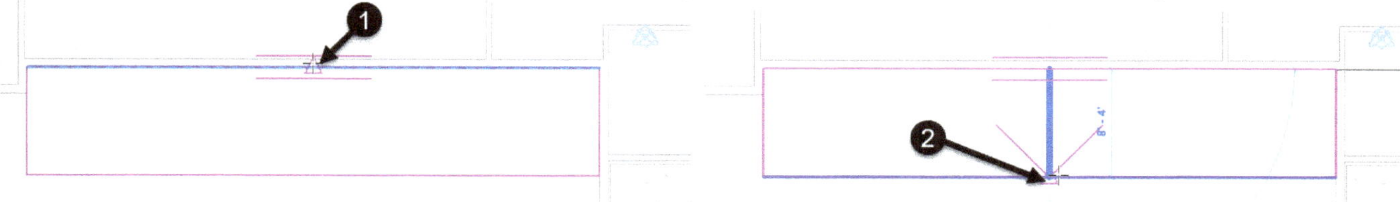

- On the **Properties** palette, select **Specify > Slope**. Next, type **0** in the **Height Offset at Tail** box.
- Type **-1/8"/12"** in the **Slope** box under the **Dimensions** section.

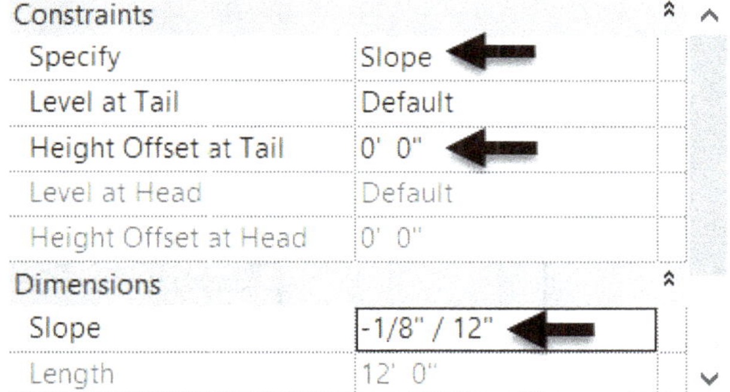

- On the ribbon, click **Modify| Create Floor Boundary** tab > **Mode** panel > **Finish Edit Mode**.

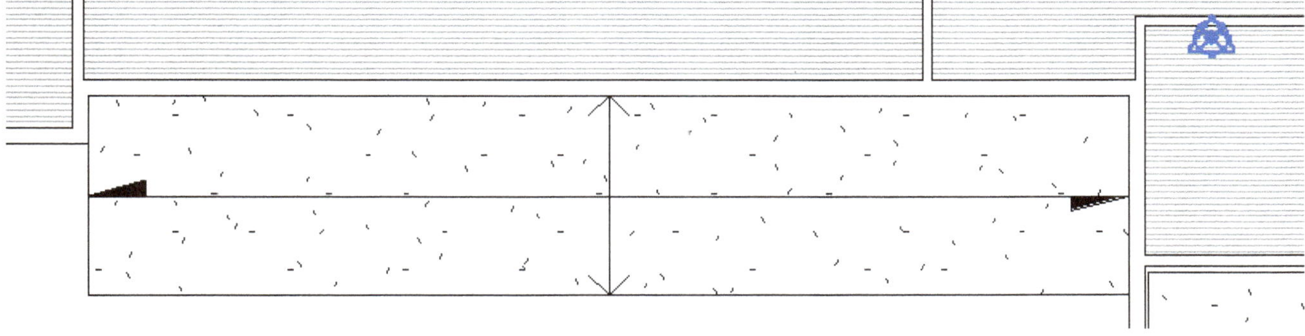

- On the ribbon, click **View** tab > **Create** panel > **Section** . Next, create a section view, as shown.
- Right-click and select **Go to View**; notice that the front and back porch are sloped outwards. It allows to drain the water.

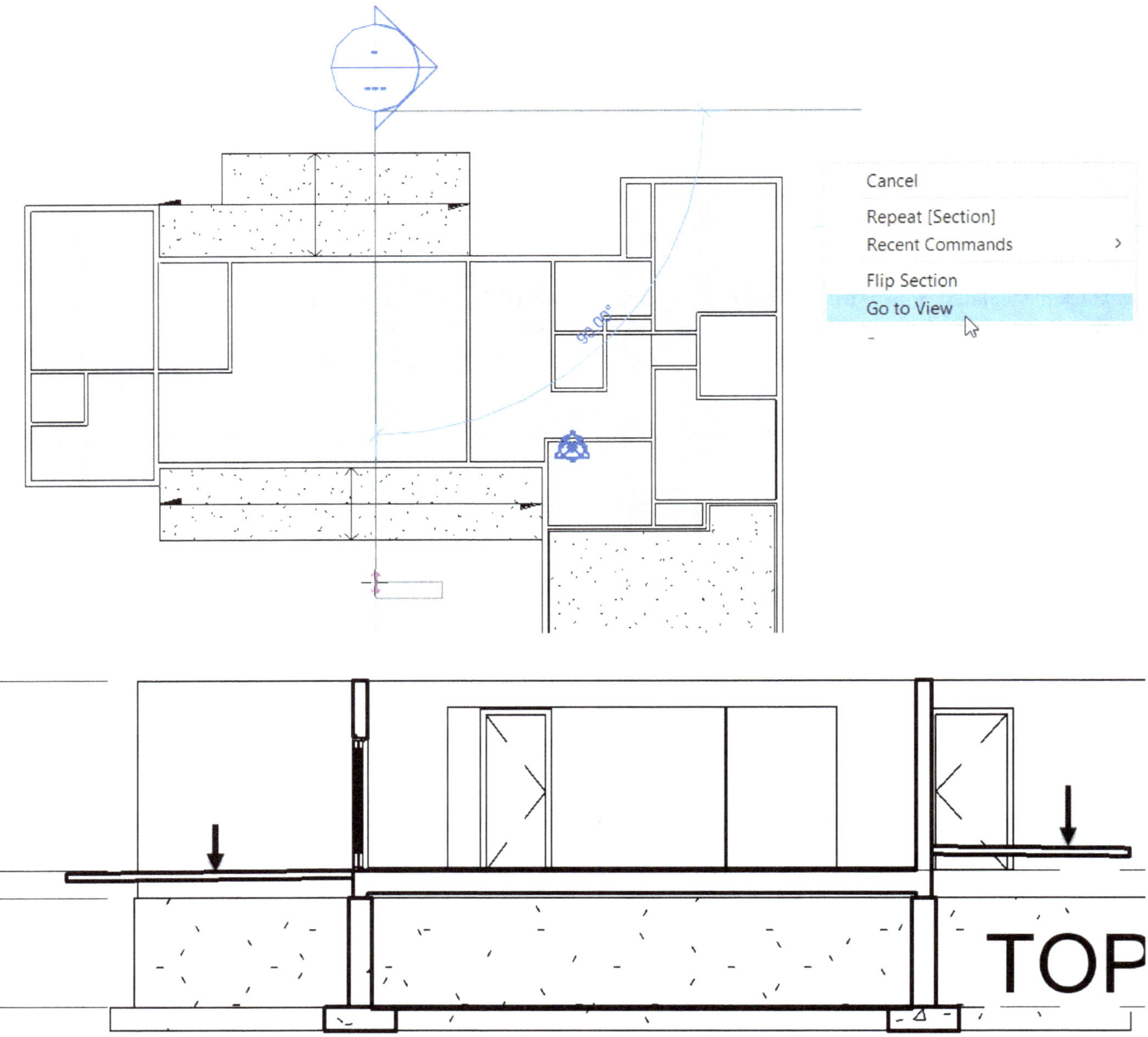

Next, you need to create a foundation to support the front and back porch.

- Double-click on the **TOP OF FOUNDATION** under the **Floor Plans** node in the **Project Browser**.

- On the ribbon, click **Architecture** tab > **Build** panel > **Wall** drop-down > **Wall Structural** .
- On the **Properties** palette, select **Basic Wall Foundation – 12" Concrete** from the **Basic Wall** drop-down.

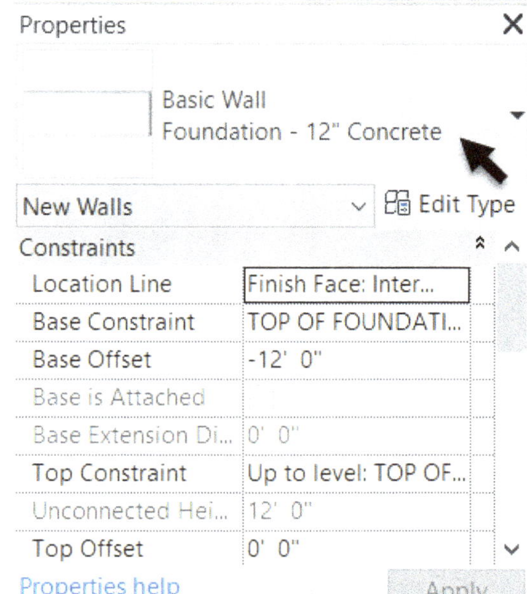

- On the Options Bar, select **Depth** drop-down > **Unconnected**. Next, select **Location Line > Finish Face: Exterior**.
- Type **3' 8"** in the **Offset** box on the Options Bar.

- Zoom to the front porch area and select the intersection point between the foundation wall and the vertical edge of the front porch.

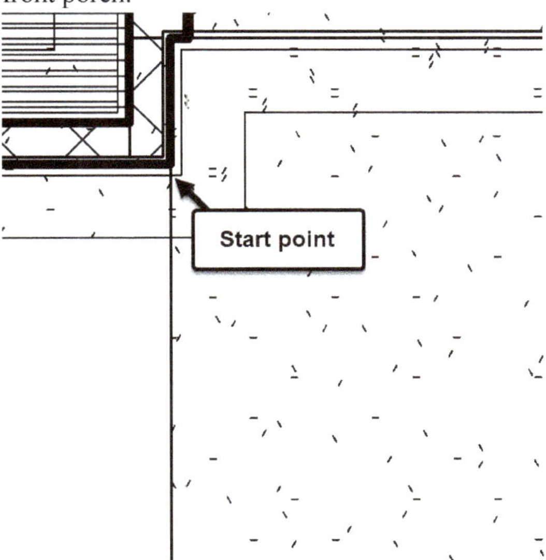

- Move the pointer vertically downward and notice that the wall is displayed outside the porch.
- Press SPACEBAR to flip the side of the wall.
- Move the pointer downward and select the corner point of the porch.

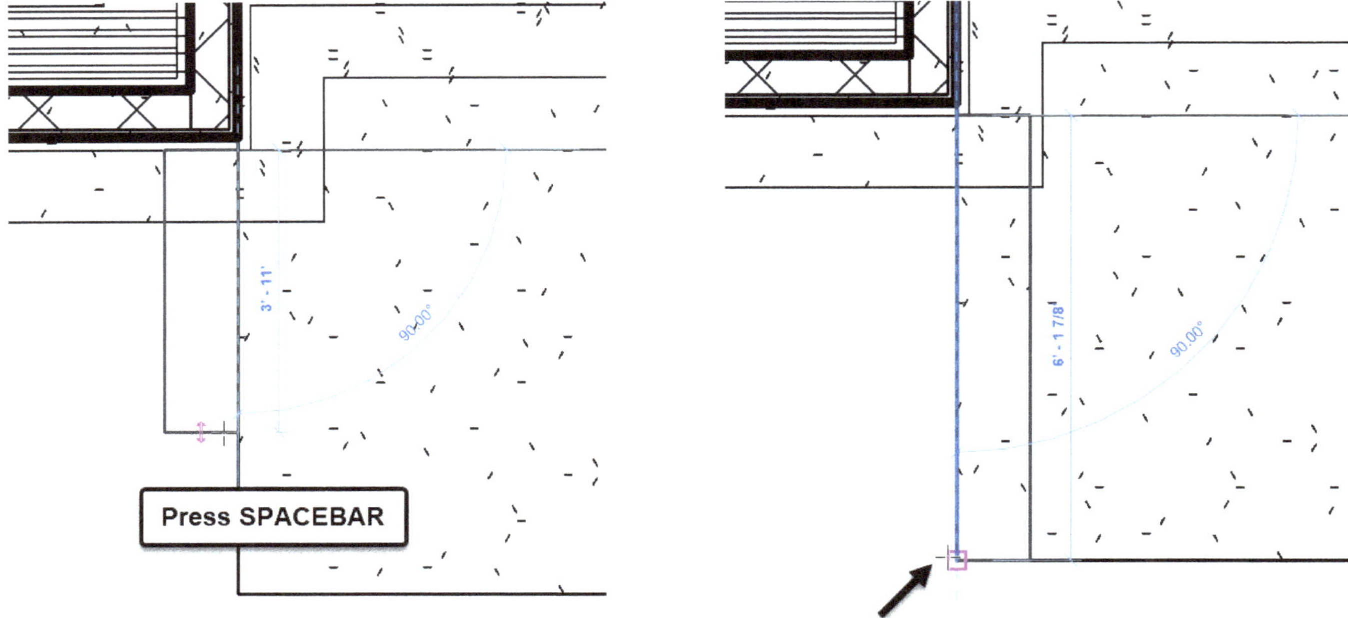

- Move the pointer horizontally toward right and select the intersection point between the porch edge and the foundation wall. Next, press ESC twice.

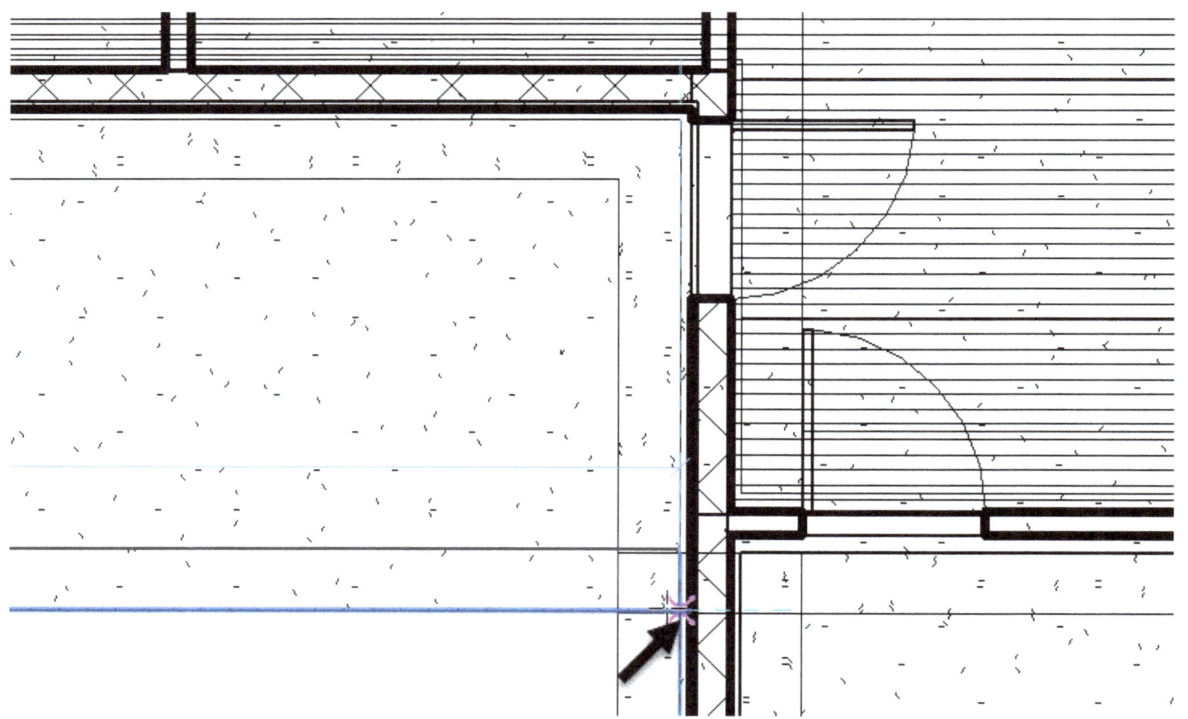

- Click the **Default 3D View** icon on the Quick Access Toolbar; notice a gap between the foundation wall and the porch.

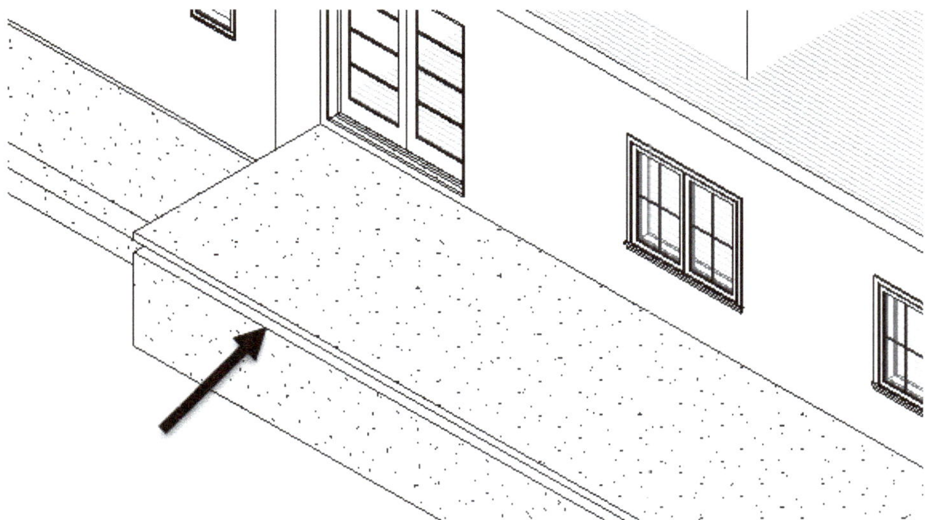

- Press and hold the CTRL key and select the two foundation walls, as shown.

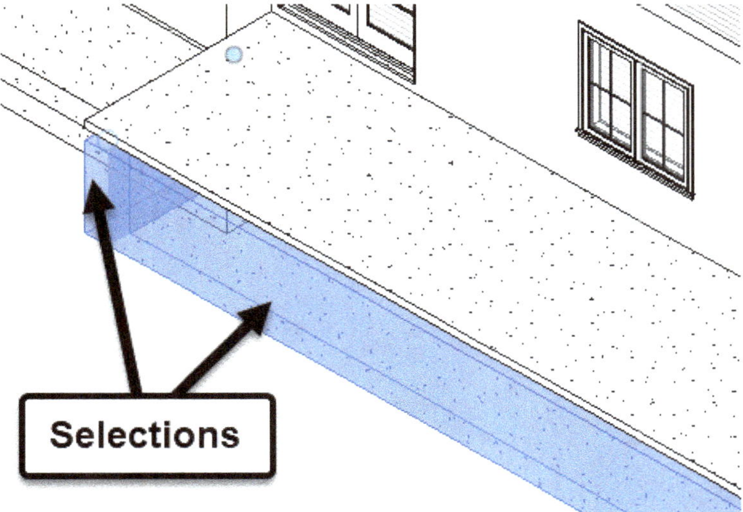

- On the ribbon, click **Modify| Walls** tab > **Modify Walls** panel > **Attach Top/Base**.
- Select the front porch; the foundation walls are attached to the front porch.

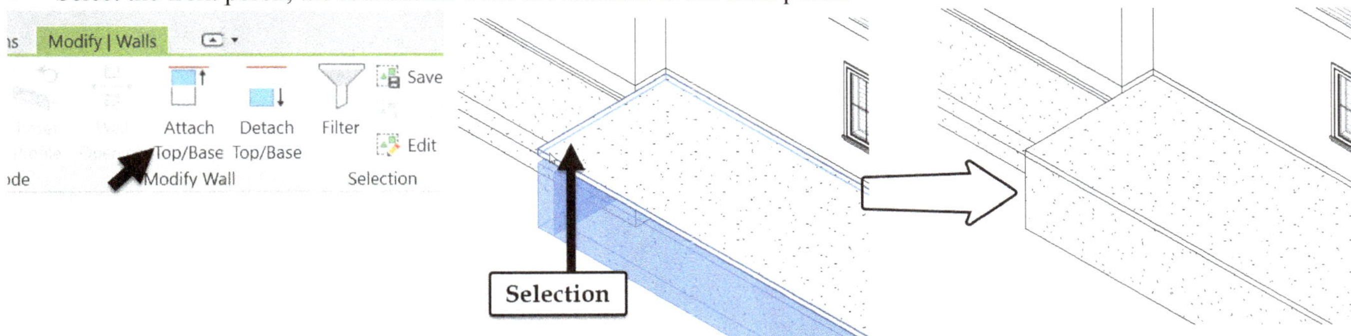

Next, you need to add footings to the foundation walls.

- On the **ViewCube**, click the lower right corner between Front and the Right faces.
- On the ribbon, click **Structure** tab > **Foundation** panel > **Wall** .
- Select the **Bearing Footing – 36" x 12"** from the **Wall Foundation** drop-down on the **Properties** palette.

- Select all the bottom faces of the foundation walls, as shown. Press ESC.

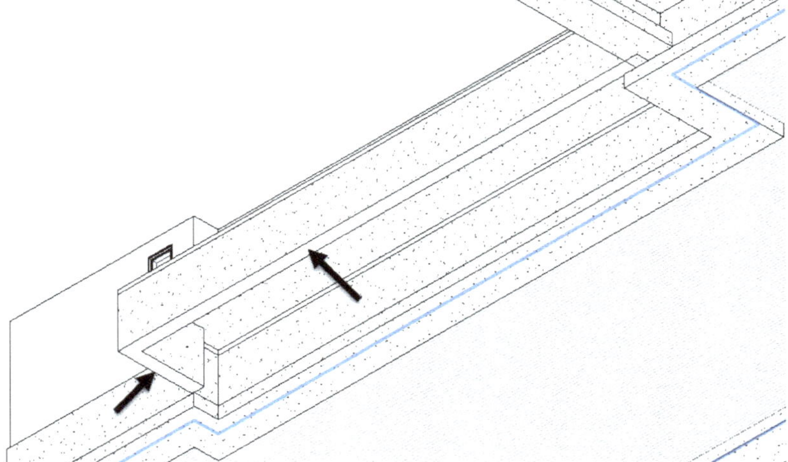

- Click the **Home** icon near the ViewCube; the orientation of the model is changed.

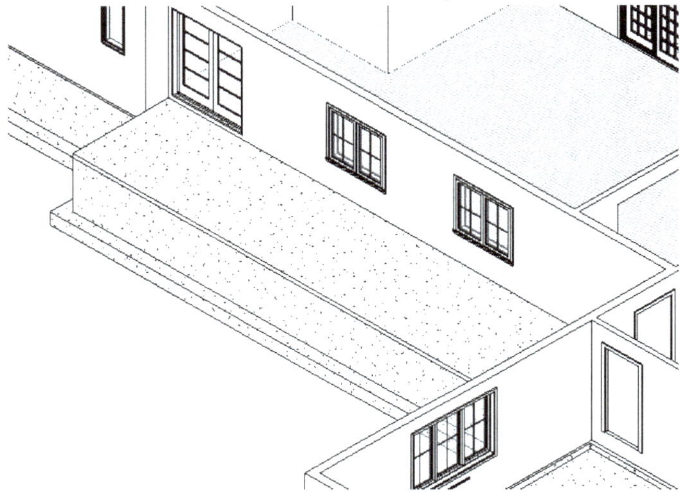

- Likewise, add a foundation and footing to the back porch.

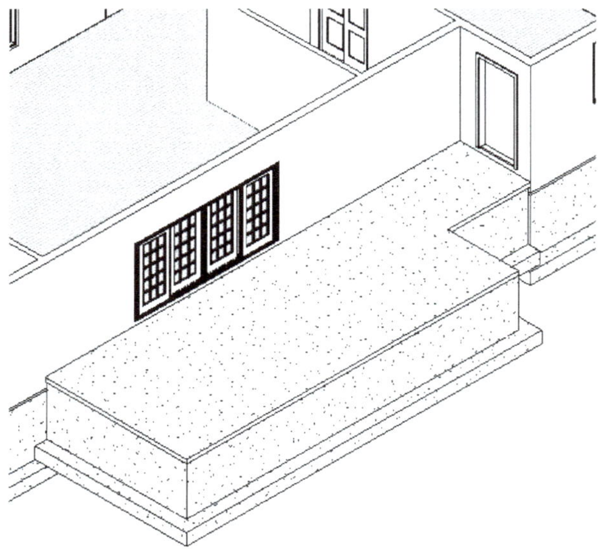

Tutorial 7: Creating Columns and Beams

- Double-click on the **TOP OF FOUNDATION** under the **Floor Plans** node in the **Project Browser**.
- On the ribbon, click **Architecture** tab > **Build** panel > **Column** drop-down > **Column: Architectural**.
- On the ribbon, click **Modify|Place Column** tab > **Mode** panel > **Load Family** .
- Go to **Local Disc C > Program Data > Autodesk > RVT 2024 > Libraries > English imperial (or metric or other base) > Columns**. Next, double-click on **Chamfered Column**.
- On the **Properties** palette, from the **Type Selector**, select the **Chamfered Column 18" X 18"** column type.
- On the Options Bar, select the **Height** and **TOP** options from the two drop-downs, respectively. The height of the column is defined up to the **TOP** level.

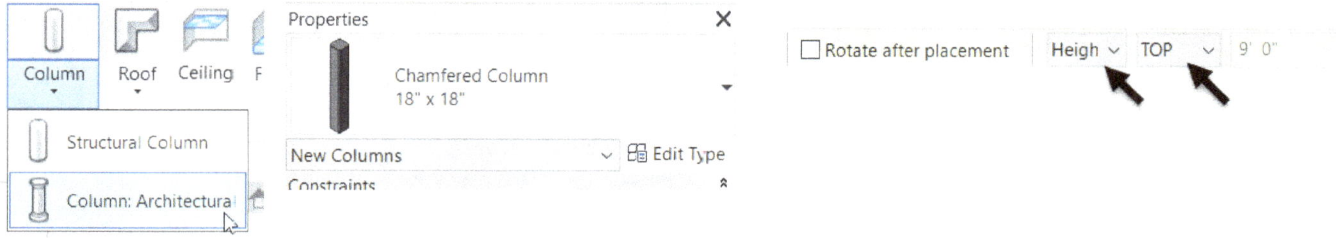

- On the ribbon, click **View** tab > **Graphics** panel > **Thin Lines**; the edges of the model are displayed as thin lines.
- Zoom to the lower-left portion of the front porch and place the pointer such that the vertical and horizontal edges of the column section is aligned with the vertical and horizontal edges of the porch, as shown.
- Click to position the column. Next, press ESC twice.

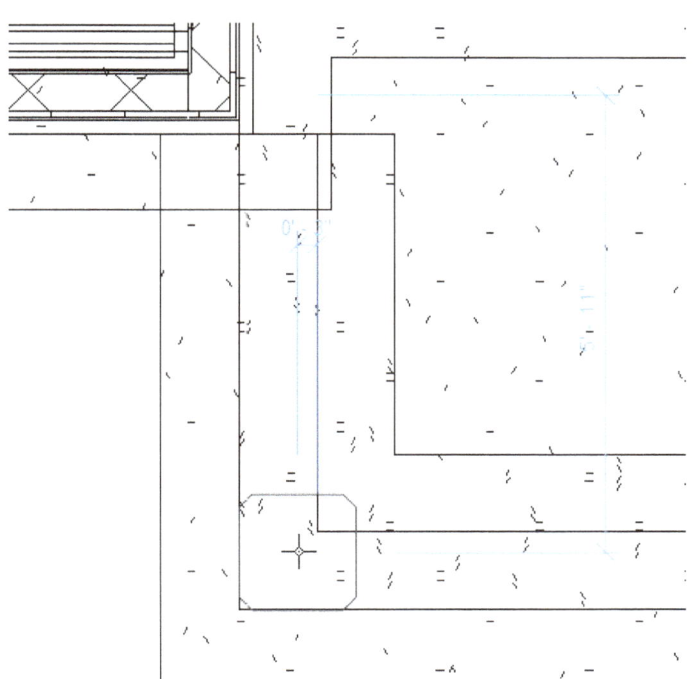

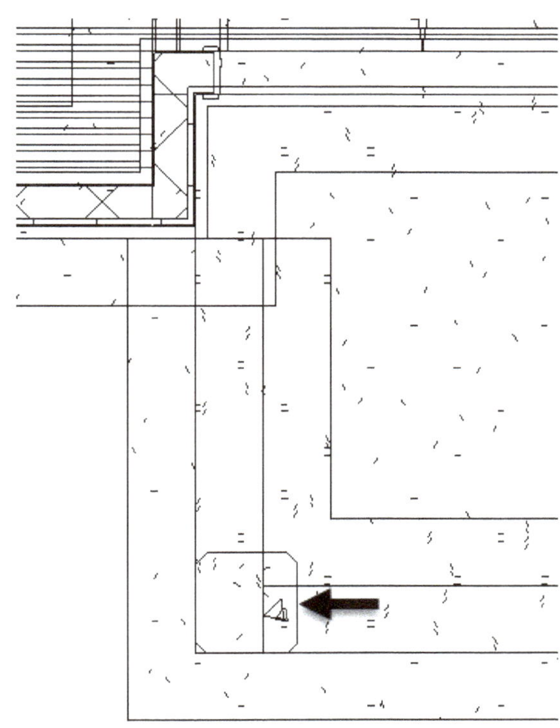

- Select the newly created columns and click the **Copy** icon on the **Modify** panel of the **Modify|Columns** ribbon tab.
- Select the lower-left corner point of the porch to define the start point.

- Move the pointer horizontally toward right. Next, type 10'9" and press ENTER.

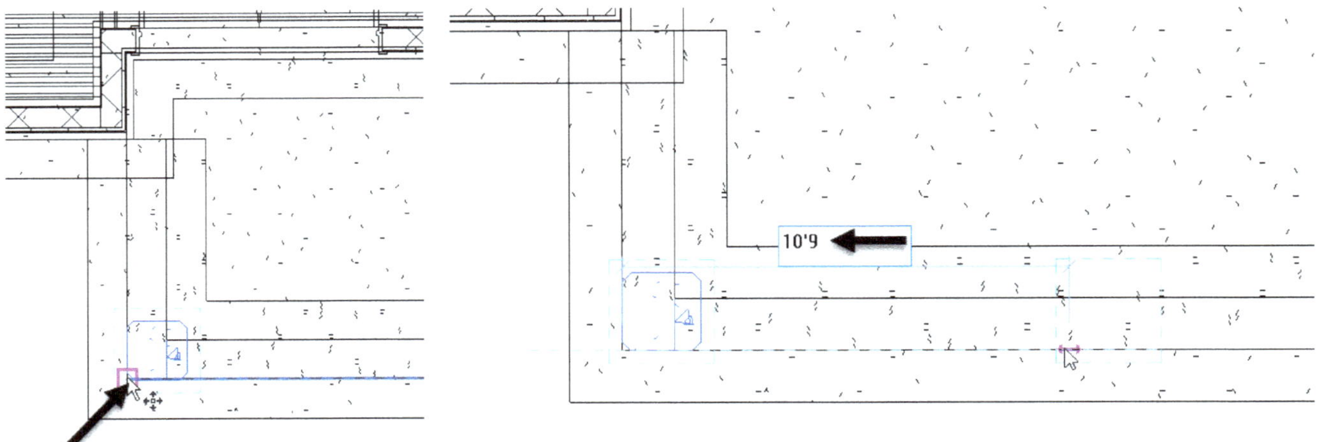

- Move the pointer horizontally toward right. Next, type 10'9" and press ENTER.

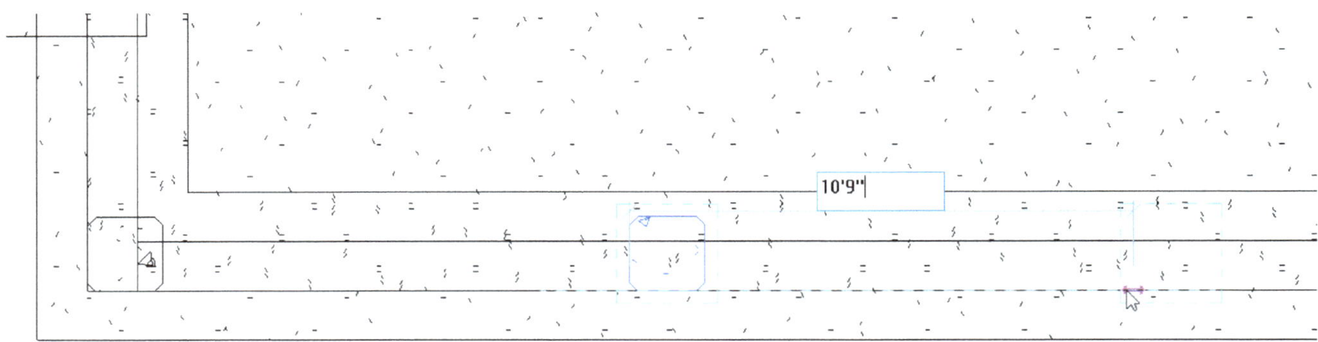

- Move the pointer horizontally toward right. Next, type 10'9" and press ENTER. Next, press ESC.

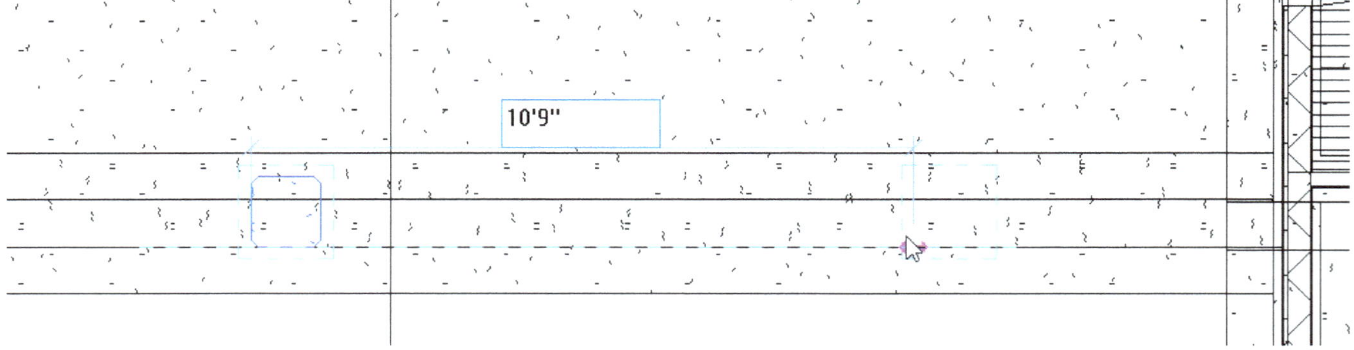

Notice that the first column is obstructing the door way. You need to move the door towards right such that it is centred between the first and second columns.

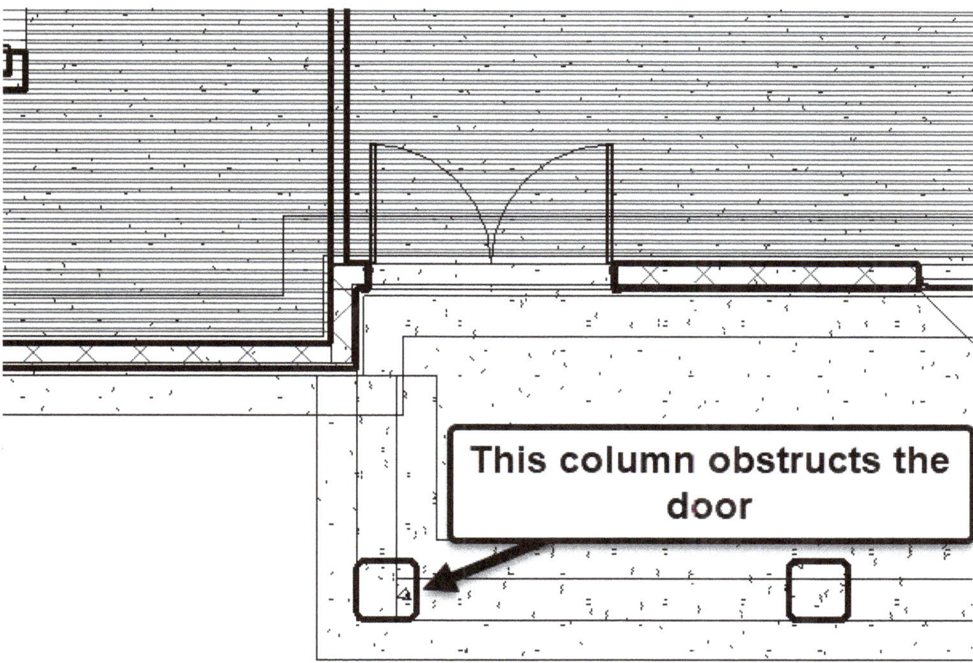

- Select the door and click on the dimension between the door and then type 6; the door is moved to the right.

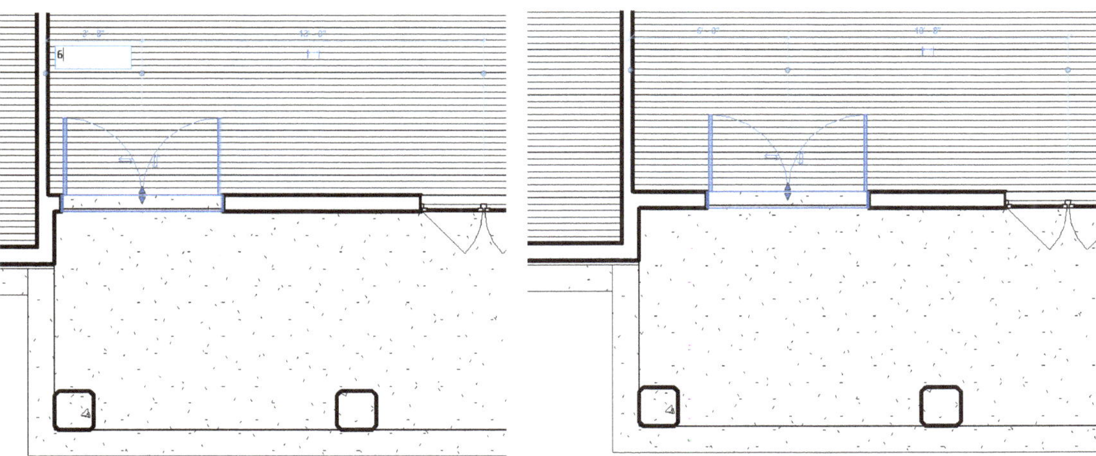

- Place two more columns at the corners of the porch.

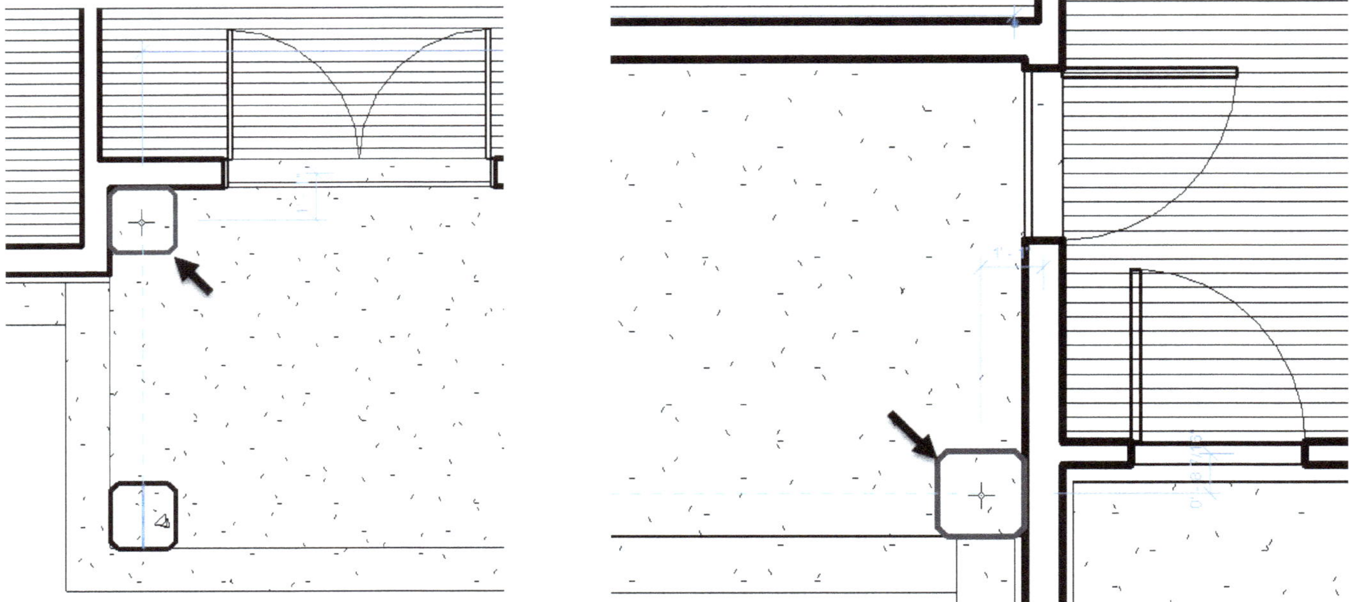

- Click the **Default 3D View** icon on the Quick Access Toolbar.
- Select anyone of the columns. Next, right-click and select **Select All Instances > Visible in View**; all the columns are selected.

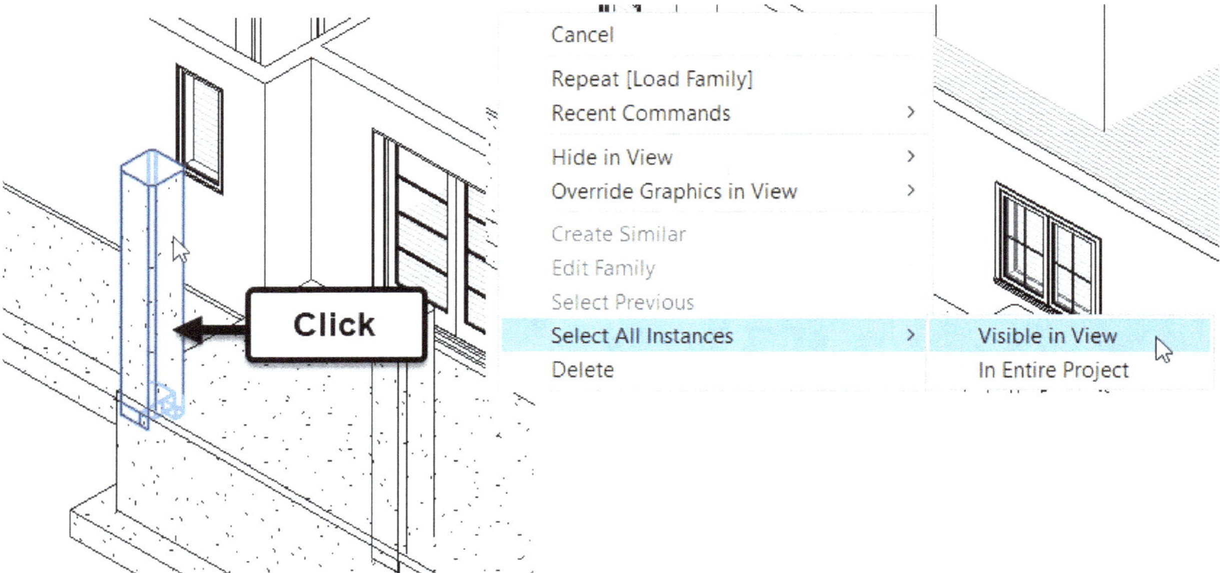

- Click **Attach Top/Base** on the **Modify Column** panel of the **Modify|Columns** ribbon tab.
- Select the **Base** option from the Options Bar. Next, select **Attachment Style > Cut Column**.
- Select the front porch and notice that the base faces of the columns are attached to the front porch.

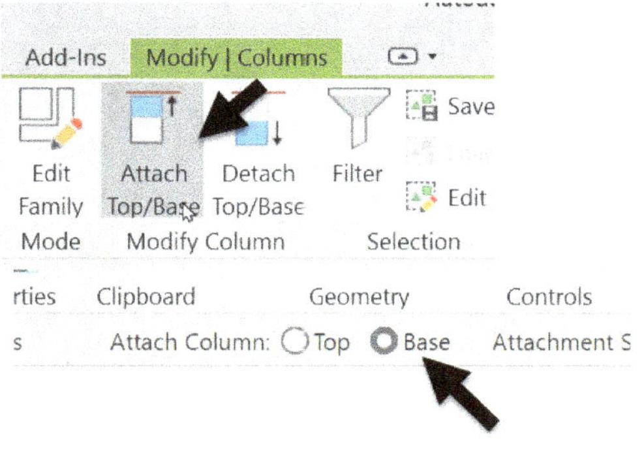

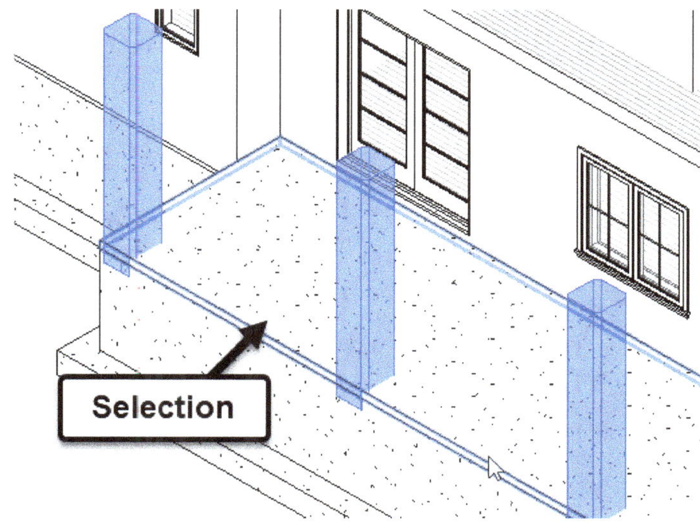

Creating the Porch Headers

- Double-click on **TOP** under the **Floor Plans** node in the **Project Browser**.
- On the **View Control Bar** located at the bottom of the drawing area, click the **Detail Level** icon, and select the **Fine** option.

- On the ribbon, click **Structure** tab > **Structure** panel > **Beam**.
- On the ribbon, click **Modify|Place Beam** tab > **Mode** panel > **Load Family**.
- Go to **Local Disc C > Program Data > Autodesk > RVT 2024 > Libraries > English imperial > Structural Framing > Wood**. Next, double-click on **Glulam-Southern Pine**.
- On the **Specify Types** dialog, select the **5X11** type, and then click **OK**.
- On the **Properties** palette, from the **Type Selector**, select the **Glulam-Southern Pine 5 X 11** beam type.

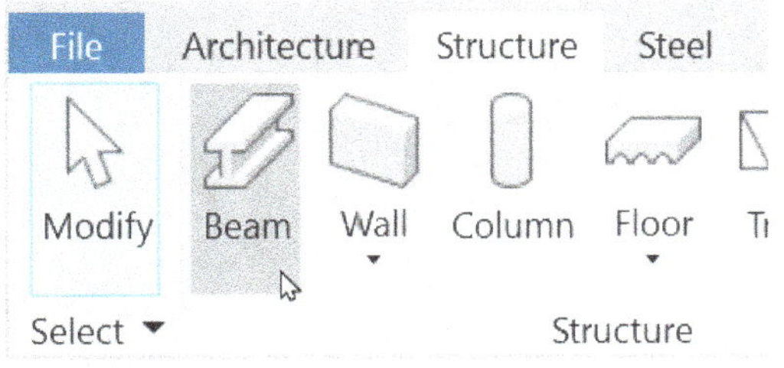 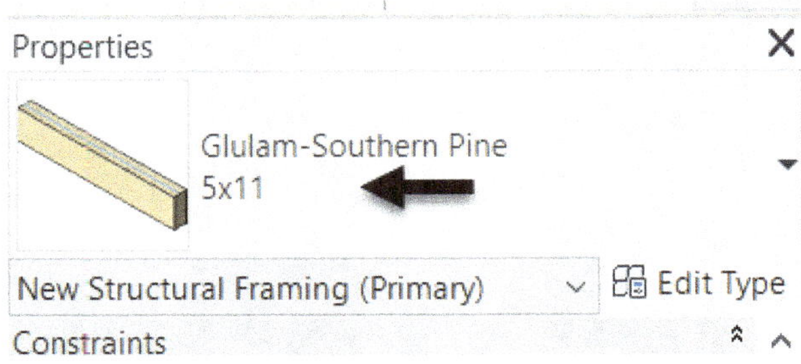

- Check the **Chain** option on the Options Bar.
- Zoom to the **Front** porch area and select the corner point of the wall, as shown.
- Move the pointer downward and select the corner point of the porch, as shown.

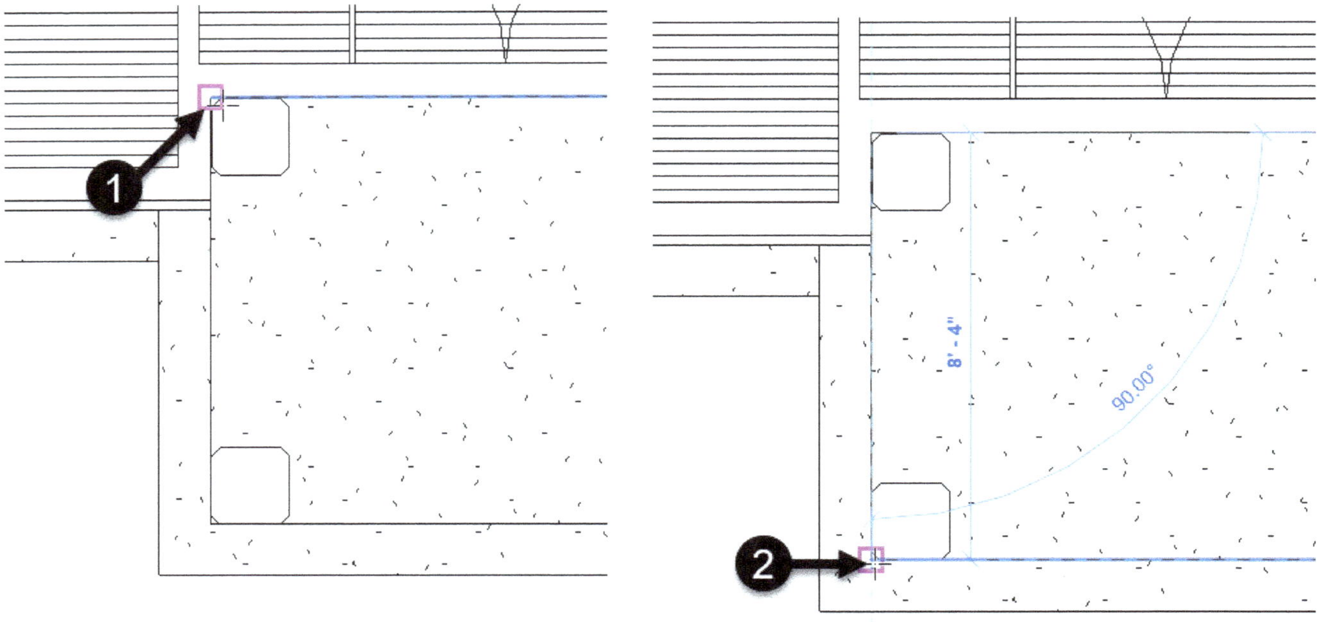

- Move the pointer horizontally toward right and select the corner point of the porch, as shown. Next, press ESC twice.

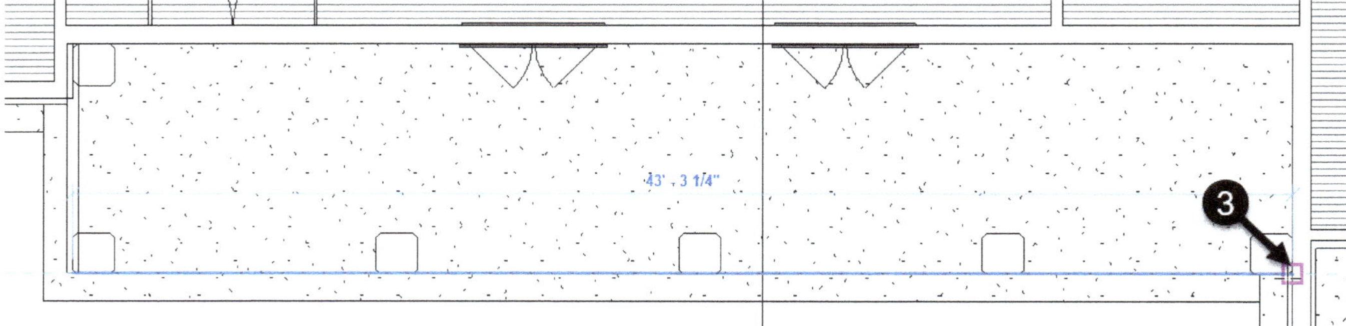

- On the **Properties** palette, scroll to the **Extents** section and click the **Edit** button next to the **View Range** parameter.
- On the **View Range** dialog, select **Bottom > Level Below (First Floor)**. Next, click **OK**.
- Select the beam located on the left-side. Next, click the **Justification Points** icon on the **Justification** panel of the **Modify | Structural Framing** ribbon tab.

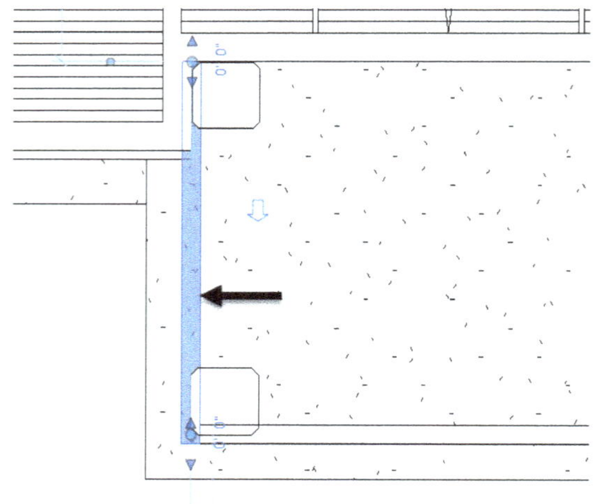

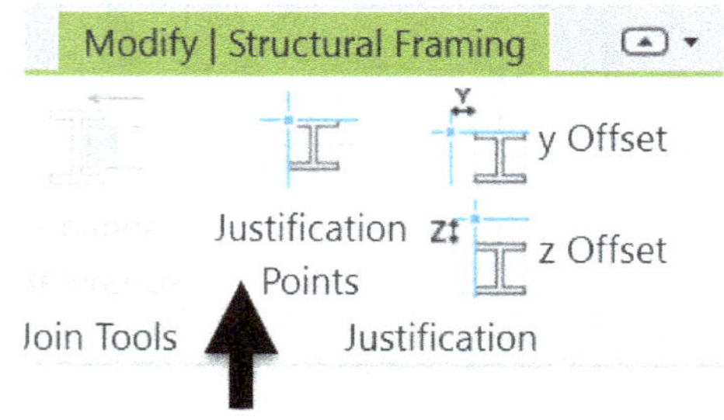

- Select the top-right edge of the beam, as shown. The justification point is changed.

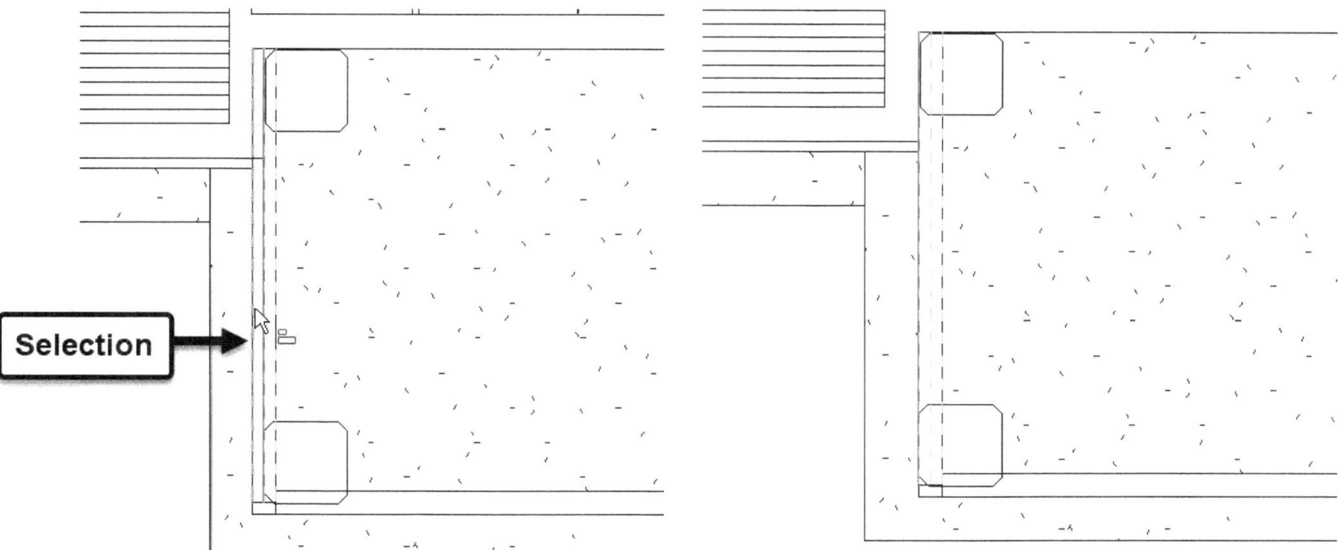

- Likewise, change the justification of the other beam, as shown.

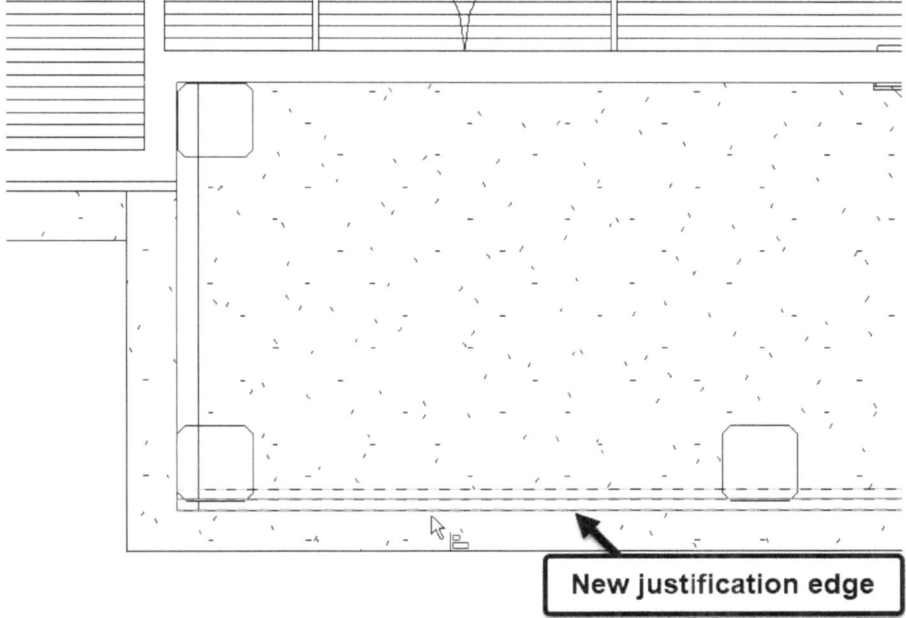

- Select the beam on the left side and click the **Beam/Column Joints** icon on the **Geometry** panel of the **Modify | Structural Framing** ribbon tab.

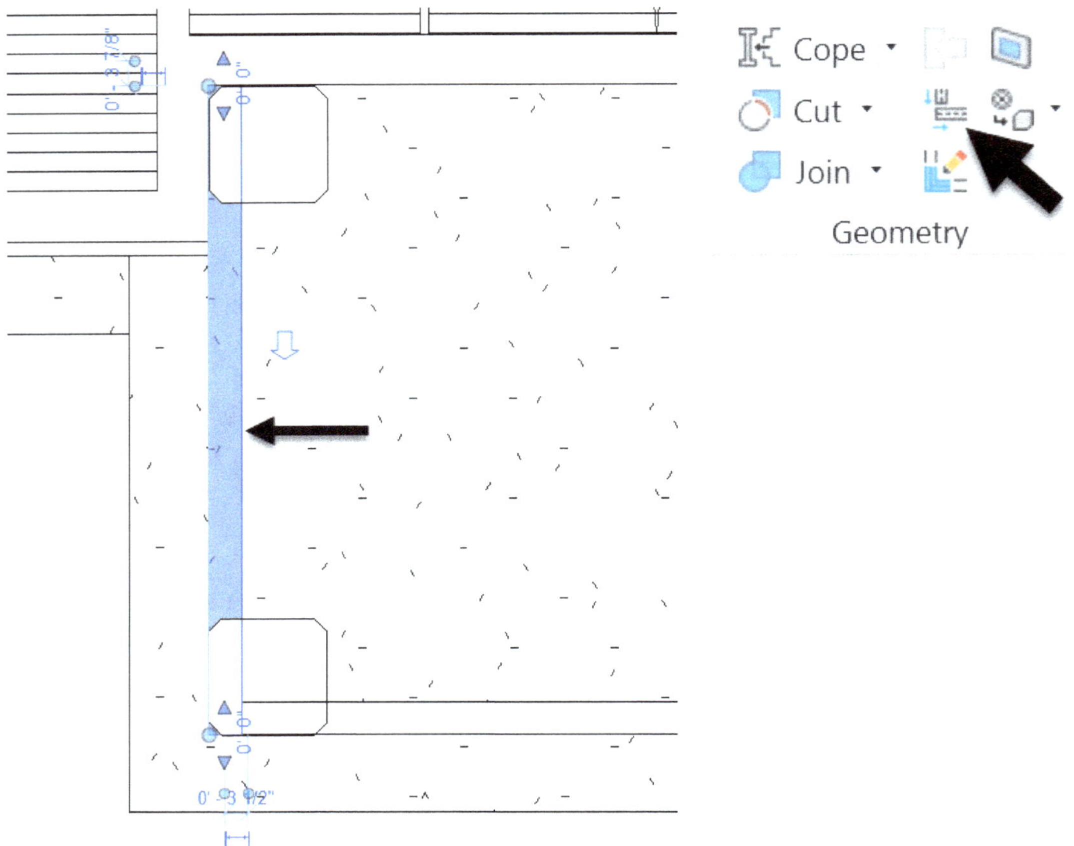

- Zoom to the lower portion of the beam and click on the arrow pointing in the downward direction; the length of the beam is reduced up to the inner edge of the horizontal beam.
- Click the arrow pointing towards left; the horizontal beam is extended up to the outer edge of the other beam.

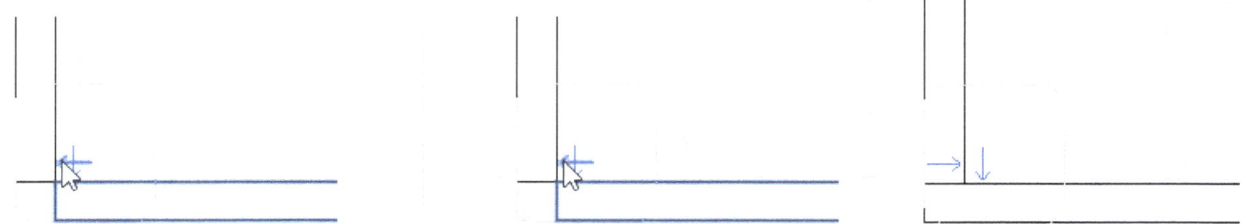

- Press ESC and click on the beam, as shown. Next, click the **Copy** icon on the **Modify** panel of the **Modify | Structural Framing** ribbon tab.

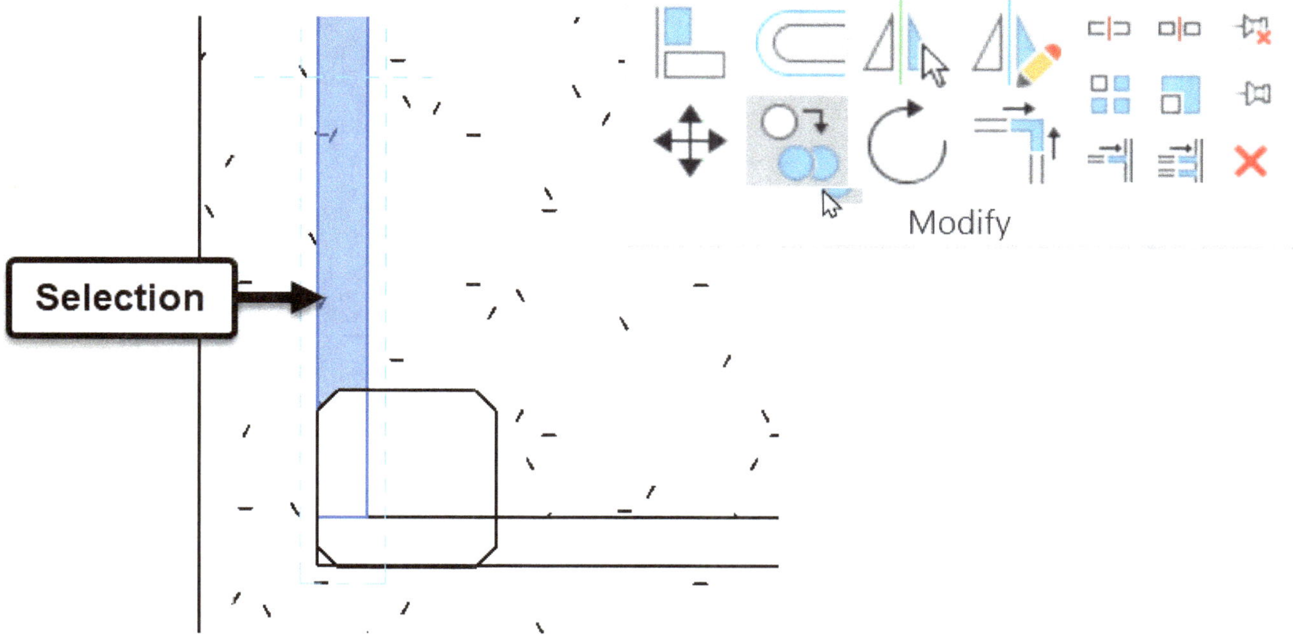

- Select the lower left corner point of the beam to define the start point.
- Move the pointer toward right and select the lower right corner point to define the end point. Press ESC and deselect the copied beam.

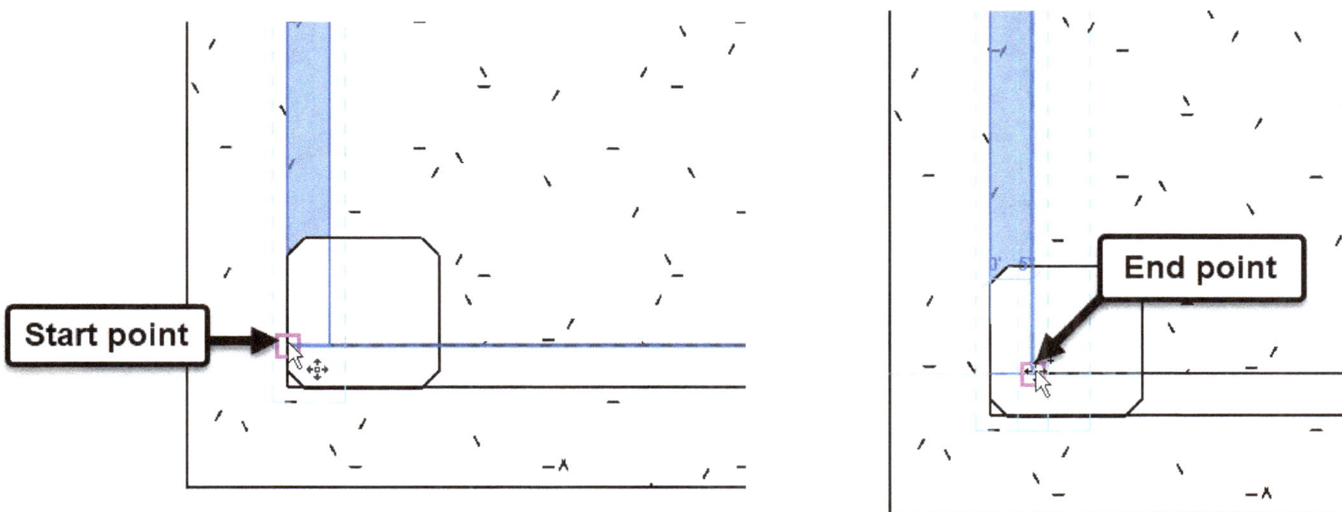

- Select the other beam and click the **Copy** icon on the **Modify** panel of the **Modify | Structural Framing** ribbon tab.
- Select the lower left corner point of the beam to define the start point.
- Move the pointer upward and select the upper left corner point to define the end point. Press ESC.

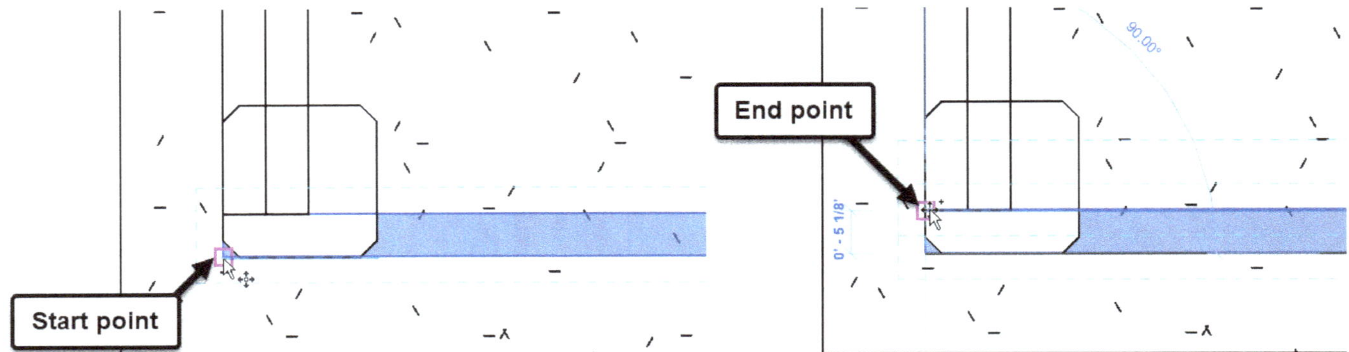

- Select the copied beam, as shown. Next, click on the arrow grip pointing in the upward direction.

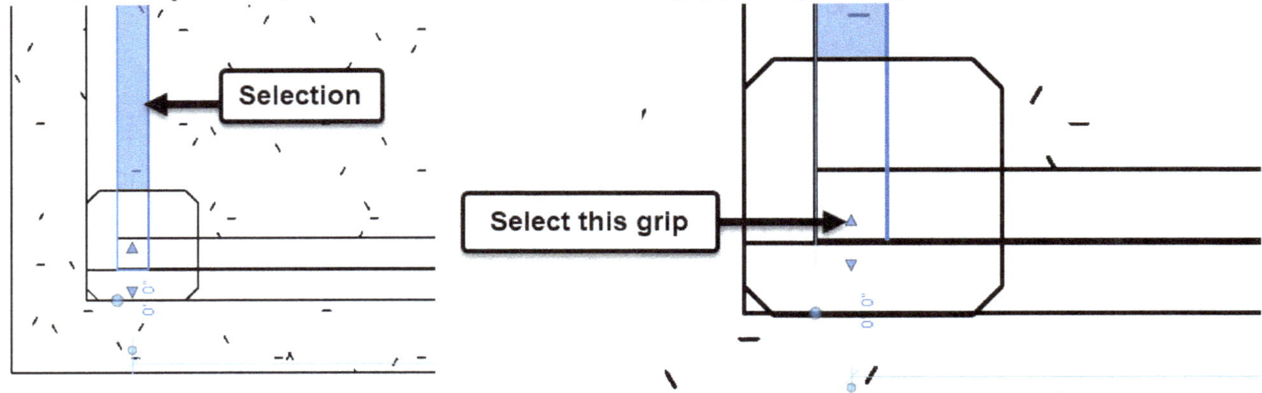

- Press and hold the left mouse button and drag the pointer upward.
- Release the pointer on the inner edge of the intersecting beam, as shown.

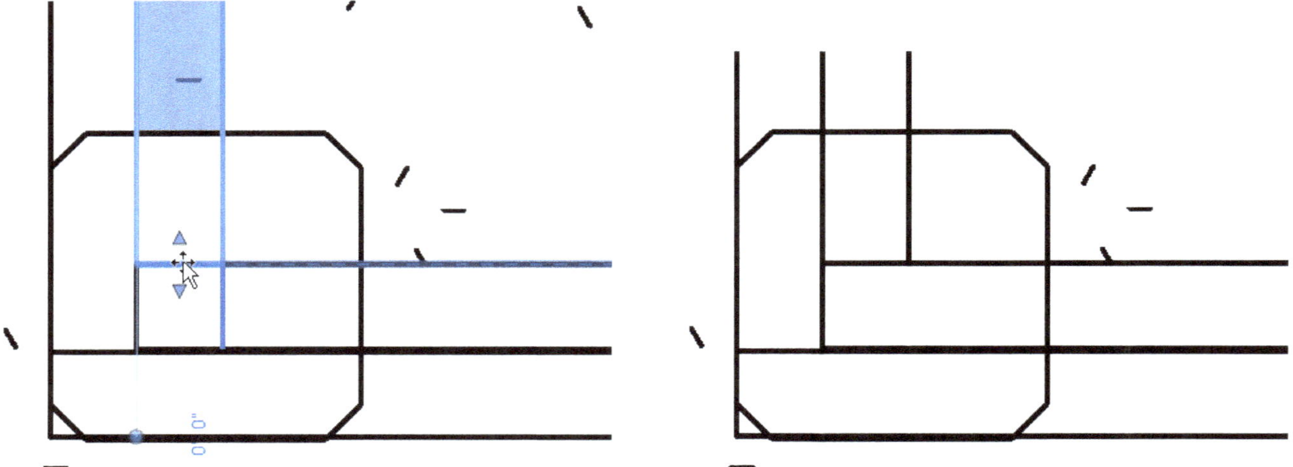

- Click the **Default 3D View** icon on the Quick Access Toolbar; the 3D view of the model is displayed.

- Press and hold the CTRL key and select the two columns, as shown.

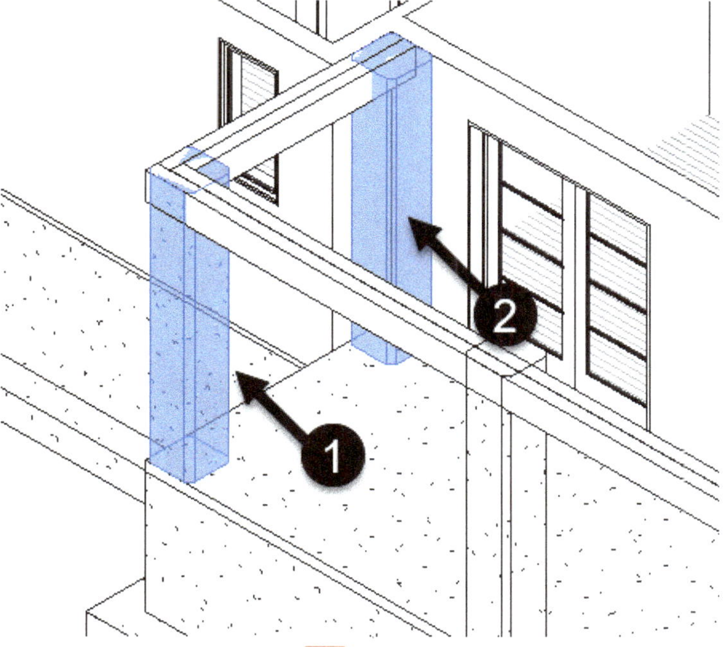

- Click **Attach Top/Base** on the **Modify Column** panel of the **Modify|Columns** ribbon tab.
- Select the **Top** option from the Options Bar. Next, select **Attachment Style > Cut Column**.
- Select the beam intersecting with the two columns, as shown. Next, press ESC.

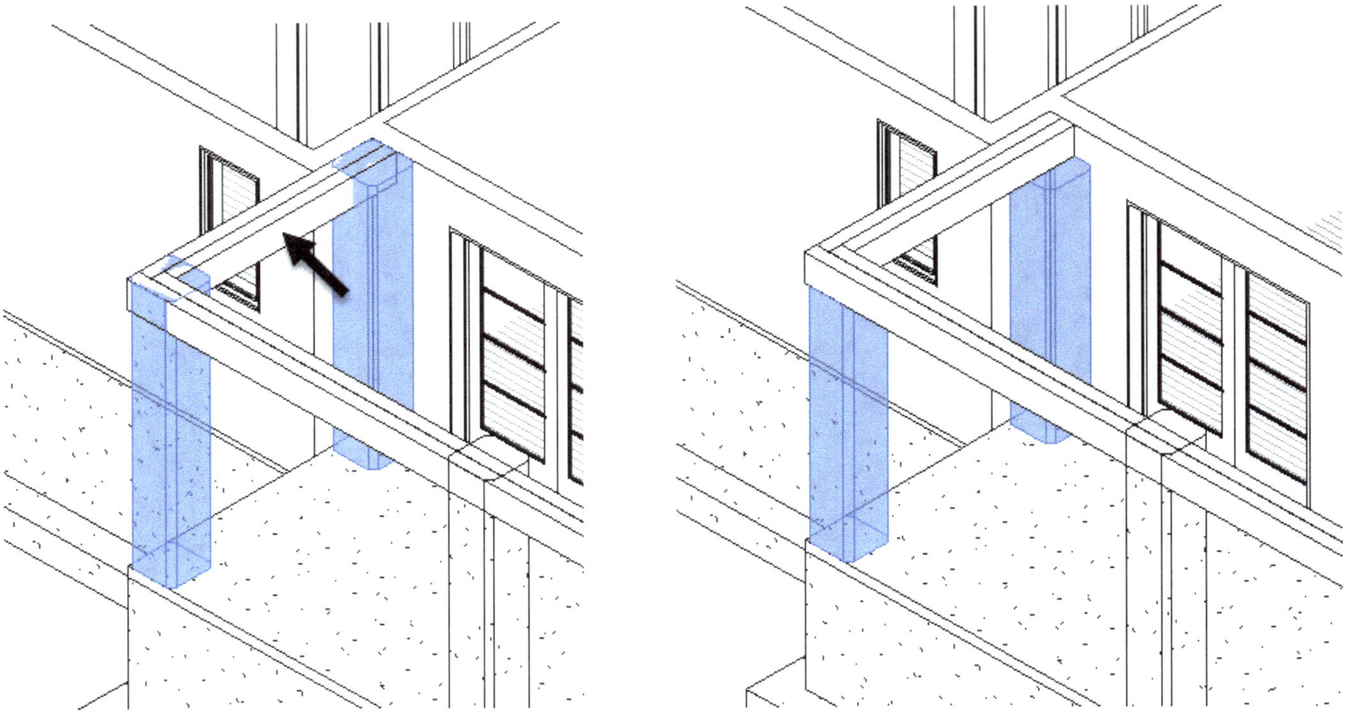

- Press and hold the CTRL key and select the remaining columns.

- Click **Attach Top/Base** on the **Modify Column** panel of the **Modify|Columns** ribbon tab.
- Select the **Top** option from the Options Bar. Next, select **Attachment Style > Cut Column**.
- Select the beam intersecting with the selected columns, as shown. Next, press ESC.

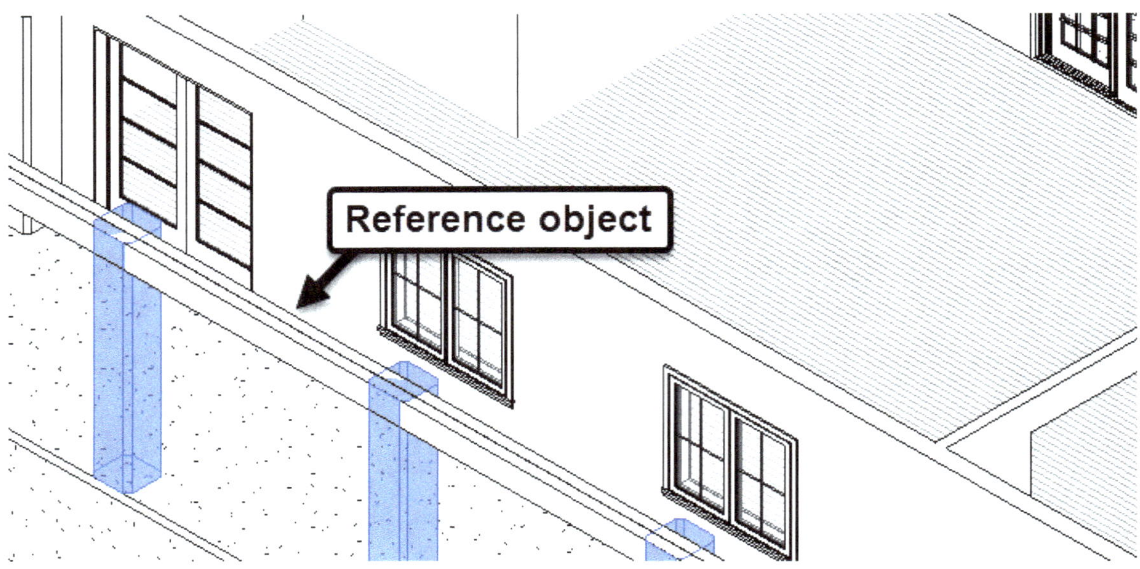

- Likewise, add columns and beams to the back porch, as shown.

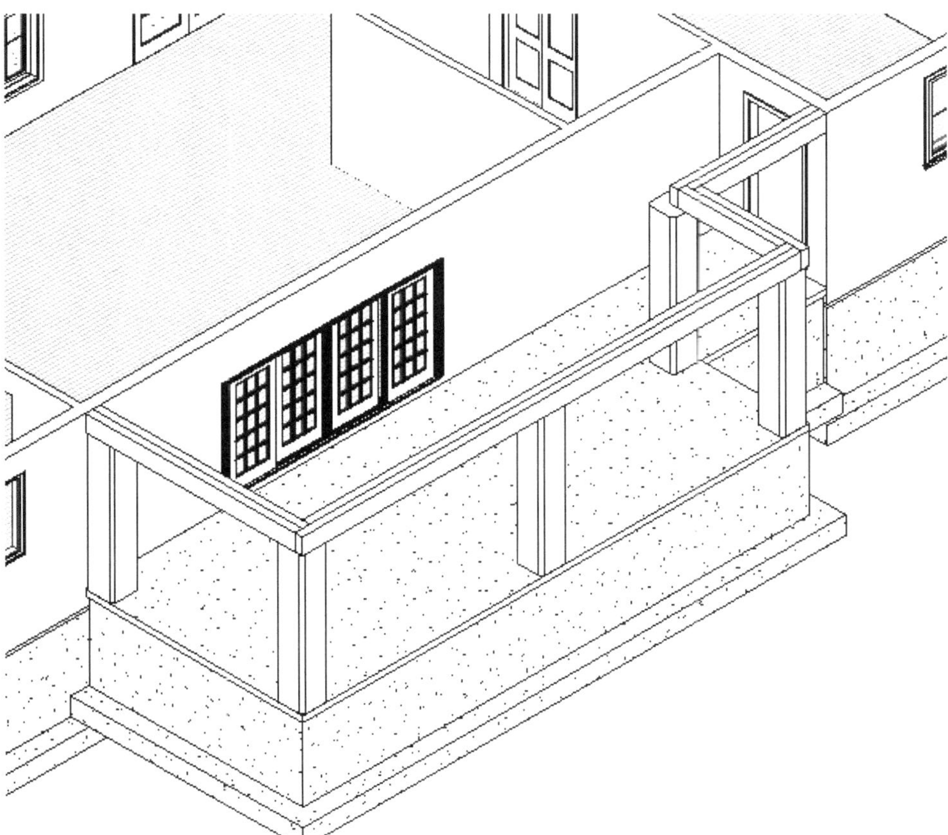

Tutorial 8: Creating Roofs

- Double-click on the **TOP** under the **Floor Plans** node in the **Project Browser**.
- On the **Properties** palette, scroll to the **Extents** section and click the **Edit** button next to the **View Range** parameter.

- On the **View Range** dialog, select **Level > Unlimited**. Next, click **OK**.
- On the ribbon, click **Architecture** tab > **Build** panel > **Roof** drop-down > **Roof by Footprint**.
- On the **Properties** palette, from the **Type Selector**, select the **Wood Rafter 8" – Asphalt Shingle Insulated** roof type.

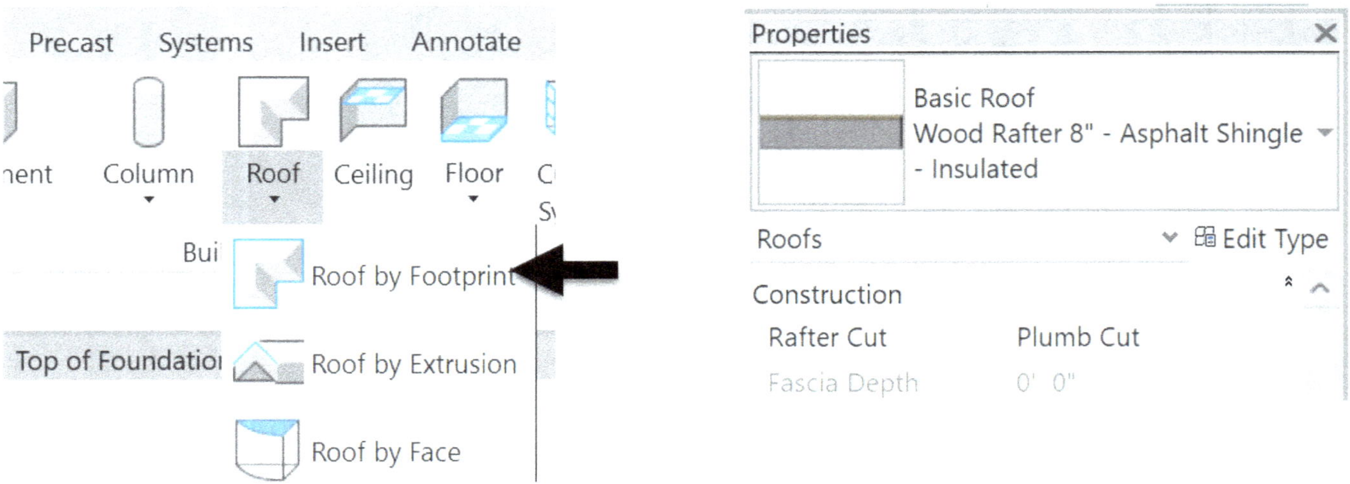

- On the Options Bar, make sure that the **Defines Slope** option is checked. Next, type **2'** in the **Overhang** box.
- Make sure that the **Boundary Line** and **Pick Walls** icons are selected on the **Draw** panel of the **Modify|Create Roof Footprint** ribbon tab.
- Zoom to the top-left corner of the floor plan and select the outer edge of the wall, as shown.
- Select the outer edges of the other two walls, as shown.

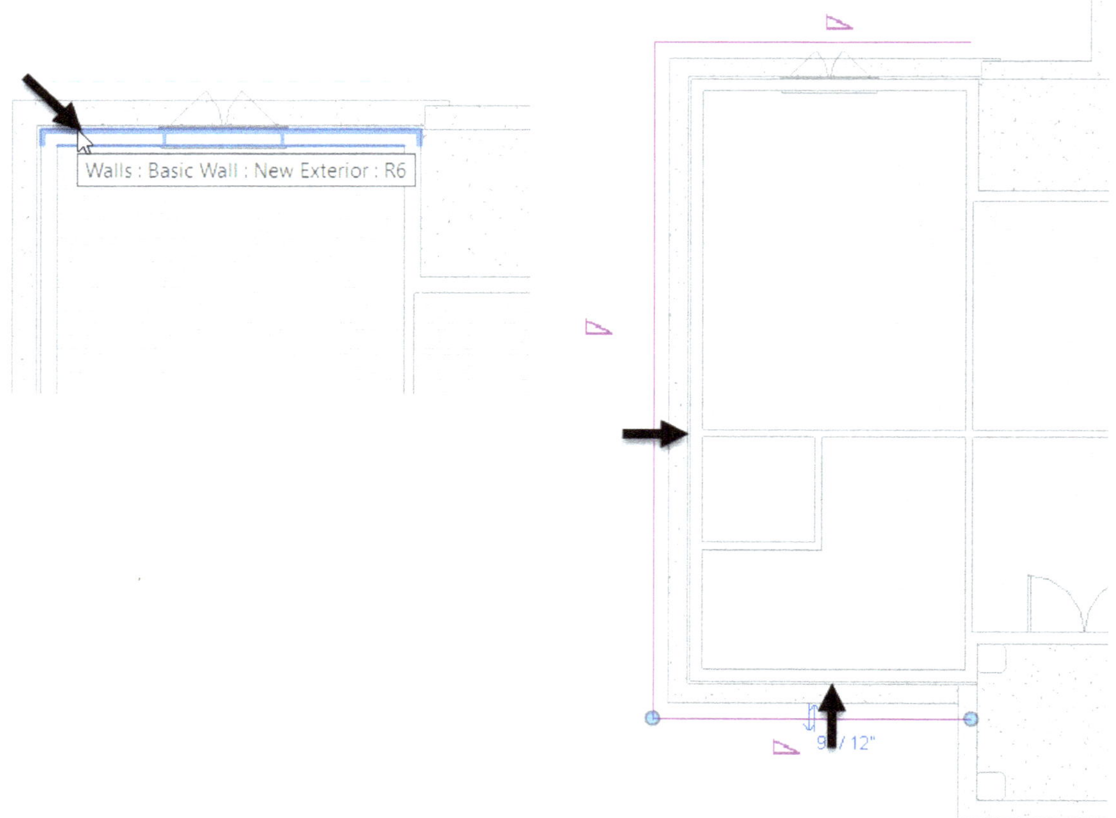

- Select the two edges of the front porch, as shown.

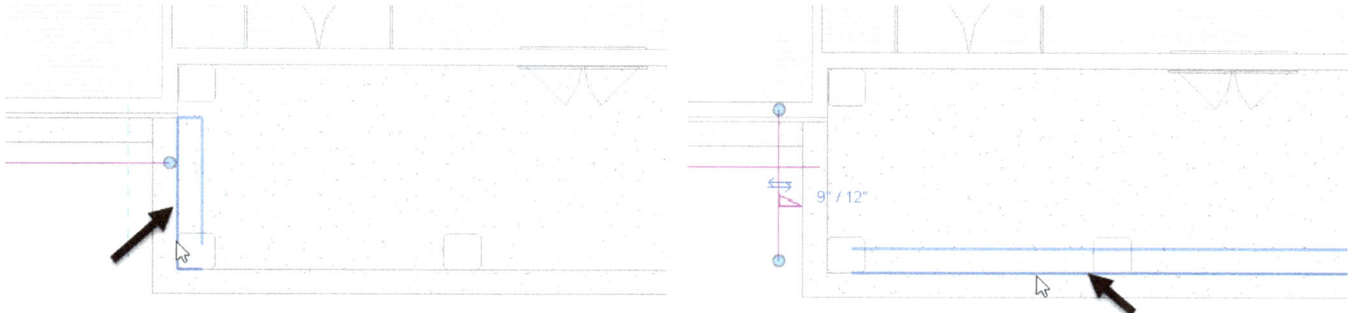

- Select the outer edges of the other walls, as shown.

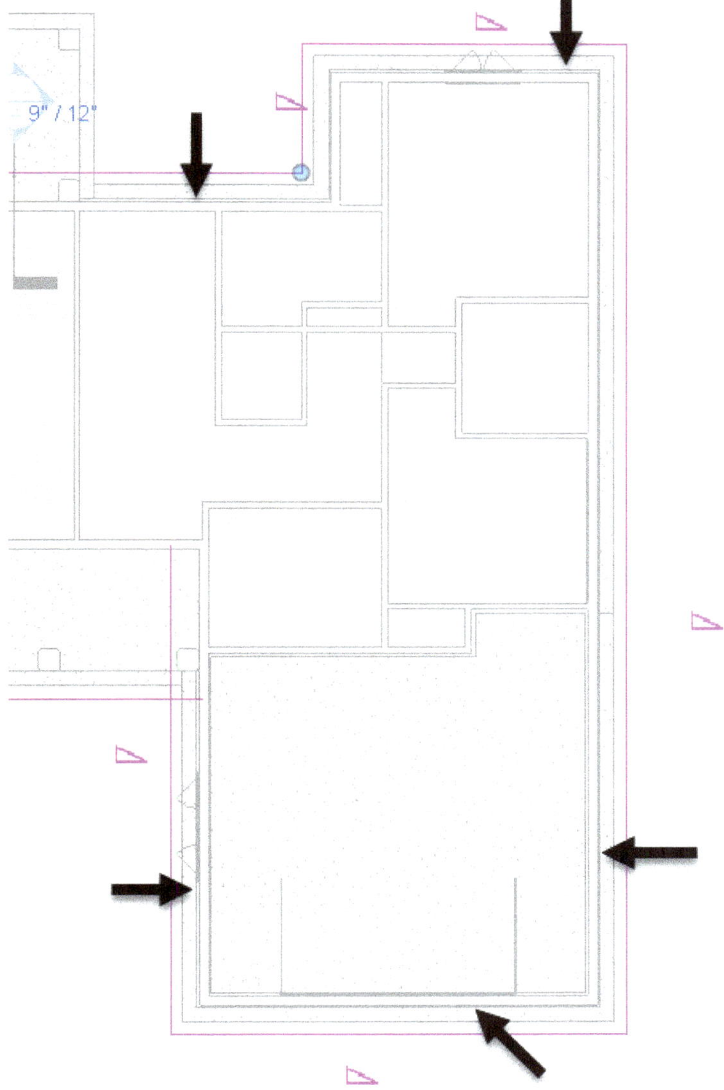

- Select the edges of the back porch, as shown.

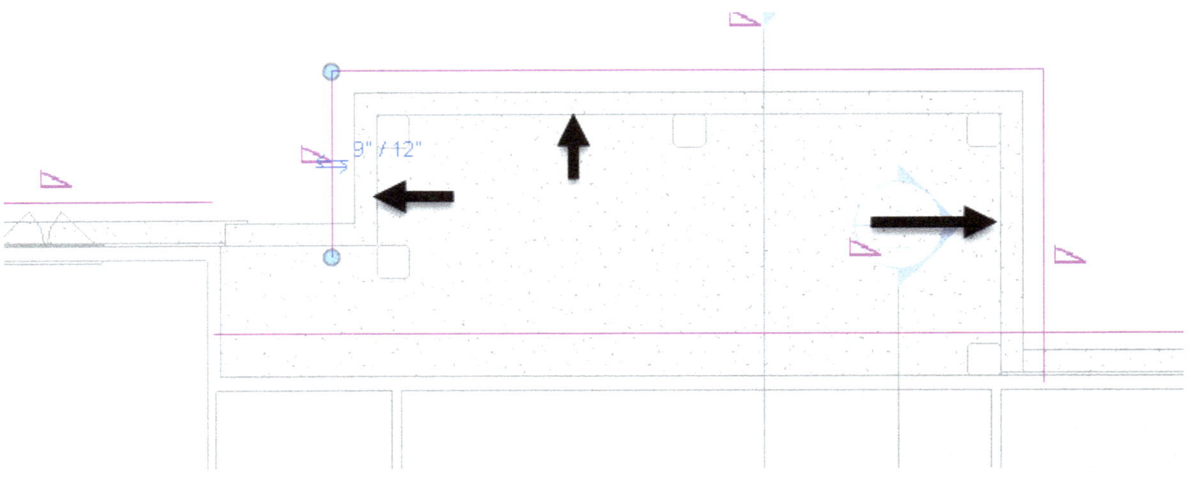

- On the ribbon, click **Modify** tab > **Modify** panel > **Trim/Extend to Corner (TR)** .
- Select the portions of the two boundary lines intersecting with each other.

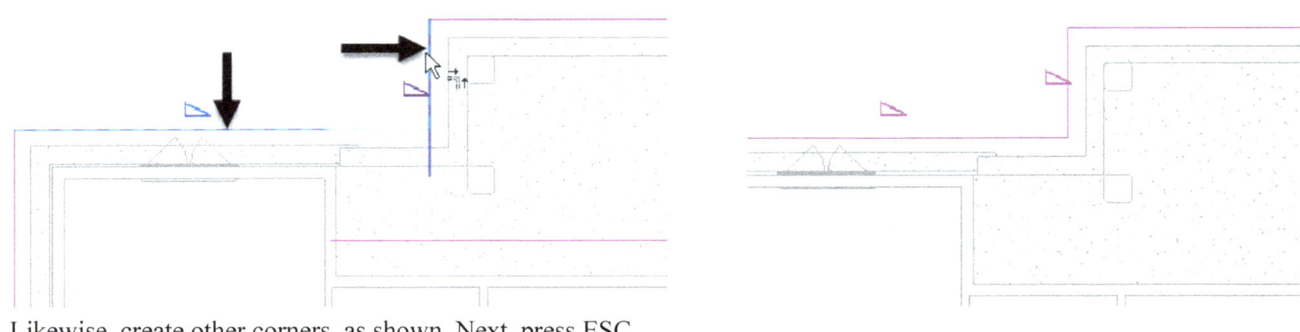

- Likewise, create other corners, as shown. Next, press ESC.

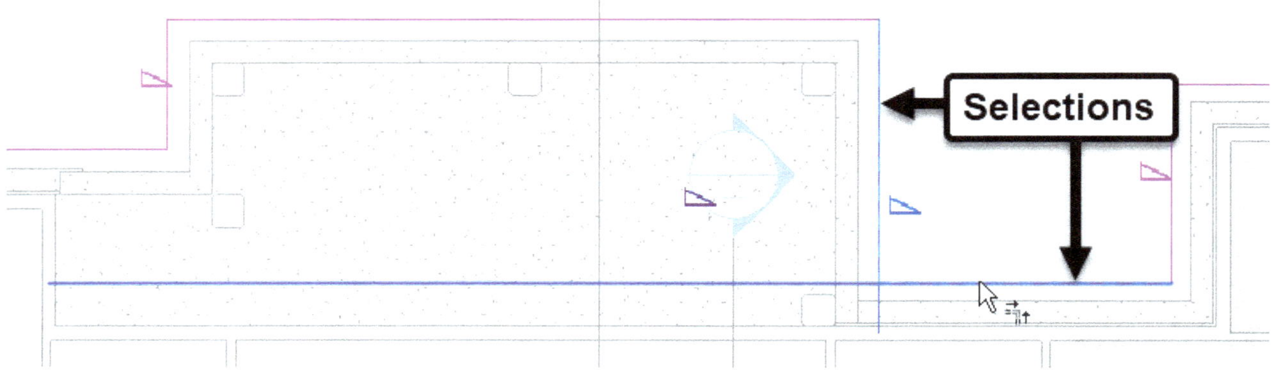

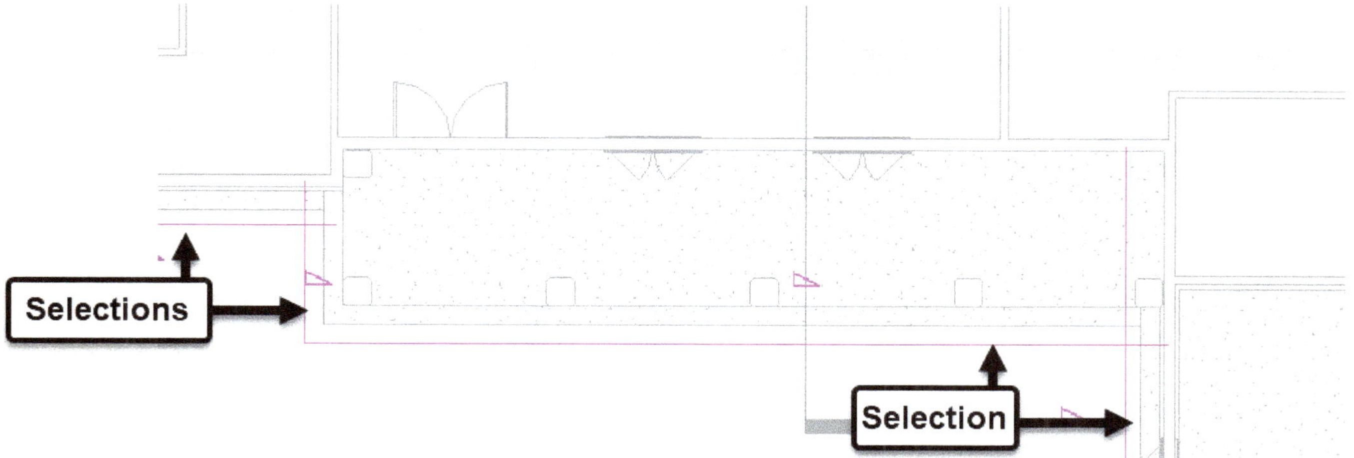

- Press and hold the CTRL key and select the lines of the boundary, as shown.

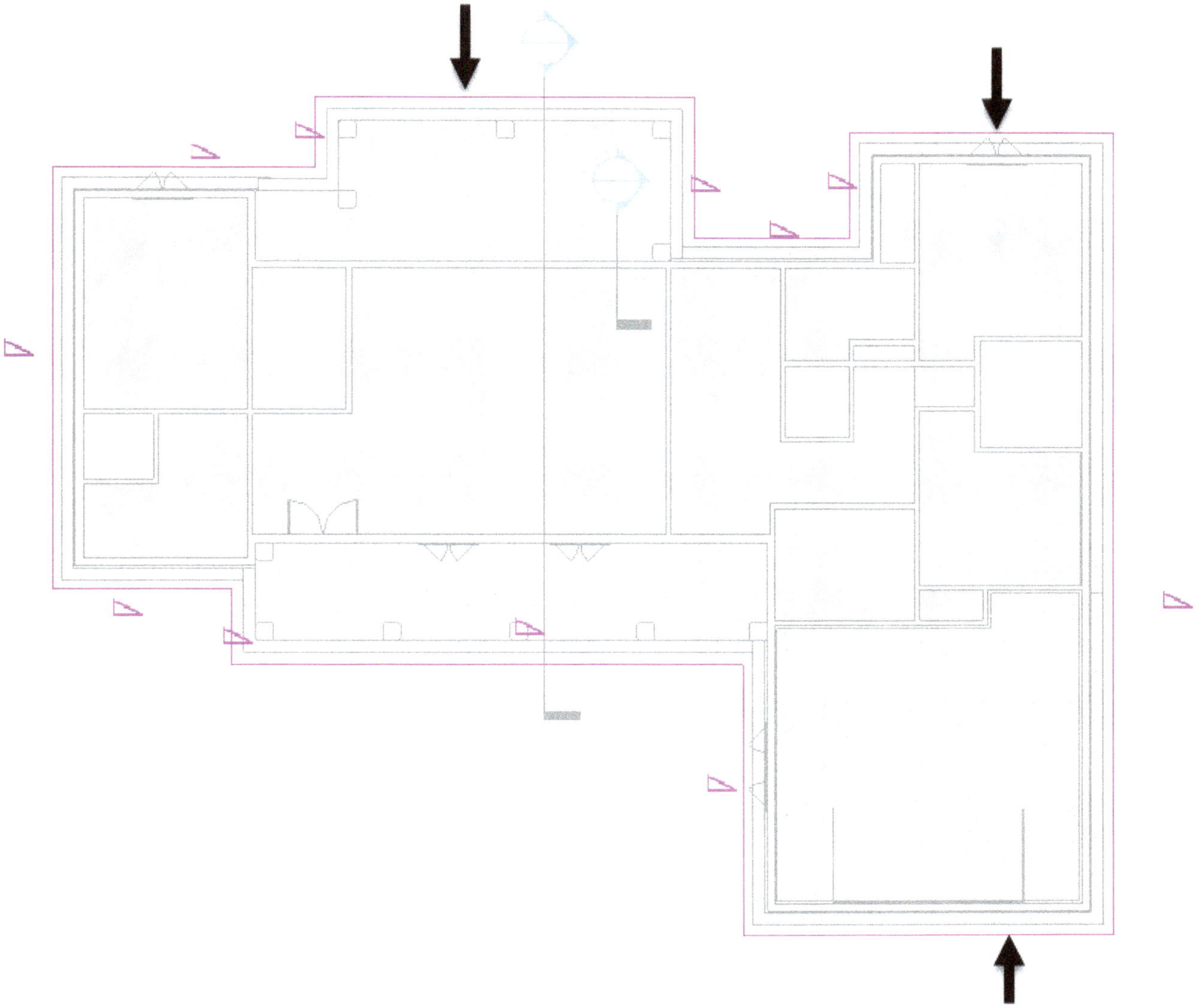

- Uncheck the **Displays Slope** option on the Options Bar. Notice that the slope symbols are not displayed on the selected boundary lines. Also, the gable openings will be created at the selected boundary lines.

- Click in the graphics window to deselect the selected boundary lines.
- Press and hold the CTRL key and select the boundary lines with slope symbols, as shown.

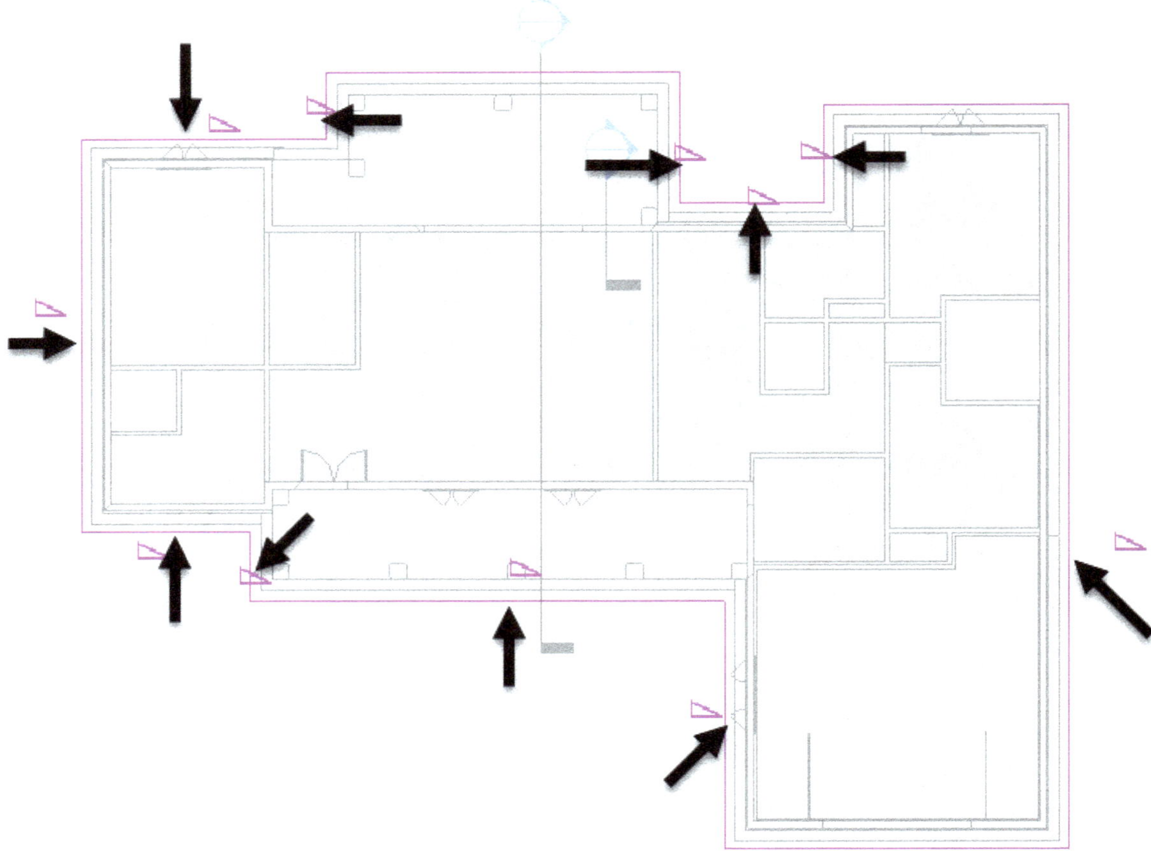

- On the **Properties** palette, type **6"/12"** in the **Slope** box under the **Dimensions** section.

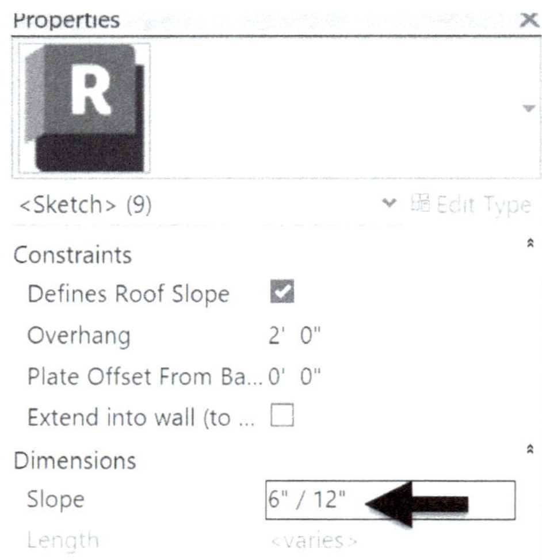

- Click the **Finish Edit Mode** ✓ icon on the **Mode** panel.
- Click the **Default 3D View** 🏠 icon on the Quick Access Toolbar.

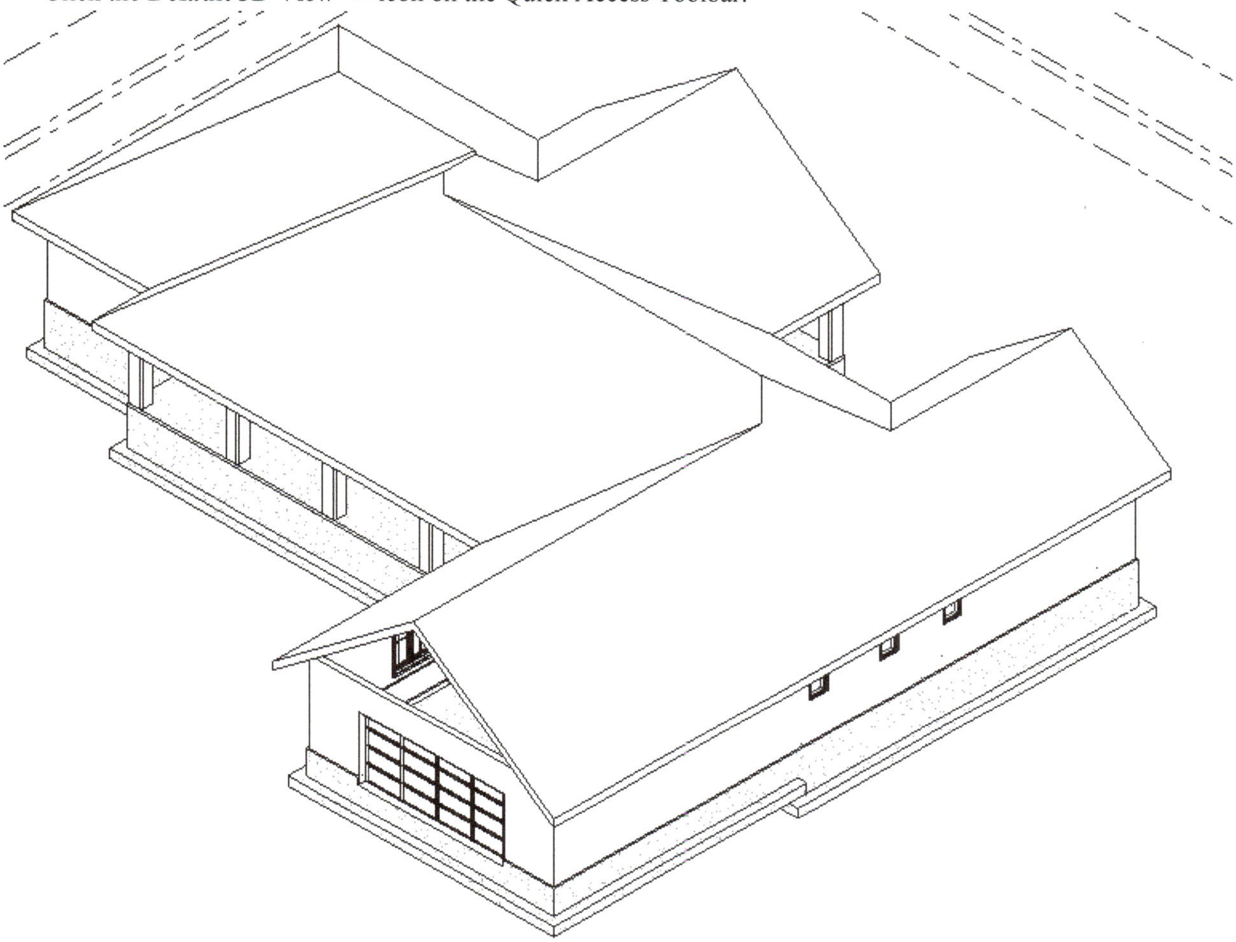

- Place the pointer on anyone of the walls, and then press the TAB key; all the walls are highlighted.

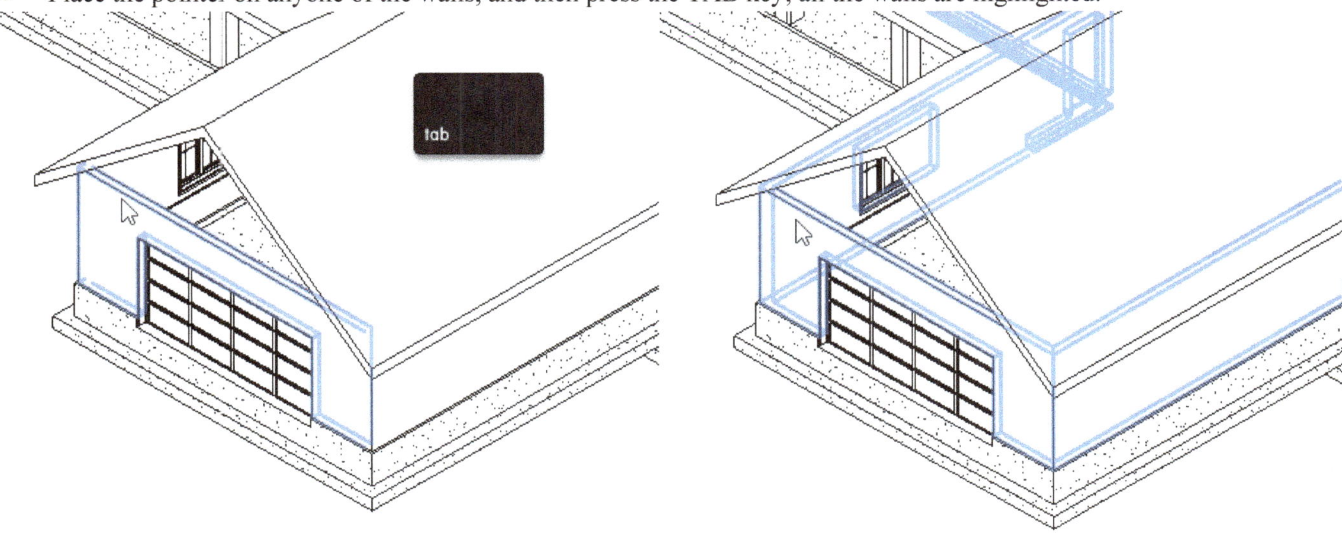

- Click to select all the walls.

- On the ribbon, click **Modify| Walls** tab > **Modify Walls** panel > **Attach Top/Base** .
- Select the **Top** option from the Options Bar. Next, select the roof; the walls are attached to the roof.

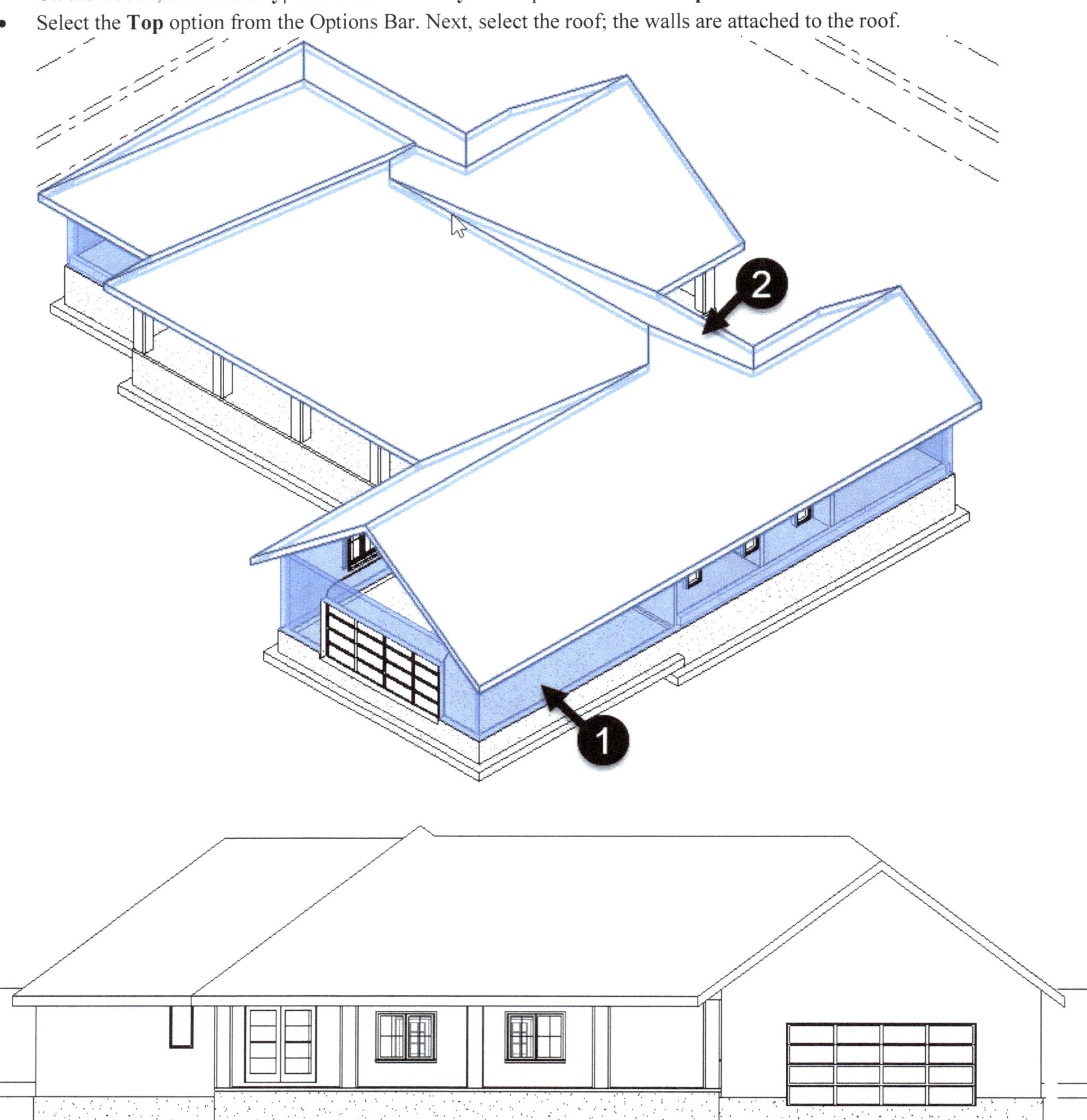

Adding a Wall on the Back Porch

- Click on the top right corner point of the Viewcube between the **Right** and **Back** faces. Notice a gap between the beam and roof.

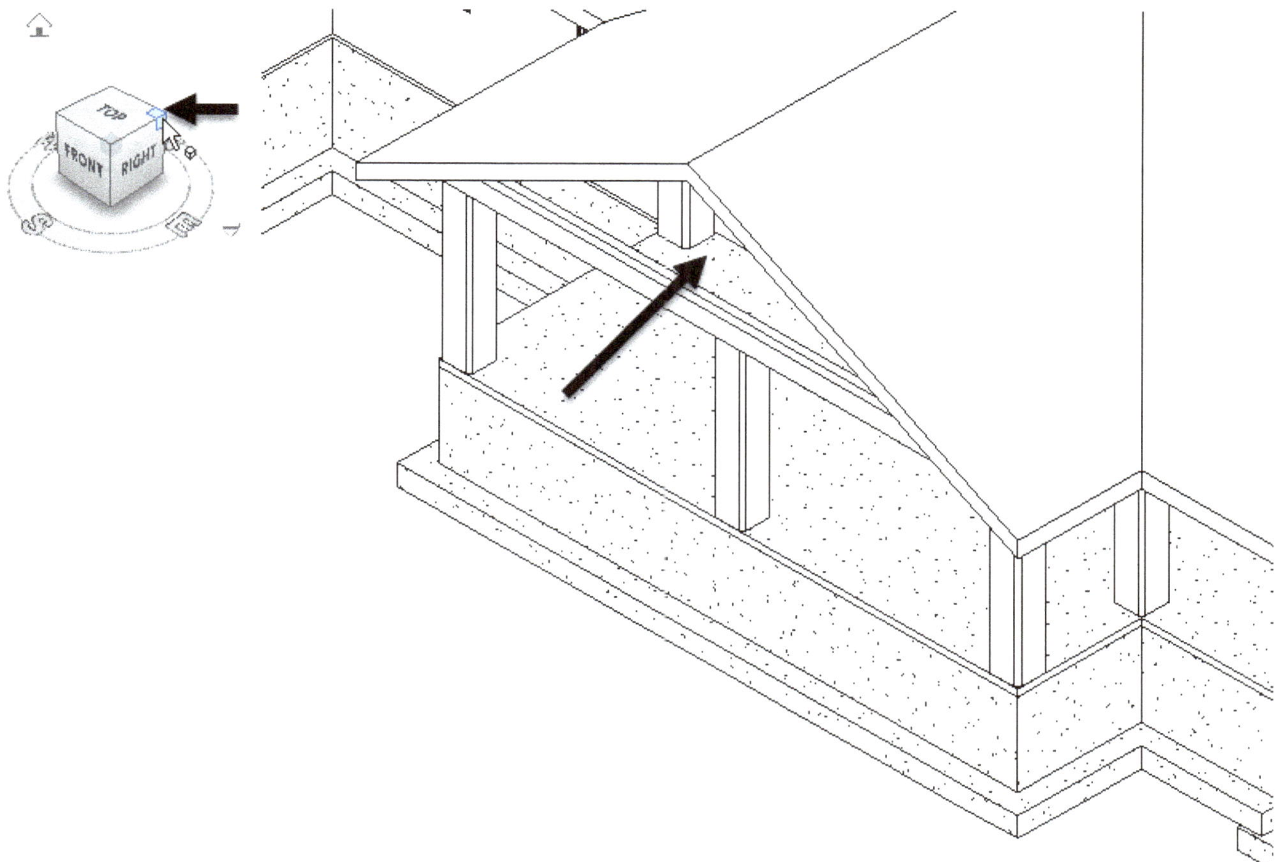

- Double-click on **TOP** under the **Floor Plans** node in the **Project Browser**.

- Click **Architecture > Build > Wall drop-down > Wall:Architectural** .
- On the **Properties** palette, from the **Type Selector** drop-down, select the **New Exterior** wall type.
- On the Options Bar, select **Height** from first drop-down. Next, select **Unconnected** from next drop-down.
- Specify the start and endpoints of the wall, as shown. Next, press ESC twice.

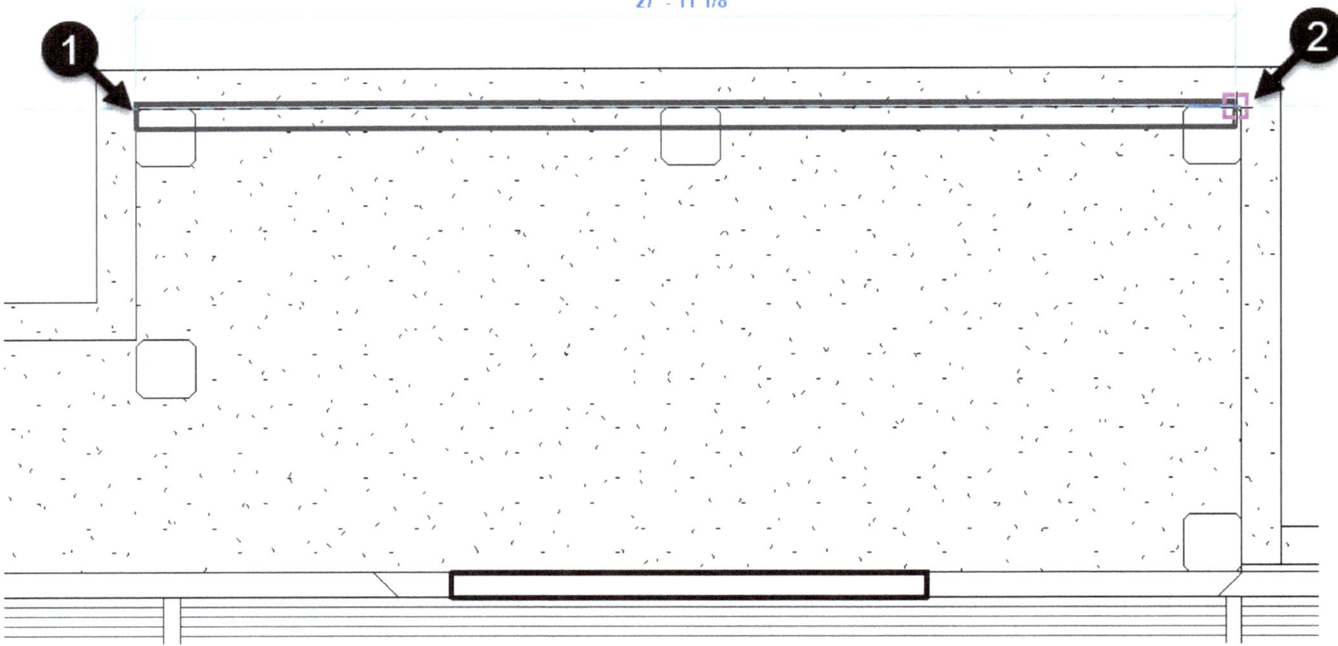

- Click the **Default 3D View** icon on the Quick Access Toolbar. Next, click on the top right corner point of the Viewcube between the **Right** and **Back** faces.
- Select the newly created wall and click **Modify| Walls** tab > **Modify Walls** panel > **Attach Top/Base** on the ribbon.
- Select the roof; the wall is attached to the roof.

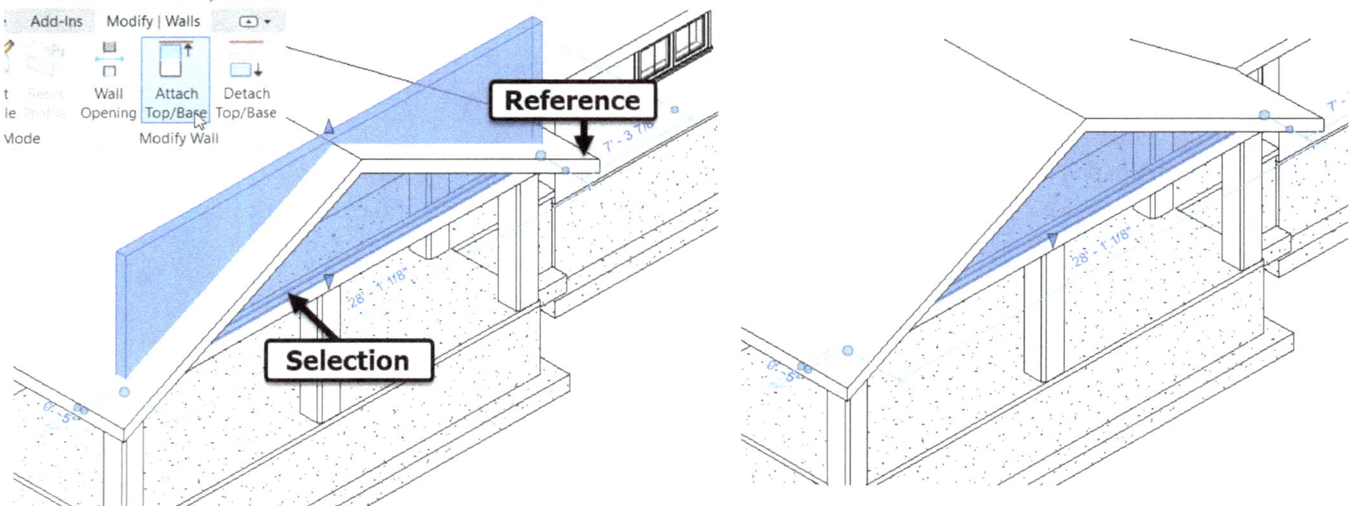

Adding Fascia and Gutters to the Roof

- Click the **Default 3D View** icon on the Quick Access Toolbar.
- On the ribbon, click **Architecture** tab > **Build** > **Roof** drop-down > **Fascia**.
- Click the **Edit Type** icon on the **Properties** palette.
- On the **Type Properties** dialog, select **Fascia Flat : 1x10** from **Profile** drop-down.
- Click in the **Material** box, and then click the **Browse** button. Next, type softwood in the search bar available on the top-left corner of the **Material Browser** dialog. Select the **Softwood, Lumber** material and click **OK** twice.

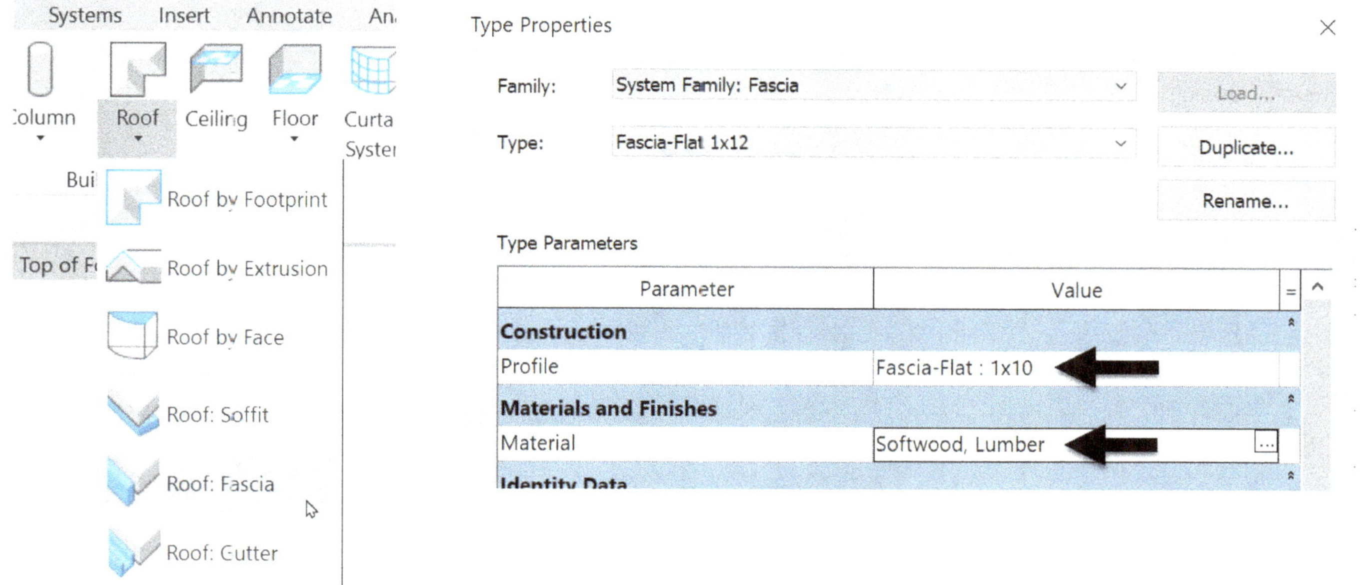

- Select the top edge of the side face of the gabble roof, as shown.
- Likewise, select the top edges of the other side faces of the roof, as shown.

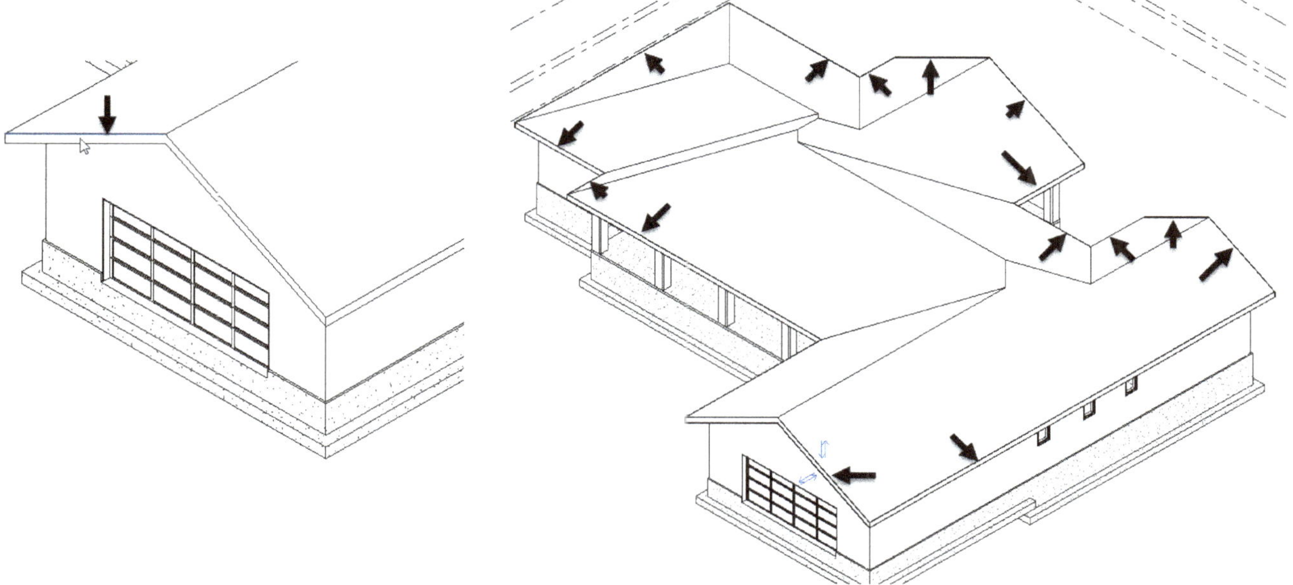

- On the ribbon, click **Architecture** tab > **Build** > **Roof** drop-down > **Gutter**.
- Click the **Edit Type** icon on the **Properties** palette.
- On the **Type Properties** dialog, select **Gutter Profile-Bevel: 5" x 5"** from **Profile** drop-down.
- Click in the **Material** box, and then click the **Browse** button. Next, type ivory in the search bar available on the top-left corner of the **Material Browser** dialog. Select the **Steel, Paint Finish, Ivory, Matte** material and click **OK** twice.

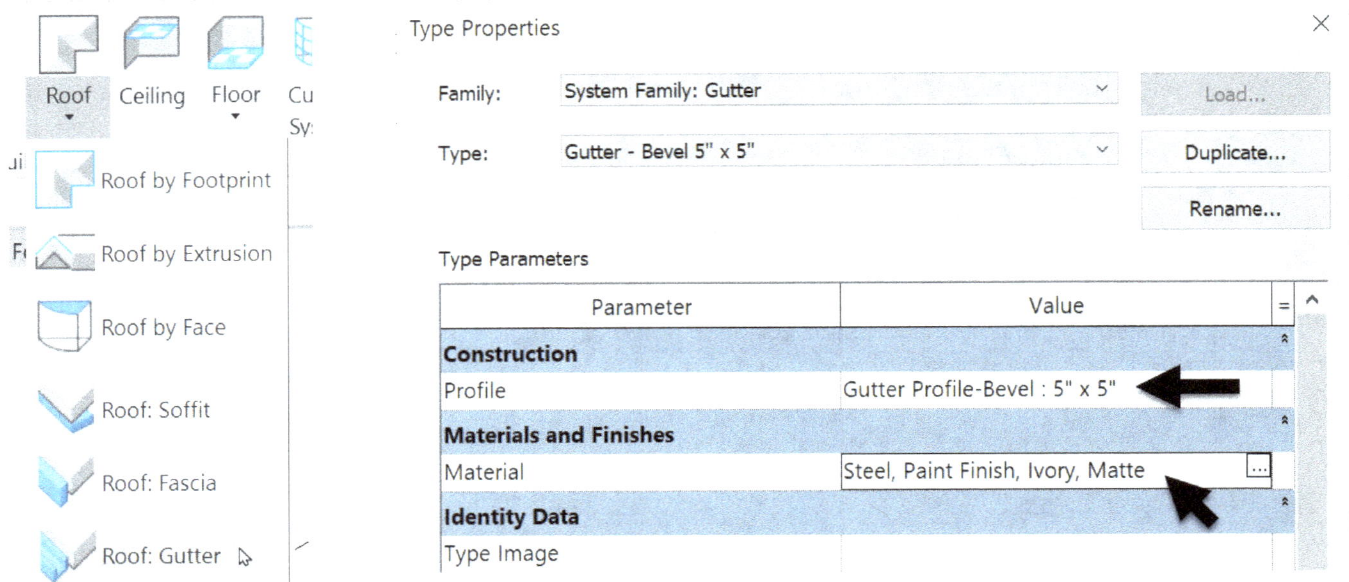

- Select the top edge of the fascia, as shown. A gutter is added to it.

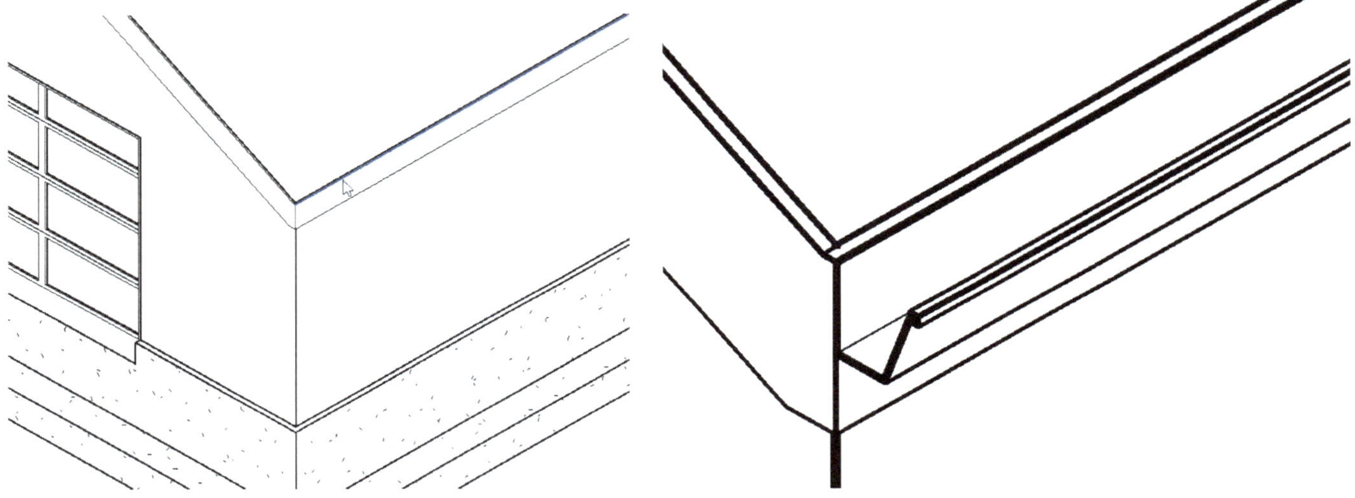

- Likewise, add gutters to the other fascias, as shown.

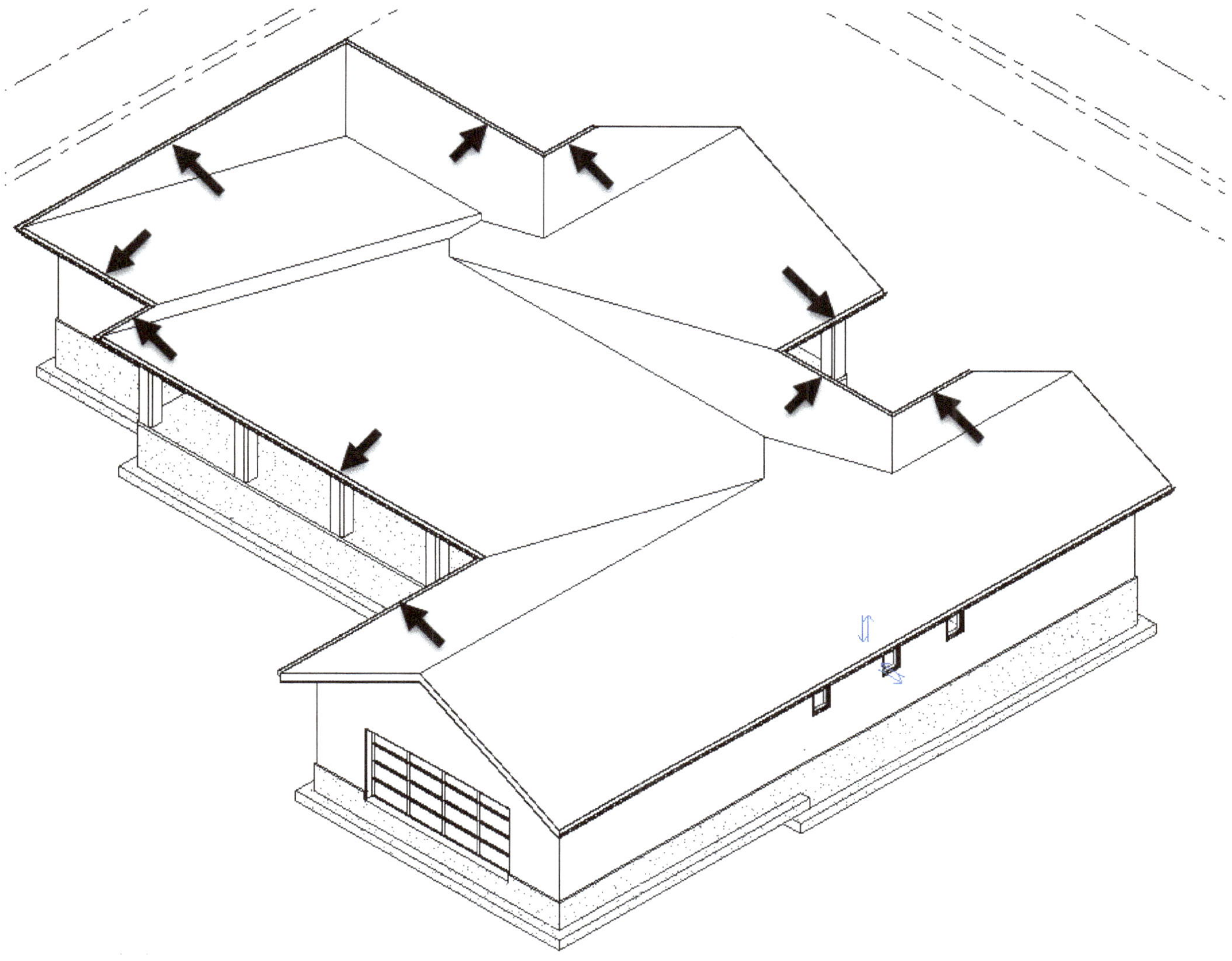

Adding Soffit to the Roof

- Double-click on the **TOP** under the **Floor Plans** node in the **Project Browser**.
- On the ribbon, click **Architecture** tab > **Build** panel > **Roof** drop-down > **Roof: Soffit**.
- On the **Properties** palette, from the **Type Selector**, select the **Generic – 4"** roof soffit type.
- Type **–1** in the **Height Offset from Level** box on the **Properties** palette.
- Make sure that the **Boundary Line** and **Lines** icons are selected on the **Draw** panel of the **Modify | Create Roof Soffit Boundary** ribbon tab.

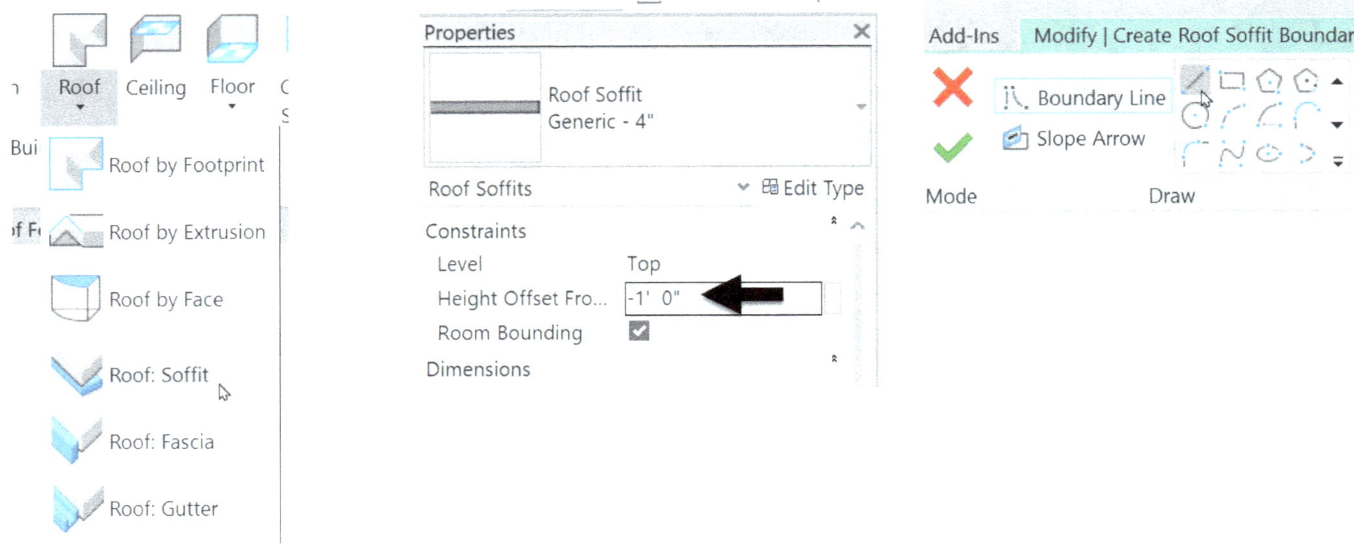

- Zoom to the top-left corner of the floor plan and select the corner point of the roof, as shown.
- Scroll the mouse wheel in the backward direction. Next, move the mouse pointer toward right, and then scroll the mouse wheel in the forward direction.
- Select the corner point of the roof, as shown.

- Move the pointer upward and place it on the corner point of the wall, as shown.
- Move the pointer toward left and notice a dashed line originating from the corner point of the wall.
- Select the intersection point between the dashed line and the roof edge, as shown.

- Press and hold the scroll wheel of the mouse pointer and drag it toward right.
- Select the intersection point between the dashed line originating from the wall edge and the roof edge, as shown.

- Move the pointer downward and select the corner point of the roof edge, as shown.

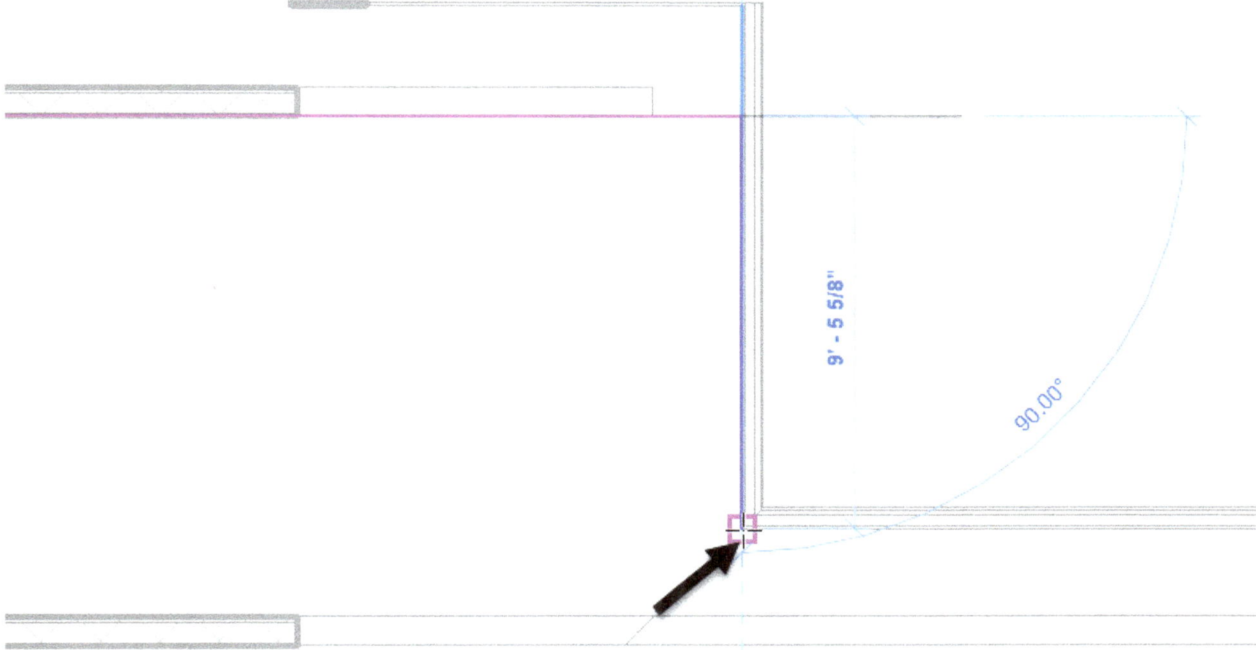

- Move the pointer horizontally toward right and select the corner point, as shown.
- Move the pointer vertically and select the endpoint of the roof, as shown.

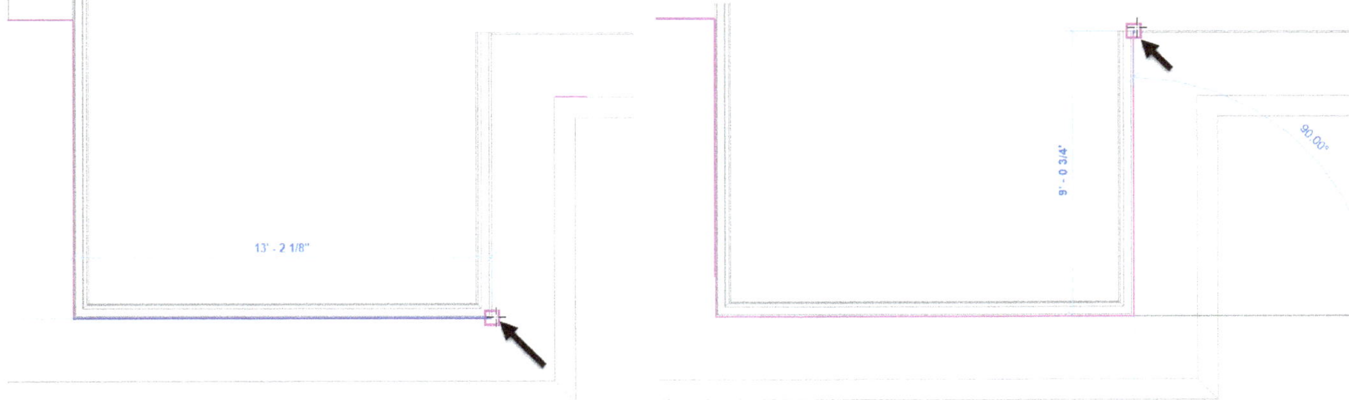

- Move the pointer toward right, type 3 and press ENTER.
- Move the pointer downward and select the intersection point between the wall edge and the dashed line, as shown.

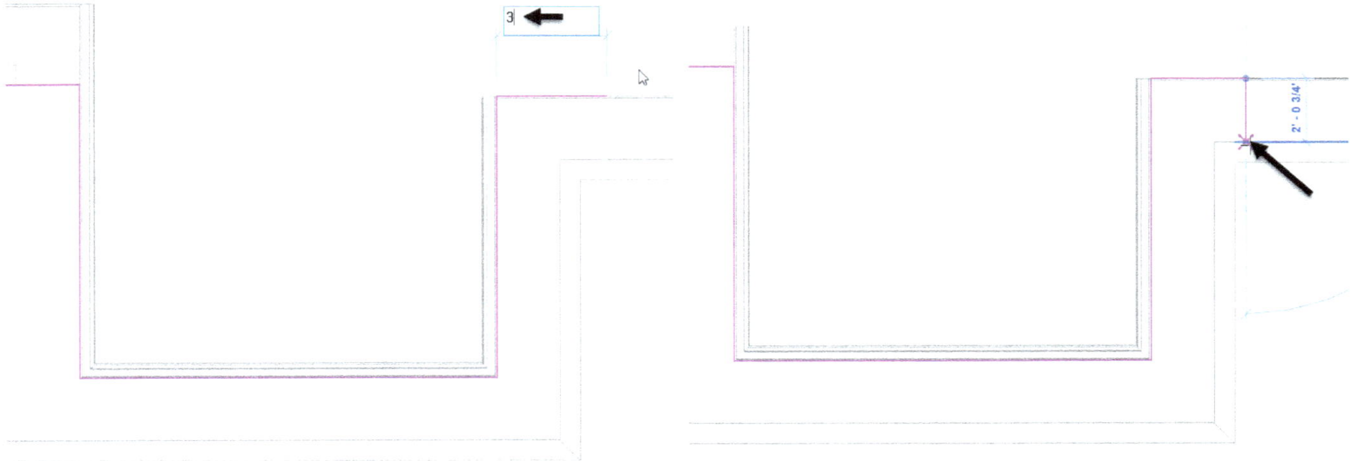

- Move the pointer toward right and select the corner point, as shown.
- Move the pointer downward and select the corner point, as shown.

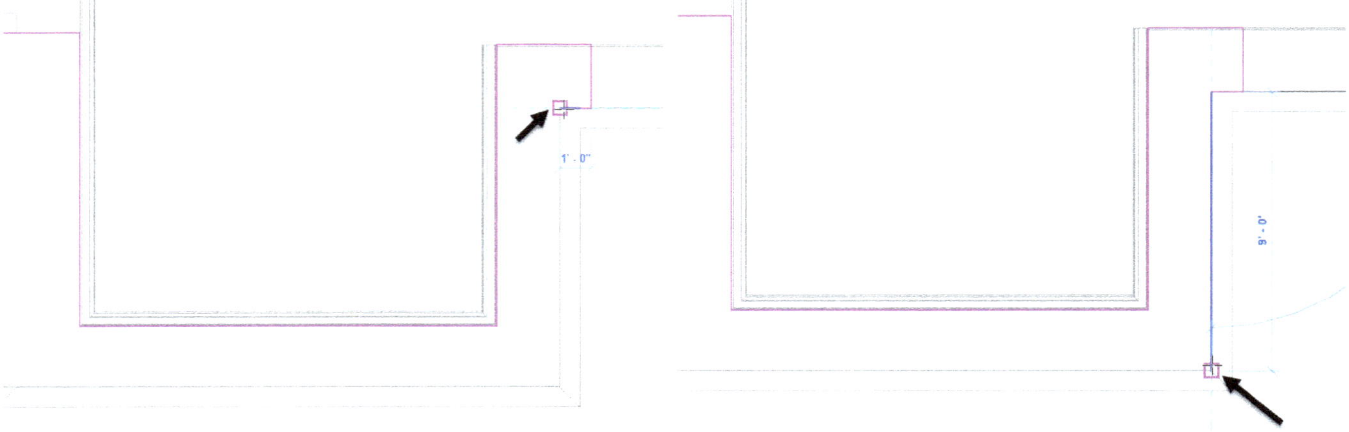

- Likewise, select the corner points of the wall edges, as shown.

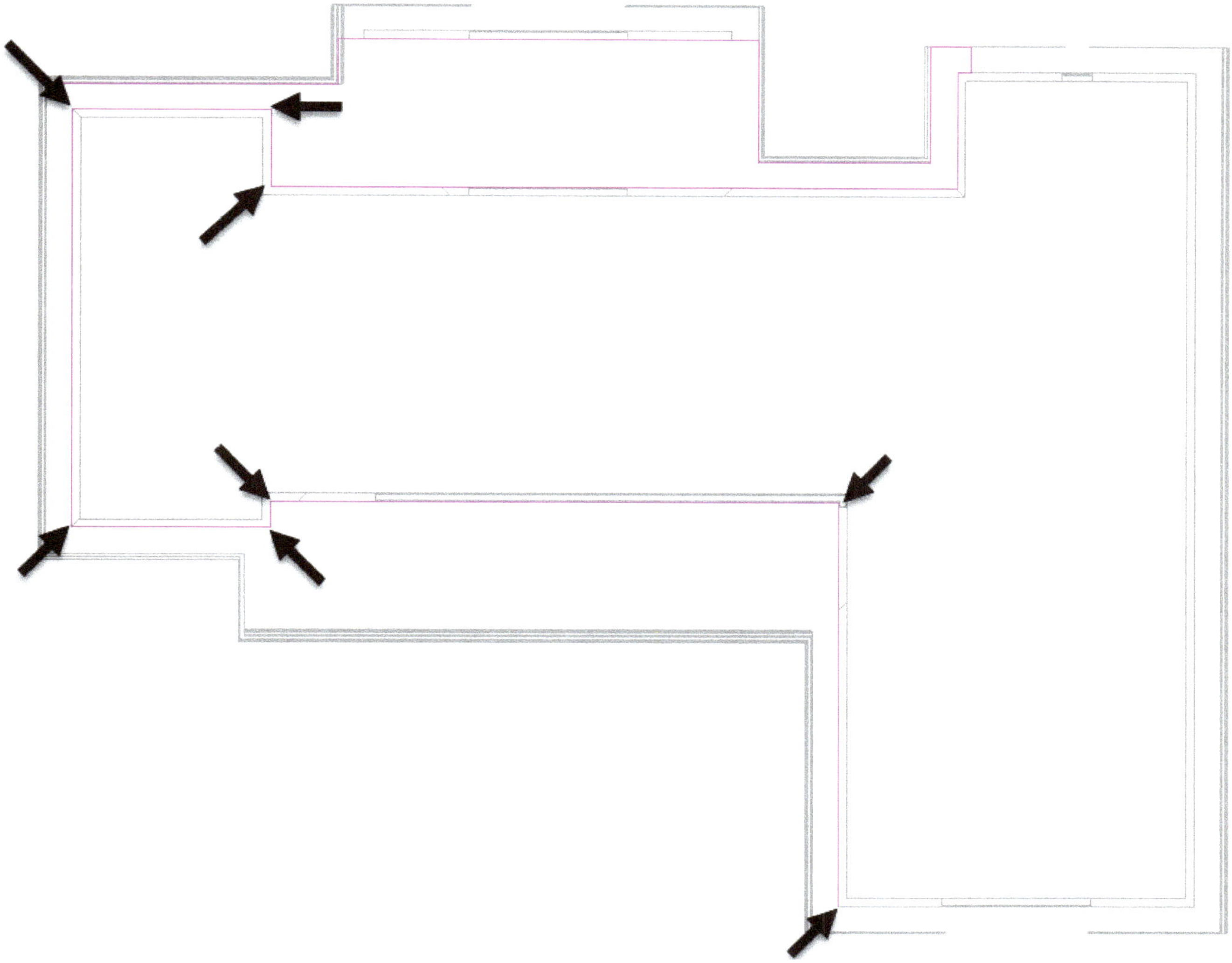

- Move the pointer toward right, type 1 and press ENTER.
- Move the pointer downward and select the intersection point between the wall edge and the roof edge, as shown.

- Move the pointer toward right and select the corner point of the roof edge, as shown.
- Move the pointer upward and select the corner point, as shown.

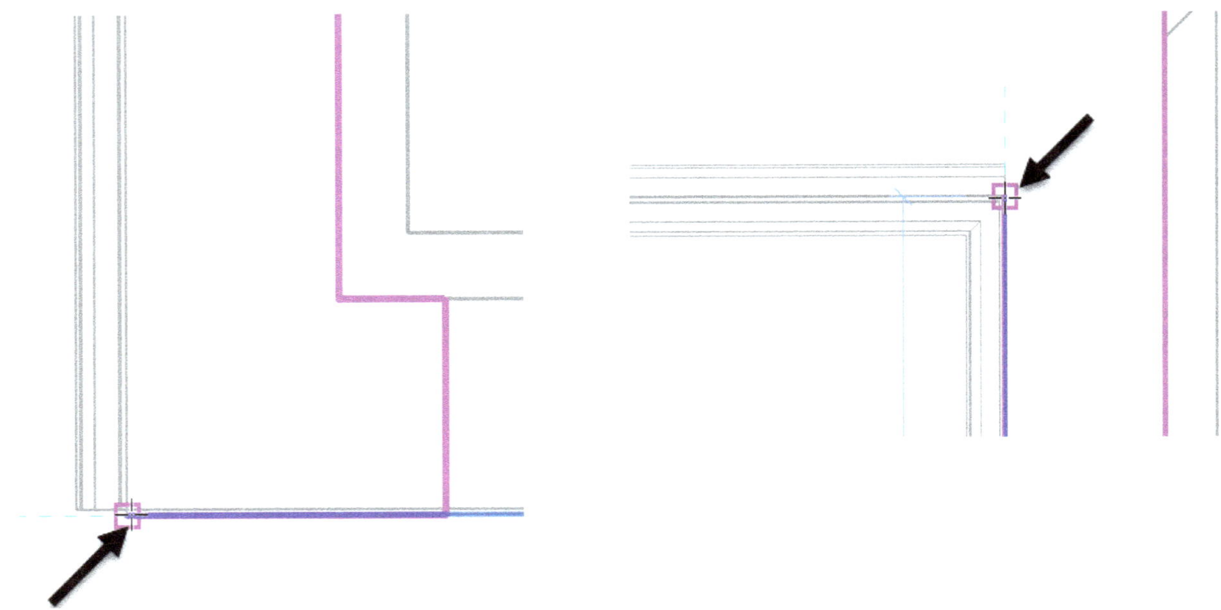

- Likewise, select the other corner points of the roof edge, as shown.

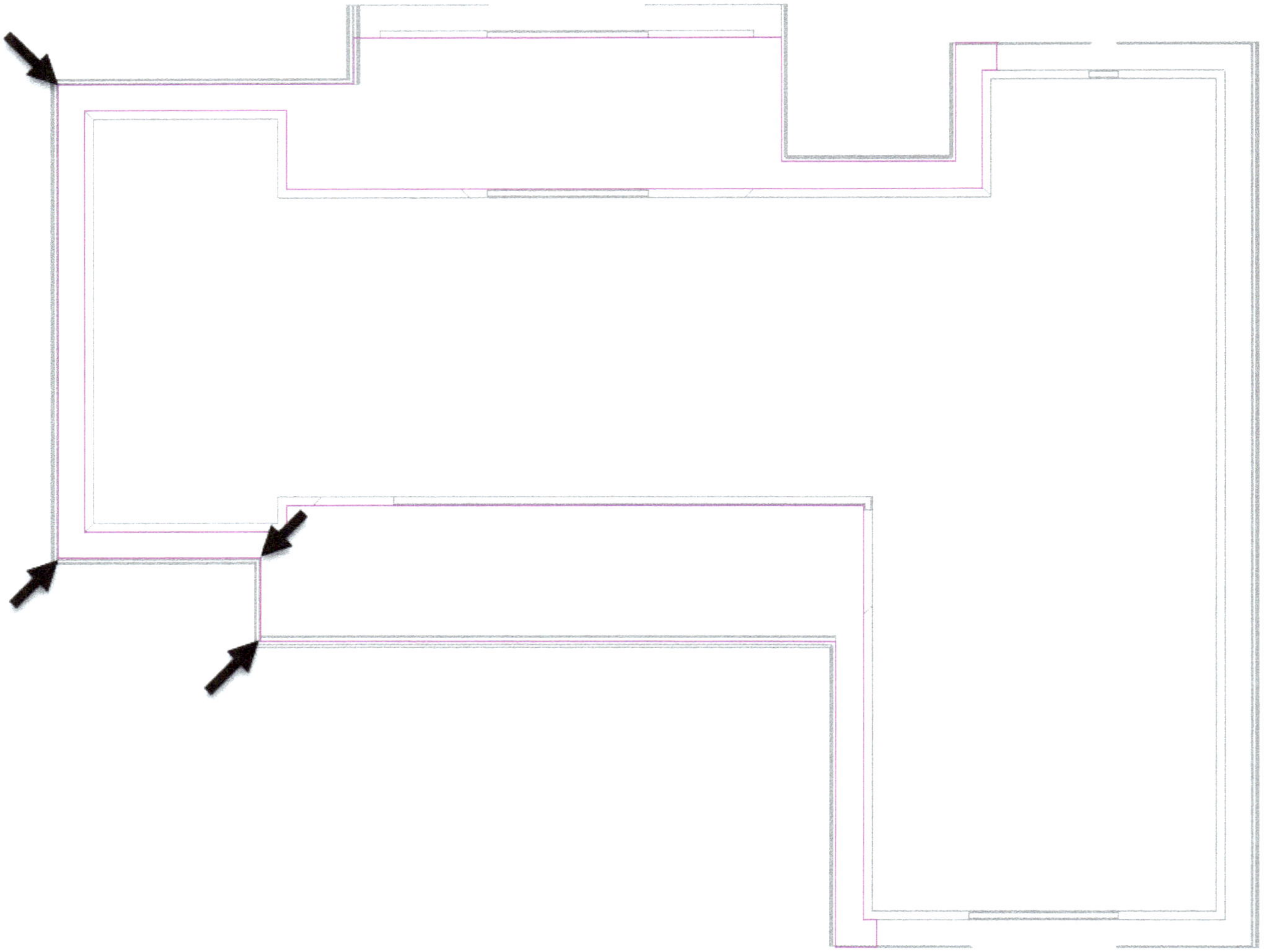

- Specify the start point of the new boundary, as shown.

- Move the pointer toward left, type 1 and press ENTER.
- Move the pointer downward and select the intersection point between the roof edge and the dashed line, as shown.

- Specify the other points of the boundary, as shown.

- Click the **Finish Edit Mode** ✔ icon on the **Mode** panel.
- Click the **Default 3D View** 🏠 icon on the Quick Access Toolbar to view the soffits.

Next, you need to close the soffits.

- Double-click on the **TOP** under the **Floor Plans** node in the **Project Browser**.
- On the ribbon, click **Architecture** tab > **Build** panel > **Wall** drop-down > **Wall Architectural**.
- On the **Properties** palette, select **Generic – 5"** wall from the **Basic Wall** drop-down.
- On the **Properties** palette, type **-1'** in the **Base Offset** box.
- Click the **Edit Type** icon on the **Properties** palette.
- Click the **Duplicate** button next to the **Type** drop-down. Next, type **Soffit Box** in the **Name** box and click **OK**.
- Click the **Edit** button next to the **Structure** parameter; the **Edit Assembly** dialog appears. Notice that there is only one layer called **Structure [1]** in the table.
- Click in the **Material** column of the **Structure[1]** layer. Next, click the **Browse** button to display the **Material Browser** dialog.
- Type **softwood** in the search box, and then select the **Softwood Lumbber** material from the search results. Next, click **OK**.
- Type **1"** in the **Thickness** column of the **Structure [1]** layer. Next, click **OK** twice.

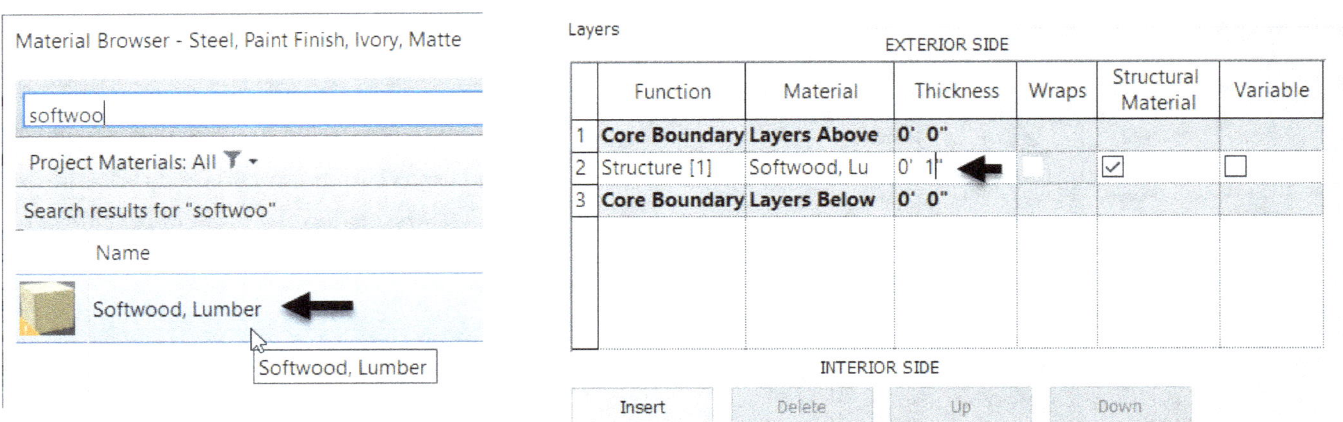

- On the Options Bar, select **Height** and **Unconnected** from the two drop-downs.
- Type **2'** as the height of the wall, and then select **Location Line > Finish Face:Interior**.

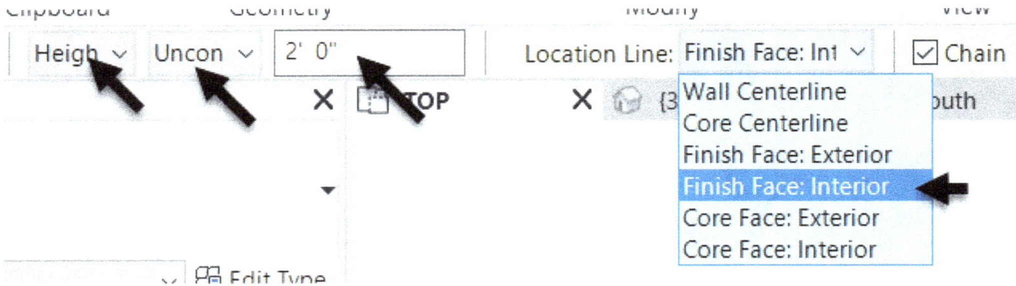

- Zoom-in to the bottom-right portion of the plan view and select the corner point of the roof, as shown.

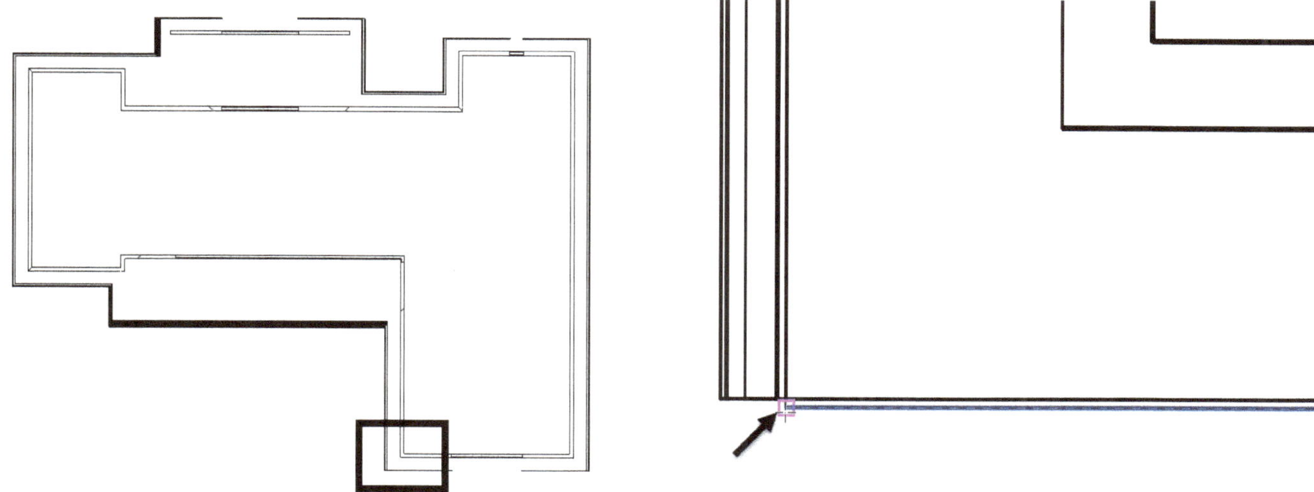

- Move the pointer toward right, type 3 and press ENTER. Next, move the pointer upward and click on the horizontal edge, as shown. Next, press ESC.

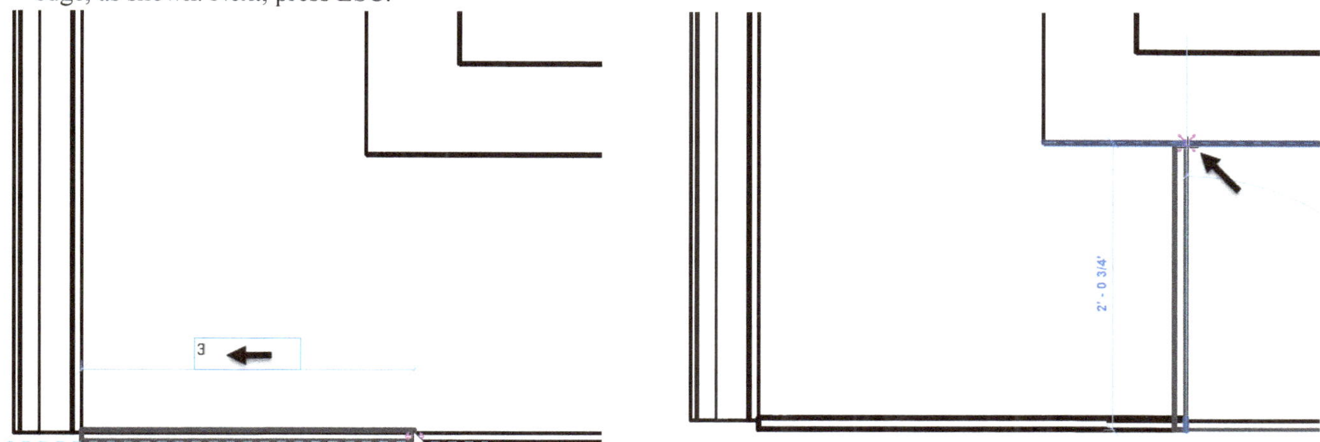

- Pan the drawing toward right and select the corner point of the roof, as shown.
- Press the SPACEBAR to reverse the side of the wall.

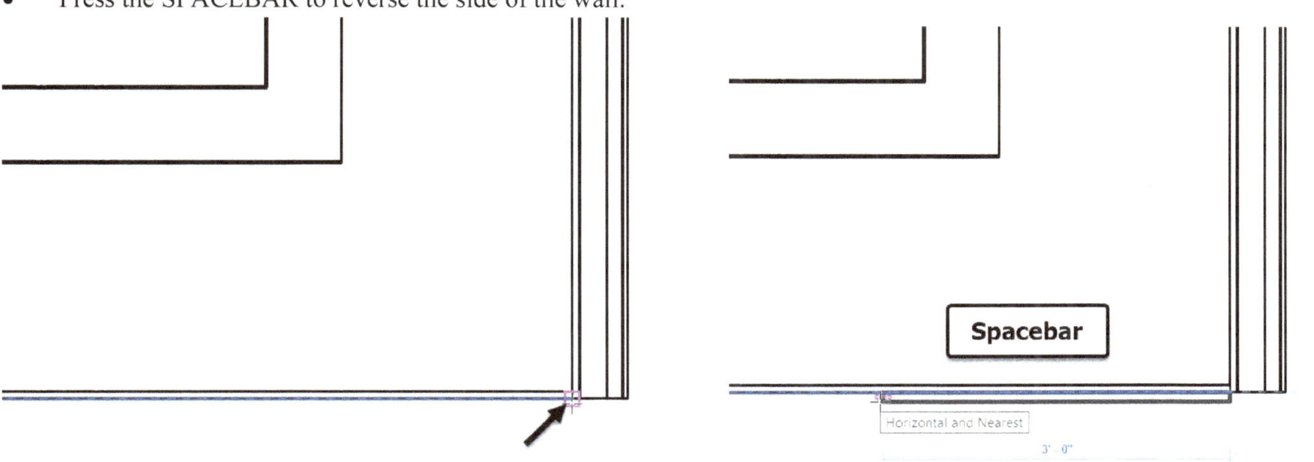

- Move the pointer toward left, type 3 and press ENTER. Next, move the pointer upward and select the horizontal edge, as shown. Next, press ESC.

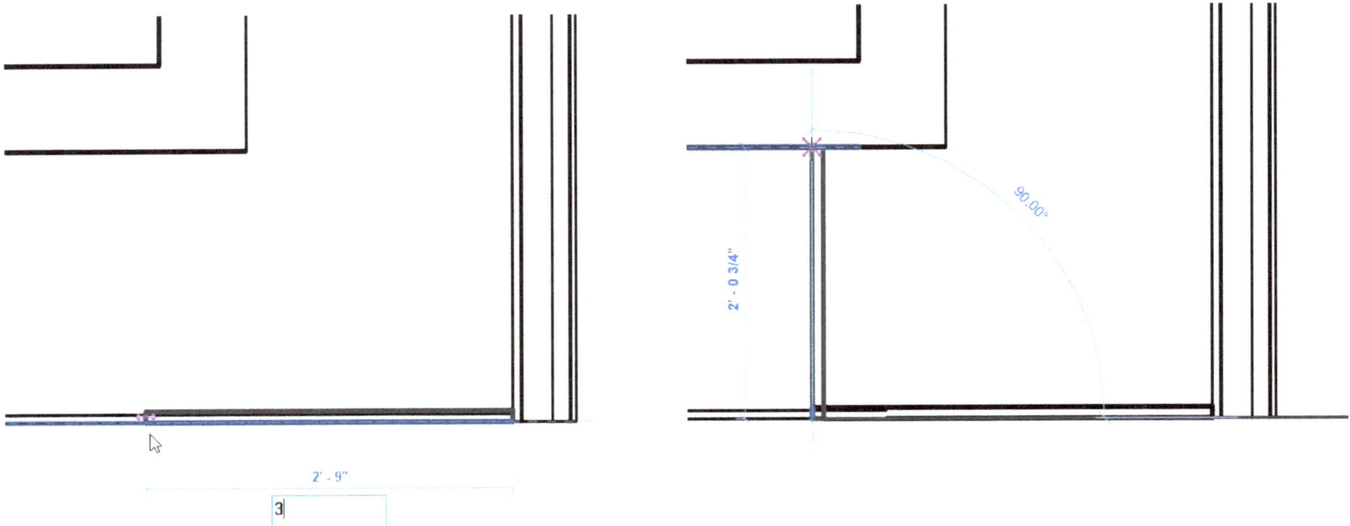

- Zoom-in to the top-right portion of the plan view and select the corner point of the roof, as shown.

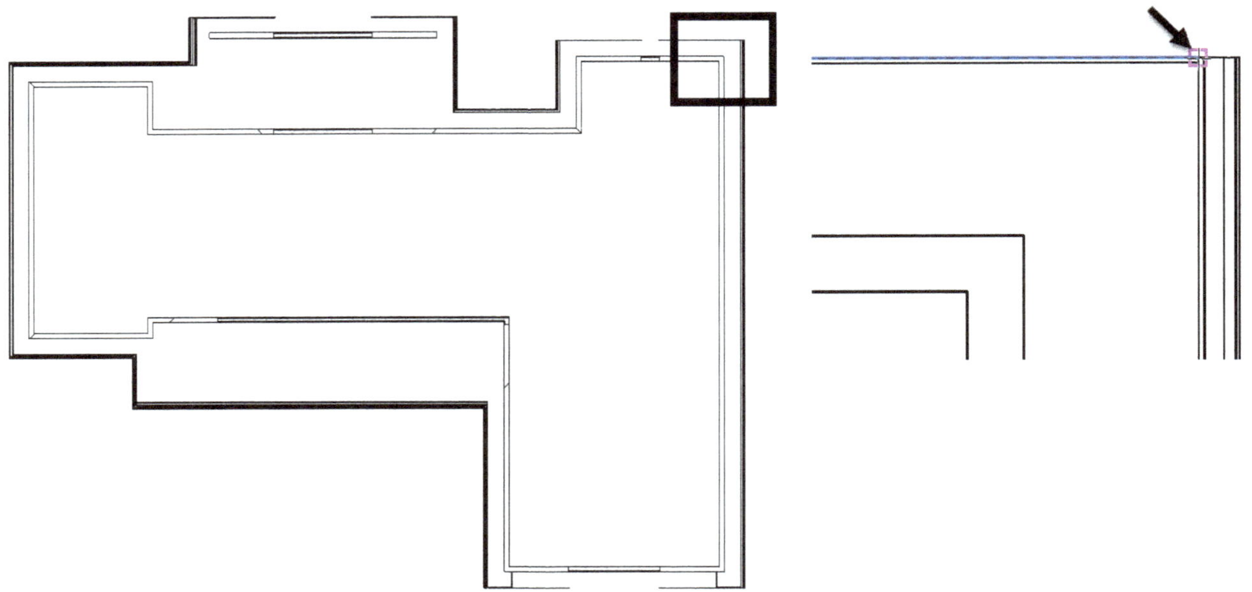

- Move the pointer toward left, type 3 and press ENTER. Next, move the pointer downward and click on the horizontal edge, as shown. Next, press ESC.

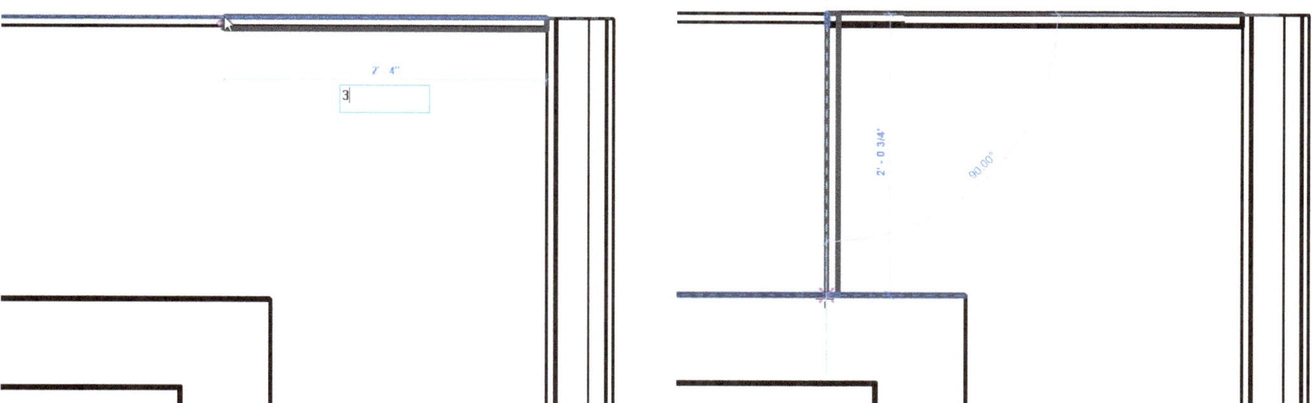

- Pan the drawing toward left and select the corner point of the roof, as shown.
- Press the SPACEBAR to reverse the side of the wall.

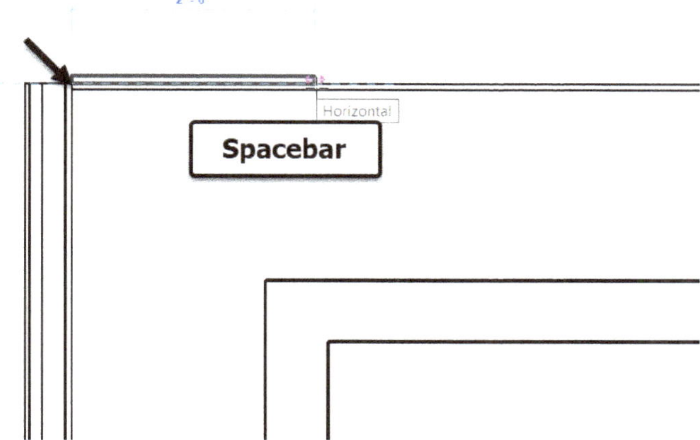

- Move the pointer toward right, type 3 and press ENTER. Next, move the pointer downward and select the horizontal edge, as shown. Next, press ESC.

- Zoom-in to the back porch area of the plan view and select the corner point wall, as shown.
- Move the pointer toward right and click on the vertical edge, as shown. Next, press ESC.

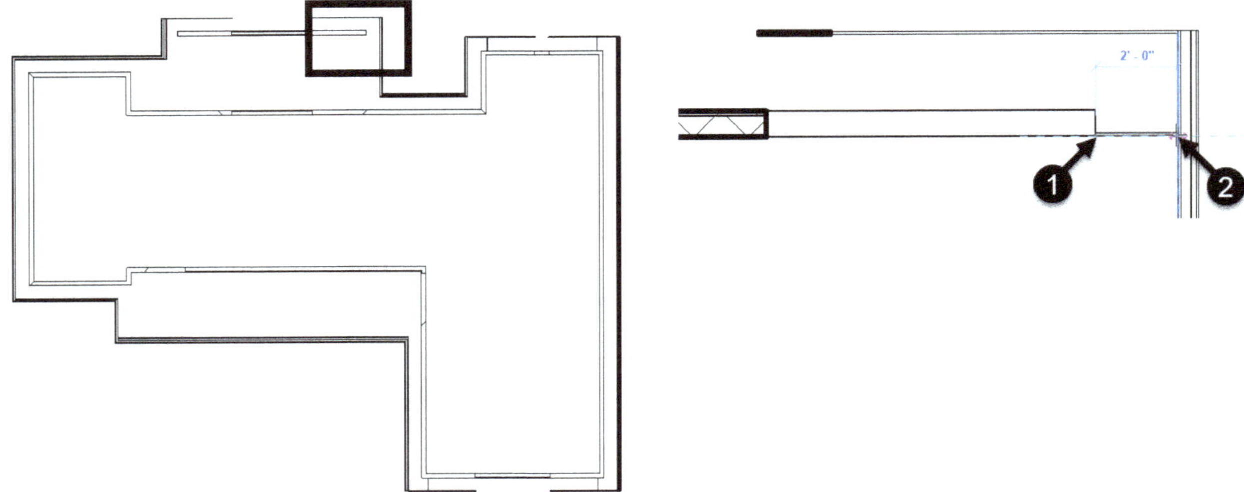

- Pan the view toward left and select the corner point of the wall, as shown.
- Press the SPACEBAR to reverse the side of the wall.

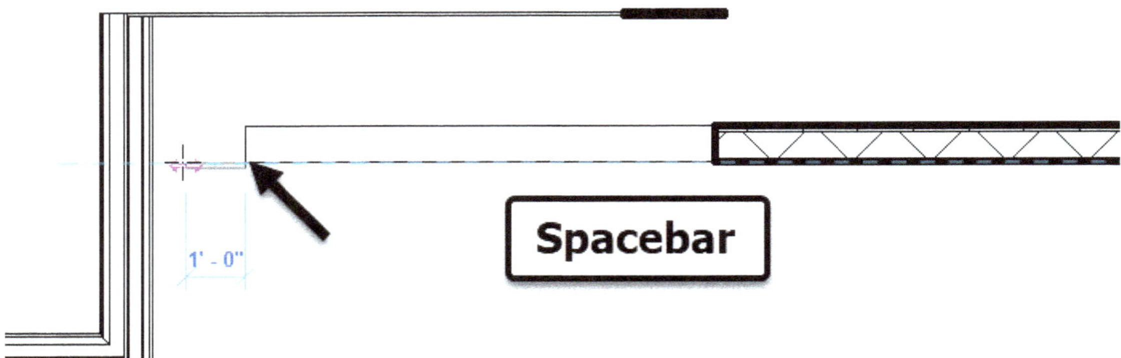

- Move the pointer toward left and click on the vertical edge, as shown. Next, press ESC twice.

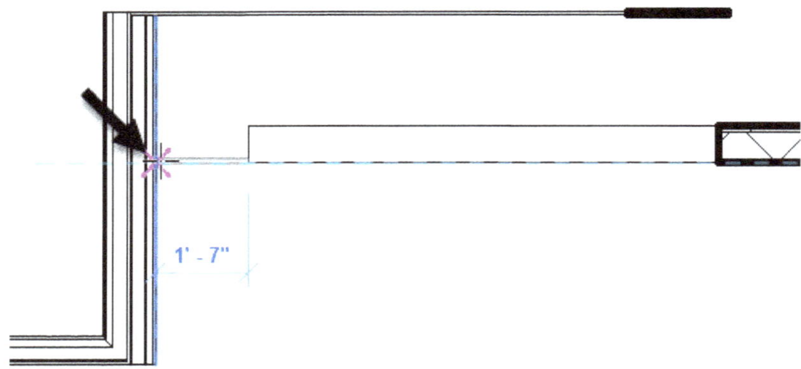

- Click the **Default 3D View** icon on the Quick Access Toolbar. Next, zoom to the front portion of the garage area.
- Press and hold the CTRL key and select the two wooden walls, as shown.
- Click the **Attach Top/Base** icon on the **Modify Wall** panel of the **Modify | Walls** ribbon tab.
- Select **Attach Wall > Top** from the Options Bar.

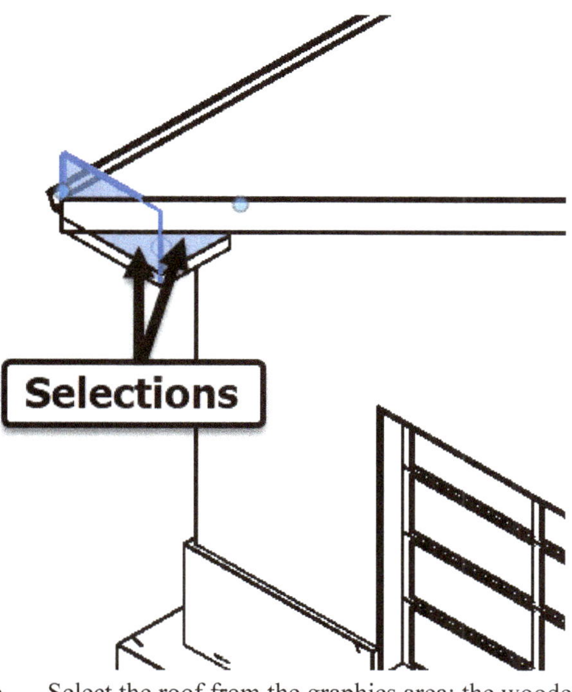

- Select the roof from the graphics area; the wooden walls are attached to the roof.

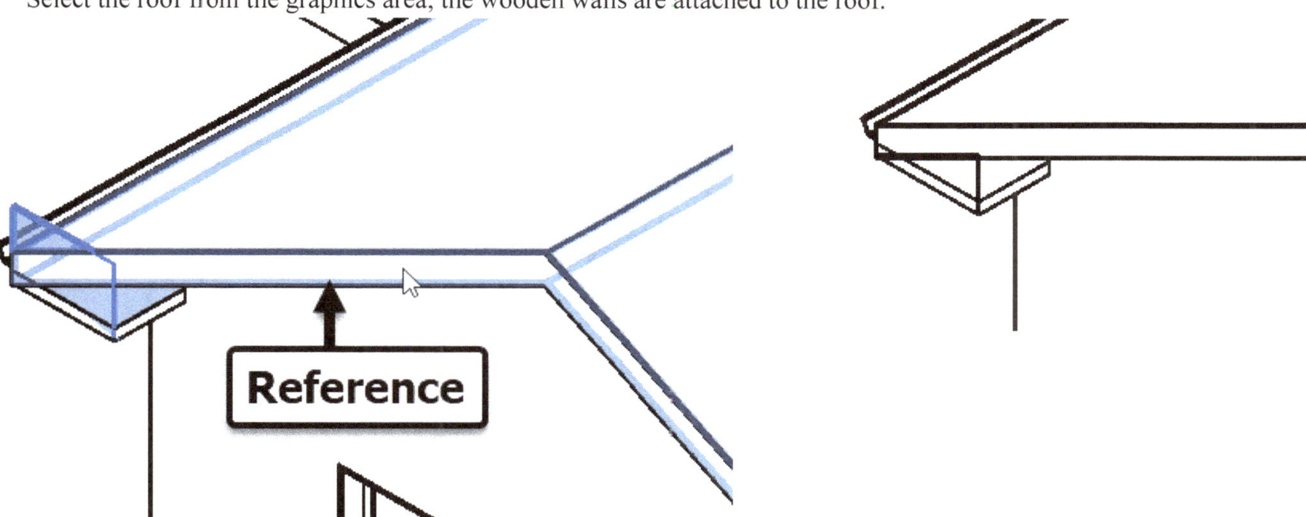

- Click the **Join** icon on the **Geometry** panel of the **Modify** ribbon tab.
- Select the fascia and the wall flushing with it; the two selected families are joined together.

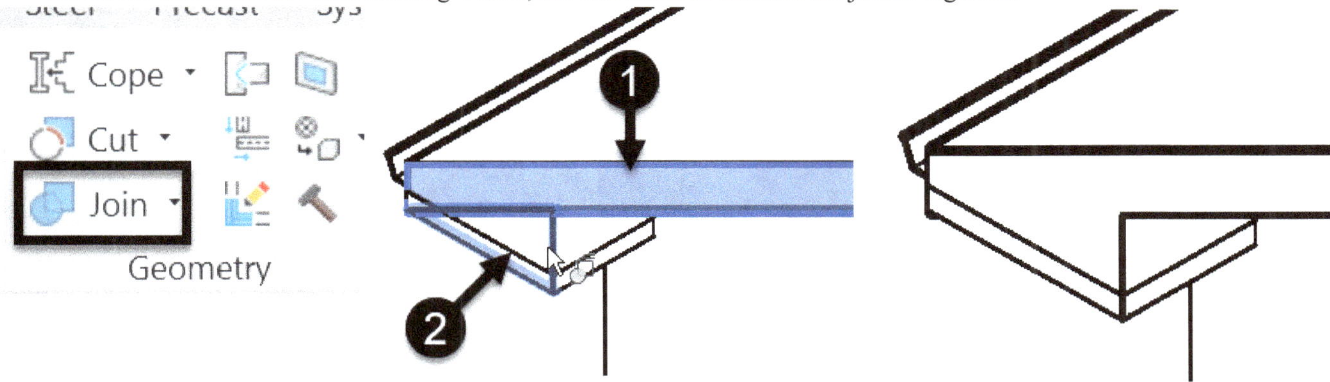

- Likewise, clean the other corners of the roof, as shown.

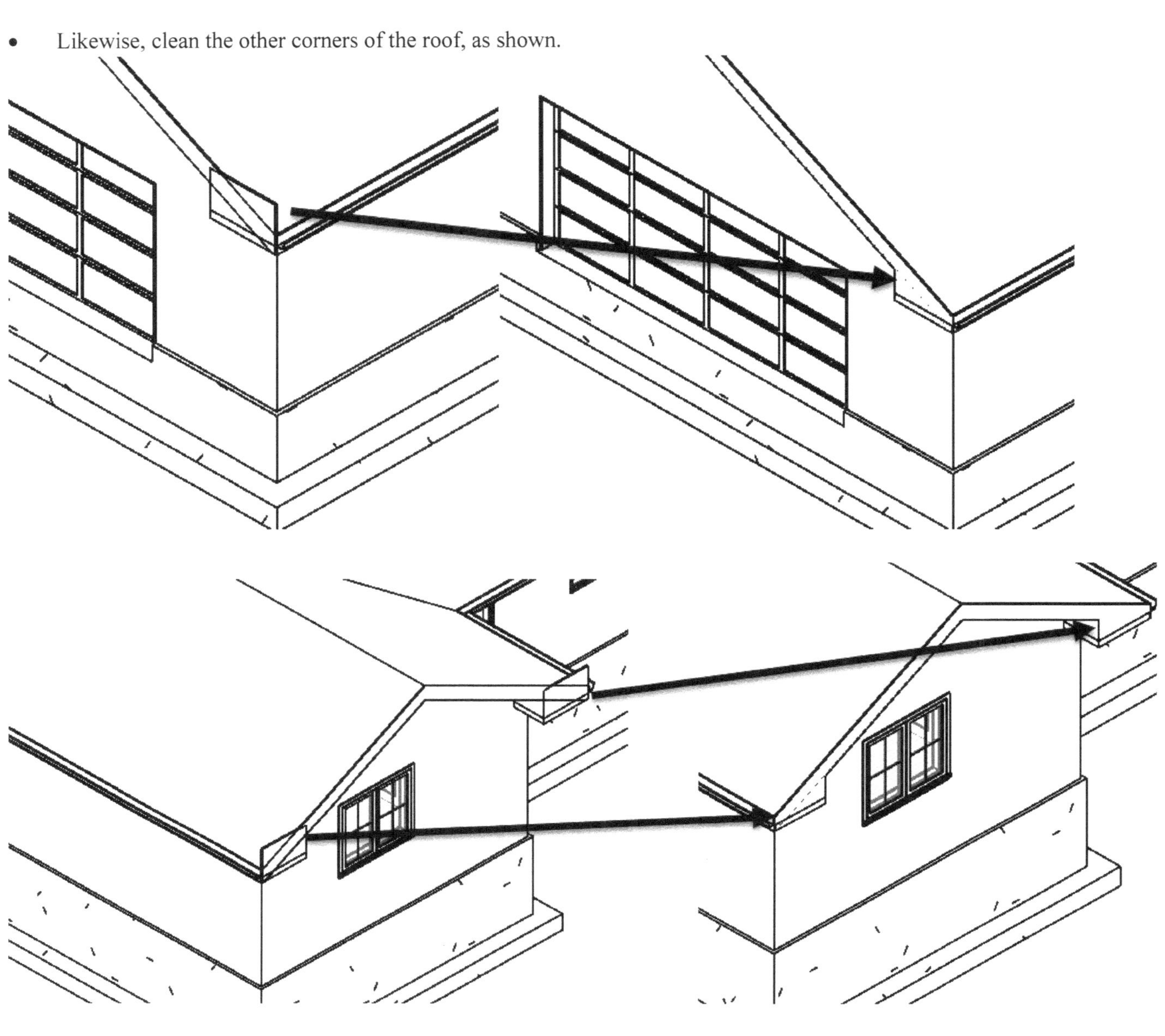

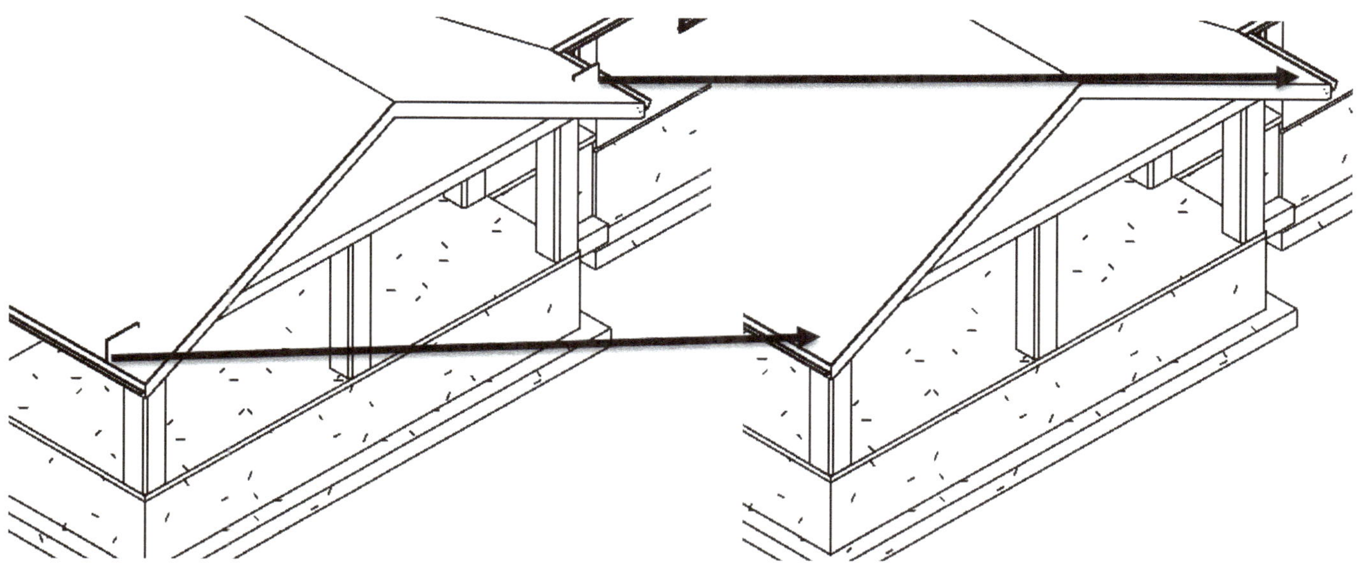

Tutorial 9: Adding Kitchen and Bathroom Fixtures

- Double-click on the **First Floor** under the **Floor Plans** node in the **Project Browser**.
- On the ribbon, click **Architecture > Build > Component** drop-down > **Place a Component**.
- On the ribbon, click **Modify | Place Component** tab > **Mode** panel > **Load Family**.
- Go to **Local Disc C > Program Data > Autodesk > RVT 2024 > Libraries > English Imperial > Casework > Counter Tops**. Next, double-click on **Counter Top w Sink Hole**.

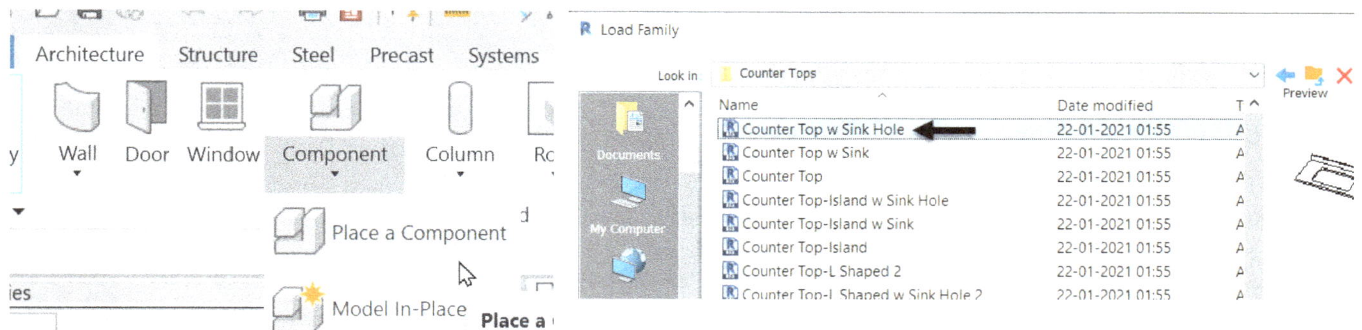

- Zoom to the kitchen area and place the counter top at the location, as shown. Next, press ESC twice.

- On the ribbon, click **Modify** tab > **Modify** panel > **Align (AL)** .
- Select the edge of the wall and the left vertical edge of the counter top, as shown. The counter top is aligned with the wall.

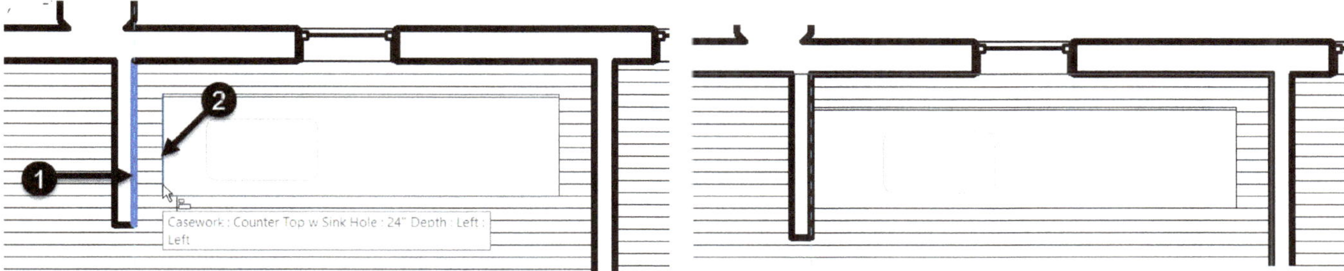

- Likewise, align the top and right edge of the counter top with the adjacent walls, as shown.

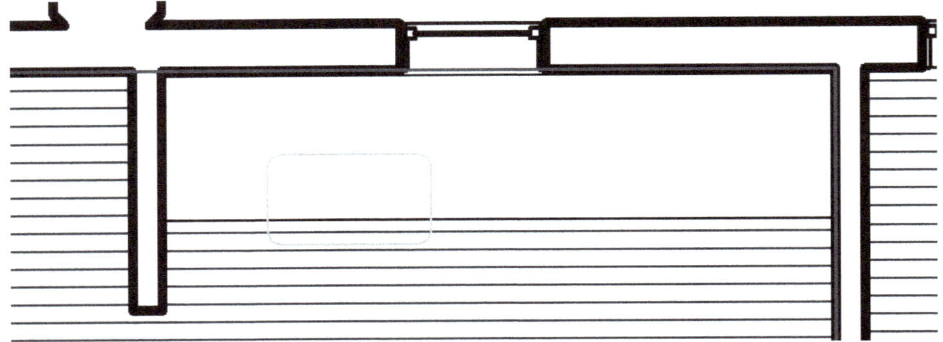

- Activate the **Align (AL)** tool and place the pointer near the center of the window, as shown. Next, click to select the centerline of the window.
- Place the pointer near the center of the sink opening, and then click to select it. The sink opening is aligned with the window.

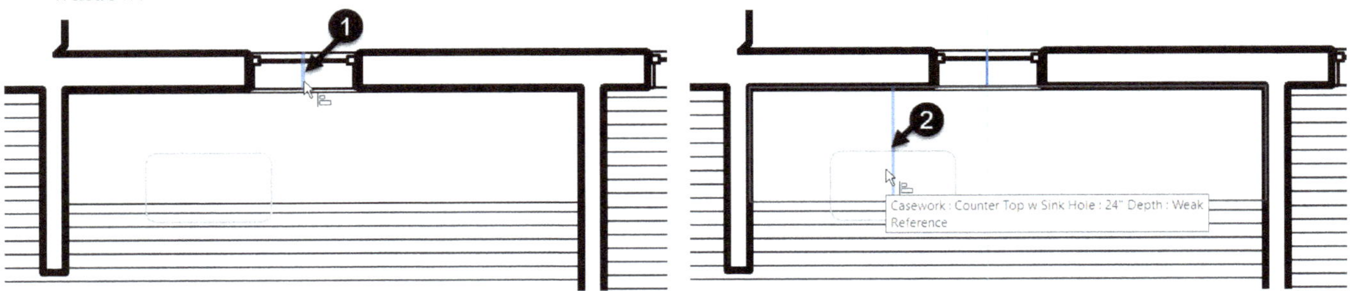

- Select the counter top and notice the arrow grips on it.
- Zoom to the top edge of the sink opening and click on the arrow grip pointing upwards; the sink opening is moved in the upward direction. Likewise, move the sink opening near to the adjacent wall.
- Zoom to the lower edge of the sink opening and click on the arrow pointing upwards. Keep clicking on the arrow until the lower edge of the sink opening is moved inside the counter top.

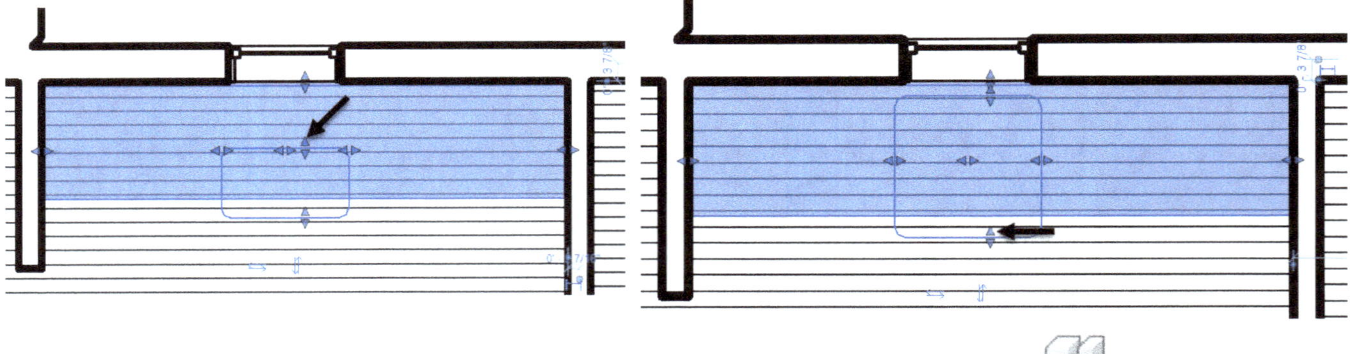

- On the ribbon, click **Architecture > Build > Component** drop-down > **Place a Component** .
- On the ribbon, click **Modify | Place Component** tab > **Mode** panel > **Load Family**.
- Go to **Local Disc C > Program Data > Autodesk > RVT 2024 > Libraries > English Imperial > Casework > Base Cabinets**. Next, double-click on the **Base Cabinet-Double Door Sink Unit**.
- On the **Properties** palette, from the **Type Selector** drop-down, select the **Base Cabinet-Double Door Sink Unit 36"** type.
- Place the pointer near the centerpoint of the window; a blue line is displayed.

- Click to place the base cabinet, as shown. Press ESC twice.

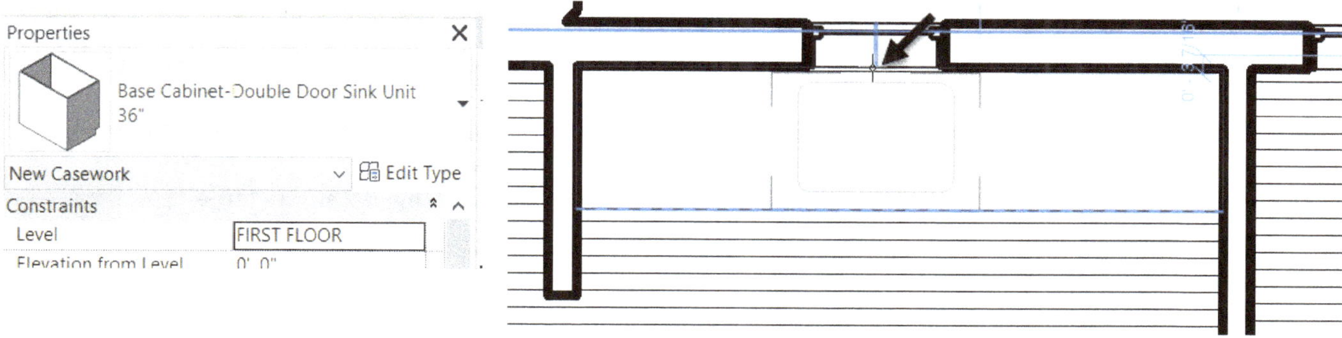

- On the ribbon, click **Architecture > Build > Component** drop-down > **Place a Component** .
- On the ribbon, click **Modify | Place Component** tab > **Mode** panel > **Load Family**.
- Go to **Local Disc C > Program Data > Autodesk > RVT 2024 > Libraries > English Imperial > Plumbing > Architectural > Fixtures > Sinks**. Next, double-click on the **Sink Kitchen-Single**.
- Move the pointer near to the centerline of the window and notice a blue line. Click to place the kitchen sink at the location, as shown.

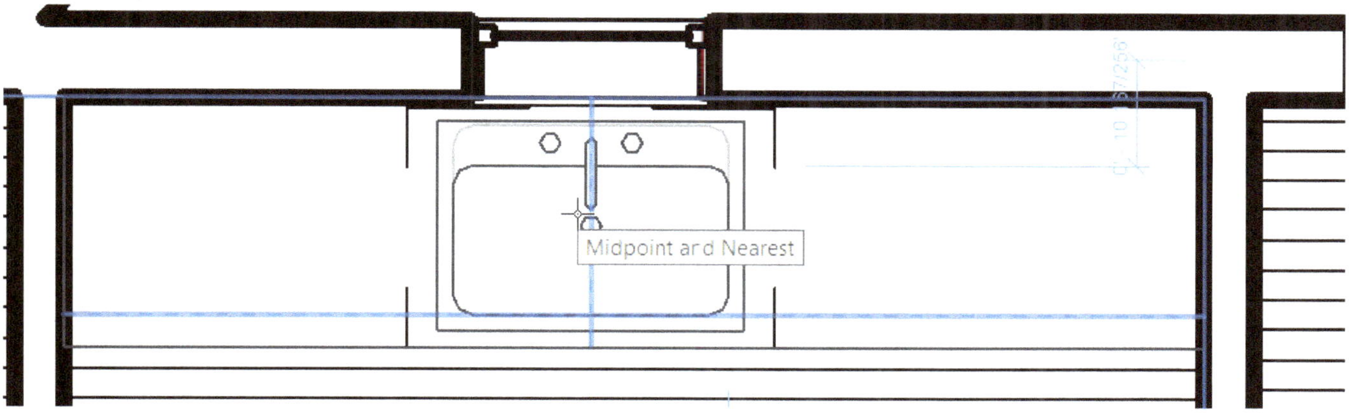

- On the ribbon, click **Architecture > Build > Component** drop-down > **Place a Component**.
- On the ribbon, click **Modify | Place Component** tab > **Mode** panel > **Load Family**.
- Go to **Local Disc C > Program Data > Autodesk > RVT 2024 > Libraries > English Imperial > Specialty Equipment > Domestic > Mid-Range**. Next, double-click on the **Dishwasher**.
- Move the pointer near to the right corner of the counter top and notice two alignment lines from the edges of the counter top. Click to place the dishwasher aligned to the edges of the counter top.

- On the ribbon, click **Architecture > Build > Component** drop-down > **Place a Component**.
- On the ribbon, click **Modify | Place Component** tab > **Mode** panel > **Load Family**.
- Go to **Local Disc C > Program Data > Autodesk > RVT 2024 > Libraries > English Imperial > Casework > Base Cabinets**.
- Press and hold the CTRL key and select the **Base Cabinet -2 Bin**, **Base Cabinet-4 Drawers**, and **Base Cabinet – Double Door & 1 Door**. Next, click **Open**.
- On the **Properties** palette, from the **Type Selector** drop-down, select the **Base Cabinet-2 Bin 18"** type.
- Move the pointer near to the right edge of the sink and notice that the base cabinet is snapped to it. Click to place the base cabinet aligned to the edge of the sink.

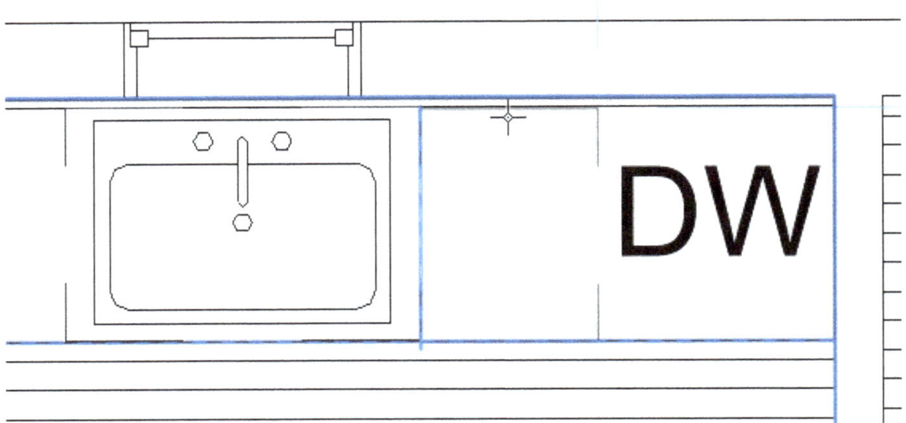

- On the **Properties** palette, from the **Type Selector** drop-down, select the **Base Cabinet-Double Door & 1 Drawer 33"** type.
- Move the pointer near to the left edge of the counter top and click to position the base cabinet.

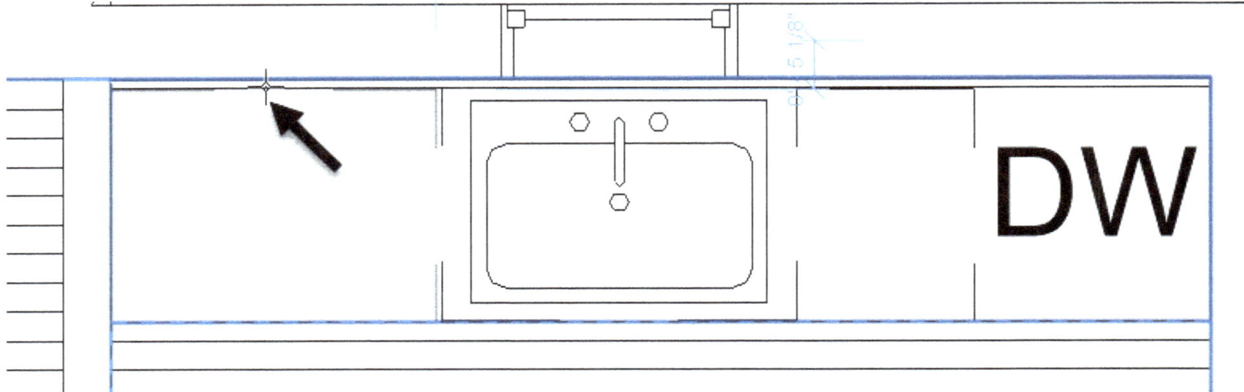

- On the ribbon, click **View > Create > Section**. Next, specify the start and end point of the section line, as shown.

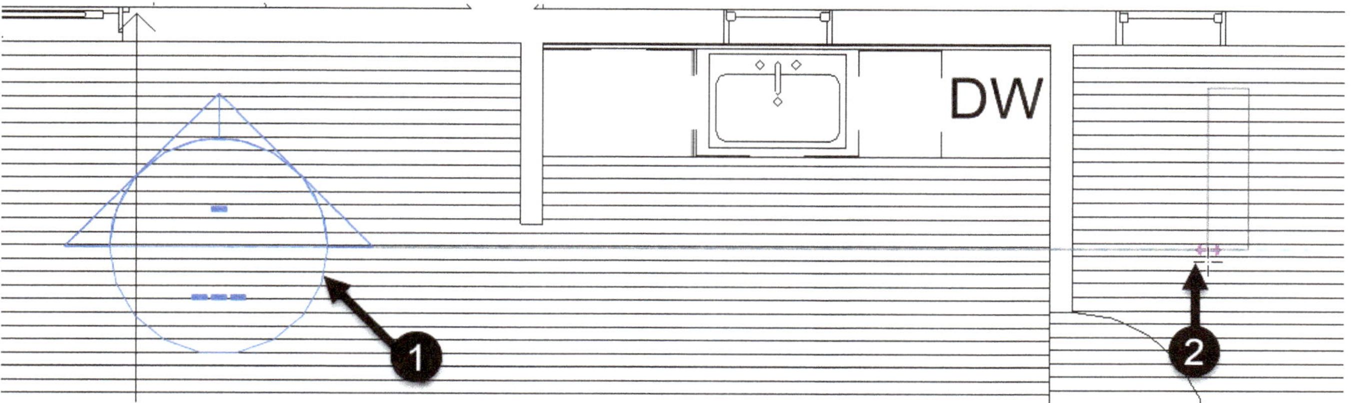

- Right-click and select **Go To View** from the shortcut menu. Notice that the counter top is obstructing the window. You need to change the window size and move it upward.

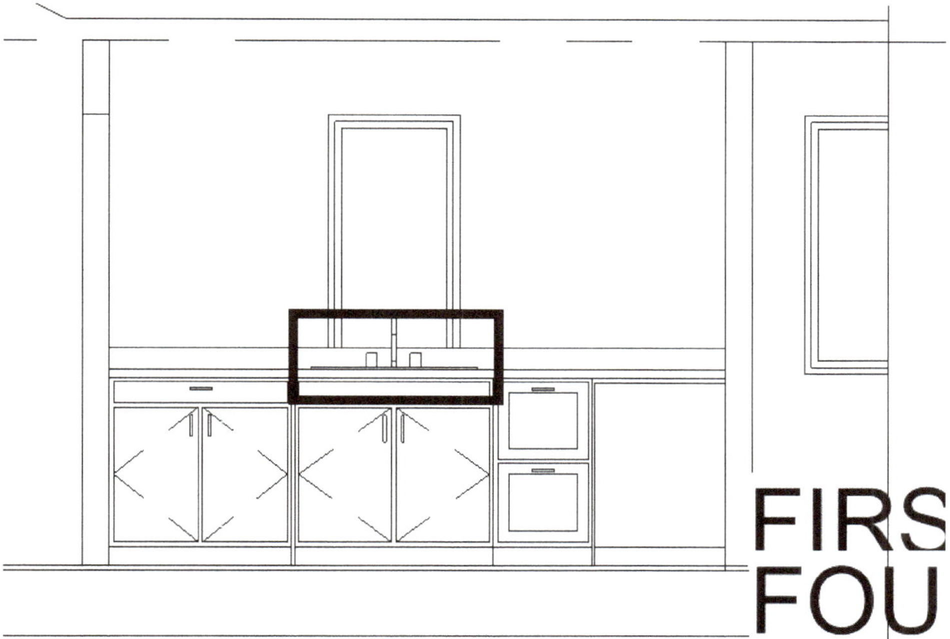

- Select the window and select **Fixed 24" x 24"** from the **Type Selector** drop-down on the **Properties** palette.
- Click on the vertical dimension between the floor and the window. Next, type 5' and then press ENTER.

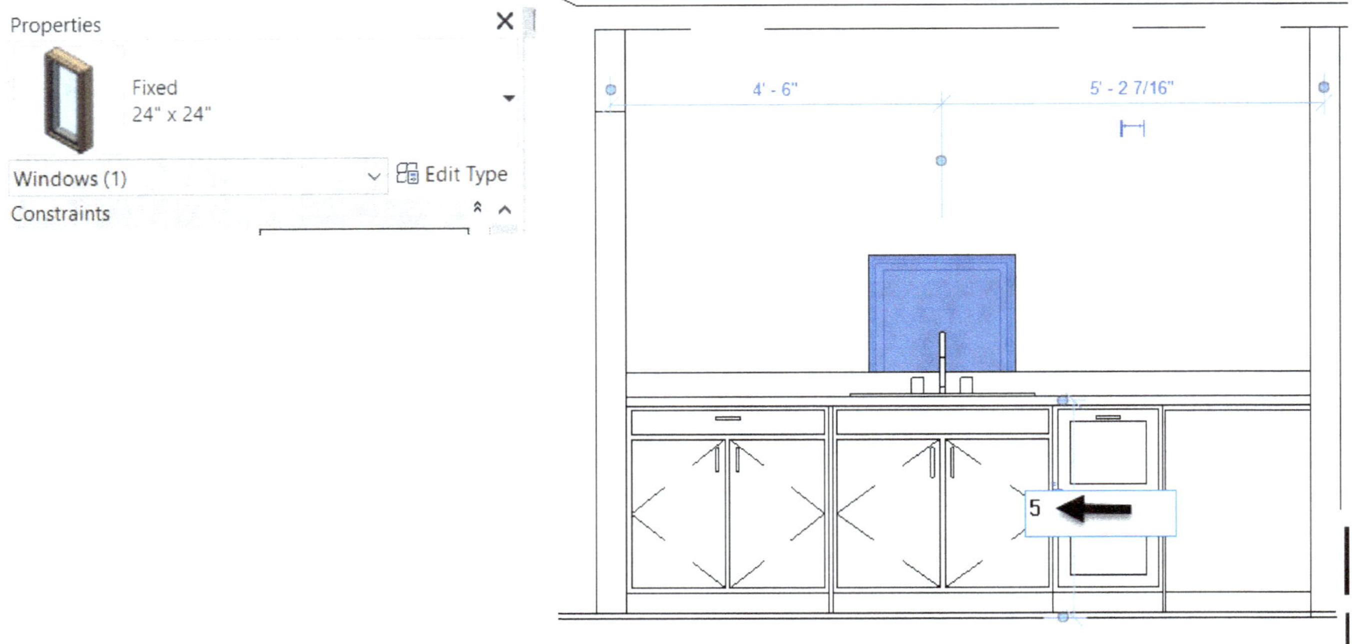

- Double-click on the **First Floor** under the **Floor Plans** node in the **Project Browser**.
- On the ribbon, click **Architecture > Build > Component** drop-down > **Place a Component**.
- On the ribbon, click **Modify | Place Component** tab > **Mode** panel > **Load Family**.
- Go to **Local Disc C > Program Data > Autodesk > RVT 2024 > Libraries > English Imperial > Specialty Equipment > Domestic > High-End**.
- Press and hold the CTRL key and select **Range-30_Inch** and **Refrigerator-French_Door**. Next, click **Open**.
- On the **Properties** palette, from the **Type Selector** drop-down, select the **Range-30_Inch Burners** type.
- Check the **Rotate after placement** option on the Options Bar.
- Position the range at the location, as shown. Next, type **-90** in the **Angle** box available on the Options bar, and then press ENTER. Next, press ESC twice.

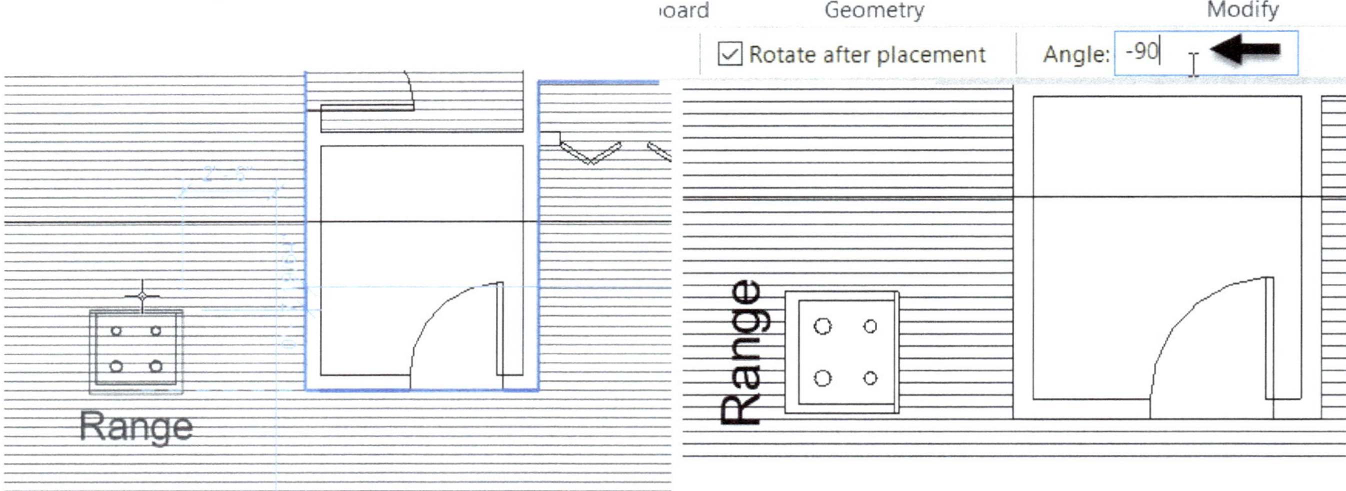

- Align the edges of the range to the wall edges, as shown.

- On the ribbon, click **Architecture > Build > Component** drop-down > **Place a Component** .
- On the **Properties** palette, from the **Type Selector** drop-down, select the **Base Cabinet-Double Door & 1 Drawer 36"** type.
- Press the SPACEBAR until the cabinet is oriented, as shown.
- Move the pointer near to the wall edge and click to position the base cabinet.

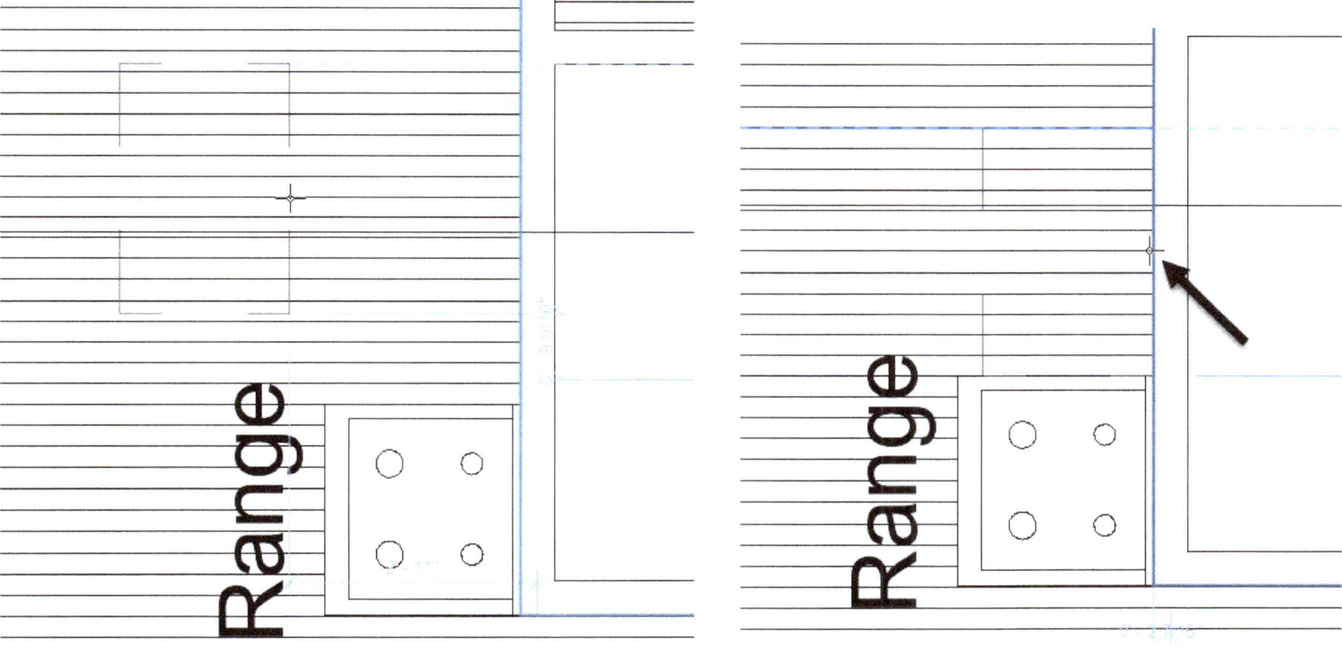

- Press the SPACEBAR until the cabinet is oriented, as shown. Next, position the base cabinet at the location, as shown.

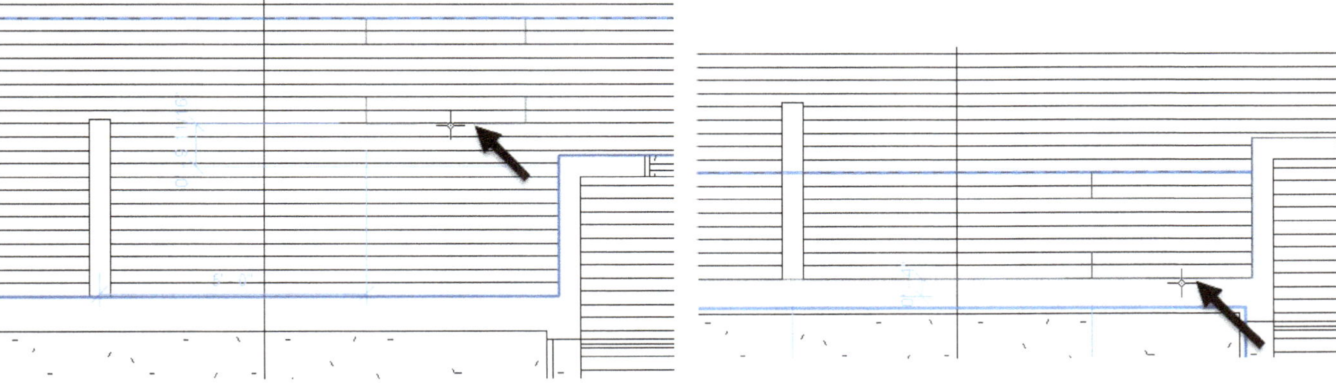

- On the **Properties** palette, from the **Type Selector** drop-down, select the **Base Cabinet-Double Door & 1 Drawer 27"** type.
- Press the SPACEBAR until the cabinet is oriented, as shown. Next, position the base cabinet at the location, as shown.

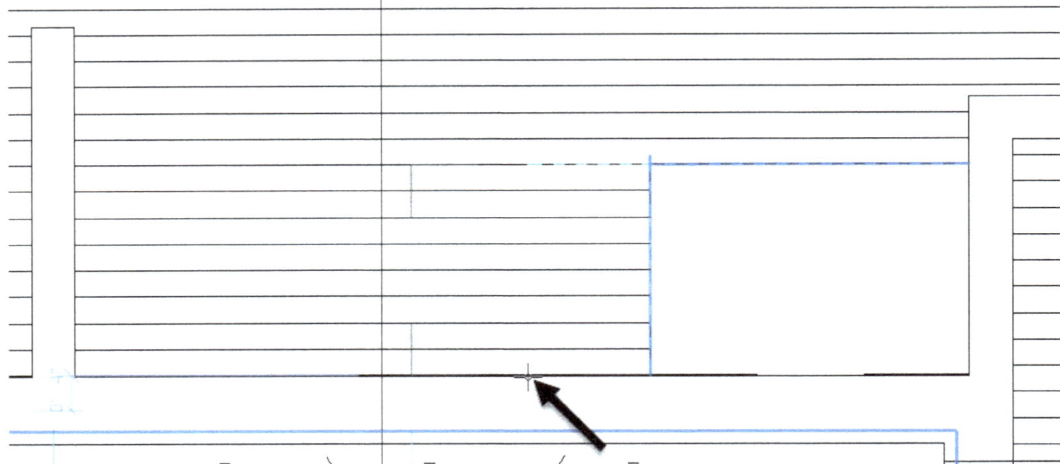

- On the **Properties** palette, from the **Type Selector** drop-down, select the **Refrigerator-French_Door 36"** type.
- Press the SPACEBAR until the refrigerator is oriented, as shown. Next, position the refrigerator at the location, as shown. Next, press ESC twice.

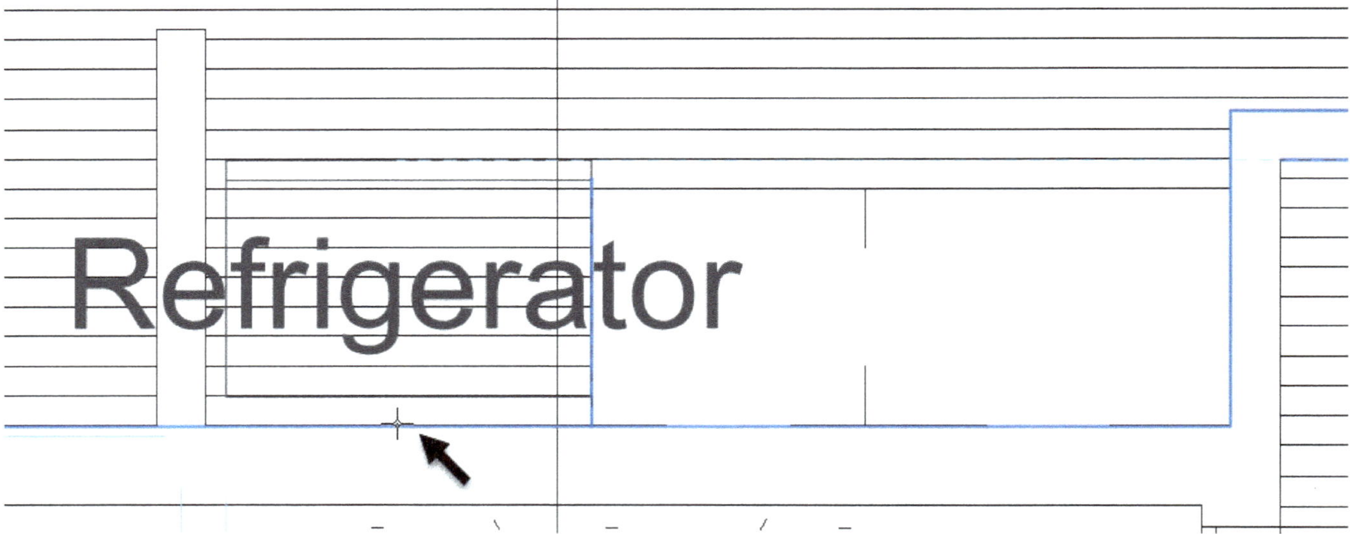

- Select the refrigerator and click the **Edit Type** icon on the **Properties** palette.

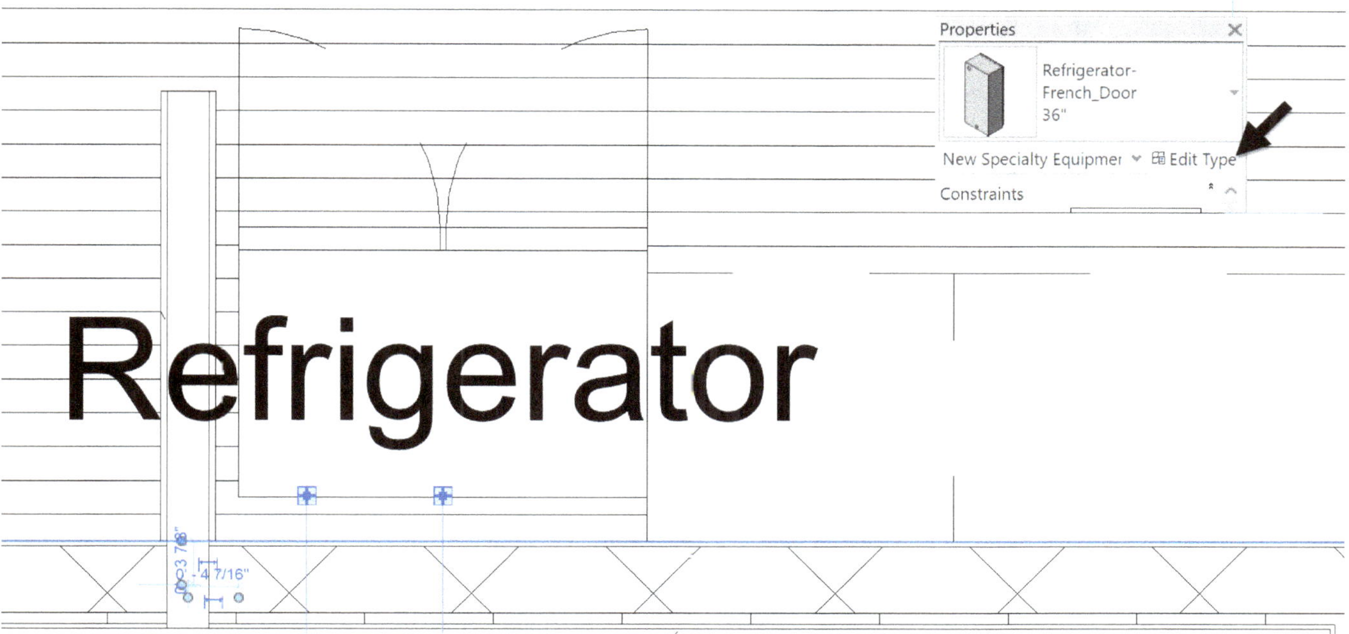

- Uncheck the **Show Label** option on the **Type Properties** dialog, and then click **OK**. The refrigerator label is hidden.

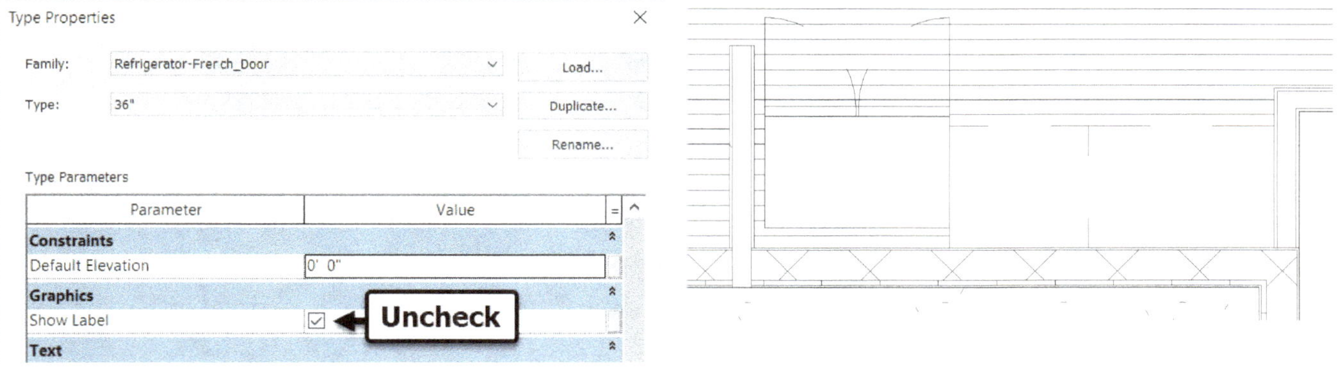

- On the ribbon, click **Architecture > Build > Component** drop-down > **Place a Component**.
- On the ribbon, click **Modify | Place Component** tab > **Mode** panel > **Load Family**.
- Go to **Local Disc C > Program Data > Autodesk > RVT 2024 > Libraries > English Imperial > Casework > Counter Tops**. Next, double-click on **Counter Top**.
- On the **Properties** palette, from the **Type Selector** drop-down, select the **Counter Top 24" Depth** type.
- Press the SPACEBAR until the counter top is oriented, as shown. Next, position the counter top at the location, as shown.

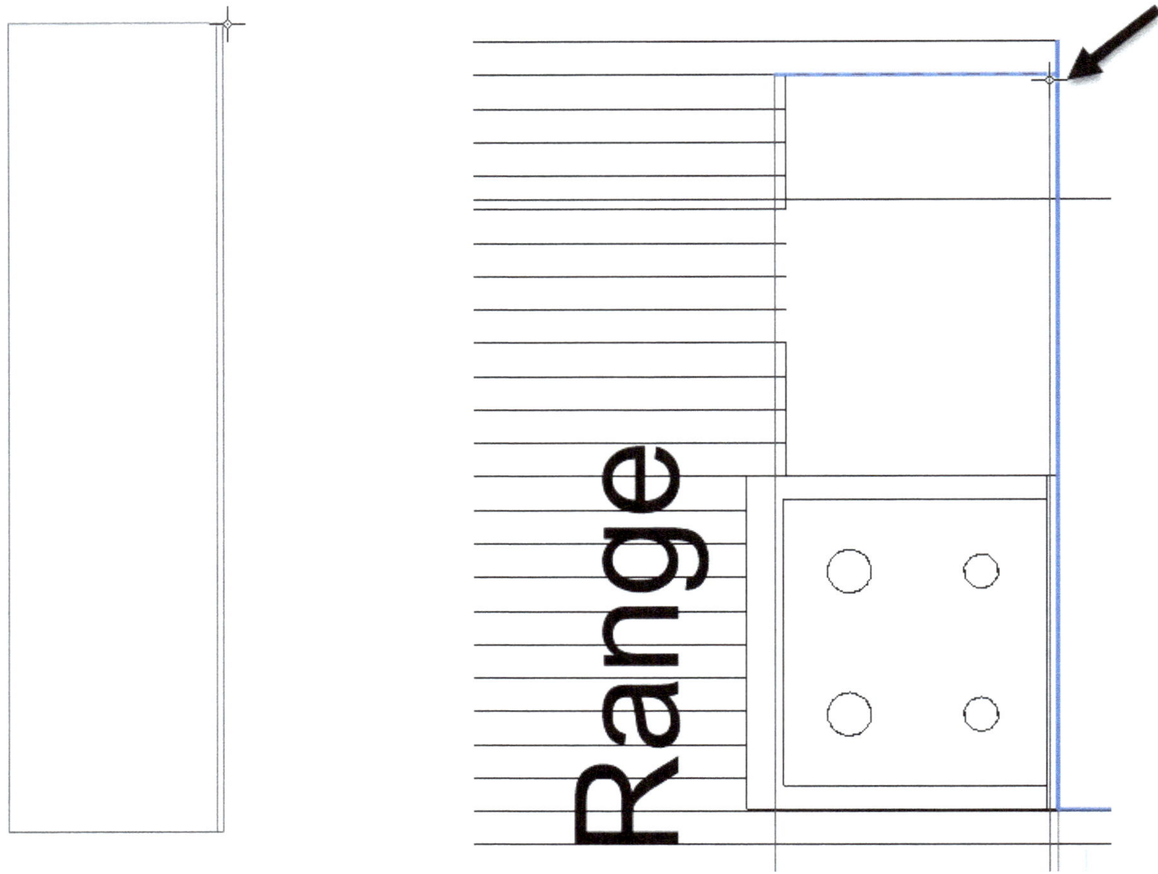

- Press the SPACEBAR until the counter top is oriented, as shown. Next, position the counter top at the location, as shown. Next, press ESC twice.

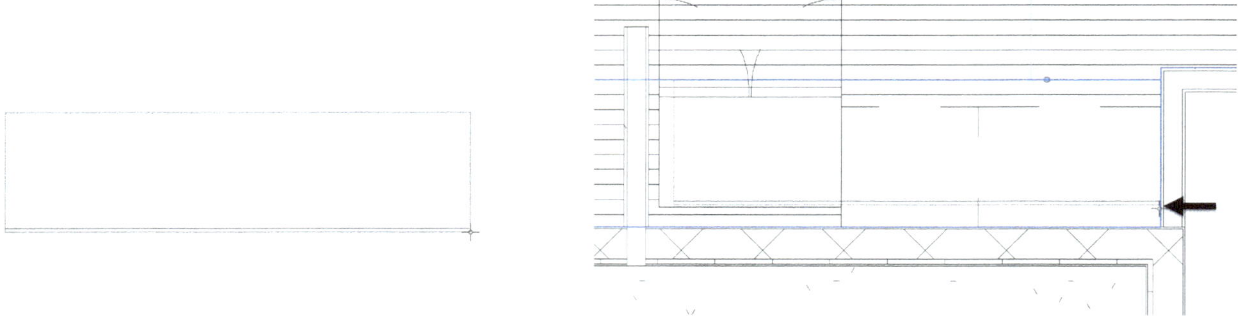

- On the ribbon, click **Modify > Modify > Align**. Next, select the inner wall edge and the counter top edge, as shown.

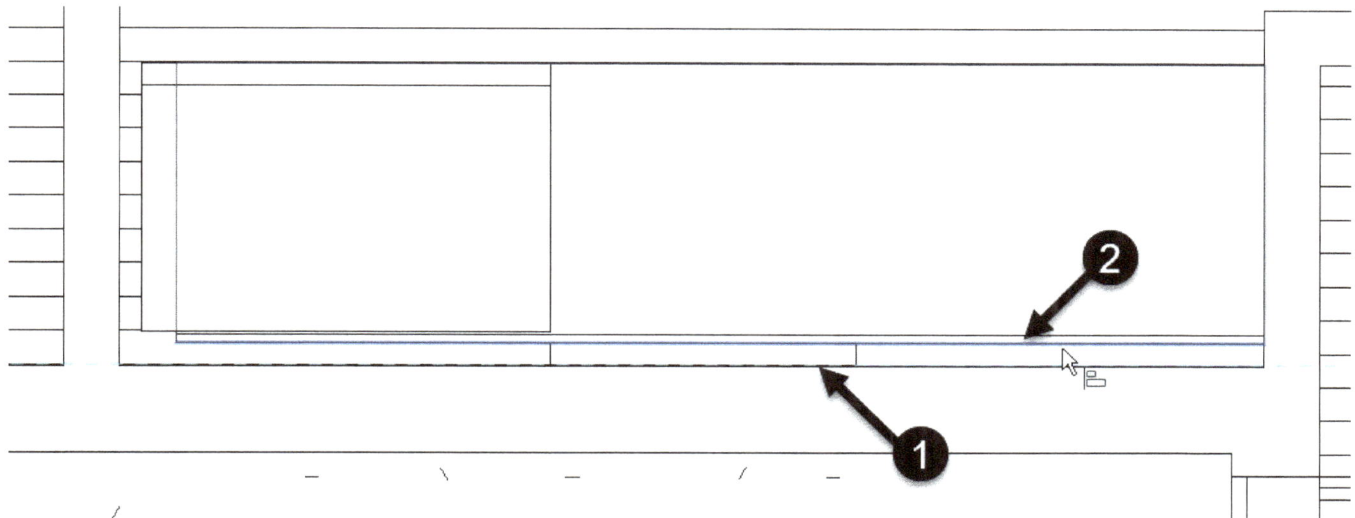

- Press ESC twice and select the counter top. Click and drag the arrow handle displayed on the left edge.
- Release the pointer on the left edge of the base cabinet, as shown.

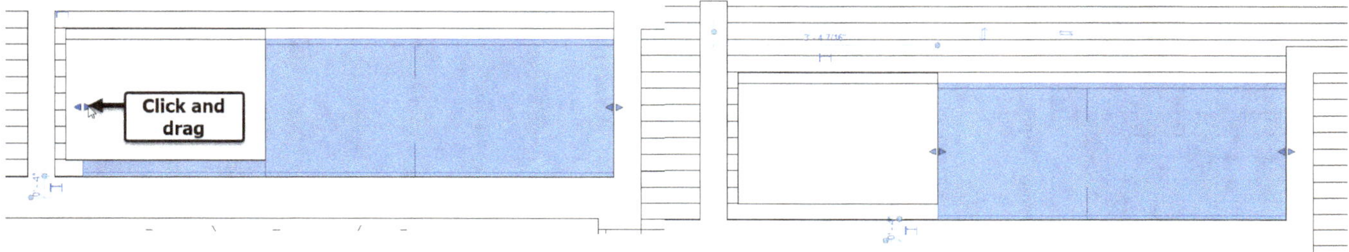

- Likewise, click and drag the arrow handle displayed on the bottom edge of the counter top next to the Range.
- Move the pointer upward and release it on the edge of the base cabinet, as shown.

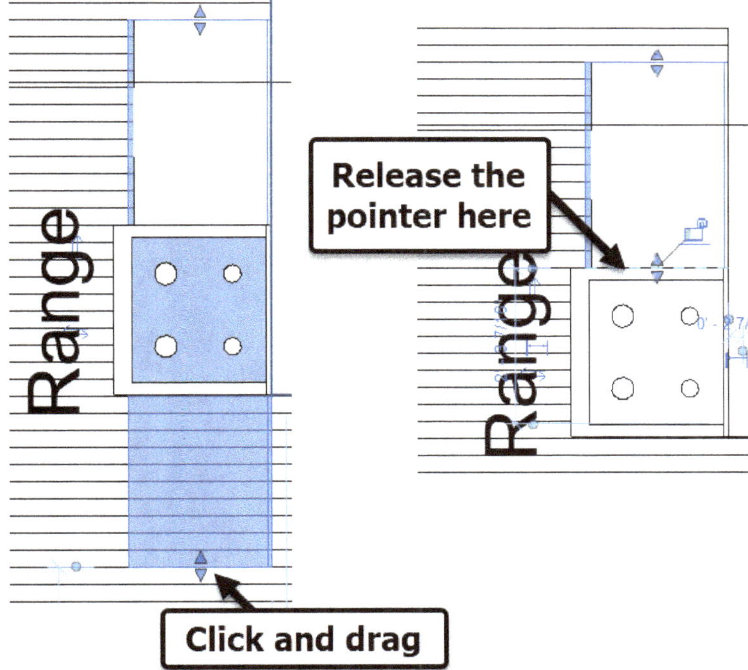

- On the ribbon, click **Architecture > Build > Component** drop-down **> Place a Component**.
- On the ribbon, click **Modify | Place Component** tab **> Mode** panel **> Load Family**.

- Go to **Local Disc C > Program Data > Autodesk > RVT 2024 > Libraries > English Imperial > Casework > Wall Cabinets**. Next, double-click on **Upper Cabinet-Double Door-Wall**.
- On the **Properties** palette, from the **Type Selector** drop-down, select the **Upper Cabinet-Double Door-Wall 33"** type.
- Place the upper cabinets at the locations, as shown.

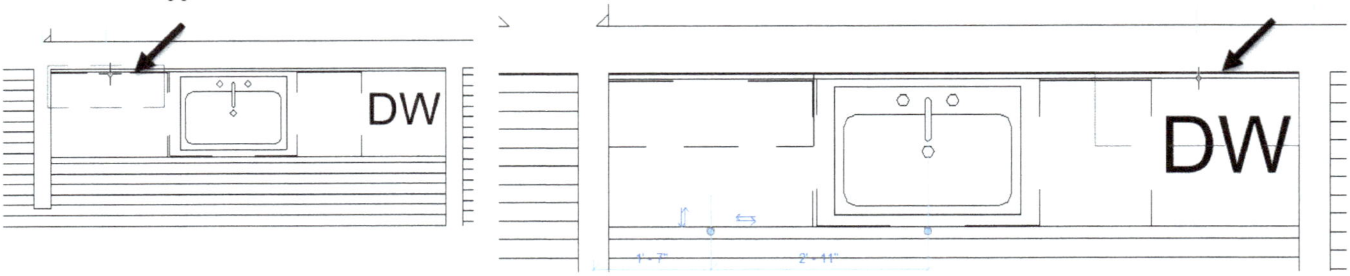

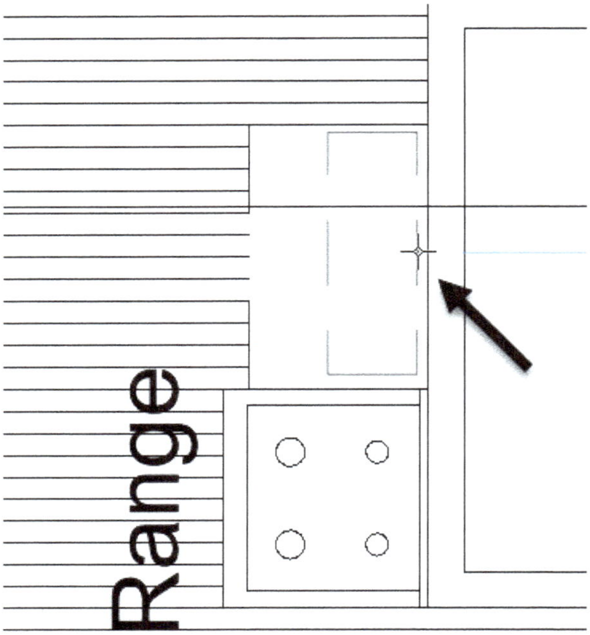

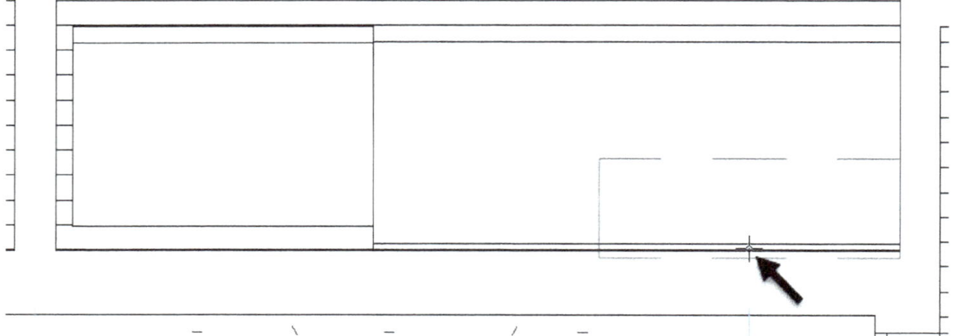

- On the **Properties** palette, from the **Type Selector** drop-down, select the **Upper Cabinet-Double Door-Wall 36"** type.
- Place the upper cabinet at the location, as shown.

- On the **Properties** palette, from the **Type Selector** drop-down, select the **Upper Cabinet-Double Door-Wall 27"** type.
- Place the upper cabinet at the location, as shown.

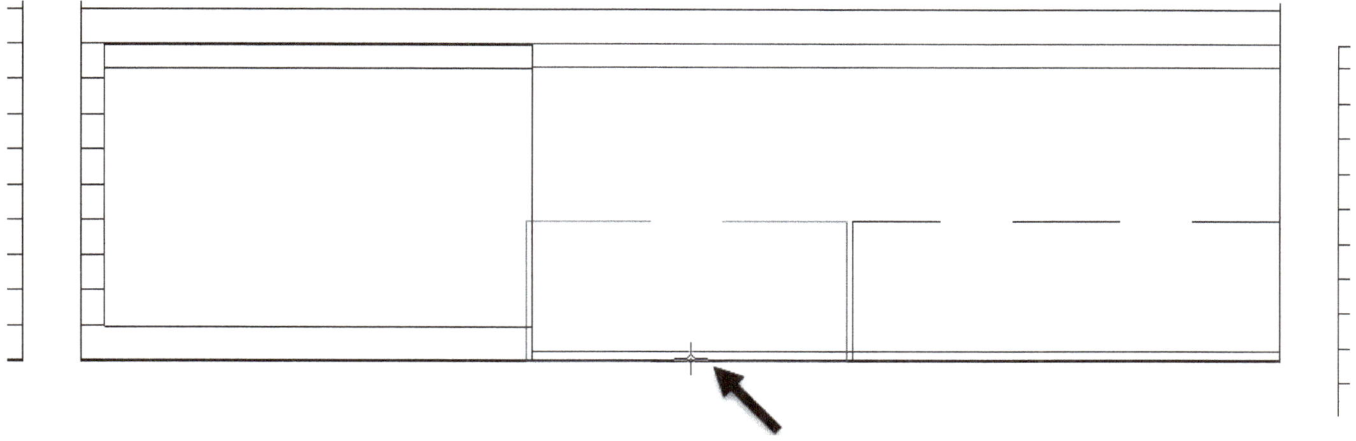

- On the ribbon, click **Modify > Modify > Align**. Next, select the edges of the upper base cabinets, as shown.

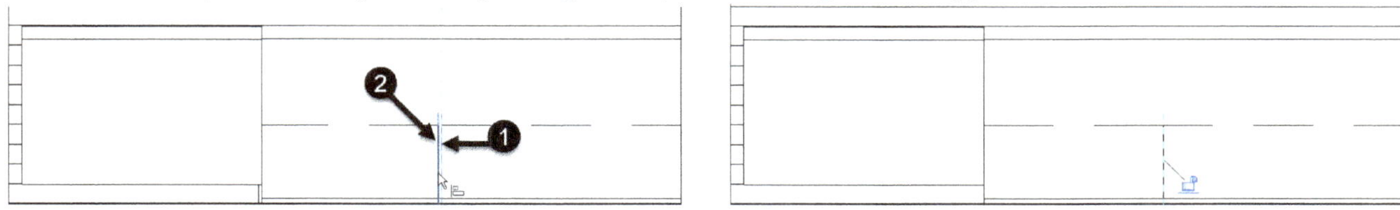

- On the ribbon, click **Architecture > Build > Component** drop-down > **Place a Component**.
- On the **Properties** palette, from the **Type Selector** drop-down, select the **Base Cabinet-Double Door & 1 Drawer 30"** type.
- Press the SPACEBAR until the base cabinet is oriented, as shown.
- Position the base cabinet at the location, as shown.

- Move the pointer upward and place another instance of the base cabinet, as shown. Again, move the pointer and upward and position the another instance.

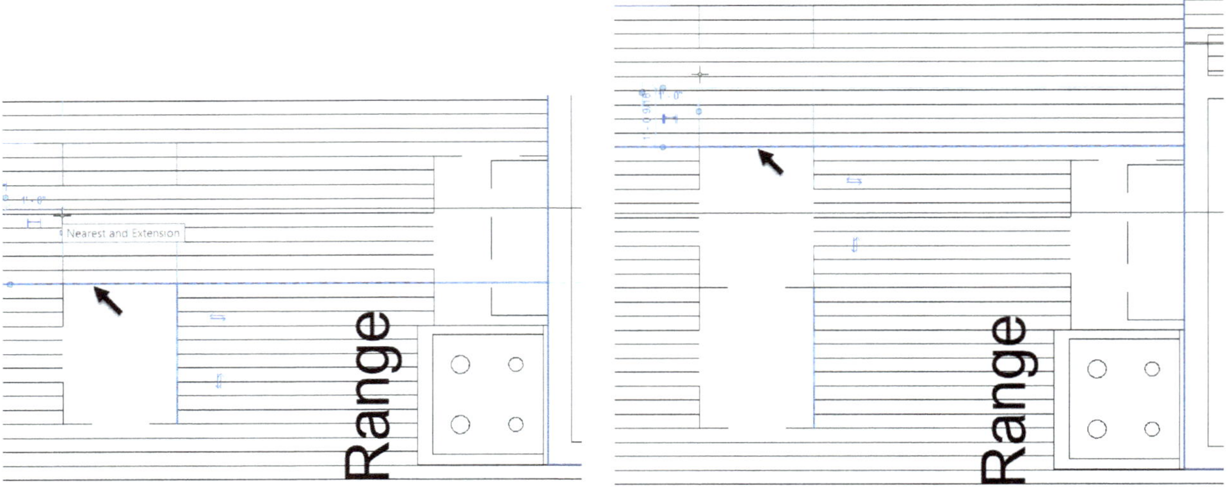

- On the ribbon, click **Architecture > Build > Component** drop-down > **Place a Component**.
- On the ribbon, click **Modify | Place Component > Mode > Load Family**.
- Go to **Local Disc C > Program Data > Autodesk > RVT 2024 > Libraries > English Imperial > Casework > Counter Tops**. Next, double-click on **Counter Top-Island**.
- On the **Properties** palette, from the **Type Selector** drop-down, select the **Counter Top-Island 48" Depth** type.
- Press the SPACEBAR until the counter top is oriented, as shown.
- Move the pointer near to the top-right corner of the base cabinet, as shown. Next, click to position the counter top.

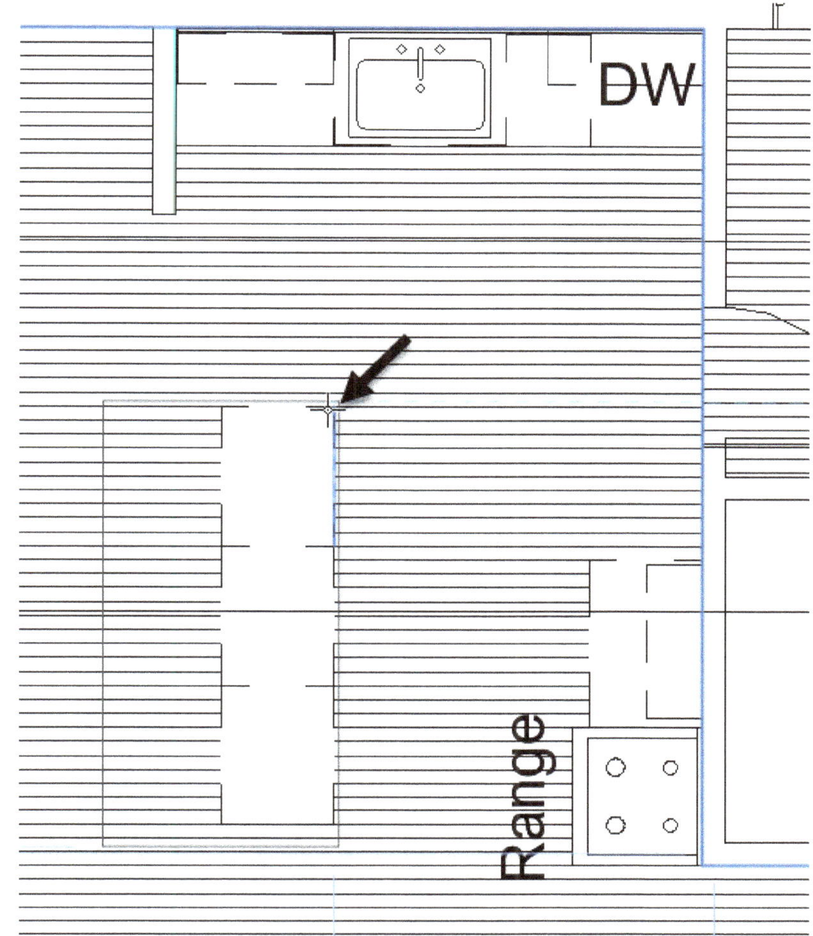

- Press ESC twice, and then select the counter top. Next, change the **Depth** and **Length** values under the **Dimensions** section of the **Properties** palette, as shown.

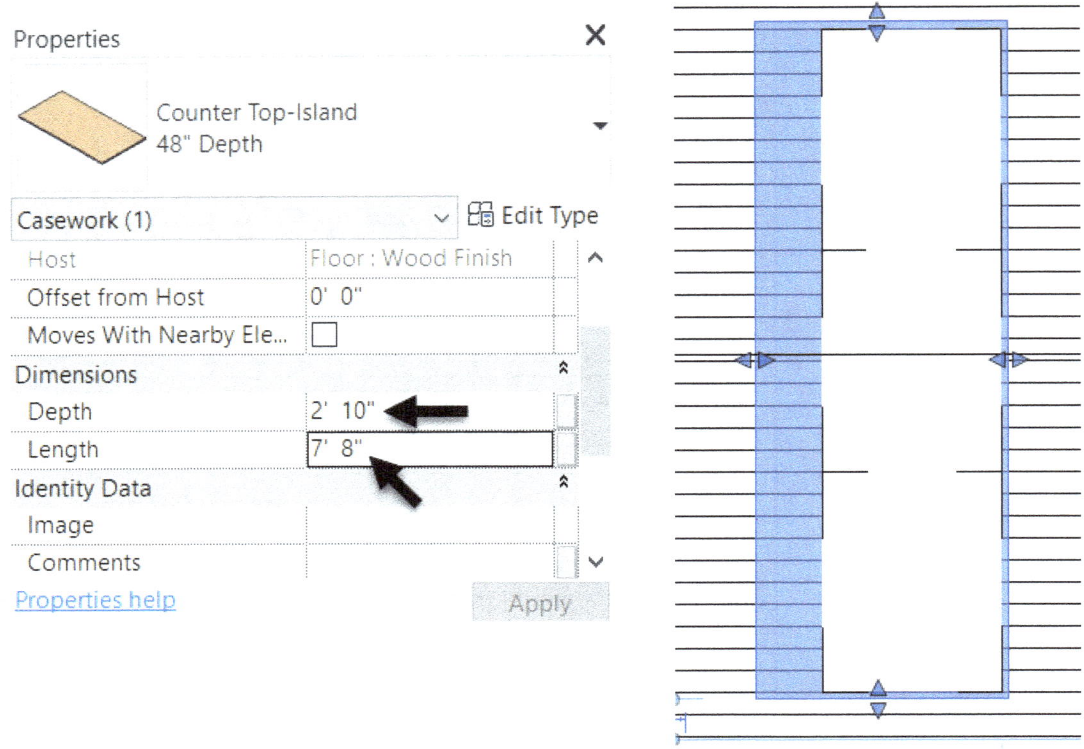

- Press and hold the CTRL key and select the counter top and the three newly created base cabinets.
- On the ribbon, click **Modify | Casework > Create > Create Group**. Next, type **Kitchen Island** in the **Create Model Group** dialog and click **OK**. The three base cabinets are combined into a group.

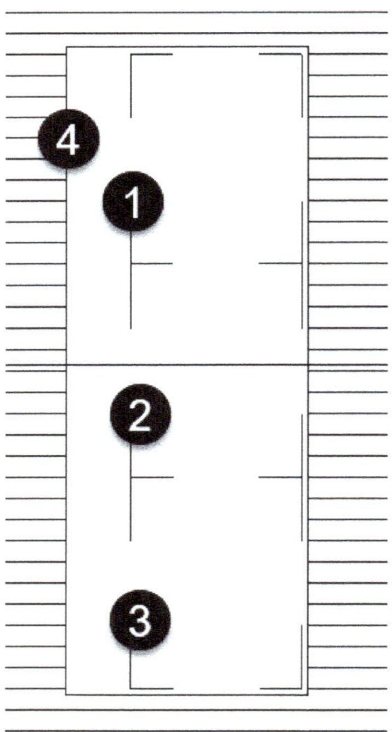

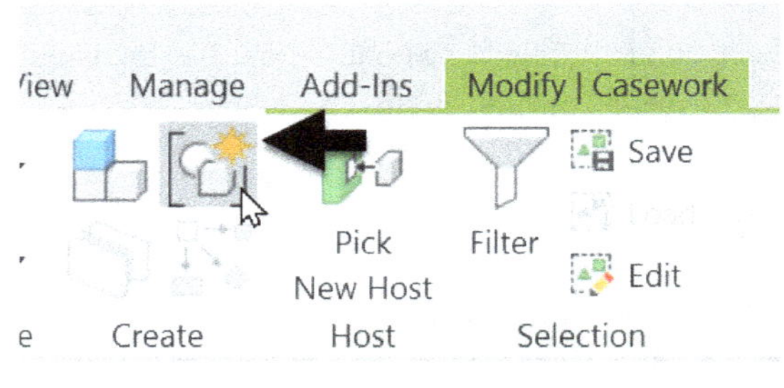

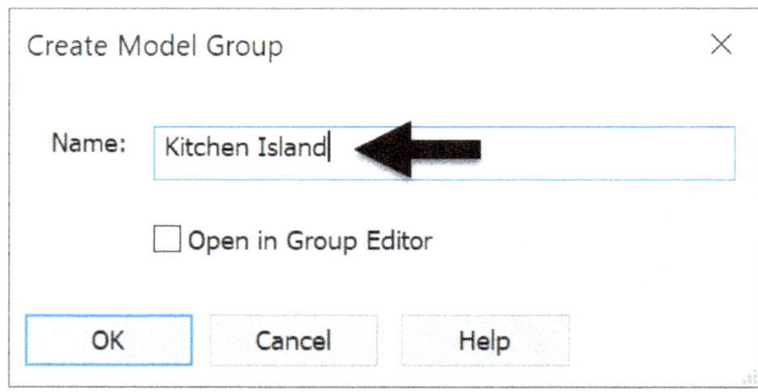

- On the ribbon, click **Modify** tab > **Modify** panel > **Align**. Next, select the right edge of the wall and the left edge of the base cabinet, as shown.

- Select the bottom edge of the Range and the bottom edge of the Kitchen Island.

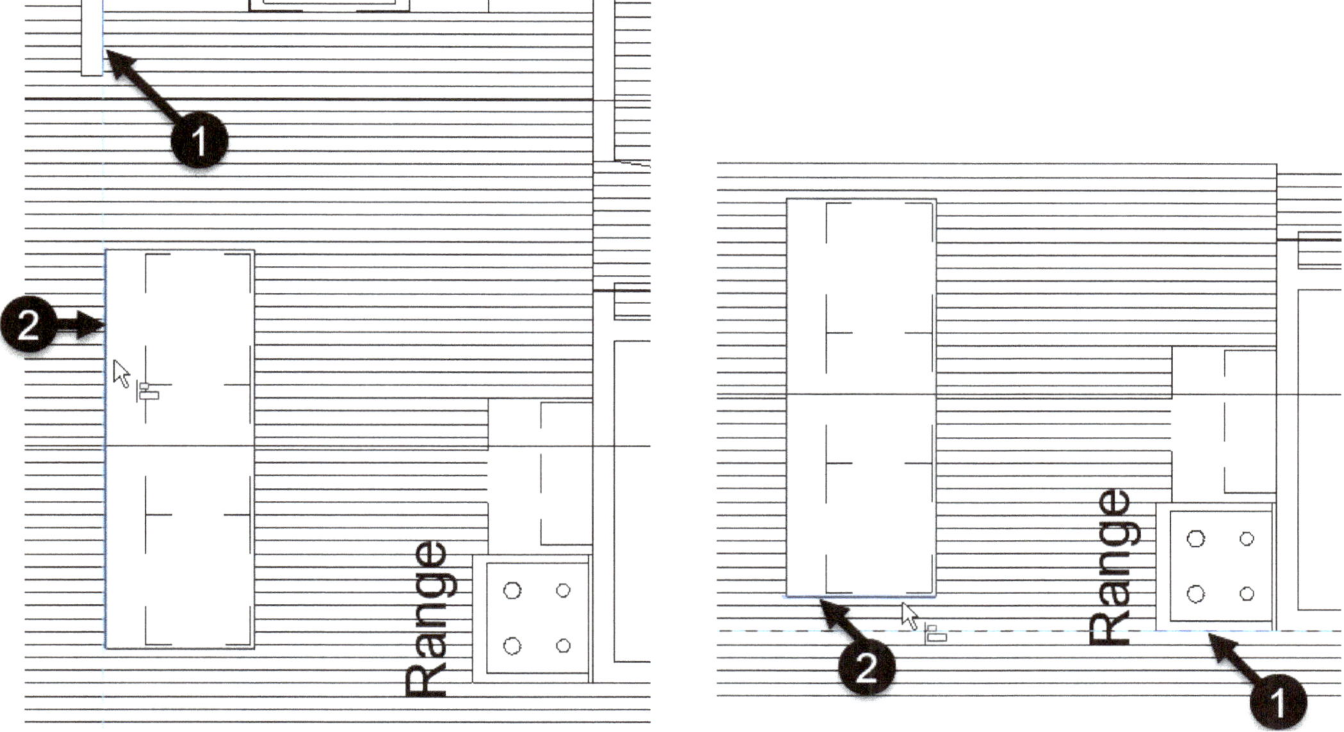

- On the ribbon, click **Insert > Load From Library > Load Family**.
- Go to **Local Disc C > Program Data > Autodesk > RVT 2024 > Libraries > English Imperial > Furniture > Seating**. Next, double-click on **Bar Stool**.
- On the ribbon, click **Architecture > Build > Component** drop-down > **Place a Component**.
- On the **Properties** palette, from the **Type Selector** drop-down, select the **Bar Stool** type.
- Press the SPACEBAR until the bar stool is oriented, as shown. Next, place the bar stool at the location, as shown.

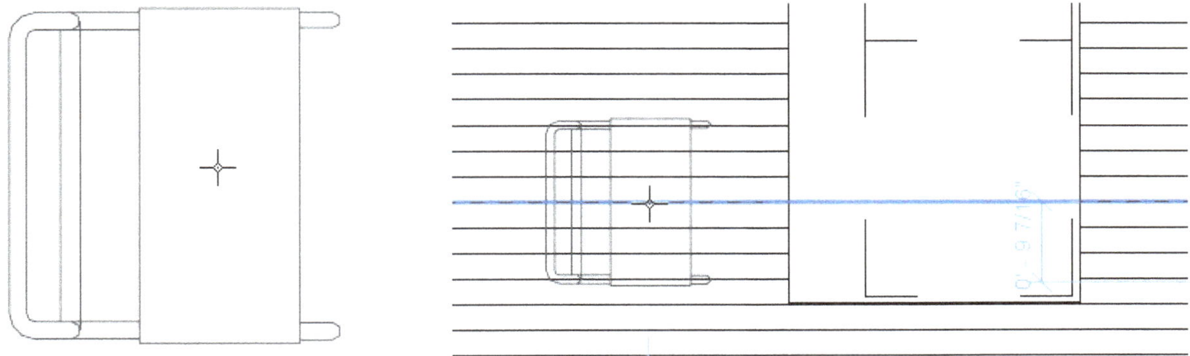

- Press ESC twice and select the bar stool. Next, click on the horizontal dimension, as shown.

- Type 6" and press ENTER. Next, click **Modify > Modify > Align** on the ribbon.
- Select the centerline of the base cabinet, as shown. Next, select the centerline of the bar stool.

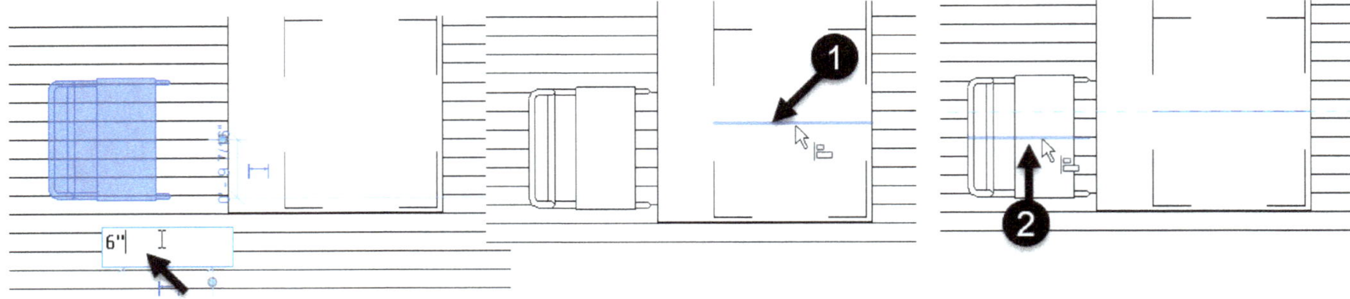

- Press ESC twice and select the bar stool. Next, click **Modify > Modify > Copy** on the ribbon.
- Select the midpoint of the bar stool to define the start point. Next, move the pointer upward, type 30", and then press ENTER.
- Move the pointer upward, type 30", and then press ENTER. Next, press ESC twice.

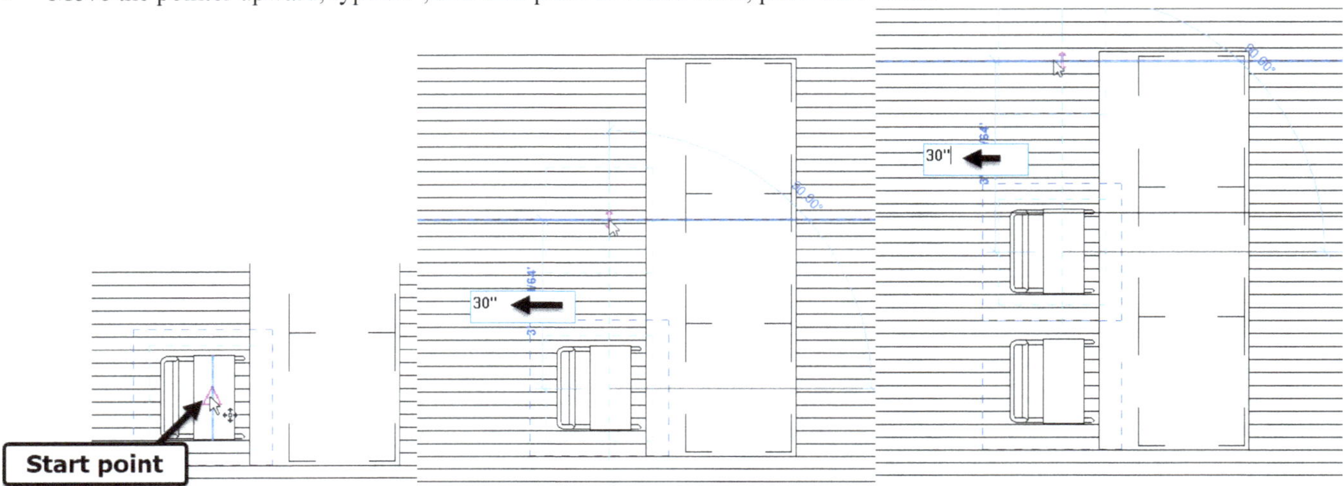

Adding Bathroom Fixtures

- On the ribbon, click **Architecture > Build > Component** drop-down > **Place a Component**.
- On the ribbon, click **Modify | Place Component > Mode > Load Family**.
- Go to **Local Disc C > Program Data > Autodesk > RVT 2024 > Libraries > English Imperial > Plumbing > Architectural > Fixtures > Bathtubs**. Next, double-click on **Tub-Rectangular-3D**.
- On the **Properties** palette, from the **Type Selector** drop-down, select the **Tub-Rectangular-3D** type.
- Zoom to the bathroom area on the right-side of the drawing.
- Place the pointer on the inner edge of the bathroom wall, as shown. Next, click to place the bathtub.
- Click **Modify > Modify > Align** on the ribbon.
- Select the bottom edge of the wall, as shown. Next, select the edge of the bathtub, as shown.

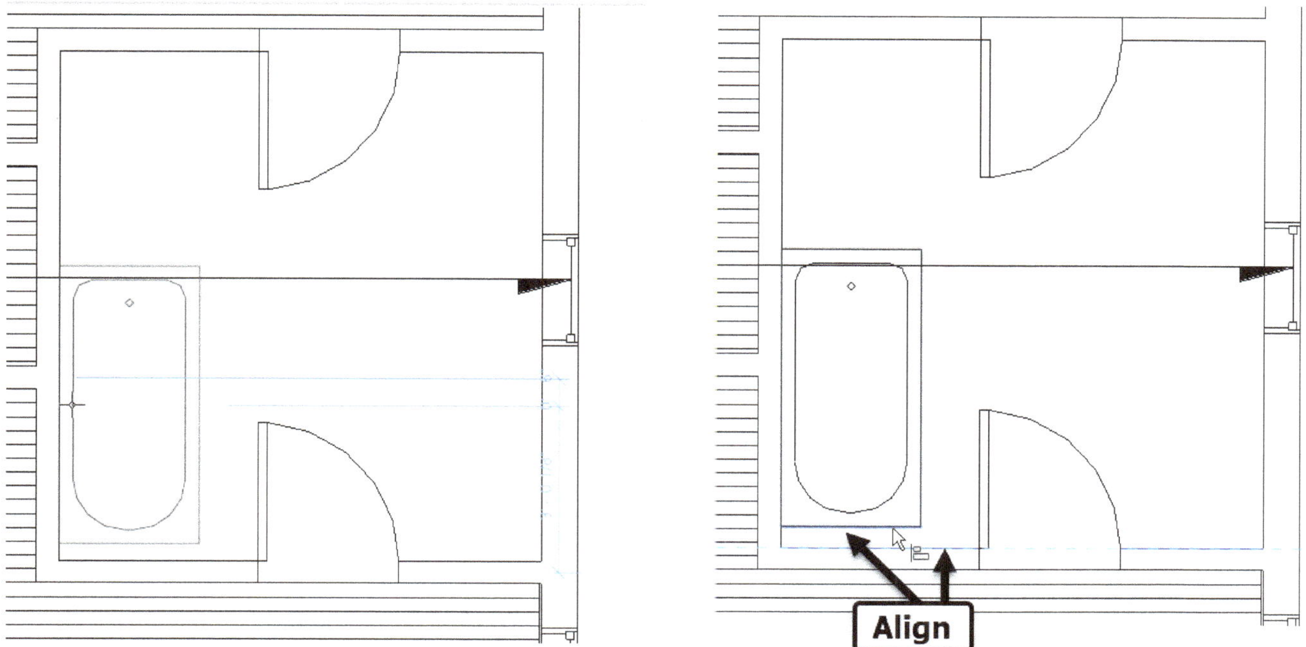

- On the ribbon, click **Architecture > Build > Component** drop-down > **Place a Component**.
- On the ribbon, click **Modify | Place Component > Mode > Load Family**.
- Go to **Local Disc C > Program Data > Autodesk > RVT 2024 > Libraries > English Imperial > Plumbing > Architectural > Fixtures > Water Closets**. Next, double-click on **Toilet-Domestic-3D**.
- On the **Properties** palette, from the **Type Selector** drop-down, select the **Toilet-Domestic-3D** type.
- Press the SPACEBAR to change the orientation of the toilet. Next, place the toilet at the location, as shown.

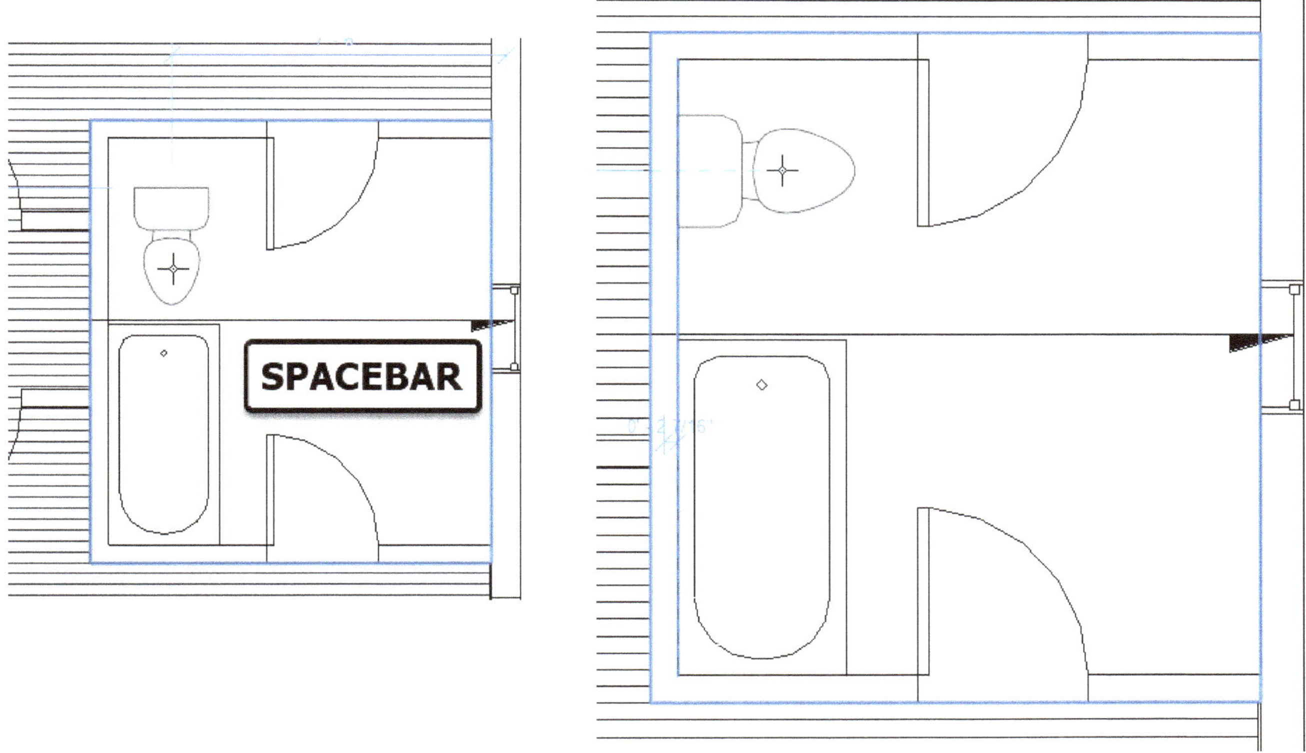

- Press ESC twice and select the toilet. Next, select the dimension, as shown. Type 1'6" and press ENTER.

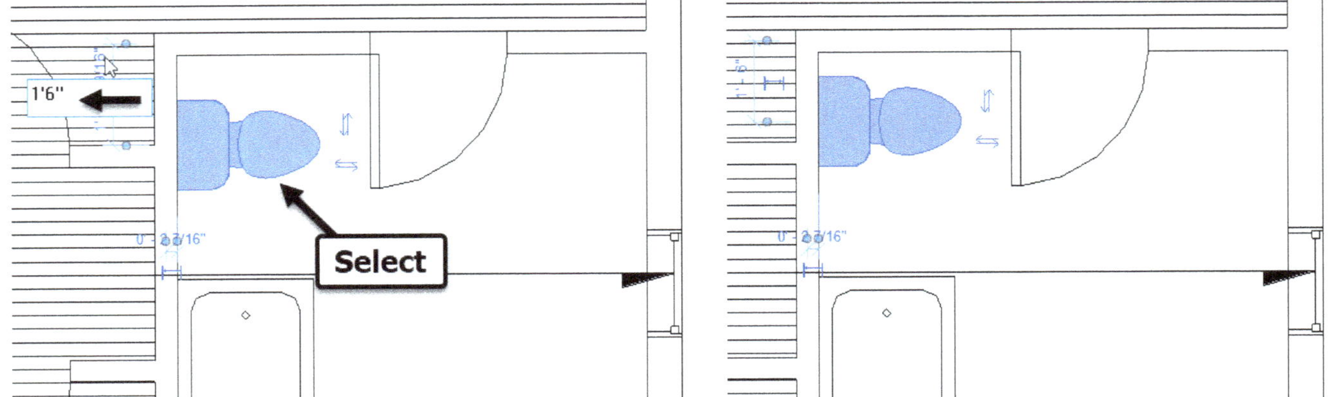

- On the ribbon, click **Architecture > Build > Component** drop-down > **Place a Component**.
- On the ribbon, click **Modify | Place Component** tab > **Mode** panel > **Load Family**.
- Go to **Local Disc C > Program Data > Autodesk > RVT 2024 > Libraries > English Imperial > Casework > Counter Tops**. Next, press and hold the CTRL key and select the **Vanity Counter Top w 2 Square Sink Holes** and **Vanity Counter Top w Square Sink Hole**. Click **Open**.
- On the **Properties** palette, from the **Type Selector** drop-down, select the **Vanity Counter Top w 2 Square Sink Holes 72"** type.
- Press the SPACEBAR until the counter top is oriented, as shown. Next, place the counter top at the location, as shown.

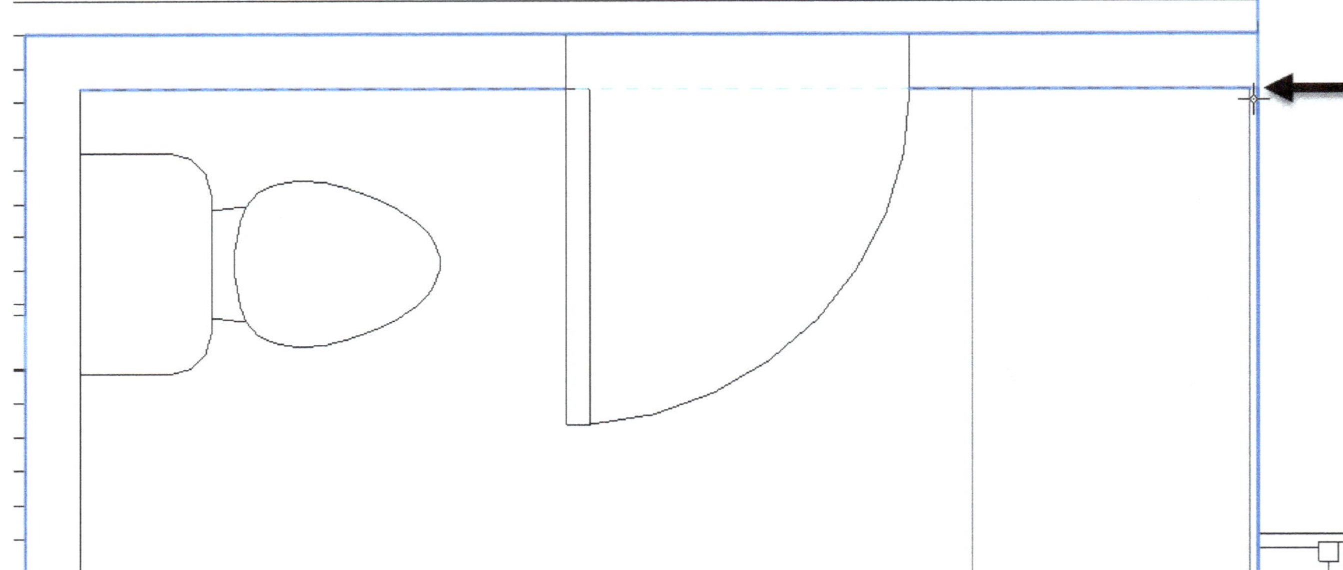

- Click **Modify > Modify > Align** on the ribbon.
- Select the edge of the wall, as shown. Next, select the edge of the counter top, as shown.

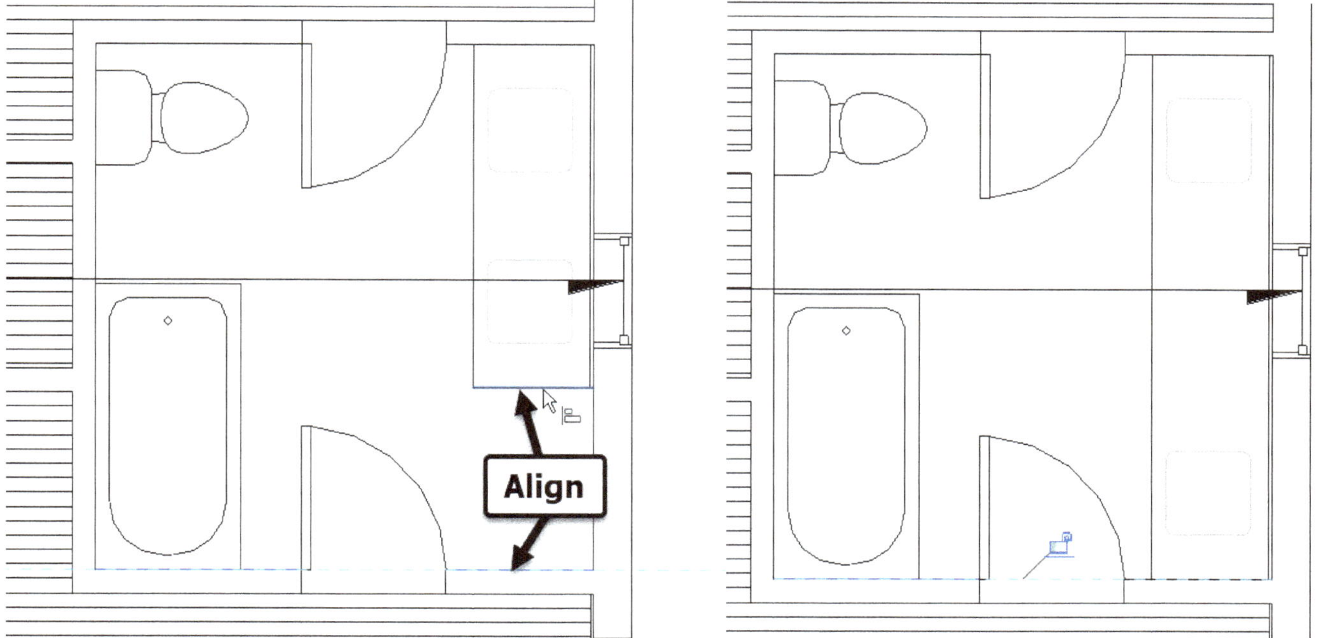

- On the ribbon, click **Architecture > Build > Component** drop-down > **Place a Component**.
- On the **Properties** palette, from the **Type Selector** drop-down, select the **Vanity Counter Top w Square Sink Hole 24"** type.
- Press the SPACEBAR to change the orientation of the counter top. Next, place the counter top at the location, as shown.
- On the **Properties** palette, from the **Type Selector** drop-down, select the **Toilet-Domestic-3D** type.
- Place the toilet at the location, as shown.

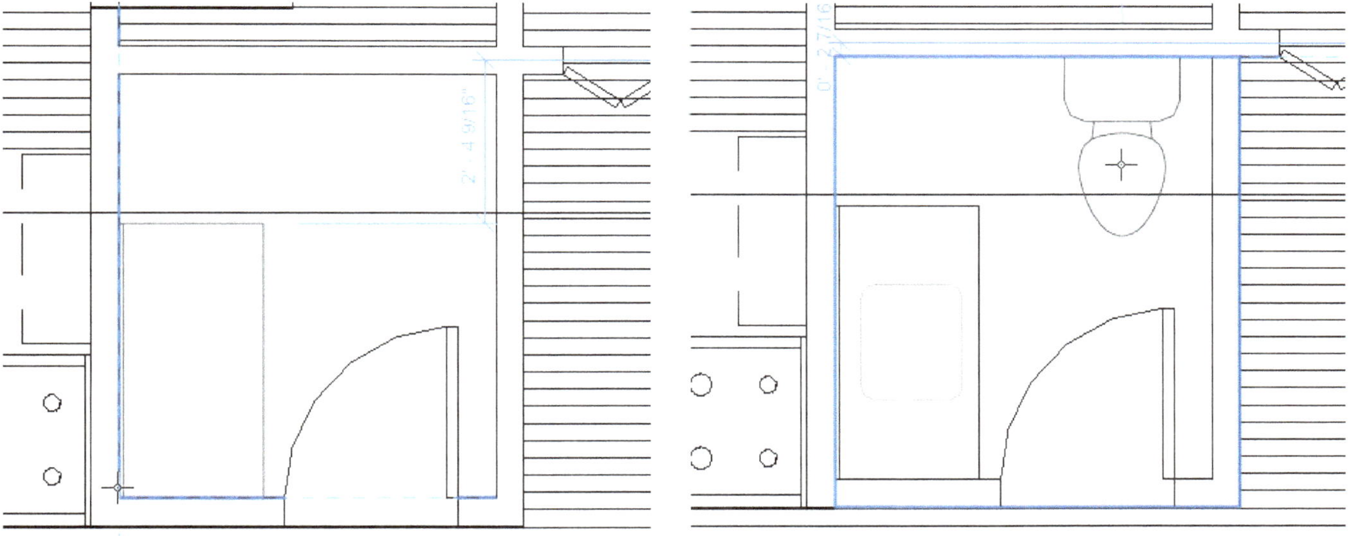

- On the **Properties** palette, from the **Type Selector** drop-down, select the **Base Cabinet-Double Door Sink Unit 36"** type.
- Place the base cabinets at the locations, as shown.

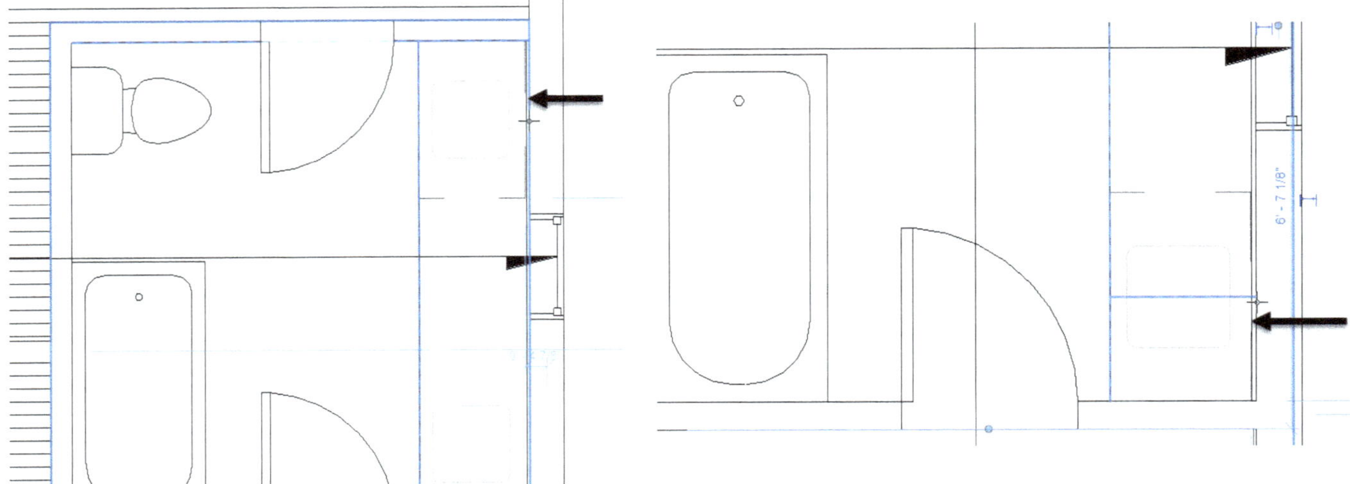

- On the **Properties** palette, from the **Type Selector** drop-down, select the **Base Cabinet-Double Door Sink Unit 48"** type.
- Place the base cabinet at the location, as shown.

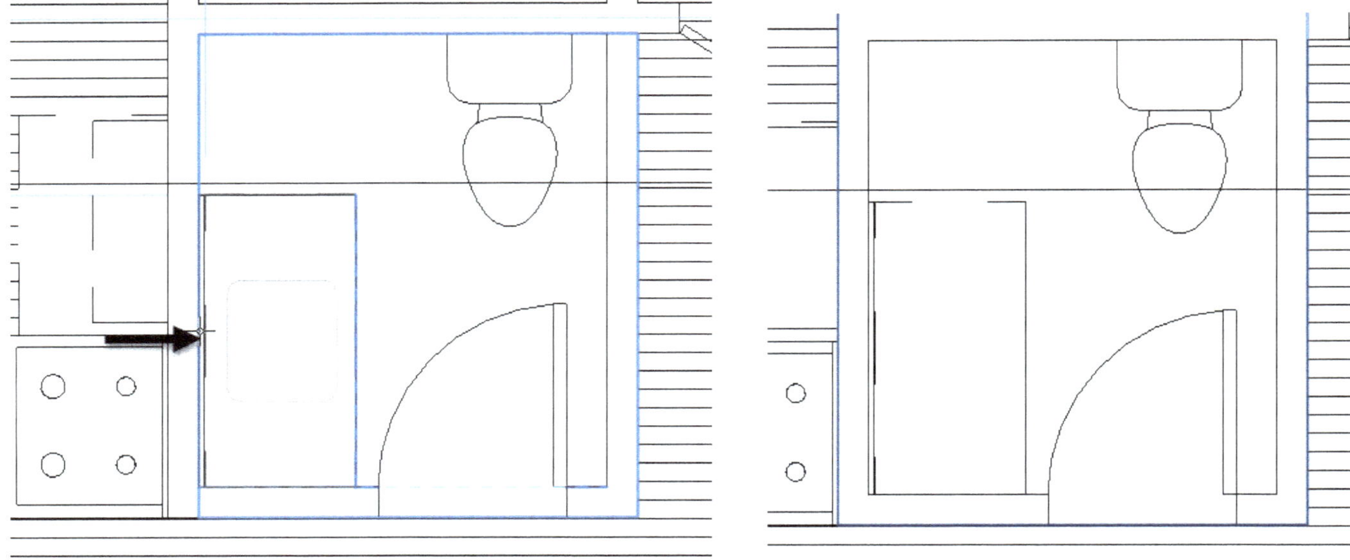

- Create a section view at the location, as shown. Next, right-click and select **Go to View**.

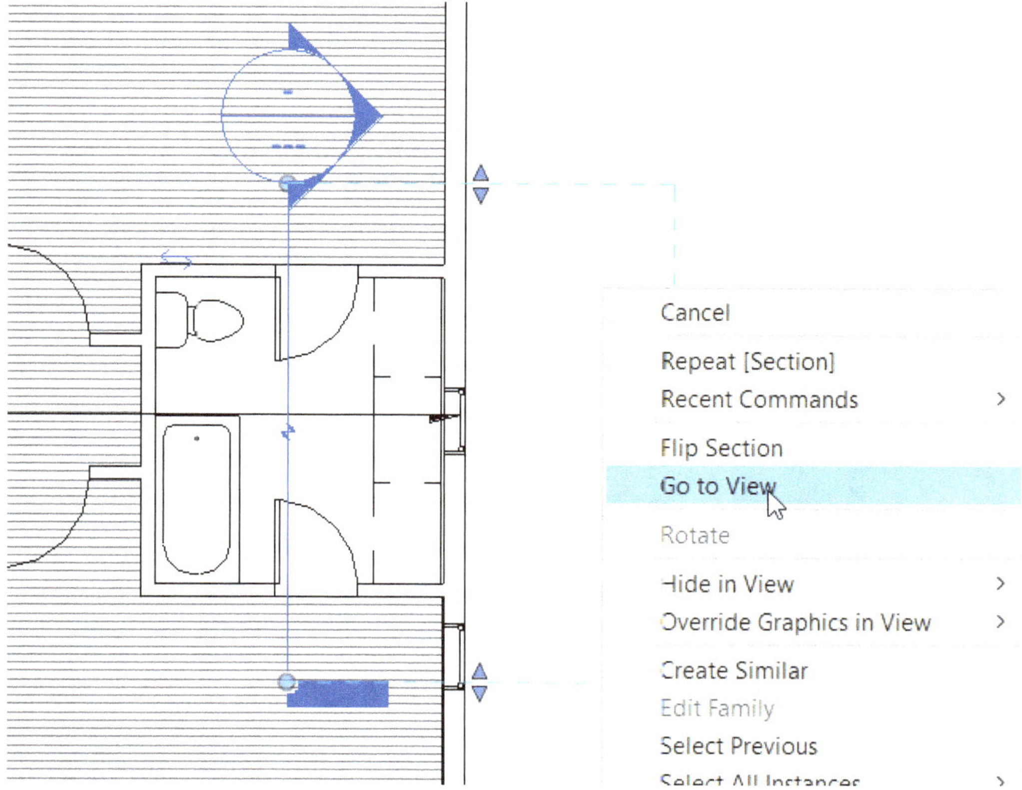

Notice that the counter top intersects with the base cabinets. You need to change the elevation of the counter top. Also, you need to change the type and elevation of the window.

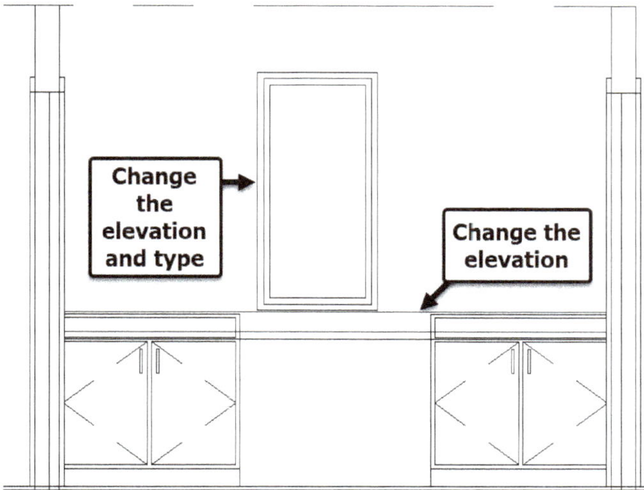

- Select the counter top and change the elevation value to 0' 5 ¾".

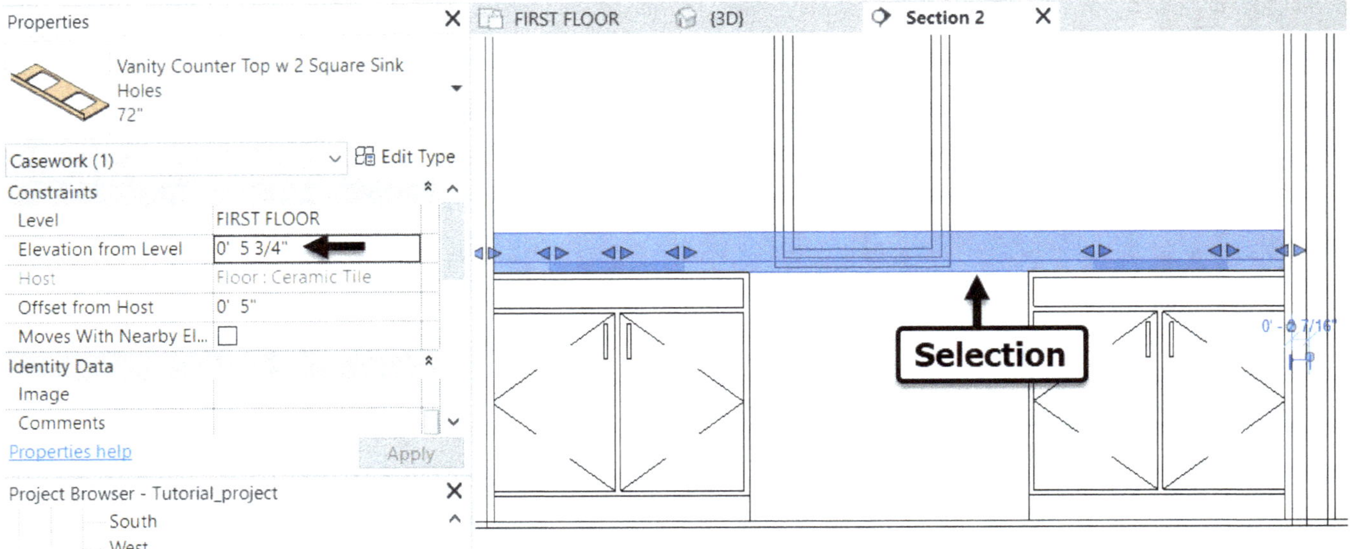

- Select the window and select **Fixed 24" x 24"** from the **Type Selector** drop-down on the **Properties** palette.
- Click on the vertical dimension between the floor and the window. Next, type 5' and then press ENTER.

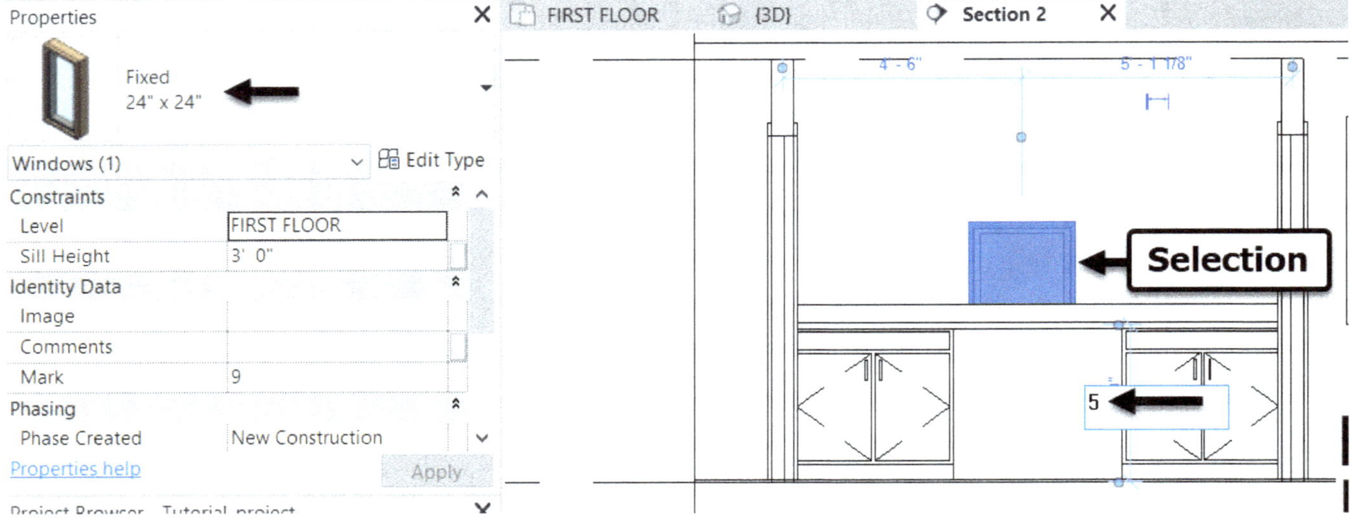

- Create a section view at the location, as shown. Next, right-click and select **Go to View**.

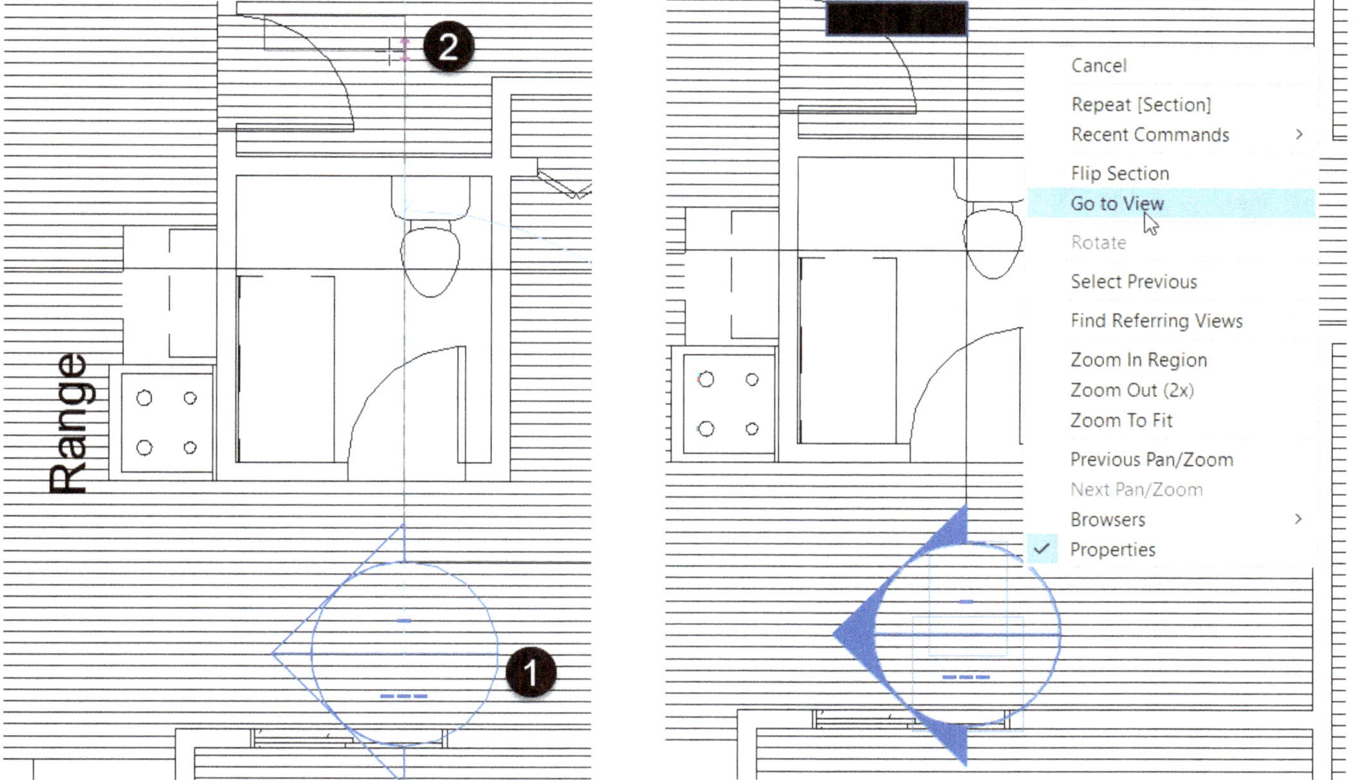

- Place the pointer on the upper portion of the base cabinet and press the TAB key; the counter top is highlighted.

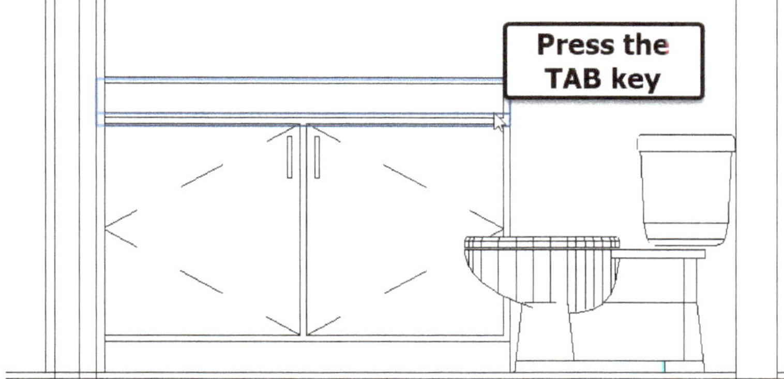

- Click to select the counter top. Next, change its elevation tc 0' 5 ¾".

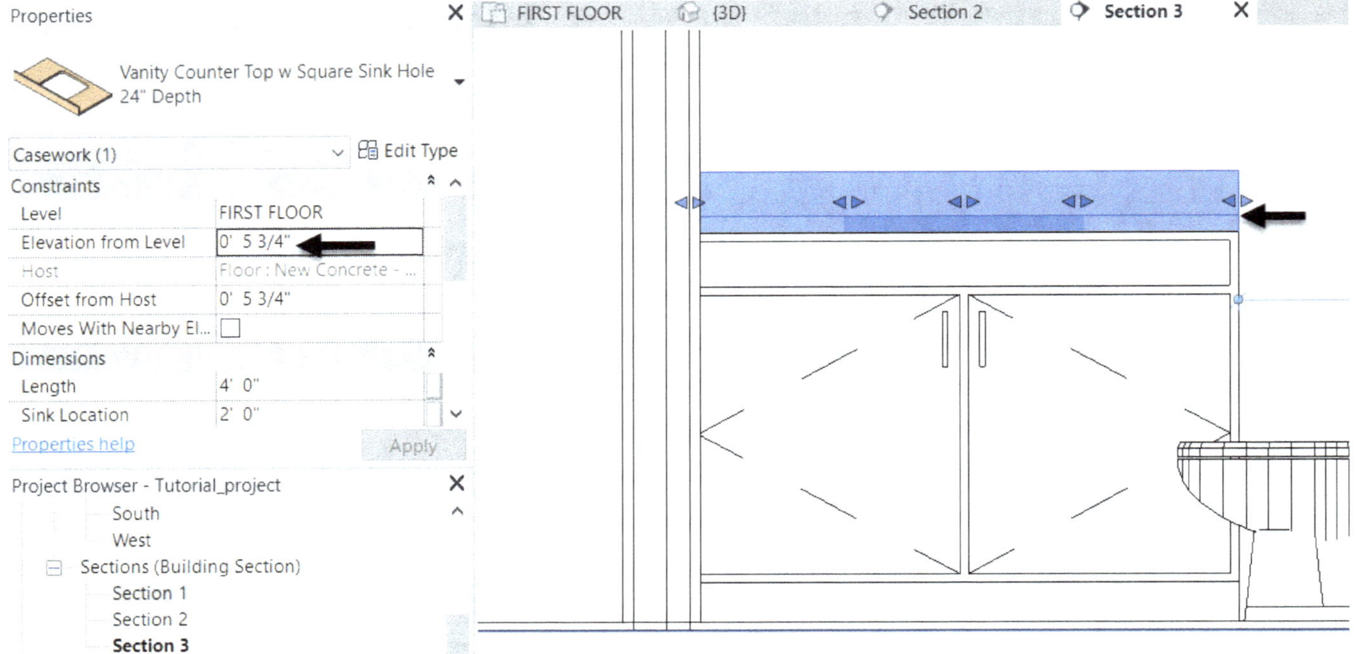

- Click the **FIRST FLOOR** view tab.
- On the ribbon, click **Architecture > Build > Component** drop-down > **Place a Component**.
- On the ribbon, click **Modify | Place Component** tab > **Mode** panel > **Load Family**.
- Go to **Local Disc C > Program Data > Autodesk > RVT 2024 > Libraries > English Imperial > Plumbing > Architectural > Fixtures > Sinks**. Next, double-click on the **Sink Vanity-Square**.
- Type **0' 5"** in the **Elevation from Level** box on the **Properties** palette.
- Press the SPACEBAR until the sink is oriented, as shown.

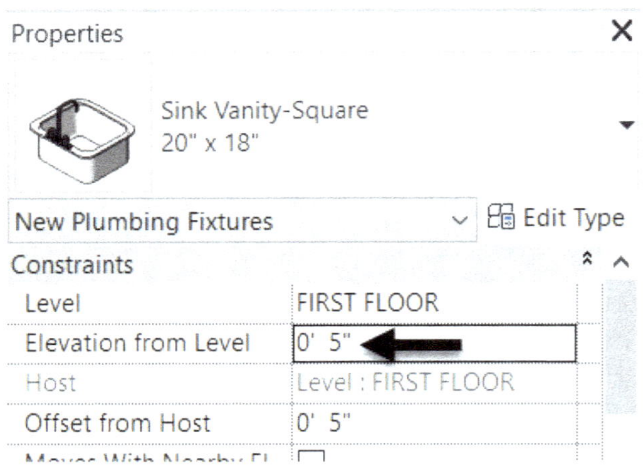

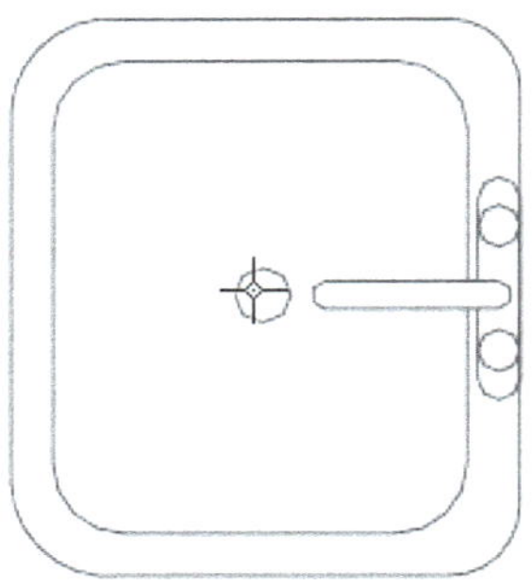

- Move the pointer near to the centerline of the sink opening and notice a blue line. Click to place the kitchen sink at the location, as shown.
- Likewise, place another instance of the sink at the location, as shown. Next, press ESC twice.

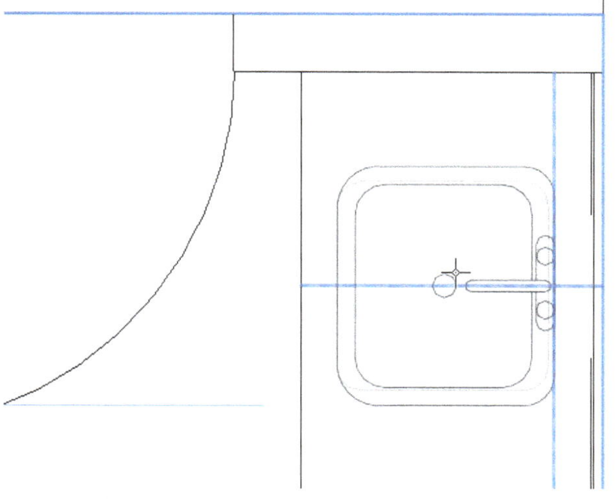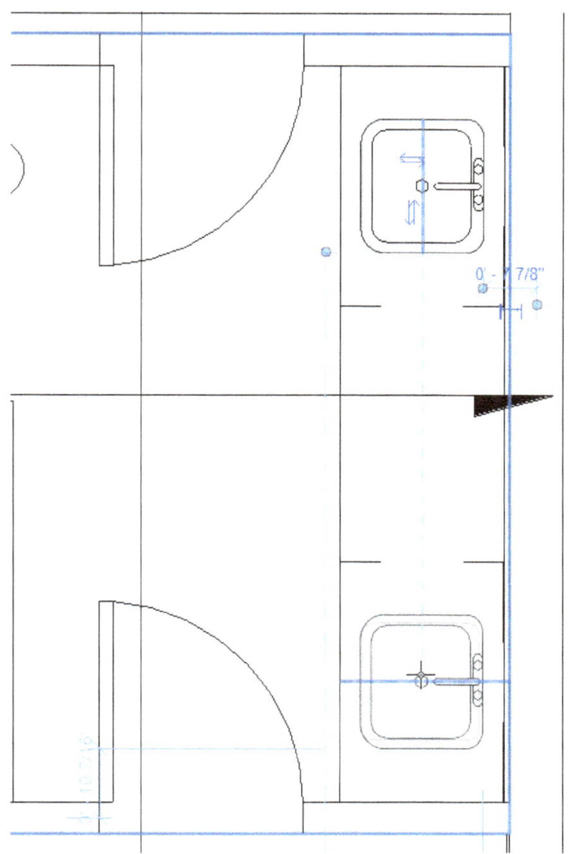

- Place the pointer on the counter top and notice that the sink opening is slightly larger than the sink. You need to reduce the size of the sink opening.

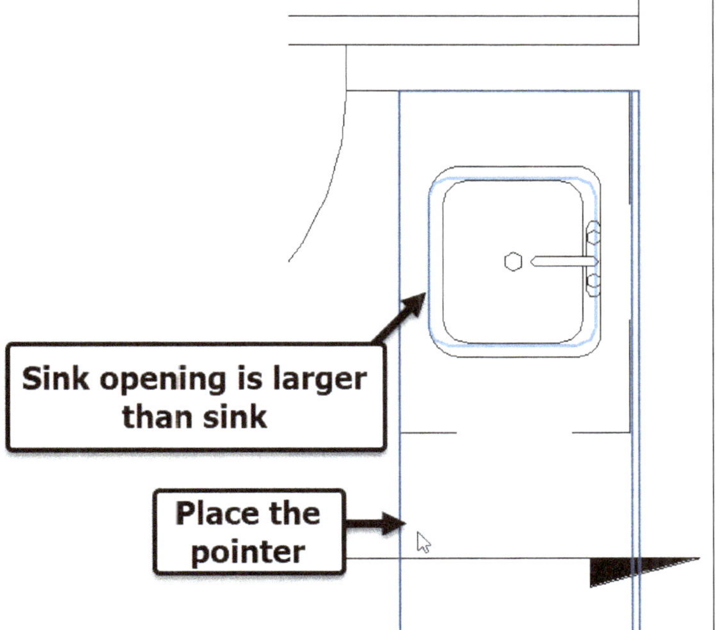

- Click on the counter top, and then click and drag the arrow grip displayed near the edge, as shown. Next, drag the pointer toward right up to a small distance and click.

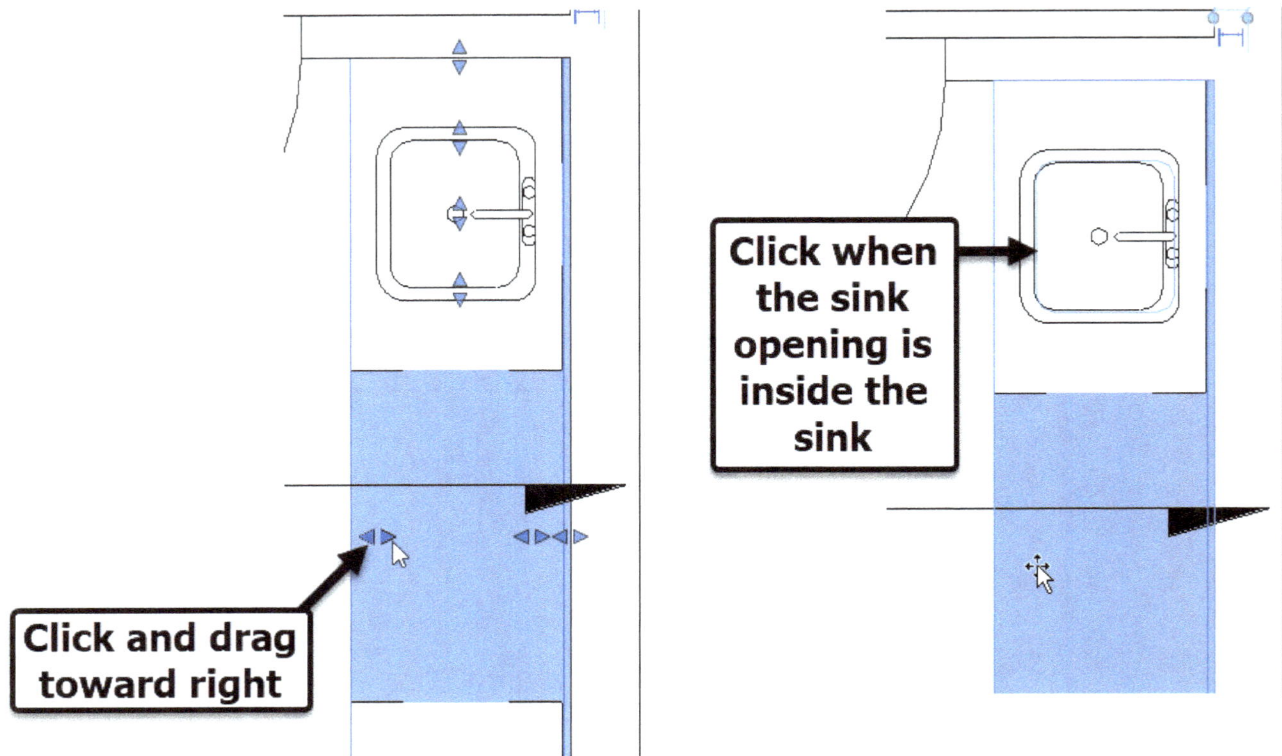

- On the ribbon, click **Architecture > Build > Component** drop-down > **Place a Component**.
- On the **Properties** palette, from the **Type Selector** drop-down, select the **Sink Vanity-Square** type.
- Type **0' 5"** in the **Elevation from Level** box on the **Properties** palette.
- Press the SPACEBAR until the sink is oriented, as shown. Next, place the sink at the location, as shown.

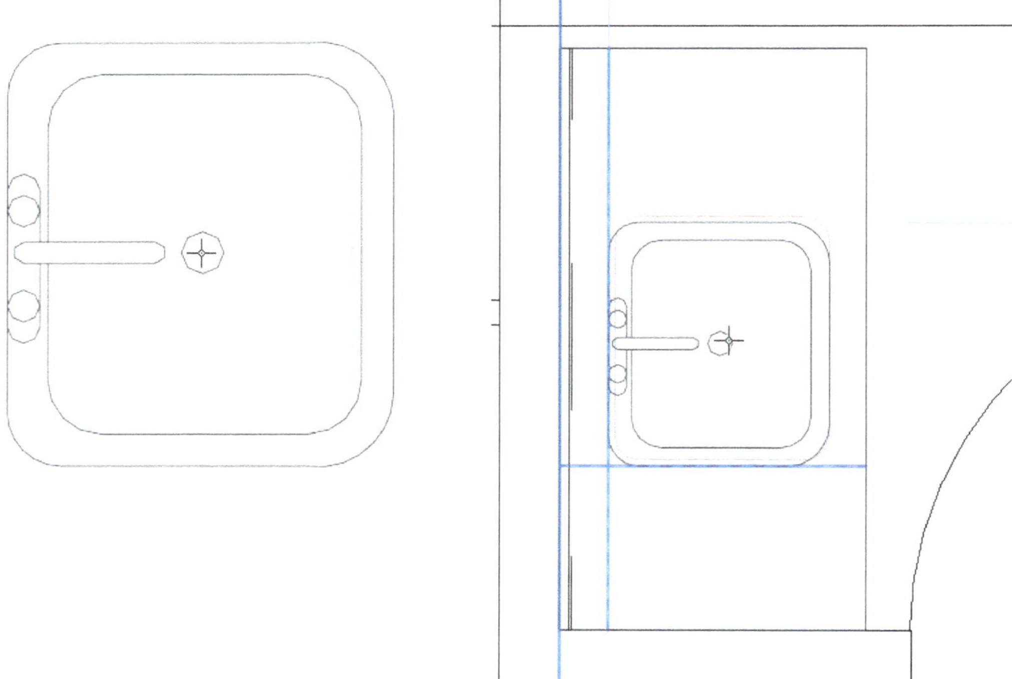

- Press Esc twice and select the counter top, as shown.
- Click twice the arrow pointing in the downward direction, as shown. Next, click on the arrow pointing in the upward

direction, as shown.

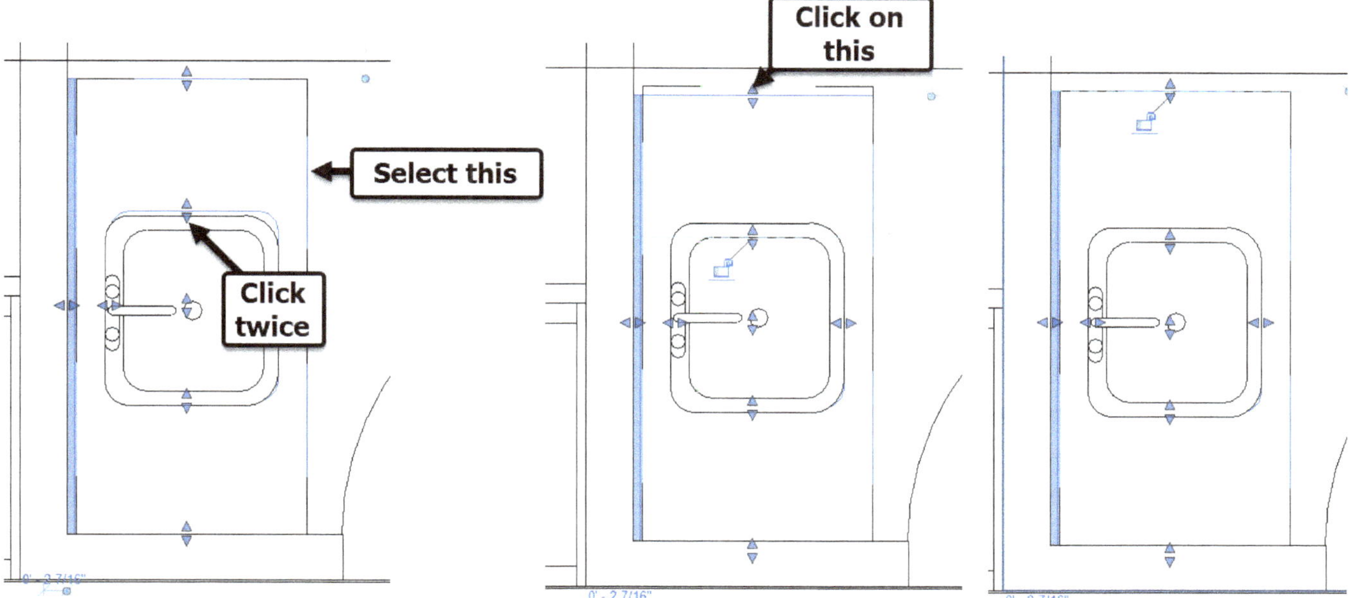

- Click on the arrow pointing upwards, as shown. Next, click and drag the arrow pointing towards left. Move the pointer toward left and release it on the inner edge of the sink.

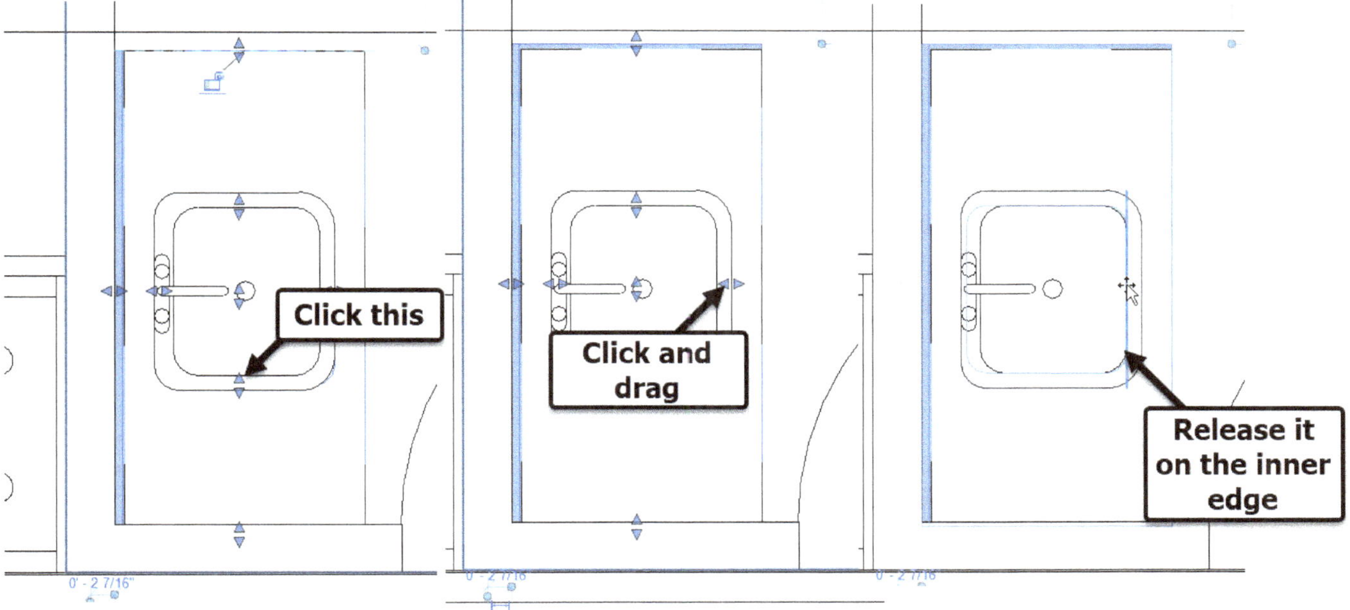

- Likewise, add bathroom fixtures to the bathroom on the left side, as shown.

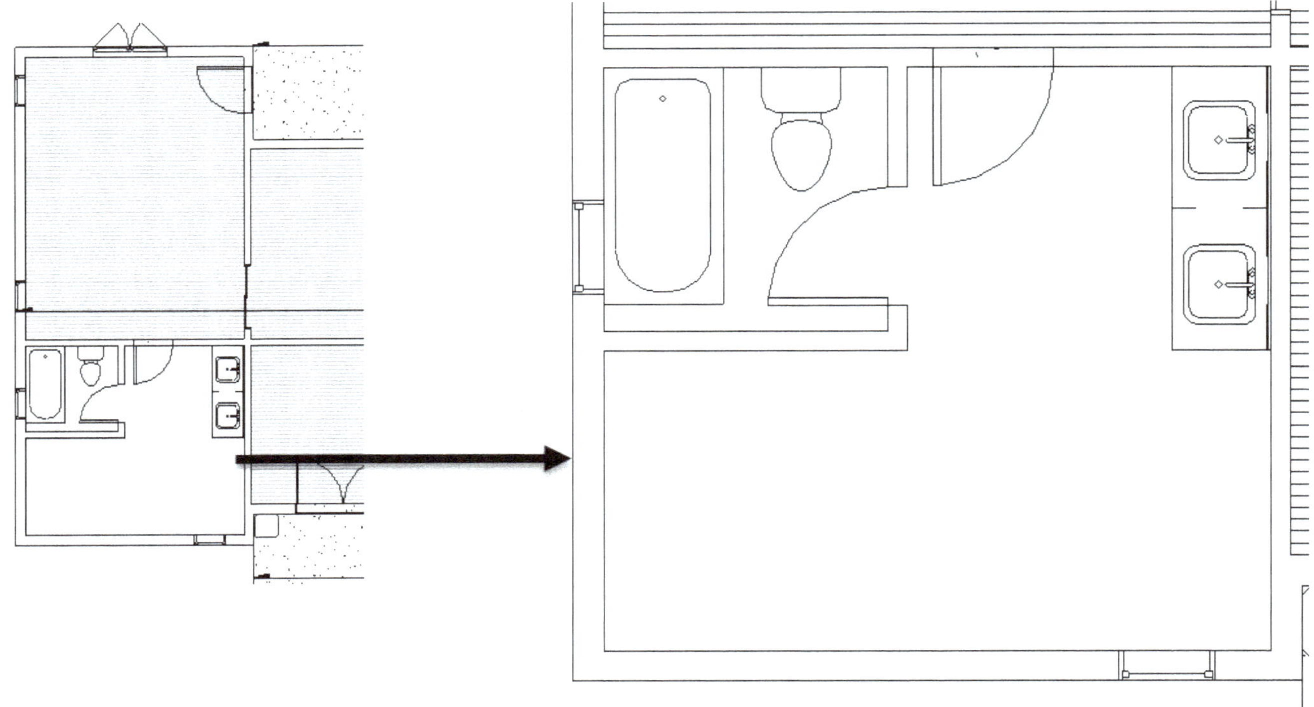

Adding Washer and Dryer

- On the ribbon, click **Architecture > Build > Component** drop-down > **Place a Component**.
- On the ribbon, click **Modify | Place Component > Mode > Load Family**.
- Go to **Local Disc C > Program Data > Autodesk > RVT 2024 > Libraries > English Imperial > Specialty Equipment > Domestic > Mid-Range**. Next, press and hold the CTRL key and select **Washer-Front_Load** and **Dryer-Front_Load**. Next, click **Open**.
- On the **Properties** palette, from the **Type Selector** drop-down, select the **Dryer-Front Load 27"** type.
- Zoom to the area on the right-side of the drawing. Next, place the dryer at the location, as shown.

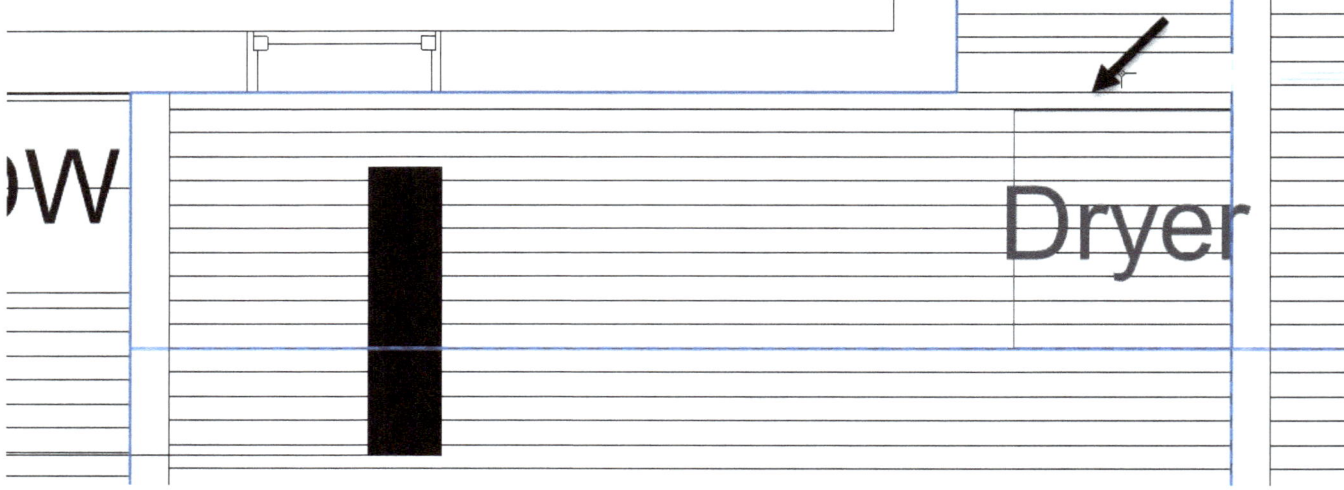

- On the **Properties** palette, from the **Type Selector** drop-down, select the **Washer-Front Load 27"** type.
- Next, place the washer next to the dryer, as shown.

Adding Room Tags

- On the ribbon, click **Architecture > Room & Area > Room**.

- Click in the bedrcom area located at the left side.

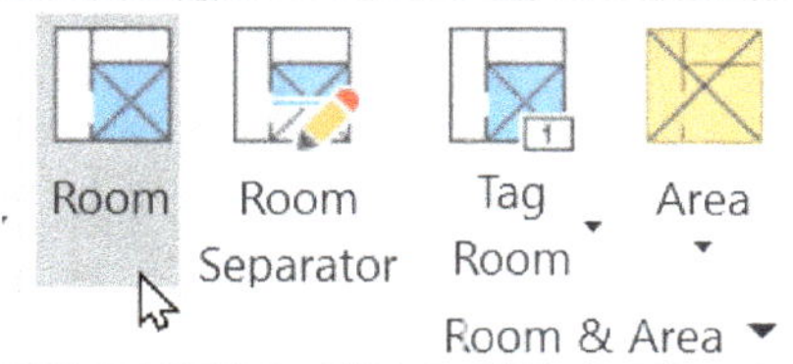

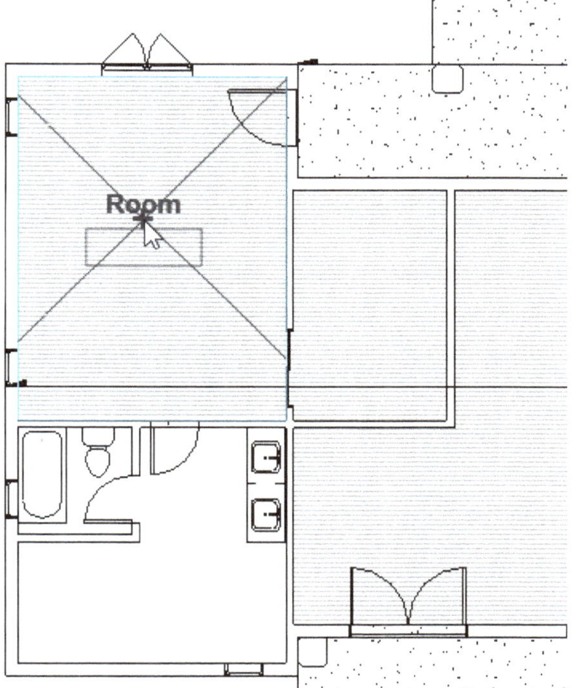

- Likewise, specify the room boundaries at the other locations. as shown.

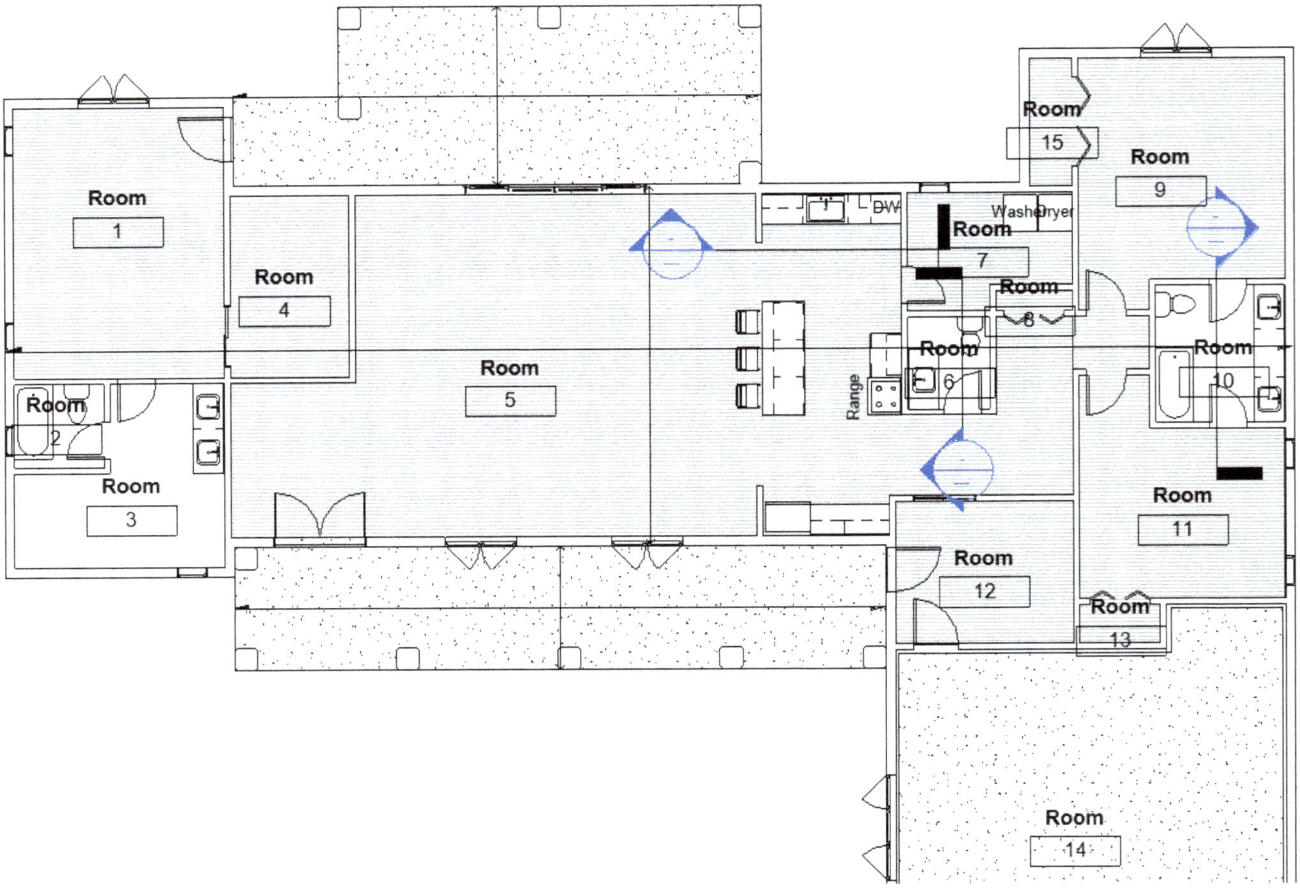

- Double-click on the room tag, as shown. Next, type Bedroom 1, and then click in the graphics window.

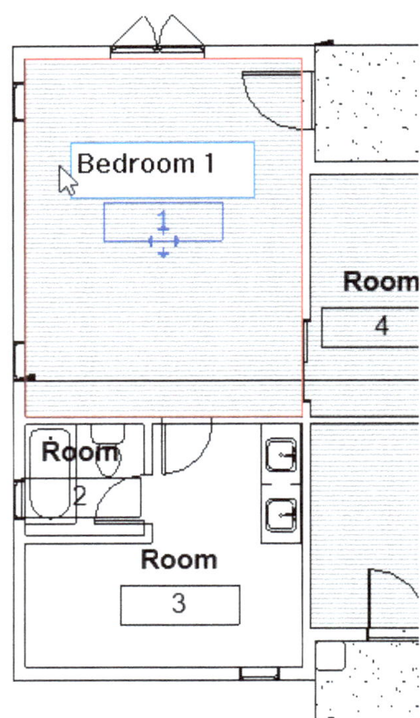

- Likewise, change the names of the other rooms, as shown.

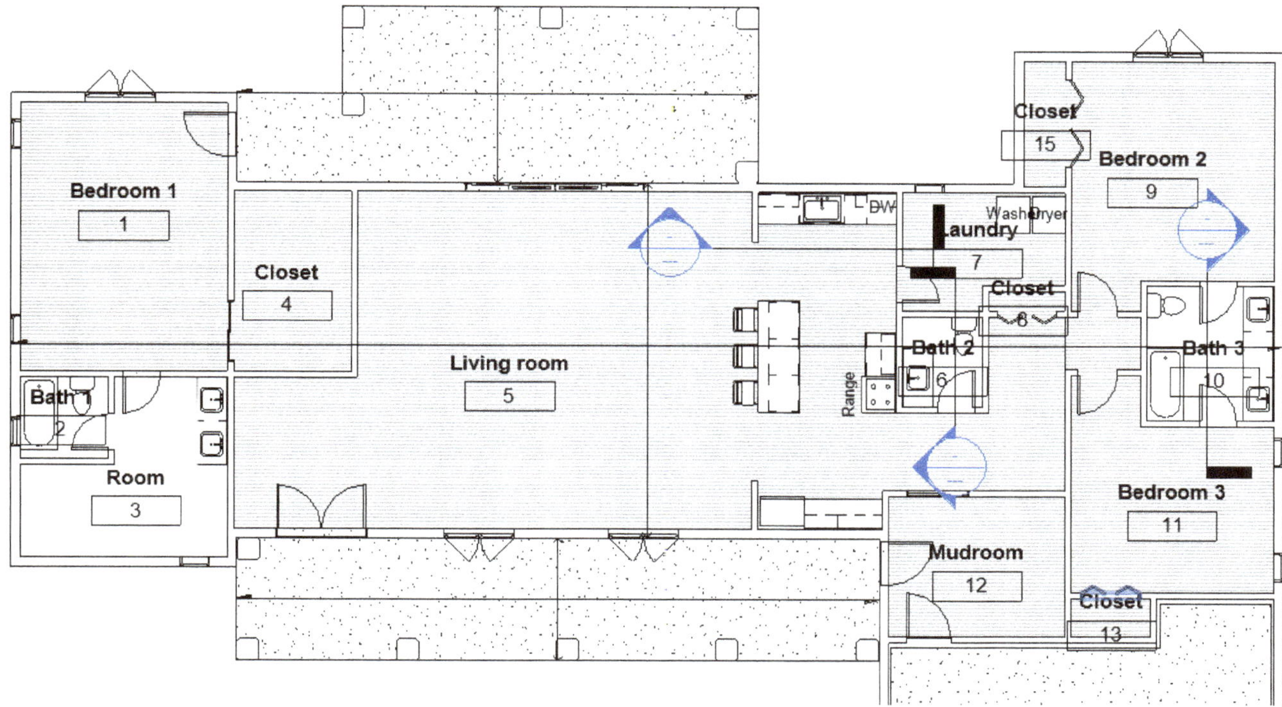

Next, you need to add room separator between the living room and kitchen area.

- On the ribbon, click **Architecture > Room & Area > Room Separator**.
- Specify the start and end point of the room separator, as shown. Next, press ESC twice.

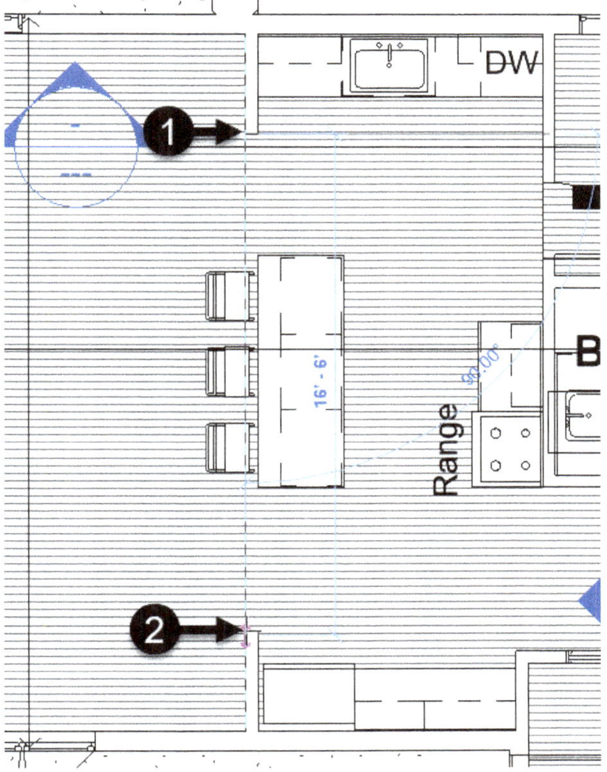

- On the ribbon, click **Architecture > Room & Area > Room**. Next, click in the kitchen area.
- Double-click on the newly placed room tag. Next, type Kitchen and click in the graphics area.

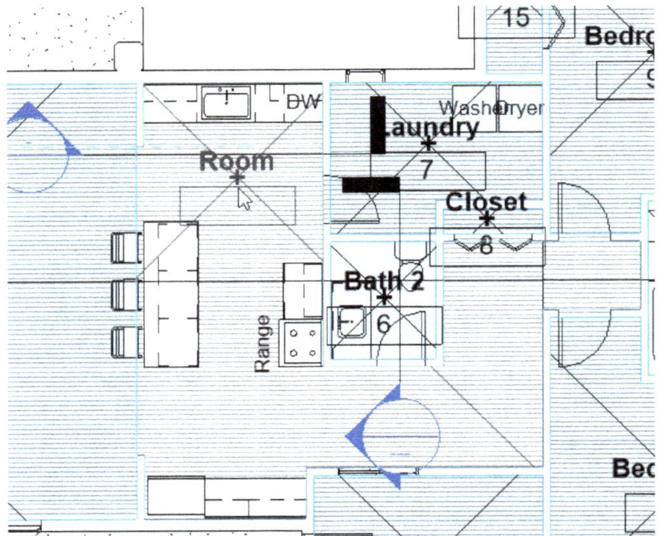

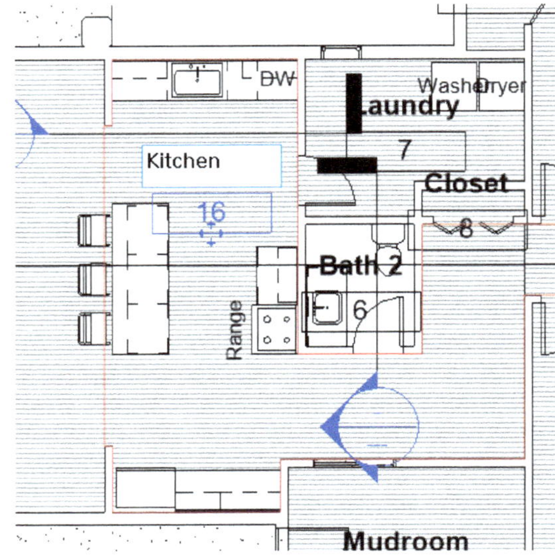

Tutorial 10: Creating Ceilings

- In the Project Browser, double-click the **FIRST FLOOR** option under the **Ceiling Plans** node.

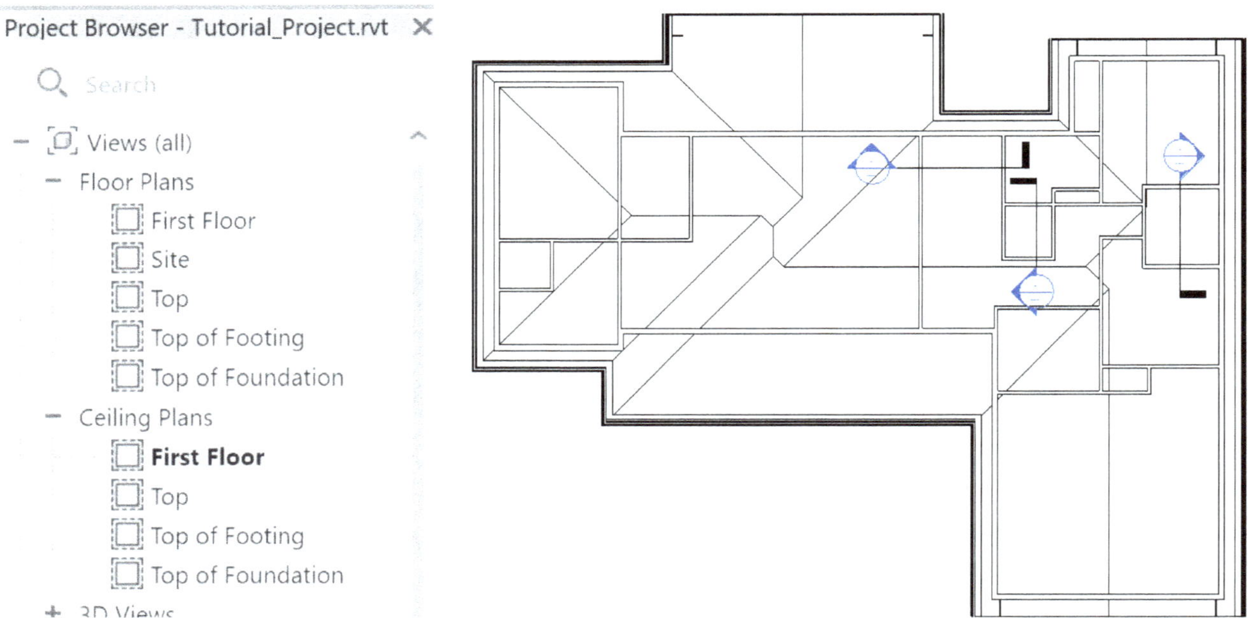

- Select the roof from the ceiling plan, and then click **Temporary Hide/Isolate > Hide Category**.

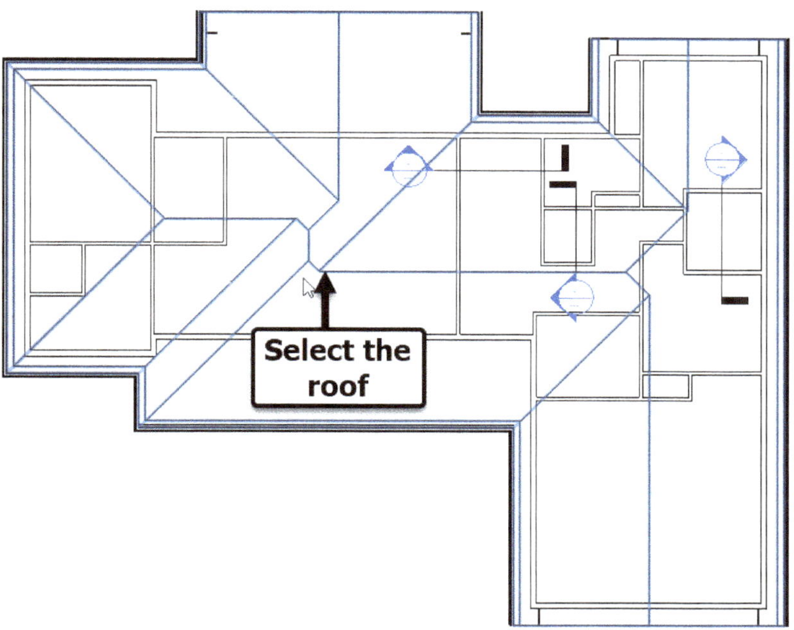

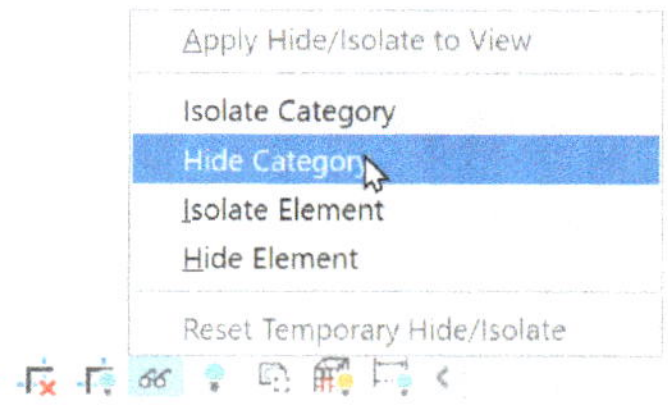

- On the ribbon, click **Architecture > Build > Ceiling**.
- On the **Properties** palette, from the **Type Selector** drop-down, select the **Compound Ceiling GWB on Mtl. Stud** type. Next, enter a value in the **Height Offset From Level** box or leave the default value.
- On the ribbon, make sure that the **Automatic Ceiling** icon on the **Modify | Place Ceiling** tab.

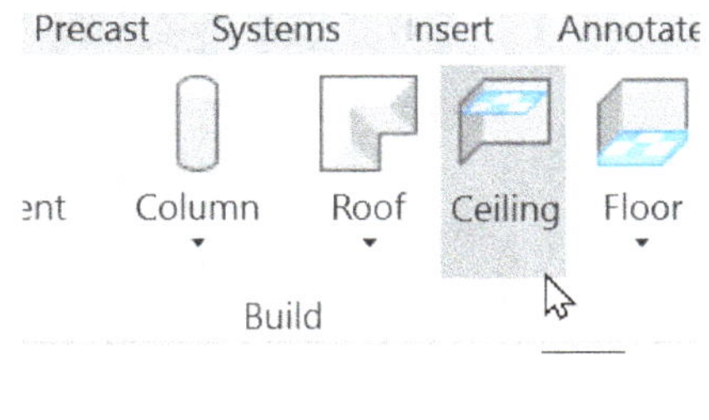

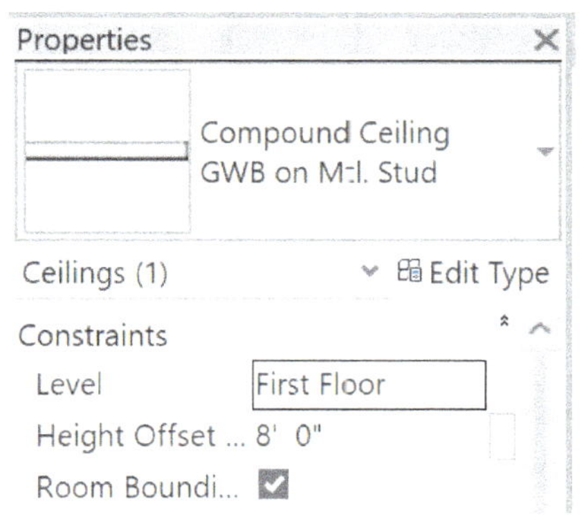

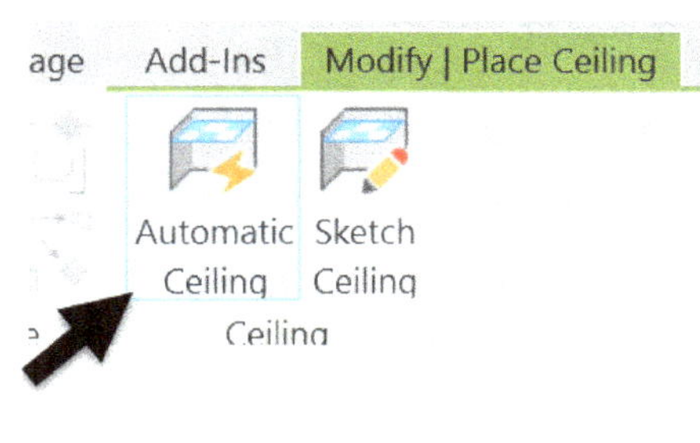

- Place the pointer in the closet area and notice a red boundary.

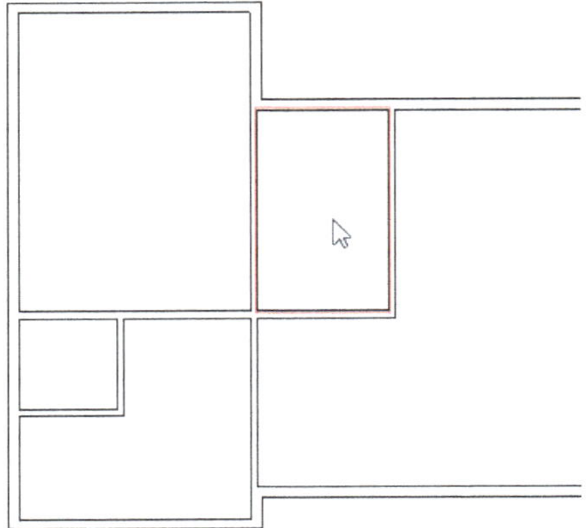

- Click in inside all the rooms except the bedroom and bathroom located at the left side. Next, press ESC twice.

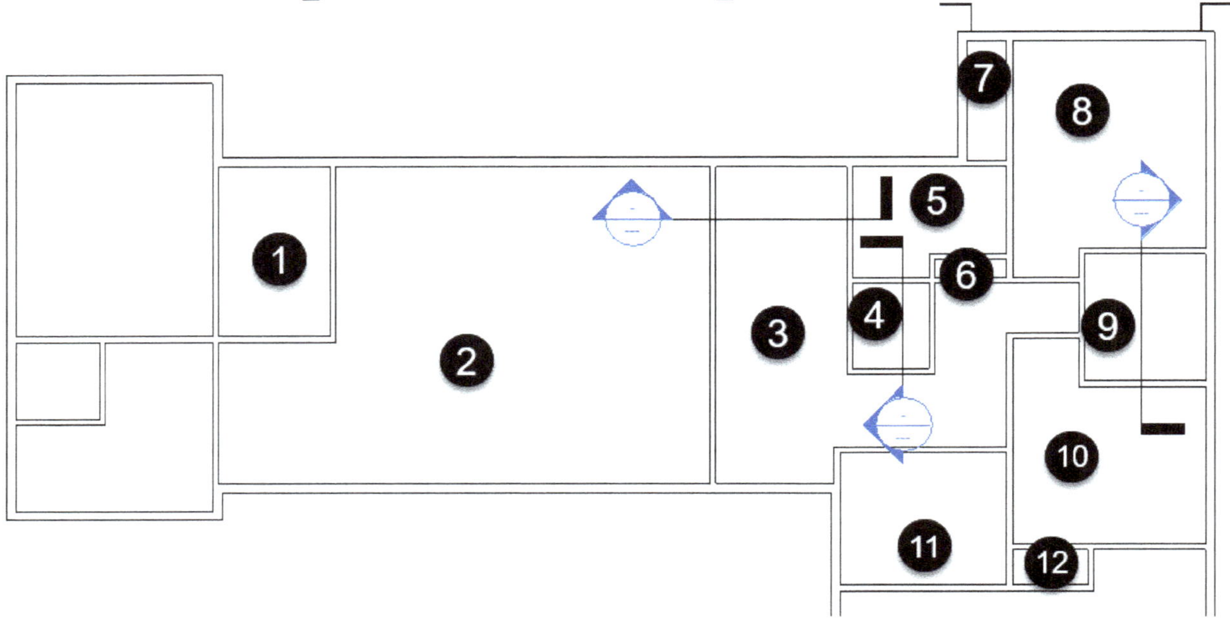

Next, you need to create a vaulted ceiling for the bedroom located at the left side.

- On the ribbon, click **Architecture > Build > Ceiling**.
- On the **Properties** palette, from the **Type Selector** drop-down, select the **Compound Ceiling GWB on Mtl. Stud** type.
- Click the **Sketch Ceiling** icon on the **Modify | Place Ceiling** tab of the ribbon.
- Click the **Rectangle** icon on the **Draw** panel of the **Modify | Create Ceiling Boundary** tab of the ribbon.

- Select top-left corner of the wall, as shown. Next, move the pointer downward and place the pointer near the midpoint of the lower horizontal edge; the midpoint grip is displayed. Click to select the midpoint of the horizontal edge.

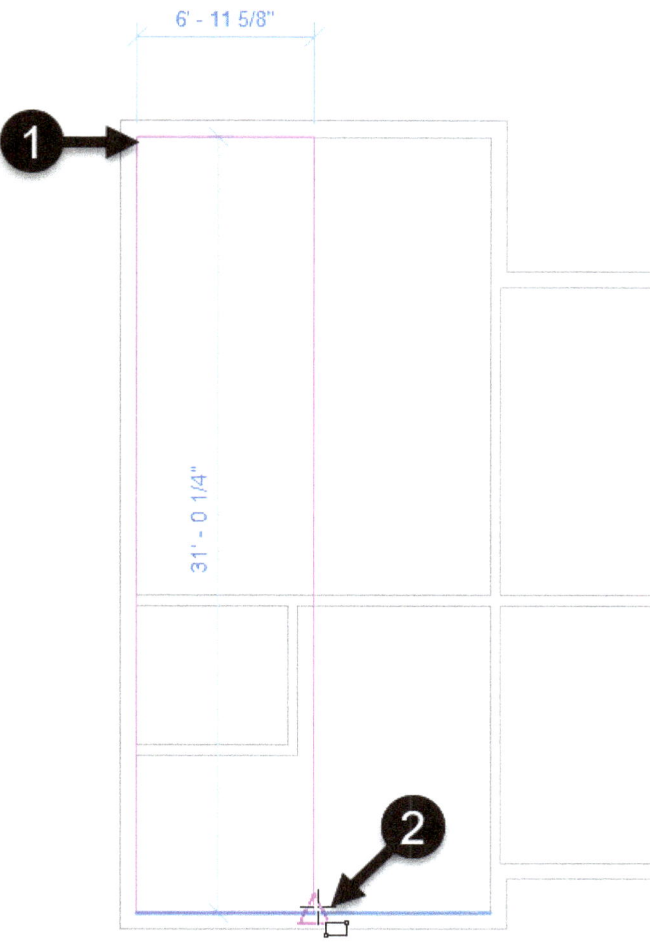

- Click the **Slope Arrow** icon on the **Draw** panel of the **Modify | Create Ceiling Boundary** tab of the ribbon.
- Select the midpoint of the right vertical line of the boundary. Next, move the pointer toward left and select the midpoint of the left vertical line.

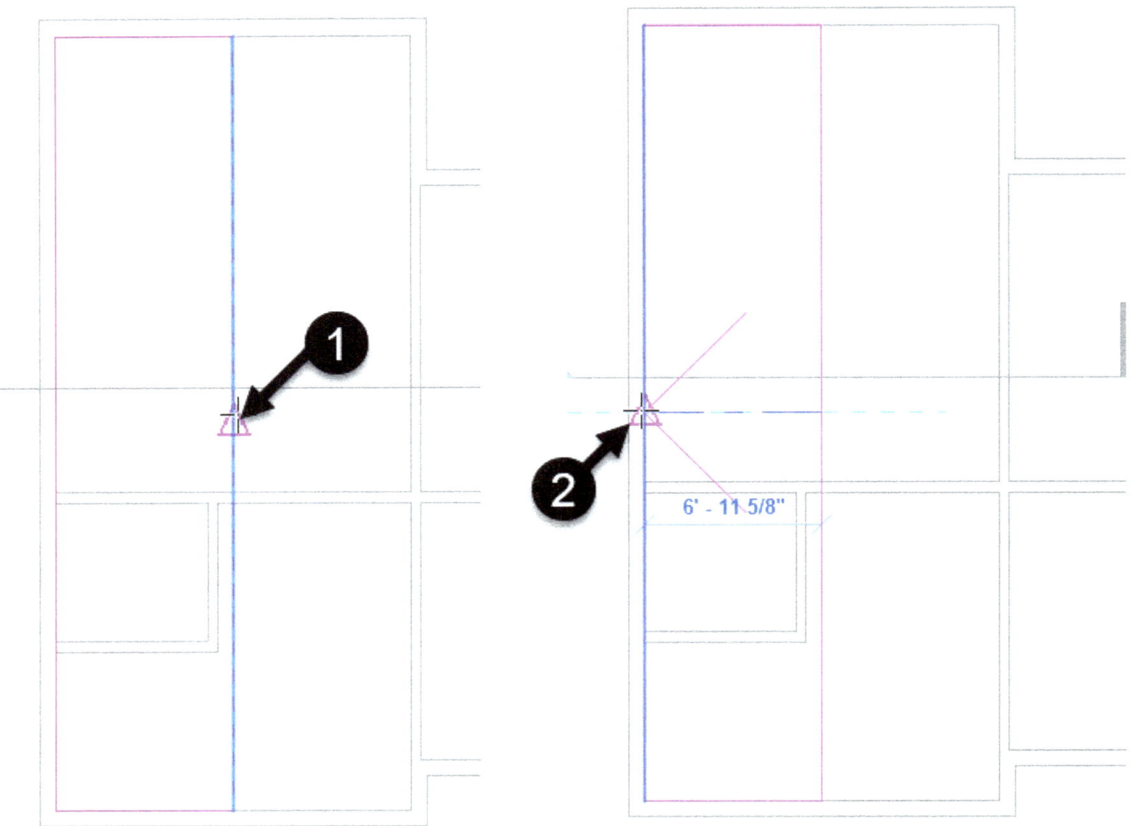

- On the **Properties** palette, type **0'8"** in the **Height Offset at Tail** box. Next, click the **Finish Edit Mode** icon on the ribbon.

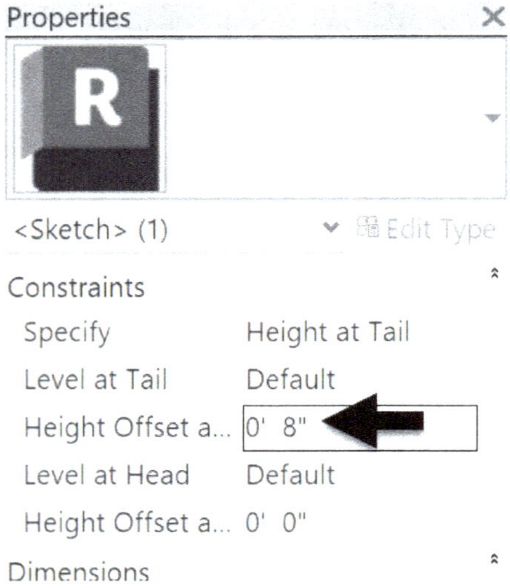

- Select the sloped ceiling and click **Modify** tab > **Modify** panel > **Mirror – Pick Axis** on the ribbon.
- Check the **Copy** option on the Options Bar. Next, select the right vertical edge of the sloped ceiling.

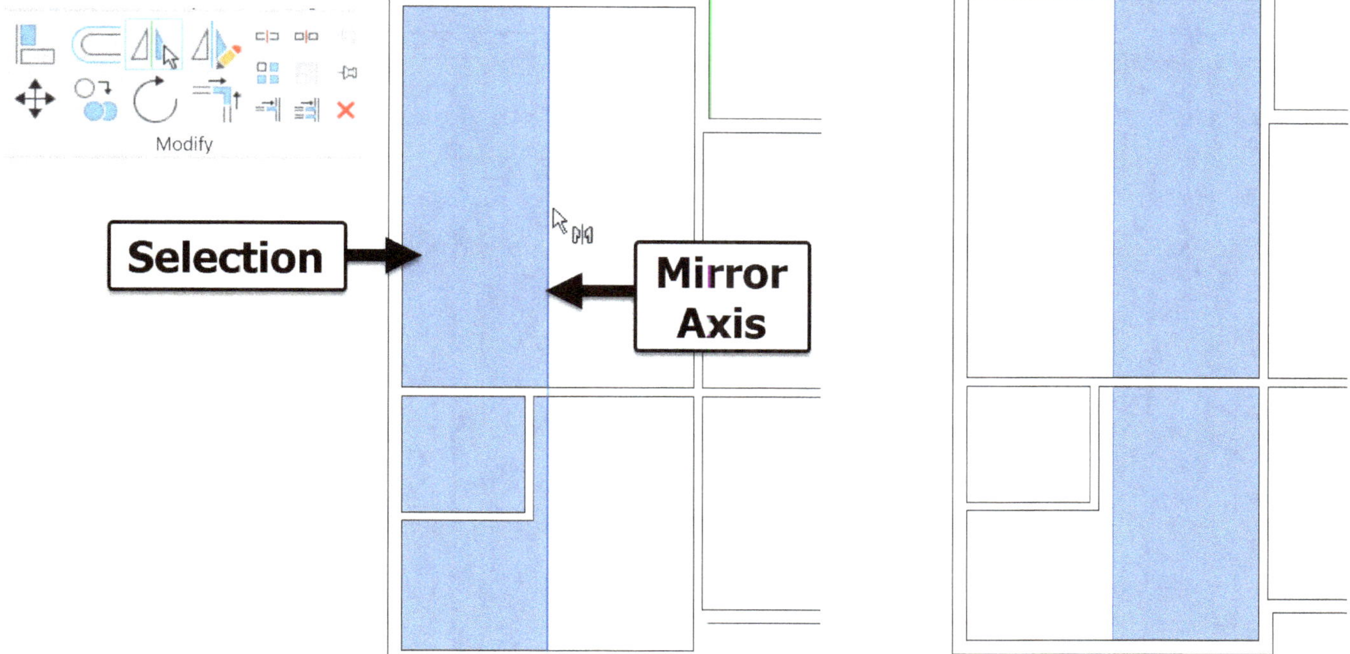

- Create section view at the location, as shown. Next, select the section view and select **Go to View**.

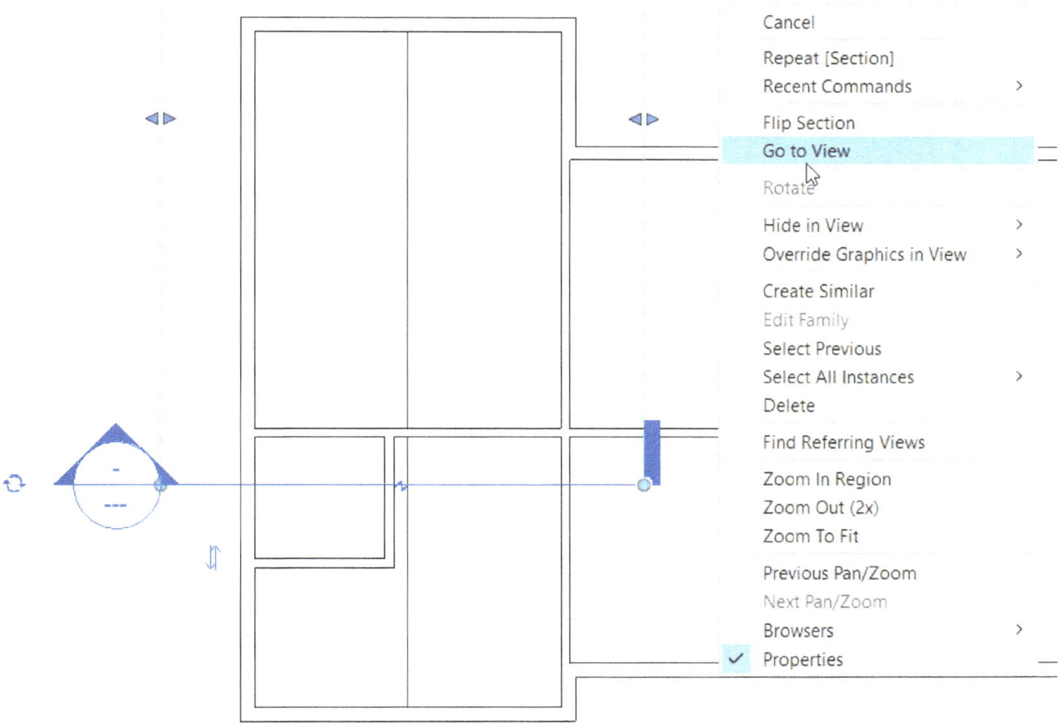

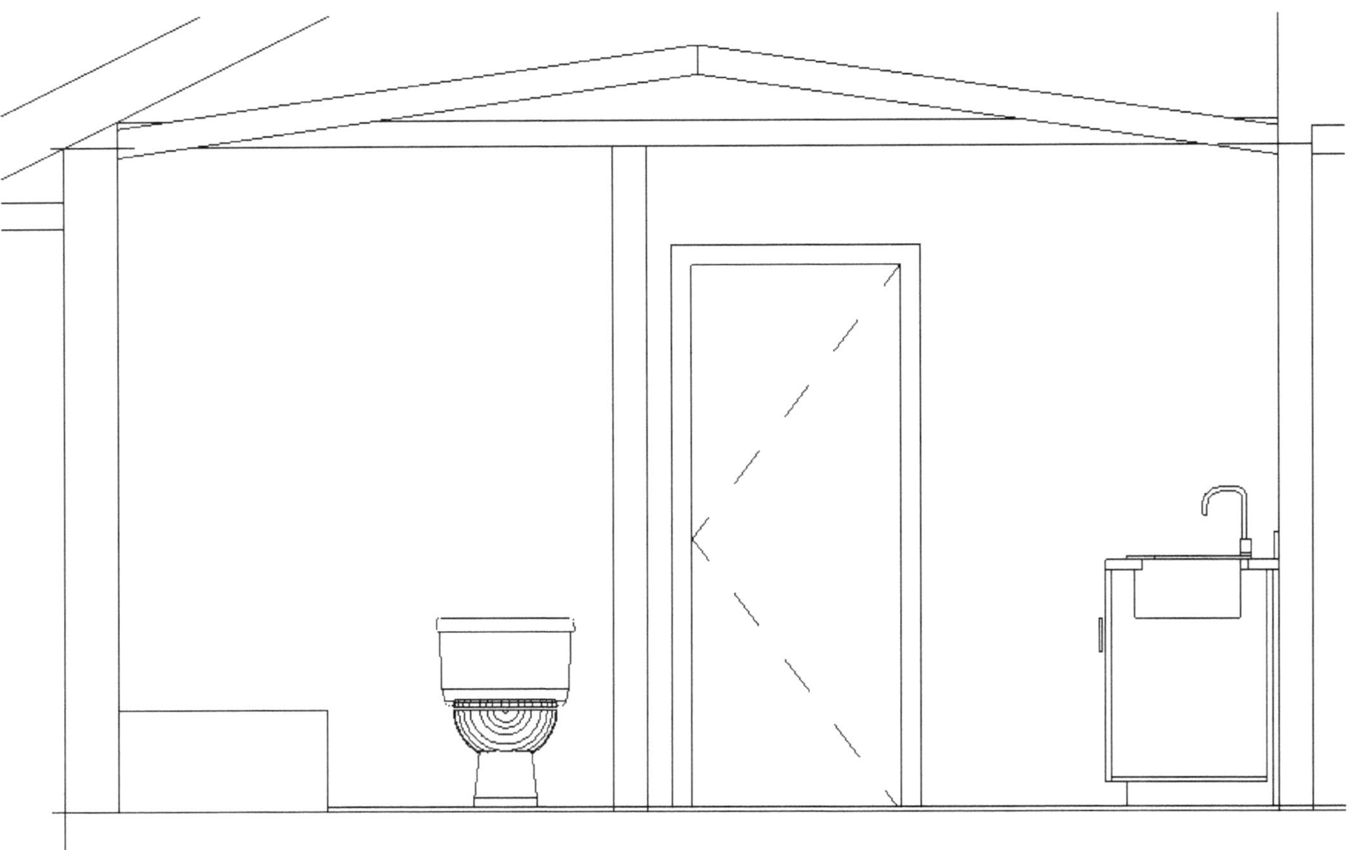

- Double-click on the **FIRST FLOOR** under the **Ceiling Plans** node on the Project Browser.
- Press and hold the CTRL key and select the three walls, as shown.
- On the ribbon, click **Modify| Walls** tab > **Modify Walls** panel > **Attach Top/Base**.
- On the Options Bar, select **Attach Wall > Top**. Next, select the left portion of the vaulted ceiling, as shown.

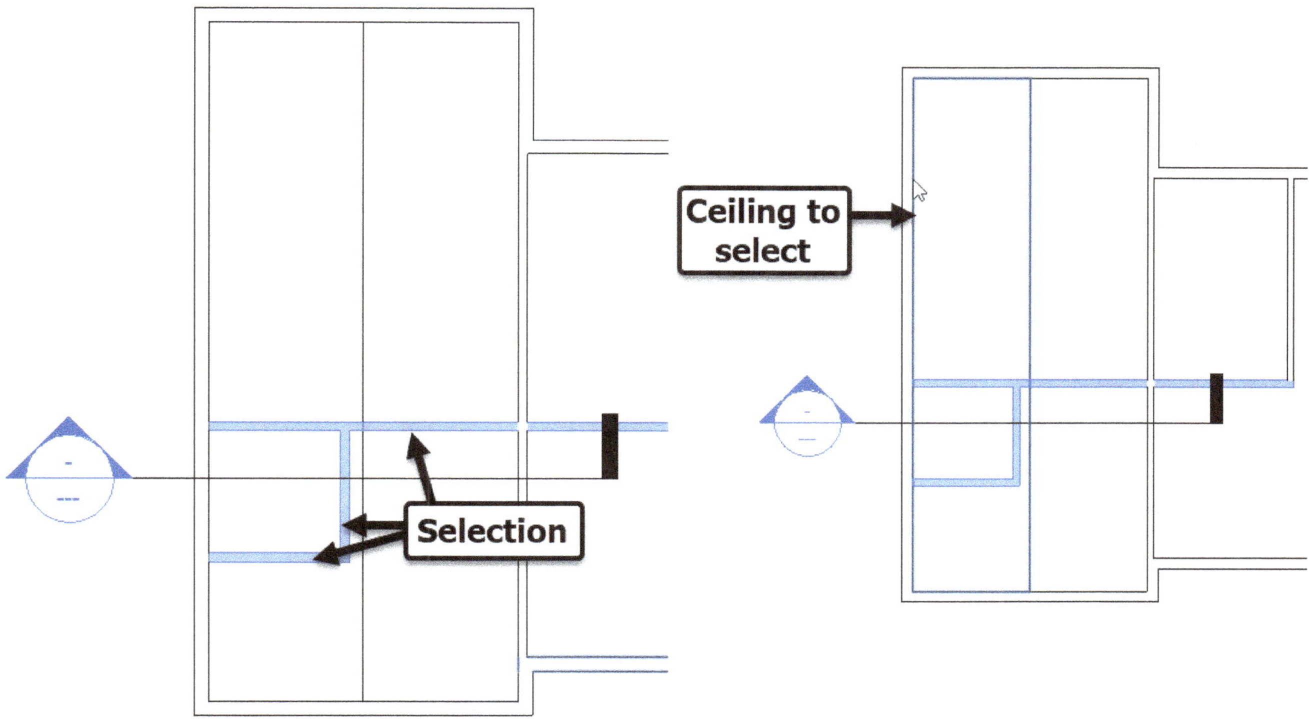

- Click in the graphic window, and then select the wall, as shown.
- On the ribbon, click **Modify| Walls** tab > **Modify Walls** panel > **Attach Top/Base**.
- On the Options Bar, select **Attach Wall > Top**. Next, select the right portion of the vaulted ceiling, as shown.

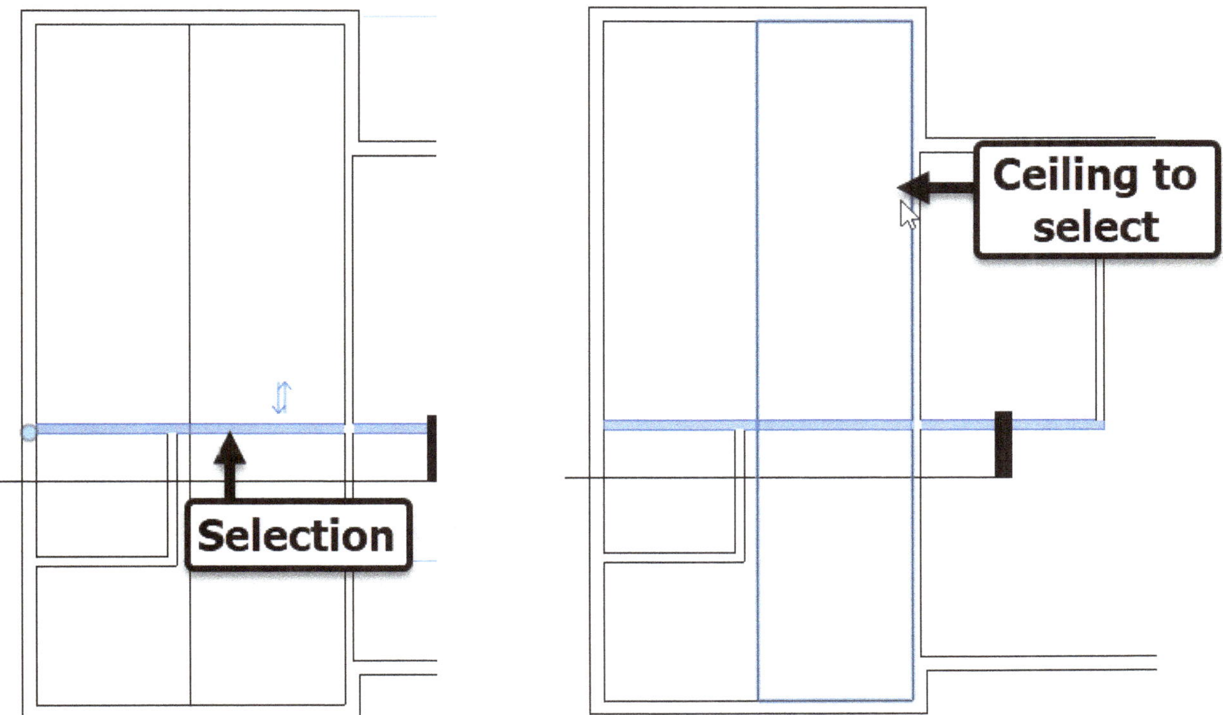

- Select the newly created Section View, right-click and then select **Go to View**. Notice that the walls are attached to the vaulted ceiling.

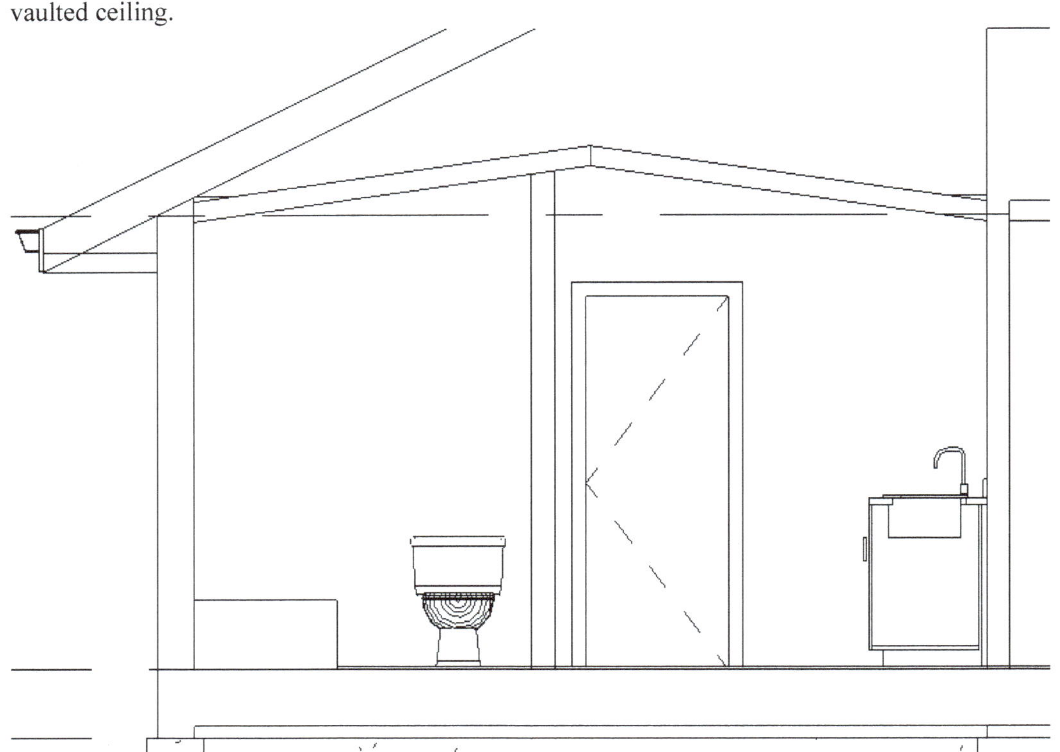

Tutorial 11: Add Lights and Electrical Fixtures

- In the Project Browser, double-click the **FIRST FLOOR** option under the **Ceiling Plans** node.
- On the ribbon, click **Systems > Electrical > Lighting Fixture**. Next, click **Yes** to load the lighting fixtures into the project.

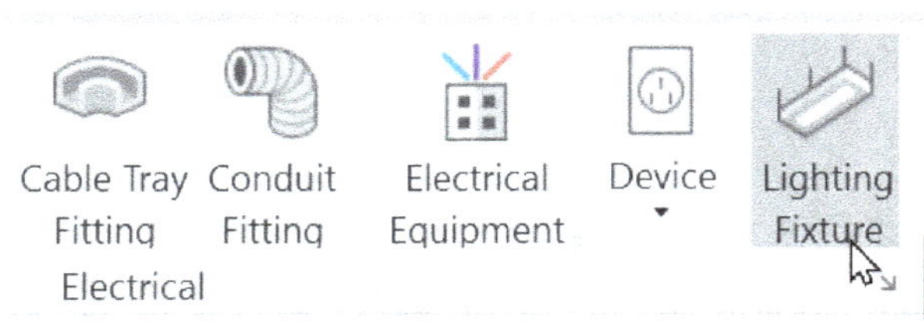

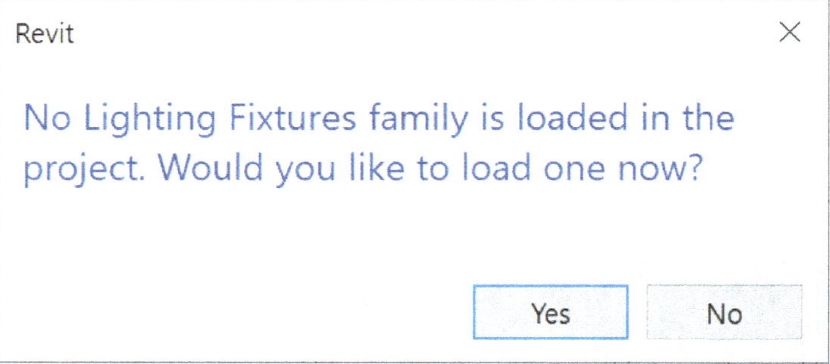

- Go to **Local Disc C > Program Data > Autodesk > RVT 2024 > Libraries > English Imperial > Lighting > Architectural > Internal**. Next, press and hold the CTRL key and select **Wall Lamp – Bracket, Pendant Light – Hemisphere, Ceiling Light – Linear Box**, and **Ceiling Light - Flat Round**. Next, click **Open**.
- On the **Properties** palette, from the **Type Selector** drop-down, select the **Ceiling Light – Linear Box 2'X2'(2 Lamp) - 120V** type.
- Zoom to the top-left corner of the floor plan and click at the location, as shown. Next, press ESC twice.
- Select the newly inserted light and click on the dimension associated with it. Next, type 16 and press ENTER.

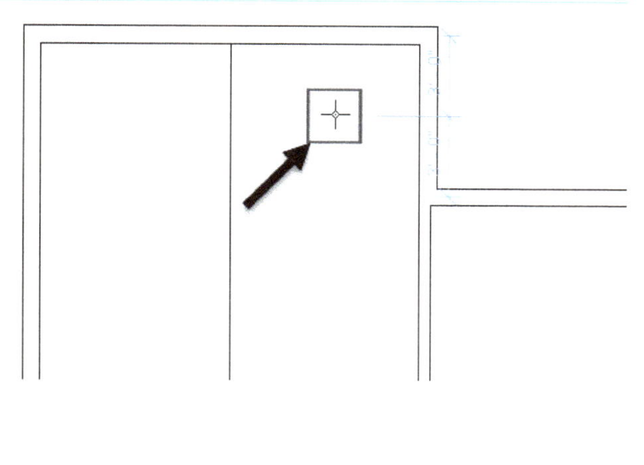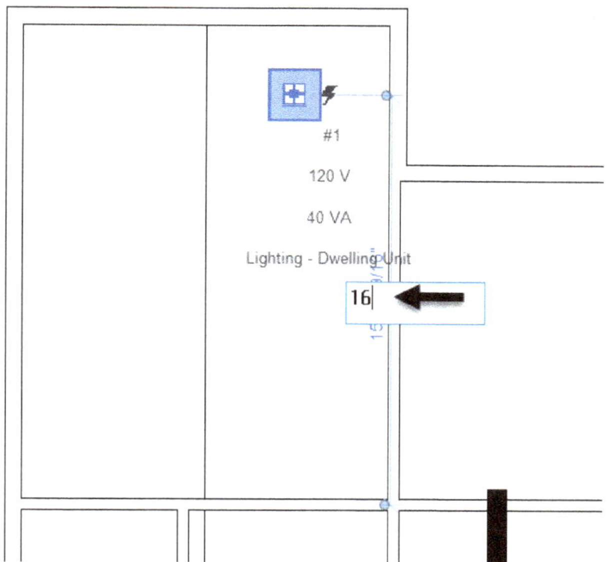

- Select the ceiling light and click **Modify | Lighting Fixtures** tab > **Modify** > **Array** on the ribbon.
- On the Options Bar, make sure that the **Linear** icon is selected.
- Type **5** in the **Number** box and select the **Last** option.

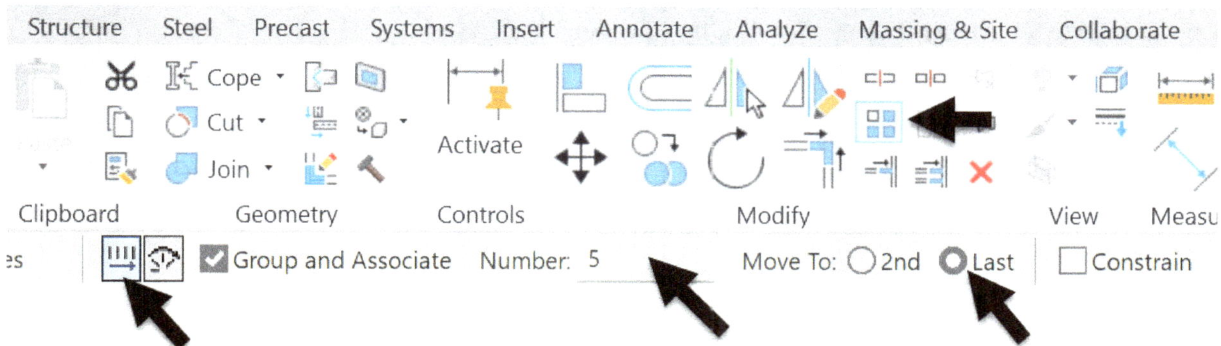

- Select the midpoint of the ceiling light to specify the start point.
- Move the pointer downward and click to the define the end point of the linear pattern. Next, click in the graphics window.

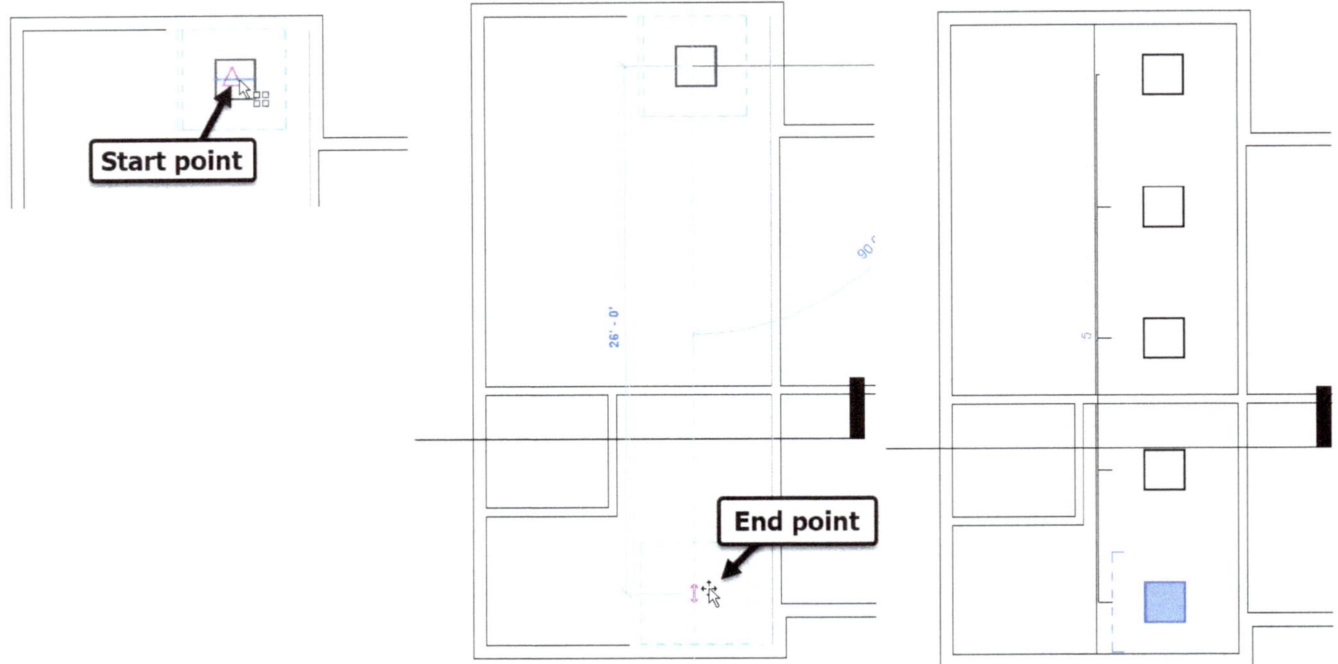

- Press and hold the CTRL key and select all the elements of the linear pattern.
- On the ribbon, click **Model | Model Groups** tab > **Modify > Mirror – Pick Axis**.
- Select the edge of the vaulted ceiling to define the mirror axis.

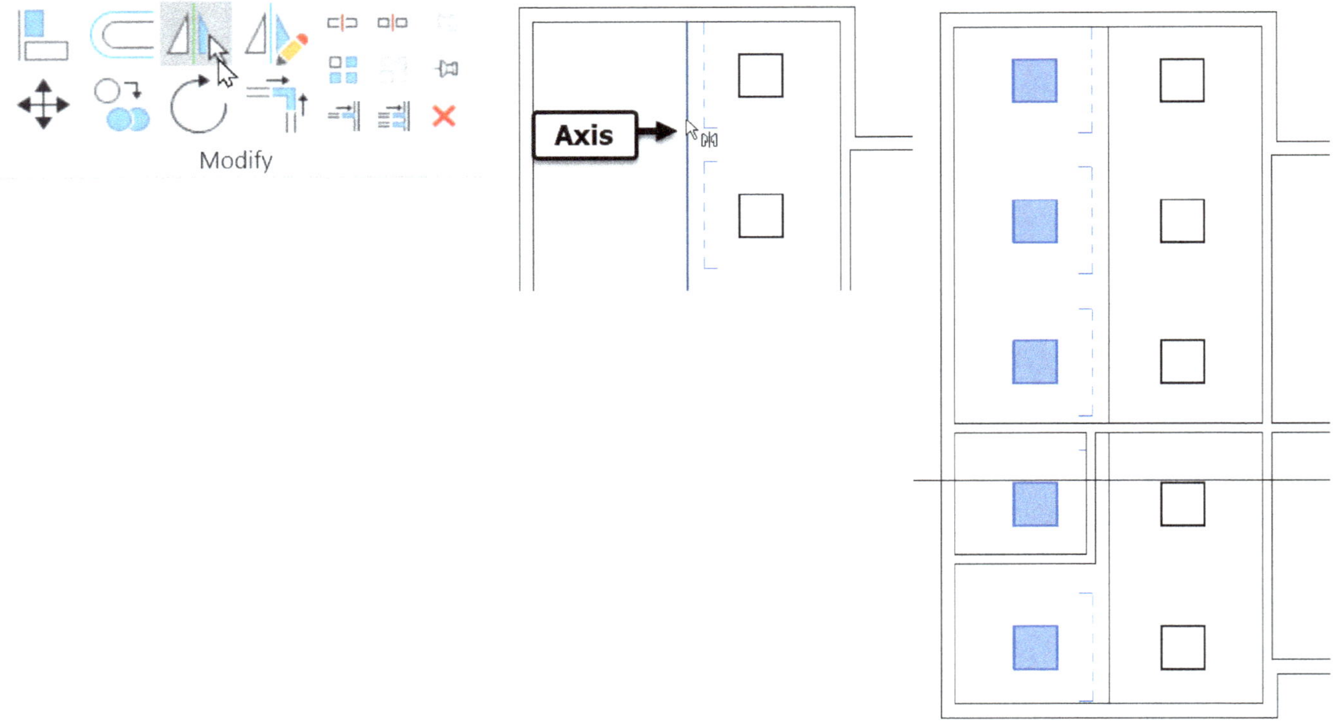

- On the ribbon, click **Systems > Electrical > Lighting Fixture**  .

- On the **Properties** palette, from the **Type Selector** drop-down, select the **Ceiling Light – Flat Round 100W - 120V** type.
- Click in the closet area next to the vaulted ceiling bedroom. Next, press ESC twice.
- Select the newly inserted light. Click the and drag the witness line downward, and then place it on the dotted line, as shown.

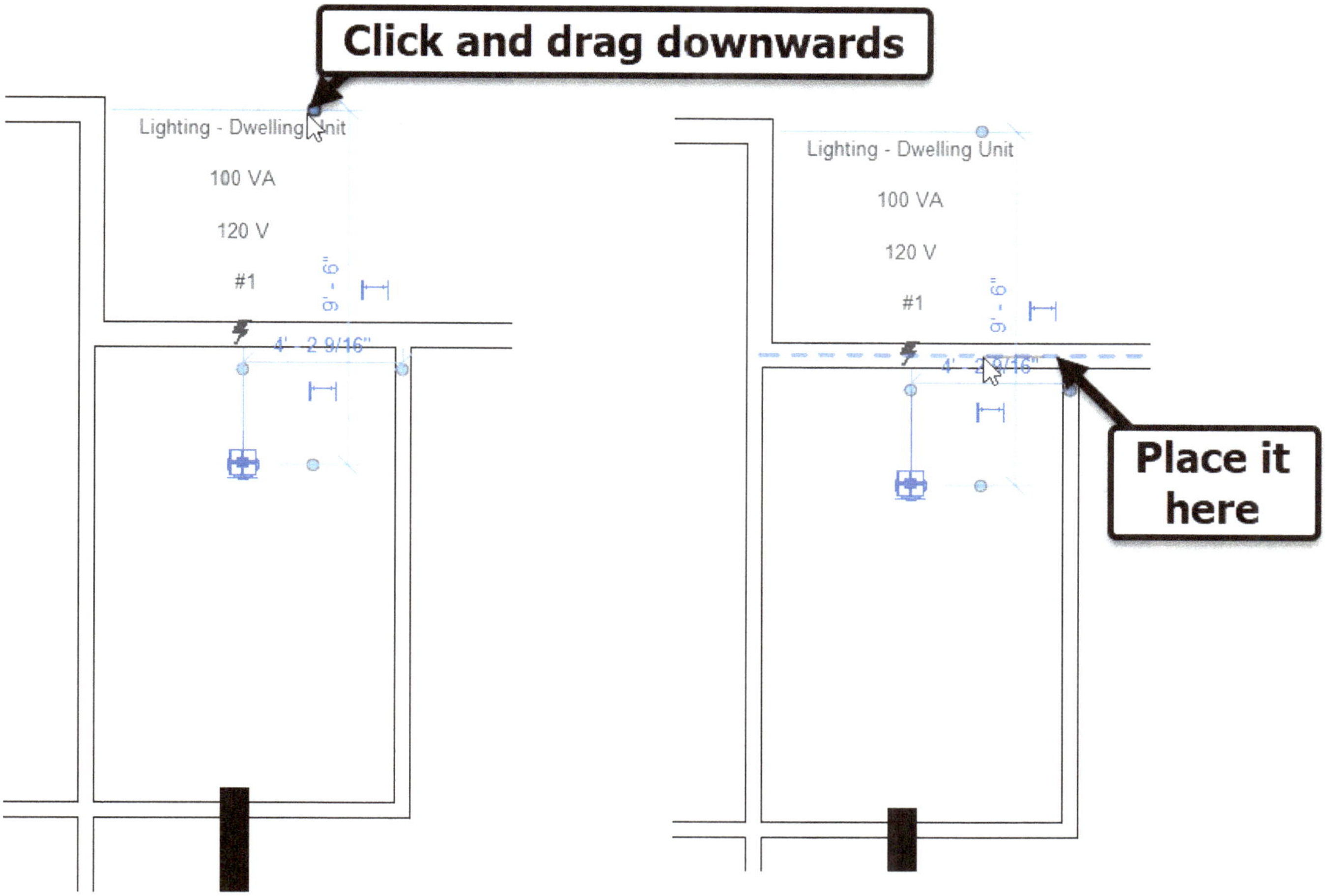

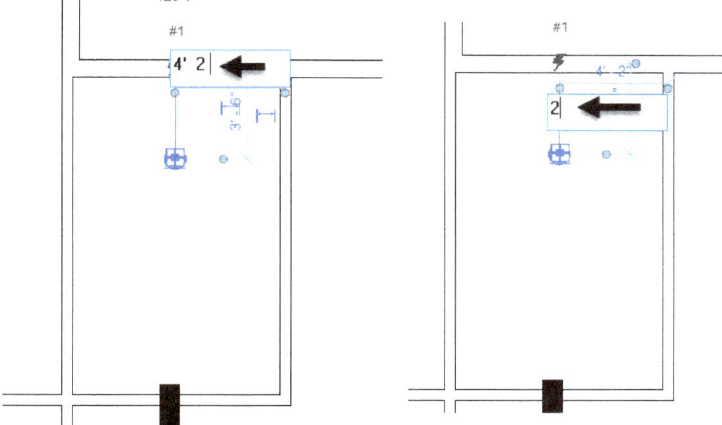

- Change the location dimensions of the light, as shown.

- Select the newly inserted light, if not already selected.
- Click **Modify | Lighting Fixtures** tab > **Modify > Array** on the ribbon.
- On the Options Bar, make sure that the **Linear** icon is selected. Type **3** in the **Number** box and select the **2nd** option

- Select the midpoint of the ceiling light to specify the start point.
- Move the pointer downward and click when the dimension between the two ceiling lights is 4'. Next, click in the graphics window.

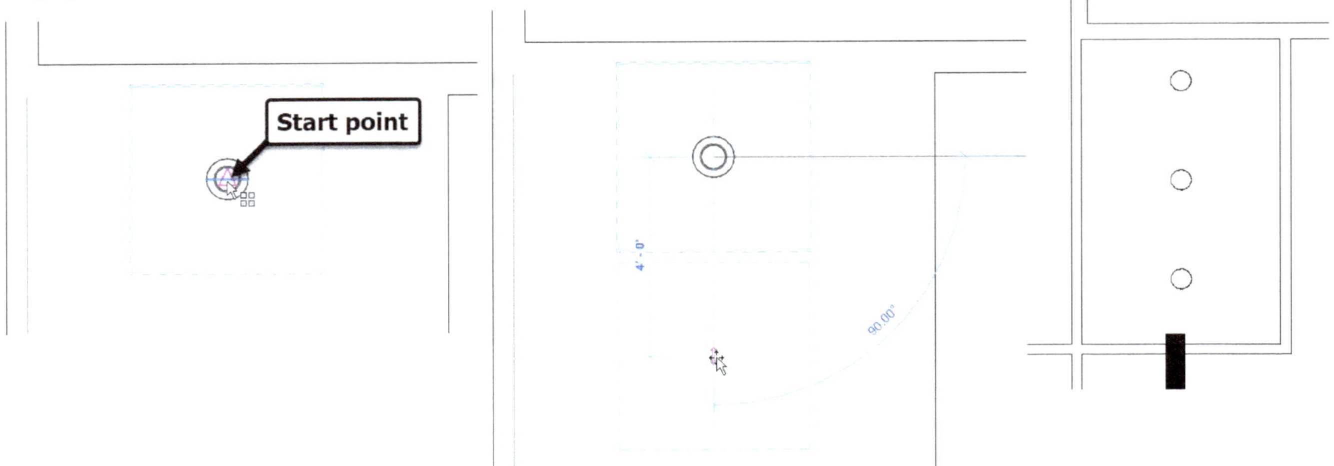

- On the ribbon, click **Systems > Electrical > Lighting Fixture**. Next, click **Yes** to load the lighting fixtures into the project.
- On the **Properties** palette, from the **Type Selector** drop-down, select the **Ceiling Light – Flat Round 100W - 120V** type.
- Click in the top left corner of the living room. Next, change its location dimensions, as shown.

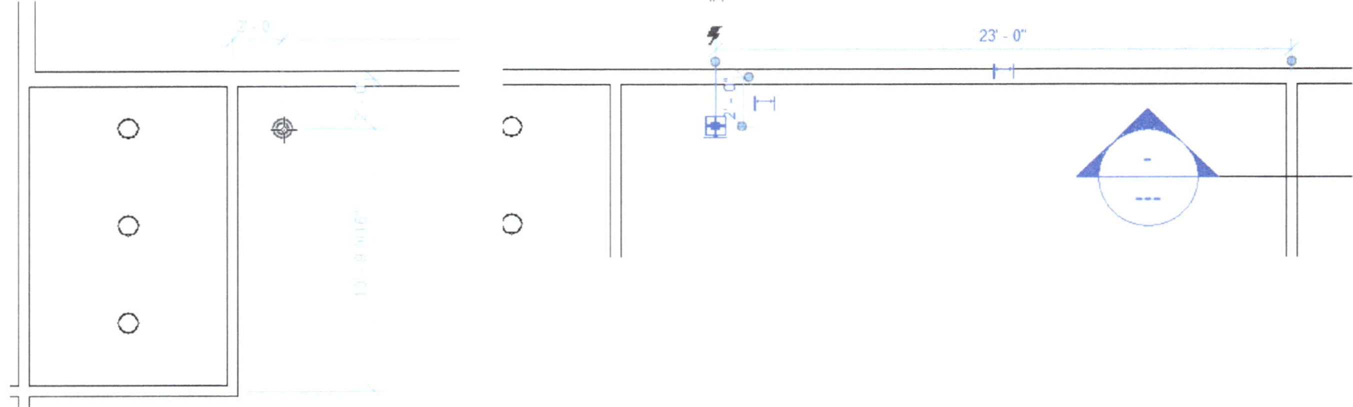

- Select the newly inserted light, if not already selected.
- Click **Modify | Lighting Fixtures** tab > **Modify > Array** on the ribbon.
- On the Options Bar, make sure that the **Linear** icon is selected. Next, select the **2nd** option
- Select the midpoint of the ceiling light to specify the start point.
- Move the pointer downward and click when the dimension between the two ceiling lights is 4'.
- Type 6 as the number of instances. Next, click in the graphics window.

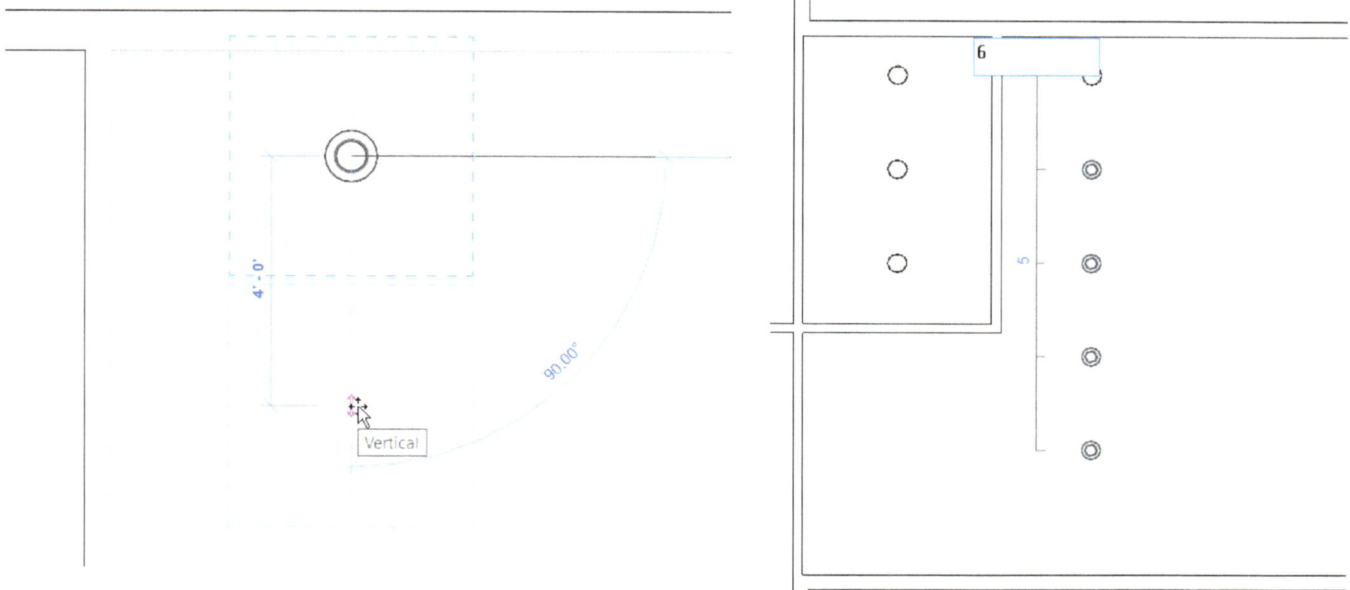

- Press and hold the CTRL key and select all the instances of the linear pattern.
- Click **Modify | Lighting Fixtures** tab > **Modify > Array** on the ribbon.
- On the Options Bar, make sure that the **Linear** icon is selected. Next, select the **2nd** option
- Select the midpoint of the ceiling light to specify the start point.
- Move the pointer toward right and click when the dimension between the two ceiling lights is 6'.

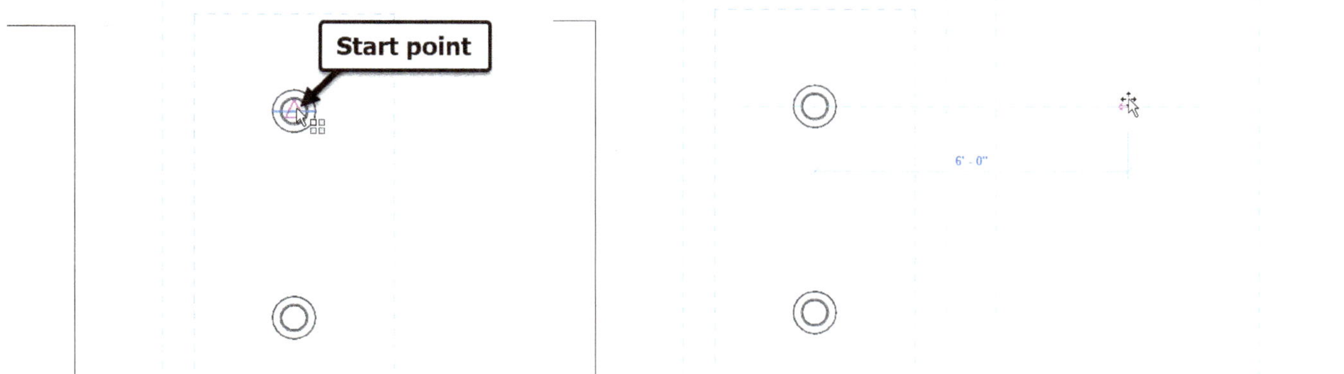

- Type 4 as the number of instances. Next, click in the graphics window.

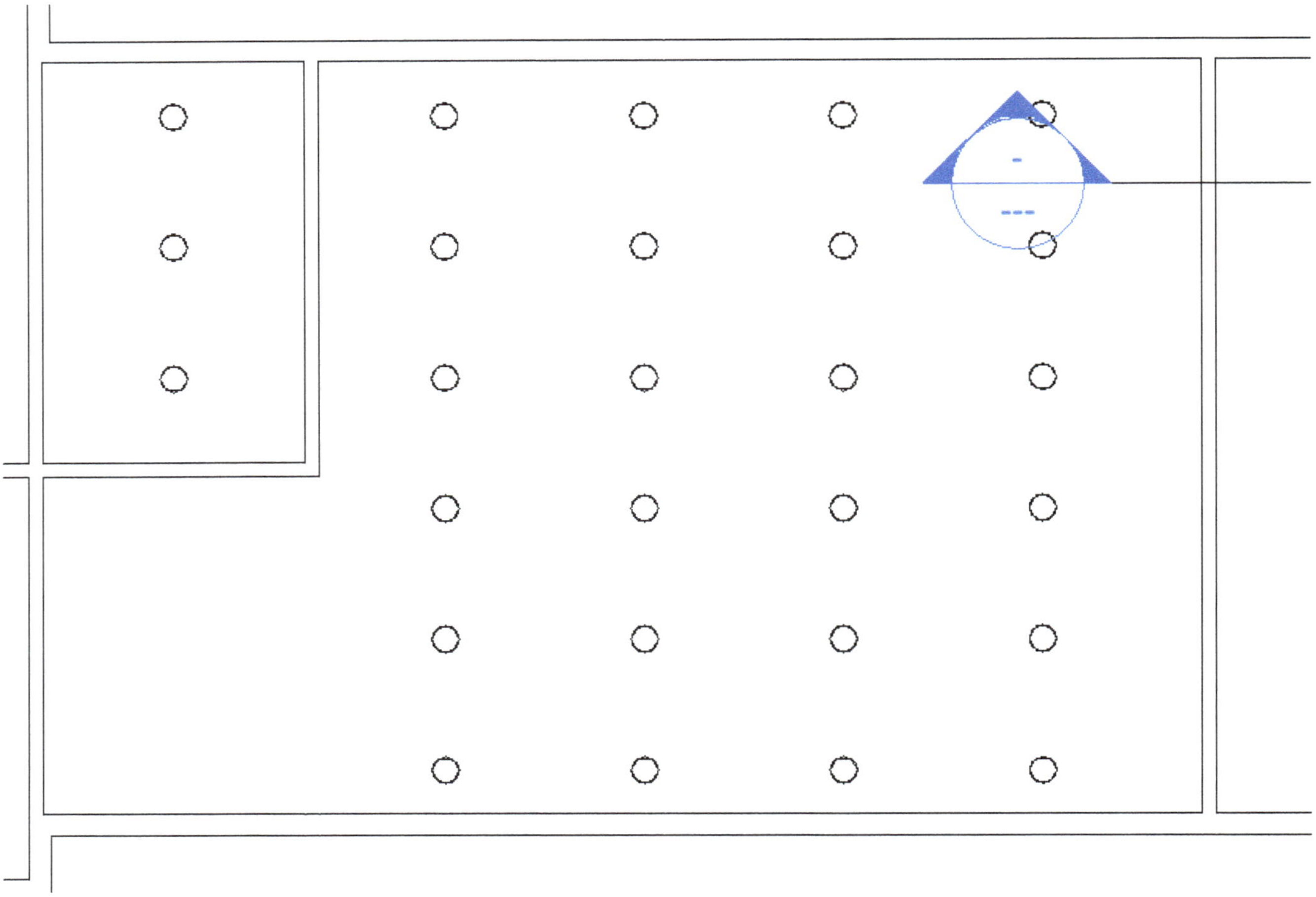

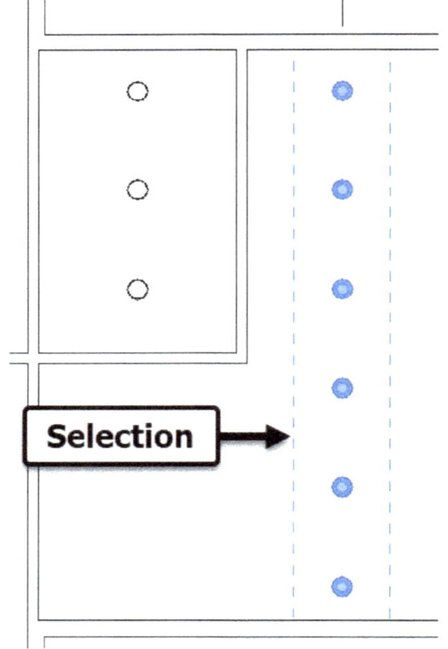

- Select the array group on the left-side and click the **Ungroup** icon on the **Modify | Model Groups** ribbon tab.

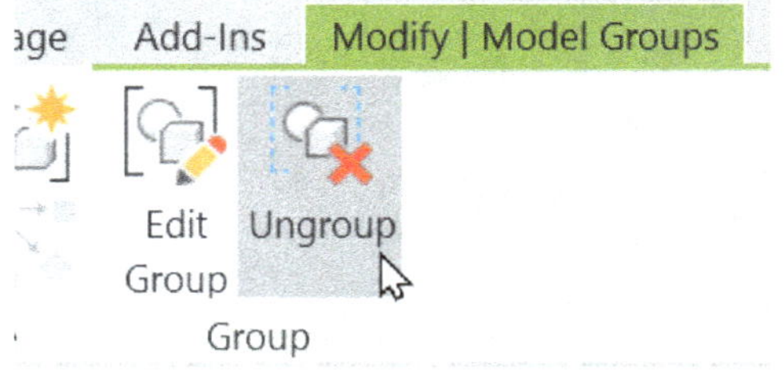

- Press and hold the CTRL key and select the bottom three lights, as shown.

- On the ribbon, click **Modify > Modify > Copy**. Next, select the midpoint of the bottom-most light.
- Move the pointer toward left and click when the dimension between the two ceiling lights is 5'.

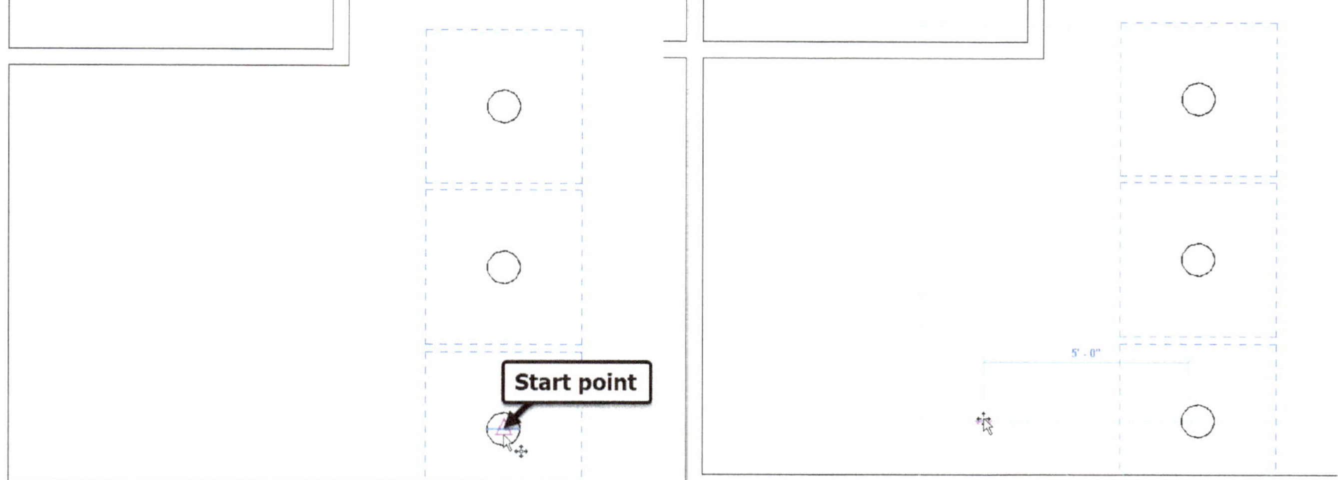

- Again, move the pointer toward left and click when the dimension between the two ceiling lights is 5'.

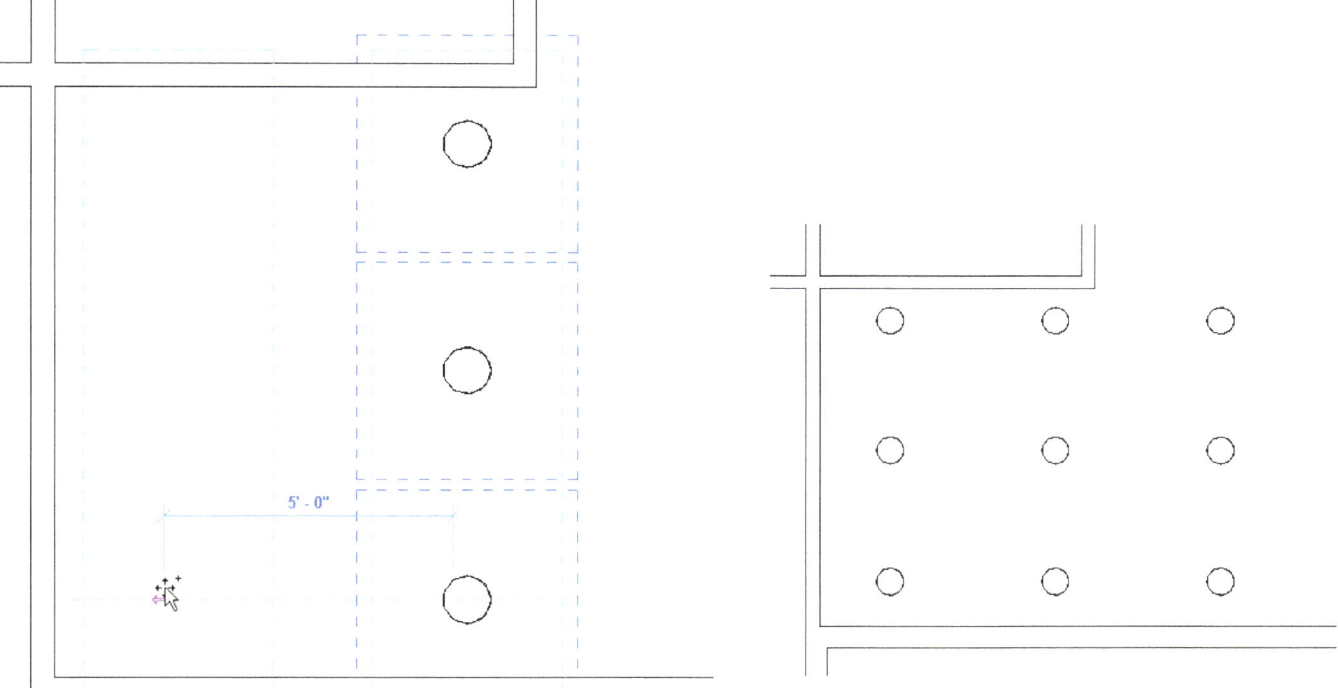

- Likewise, add ceiling lights to the kitchen, laundry, bathrooms, mudroom, and bedrooms.

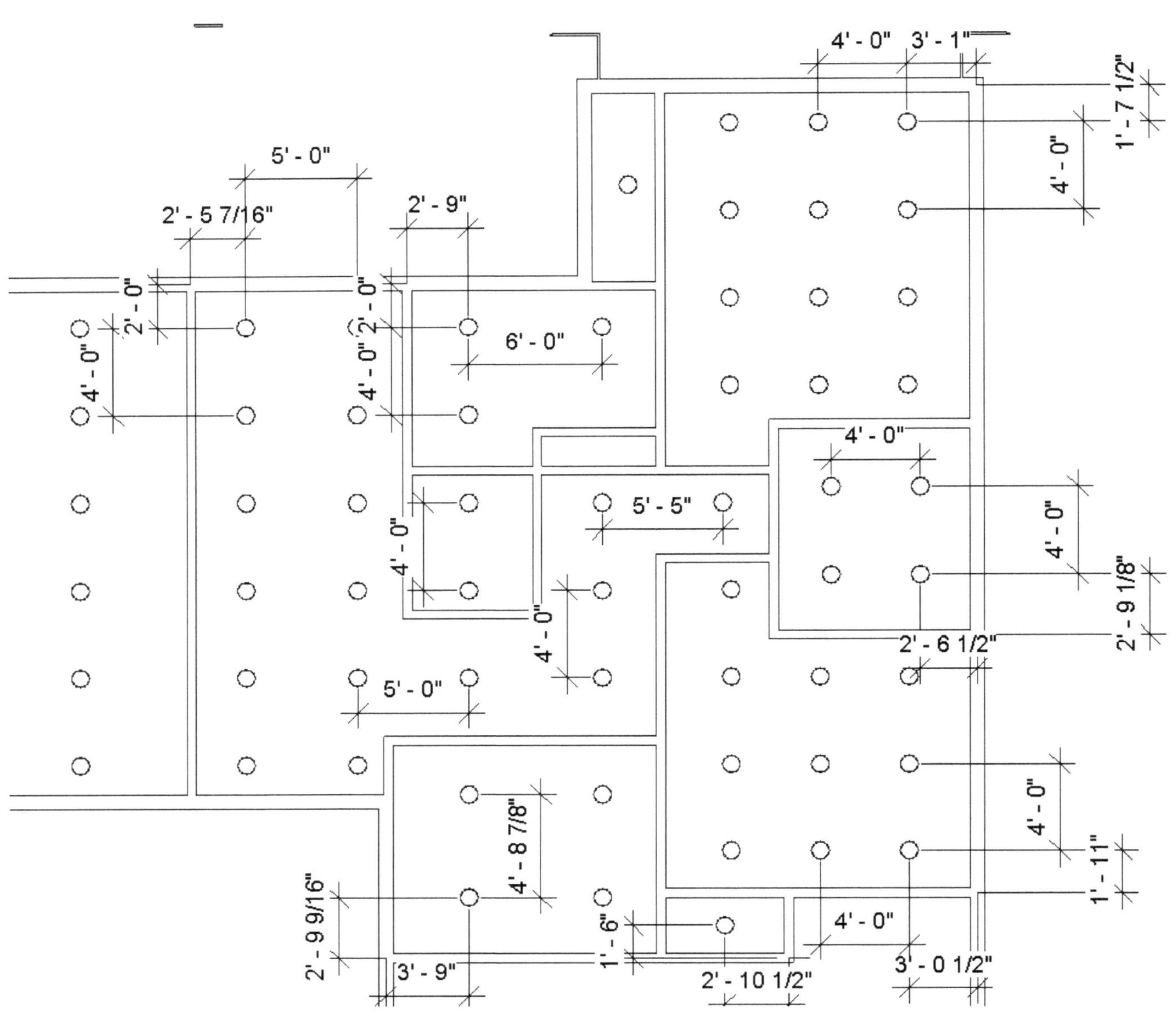

4' - 0"
3' - 1"
1' - 7 1/2"
4' - 0"
5' - 0"
2' - 5 7/16"
2' - 9"
2' - 0"
2' - 0"
4' - 0"
2' - 0"
4' - 0"
6' - 0"
4' - 0"
4' - 0"
4' - 0"
5' - 5"
4' - 0"
4' - 0"
2' - 9 1/8"
2' - 6 1/2"
5' - 0"
4' - 8 7/8"
4' - 0"
1' - 11"
2' - 9 9/16"
3' - 9"
1' - 6"
4' - 0"
2' - 10 1/2"
3' - 0 1/2"

Part 2: Creating Views

Tutorial 1: Creating Elevation Views

In Revit, the elevations are generated using the elevation tags placed in a plan view. You can notice four elevation tags around the parameter of the plan view. The elevation tag has two parts: **Body** and **Elevation Mark**.

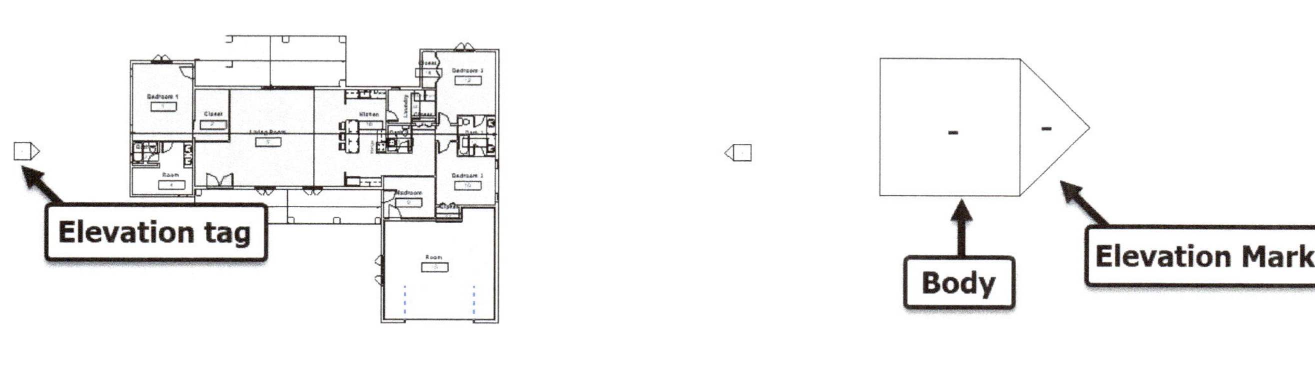

You can add a new elevation mark to the elevation tag. To do this, select the body of the elevation tag; the elevation marks are displayed on all its sides. Next, select anyone of the check boxes displayed above the elevation marks, and then click in the graphics window. On doing so, a new elevation view is added to the **Elevations** section of the Project Browser.

To remove the newly created elevation view, select the body of the elevation tag and uncheck the check box. Next, click **OK** and click in the graphics window.

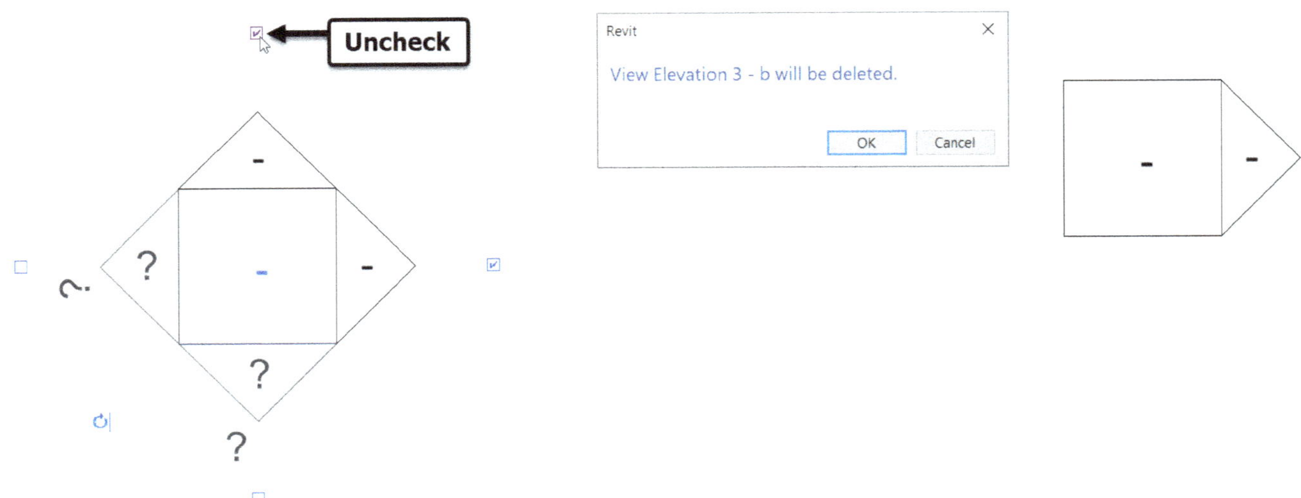

Zoom-out and select the elevation mark arrow and notice a line. It defines the extents of the elevation view.

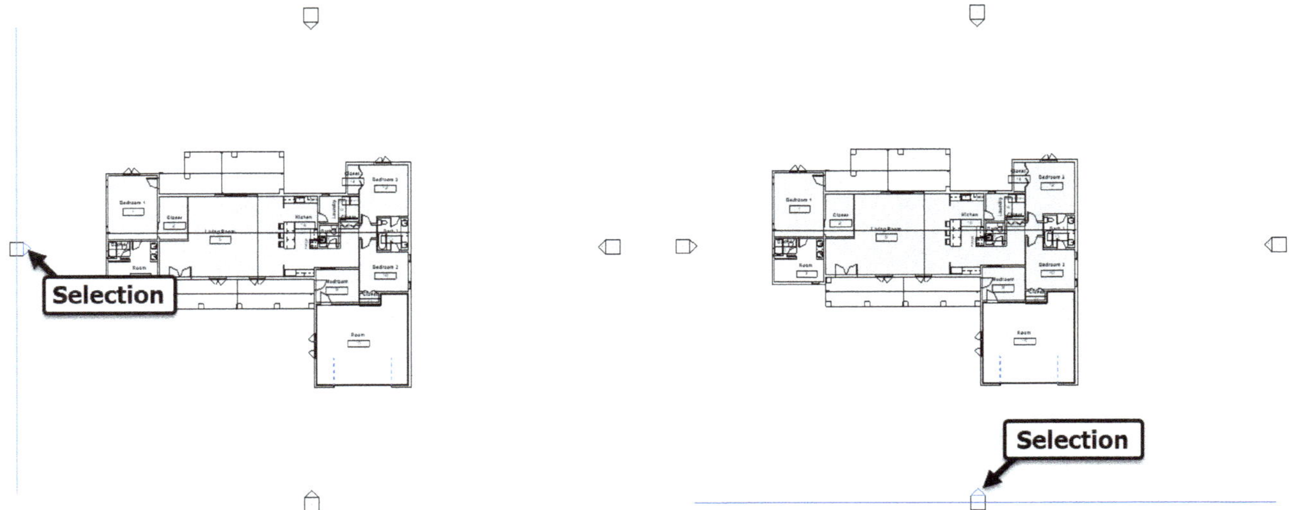

To view anyone of the existing elevation views, double-click on their elevation marks (or) double-click on anyone of the views under the **Elevations** node in the Project Browser.

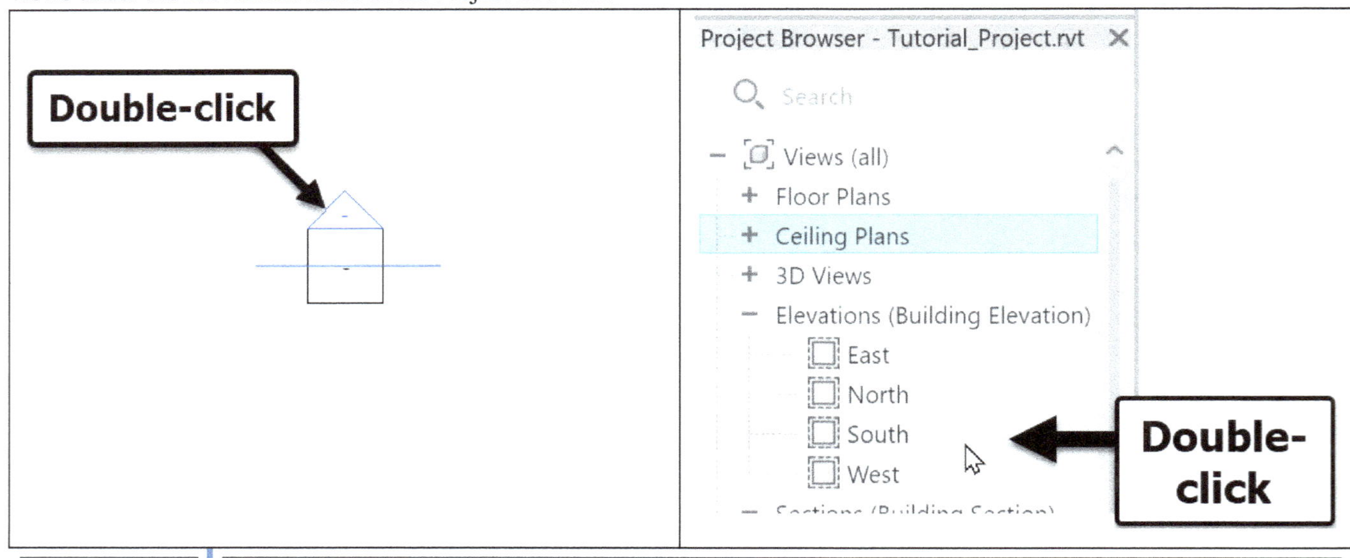

Close the South elevation tab to close the south elevation.

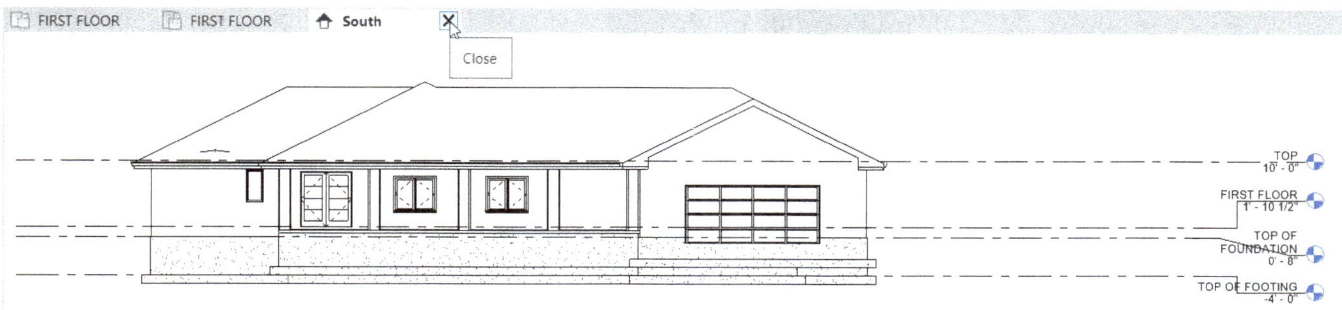

In addition to the existing elevation views, you can also create new elevation views.

- On the ribbon, click the **View** tab > **Create** panel > **Elevation**.
- On the Properties palette, from the **Type Selector**, select **Elevation: Building Elevation**.

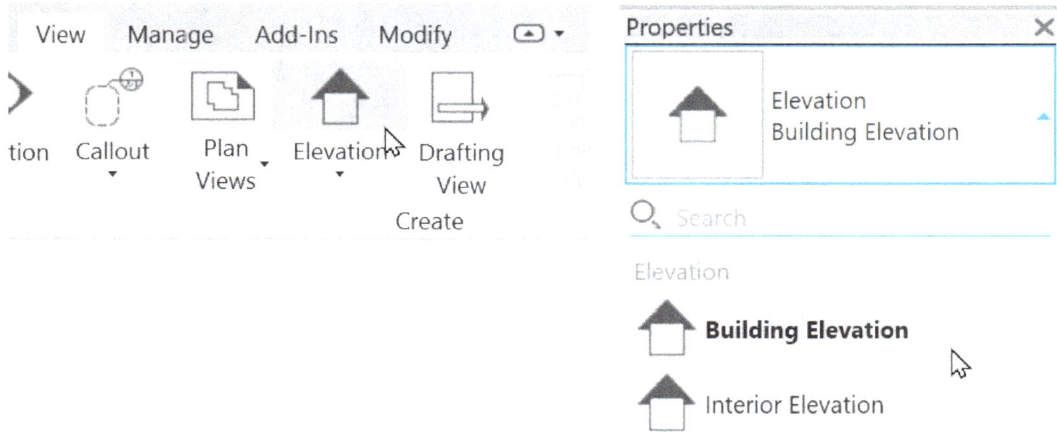

Next, move the pointer around the building and notice that the elevation tag always points to the closest wall.

- Place the pointer near the front porch of the building. Next, press ESC twice.

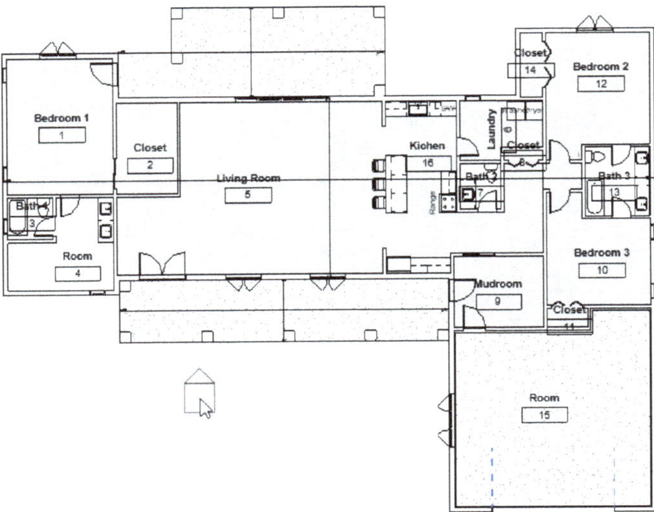

- Select the elevation mark and notice a horizontal line and the dashed boundary. The dashed boundary defines the view depth of the elevation view.

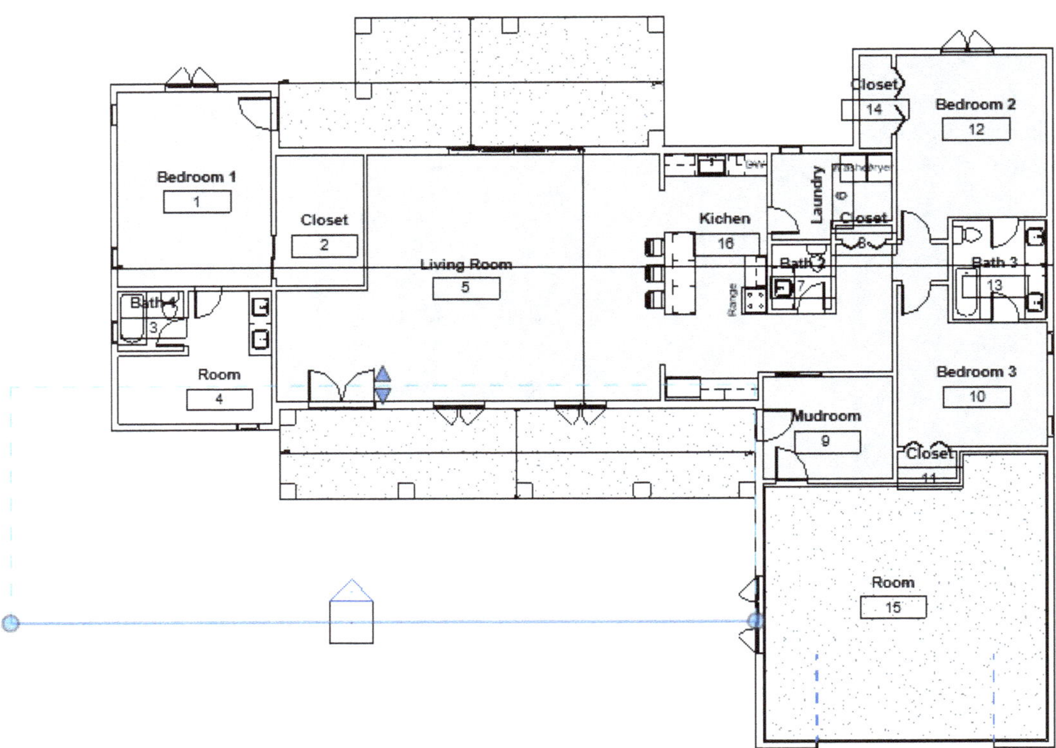

You can change the extents of the elevation view by scrolling down to the **Extents** section of the **Properties** palette and changing the **Far Clip Offset** value (or) clicking and dragging the arrow handle displayed on the dashed line.

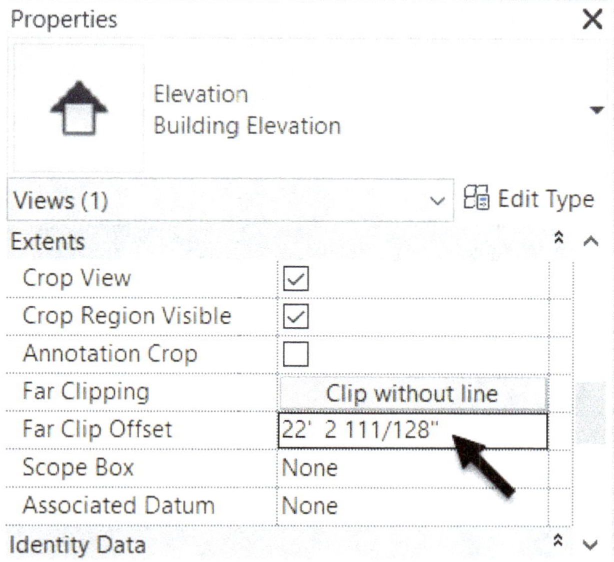

- Double-click on the elevation mark of the elevation tag; the elevation view is displayed. Notice that the only the portion of the roof that is inside the dashed boundary is displayed.
- Close the **Elevation 1 – a** tab.

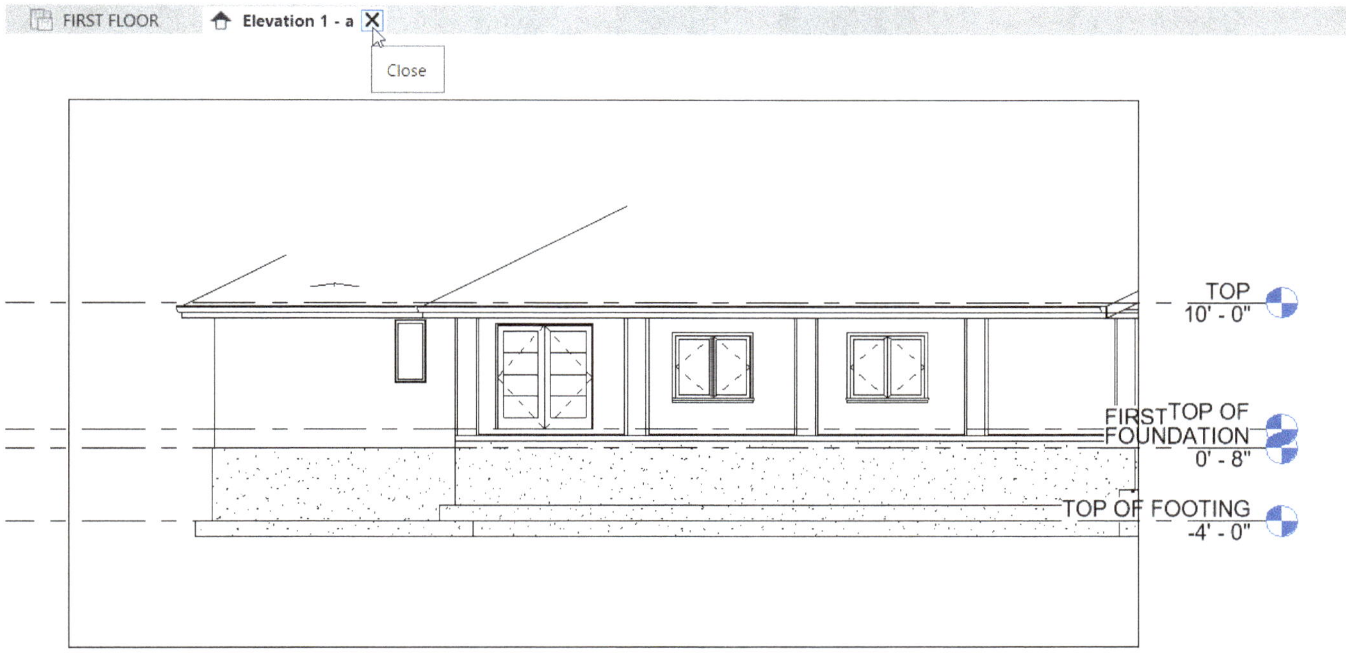

- Select the elevation mark and scroll down to the **Extents** section of the **Properties** palette.
- Click the **Clip without Line** button; the **Far Clipping dialog** pops up on the screen. It has three options: **No clip, Clip without Line**, and **Clip with line**. The **No Clip** option will create an elevation view without clipping it. The **Clip without Line** clips the elevation view using the boundary line. The **Clip with line** option clips the view and displays a line at the intersection of the model and the clipping plane.

Properties
Elevation
Building Elevation
Views (1)
Edit Type
Extents
Crop View
Crop Region Visible
Annotation Crop
Far Clipping   Clip without line
Far Clip Offset   36' 2 59/128"
Scope Box   None
Associated Datum   None
Identity Data

Far Clipping   ?   X
No clip
Clip without line
Clip with line
OK   Cancel

No clip

TOP
10' - 0"
FIRST TOP OF
FOUNDATION
0' - 8"
TOP OF FOOTING
-4' - 0"

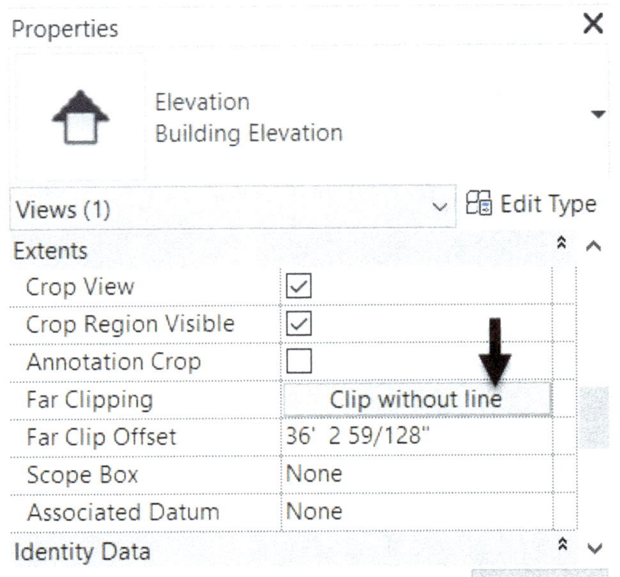

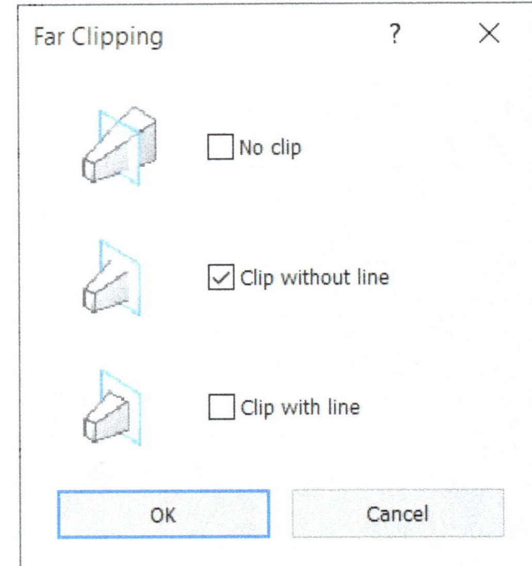

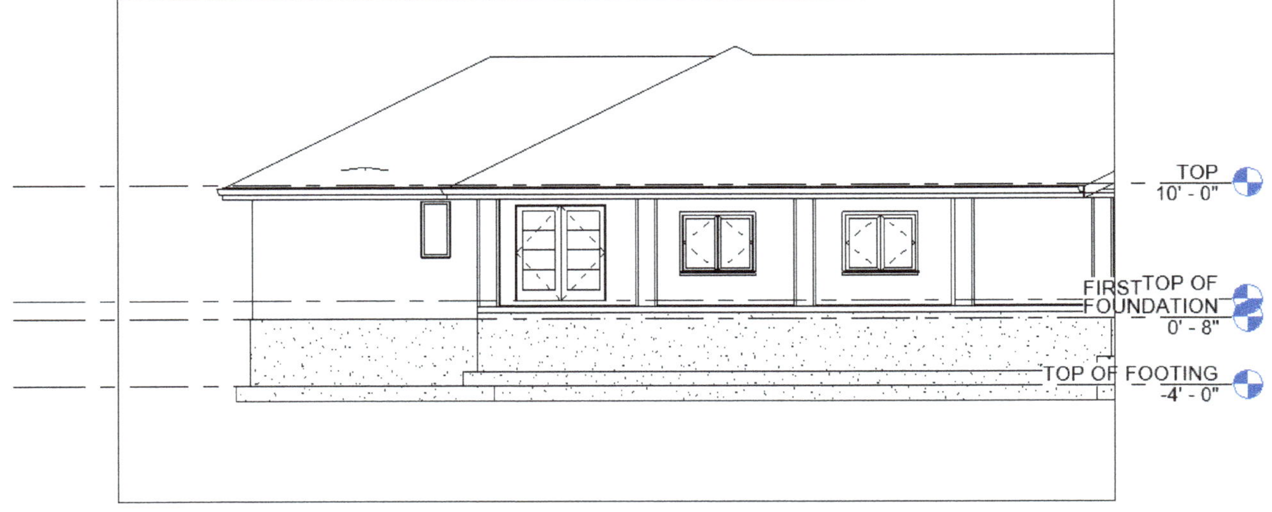

Clip without line

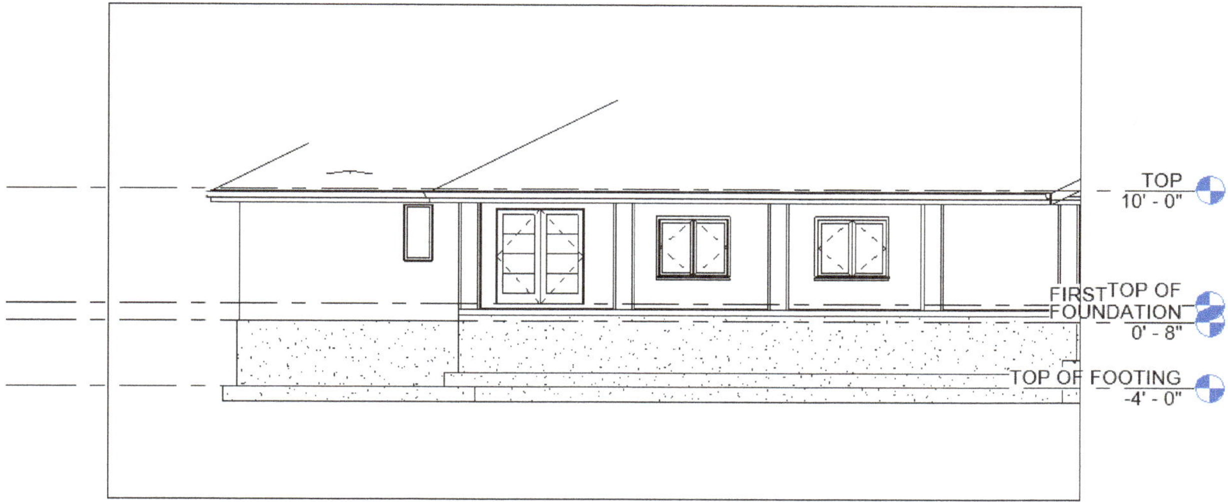

Clip with line

- Select the **Clip with line** option and click **OK**.
- Double-click on the elevation mark to open the elevation view window.
- Click and drag the segment handles of the elevation view boundary, as shown.

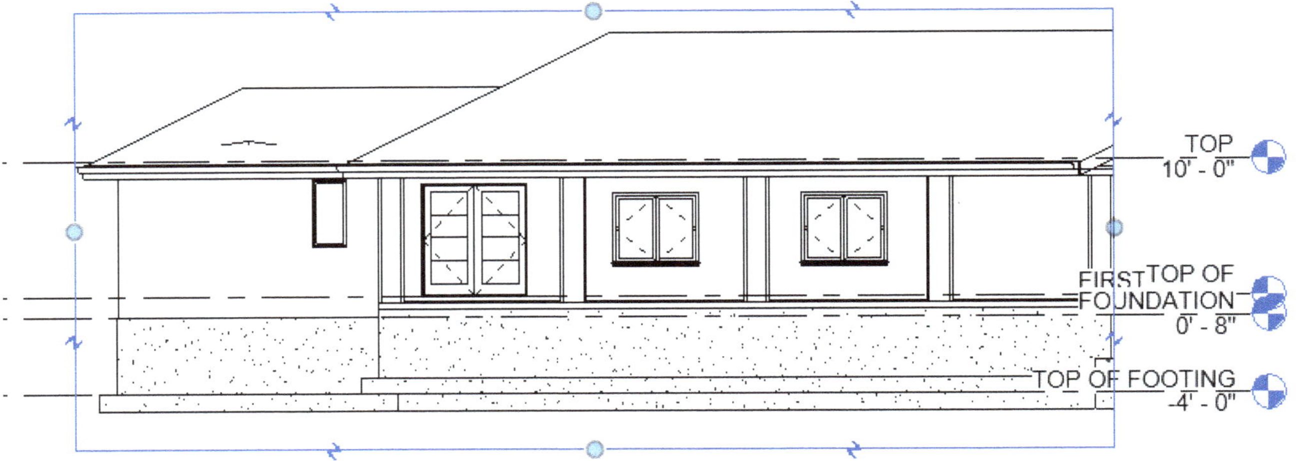

- On the Project Browser, under the **Elevations (Building Elevation)** node, right-click on the **Elevation 1 – a**, and then select **Rename**.
- Type **Front Porch** and press ENTER.

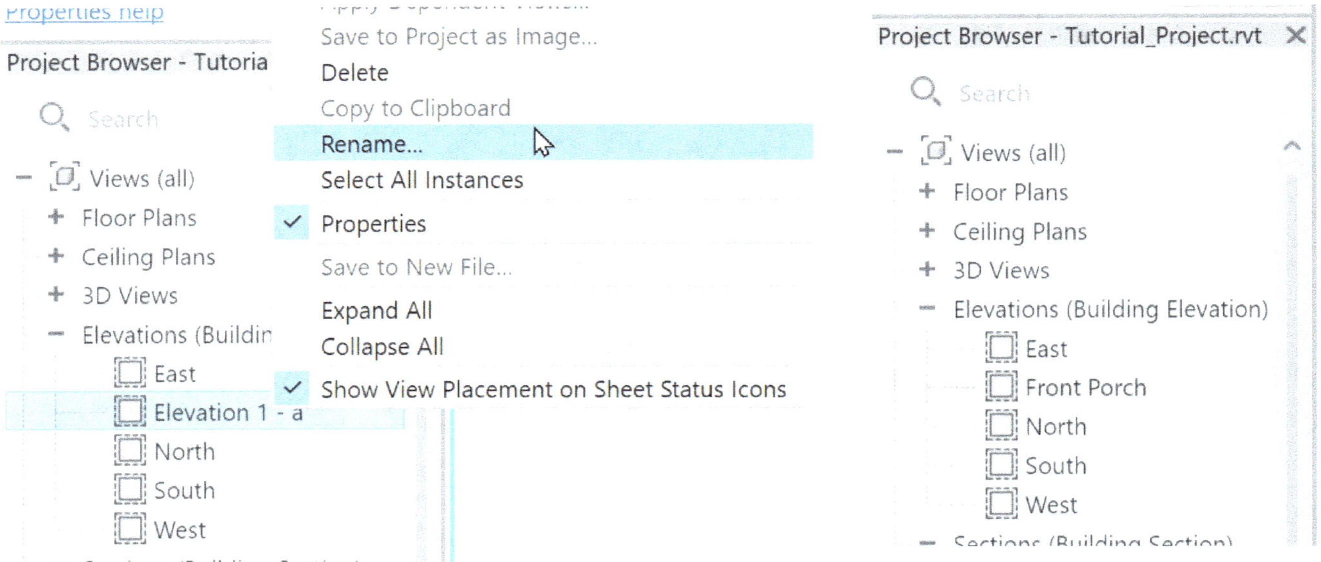

Adding Notes and Dimensions

- On the ribbon, click **Annotate > Text > Text**. Next, click the **Curved** icon on the **Leader** panel of the **Modify | Place Text** tab of the ribbon.
- On the **Properties** palette, select **¼" Arial** from the **Type Selector** drop-down.

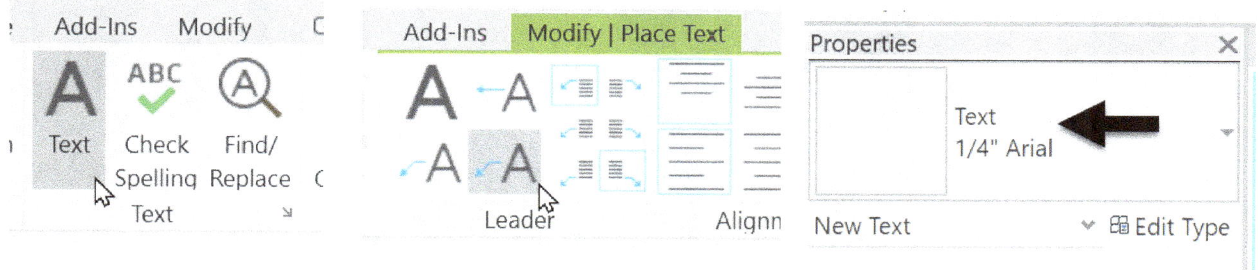

- Click on the roof, move the pointer toward right and click. Next, type **Asphalt Shingles** and click in the graphics window.

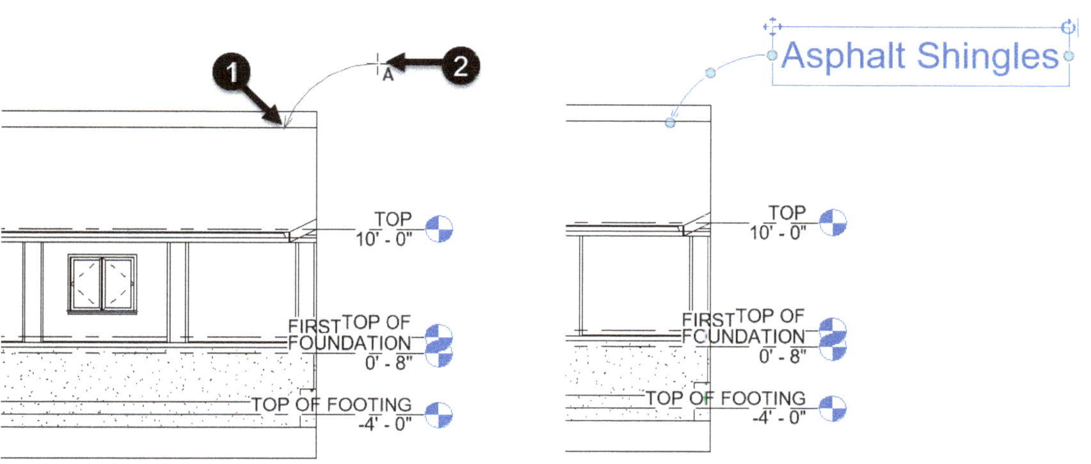

- Select the Top level; a grip is displayed at the endpoint of the top level. Also, a dotted alignment line is displayed. It means that endpoints of all the levels are aligned.
- Click and drag the endpoint of the Top level toward right; the endpoints of all the levels are move to right.

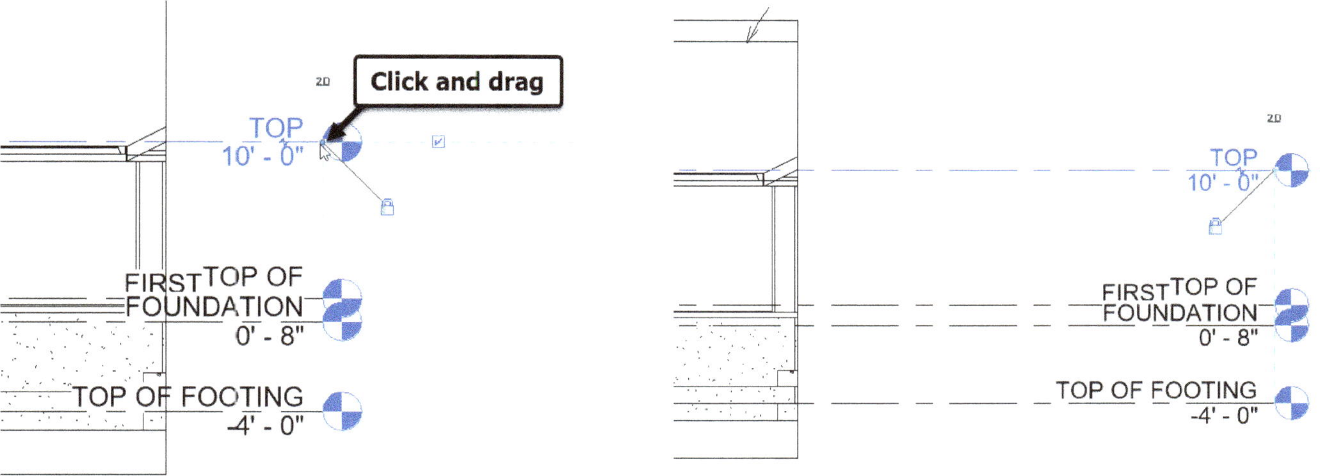

- Select the TOP OF FOOTING level and click on the Add Elbow grip; an elbow is added to the level.

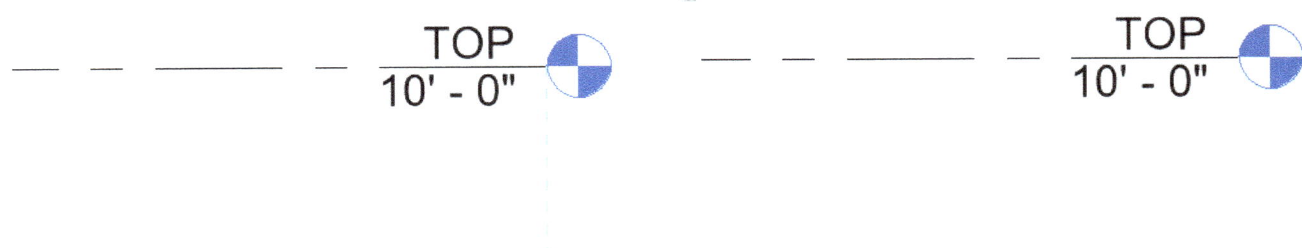

- Likewise, add an elbow to the TOP OF FOUNDATION level. Next, select the TOP OF FOUNDATION level, and then drag the lower grip of the elbow towards left.

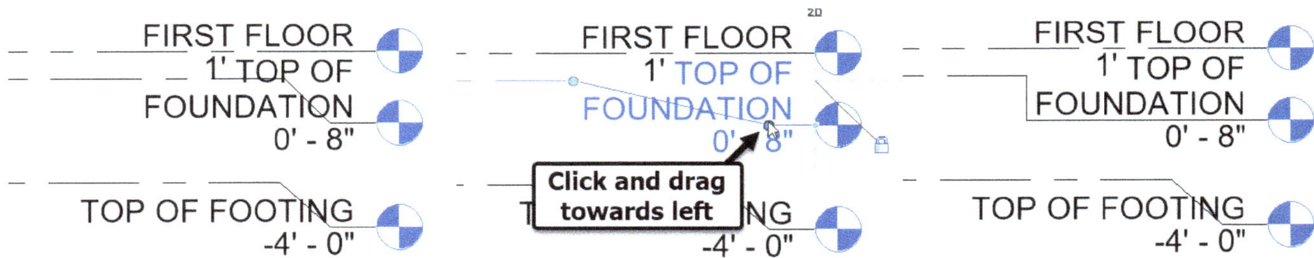

- Likewise, add elbow to the FIRST FLOOR level, and then modify it.

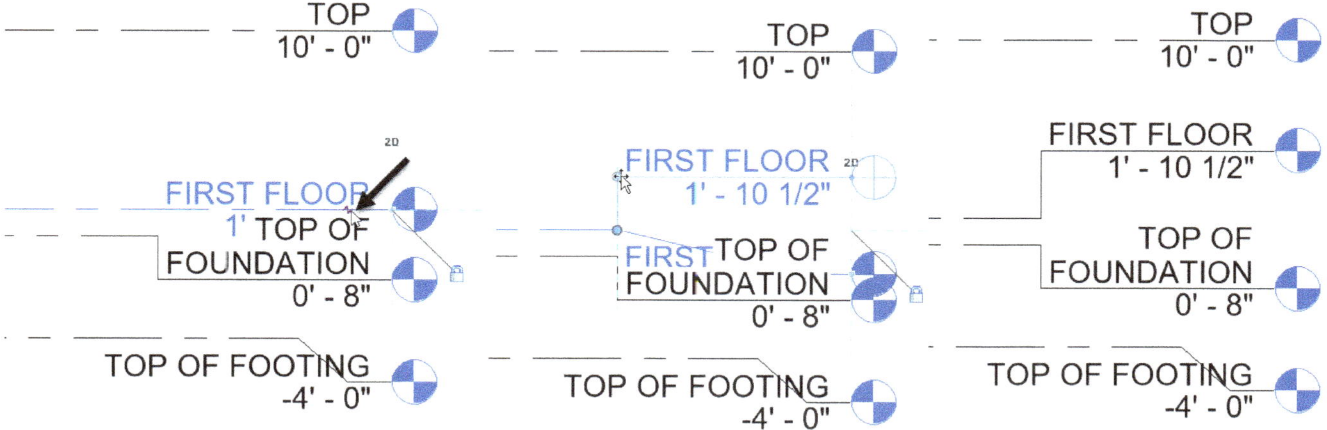

- On the ribbon, click **Annotate > Dimensions > Aligned**. Next, select the levels from top to bottom.
- Move the pointer upward and click on a dimension to specify the location of the dimensions.

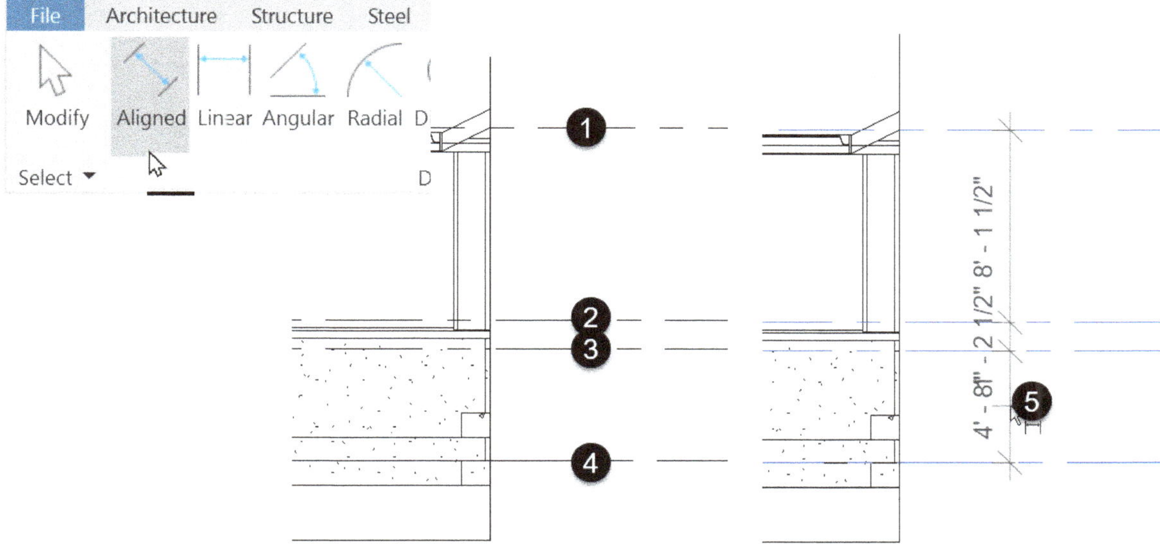

Creating Interior Elevations

- Double-click on the **FIRST FLOOR** plan under the **Floor Plans** node in the Project Browser.
- On the ribbon, click **View > Create > Elevation**. Next, select **Interior Elevation** from the Type **Selector** drop-down on the **Properties** palette.

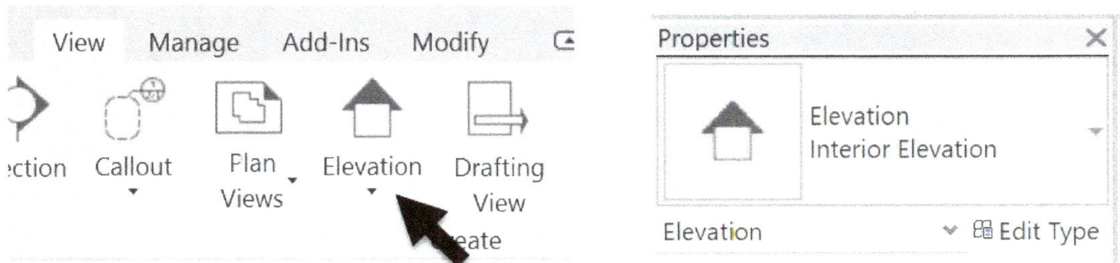

- Zoom to the kitchen area and click at the location, as shown. Next, press ESC twice.
- Zoom-in to the interior elevation mark and click on its edge to select it.

- Uncheck the check box displayed at the right side of the elevation mark. Next, click **O**K to delete the elevation mark.

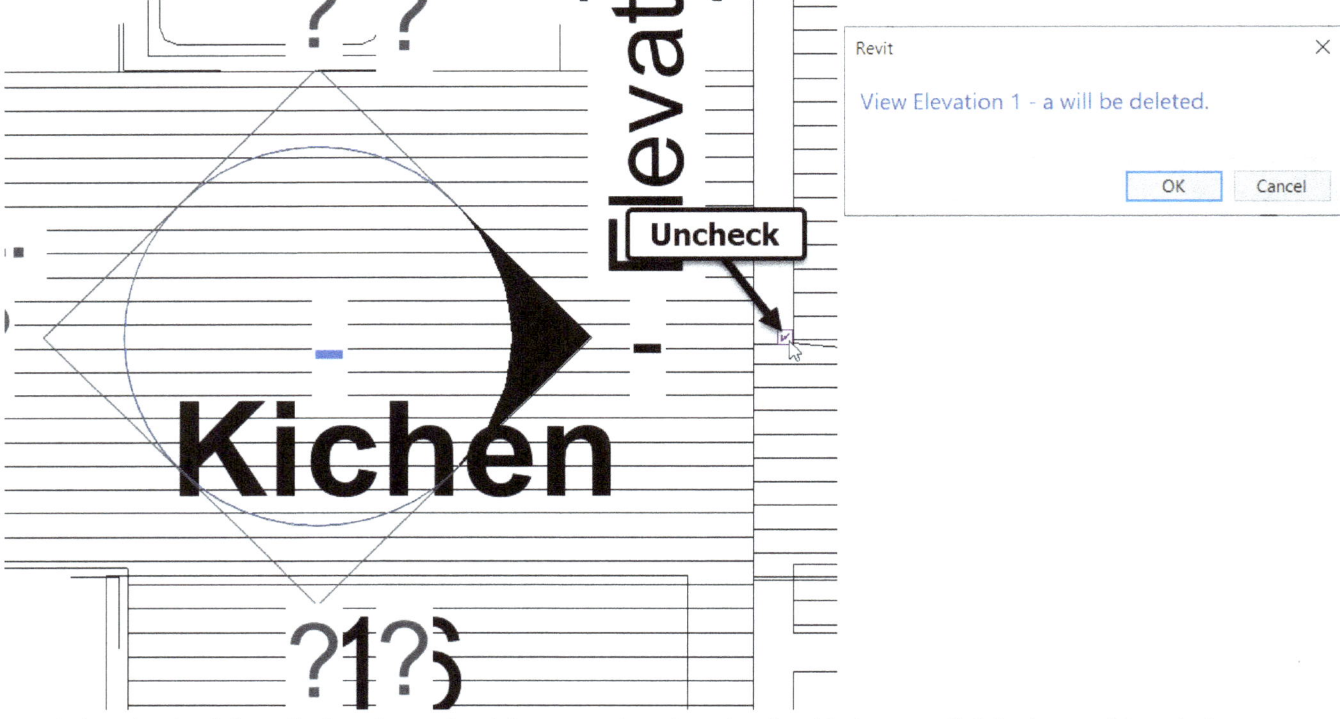

- Select the check box displayed near the sink; a new elevation view is added. Next, click in the graphics window.

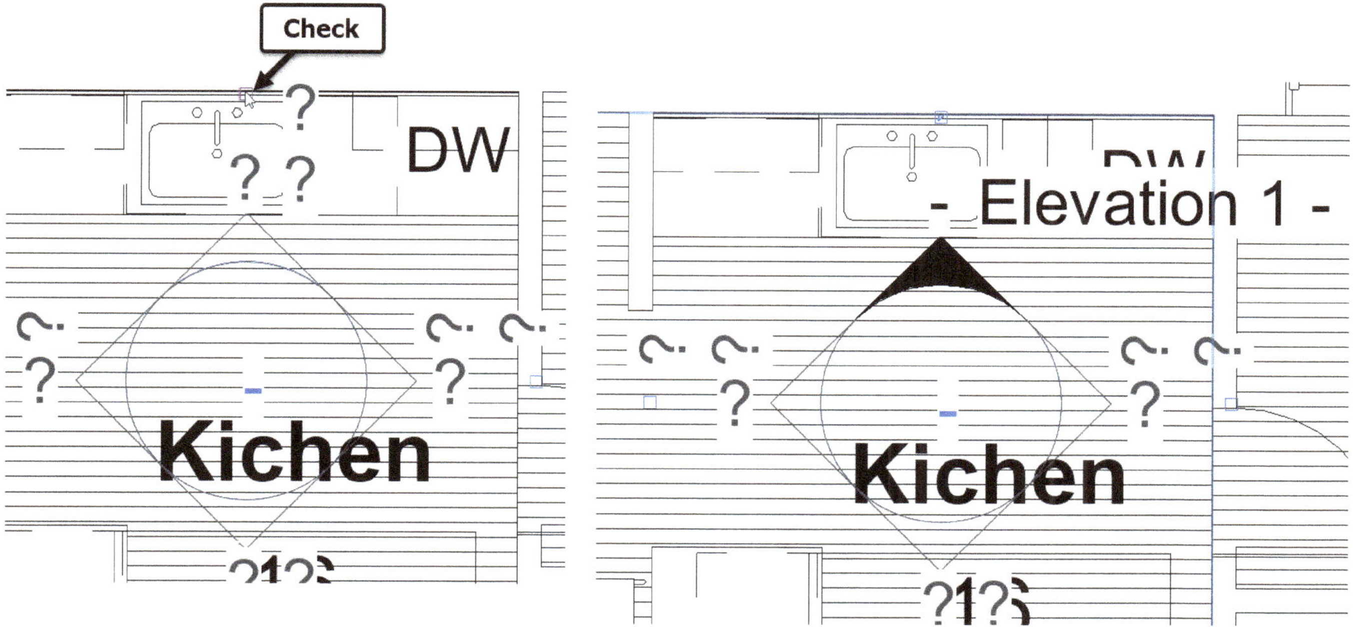

- Zoom-in to the elevation mark and select the elevation arrow: a line is displayed defining the extents of the elevation view.
- Zoom-out of the elevation mark and notice the dashed boundary. Click and drag the arrow grip displayed on the boundary in the downward direction.

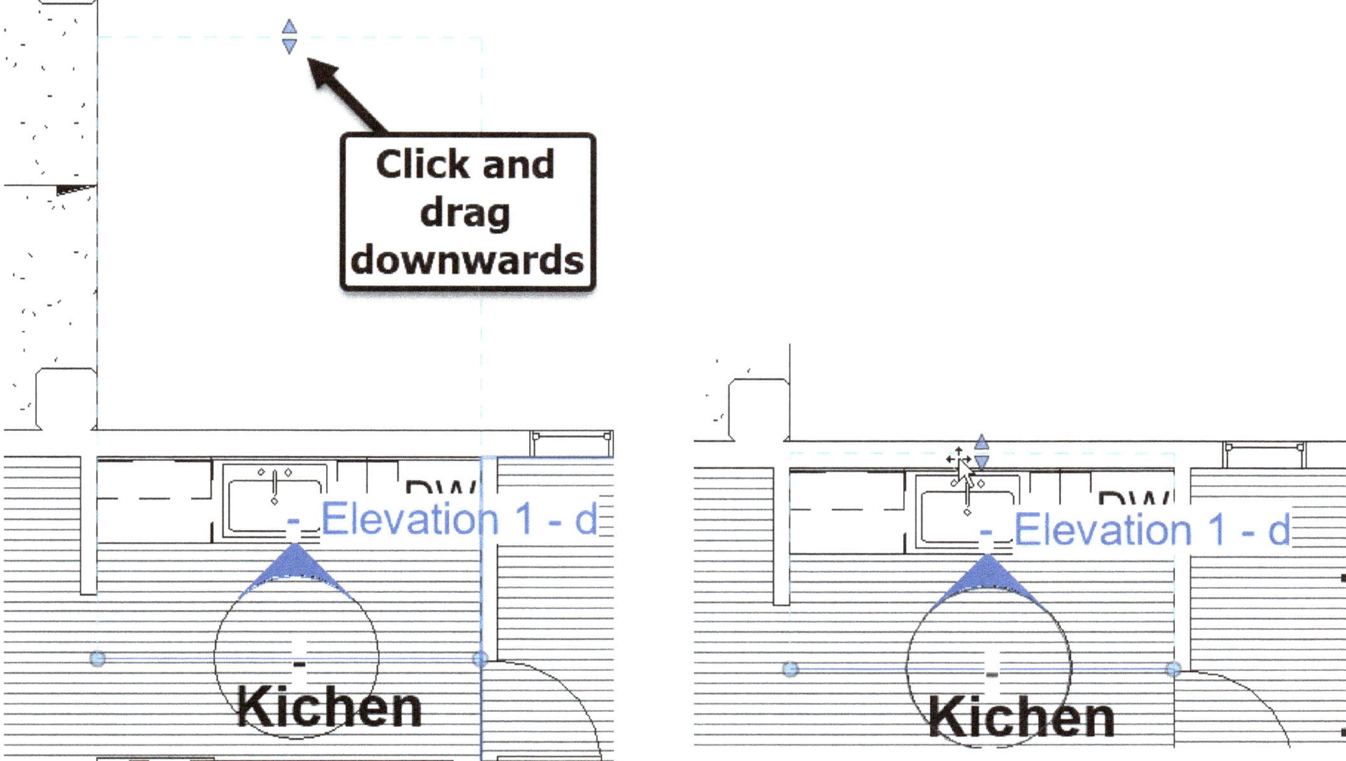

- Double-click on the arrow of the elevation mark; the elevation view is opened.

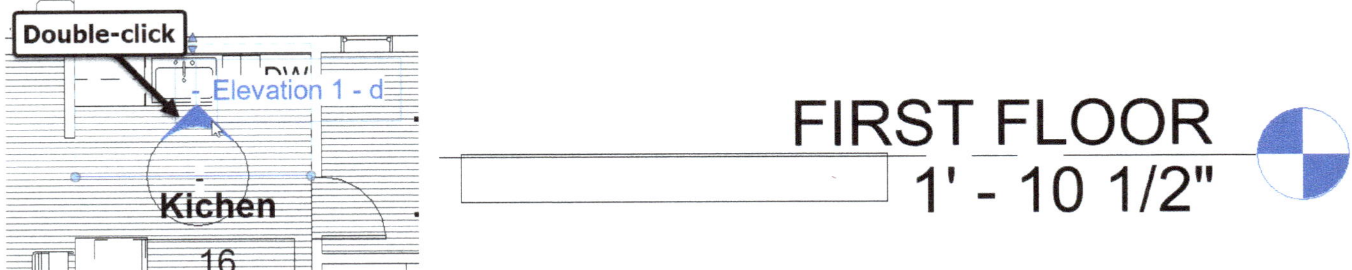

- Select the boundary of the elevation view. Next, select the midpoint grip of the top horizontal edge of the boundary.
- Press and hold the left-mouse button and drag the pointer upward. Next, release the pointer when the ceiling is displayed.

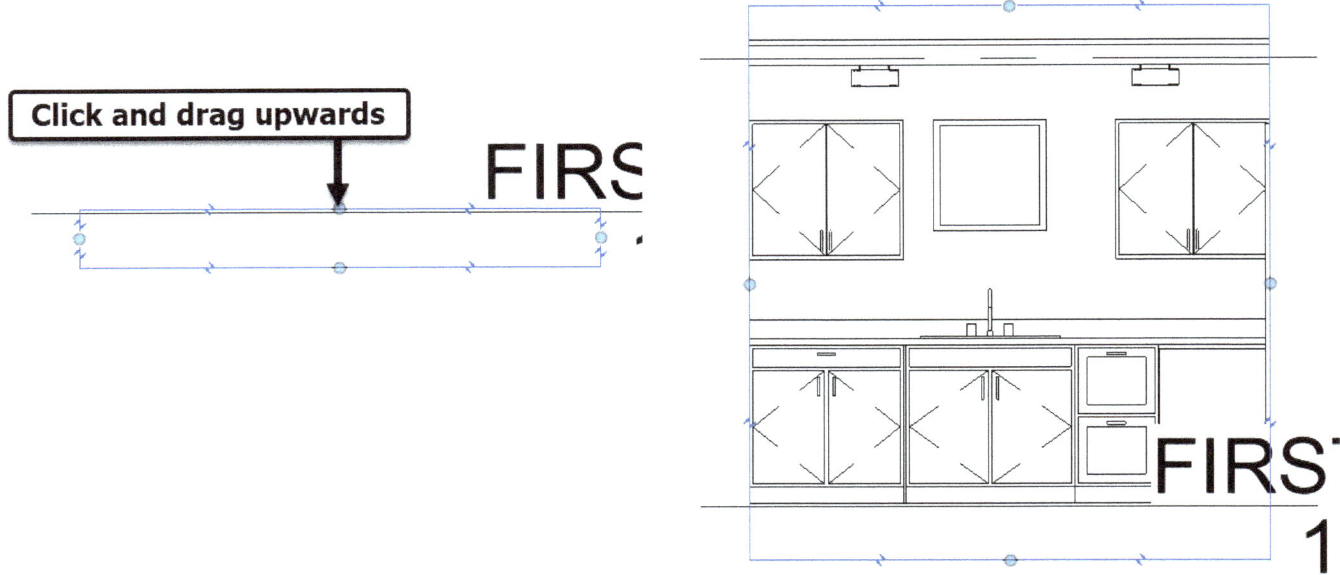

- Likewise, create another interior elevation in the Bathroom, as shown.

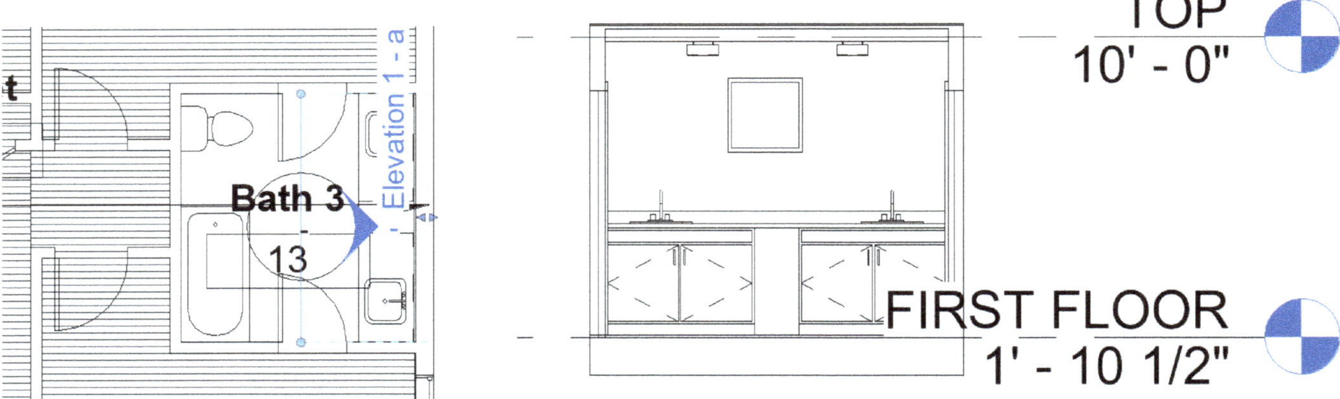

Tutorial 2: Creating Callout and Section Views

The **Callout** tool is used to create an enlarged view of an area.

- Double-click on the **FIRST FLOOR** under the Floor Plans node in the Project Browser.
- On the ribbon, click the **View** tab > **Create** panel > **Callout drop-down** > **Rectangle.**

- Specify the first and second corners of the callout, as shown.

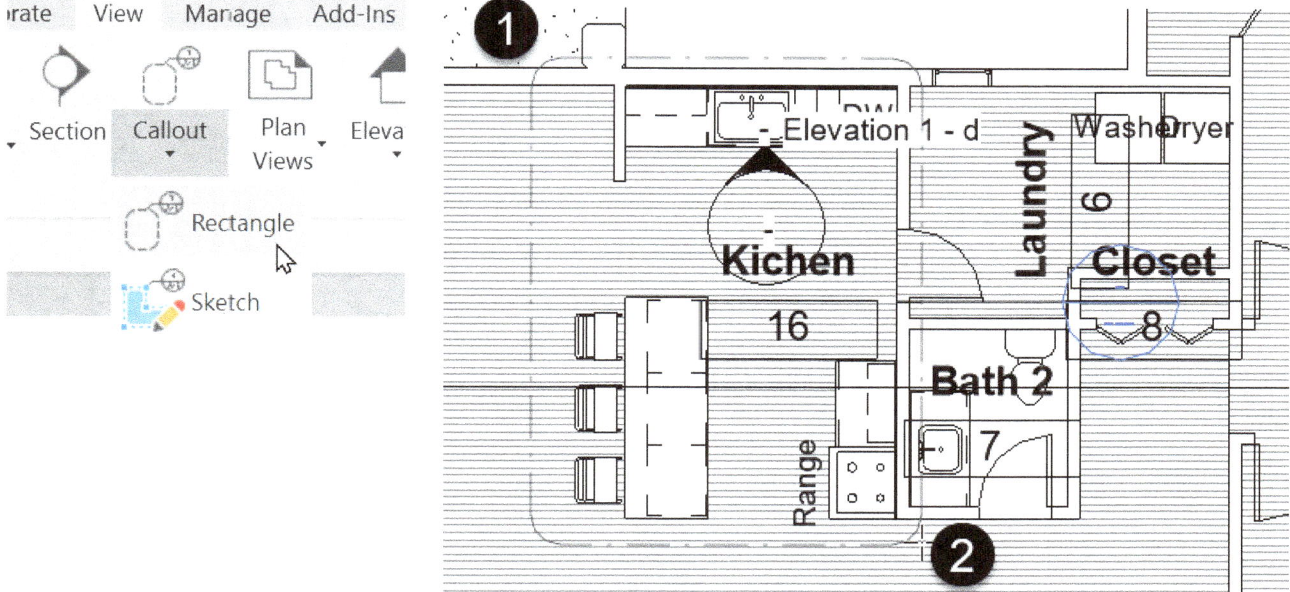

- Select the boundary of the callout. Next, click and drag the grip attached to the balloon, as shown.
- Release the pointer in the free space, as shown. Next, click in the graphics window.
- On the Project Browser, under the Floor Plans node, and then select Rename.
- Type Kitchen and press ENTER.

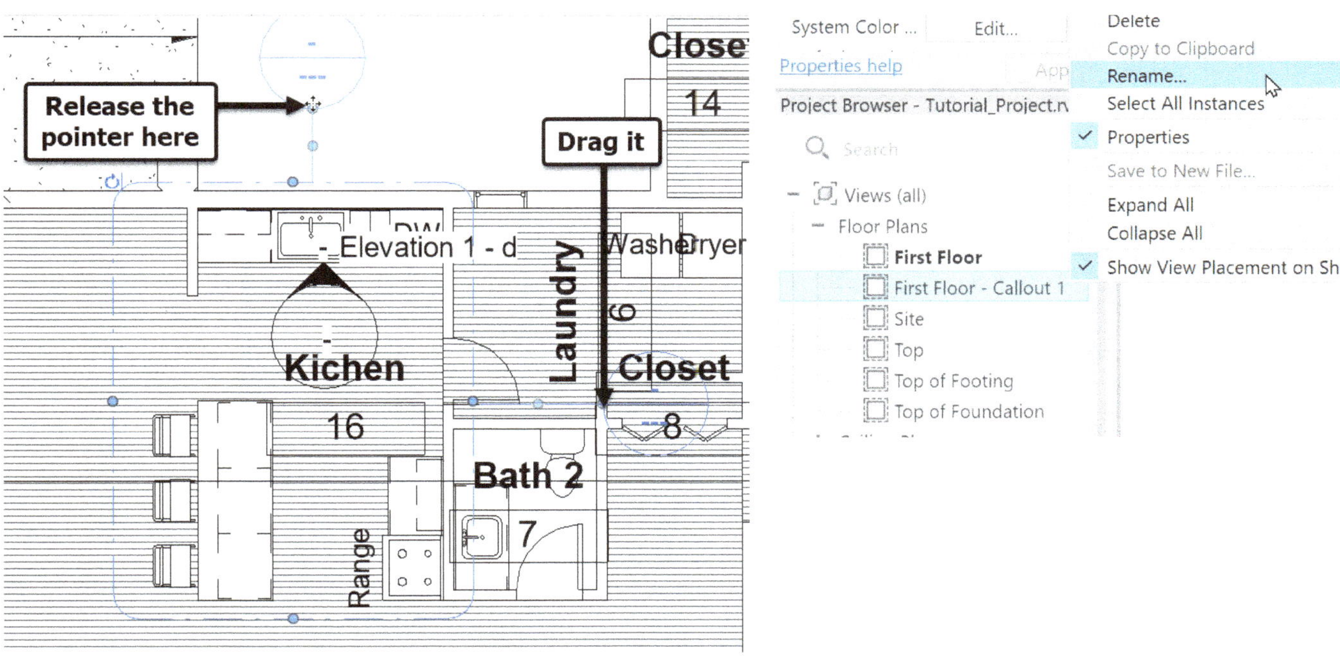

- Select the balloon of the Kitchen callout view, right-click, and then select **Go to View**; the enlarged callout view is displayed in a separate window.

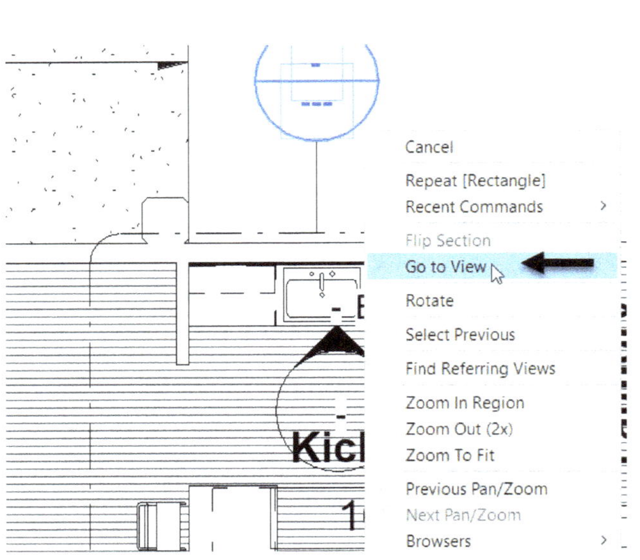

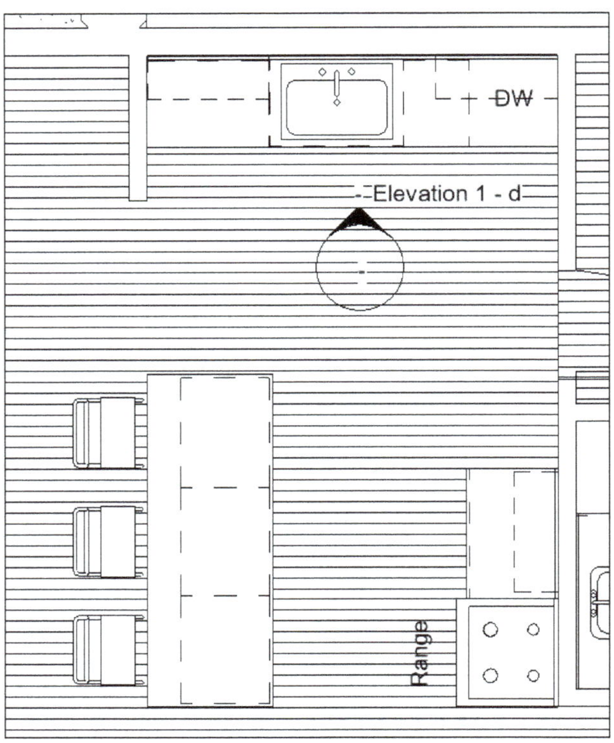

Creating a Wall Section

- Double-click on the **FIRST FLOOR** under the **Floor Plans** node in the Project Browser.
- On the ribbon, click the **View** tab > **Create** panel > **Section**.
- On the **Properties** palette, select **Wall Section** from the **Type Selector** drop-down.
- Specify the start and end points of the section line, as shown.

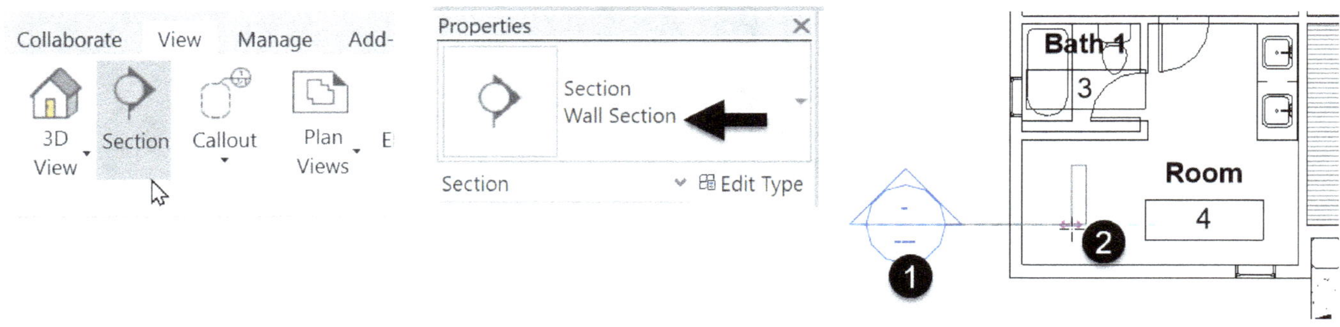

- Right-click and select **Go to View**. Next, change the scale of the section view to ¾" = 1'-0".
- Set the **Detail level** to **Fine**.

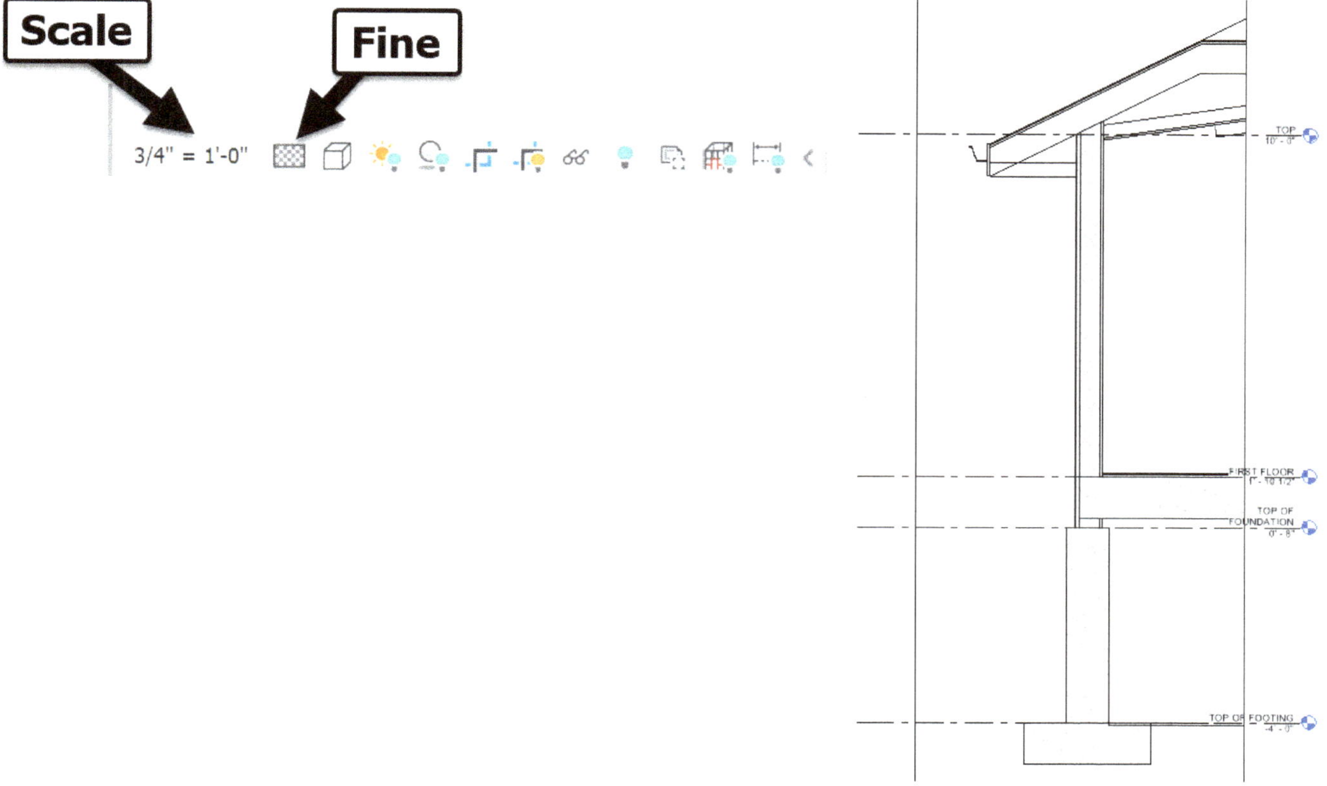

Creating Schedules

- Double-click on the **FIRST FLOOR** under the **Floor Plans** node in the Project Browser.
- On the ribbon, click the **View** tab > **Create** panel > **Schedules drop-down** > **Schedules/Quantities**.
- Select the **Doors** option from the **Category** list on the **New Schedule** dialog. Next, click **OK**.

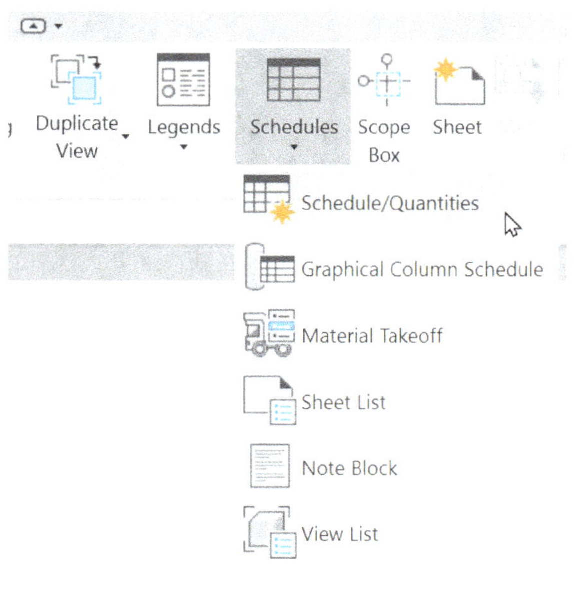

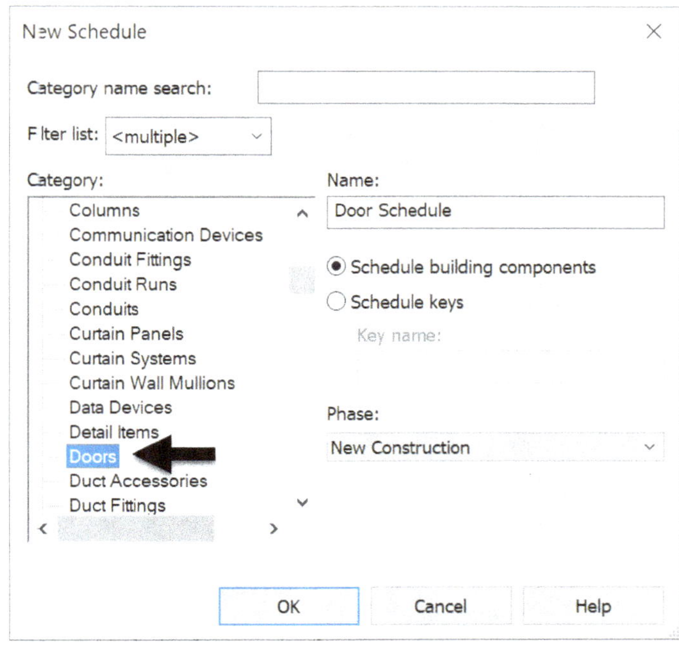

- On the **Schedule Properties** dialog, select **Mark** from the **Available fields** list and click the **Add Parameter(s)** icon. The Mark field is added to the **Scheduled fields (in order)** list.
- Likewise, add the **Width** and **Height** fields to the **Scheduled fields (in order)** list.

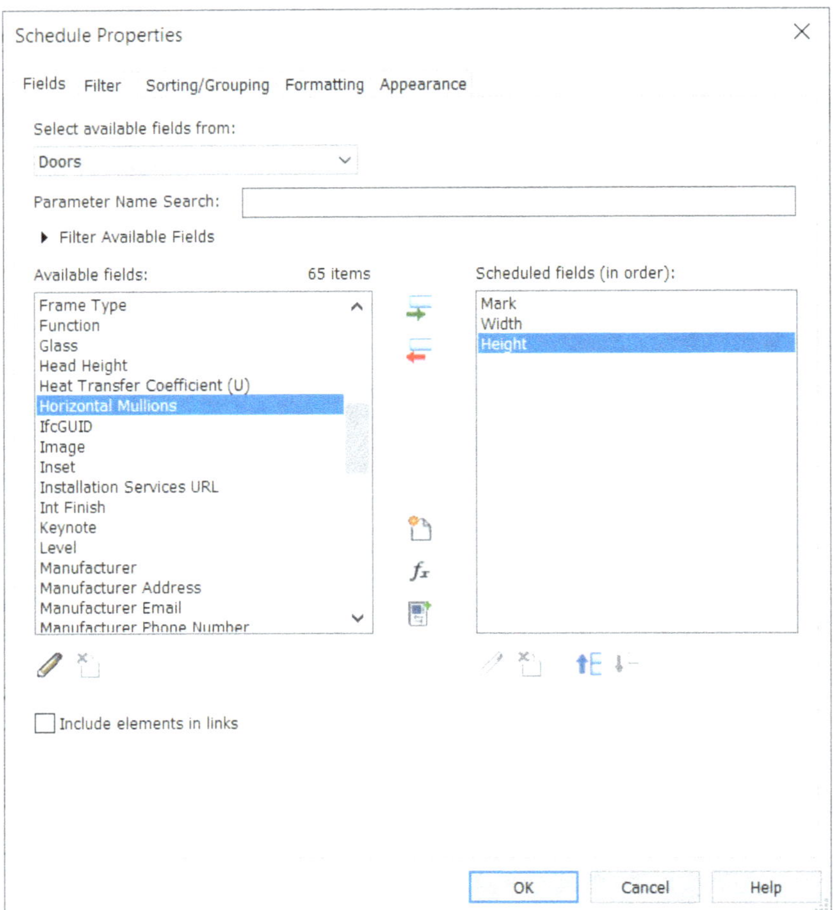

- Click the **Sorting/Grouping** tab on the **Schedule Properties** dialog. Next, select **Mark** from the **Sort by** drop-down.
- Make sure that the **Itemize every instance** option is selected. On doing so, two or more doors with same properties are displayed on the schedule.
- Click **OK** to create the Door Schedule.

	A	B	C
	Mark	Width	Height
3		6' - 0"	6' - 8"
4		3' - 0"	6' - 8"
5		3' - 0"	6' - 8"
6		3' - 0"	6' - 8"
7		2' - 8"	7' - 0"
8		2' - 8"	7' - 0"
9		2' - 6"	6' - 8"
10		2' - 6"	6' - 8"
11		2' - 6"	6' - 8"
12		2' - 6"	6' - 8"
13		2' - 6"	6' - 8"
15		12' - 0"	5' - 8"
16		2' - 6"	6' - 8"
17		4' - 0"	6' - 8"
19		4' - 0"	6' - 8"
20		4' - 0"	7' - 0"
21		6' - 0"	7' - 0"
22		4' - 0"	7' - 0"
28		16' - 0"	7' - 0"

(Door Schedule) title row spans above columns A, B, C.

The door schedule is updated automatically if you add a new door to the model. In addition to that, you can highlight any door in the model using the door schedule. To do this, select any one of the door from the door schedule and click the **Highlight in model** icon on the ribbon.

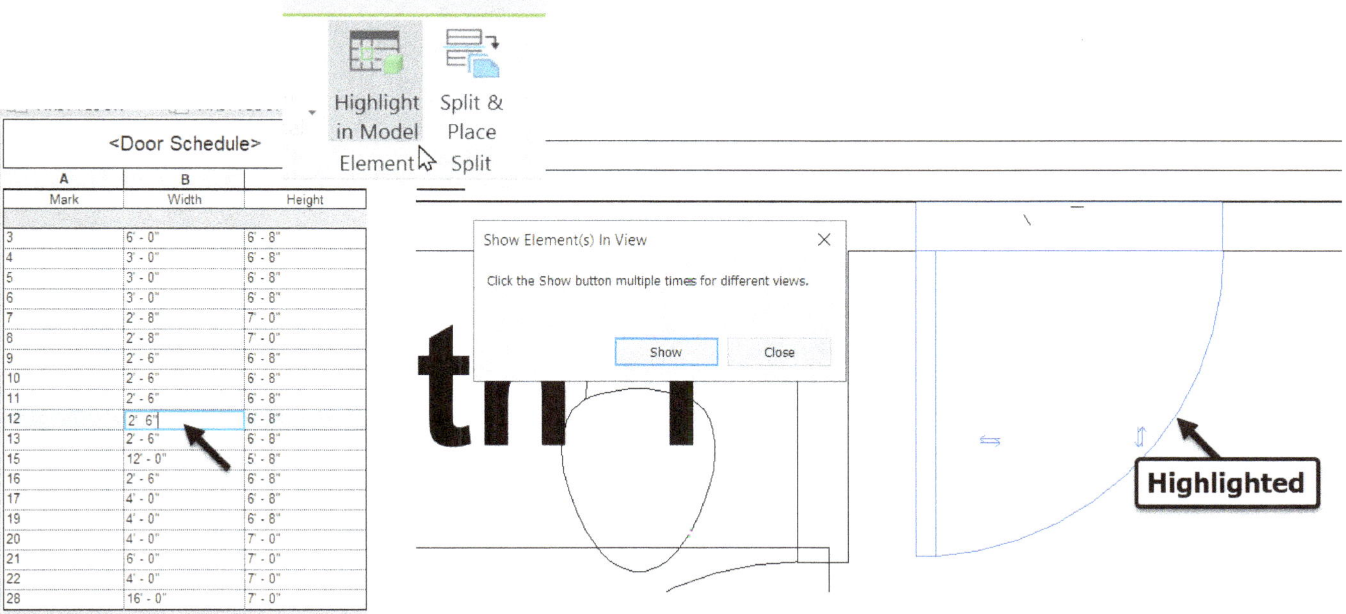

- Click **Close** on the **Show Elements(s) in View** dialog.
- Double-click on the **FIRST FLOOR** plan under the **Floor Plans** node of the Project Browser.
- Change the view scale to ¼"=1'-0".
- On the ribbon, click **Annotate > Tag > Tag All**.

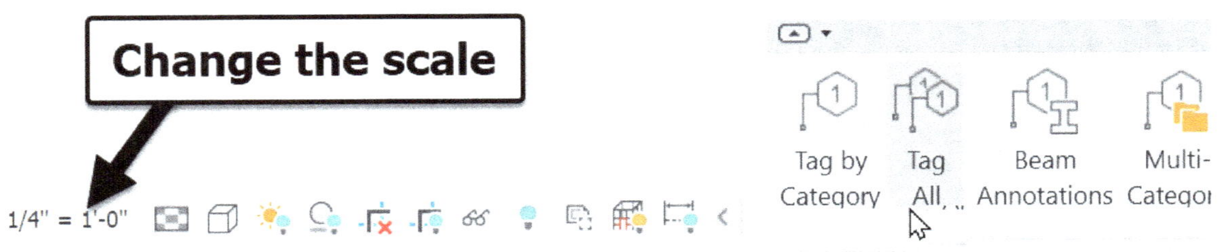

- Select the **Door Tags** option from the **Tag all Not Targeted** dialog, and then click **OK**. The door tags are added to the door.

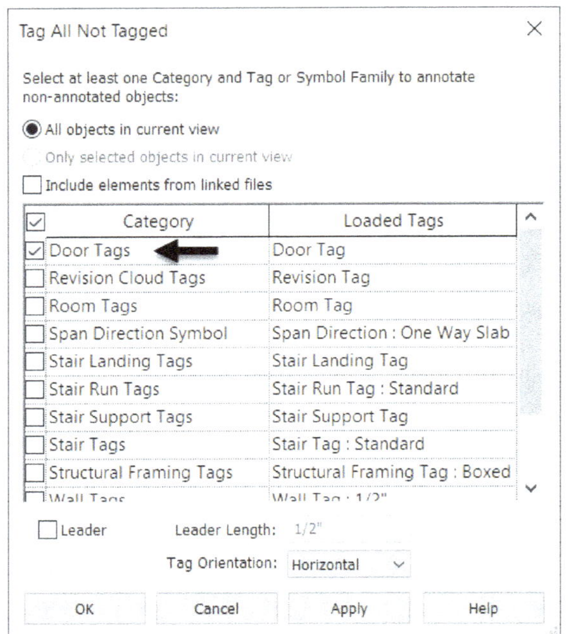

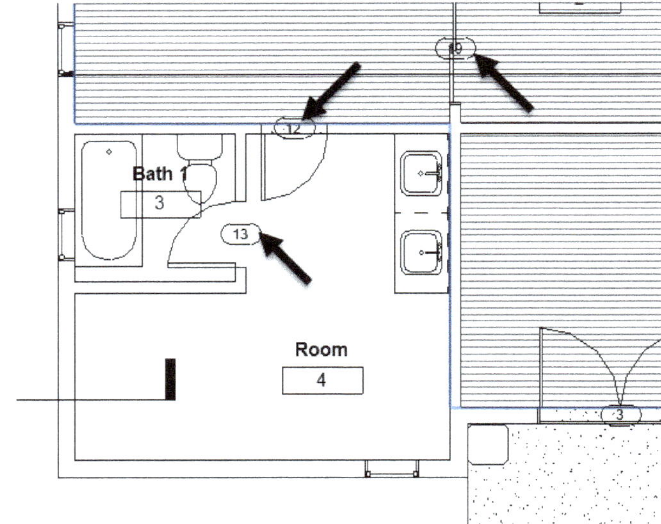

Part 3: Publishing

Tutorial 1: Creating a Site Plan

In this tutorial, you create a site plan.

- Double-click on the **Site** under the **Floor Plans** node in the Project Browser.
- On the ribbon, click the **Massing & Site** tab > **Model Site** panel > **Toposolid**.

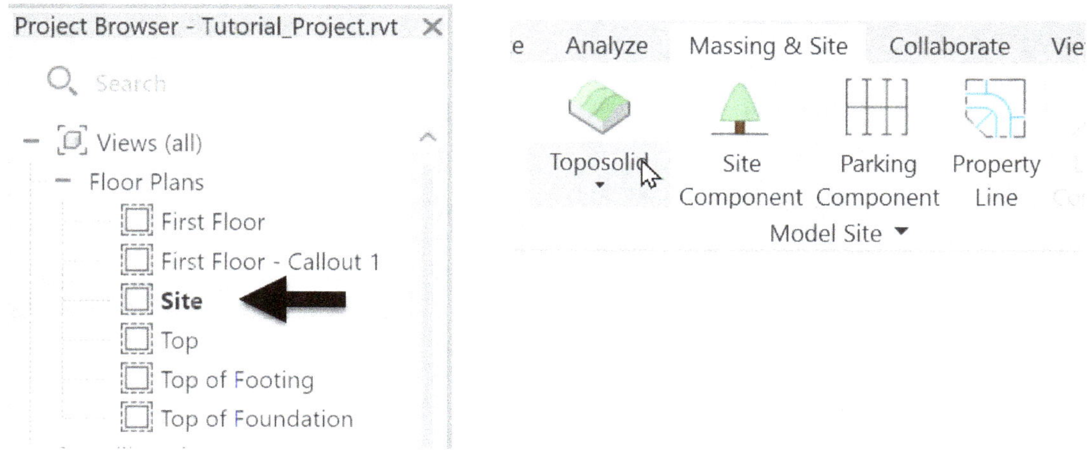

- Type **1'** in the **Offest** box available on the Options Bar; the toposolid will be offset from the selected level by **1'**.

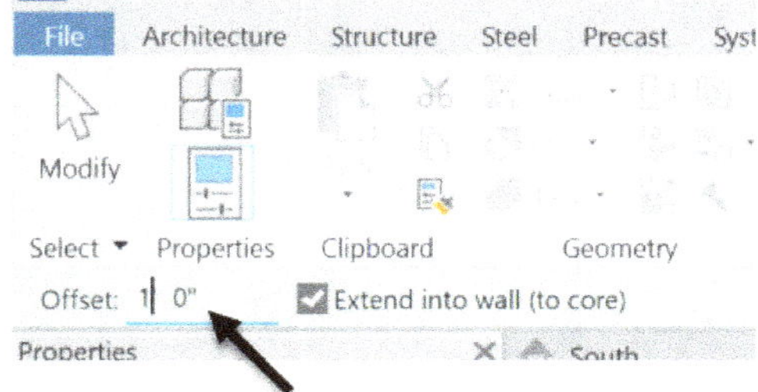

- On the **Properties** palette, select **Grassland – 20"** from the **Type Selector** drop-down. Next, click the **Edit Type** button.
- Click the **Duplicate** button next to the **Type** drop-down. Next, type **New Grassland** in the **Name** box and click **OK**.

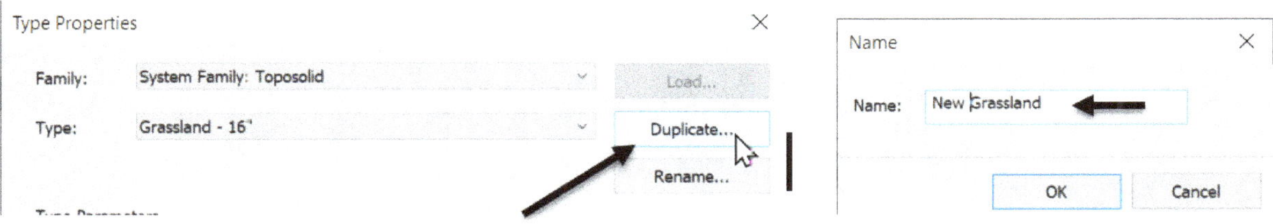

- Click the **Edit** button next to the **Structure** column.
- Type **20'** in the **Thickness** column of the **Structure (1)** Function. Next, click **OK** twice.

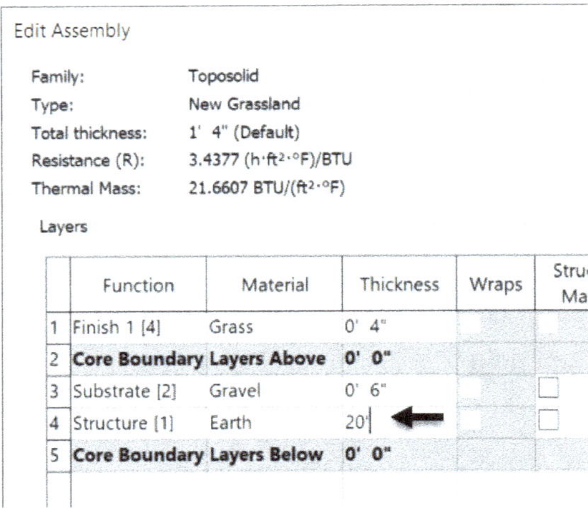

Edit Assembly

Family:	Toposolid
Type:	New Grassland
Total thickness:	1' 4" (Default)
Resistance (R):	3.4377 (h·ft²·°F)/BTU
Thermal Mass:	21.6607 BTU/(ft²·°F)

Layers

	Function	Material	Thickness	Wraps	Struc Ma
1	Finish 1 [4]	Grass	0' 4"		
2	**Core Boundary**	**Layers Above**	**0' 0"**		
3	Substrate [2]	Gravel	0' 6"		
4	Structure [1]	Earth	20'		
5	**Core Boundary**	**Layers Below**	**0' 0"**		

- On the **Modify|Create Toposolid Baundary** tab of the ribbon, click **Draw** panel > **Rectangle**. Next, specify the corner points of the rectangle, as shown.

- Click **Finish Edit Mode** ✔ on the Mode panel of the **Modify|Create Toposolid Baundary** tab of the ribbon; the Warning message box appears showing that the Highlighted toposolid and floor overlap. Close the **Warning** message box.

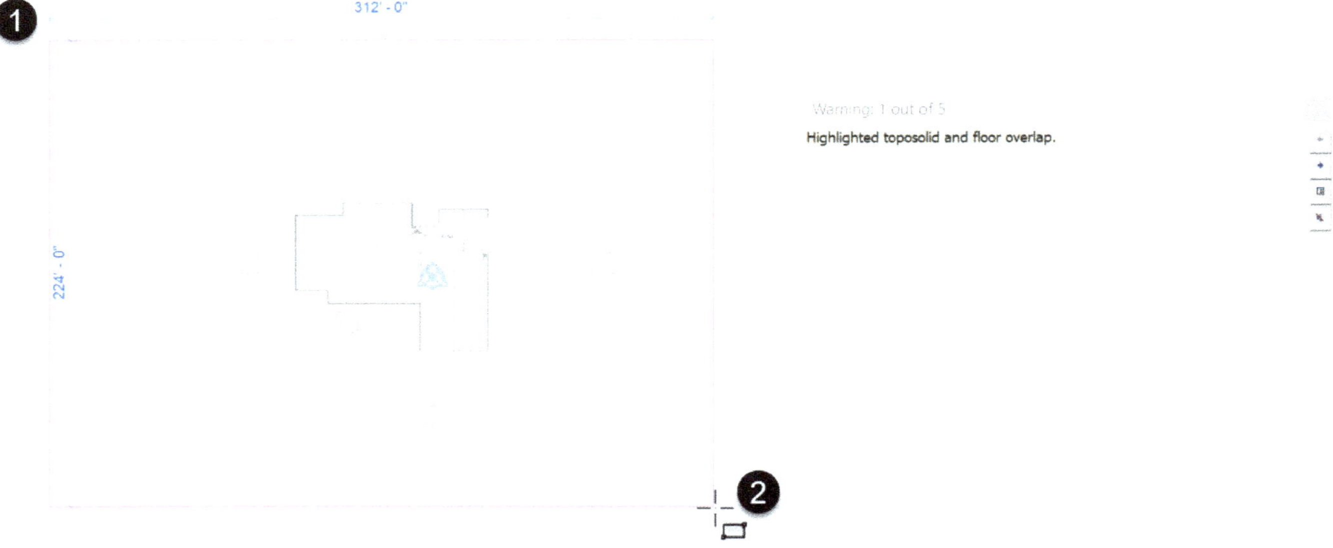

- Select the toposolid if not already selected.
- On the **Modify|Toposolid** tab of the ribbon, click **Shape Editing** panel > **Modify Sub Elements**. Next, select the bottom edge of the rectangle, as shown.
- On the ribbon, type **-2'** in the **Elevation** box of the **Modify Sub Elements** panel.

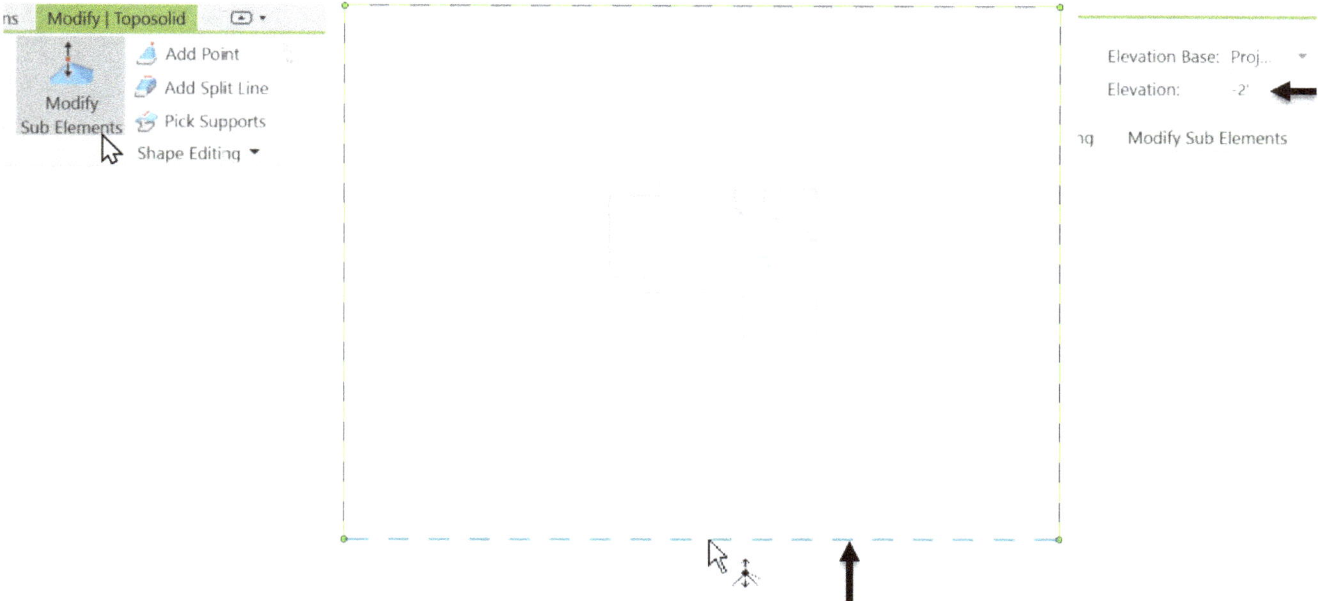

Creating Driveway and Sidewalk

- Select the Toposolid if not already selected. Next, select **Visual Style > Wireframe**.

- On the **Modify|Toposolid** tab of the ribbon, click **Topology Shaping** panel > **Sub-Divide**. Next, select the bottom edge of the rectangle, as shown.

- Zoom to the garage area and specify the start point of the driveway on the left side of the garage door.

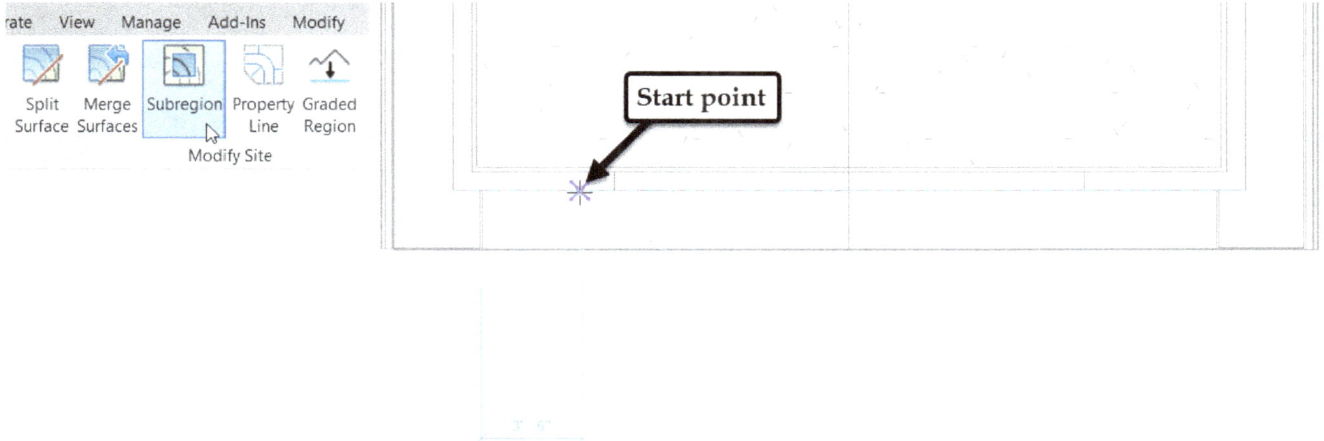

- Move the pointer vertically downward and click when the length of the line is 11'0".
- Move the pointer horizontally toward left and click when the length of the line is 31'6".

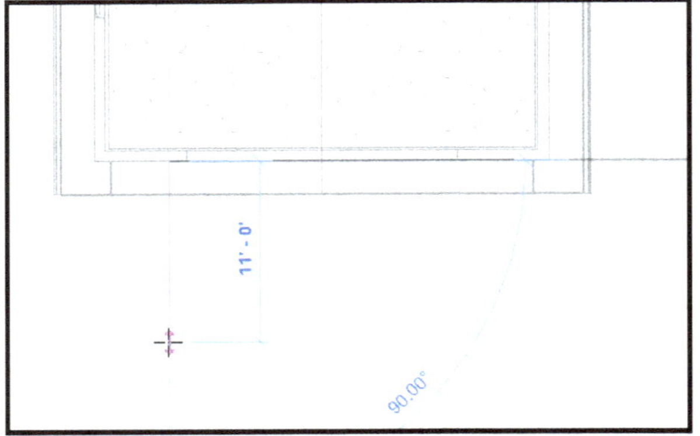

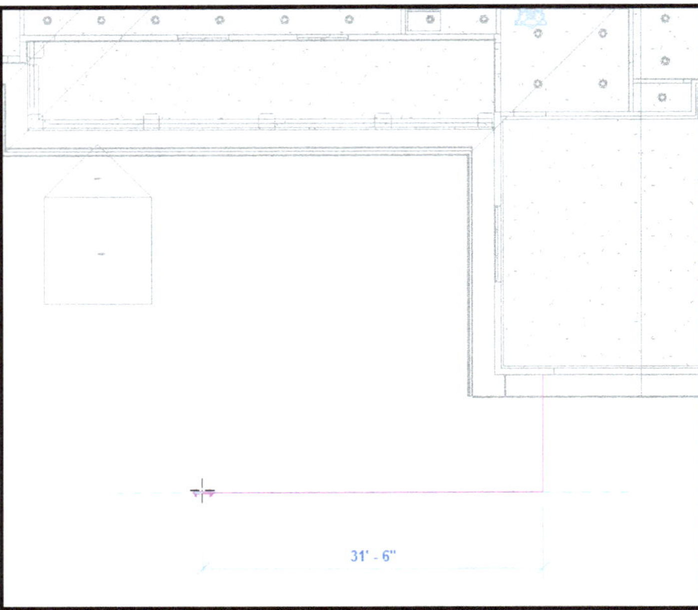

- Move the pointer vertically upward and click on the edge of the front porch.
- Move the pointer toward left and select the corner point of the front porch.

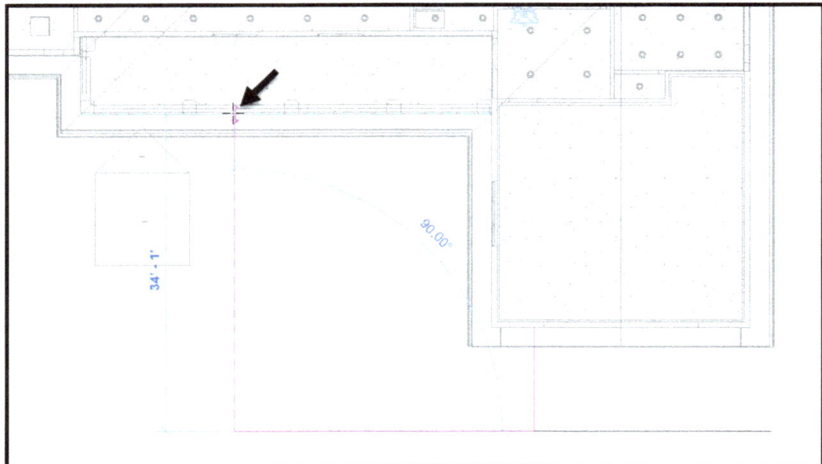

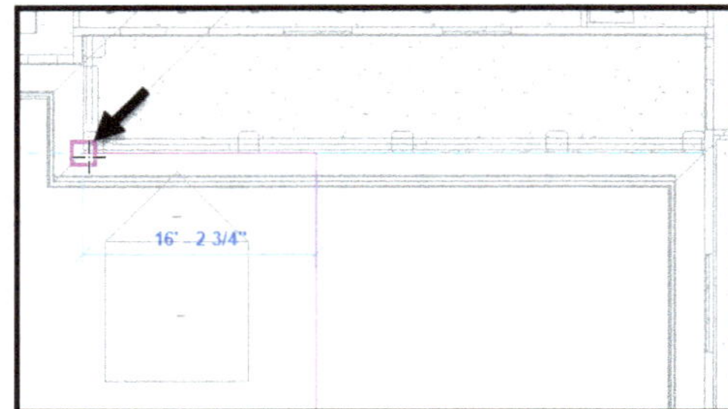

- Move the pointer vertically downward and click when the length of the line is 50'0".
- Move the pointer horizontally toward left and click when the length of the line is 47'6". Press ESC twice.

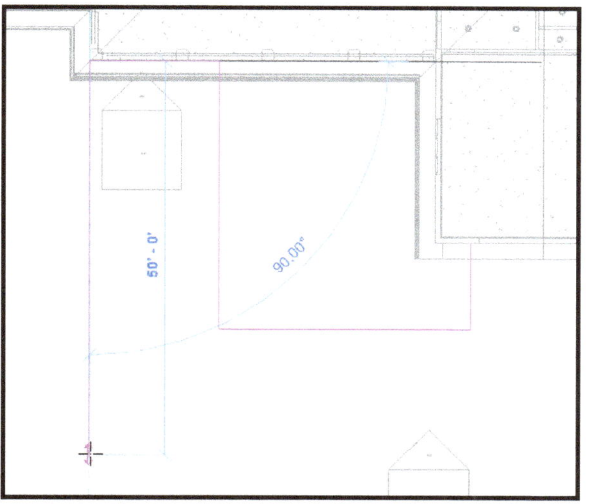

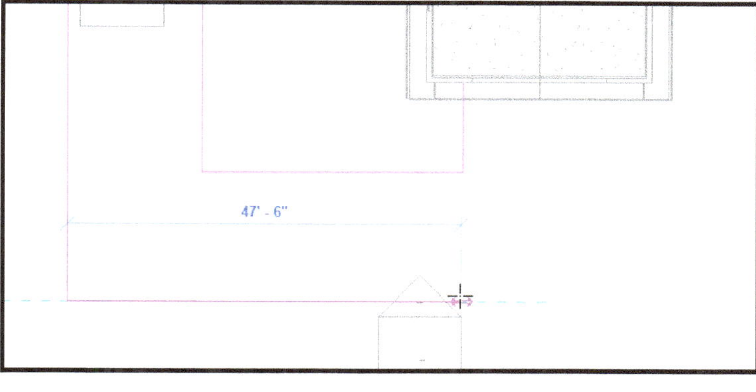

- On the ribbon, click **Modify|Create Sub-Division Boundary** tab > **Modify** panel > **Trim/Extend Single Element** .

- Select the vertical line, as shown. The boundary is defined.
- Select the horizontal line; the horizontal line is extended up to the select edge.

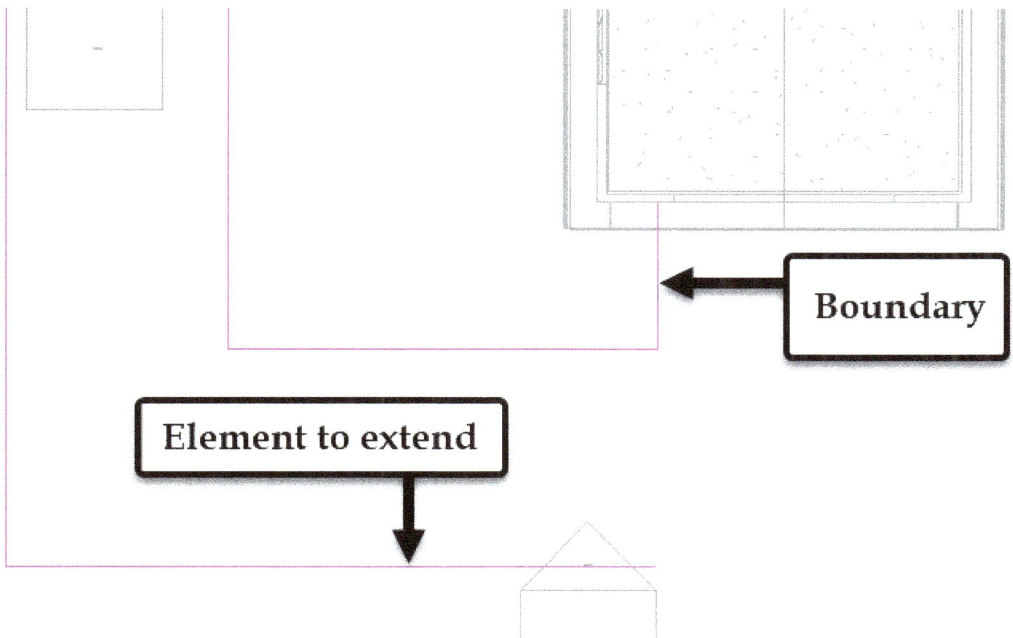

- Click the **Line** tool on the **Draw** panel of the **Modify|Create Sub-Division Boundary** ribbon tab.
- Select the endpoint of the horizontal line. Next, move the pointer downward and select the boundary edge of the toposolid.
- Move the pointer toward right, and then type 19'1 ¾". Next, press ENTER.

- Move the pointer vertically upward and click on the outer edge of the garage wall, as shown.
- Move the pointer toward left and select the start point of the first line.

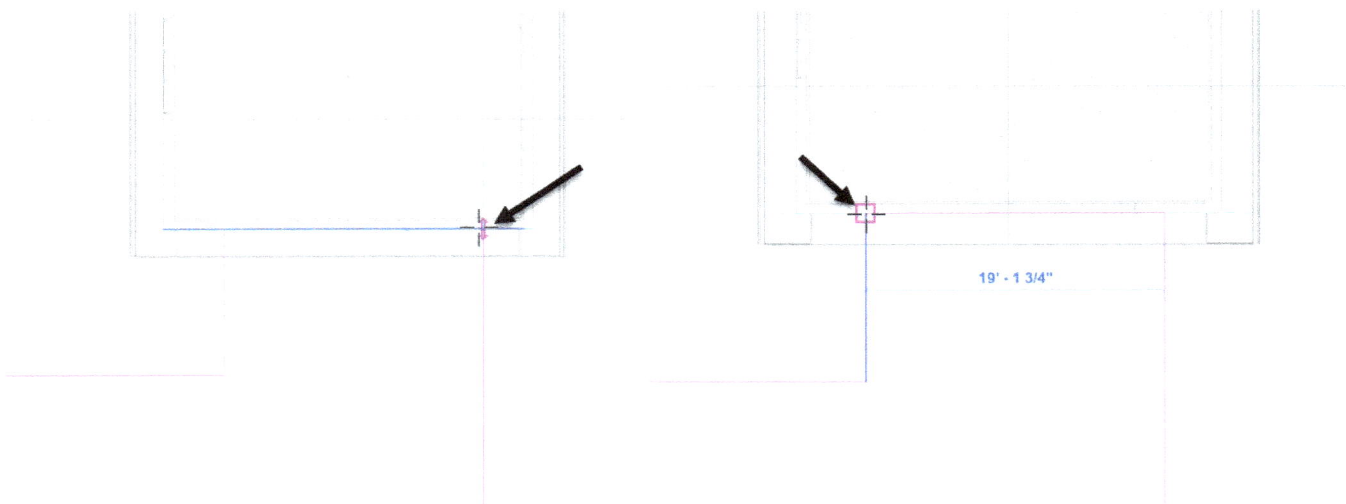

- Click the **Finish Edit Mode** icon on the **Mode** panel of the **Modify | Create Sub-Division Boundary** ribbon tab.
- Select the toposolid subregion from the graphics window.
- On the **Properties** palette, click in the **Material** box, and then click the button displayed on the right-side.

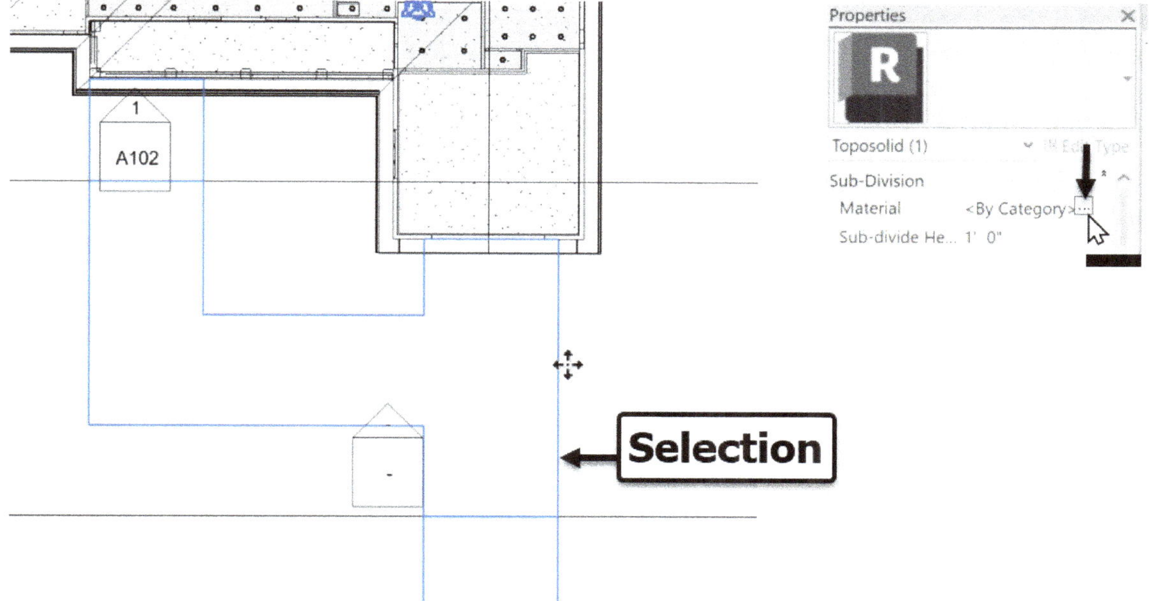

- Type site in the search box available on the **Material Browser** dialog.
- Place the pointer on the **Asphalt, Pavement, Dark Grey** material in the **Search Result** section.
- Click the **Add material to document** icon. Next, click **Apply** and **OK**.

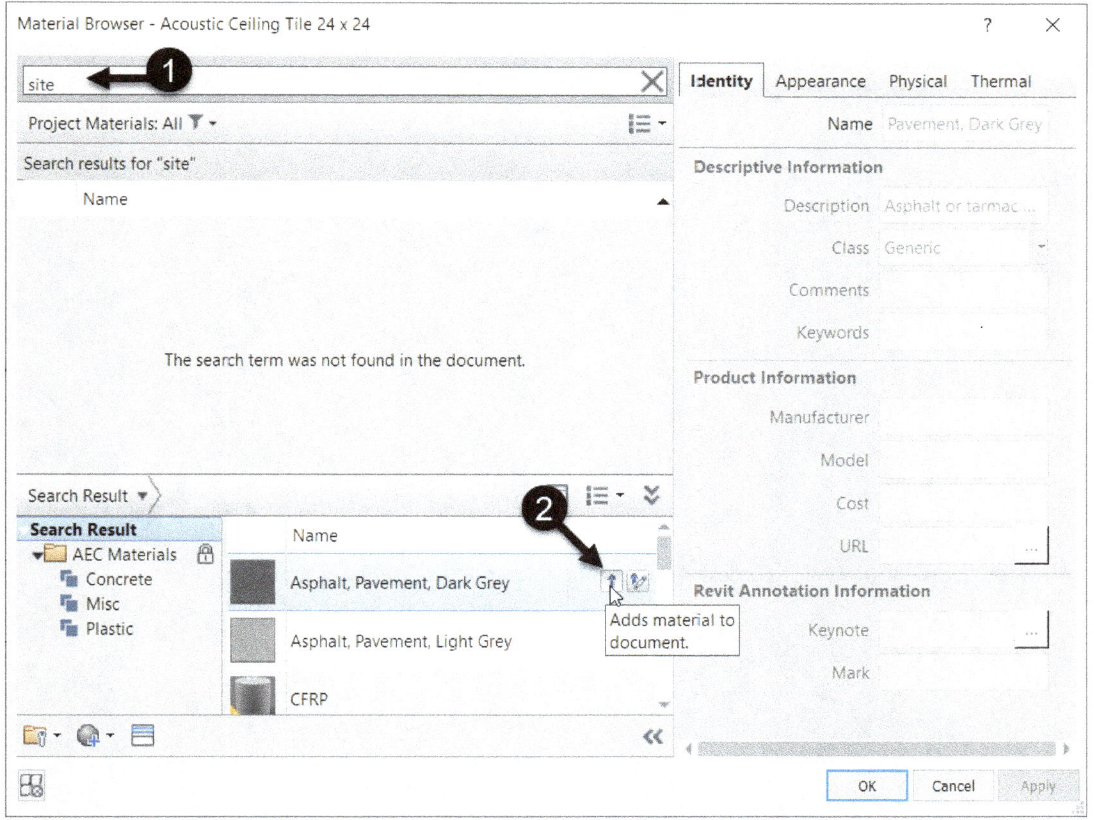

- Type **1"** in the **Sub-Divide Height** box and press ENTER; the height of the sub division region is changed.

- Select the toposolid and click the **Show Related Warnings** button on the **Warnings** panel of the **Modify | Toposolid** tab of the ribbon; the **Autodesk Revit 2024** dialog appears showing that the toposolid overlaps with the floor. You need to remove material from the toposolid to solve these errors.
- Click **Close** on the **Autodesk Revit 2024** dialog.
- On the ribbon, click **Modify | Toposolid** tab > **Mode > Edit Sketch** .
- On the ribbon, click **Modify | Toposolid** > **Edit Boundary** tab > **Draw > Line**.
- Create a closed sketch by selecting the corner points of the foundation walls, as shown. Next, click **Finish Edit Mode** . Notice that the **Warnings** panel disappears from the ribbon.

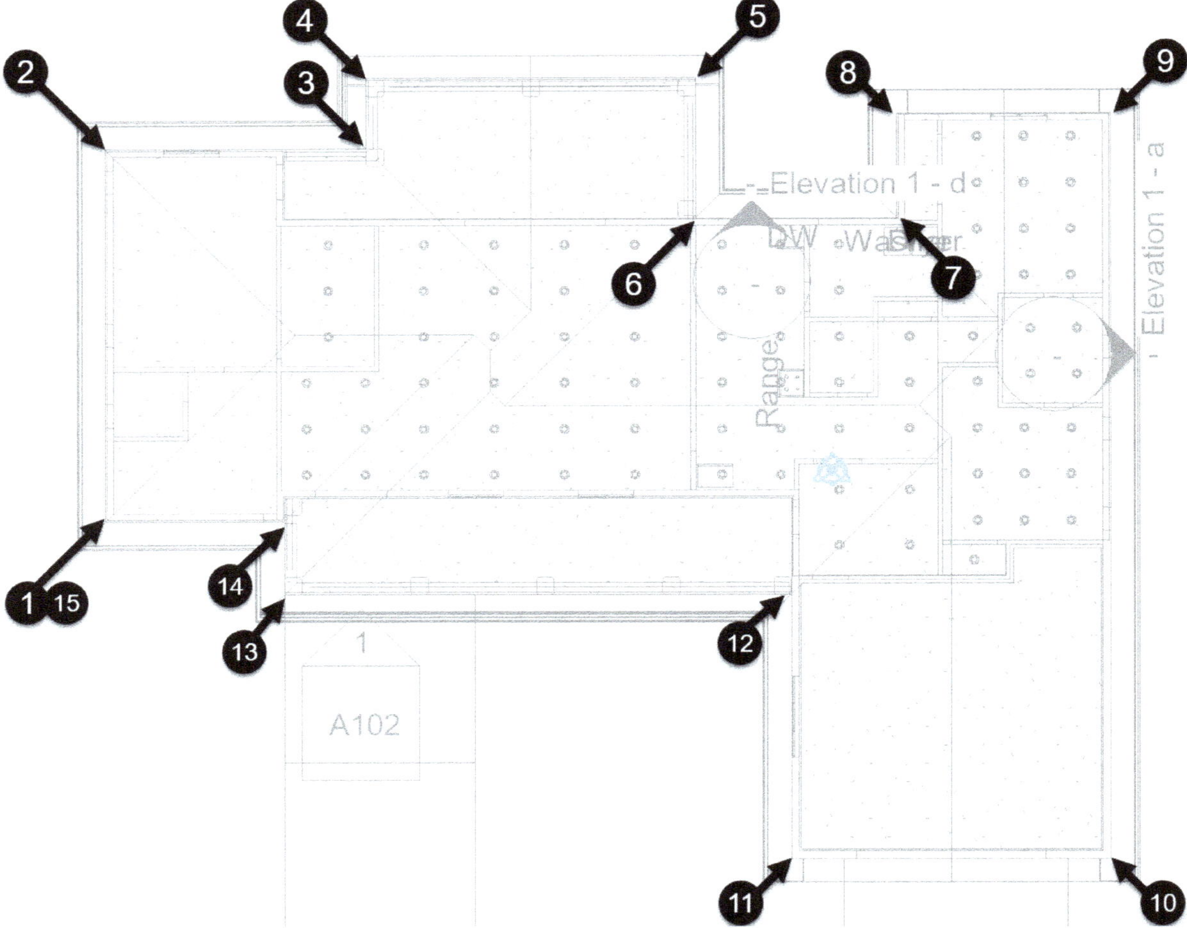

- Click the **Default 3D View** icon on the Quick Access Toolbar; the toposolid is displayed in the 3D view.
- Set the **Visual Style** to **Realistic**.

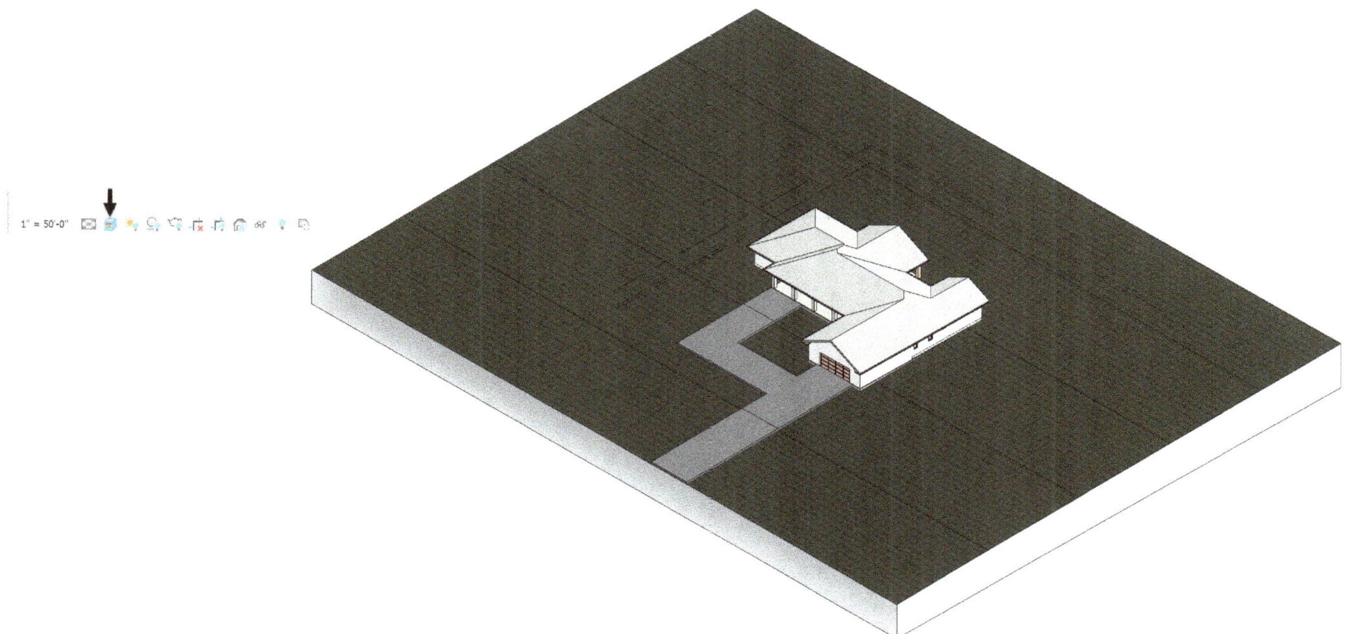

- Select the toposolid and click **Modify | Toposolid** tab > **Shape Editing > Add Point**. Next, type **-3'** in the **Offset from Surface** box.

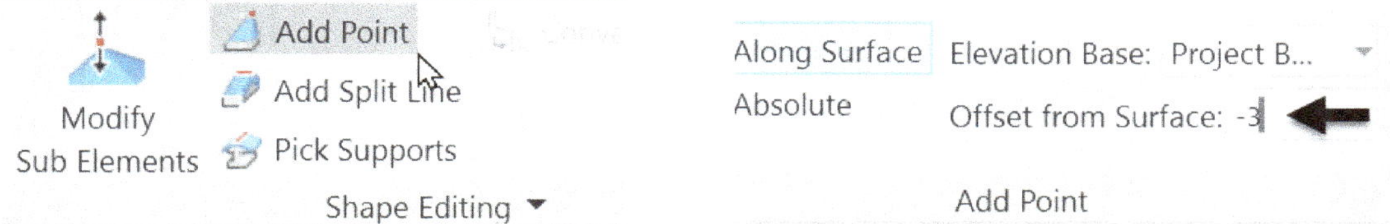

- Zoom-in to the garage entrance and select the corner points of the walls, as shown.

- Type **-2' 3"** in the **Offset from surface** box and select the corner point on the back side of the model, as shown.

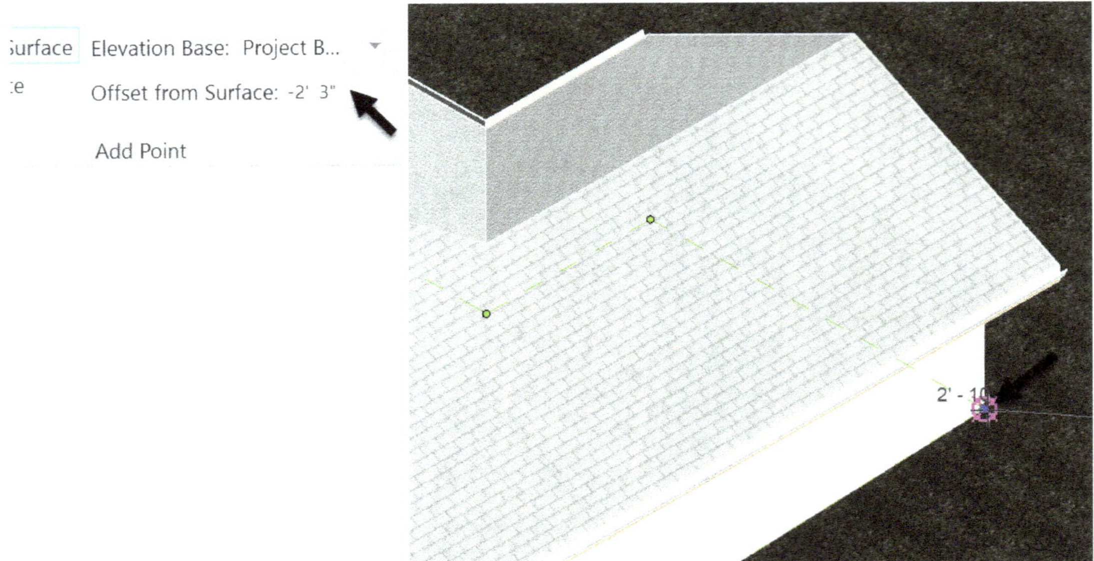

- Click the top-left corner of the Front face of the ViewCube.
- Type -2' in the **Offset from Surface** box and select corner points of the toposolid, as shown.

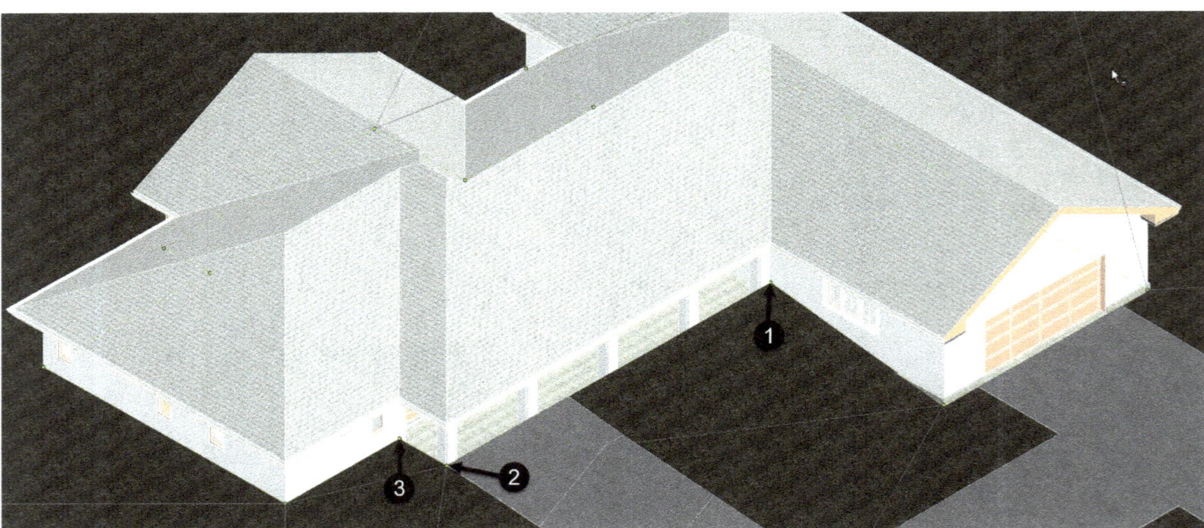

- Type -2' 3" in the **Offset from Surface** box and select corner points of the toposolid, as shown.

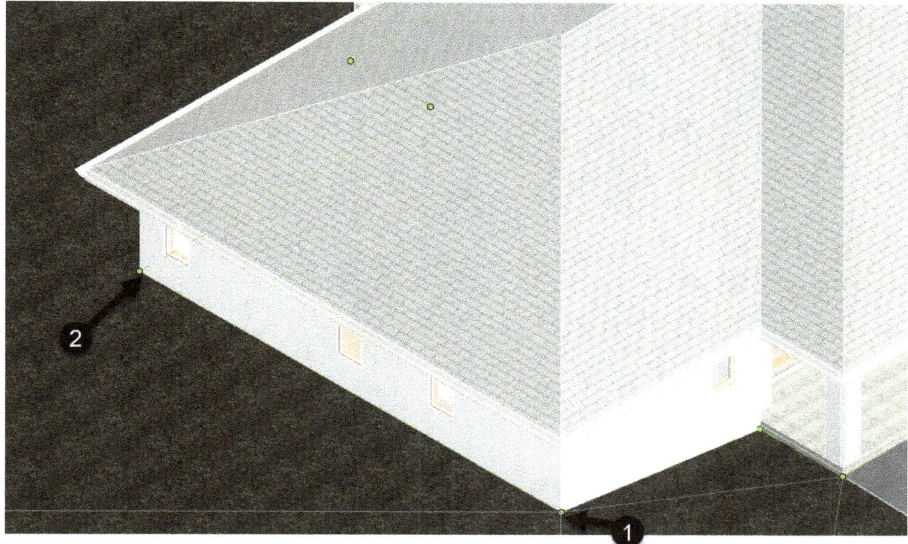

- Click the top-left corner of the Left face of the ViewCube, as shown.
- Select the corner points of the toposolid, as shown.

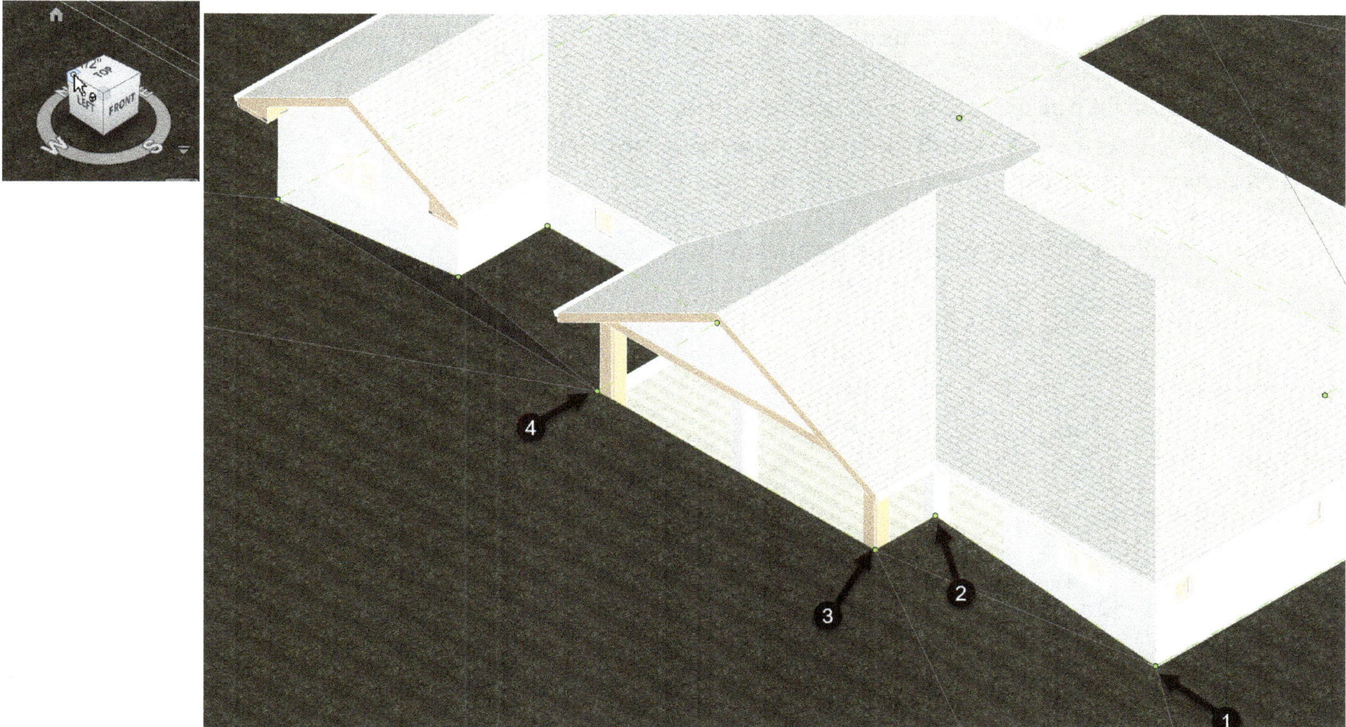

- Click the Top-left corner of the Back face of the ViewCube, as shown.
- Type -2' in the **Offset from Surface** box and select corner points of the toposolid, as shown. Next, press ESC twice.

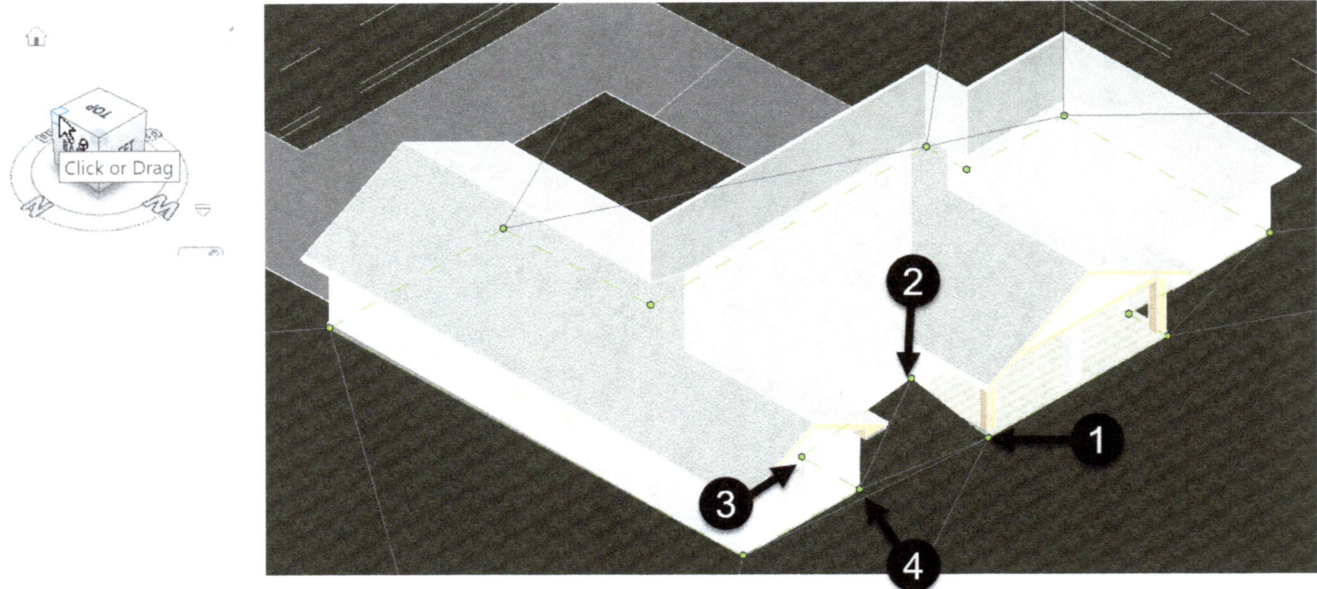

Tutorial 2: Create Cameras and Renderings

In this tutorial, you create camera views, then render the model.

- Double-click on the **Site** under the **Floor Plans** node in the Project Browser.
- Click **View > Create > 3D View drop-down > Camera** on the ribbon.
- On the Options Bar, make sure that the Perspective option is checked. In addition, make sure that 5'6" is entered in the Offset box.
- Select TOP OF FOUNDATION from the **From** drop-down.

- Click at the location on the toposolid, as shown.
- Specify the camera target, as shown.

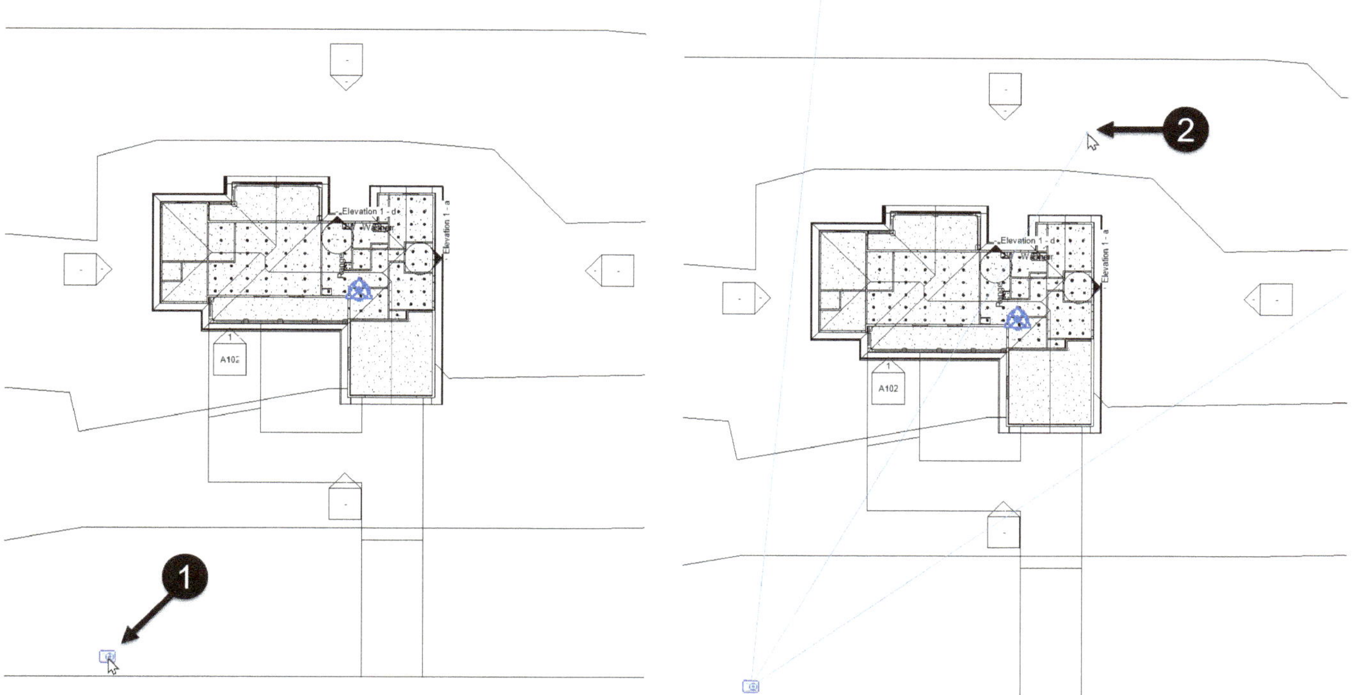

The camera view is displayed in a new tab.

- On the **Properties** palette, scroll down to the **Camera** section and change the **Eye Elevation** value to **30'**.
- Click **Apply** and notice that the elevation of the camera is changed. Likewise, you can change the target elevation.

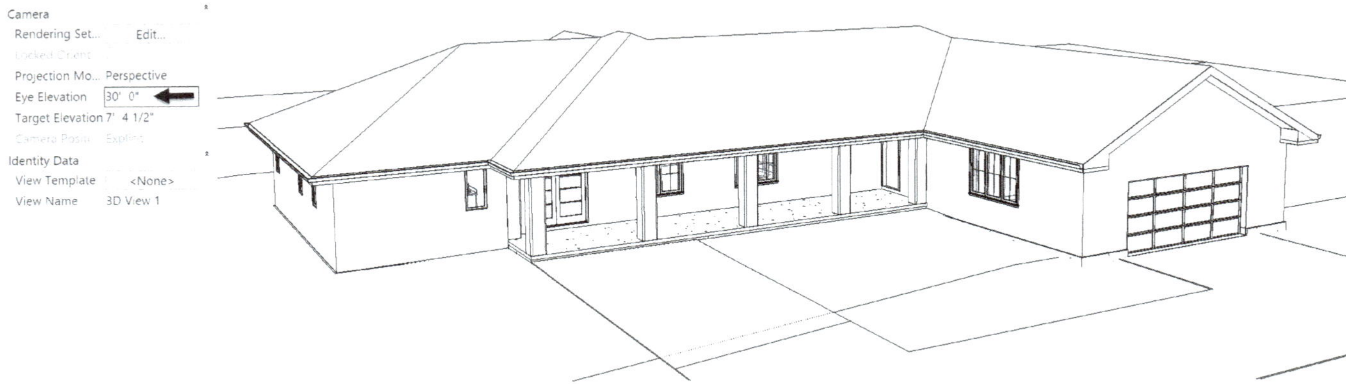

- Click the **Show Rendering Dialog** icon on the **View Control Bar** located at the bottom of the drawing area.

- In the **Rendering** dialog, set the **Setting** to **Best** under the **Quality** section. Note that the processing time will increase as you increase the image quality.
- Under the **Lighting** section, select **Scheme > Exterior: Sun Only**.
- Click the **Choose Sun Location** button next to the **Sun Setting** box.
- On the **Sun Settings** dialog, select the **Still** option from the **Solar Study** section. Next, click the button next to the **Location** box.

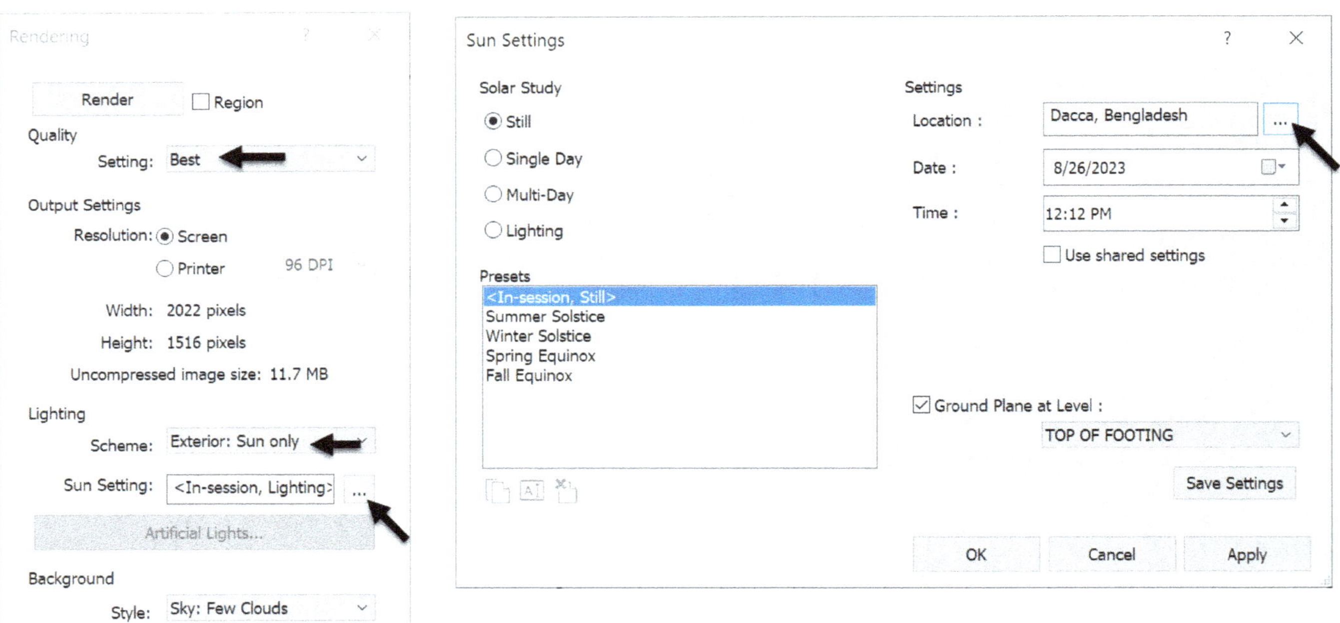

- On the **Location and Site** dialog, select the **Default City List** option from the **Define Location by** drop-down.
- Select a city near to your location from the **City** drop-down. Next, check the **Day Light Savings time** option.
- Leave the other default options and click **OK**.

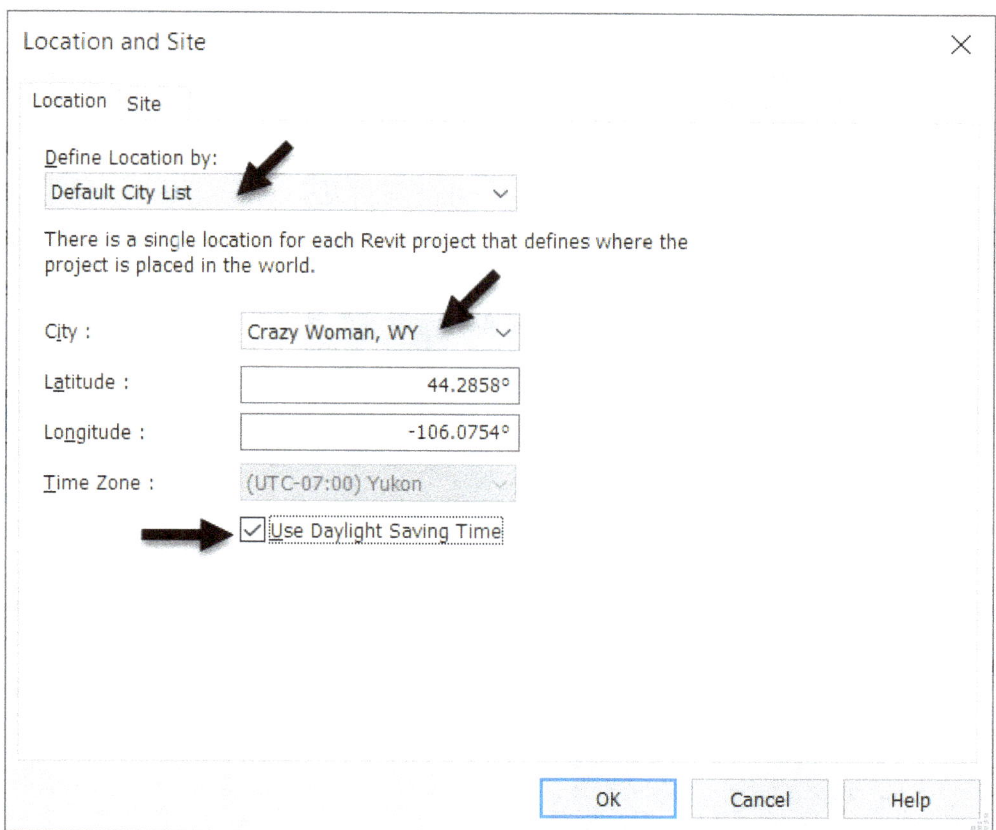

- Specify the **Date** and **Time** under the **Settings** section of the **Sun Settings** dialog. Next, click **OK**.

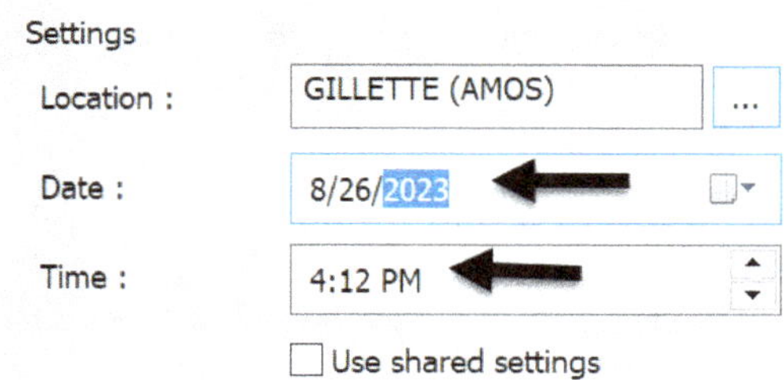

- Click the **Render** button on the **Rendering** dialog; the camera view is rendered.
- Click the **Save to Project** button on the **Rendering** dialog. Next, type **Rendering 1** in the **Save to Project** dialog and click **OK**.

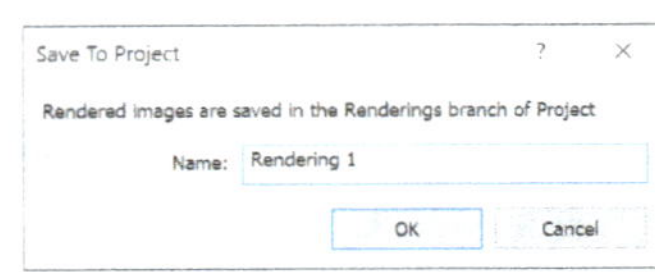

- Click the **Show the Model** button located at the bottom of the **Rendering** dialog.
- Type **7' 4 1/2"** in the **Eye Elevation** box on the **Properties** palette.
- Click the **Choose Sun Location** button next to the **Sun Setting** box.
- Type **10:31 AM** in the **Time** box and then click **OK**.
- Click the **Render** button on the **Rendering** dialog.

- Click the **Save to Project** button on the **Rendering** dialog. Next, type **Rendering 2** in the **Save to Project** dialog and click **OK**.
- Close the **Rendering** dialog.

Tutorial 3: Create Sheets and Print Drawings

In this tutorial, you add sheets, place drawing views, and then print sheets.

- Click **View > Sheet Composition > Sheet** on the ribbon.
- On the **New Sheet** dialog, click the **Load** button.

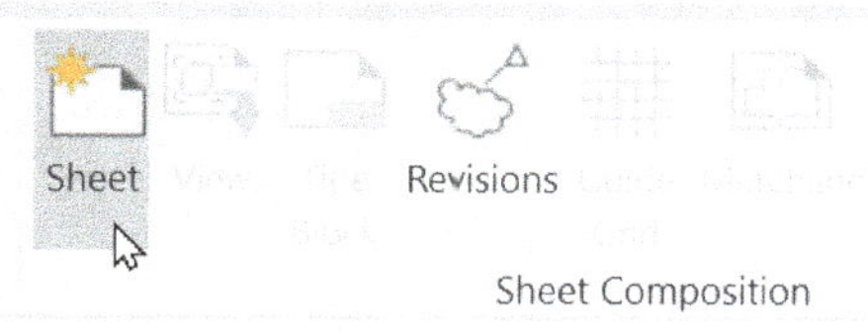

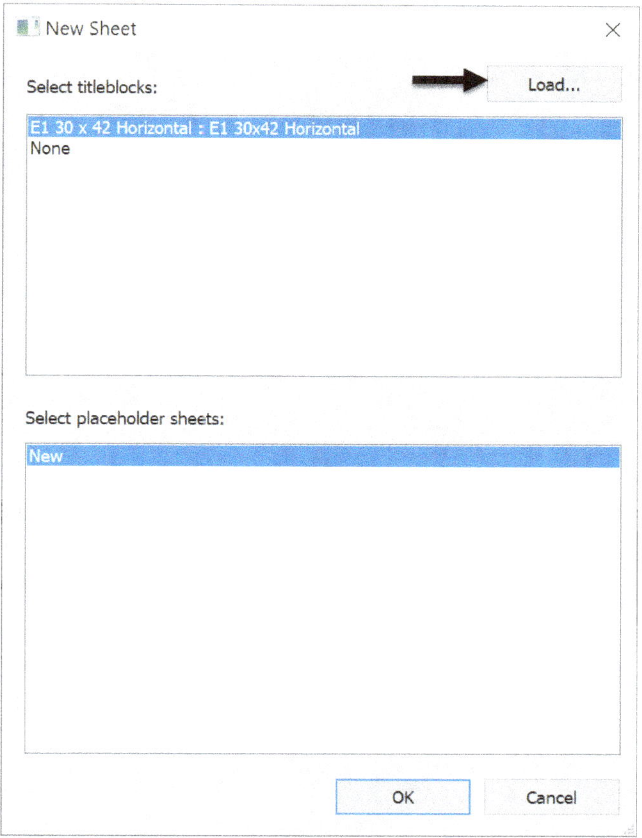

- Go to **Local Disc C > Program Data > Autodesk > RVT 2022 > Libraries > English Imperial > Titleblock**. Next, double-click on **E1 30 x 42 Horizontal**. Next, click **OK**.

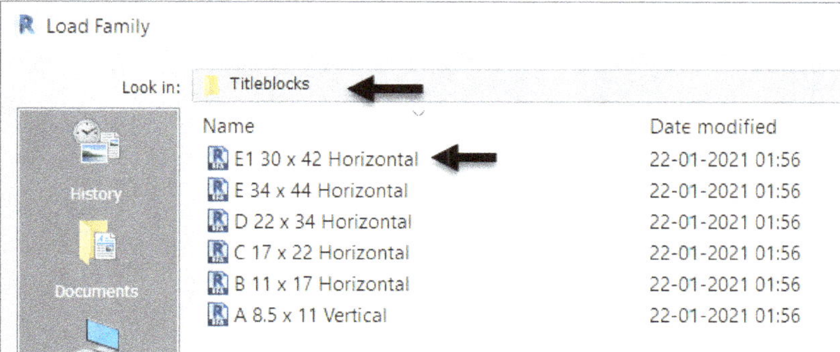

- Expand the **Sheets** node in the **Project Browser** and notice that the newly created sheet is added under it.
- Right-click on the **Sheets** node and then select **New Sheet**. Next, click **OK** on the **New Sheet** dialog.

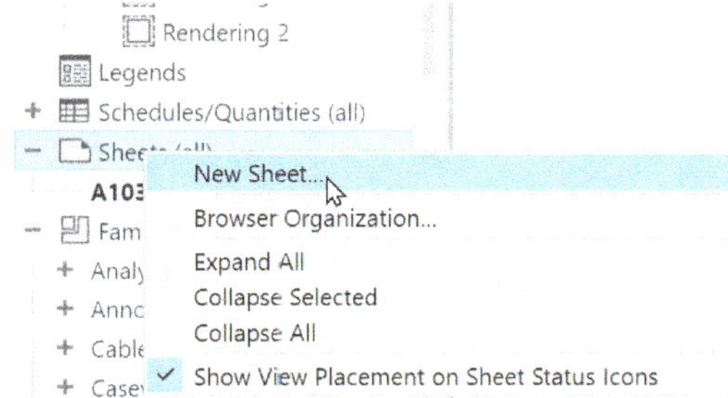

- Right-click on the **A101-Unamed** sheet and then select **Rename**. Next, type **Floor Plan** in the **Name** box and click **OK**.

- Likewise, rename the second sheet to **A101-Elevation**.

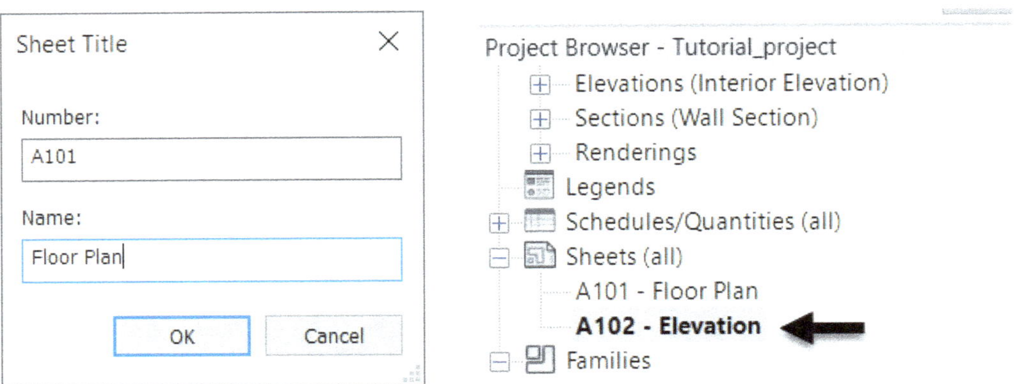

- Double-click on **A101-Floor Plan** sheet. Next, zoom-in to the bottom-right corner of the sheet and notice that the sheet name and other details are displayed. You can change the details one-by-one by clicking on them.

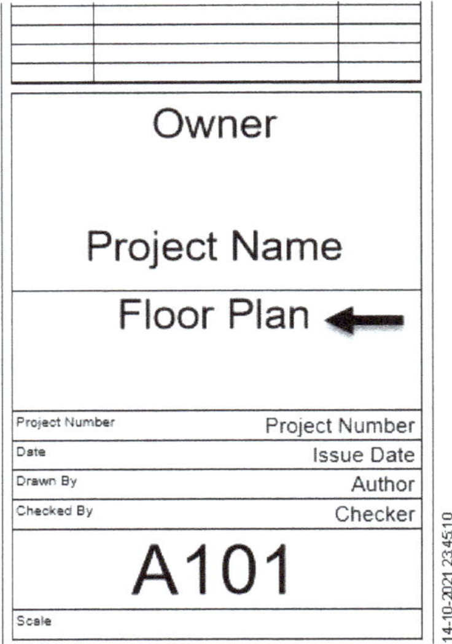

- Right-click and select **Zoom-to-Fit**.
- On the Project Browser, expand the **Floor Plans** node and drag the **FIRST FLOOR** view onto the drawing sheet. Next, click to position the view.

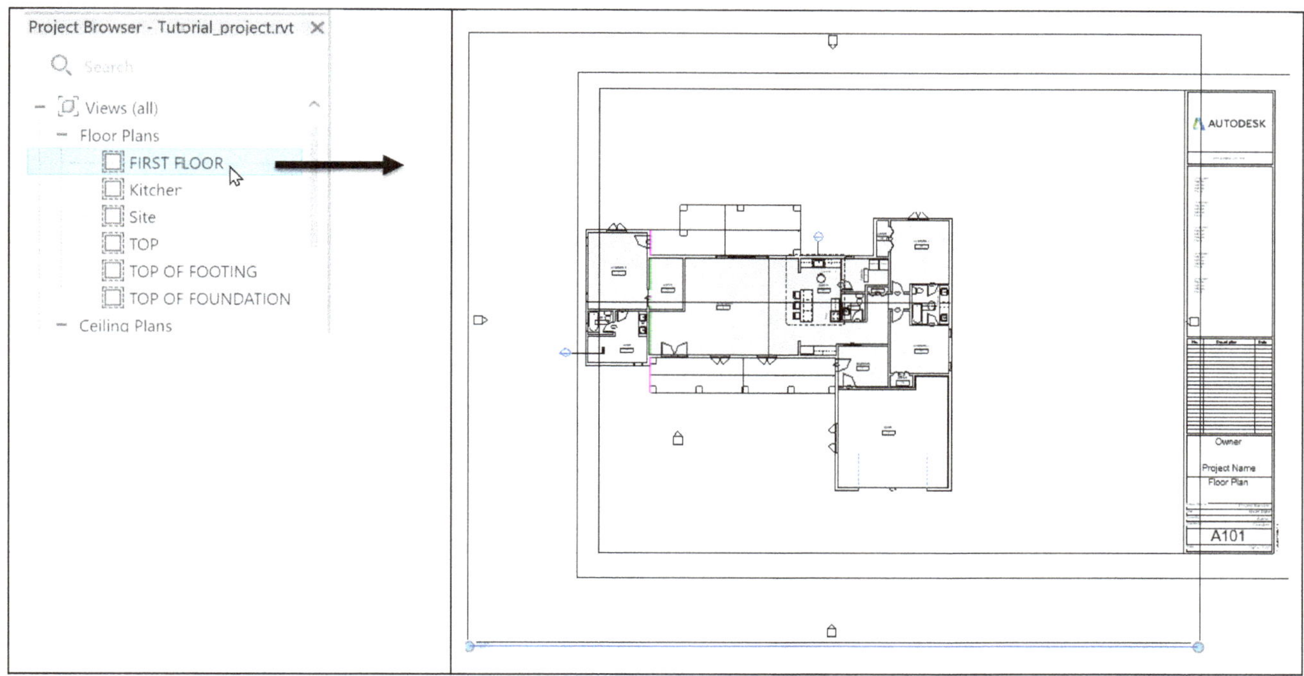

- On the **Properties** palette, scroll down to the **Extents** section and check the **Crop view** option.
- On the ribbon, click **Modify | Viewports > Crop > Size Crop**.

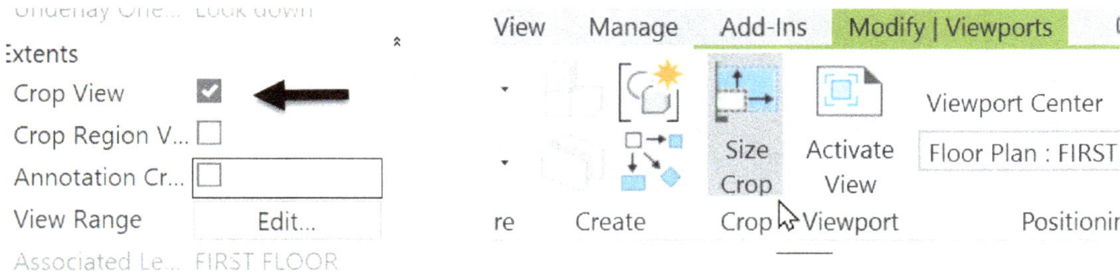

- Type **30"** and **22"** in the **Width** and **Height** boxes, respectively. Next, click **OK**.

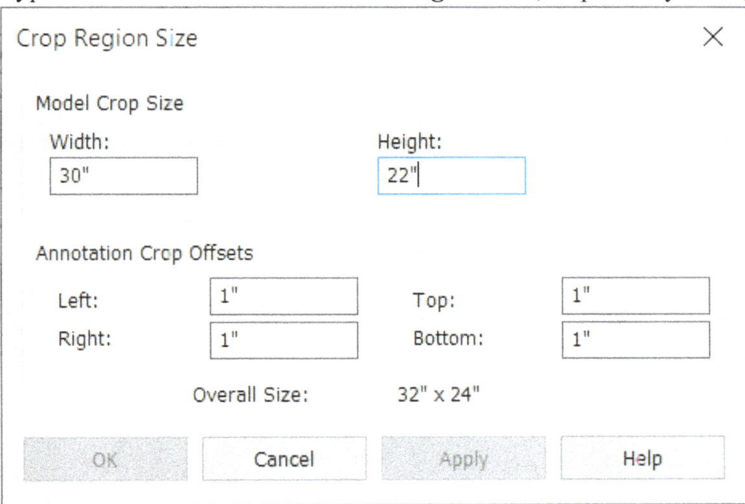

- Select the view title, press and hold the left mouse button, and then drag the pointer upward. Next, release the pointer to place the view title.

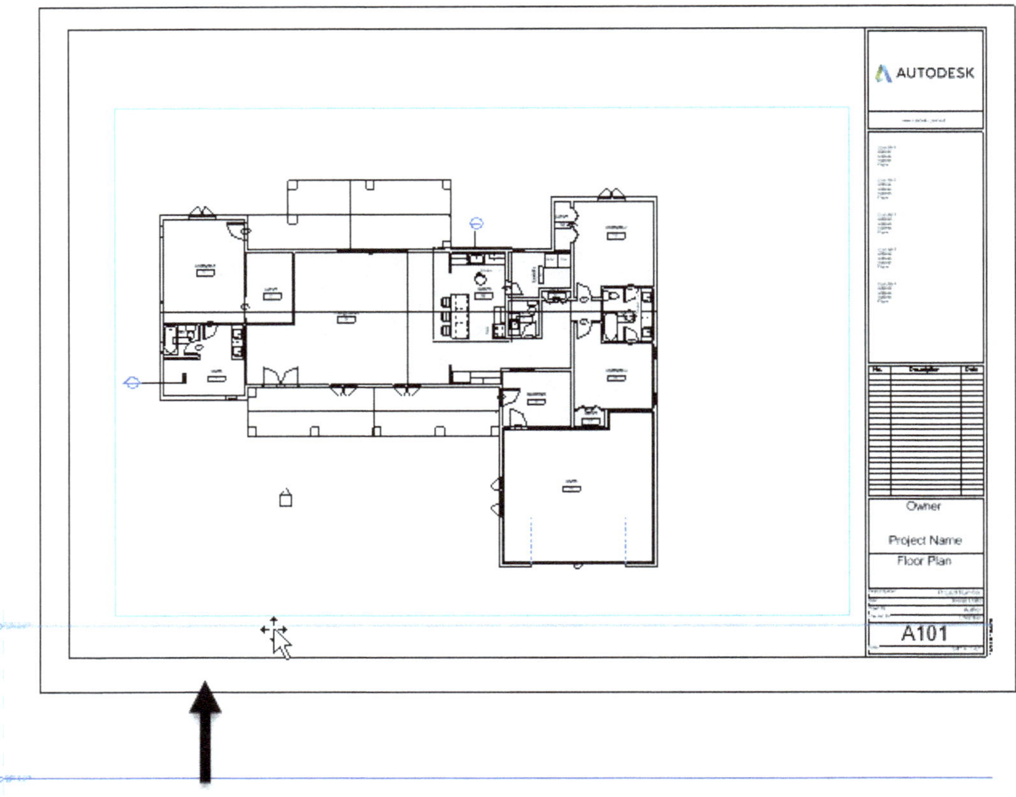

- Double-click in the viewport and notice the grip handles at the endpoints of the view title.
- Click on the left grip of the view title. Next, press and hold the left mouse button, drag the pointer toward right, and release the pointer.
- Click on the right grip of the view title. Next, press and hold the left mouse button, drag the pointer toward left, and then release the pointer.

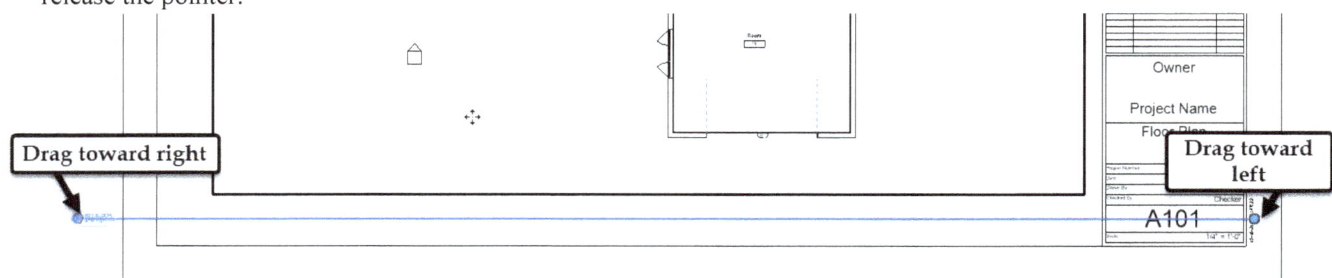

- Double-click in the viewport and click the **Show Crop Region** icon on the **View Control Bar** located at the bottom of the drawing area.

- Click on the viewport boundary and select the grip displayed on the midpoint of the right vertical edge.
- Press and hold the left mouse button and drag the pointer toward left. Next, release the mouse button.

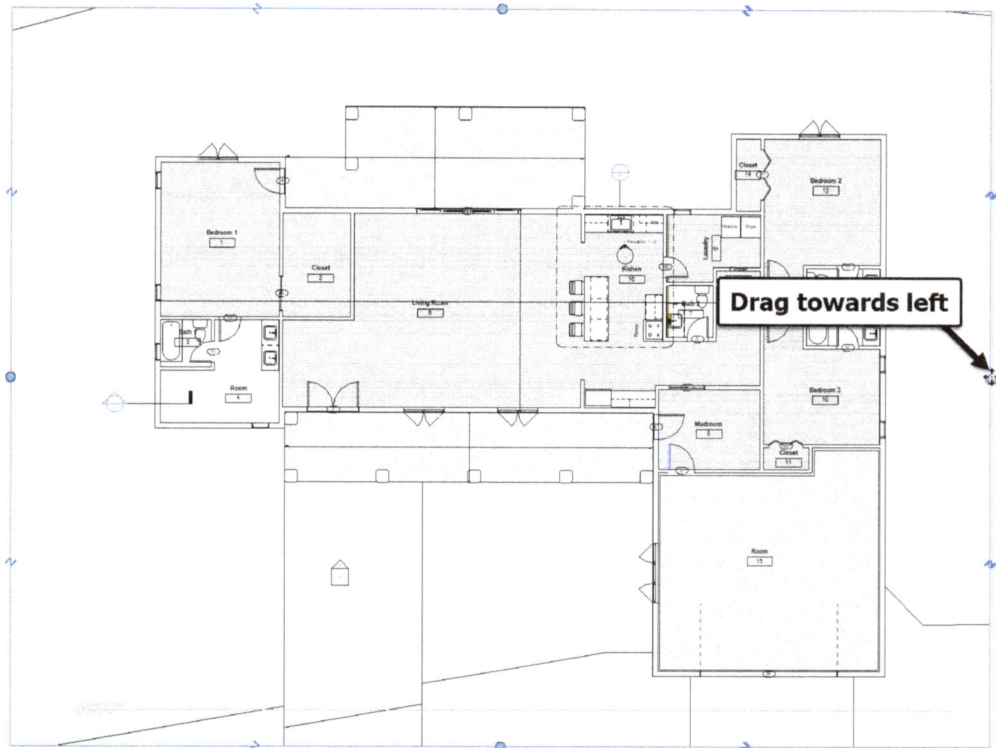

- Likewise, crop the other boundary edges, as shown.

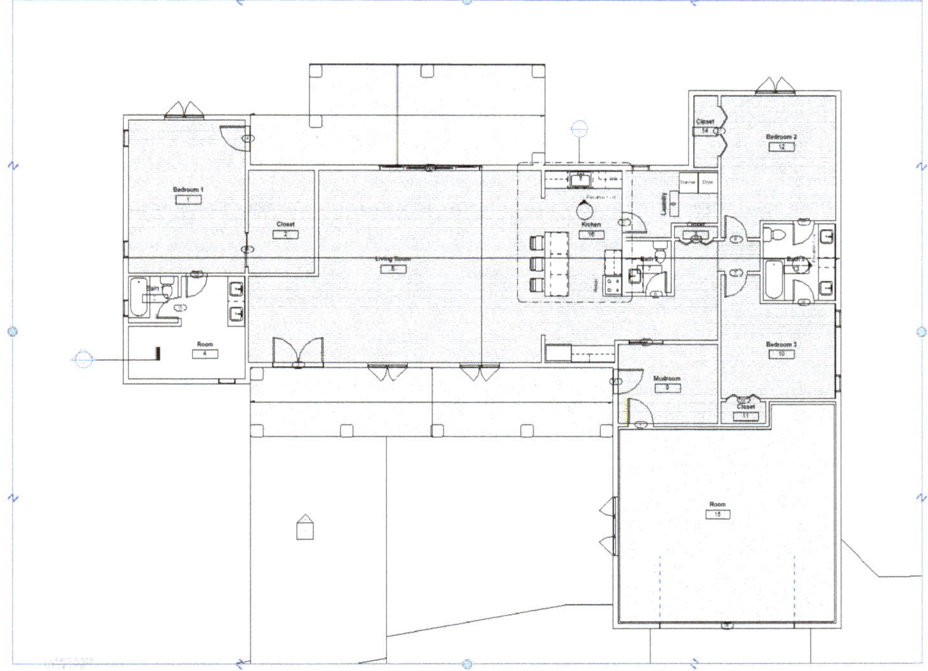

- Click the **Hide Crop Region** 🔲 icon on the **View Control Bar**.
- Double-click outside the viewport to deactivate the view.
- On the Project Browser, expand the **Elevations** node and drag the **Front Porch** view onto the drawing sheet. Next, click to position the view.

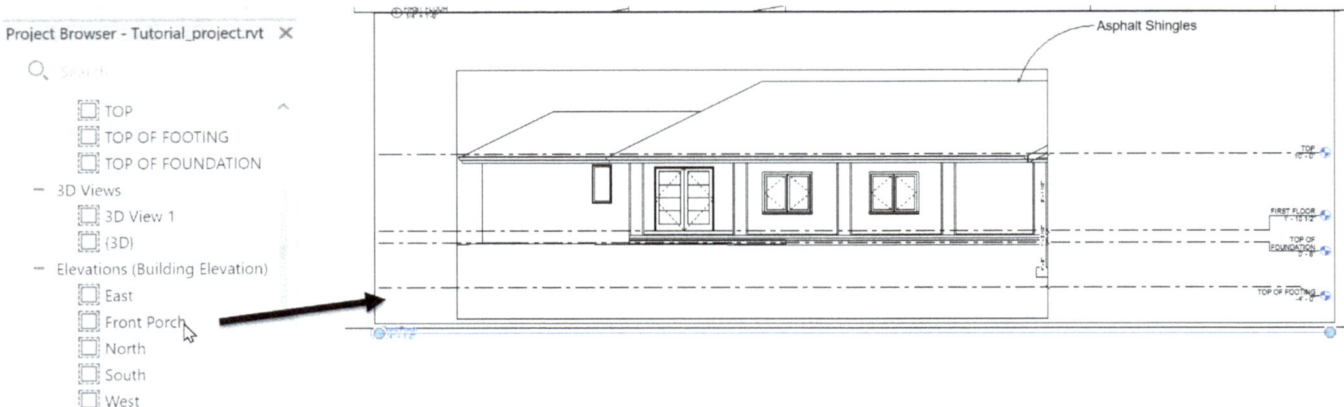

- On the **Properties** palette, change the View Scale to ¼" = 1'-0".

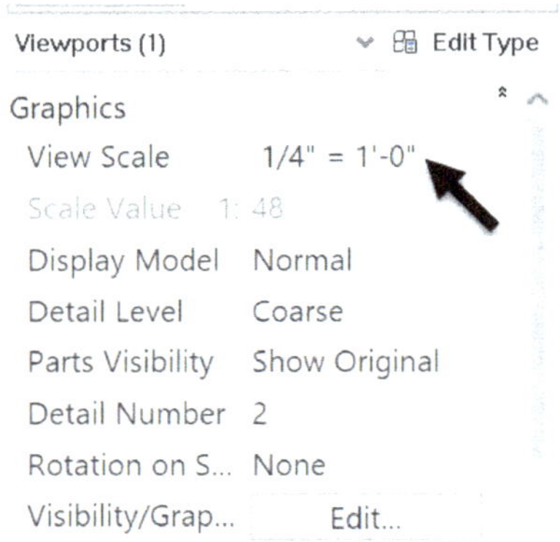
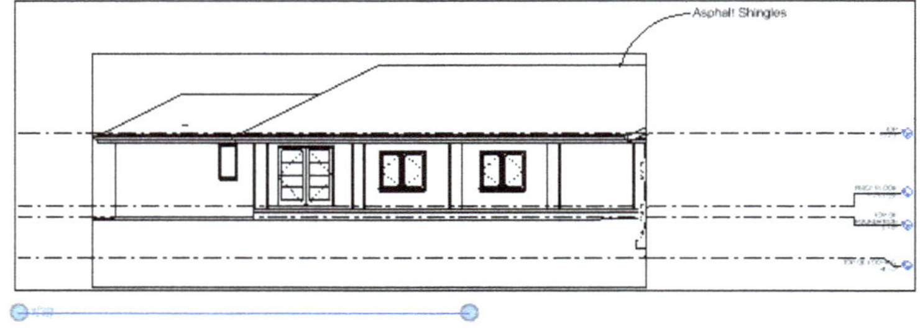

Printing Sheets

- Click **File Menu > Print > Print**. Next, select the printer from the **Name** drop-down on the **Print** dialog.
- Click the **Setup** button to the open the **Print Setup** dialog. Next, specify the settings on this dialog such as Paper size, placement, orientation, appearance, and zoom factor. You can save the specified settings by clicking the **Save As** button/
- Click **OK** on the **Page Setup** dialog.

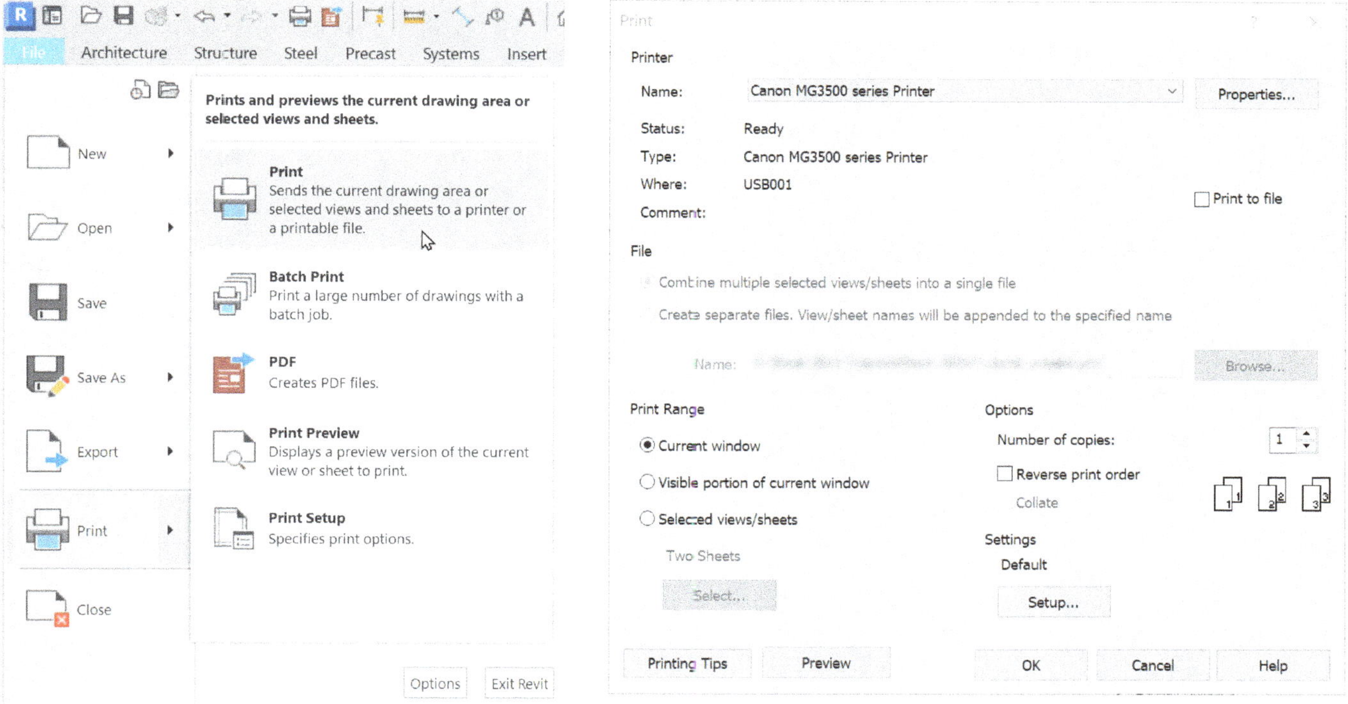

- On the **Print** dialog, select **Print Range > Selected view/sheets**. Next, click the **Select** button under the **Print Range** section.
- On the **Select Views/Sheets** dialog, select the two sheets that you have created in this tutorial from the list, and then click the **Save As** button.
- Type **Two Sheets** in the **New** dialog and click **OK**. Next, select **Two Sheets** from the **Name** drop-down and click **Select**.
- Click **OK** to print the sheets.